MARSILIUS OF PADUA

DISPUTATIO

VOLUME 36

Editorial Board
Clare Monagle, *Macquarie University*
Cary J. Nederman, *Texas A&M University*

Founding Editors
Georgiana Donovin, *Westminster College*
Richard Utz, *Western Michigan University*

Marsilius of Padua

Between History, Politics, and Philosophy

Edited by
ALESSANDRO MULIERI, SERENA MASOLINI,
AND JENNY PELLETIER

BREPOLS

© 2023, Brepols Publishers n.v., Turnhout, Belgium.

All rights reserved. No part of this publication may
be reproduced, stored in a retrieval system, or
transmitted, in any form or by any means, electronic,
mechanical, photocopying, recording, or otherwise
without the prior permission of the publisher.

D/2023/0095/24
ISBN 978-2-503-60133-5
eISBN 978-2-503-60134-2
DOI 10.1484/M.DISPUT-EB.5.130726
ISSN 1781-7048
eISSN 2294-8481

Printed in the EU on acid-free paper.

Contents

Preface   7

Introduction
Alessandro MULIERI   9

Part 1
Marsilius's Sources

Marsilius of Padua. A Reader of Aristotle's *Politica*
Roberto LAMBERTINI   31

'What More Do You Want?'. The Use of the Roman Trial of Jesus by Augustine and Marsilius of Padua
Gert-Jan VAN DE VOORDE   49

The Early *Politics* Commentaries as the Missing Link between Marsilius and Aristotle
Marco TOSTE   75

Marsilius of Padua on Human Acts, Law, and the (Toothless) Law of Christ
Iacopo COSTA   103

Marsilius of Padua and Collective Prudence
Alessandro MULIERI   123

Part 2
Marsilius's Thought and his Contemporaries

The Social and Political Functions of Emotions in Marsilius of Padua's *Defensor pacis* (and *Defensor minor*)
Juhana TOIVANEN   149

The Good Life and the Perfect Life in the *Defensor pacis*
Ferdinand DEANINI   179

Ghibelline Marsilius. Remarks on Marsilius of Padua's
Ghibelline Politico-Institutional Theory
Gianluca BRIGUGLIA   197

Defenders of the Peace. The Political Thought of Marsilius's
Italian Dominican Contemporaries
Charles F. BRIGGS   215

How History Happens. Contingency and Finality in the
Political Philosophy of Marsilius of Padua, with a View on John
Quidort of Paris and Dante Alighieri
Jacob LANGELOH   253

'The Great Refusal'. Pilate and Jesus in the Political Theologies
of Dante, Valla, and Marsilius
David Lloyd DUSENBURY   285

Part 3
The Marsilian Moment

Between Venice and Sant'Elmo. Tommaso Campanella,
Marsilius of Padua, and a 'Modern Theologian'
Serena MASOLINI   323

Papacy, Peace, and Political Science. Collective Action
Problems in Marsilius of Padua's *Defensor pacis*
Cary J. NEDERMAN   359

The *Defender of Peace* during the Third Reich
Frank GODTHARDT   383

Marsilius of Padua in *The Name of the Rose*. Between Historical
Fiction and Post-1968 Ideology
Gregorio PIAIA   409

Index of Names, Places, and Events   431

Preface

This volume was born out of a conference that we held in the summer of 2018 in Leuven called 'Marsilius of Padua between History, Philosophy and Politics'. We would like to thank all the participants at the conference for their invaluable feedback on the presentations that were given there, most of which have been included in this volume after much revision. We would also like to warmly thank Andrea Aldo Robiglio for his enthusiastic help in organizing the conference.

We are grateful to Cary Nederman, Clare Monagle, Deborah A. Oosterhouse, and the Brepols team for making the preparation of the manuscript for publication as easy and efficient as could be expected given the pandemic. They were patient and understanding of delays. We are also grateful to the anonymous reader who took on the responsibility of reading the entire manuscript and sent back a thorough and careful assessment of each contribution.

As regards our division of labour, Alessandro Mulieri wrote the introduction (while some summaries of the book chapters towards the end were written by Jenny Pelletier and Serena Masolini) and his own contribution. Serena Masolini copy-edited and formatted the manuscript in addition to writing her own contribution. Jenny Pelletier provided substantive and comprehensive content editing for the volume as a whole and proofread the English.

Alessandro Mulieri would like to thank his co-editors for their support and enthusiasm in pursuing the project and for working on any step of the editing process with a good mix of intellectual rigour and human generosity. He gratefully acknowledges the funding he received from the FWO (Research Foundation – Flanders) while preparing this volume. Serena Masolini would like to thank her co-editors for their support during these years. Her research and her share in the preparation of the volume was funded by the KU Leuven Research Council (project no. 3H170335, directed by Gert Partoens, Anthony Dupont, and Andrea Aldo Robiglio), and by the Academy of Finland ('Augustinian Natural Philosophy at Oxford and Paris ca. 1277', directed by Filipe Pereira da Silva). Jenny Pelletier would like to thank her co-editors for their generosity, good humour, and easy collaboration. Preparing this volume was enjoyable largely because of them. She is grateful to the FWO and the Swedish Research Council for their financial support.

A special thanks goes to Matthew S. Champion, who brought to our attention the image of the bombed copy of the *Defensor pacis,* which we chose as the cover image. The image conveys a sense of the *DP* as a living text throughout history and evokes the encounter between philosophy and real political conflict.

ALESSANDRO MULIERI

Introduction*

We do not know much about the life of Marsilio de' Mainardini (henceforth, Marsilius of Padua). He was born in Padua to a family of notaries, perhaps between 1275 and 1285, and had a very adventurous life that led him to study and teach in Paris (from where he probably went back and forth to Padua a number of times).[1] Marsilius lived during the first half of the fourteenth century, a time of great political, social, and cultural transformation. After the crisis of the Holy Roman Empire, which developed with the death of Frederick II Hohenstaufen in 1250, the very ideal of the empire had suffered considerably vis-à-vis an increasingly aggressive papal policy centring on the idea of *plenitudo potestatis*.[2] The clash between the papacy and the empire reached its climax at the beginning of the fourteenth century, when there was an important attempt by the emperor, Henry VII of Luxembourg, to reclaim his power in Germany and in Italy.

It is in this context that we have to understand the action of Ludwig IV (Ludwig von Wittelsbach), also called the Bavarian, who was elected emperor in Bavaria from among five of the eight elector princes and had to face the other claimant to the imperial throne, Frederick von Aubsburg, who was appointed by the three remaining electors. After the latter's defeat in 1322, Ludwig encountered Pope John XXII's strong opposition (John had considered the imperial throne vacant and taken its office). Ludwig's behaviour led to his excommunication by John in 1324, which was immediately followed by the Sachsenhausen Appeal in which the Germanic ruler reclaimed the validity of his appointment against the pope. Following this reaction, Ludwig went to Italy in 1327 — followed by

---

* While Alessandro Mulieri was the main author of the introduction, Serena Masolini and Jenny Pelletier contributed to the summaries of the volume's contents. Jenny Pelletier comprehensively and substantially edited the introduction.

1 For a reconstruction of Marsilius's life, see Godthardt, 'The Philosopher as Political Actor'; Courtenay, 'Marsilius of Padua at Paris'; Brett, 'Introduction'; Briguglia, *Marsilio da Padova*, pp. 25–62.

2 Lee, *Humanism and Empire*.

Marsilius of Padua, ed. by Alessandro Mulieri, Serena Masolini, and Jenny Pelletier, Disputatio, 36 (Turnhout: Brepols, 2023), pp. 9–28

BREPOLS ❦ PUBLISHERS   10.1484/M.DISPUT-EB.5.132905

Marsilius himself and John of Jandun — and allied himself with the Italian Ghibelline faction, to then be crowned in Rome upon which he then appointed an anti-pope named Niccolò V.

In this context, the divisions between Guelphs and Ghibellines in the Italian Peninsula continued to characterize the internal equilibria of the Italian *comuni*, which had in fact lost their effective and usual ideological nature to adapt to the patterns of international power.[3] Ghibellinism was partly emptied of some of its original ideological meaning, which consisted in its endorsement of the empire and the imperial idea. Guelphism was decisively reinstated in the aggressive policy of John XXII, the Avignon pope against whom Marsilius wrote the *Defensor pacis*. It is important to understand this specific Guelph tendency in fourteenth-century Italy in light of the fact that the papacy had previously moved its main centre of power from Rome to Avignon under the pontificate of Clement V, a move that had also brought the papacy under the influence of the French political monarchy. The ascendance of John XXII to the pontificate in 1316 had enhanced an assertive policy of reclaiming temporal power that had been the distinctive mark of the Church under such different popes as Innocent III, Gregory IX, Innocent IV, and Boniface VIII from the beginning of the thirteenth century. However, John had moved the centre of the political axis to a close alliance with the French monarchy and in opposition both to the usual attempts of the Italian city-states to gain more independence and of the rising importance of Aragon's monarchy in the south. At the beginning of the fourteenth century, the political claims of both the papacy and the French monarchy also represented the core of the political and institutional equilibria in the Italian context.

A quick glimpse at this history suggests an important point about Marsilius of Padua's biography and political ideas. He lived between three of the most important centres of European power of the time, Padua, Paris, and Munich, in which this complex dialectic between the two major powers of the Middle Ages and their impact on the complex equilibria of the Italian city-states was crucial. In fact, his thought reflects the very vivid intellectual and cultural lives that characterized these three important centres of power at the beginning of the fourteenth century in interesting ways. Marsilius's active participation in the Ghibelline league (as we will see, he was actively militant within the Ghibelline milieu) certainly links his thought closely to this historical context. So, we can imagine that when he returned to Paris sometime before 1321 and he likely started to work on the *Defensor*, this played an important role in his intellectual development. His reference to the necessity of achieving peace in Italy in the *Defensor* must also be read in light of the above circumstances.

---

3 Jones, *The Italian City-State*; Hyde, *Society and Politics in Medieval Italy*; Black, *Political Thought in Europe*.

In Padua, Marsilius would have started his education at a very young age, probably in the first years of the fourteenth century. Albertino Mussato tells us that Marsilius asked him for advice on whether to study law or medicine and then decided to study medicine.[4] In the late medieval period, Padua had become the centre of two crucial intellectual developments. One was the development of a pre-humanist literature that had seen important representatives in Lovato Lovati and Albertino Mussato, the latter of whom Marsilius knew well.[5] Moreover, starting from the thirteenth century, Padua had also become an important centre for discussing the ideas of Aristotelian natural philosophy, leading to important studies in medicine, astrology, etc.[6] Peter of Abano, who was probably one of Marsilius's teachers, is an important representative of this tradition.

Marsilius went to Paris where he first studied and then taught in the years between 1310 and 1315, serving as the rector of the university between December 1312 and March 1313.[7] At that time, the University of Paris was one of the liveliest cultural and intellectual milieux in the late medieval period. In the same years as Marsilius several *magistri* were present at the university, ranging from Bartholomew of Bruges and Walter Burley to Thomas Wilton, Radulphus Brito, John of Jandun, Thomas de Bailly, William Bernard of Narbonne, Jean de Pouilly, but also many others. Marsilius might have attended the classes of some of them, known some of their texts, or exchanged ideas with them on a variety of subjects that were the typical topics of university *magistri* in those years.[8] The context of the University of Paris at the beginning of the fourteenth century was especially dynamic, and various new and original streams of research were

---

4 Briguglia, *Marsilio da Padova*, p. 59.

5 For more on this, see Billanovich, 'Il preumanesimo padovano'. While scholars agree that this context is not reflected in the *Defensor*, the Paduan tradition of natural philosophy is clearly echoed in the *Defensor*. On the Paduan context being one of Marsilius's sources, see Marangon, 'Marsilio tra preumanesimo e cultura della arti'.

6 For a general introduction to the Paduan school of natural philosophy, see Siraisi, *Arts and Sciences at Padua*.

7 *Chartularium Universitatis Parisiensis*, ed. by Denifle and Chatelain, II, p. 158; cf. Godthardt, 'The Life of Marsilius of Padua', p. 14. Courtenay claims that he could have been in Paris already at the beginning of the fourteenth century between 1300 and 1306. See Courtenay, 'Marsilius of Padua at Paris'.

8 Courtenay, 'Marsilius of Padua at Paris', pp. 69–70. In this contribution Courtenay provides an excellent and detailed reconstruction of the Parisian context in Marsilius's time. Among the studies on the general context and topics discussed at the University of Paris at the beginning of the fourteenth century, see for instance Courtenay, *Parisian Scholars in the Early Fourteenth Century*, Weijers, *Le travail intellectuel à la Faculté des arts de Paris*, and Schabel, *Theological Quodlibeta in the Middle Ages*.

taking place, substantively renewing the already rich environment of the thirteenth century.[9]

Thanks to the will of one of Marsilius's possible teachers, Peter of Abano (the will being a document compiled by the same Mussato),[10] we know that in May 1315 Marsilius was in Padua. Peter was on trial for heterodoxy, and Marsilius was one of the witnesses who testified to Peter's orthodoxy.[11] In the years between 1316 and 1319, Marsilius was also in Italy, and actually in March 1319, he served as an ambassador for the Ghibelline league that had been formed against the pope.[12] In this period, he was close to the Ghibelline league and served as an envoy of Cangrande della Scala and Matteo Visconti. We also have evidence that he must have returned to Paris before 1321 because John of Jandun informs us that Marsilius had brought the manuscript of Peter of Abano's *Expositio* of the Pseudo-Aristotle *Problemata* from Padua to the French capital.[13] This may have been the period in which Marsilius worked on his masterpiece, the *Defensor pacis*. From several manuscripts of the *Defensor*, we know that he must have completed this work on 24 June 1324,[14] but scholars are divided on whether he immediately left Paris after this date — as he feared that his life was in danger because of the ideas he presented in the *Defensor* — or whether he actually left the city one year later, in 1325, to go to the imperial court in Munich and seek protection with Ludwig the Bavarian.[15] In 1327–1328, Marsilius accompanied Emperor Ludwig the Bavarian on his expedition to Italy where Ludwig was crowned in Rome as the Holy Roman Emperor in 1328. In his time with the emperor, Marsilius was also *vicarius in spiritualibus* in Milan and was excommunicated in 1327 by Pope John XXII in Avignon.[16] After the failure of Ludwig's expedition,

---

9 Of course, Marsilius could also find a specific political stream of thought represented around the beginning of the fourteenth century, as witnessed by the proliferation of important political treatises authored by Giles of Rome, John of Paris, and other theorists. On the possible impact of these sources on Marsilius, see Briguglia, 'The Minor Marsilius'.

10 A short description of Mussato's texts where Marsilius is mentioned can be found in Briguglia, *Marsilio da Padova*, pp. 56–60, and in Godthardt, 'The Life of Marsilius of Padua', pp. 45–49.

11 See Pesenti, 'Per la tradizione del testamento di Pietro d'Abano', esp. pp. 541–42; Courtenay, 'Marsilius of Padua at Paris', p. 65.

12 Godthardt, 'The Life of Marsilius of Padua', pp. 17–19.

13 Siraisi, *Arts and Sciences at Padua*, p. 164.

14 However, Collodo suggests that some parts of the *Defensor* could have already been composed separately far before Marsilius's stay in Paris that took place between 1310 and 1315. He may have composed some of it, for example, in Padua. See Collodo and Simonetti, eds, *Filosofia naturale e scienze dell'esperienza*, pp. 15–240.

15 On this matter, see Godthardt, 'The Philosopher as Political Actor'.

16 On Marsilius's office of *vicarius* in Milan, see Cadili, 'Marsilio da Padova amministratore della Chiesa ambrosiana'. The bull *Licet iuxta doctrinam* by Pope John XXII can be found in Du Plessis d'Argentré, *Collectio judiciorum de novis erroribus*, I, cols 304–11.

Marsilius returned to Munich where he spent most of the remainder of his life. He must have died sometime before 1343.[17] We are certain that Marsilius authored three main works: the *Defensor pacis* (which is his masterpiece and by far his longest work), the *Defensor minor* (a shorter restatement of many of the ideas of the previous work with a stronger pro-empire sentiment, which he probably composed around 1340), and the *De translatione imperii* (in which he copies Landulphus Colonna's analogous treatise on the *translatio imperii* with some small but substantive differences). His authorship of a few other works, which are not directly political, remains controversial in most cases.[18]

The *Defensor pacis* is Marsilius's work that has received most attention from scholars. This work is composed of three main *dictiones*: a first *dictio* in which Marsilius states that he will present his ideas according to human reason, a second *dictio* in which he declares that he will draw on the truth of revelation, and a third short *dictio* in which he sums up the main positions discussed in the two previous *dictiones*. The relationship between the first two *dictiones* has been one of the most controversial points both in the reception of Marsilius's work and in discussions of his thought in the modern scholarly literature.[19] In contrast to a tendency in the early modern period (especially during the European religious wars in the sixteenth and seventeenth centuries) to draw on Marsilius's ecclesiological and theological ideas that are discussed especially in the second *dictio* of the *Defensor*,[20] a considerable part of the scholarship in the twentieth century has paid greater attention to the first *dictio* of Marsilius's work. Ideas such as law, self-government, sovereignty, and rights that are discussed in this part of the *Defensor* found an especially fertile ground among scholars who read Marsilius's work as anticipating modern, democratic ideas. This was already the case in the approach of George

---

17 On 10 April 1343, Pope Clement VI commented on Ludwig the Bavarian's heresies and informs us that both Marsilius and John had already died. See Godthardt, 'The Life of Marsilius of Padua', p. 55; Briguglia, *Marsilio da Padova*, p. 61.

18 Marsilius might have authored two *sophismata* on the question of universals, but he is confirmed as the author of only one of them; see Lambertini, 'The "Sophismata" Attributed to Marsilius of Padua'. The authorship of the *Quaestiones super metaphysice libros I–VI*, which had been ascribed to Marsilius, is now confirmed to be that of John of Jandun. See Lambertini and Tabarroni, 'Le "Quaestiones super Metaphysicam" attribuite a Giovanni di Jandun'. Marsilius also authored three short documents concerning the role of the human legislator in deciding about marriage and separation. Briguglia underlines the close correspondence between these texts and Chapters 13–15 of the *Defensor minor*; see Briguglia, 'The Minor Marsilius', pp. 287–90.

19 A very good overview of the most recent literature on Marsilius is Briguglia, 'Note sulle tendenze attuali'.

20 On this matter, see especially the study of Piaia, *Marsilio da Padova nella Riforma e nella Controriforma*.

de Lagarde who, in the 1930s, was reading Marsilius as a precursor of the modern idea of secularism, seeing in the Paduan a premodern version of the French idea of *laicité*.[21] The subsequent debate on the presumed 'modernity' of Marsilius's political thought continued to focus on the first *dictio*, either stressing with Walter Ullmann the view that Marsilius was a theorist *ex ante* of the modern idea of sovereignty or with Alan Gewirth the idea of Marsilius as a precursor of the modern notion of consent as based on individual rights.[22] While Ullmann stresses that Marsilius played a key role in the development of modern political theories of ascending power, Gewirth sees in Marsilius's work a representation *ex ante* of modern theories of democracy and liberalism. Gewirth goes so far as to suggest that the two *dictiones* could have been written by two different authors, such as Marsilius and John of Jandun. These interpretations prepared the ground for those who, still emphasizing the importance of the first *dictio* of the *Defensor*, read Marsilius as a republican author; a view that has been especially common among theorists of the so-called Cambridge School.[23]

In contrast to these views, other scholars have tried to soften the presumedly 'republican nature' of the first part of the *Defensor*, by providing interpretations that would also take into consideration the more clearly pro-imperial ideas of the second *dictio*. For example, in Jeannine Quillet's studies on Marsilius, the concepts that are present in the first *dictio* must be considered as functional to those in the second where there is a clearer defence of the prerogatives of imperial power.[24] Therefore, the theories of the legislator and popular sovereignty should be interpreted as providing a strong and alternative ground to the imperial prerogatives vis-à-vis the temporal claims of the *plenitudo potestatis*. Similarly, from different perspectives, other authors such as Gregorio Piaia, Carlo Pincin, and Jürgen Miethke have stressed the importance of the continuity between the two *dictiones*.[25]

This tendency to stress one of the two *dictiones* as the focal point of analysis is still present in the most recent Marsilian studies. As for the first *dictio*, this is the case for the important studies of Vasileios Syros, who has authored one book in German and one in English on Marsilius that open up a new vista onto studies in comparative political thought.[26] Syros reads the *Defensor*, and Marsilius's thought in the first *dictio*, against

---

21 De Lagarde, *La naissance de l'esprit laïque*, vols II and III.
22 Ullmann, *Principles of Government and Politics*, p. 232, and Ullmann, *A History of Political Thought*, ch. 2; Gewirth, *Marsilius of Padua*.
23 Skinner, *The Foundations of Modern Political Thought*, I, pp. 60–66; Viroli, *From Politics to Reason of State*, pp. 50–52.
24 Quillet, *La philosophie politique de Marsile de Padoue*.
25 Piaia, *Marsilio e dintorni*; Pincin, *Marsilio*; Miethke, *Politiktheorie im Mittelalter*.
26 Syros, *Die Rezeption der aristotelischen politischen Philosophie* and Syros, *Marsilius of Padua at the Intersection*.

the backdrop of Jewish, Islamic, and Byzantine sources that could have reached this author through a variety of Latin sources. Similarly, the French scholar Didier Ottaviani explores the possible influence of a variety of Aristotelian sources on the development of Marsilius's political science. He focuses especially on the first *dictio* of the *Defensor* as the space in which Marsilius develops a new idea of political science.[27] On the other hand, George Garnett and Riccardo Battocchio have produced studies that focus more on the second *dictio*.[28] In an open critique of those approaches that read the Marsilian work only in light of themes focused on the first *dictio*, Garnett rediscovers the relationship that links the *Defensor* to the prophetical and apocalyptic literature of his own context. Similarly, Battocchio pays attention to a series of different ecclesiological and theological problems in Marsilius's context and investigates their relevance for the *Defensor*.

Along with this literature, which has selectively focused on either the first or the second *dictio* of the *Defensor*, a parallel wave of studies gradually developed stressing the various philosophical, historical, and political sources that influenced Marsilius's *Defensor*. This trend had already started in the 1960s and 1970s and is well represented in a special issue of the Italian journal *Medioevo*, which was published at the beginning of the 1980s by experts from different national traditions.[29] The tendency to approach the *Defensor* in light of the different sources and contexts in which Marsilius worked and studied has been more recently pursued by two different volumes that were published in English for the publishers Brepols and Brill. The 2006 volume edited by Gerson Moreno-Riaño contains studies on Marsilius that range from the traditional problems of power and sovereignty in the first *dictio* to the importance of medical sources, but also includes several studies of key theological and ecclesiological arguments in the second *dictio* of the *Defensor*.[30] Likewise, the Brill volume edited by Cary J. Nederman and Gerson Moreno-Riaño in 2012 includes contributions that aim to cover different aspects that belong to the first and the second *dictiones* of the *Defensor* in an equal way.[31] More and more scholars follow this path and interpret the *Defensor* as a unified work, thereby adopting a more integrated perspective based on the variety of contexts and sources that shape Marsilius's work. For example, both Cary J. Nederman and Conal Condren have emphasized the importance of an integrated approach to the *Defensor* in which the core ideas in the first

---

27 Ottaviani, *La naissance de la science politique*.
28 Garnett, *Marsilius of Padua and 'the Truth of History'*; Battocchio, *Ecclesiologia e politica in Marsilio da Padova*.
29 See the two special issues of *Medioevo*, 5 (1979) and 6 (1980).
30 Moreno-Riaño, ed., *The World of Marsilius of Padua*.
31 Moreno-Riaño and Nederman, eds, *A Companion to Marsilius of Padua*.

two *dictiones* must be read in a unitary logic.[32] In their studies, it emerges that some key normative notions described in the first *dictio* (for example, that of the legislator) are designed to be functional to the overall thesis of the work, namely, to oppose the idea of the *plenitudo potestatis*. This same approach can be found in Gianluca Briguglia's studies on Marsilius of Padua, in which the Paduan's message is reconstructed in light of different sources that range from theology to ecclesiology, political theory, and history.[33]

Once again showing the importance of considering the variety of sources that influenced the *Defensor*, scholars in the recent literature have especially focused on four areas of study. First, studies that focus on the possible impact of the Paduan tradition of natural philosophy have considered the influence that medical and astrological thought might have had on the *Defensor*. This is the case for Takashi Shogimen, Alexander Aichele, and my focus on Peter of Abano's influence on Marsilius,[34] as well as Joel Kaye's reconstruction of the impact of Galenic medical discourse on balance on the *Defensor*.[35] Second, important studies by Roberto Lambertini, Brian Tierney, and Annabel Brett have focused on the contextual importance of Marsilius in genealogies of the modern concept of rights and some problems that were debated among the intellectual circle around Ludwig in Munich, that is, the question of evangelical poverty that was at the centre of Franciscan debates (which included Michael of Cesena, Bonagratia of Bergamo, William of Ockham, etc.).[36] Third, increasing attention has being paid to the specific nature of Marsilius's republicanism within the history of premodern republicanism, with more and more scholars stressing the anti-republican or post-republican nature of Marsilius's political thought or Marsilius's proximity to Ghibellinism.[37] Important advancements in the Marsilian literature have also been made in tracing the influence of the ideas in the *Defensor* on early modern authors such as Thomas Hobbes or the complex religious discussions in the early modern and modern periods.[38] Finally, the comparative political thought approach inaugurated by Vasileios Syros and Antony Black is also implicitly contained in some recent attempts by Jean-Baptiste Brenet and myself to reopen the possible

---

32 Nederman, *Community and Consent*; Condren, 'Democracy and the *Defensor Pacis*'.

33 Briguglia, *Marsilio da Padova*.

34 Shogimen, 'Medicine and the Body Politic'; Aichele, 'Heart and Soul of the State'; Mulieri, 'Marsilius of Padua and Peter of Abano'.

35 Kaye, *A History of Balance*.

36 Lambertini, 'Marsilius and the Poverty Controversy'; Tierney, 'Marsilius on Rights'; Tierney, *Liberty and Law*; Brett, 'Political Right(s) and Human Freedom'.

37 Briguglia, *Marsilio da Padova*.

38 Piaia, *Marsilio da Padova nella Riforma e nella Controriforma*; Koch, *Zur Dis-/Kontinuität mittelalterlichen politischen Denkens*; Simonetta, *Marsilio in Inghilterra*.

path of the influence of Ibn Rushd's work on Marsilius's *Defensor* through
the filter of Marsilius's close friend and colleague, John of Jandun.[39]

The present volume builds upon all the lines of research noted above,
bringing together a range of younger and established scholars for a new
generation of research on Marsilius of Padua. It is divided into three
different parts.

The first part devotes some attention to the relationship between Marsilius's thought and its possible sources. In his chapter, Roberto Lambertini
reconstructs the complex textual relationship between Marsilius's *Defensor*
and Aristotle's *Politics*, enumerating the manuscript(s) from which Marsilius likely took his reading of Aristotle's text, and examines Marsilius's
engagement with the different books of Aristotle's *Politics* in depth. In
the first of two chapters on the Roman trial of Christ, Gert-Jan Van de
Voorde returns to a problem that was a long-standing focus of attention in
the Anglophone literature on Marsilius, namely, the relationship between
the *Defensor* and Augustine or Augustinianism, which is filtered either
directly or indirectly through Thomas Aquinas's *Catena aurea*. He analyses
Marsilius's discussion of Christ's Roman trial in the *Defensor*, focusing on
the scriptural passages used to argue, ultimately, that Christ recognized
the legitimacy of Roman temporal power. He also argues that Bernard of
Clairvaux is one of Marsilius's sources on the trial. Marco Toste devotes
attention to the influence of Peter of Auvergne, who authored the continuation of Thomas Aquinas's commentary on Aristotle's *Politics* and also
wrote *Questiones* on this text. Peter is a source that surfaces now and then
in the scholarly literature on Marsilius,[40] but given that his two main works
had remained unedited until today, no scholar had provided a systematic
study of the impact of his ideas on Marsilius.

In the remaining two chapters of this first part of the volume, the
approach taken to the sources of the *Defensor* is more indirect. Iacopo
Costa's and Alessandro Mulieri's chapters return to a question that was
essential in the past scholarship on Marsilius, that is, the relationship
between Marsilius and Thomas Aquinas's thought, especially the *Summa
theologiae*. Picking up the theme of the relationship between immanent
('internal') and transient ('external') acts contained in Chapter 12 of the
second *dictio* of the *Defensor*, Costa shows that Marsilius's thought on this
topic is characterized by a strong anti-Thomistic dimension. According
to Marsilius, Costa shows, the law of Christ has the status of counsel

---

39 Black, *The West and Islam*, pp. 51–57 and 166 (Appendix); Syros, 'Did the Physician from
Padua Meet the Rabbi from Cordoba?'; Brenet, 'Multitude et *bene esse* chez Averroès et
Dante'; Mulieri, 'Against Classical Republicanism'. See note 44, below.
40 For example, see Toste, 'The Parts and the Whole, the Few Wise Men and the Multitude',
and Lanza, 'Comprendere il consenso esaminando il dissenso'.

and without any coercive force. Along similar lines, Mulieri focuses on a concept that has surprisingly not received any attention in the scholarly literature on Marsilius, that is, the topic of collective prudence. Aristotle mentions this topic in the *Politics* but never develops it, whereas bits and pieces of the idea of collective prudence are hinted at in the works of some Aristotelian commentators. Mulieri's chapter shows that Marsilius built a comprehensive theory of collective prudence that serves as a substitute for natural law with respect to the legitimacy of human laws, therefore challenging the Thomistic idea of the dependence of human laws on natural law.

The second part of the volume explores the relationship between Marsilius's thought and other important traditions or authors who were his prominent contemporaries. Juhana Toivanen's chapter examines the role of emotions and their complex relationship with rationality in the *Defensor*. Toivanen focuses on the social and political function of emotions in two different ways. First of all, he claims that emotions have a crucial role in the emergence and structure of social and political institutions and are the result of a combined influence of both the Ciceronian and Aristotelian traditions. Second, he focuses on the function that emotions play in the political community of the *Defensor* once it has been instituted. In Marsilius's work, emotions act both as mechanisms that must be handled and reduced to moderation (avoiding excessive manifestations), especially in light of human laws, but also as key motivators for the polity as such. Ferdinand Deanini aims to analyse the function of the concept of the good life in the *Defensor*. He stresses how in Marsilius's work there seem to be two different ideas of the good life: one grounded in the pursuit of civil life and founded in the desire for living and living well, and the other based on the life of the *perfecti* and on Marsilius's praise of the doctrine of evangelical poverty, which entails the rejection of worldly property and power. Deanini's goal is to find a way to reconcile these two different models of lives.

The focus of Gianluca Briguglia's chapter is concerned with the Ghibelline nature of Marsilius's ideas. The republican scholarship on Marsilius has particularly insisted on the fact that the ideas of self-government play a crucial role in interpreting Marsilius's thought as republican. Drawing on very recent important revisionist literature in the history of republicanism, Briguglia questions the divisive opposition between empire and self-government that can be found in this literature in order to defend the claim that Marsilius did not simply have Ghibelline ideas but was actually a philosopher of Ghibellinism. According to Briguglia, Marsilius's political philosophy of Ghibellinism is based on the combination of two different layers, one pertaining to the institutional and political life of late medieval Italian city-states, and the other based on the two great medieval powers of the empire and the papacy. A similar intention characterizes Charles F.

Briggs's chapter. Briggs analyses the web of Italian Dominican sources in the late thirteenth and early fourteenth centuries, many of whom were largely influenced by Aristotle and Aquinas's ethical and political writings. Briggs aims to show that the beginning of the fourteenth century witnesses a flowering of political thought, expressed in various genres, in the writings of Dominican authors in response to what he considers their 'distinctive' pastoral and educational mandate as well as the concrete historical conditions in which they lived. He accomplishes this by focusing on the questions of the common good and of peace or 'tranquillity of order' in such authors as Remigio de' Girolami of Florence, Ptolemy of Lucca, Bartolomeo da San Concordio, Enrico da Rimini, and others.

Jacob Langeloh reads Marsilius's *Defensor* against the backdrop of two other theorists of the beginning of the fourteenth century, namely John Quidort and Dante Alighieri, and discusses the complex relationship between apocalyptic thought and Aristotelian political thought in these authors' works. Langeloh questions George Garnett's interpretation of Marsilius as an apocalyptic thinker, but nevertheless embraces his claim that Marsilius presents an idea of history based on the notion of truth. To prove this point, Langeloh reads Marsilius against Quidort and Dante, showing that their accounts of history are based on a complex relationship between contingency and divine intervention which can be then read as apocalyptic. David Lloyd Dusenbury, in the second of the two chapters devoted to the Roman trial of Christ, investigates the role of Pilate's trial in the Augustinian and in the Latin Christian tradition in the works of three different authors: Marsilius of Padua, Dante Alighieri, and Lorenzo Valla. Dusenbury finds late medieval theories of secular power in these authors and focuses on the tension between Pilate's condemnation of Jesus as a king and the latter's ideas on renouncing any kingship. He claims that this unresolved tension, which characterizes Pilate's trial, can be considered an unnoticed element in Marsilius of Padua's radical rejection of the idea of papal monarchy in the *Defensor*.

The third part of the volume focuses on 'The Marsilian Moment' and sheds light on some examples of the presence of Marsilius's thought in the (early) modern period, while also focusing on some aspects of Marsilius's text that are relevant for contemporary debates. In her chapter, Serena Masolini considers how Tommaso Campanella referred to Marsilius — alongside other authors considered deplorable either for their Aristotelianism or for having denied the *potestas directa in temporalibus* of the pope — as a negative model suitable to better express, by counter-position, his own political vision. A particular focus is devoted to the writings that Campanella composed in the context of the pamphlet war generated by the conflict between Pope Paul V and the Republic of Venice in 1605–1607, putting them into dialogue with those composed by Giovanni Marsilio and Robert Bellarmine on the same occasion. In the context of the

Venetian Interdict, Marsilius's condemnation of heresy was indeed referred to by the supporters of the Holy See as a warning against the pro-Venetian writers, who were accused of taking inspiration from Marsilian doctrines.

Cary J. Nederman reads Marsilius against the backdrop of contemporary social science debates on the status of political science. Noting that it is hard to characterize the foundations of Marsilius's thought on political science in the Aristotelian tradition, Nederman makes two different arguments. First, he claims that in order to understand Marsilius's distance from the term 'political science', we have to consider the strong anti-papal dimension of his agenda in the *Defensor*. Second, and related to this claim, Nederman reads Marsilius's project in light of some important debates in contemporary social sciences. For him, Marsilius provides a theory of society that is grounded in a notion of individual choice and rational self-interest as compatible with the social settings in which they emerge. He thus reads Marsilius as a progenitor of modern theories of communitarianism.

Paying attention to the German reception of Marsilius's work, Frank Godthardt's chapter explores a theme that has received no attention at all, that is, the impact and development of Marsilius's ideas in the debates of the Third Reich under National Socialism. Analysing the work of three German academic scholars who lived in the first half of the twentieth century — Wilhelm Schneider-Windmüller, Richard Scholz (the editor of one of the modern Latin editions of Marsilius's text), and Friedrich Bock — Godthardt proves how these three figures read the *Defensor* as a work in which they could find ideas presenting many affinities with Germany's political order in the 1930s. Finally, Gregorio Piaia explores the intriguing role of the figure of Marsilius in Umberto Eco's famous novel, *The Name of the Rose*. He claims that within the context of the *anni di piombo* and the radical, violent ideas that characterized the Italian debate of the 1970s and early 1980s, many progressive intellectuals shifted to writing fiction in order to sublimate the defeat that they suffered on the ideological and political level. This is reflected in Eco's treatment of the figure of Marsilius who in the novel is a positive progressive figure whose actions are described as reflecting his intention to provide a programme based on the ideas of democracy and liberty.

The aim of the contributions that are collected in this edited volume pursues the generally acknowledged purpose, which is present in the most recent literature, that Marsilius studies should take into account the complex set of different contexts and milieux in which the Paduan was trained and out of which the *Defensor* emerged. At the same time, the volume has the ambition of opening several areas of exploration that can be addressed in future research on Marsilius. Among others, four can be listed.

The first important theme that requires more research lies in the Italian context from which the *Defensor* emerged. We saw Marsilius's affinity with one of his teachers, Peter of Abano, who was in Padua and in Paris, and his commitment to important Ghibelline leaders. Future research on Marsilius will have to further deepen two aspects that have remained relatively unexplored in the impact of the Italian context on the Paduan *magister*. The first is concerned with Marsilius's relationship with the Paduan milieu and Peter of Abano, which deserves a specific study of its own. Given the likelihood that Marsilius knew Peter's *Expositio* of the Pseudo-Aristotelian *Problemata*, Peter's naturalist approach to ethical and political problems may well be reflected in Marsilius's *Defensor*. In addition to this path of research, the other theme that connects Marsilius to the Italian context deals with his affinity to Italian late medieval and early modern republican thought. The possible implications of this relationship for debates on the republicanism of Marsilius's political thought is a crucial topic that fits with the most recent attempts to renew the very category of late medieval and early modern republicanism.[41]

The second important area of study that requires more research in the future is concerned with the Parisian context of Marsilius's political thought, which is still in its infancy, due in part to the fact that many of these sources remain unedited and difficult to access. Future research on this topic will have to consider, on the one hand, the link between the *Defensor* and seminal texts in theology and moral philosophy from the previous century that were widely available in the first years of the fourteenth century. On the other hand, future research should take up the possible influence of those *magistri* who were active in Paris at the beginning of the fourteenth century: among them, Walter Burley, Godfrey of Fontaines, Radulphus Brito, Bartholomew of Bruges, Thomas Wilton, John of Jandun, Thomas de Bailly, Jean de Pouilly, and many others. The recent publications of Peter of Auvergne's *Continuatio* and *Questiones* to Aristotle's *Politics*, edited respectively by Lidia Lanza and Marco Toste,[42] will also certainly contribute to a more comprehensive exploration of the relationship between Marsilius's *Defensor* and Peter of Auvergne's Aristotelian political ideas.

The third possible, and very rich, scenario for future research pertains specifically to Marsilius's relationship to the thought of his friend and colleague, John of Jandun. Surprisingly, the relationship between the two

---

41 For studies that substantively revise the notion of late medieval and early modern republicanism, see especially Hankins, *Virtue Politics*; Hankins, 'Exclusivist Republicanism and the Non-Monarchical Republic'; Pedullà, 'Humanist Republicanism'; as well as the recent study by Nederman, 'Post-Republicanism and Quasi-Cosmopolitanism'.

42 See Peter of Auvergne, *Scriptum super III–VIII libros*, ed. by Lanza, and Peter of Auvergne, *Questiones super I–VII libros Politicorum*, ed. by Toste.

has been the subject of very little research, probably because most of Jandun's works are still unedited.[43] Yet, the similarities and analogies between the two are likely far stronger than most Marsilian scholars have so far understood in both directions. Even if it seems that he did not directly comment on the *Nicomachean Ethics* and the *Politics*, Jandun discusses several ethical and political ideas in his philosophical works, for example, in his commentaries on the *Metaphysics*, on the *De anima*, and on the *Rhetoric*. Some of these discussions are quite similar to those of Marsilius, as is his overall approach to the relationship between reason and faith as well as to the relationship between religion and philosophy, which has important parallels in the *Defensor*.[44] In addition to this, John was very well acquainted with Jewish and Islamic sources that were widely available in the Parisian milieu. Jewish and Islamic sources — for example, al-Fārābī, Maimonides, and Ibn Rushd — might have had a far stronger impact on Marsilius than scholars have ever suggested, with the exception of Vasileios Syros's work.

The fourth and final avenue of future research on Marsilius that deserves further scrutiny is the question of the Marsilian moment. This volume explores some possible avenues of research. It pays attention to the appeal of Marsilius's theory in the context of the Venetian Interdict and on contemporary social science, and his influence on the thought of the Germany of the Third Reich along with the Italian leftist movements of the 1970s. However, the question of the influence of Marsilius's thought in the early modern period has remained relatively unexplored, above all in the literature available in English. Marsilius's text was widely read and known in certain Protestant contexts. What was the weight of his ideas in the Protestant movements of the sixteenth and seventeenth centuries? Did his ideas have any impact on thinkers such as Niccolò Machiavelli, Thomas Hobbes, and John Locke?[45] The hope is that this volume can represent a first and an early attempt to start grappling with some of the questions that still need to be addressed concerning one of the greatest political thinkers of the Middle Ages.

---

43 Within this first promising area of research, the relationship with John of Jandun is certainly an area that deserves further scrutiny in future research. Undoubtedly, Iacopo Costa and Jean-Baptiste Brenet's intention to edit John of Jandun's *Opera Omnia* can be a welcoming and helpful contribution to shed more light on the relationship between this author and Marsilius.

44 Some similarities between Marsilius's and John's ideas are already highlighted by Brenet, 'Multitude et *bene esse* chez Averroès et Dante'; Lambertini, 'Jandun's Question-Commentary'; Mulieri, 'Against Classical Republicanism'.

45 Aside from Piaia, *Marsilio da Padova nella Riforma e nella Controriforma*, an important piece of literature on the relationship between Marsilius and Hobbes can be found in Koch, 'Marsilius and Hobbes on Religion and Papal Power'. On the English reception of Marsilius,

Works Cited

Primary Sources

Chartularium Universitatis Parisiensis, ed. by Heinrich Denifle and Emile Chatelain, 4 vols (Paris: Delalain, 1889–1897)

Dante Alighieri, *Monarchia*, ed. by Prue Shaw, Le Opere di Dante Alighieri, 5 (Florence: Le Lettere, 2009)

Du Plessis d'Argentré, Carolus, *Collectio judiciorum de novis erroribus, qui ab initio duodecimi seculi post Incarnationem Verbi, usque ad annum 1713, in Ecclesia proscripti sunt & notati, censoria etiam judicia insignium academiarum, inter alias Parisiensis & Oxoniensis, tum Lovaniensis & Duacensis in Belgio, aliorumque Collegiorum Theologiae apud Germanos, Italos, Hispanos, Polonos, Hungaros, Lotharos, &c. cum notis, observationibus, & variis monumentis ad theologicas res pertinentibus*, 3 vols (Paris: Lambertus Coffin, 1724–1736)

John of Jandun, *Quaestiones perspicacissimi peripatetici Ioannis de Ianduno in duodecim libros metaphysicae* (Venice: apud Hieronymum Scotum, 1554; repr. Frankfurt a.M.: Minerva, 1966)

Mussato, Albertino, *Epistola ad magistrum Marsilium phisicum Paduanum*, in Jürgen Miethke, 'Die Briefgedichte des Albertino Mussato an Marsilius von Padua', *Pensiero politico medievale*, 6 (2008), 49–65 (pp. 62–64)

Peter of Auvergne, *Scriptum super III–VIII libros Politicorum Aristotelis*, ed. by Lidia Lanza (Wiesbaden: Reichert, 2021)

Peter of Auvergne, *Questiones super I–VII libros Politicorum: A Critical Edition and Study*, ed. by Marco Toste, Ancient and Medieval Philosophy, Ser. 1, 61 (Leuven: Leuven University Press, 2022)

Secondary Works

Aichele, Alexander, 'Heart and Soul of the State: Some Remarks Concerning Aristotelian Ontology and Medieval Theory of Medicine in Marsilius of Padua's *Defensor Pacis*', in *The World of Marsilius of Padua*, ed. by Gerson Moreno-Riaño, Disputatio, 5 (Turnhout: Brepols, 2006), pp. 163–86

Battocchio, Riccardo, *Ecclesiologia e politica in Marsilio da Padova*, Fonti e ricerche di storia ecclesiastica padovana, 31 (Padua: Istituto per la storia ecclesiastica padovana, 2005)

Billanovich, Giuseppe, 'Il preumanesimo padovano', in *Storia della cultura veneta*, II: *Il Trecento* (Vicenza: Neri Pozza, 1976), pp. 19–110

---

see also Simonetta, *Marsilio in Inghilterra*; Simonetta, *Dal Difensore della pace al Leviatano*. On the relationship between Machiavelli and Marsilius, see Condren, 'Marsilius of Padua and Machiavelli'. Some scholars are convinced that Machiavelli read Marsilius. See, for example, Cutinelli-Rèndina, *Chiesa e religione in Machiavelli*, pp. 295–301.

Black, Antony, *Political Thought in Europe, 1250–1450* (Cambridge: Cambridge University Press, 1992)

——, *The West and Islam: Religion and Political Thought in World History* (Oxford: Oxford University Press, 2008)

Brenet, Jean-Baptiste, 'Multitude et *bene esse* chez Averroès et Dante: Retour sur la *Monarchie* I, 3', in *Dante et l'averroisme*, ed. by Alain de Libera, Jean-Baptiste Brenet, and Irène Rosier-Catach, Docet omnia (Paris: Les Belles Lettres, 2019), pp. 357–83

Brett, Annabel, 'Introduction', in Marsilius of Padua, *The Defender of the Peace*, trans. by Annabel Brett, Cambridge Texts in the History of Political Thought (Cambridge: Cambridge University Press, 2005), pp. xi–lxi

——, 'Political Right(s) and Human Freedom in Marsilius of Padua', in *Transformations in Medieval and Early-Modern Rights Discourse*, ed. by Virpi Mäkinen and Petter Korkman, The New Synthese Historical Library, 59 (Dordrecht: Springer, 2006), pp. 95–116

Briguglia, Gianluca, *Marsilio da Padova*, Pensatori, 31 (Rome: Carocci, 2013)

——, 'The Minor Marsilius: The Other Works of Marsilius of Padua', in *A Companion to Marsilius of Padua*, ed. by Gerson Moreno-Riaño and Cary J. Nederman, Brill's Companions to the Christian Tradition, 31 (Leiden: Brill, 2012), pp. 265–303

——, 'Note sulle tendenze attuali della storiografia su Marsilio da Padova', *Giornale critico della filosofia italiana*, 1 (2020), 149–60

Cadili, Alberto, 'Marsilio da Padova amministratore della Chiesa ambrosiana', *Il Pensiero politico medievale*, 3–4 (2005–2006), 193–225

Collodo, Silvana, and Remy Simonetti, eds, *Filosofia naturale e scienze dell'esperienza fra medioevo e umanesimo: Studi su Marsilio da Padova, Leon Battista Alberti, Michele Savonarola*, Contributi alla storia dell'Università di Padova, 47 (Treviso: Antilia, 2012)

Condren, Conal, 'Democracy and the *Defensor Pacis*: On the English Language Tradition of Marsilian Interpretation', *Il Pensiero Politico*, 13 (1980), 301–06

——, 'Marsilius of Padua and Machiavelli', in *Comparing Political Thinkers*, ed. by Ross Fitzgerald (Oxford: Pergamon Press, 1980), pp. 94–115

Courtenay, William J., 'Marsilius of Padua at Paris', in *A Companion to Marsilius of Padua*, ed. by Gerson Moreno-Riaño and Cary J. Nederman, Brill's Companions to the Christian Tradition, 31 (Leiden: Brill, 2012), pp. 57–70

——, *Parisian Scholars in the Early Fourteenth Century: A Social Portrait*, Cambridge Studies in Medieval Life and Thought, Ser. 4, 41 (Cambridge: Cambridge University Press, 1999)

Cutinelli-Rèndina, Emanuele, *Chiesa e religione in Machiavelli*, Piste, 2 (Rome: Istituti editoriali e poligrafici internazionali, 1998)

De Lagarde, George, *La naissance de l'esprit laïque au déclin du moyen âge*, II: *Marsile de Padoue, ou, le premier théoricien de l'état laïque* (Saint-Paul-Trois-Châteaux: Drome; Vienna: Nauwelaerts, 1934); and III: *Le Defensor Pacis* (Louvain: Nauwelaerts, 1970)

Garnett, George, *Marsilius of Padua and 'the Truth of History'* (Oxford: Oxford University Press, 2006)

Gewirth, Alan, *Marsilius of Padua: The Defender of Peace*, I: *Marsilius of Padua and Medieval Political Philosophy*, Records of Civilization, Sources and Studies, 46 (New York: Columbia University Press, 1951)

Godthardt, Frank, 'The Life of Marsilius of Padua', in *A Companion to Marsilius of Padua*, ed. by Gerson Moreno-Riaño and Cary J. Nederman, Brill's Companions to the Christian Tradition, 31 (Leiden: Brill, 2012), pp. 13–55

——, 'The Philosopher as Political Actor — Marsilius of Padua at the Court of Ludwig the Bavarian: The Sources Revisited', in *The World of Marsilius of Padua*, ed. by Gerson Moreno-Riaño, Disputatio, 5 (Turnhout: Brepols, 2006), pp. 29–46

Hankins, James, 'Exclusivist Republicanism and the Non-Monarchical Republic', *Political Theory*, 38.4 (2010), 452–82

——, *Virtue Politics: Soulcraft and Statecraft in Renaissance Italy* (Cambridge, MA: Belknap Press of Harvard University Press, 2019)

Hyde, John K., *Society and Politics in Medieval Italy: The Evolution of Civil Life, 1000–1350*, New Studies in Medieval History (London: Springer, 1973)

Jones, Philip J., *The Italian City-State: From Commune to Signoria* (Oxford: Oxford University Press, 1997)

Kaye, Joel, *A History of Balance, 1250–1375: The Emergence of a New Model of Equilibrium and its Impact on Thought* (Cambridge: Cambridge University Press, 2014)

Koch, Bettina, 'Marsilius and Hobbes on Religion and Papal Power: Some Observations on Similarities', in *The World of Marsilius of Padua*, ed. by Gerson Moreno-Riaño, Disputatio, 5 (Turnhout: Brepols, 2006), pp. 189–209

——, *Zur Dis-/Kontinuität mittelalterlichen politischen Denkens in der neuzeitlichen politischen Theorie: Marsilius von Padua, Johannes Althusius und Thomas Hobbes im Vergleich*, Beiträge zur Politischen Wissenschaft, 137 (Berlin: Duncker & Humblot, 2005)

Lambertini, Roberto, 'Jandun's Question-Commentary on Aristotle's *Metaphysics*' in *A Companion to the Latin Medieval Commentaries on Aristotle's Metaphysics*, ed. by Fabrizio Amerini and Gabriele Galluzzo, Brill's Companions to the Christian Tradition, 43 (Leiden: Brill, 2013), pp. 385–411

——, 'Marsilius and the Poverty Controversy in *Dictio* II', in *A Companion to Marsilius of Padua*, ed. by Gerson Moreno-Riaño and Cary J. Nederman, Brill's Companions to the Christian Tradition, 31 (Leiden: Brill, 2012), pp. 229–63

————, 'The "Sophismata" Attributed to Marsilius of Padua', in *Sophisms in Medieval Logic and Grammar*, ed. by Stephen Read, Nijhoff International Philosophy Series, 48 (Dordrecht: Springer, 1993), pp. 86–102

Lanza, Lidia, 'Comprendere il consenso esaminando il dissenso: Aristotele e i commenti alla Politica di Pietro d'Alvernia', *Storia del pensiero politico*, 9.2 (2020), 233–50

Lee, Alexander, *Humanism and Empire: The Imperial Ideal in Fourteenth-Century Italy* (Oxford: Oxford University Press, 2018)

Marangon, Paolo, 'Marsilio tra preumanesimo e cultura della arti, ricerca sulle fonti padovane del I discorso del "Defensor Pacis"', in *Ad cogitationem scientiae festinare: Gli studi delle università e nei conventi di Padova nei Secoli XIII e XIV*, ed. by Paolo Marangon (Trieste: LINT, 1997), pp. 89–119

Miethke, Jürgen, *Politiktheorie im Mittelalter: Von Thomas von Aquin bis Wilhelm von Ockham* (Tübingen: Mohr Siebeck, 2008)

Moreno-Riaño, Gerson, ed., *The World of Marsilius of Padua*, Disputatio, 5 (Turnhout: Brepols, 2006)

————, and Cary J. Nederman, eds, *A Companion to Marsilius of Padua*, Brill's Companions to the Christian Tradition, 31 (Leiden: Brill, 2012)

Mulieri, Alessandro, 'Against Classical Republicanism: The Averroist Foundations of Marsilius of Padua's Political Thought', *History of Political Thought*, 40.2 (2019), 218–45

————, 'Marsilius of Padua and Peter of Abano: The Scientific Foundations of Law-Making in *Defensor Pacis*', *British Journal for the History of Philosophy*, 26.2 (2018), 276–96

Nederman, Cary J., *Community and Consent: The Secular Political Theory of Marsiglio of Padua's 'Defensor Pacis'* (Lanham, MD: Rowman & Littlefield, 1995)

————, 'Post-Republicanism and Quasi-Cosmopolitanism in Marsiglio of Padua's *Defensor pacis*', in *Al di là del Repubblicanesimo: Modernità politica e origini dello Stato*, ed. by Guido Cappelli, with the assistance of Giovanni De Vita, Quaderni della ricerca, 5 (Naples: UniorPress, 2020), pp. 131–46

Ottaviani, Didier, *La naissance de la science politique: Autour de Marsile de Padoue*, Politiques, 16 (Paris: Classiques Garnier, 2018)

Pedullà, Gabriele, 'Humanist Republicanism: Towards a New Paradigm', *History of Political Thought*, 41.1 (2020), 43–95

Pesenti, Tiziana, 'Per la tradizione del testamento di Pietro d'Abano', *Medioevo*, 6 (1980), 533–42

Piaia, Gregorio, *Marsilio da Padova nella Riforma e nella Controriforma: Fortuna ed interpretazione*, Pubblicazioni dell'Istituto di storia della filosofia e del Centro per ricerche di filosofia medioevale, Università di Padova, n.s., 24 (Padua: Antenore, 1977)

————, *Marsilio e dintorni: Contributi alla storia delle idee*, Miscellanea erudita, 61 (Padua: Antenore, 1999)

Pincin, Carlo, *Marsilio*, Pubblicazioni dell'Istituto di scienze politiche dell'Università di Torino, 17 (Turin: Giappichelli, 1967)

Quillet, Jeannine, *La philosophie politique de Marsile de Padoue*, L'Église et l'État au Moyen-Age, 14 (Paris: Vrin, 1970)

Schabel, Christopher D., *Theological Quodlibeta in the Middle Ages: The Fourteenth Century*, Brill's Companions to the Christian Tradition, 7 (Leiden: Brill, 2007)

Shogimen, Takashi, 'Medicine and the Body Politic in Marsilius of Padua's *Defensor pacis*', in *A Companion to Marsilius of Padua*, ed. by Gerson Moreno-Riaño and Cary J. Nederman, Brill's Companions to the Christian Tradition, 31 (Leiden: Brill, 2012), pp. 71–115

Simonetta, Stefano, *Dal Difensore della pace al Leviatano: Marsilio da Padova nel Seicento inglese*, Testi e studi, 155 (Milan: UNICOPLI, 2000)

——, *Marsilio in Inghilterra: Stato e Chiesa nel pensiero politico inglese fra XIV e XVII secolo*, Il Filarete, 195 (Milan: LED, 2000)

Siraisi, Nancy G., *Arts and Sciences at Padua: The Studium of Padua Before 1350*, Studies and Texts, 25 (Toronto: Pontifical Institute of Mediaeval Studies, 1973)

Skinner, Quentin, *The Foundations of Modern Political Thought*, 2 vols (Cambridge: Cambridge University Press, 1978)

Syros, Vasileios, 'Did the Physician from Padua Meet the Rabbi from Cordoba?', *Revue des études juives*, 170.1–2 (2011), 51–71

——, *Marsilius of Padua at the Intersection of Ancient and Medieval Traditions of Political Thought* (Toronto: University of Toronto Press, 2012)

——, *Die Rezeption der aristotelischen politischen Philosophie bei Marsilius von Padua: Eine Untersuchung zur ersten Diktion des 'Defensor pacis'*, Studies in Medieval and Reformation Traditions, 134 (Leiden: Brill, 2007)

Lambertini, Roberto, and Andrea Tabarroni, 'Le "Quaestiones super Metaphysicam" attribuite a Giovanni di Jandun: Osservazioni e problemi', *Medioevo*, 10 (1984), 41–104

Tierney, Brian, *Liberty and Law: The Idea of Permissive Natural Law, 1100–1800*, Studies in Medieval and Early Modern Canon Law, 12 (Washington, DC: Catholic University of America Press, 2014)

——, 'Marsilius on Rights', *Journal of the History of Ideas*, 52.1 (1991), 3–17

Toste, Marco, 'The Parts and the Whole, the Few Wise Men and the Multitude: Consent and Collective Decision Making in Two Medieval Commentaries on Aristotle's *Politics*', *Storia del pensiero politico*, 9.2 (2020), 209–32

Ullmann, Walter, *A History of Political Thought: The Middle Ages* (Harmondsworth: Penguin, 1965)

——, *Principles of Government and Politics in the Middle Ages* (London: Methuen, 1961)

Viroli, Maurizio, *From Politics to Reason of State: The Acquisition and Transformation of the Language of Politics, 1250–1600* (Cambridge: Cambridge University Press, 1992)

Weijers, Olga, *Le travail intellectuel à la Faculté des arts de Paris: Textes et maîtres (ca. 1200–1500)*, Studia artistarum (Turnhout: Brepols, 1994–)

PART 1

Marsilius's Sources

ROBERTO LAMBERTINI

Marsilius of Padua[*]

A Reader of Aristotle's Politica

Introduction

'Marsilius reads the writings of Aristotle with medieval eyes'. This metaphorical remark is taken from one of Jürgen Miethke's most recent works devoted to the Paduan thinker, and it can be seen as the starting point of the present chapter.[1] In 2012 in their own contribution to the Brill *Companion to Marsilius of Padua*, Gerson Moreno-Riaño and Cary J. Nederman recalled that 'the numerous references to Aristotle found within the *Defensor pacis* seem to weigh heavily in favour of reading Marsilius as a medieval Aristotelian'. They observed that Conal Condren, by contrast, had argued that Marsilius's references to ancient authors are rather rhetorical tools, and 'not evidence of any philosophical impulse'. Moreover, they pointed out that other scholars considered an Augustinian influence or a 'Ciceronian impulse' more effective than the Stagirite in influencing the *Defensor pacis*.[2] Gianluca Briguglia was therefore quite right in pointing out that the issue of the relation between Marsilius and Aristotle is still open and closely connected to the debate about so-called 'political Aristotelianism'.[3] Indeed, Briguglia's remark was confirmed when, a year later, Marco Toste suggested that Marsilius's treatment of the naturalness of human

---

[*] With minor modifications this is the text presented in Leuven in July 2018, with the addition of footnotes that do not aim at examining the enormous Marsilian bibliography but only at providing the most essential support to the claims contained in this chapter. There is, however, one exception: I had access to Toledo, Bib. Cap., MS 47.9 after July 2018. I am deeply indebted to Russell Friedman for this opportunity.

[1] Miethke, 'Einleitung', p. lii.

[2] Moreno-Riaño and Nederman, 'Marsilius of Padua's Principles of Secular Politics', p. 120.

[3] Briguglia, *Marsilio da Padova*, p. 68.

> **Roberto Lambertini** teaches Medieval History at the University of Macerata, Department of Studi Umanistici. His main field of interest is medieval intellectual history. One of his recent publications is *Francis, his Friars, and Economic Ethics: An Introduction* (2020).

Marsilius of Padua, ed. by Alessandro Mulieri, Serena Masolini, and Jenny Pelletier, Disputatio, 36 (Turnhout: Brepols, 2023), pp. 31–48

BREPOLS ❧ PUBLISHERS 10.1484/M.DISPUT-EB.5.132906

association is entirely consistent with the tradition of Latin commentaries on the *Politica*, and that Marsilius's position need not be traced back to any sources other than Aristotle as he was read and interpreted at the Arts Faculty in Paris.[4]

It goes without saying that in this ongoing discussion divergent interpretations of 'medieval Aristotelianism' are also at stake.[5] It is not the ambition of the present chapter to intervene directly in the discussion of whether Marsilius is or is not Aristotelian in some sense of the word.[6] It approaches the multifaceted issue of Marsilius's political Aristotelianism from a particular angle, focusing on some features of his attitude to the actual text of the *Politica*, or, to continue with the opening metaphor, on the perspective from which his 'medieval eyes' looked at Aristotle's political masterpiece in its Latin translation. To this purpose, I will first offer an overview of Marsilius's explicit references to the actual text of the *Politica* in the *Defensor pacis*, distinguishing among the different ways in which the Paduan philosopher appeals to Aristotle's text, for example, quoting literally or *ad sensum*. Second, I will formulate an explanation of the recurrent mismatches between the numbering of chapters of the *Politica* according to the standard edition and Marsilius's references. Finally, I offer some considerations on the strategy that Marsilius adopts in using the *Politica* in support of his claims.

References

Some features of Marsilius as a reader of the *Politica* can be obviously reconstructed only in an indirect way, from the writings where he shows himself to be acquainted with the text. This limits our field of investigation essentially to the *Defensor pacis*,[7] where I could identify roughly one hundred references to the *Politica*, including literal quotations, quotations *ad sensum*, mentions of a word or phrase, and references to book and chapter (without quoting a precise passage). For the present purpose, I will limit myself to passages where the reference is made explicit by Marsilius. A thorough analysis of implicit references to the *Politica* contained in the

---

4 Toste, 'The Naturalness of Human Association', pp. 165–68.

5 It obviously makes a great difference whether a scholar identifies a 'pattern of thought' as Aristotelian and studies the extent to which a given author conforms to such a pattern or investigates the textual relationships between certain medieval writings and the *Politica*. For various remarks on method, see Flüeler, 'Politischer Aristotelismus im Mittelalter'.

6 To mention only some examples: Nederman, *Community and Consent*; Nederman, 'The Meaning of "Aristotelianism"'; Piaia, '"Aristotelicus magis quam christianus"'; Toste, 'The Naturalness of Human Association', esp. pp. 165–68; now, Toste, 'La socievolezza umana'.

7 I will be using Scholz's edition.

Defensor pacis would be of great interest too but cannot be offered in the present contribution.

The sheer number of references (in a broad sense, from literal quotations to mentions in passing) is divided in a very unbalanced way between the three *dictiones* of the *Defensor*. Rather unsurprisingly, there are no quotations in *Dictio* III, a meagre five percent is found in *Dictio* II, which is twice as long as *Dictio* I, where all the rest are concentrated. References to the *Politica* are not distributed equally among the nineteen chapters of *Dictio* I either. To sum up, the bulk of references is to be found in the second part of *Dictio* I (more precisely Chapters 9 to 16), where Marsilius develops the most important tenets of his theory on law-making and on the election of rulers. Thanks to its dialectical structure (it is in fact structured as a *quaestio*, with *rationes quod sic* and *rationes quod non*), Chapter 16 has the most references (sixteen), while Chapters 6 (dealing with 'the origin of Christian priesthood'), 10, and 17 have none.[8]

Quotations

I consider 'literal quotations' all the passages of the *Defensor pacis* where Marsilius inserts a shorter or longer text taken from the *Politica*. According to my survey, more than half of the quotations contained in the *Defensor* fall in this category. It is, therefore, extremely unlikely that Marsilius was acquainted with the *Politica* only by means of a *florilegium*. I must admit that my knowledge of the *florilegia* from the *Politica* circulating especially in the Parisian milieu in the first decades of the fourteenth century is extremely limited.[9] However, as of now, I can declare that I have found no compelling evidence of the use of the *Auctoritates Aristotelis* or of any other *florilegium* that summarizes the main contents in the *Politica* in quasi-aphoristic statements.[10] If Marsilius had ever used such a collection,

---

8 In more detail, Chapter 16 ('Whether it is better for a polity to adopt a monarch by a new election each time, or to elect only one man together with his entire posterity, which is usually called hereditary succession') has sixteen references. Chapter 11 ('On the necessity of making laws'), Chapter 14 ('On the qualities of the perfect prince'), and Chapter 15 ('On the best way of instituting a principate') contain ten references each. Chapter 5 ('On the parts of the city'), Chapter 9 ('On the modes of instituting a royal monarchy'), Chapter 12 ('On the demonstrable efficient cause of human law'), and the tightly connected Chapter 13 ('Objections to what was said in the previous chapter') contain between five and ten references. Chapters 1 to 4, 18, and 19 have less than five references. Chapter 6 ('On the origin of Christian priesthood') unsurprisingly lacks any reference to the *Politica*, but the same holds true for Chapter 10 ('On differentiating and identifying this term "law"') and for Chapter 17 ('On the numerical unity of the supreme principate').
9 Cf. *Auctoritates Aristotelis*, ed. by Hamesse; Hamesse and Meirinhos, eds, *Les Auctoritates Aristotelis, leur utilisation et leur influence*.
10 Flüeler, *Rezeption und Interpretation*, esp. pp. 50–91, lists several examples of such *florileges*.

it must have been a list of literal excerpts, not of '*flores*'. As will be the case some decades later for William of Ockham's *Dialogus*, the most economical explanation of his relations to the *Politica* is that the author of the *Defensor pacis* had direct access to the text.[11]

Evidence strongly suggests, therefore, that the Paduan master had acquaintance with the text of the *Politica*. We must stress that scholars must still rely on Susemihl's critical edition of the *Politica*, which was designed mainly in support of his edition of the Greek text. As the German philologist active at the University of Greifswald remarked, the main reason for his choice is that William of Moerbeke's translation method allows us to infer what his Greek model was on the basis of his Latin rendering.[12] The outstanding Leonina edition of Aquinas's *Sententia libri Politicorum* includes a partial edition of the text of the *Politica*, which is planned as a reconstruction of the text actually used by Aquinas, and is therefore limited to the first two books and a fragment of the third.[13] The *translatio prior imperfecta* is even more limited and, according to my comparison, did not play any role in Marsilius's access to the *Politica*, as expected.[14] Very recently, publishing her critical edition of Peter of Auvergne's *Scriptum super III–VIII libros Politicorum*, Lidia Lanza has made available to the scholarly world an edition of the *Politica* (Books III to VIII) too, which does not claim to be critical, but is excellent and extremely useful.[15]

In anticipation of the Aristoteles Latinus Project producing a complete critical edition of the whole *Politica*,[16] I have had to content myself with Susemihl's groundbreaking accomplishment, although his idea of introducing a different order among the books (that is I–III, VII–VIII, IV, VI, V) is torturous for medievalists. Leaving aside the question of the correctness

---

11 Lambertini, 'Wilhelm von Ockham als Leser der "Politica"'.

12 The lack of an updated critical edition of William of Moerbeke's translation of Aristotle's *Politica* is one of the major obstacles for contemporary scholarship. I had to rely on Aristotle, *Politicorum libri Octo cum vetusta translatione Guilelmi de Moerbeka*, ed. by Susemihl, where the Latin text is edited mainly as a further witness for the Greek original. For Susemihl's remarks, cf. his introduction, p. vi, pp. xxxi–xxxiv. Only occasionally do I refer to other available partial editions of the *Politica*.

13 Thanks to the efforts of Hyacinthe-F. Dondaine and Louis-J. Bataillon in Thomas Aquinas, *Sententia libri Politicorum*.

14 Aristotle, *Politica, Translatio prior imperfecta*; about the relationship between the two translations, which are both attributed to William of Moerbeke, cf. Schütrumpf, *The Earliest Translations of Aristotle's Politics*, esp. pp. 9–25.

15 Peter of Auvergne, *Scriptum super III–VIII libros Politicorum*, published after I had submitted the first draft of the present chapter to the editors. Therefore, I could profit only in part from Lidia Lanza's important achievement, which supersedes Peter of Auvergne's editions by Spiazzi (as continuation of Thomas Aquinas's commentary on the *Politics*) and by Grech, *The Commentary of Peter of Auvergne*.

16 For the Aristoteles Latinus Project, see <https://hiw.kuleuven.be/dwmc/research/al> [accessed 5 April 2023].

of this reconstruction of the Greek original, it is certain that the order of the books adopted by Susemihl was unknown to William of Moerbeke and the following tradition. The rather obvious result of my preliminary research, which is provisional at this point, is that Marsilius's quotations match Moerbeke's translation very well, with some unsurprising variants. In the current state of our knowledge, it is almost impossible to ascertain whether these variants stem from the copy of the *Politica* that Marsilius would have used, or whether they are due to the manuscript tradition of the *Defensor* itself.

The *Defensor pacis* is an extremely structured text, unusually full of internal cross-references to preceding chapters and to following chapters and paragraphs of the work on occasion as well. One of the most extreme cases is represented by a passage where Marsilius refers to a following chapter. In that chapter the reader will find the complete text from the *Politica*, which the previous chapter mentions only by book and chapter.[17] Such features reveal very careful redactional work. Richard Scholz traced back the French and the German family of manuscripts to two editorial stages. Marsilius is, therefore, very likely to have continued his careful editing even after leaving Paris to find a more secure haven at the court of Louis of Bavaria.[18]

Books, Chapters, and Manuscripts: A New Hypothesis

Marsilius is very careful in referring to the *Politica*; most quotations are accompanied by a reference to book and chapter. I noticed only one mistake, which Scholz had already detected, where Marsilius refers to Book II while the quoted text is actually contained in Book I.[19] This holds true for the books. The chapters, on the contrary, lead to a question which is much more complex and intriguing. In almost all cases, the numbering of the books matches the standard modern editions of the *Politica*, but the numbers of the chapters are almost always different. It is unlikely that this can be explained as an accident in the manuscript tradition because of the extension and consistency of the mismatch. In some cases, moreover, Marsilius repeats the reference to the same passage in identical terms. The existence of different internal divisions of the books into chapters is not

---

17 *DP*, I, 5.8, ed. by Scholz, p. 24.
18 Scholz, 'Einleitung' in Marsilius of Padua, *Defensor Pacis*, pp. xlvi–xlviii; Miethke, 'Einleitung', pp. xliii–xlviii; cf. Fidora and Tischler, 'Zwischen Avignon, München und Tortosa'.
19 *DP*, I, 16.4, ed. by Scholz, p. 97.

36 ROBERTO LAMBERTINI

surprising.[20] A comparison between Albert the Great's commentary and the commentaries by Thomas Aquinas and Peter of Auvergne on Book III shows that they do not use the same chapter numbering.[21] Unexpectedly, then, Marsilius's division of books into chapters not only differs from the one adopted by Albert,[22] but also from what we could call the 'standard' commentary that resulted from the merging of Aquinas's fragment with Peter's 'continuation'.[23] Many clues point to the fact that Marsilius used a copy of the *Politica* first-hand that contained different chapter divisions. In particular, he seems to have had at his disposal a version that includes fewer but longer chapters. A thorough examination of the manuscript tradition of William of Moerbeke's translation would be necessary to corroborate this hypothesis. As of now, however, I can point to a manuscript, namely Toledo, Biblioteca Capitular (formerly known as del Cabildo), 47.9, folios 98^r–211^v,[24] whose chapter divisions almost entirely overlap with the one presupposed by the *Defensor pacis*.[25] For example, in *DP*, I, 9.5, Marsilius quotes the following sentence: 'Unde 4° Politice, 8° capitulo scribitur: *Erant autem propterea quod secundum legem regales*, monarchie

---

20 Franz Susemihl himself pointed to this feature of the Latin manuscript tradition; see his introduction to *Politica*, p. xxxix.

21 Book III provides a striking example: Albert divides it into ten chapters (cf. Albertus Magnus, *Politicorum Lib. VIII*, ed. by Borgnet, pp. 201–311), while Peter of Auvergne has sixteen: Peter of Auvergne, *Scriptum*, ed. by Lanza, pp. 5–137. As is well known, Aquinas is incomplete: *Sententia libri Politicorum*, III, ed. by Dondaine and Bataillon, pp. A185–A205.

22 About Albert's commentary on the *Politica*, see the groundbreaking and still unsurpassed Fioravanti, '"Politiae Orientalium et Aegyptiorum"'; see also, among many other contributions, Miethke, 'Praktische Bedürfnisse'; Bertelloni, 'Die "Philosophia Moralis" als Enzyklopädie menschlicher Handlungen'.

23 In addition to what happens for Book III, divergences emerge also for Book II: Albert's commentary on Book II is divided into twelve chapters (*Politicorum Lib. VIII*, II, ed. by Borgnet, pp. 83–200); Aquinas's *Sententia* on Book II includes seventeen chapters (*Sententia libri Politicorum*, II, ed. by Dondaine and Bataillon, pp. A119–A183); Marsilius refers to nine chapters, and the Toledo manuscript (see following note) divides Book II into nine chapters as well.

24 I owe the possibility of working on the digitized copies of a microfilm of this manuscript to the generosity of Russell Friedman. Unfortunately, due to technical difficulties, I am not able to give a reliable pagination. I hope to be able to do so in a future publication. The Toledo manuscript is, so to speak, an 'old acquaintance' of the studies about the reception of Aristotle and Aristotelianism in the Latin West. Cf. Alexander of Aphrodisia, *Commentaire sur les Météores d'Aristote*, ed. by Smet, pp. xlix–lix; Hyacinthe Dondaine and Louis-J. Bataillon ('Préface' to Thomas Aquinas, *Sententia libri Politicorum*, p. A50, p. A53, p. A57) regard this thirteenth-century manuscript of Italian origin as very important for the textual tradition of Moerbeke's translation. An interesting contribution of an art historian contains further remarks and references to previous bibliography: Salvatelli, 'Suggestioni da una libraria cardinalizia'.

25 Mismatches amount roughly to 10 percent of the total.

MARSILIUS OF PADUA 37

scilicet *et quia monarchizabant voluntariis*', attributing it to *Politica*, IV, 8.[26] In Susemihl's edition, the same sentence is in Chapter 10.[27] In the copy of the *Politica* preserved in Toledo, it is in Chapter 8. Again, in *DP*, I, 9.2, Marsilius literally quotes the *Politica*, inserting his own explanations according to the pattern of an *expositio litterae*: 'Valencius autem — id est prestancius ad iudicandum — cui non adest, quod passionale omnino id est affeccio que iudicium pervertere potest, quam cui connaturale'.[28] According to the Paduan philosopher, this sentence can be read in *Politica*, Book III, Chapter 9. In Susemihl's edition, the passage is in Chapter 15,[29] but in the Toledo manuscript it is contained in Chapter 9. Finally, while formulating arguments in favour of hereditary monarchy (to refute them) in *DP*, I, 16.1, Marsilius resorts to some of Aristotle's remarks in the context of Aristotle's criticism of Plato's *Republic*. Marsilius writes: 'Unde 2° Politice, capitulo 1° circa medium inquit Aristoteles: *Minime enim cura sortitur, quod plurimorum est commune*'.[30] According to Susemihl, this is in Chapter 3,[31] but in the Toledo manuscript can be found in a very long Chapter 1. Examples could be multiplied, but they would not add much to the reasonable assumption that, while working on the *Defensor pacis*, Marsilius had access to a copy of the *Politica* that carried a chapter division at least very similar to the one witnessed by Toledo, Biblioteca Capitular, MS 47.9. To my knowledge, this hypothesis was not previously formulated in the field of Marsilian studies. The scrutiny of the whole manuscript tradition of Moerbeke's translation, essential to the critical edition of the *Politica*, could be decisive in verifying it.

Building on the assumption that Marsilius did indeed have a copy of the *Politica* available and read it carefully, one can observe that he quotes from all of its eight books. Some of them, namely Book VI (in which Aristotle discusses constitutions where the basic forms of government are mixed) and Book VIII (the second book devoted to the 'ideal' *polis*), receive far less attention than others. Book III (where Aristotle discusses citizenship, classifies different forms of constitutions, and compares their

---

26 *DP*, I, 9.5, ed. by Scholz, p. 44; trans. by Brett, p. 47: 'Hence Aristotle writes in *Politics* IV, chapter 8: they were royal (sc. monarchies) because they were according to law and because they exercise monarchies over the voluntary'.

27 Aristotle, *Politica*, IV, 10, 1295a15–16, ed. by Susemihl, p. 415; ed. by Lanza, p. 194 (according to Peter of Auvergne's division into chapters, this passage is in Ch. 9).

28 *DP*, I, 9.2, ed. by Scholz, p. 52; trans. by Brett, p. 57: 'That has the advantage i.e. is superior for the purpose of judging which entirely lacks an element of passion, i.e. the affection that can corrupt a judgement over to which it is innate'.

29 Aristotle, *Politica*, III, 15, 1286a17–18, ed. by Susemihl, p. 221; ed. by Lanza, p. 113 (according to Peter of Auvergne's division in chapters, this passage is in Ch. 14).

30 *DP*, I, 16.1, ed. by Scholz, p. 95; trans. by Brett, p. 99: 'Hence Aristotle says, *Politics* II, chapter 1, about half-way through: That which is in common to many receives little care'.

31 Aristotle, *Politica*, II, 3, 1261b33–34, ed. by Susemihl, p. 65; ed. by Dondaine and Bataillon, p. A124.

advantages and disadvantages), by contrast, by far outnumbers the quotations from all the other books. One third of the quotations to the *Politica* refer to Book III. Of these, Marsilius quotes considerably more from the final chapters of Book III, where the discussion on the relationship between law and ruler, monarchy, and rule of the many, and of the different kinds of monarchy provide Marsilius with interesting material. He quotes less from its opening chapters containing Aristotle's famous classification of constitutions. Some years later, in the third part of his *Dialogus*, Ockham's preference is also for Book III of the *Politica*, where he finds arguments for and against the monarchical government of the Church.[32] At second place for most frequently quoted, we find Book V (on the causes of political revolutions and the means of preserving the existing regime). At third place, with almost the same number of quotations, is Book I (devoted to the origin of political community, slavery, and household), understandably represented by its opening chapters.

It is expected that a medieval author approaching an Aristotelian text also makes use of a literal commentary, if available, and then often without quoting it explicitly. Within the field of the reception of Aristotle's *Politica* we can see this in Giles of Rome's *De regimine principum*,[33] in Ockham's *Dialogus*,[34] and in Walter Burley.[35] In all these cases, the Aquinas–Auvergne commentary plays a pivotal role that made it the 'standard-commentary' on the *Politica*, overshadowing Albert's exposition.[36] Besides having prepared a badly needed critical edition of the text, Lidia Lanza has written interesting chapters on the long history of the reception of the Aquinas–Auvergne commentary.[37] It is legitimate to think that Marsilius also made use of that commentary, and many scholars including Flüeler, Syros, and Toste have pointed to the influence of Peter of Auvergne's question commentary on the *Defensor pacis*.[38] The search for texts that have or could have been used by Marsilius while writing his *Defensor pacis* does not amount to 'dissolv[ing] his thought into its medieval context',[39] since a medieval author can make intensive use of *auctoritates* and commentaries and, at the same time, be innovative in

---

32 Lambertini, 'Wilhelm von Ockham als Leser der "Politica"'; William of Ockham, *Dialogus*, 3, 1, ed. by Kilcullen and others, p. 172; cf. William of Ockham, *De potestate papae*, trans. by Miethke, p. 222.

33 Lambertini, '*Philosophus videtur tangere tres rationes*'.

34 Cf. note 32, above.

35 Lambertini, 'Burley's Commentary on the Politics'.

36 Cf. Lanza, '*Ei autem qui de politia considerat…*'.

37 Lanza, 'The "Scriptum super III–VIII libros Politicorum"'.

38 Cf. Flüeler, *Rezeption und Interpretation*, pp. 120–31; Syros, 'The Sovereignty of the Multitude'; Toste, 'An Original Way of Commenting', esp. pp. 348–53; Peter of Auvergne, *Questiones super I–VII libros Politicorum*, ed. by Toste.

39 Moreno-Riaño and Nederman, 'Marsilius of Padua's Principles of Secular Politics', p. 120.

his conclusions.[40] Marsilius, however, shows a remarkable unequivocal independence already as a reader of the *Politica*, and it is not easy to detect his borrowings from any literal commentary that I know of. This can be shown with an example taken from *DP*, I, 13.2, where Marsilius writes that 'eo quod *impossibilium* est *civitatem aristocratizantem*, id est secundum virtutem gubernatam, *non bene legibus disponi* ut habetur 4° Politice, capitulo 7°'.[41] A literal quotation of the *Politica* is embedded here, namely: 'Impossibilium civitatem aristocratizantem, non bene legibus disponi',[42] where Marsilius has inserted his own gloss to 'aristocratizantem', 'id est secundum virtutem gubernatam'. Commenting on the same passage, Peter of Auvergne had interpreted 'aristocratizantem' in a different way, which is most probably a more accurate rendering of Aristotle's text: 'que regitur principatu aristocratico'.[43] Albert too, before Peter of Auvergne, had moved in the same line of interpretation.[44] One can find more cases where the Paduan master adds a personal gloss after expressions such as 'id est' or 'supple' that are typical of the language of the literal commentary. The passage quoted above is an example of him bending the *Politica* to meet the needs of his own argument in favour of a key tenet of his theory, namely that the authority to legislate belongs to the multitude of the citizens.

An Attentive and Skilful Reader

So far, I have devoted my attention to literal quotations. As already noted, however, the *Defensor* also contains several references to the *Politica* that are merely passing references to book and chapter, as is the case, for example, in *DP*, I, 5.1: 'secundum Aristotelis sentenciam 7° Politice, capit-

---

40 Many interpreters have insisted on the originality of Marsilius's contribution to political thought. Besides Dolcini, *Introduzione a Marsilio da Padova*, pp. 18–19, 28–29, one can mention, among others, Nederman in many contributions and Briguglia, *Il pensiero politico medievale*, p. 155, whose description of Marsilius as 'pensatore ghibellino' is not meant to question Marsilius's originality, since no other supporter of Italian Ghibellinism was able to offer a comparable contribution to political theory.

41 *DP*, I, 13.2, ed. by Scholz, p. 71; trans. by Brett, pp. 74–75: 'it is impossible for a city which is aristocratic, i.e. governed according to virtue, not to be well ordered with laws, as is maintained in *Politics* IV, chapter 7'.

42 Aristotle, *Politica*, IV, 8, 1294a1, ed. by Susemihl, p. 408; ed. by Lanza, p. 183. It should be noted that, according to the standard numbering and to Susemihl's edition, the literal quotation refers to Book IV, Chapter 8; for Marsilius, as in the Toledo manuscript, the chapter is 7.

43 Peter of Auvergne, *Scriptum super III–VIII libros Politicorum*, IV, 7, p. 186.

44 Albertus Magnus, *Politicorum Lib. VIII*, IV, 7, ed. by Borgnet, p. 363: 'id est principatu aristocratico gubernatam'.

ulo 7°',[45] or, even less precisely to books alone: 'De hiis sufficienter tradidit Aristoteles 3° et 4° sue Politice'.[46] Sometimes it is not difficult to identify the passage Marsilius must have had in mind, but in other cases this can be very puzzling to scholars. The most telling example is the passage in *DP*, I, 12.4, where the Paduan philosopher, speaking of the *valencior pars*, refers to Book VI, Chapter 2 of the *Politica*: 'Valenciorem verum partem oportet attendere secundum policiarum consuetudinem honestam, vel hanc determinare secundum sentenciam Aristotelis, 6° *Politice*, capitulo 2°'.[47] Not only are specialists divided on the interpretation of this 'prevailing part', that is to say whether it should be understood qualitatively or quantitatively,[48] but they are also at odds when it comes to identifying the passage in the *Politica* that Marsilius is referring to, since he limits himself to giving the number of the chapter without quoting a specific passage. Different solutions to the problem have been put forward, including an error in the manuscript tradition or even, as Carlo Dolcini does, to adopt Susemihl's thesis that the books of the *Politica* had a different order, at least in the case of the copy that was available to Marsilius.[49] I would rather point to the fact that in the same chapter Marsilius refers again to Book VI of the *Politica*, which he quotes literally: 'Idem 6° eiusdem capitulo 6° *Nullus profectus est fieri quidem sentencias de iustis, has autem non accipere finem*'.[50] In this case, Marsilius's reference to the book corresponds to the standard division while the chapters do not match: the *Defensor* has 6, which in the usual numbering is Chapter 8. This discrepancy can be explained by having recourse to the Toledo manuscript, where in fact the passage is contained in Chapter 6. This second quotation, which occurs only two paragraphs after the puzzling reference related to the concept of *valencior pars*, strongly suggests that Marsilius indeed meant Book VI also in the first case, making it rather unlikely that he was following a different order of the books or that an error affected the whole manuscript tradition.

If we take Marsilius's reference at face value and assume that he had indeed a copy of the *Politica* at hand in which the numbering of the

---

45 *DP*, I, 5.1, ed. by Scholz, p. 20; trans. by Brett, p. 22: 'according to the opinion of Aristotle in Politics VII, chapter 7'.

46 *DP*, I, 8.2, ed. by Scholz, p. 37; trans. by Brett, p. 41: 'For Aristotle said enough on the subject of them in books III and IV of his Politics'.

47 *DP*, I, 12.4, ed. by Scholz, pp. 64–65; trans. by Brett, pp. 67–68: 'The prevailing part of the citizens should be identified from the honourable custom of polities, or determined according to the opinion of Aristotle, Politics VI, chapter 2'.

48 Cf. Briguglia, *Marsilio da Padova*, pp. 103–04.

49 Dolcini, *Introduzione a Marsilio da Padova*, pp. 30–31.

50 *DP*, I, 12.6, ed. by Scholz, pp. 66–67; trans. by Brett, pp. 69–70: 'And in book VI, chapter 5: There is no profit — says Aristotle — if sentences are passed about what is just, but these are not carried out'. Note that Brett refers to Chapter 5 instead of Chapter 6, as Scholz does; for Aristotle's text, cf. Aristotle, *Politica*, VI, 8, 1322a5–6, ed. by Susemihl, p. 488; ed. by Lanza, p. 421.

chapters was close to that witnessed by the Toledo manuscript, the result would be that he is pointing to Chapter 3 in the standard chapter division of Book VI, that is, the text between 1318a10 and 1318b5.[51] In these lines, Aristotle discusses whether decisions should be taken according to the arithmetic majority, or modifications should be introduced, which take into account differences in wealth. This is not an explicit definition of the *valencior pars*, but Aristotle tackles an issue here that is indeed related. In commenting on this passage of the *Defensor*, scholars such as Cesare Vasoli had already suggested that Marsilius, despite writing Chapter 2, ought to have meant Chapter 3 or 4 of Book VI.[52] As shown above, Marsilius is likely to have used a copy of the *Politica* similar to that witnessed by Toledo, Biblioteca Capitular, MS 47.9, where Chapter 2 of Book VI corresponds to Chapter 3 of the standard division. One could observe that Aristotle does not explain how to determine 'the prevailing part of the citizen' in Chapter 3 of Book VI either, but rather leaves the discussion open,[53] so that the puzzle of the *valencior pars* remains at least in part unsolved.

An answer to this reasonable objection should take into consideration Marsilius's general attitude towards the *Politica*. As we have seen, the author of the *Defensor pacis* has no difficulty in quoting Moerbeke's translation literally with noteworthy precision. Sometimes he refers to passages only *ad sensum*. In other cases, he chooses to refer to a larger portion of the text, to one chapter, or even to more chapters. For example, in *DP*, I, 2.3, Marsilius writes 'Suscipiamus cum Aristotele primo et quinto Politice sue, capitulis 2 et 3, civitatem esse velut animal seu animalem naturam quandam'.[54] This, incidentally, is an assertion that recent scholarship has particularly underscored as an important principle in Marsilian political thought,[55] suggesting that the source of this organistic approach can be found in Marsilius's studies in medicine.[56] Scholarship has so far identified two passages in the *Politica* that can match Marsilius's references:[57] in Book I, the passage where Aristotle maintains that in all composite bodies,

---

51 Aristotle, *Politica*, VI, 2, 1318a10–1318b5, ed. by Susemihl, pp. 463–66; ed. by Lanza, pp. 389–90.

52 Cf. *DP*, ed. by Vasoli, in particular the notes on pp. 362–65.

53 Cf. e.g., Geiger, 'Die Einrichtung von Demokratien und Oligarchien'.

54 *DP*, I, 2.3, ed. by Scholz, p. 11; trans. by Brett, p. 12: 'Let us suppose with Aristotle in the first and fifth books of his *Politics*, chapters 2 and 3 respectively, that the city is like a kind of animal or animal nature'.

55 Cf. Syros, *Marsilius of Padua at the Intersection*, esp. pp. 21–22, pp. 108–13; Kaye, *A History of Balance*, pp. 299–322. For critical remarks, see Toste, 'La socievolezza umana', esp. p. 27.

56 Cf. e.g. Shogimen, 'Medicine and the Body Politic', who discusses this passage esp. at pp. 83–84.

57 Cf. *DP*, ed. by Vasoli, p. 354; Richard Scholz had already pointed to these two references in his critical edition of the *Defensor pacis*, cf. p. 11 n. 1.

and therefore in all animated bodies, parts can be kept together only if there is a hierarchical relation among them;[58] as for Book v, Marsilius is likely to have had in mind the text where Aristotle writes that the unbalanced growth of one part of the city jeopardizes the harmony of the whole, just as in living bodies.[59] As a matter of fact, Aristotle does not explicitly state in either passage that the city is like a living body. Rather, he uses analogies from which one might draw the conclusion that the city can be considered to be like an animal.

Except for the cases where Marsilius wants to avoid needless repetition for brevity's sake, it is therefore arguable that he opts for a generic reference when he has no literal quotation available but is persuaded (or wants to persuade his own readers) that the Aristotelian text as a whole supports his claim. This is not surprising, since many medieval authors tend to look for confirmation of their own positions in the *Politica*. This is true for Giles of Rome, who presents Aristotle as a supporter of the view that monarchy is the very best constitution. Marsilius shares this attitude towards the Philosopher although he reads Aristotle from a very different perspective than Giles's, holding political positions that diverge from those held by the author of the *De regimine principum*.[60]

Conclusions

In conclusion, Marsilius emerges as an attentive and knowledgeable reader of the *Politica*. He mastered almost the entire text, unlike other authors, who seem to have focused their attention on a few, well-known passages. In his effort to trace back his position to the teachings of the Philosopher, Marsilius could also be very precise in referring to the text of the *Politica*. The discrepancies in his numbering of the chapters can be explained by the use of a manuscript that witnesses a chapter division that differs from the division that scholars consider 'standard' today. When he opts for more

---

58 Aristotle, *Politica*, I, 5, 1254a31–32, ed. by Susemihl, p. 17: 'quaecumque enim ex pluribus constituta sunt et fit unum aliquod commune, sive ex coniunctis sive ex divisis, in omnibus videtur principans et subiectum. Et hoc ex omni natura inest animatis: et enim in non participantibus vita est quidam principatus'; ed. by Dondaine and Bataillon, p. A85.

59 Aristotle, *Politica*, v, 3, 1302b33–36, ed. by Susemihl, pp. 506–07: 'Fiunt autem et propter excrescentiam que praeter proportionem transmutationes politiarum sicut enim corpus ex partibus componitur et oportet augeri proportionaliter, ut maneat commensuratio, si autem non, corrumpitur'; ed. by Lanza, p. 256.

60 For instance, they disagree on hereditary monarchy. See e.g. Lambertini, '*Philosophus videtur tangere tres rationes*', pp. 316–18, and Nederman, *Community and Consent*, pp. 109–15.

generic references, this is arguably a sign that he is persuaded that his claim can be potentially supported by a general reference to a chapter or even a larger section of the *Politica*. In sum, Marsilius had read Aristotle's *Politica* very well and could just as well read into it.

Works Cited

Manuscripts and Archival Sources

Toledo, Biblioteca Capitular (formerly del Cabildo), MS 47.9

Primary Sources

Albertus Magnus, *Politicorum libri VIII*, vol. VIII of *Opera Omnia*, ed. by Auguste Borgnet (Paris: Vivès, 1891)

Alexander of Aphrodisia, *Commentaire sur les Météores d'Aristote*, ed. by Alfonz J. Smet, Corpus Latinum Commentariorum in Aristotelem Graecorum, 4 (Louvain: Publications Universitaires de Louvain; Paris: Nauwelaerts, 1968)

Aristotle, *Politica, Translatio prior imperfecta interprete Guillelmo de Moerbeka (?)*, ed. by Pierre Michaud-Quantin, Aristoteles Latinus, 29.1 (Bruges: Desclée de Brouwer, 1961)

——, *Politicorum libri octo cum vetusta translatione Guilelmi de Moerbeka*, ed. by Franz Susemihl (Leipzig: Teubner, 1872)

Auctoritates Aristotelis, in *Les Auctoritates Aristotelis: Un florilège médiéval. Étude historique et édition critique*, ed. by Jacqueline Hamesse, Philosophes médiévaux, 17 (Louvain: Publications Universitaires; Paris: Nauwelaerts, 1974), pp. 111–335

Marsilius of Padua, *The Defender of the Peace*, trans. by Annabel Brett, Cambridge Texts in the History of Political Thought (Cambridge: Cambridge University Press, 2005)

——, *Defensor pacis*, ed. by Richard Scholz, Monumenta Germaniae Historica: Fontes iuris germanici antiqui in usum scholarum separatim editi, 7.2 (Hannover: Hahn, 1933)

——, *Il difensore della pace: Primo discorso*, trans. and commented by Cesare Vasoli (Venice: Marsilio, 1991)

Peter of Auvergne, *Questiones super I–VII libros Politicorum: A Critical Edition and Study*, ed. by Marco Toste, Ancient and Medieval Philosophy, Ser. 1, 61 (Leuven: Leuven University Press, 2022)

——, *Scriptum super III librum*, in *The Commentary of Peter of Auvergne on Aristotle's 'Politics', the Inedited Part, Book III, less. I–VI. Introduction and Critical Text*, ed. by Gundisalvus Maria Grech (Rome: Desclée, 1967), pp. 73–129

——, *Scriptum super III–VIII libros Politicorum Aristotelis*, ed. with an introduction by Lidia Lanza, Scrinium Friburgense, 50 (Wiesbaden: Reichert, 2021)

Thomas Aquinas, *In libros politicorum Expositio*, ed. by Raimondo M. Spiazzi (Turin: Marietti, 1951)

————, *Sententia libri Politicorum*, [ed. by Hyacinthe Dondaine and Louis-J. Bataillon], in *Opera Omnia iussu Leonis XIII edita*, vol. XLVIII (Rome: Thomas Aquinas Foundation, 1971), pp. A69–A205

William of Ockham, *De potestate papae et cleri / Die Amtsvollmacht von Papst und Klerus, III.1: Dialogus*, vol. I, trans. and commented by Jürgen Miethke (Freiburg. i.B.: Herder, 2015)

————, *Dialogus, Part 2, Part 3, Tract 1*, ed. by John Kilcullen, John Scott, Jan Ballweg, and Volker Leppin (Oxford: Oxford University Press, 2011)

Secondary Works

Bertelloni, Francisco, 'Die "Philosophia Moralis" als Enzyklopädie menschlicher Handlungen: Zu Alberts des Großen Kenntnisnahme von der Aristotelischen "Politik"', in *Handlung und Wissenschaft: Die Epistemologie der praktischen Wissenschaften im 13. und 14. Jahrhundert / Action and Science: The Epistemology of the Practical Sciences in the 13th and 14th Century*, ed. by Matthias Lutz-Bachmann and Alexander Fidora, Wissenskultur und gesellschaftlicher Wandel, 29 (Berlin: Akademie Verlag 2008), pp. 45–59

Briguglia, Gianluca, *Marsilio da Padova*, Pensatori, 31 (Rome: Carocci 2013)

————, *Il pensiero politico medievale*, Piccola biblioteca Einaudi: Mappe, 68 (Turin: Einaudi, 2018)

Dolcini, Carlo, *Introduzione a Marsilio da Padova*, I filosofi, 63 (Rome: Laterza, 1995)

Fidora, Alexander, and Matthias M. Tischler, 'Zwischen Avignon, München und Tortosa: Die Defensor-Pacis-Handschrift des Marsilius von Padua in der Bibliothek Benedikts XIII.', *Scriptorium*, 69 (2015), 179–89

Fioravanti, Gianfranco, '"Politiae Orientalium et Aegyptiorum": Alberto Magno e la Politica aristotelica', *Annali della Scuola Normale Superiore di Pisa*, Ser. 3, 9 (1979), 195–246; repr. in Gianfranco Fioravanti, *Da Parigi a San Gimignano: Un itinerario del pensiero filosofico medievale* (Rome: Aracne 2021), pp. 169–229

Flüeler, Christoph, 'Politischer Aristotelismus im Mittelalter: Einleitung', *Vivarium*, 40.1 (2002), 1–13

————, *Rezeption und Interpretation der aristotelischen 'Politica' im späten Mittelalter*, vol. II, Bochumer Studien zur Philosophie, 19 (Amsterdam: Grüner, 1992)

Geiger, Rolf, 'Die Einrichtung von Demokratien und Oligarchien (VI 1–8)', in *Aristoteles: Politik*, ed. by Otfried Höffe (Berlin: Akademie Verlag, 2001), pp. 151–67

Grech, Gundisalvus Maria, *The Commentary of Peter of Auvergne on Aristotle's 'Politics', the Inedited Part, Book III, less. I–VI: Introduction and Critical Text* (Rome: Desclée, 1967)

Hamesse, Jacqueline, and José Meirinhos, eds, *Les Auctoritates Aristotelis, leur utilisation et leur influence chez les auteurs médiévaux: État de la question 40 ans après la publication*, Textes et études du moyen âge, 83 (Turnhout: Brepols, 2017)

Kaye, Joel, *A History of Balance, 1250–1375: The Emergence of a New Model of Equilibrium and its Impact on Thought* (Cambridge: Cambridge University Press, 2014)

Lambertini, Roberto, 'Burley's Commentary on the Politics: Exegetic Techniques and Political Language', in *A Companion to Walter Burley: Late Medieval Logician and Metaphysician*, ed. by Alessandro D. Conti (Leiden: Brill, 2013), pp. 347–73

——, '*Philosophus videtur tangere tres rationes*: Egidio Romano lettore ed interprete della *Politica* nel terzo libro del *De regimine principum*', *Documenti e studi sulla tradizione filosofica medievale*, 1 (1990), 277–325

——, 'Wilhelm von Ockham als Leser der "Politica": Über die Rezeption der politischen Theorie des Aristoteles in der Ekklesiologie Ockhams', in *Das Publikum politischer Theorie im 14. Jahrhundert*, ed. by Jürgen Miethke with the help of Arnold Bühler (Munich: Oldenbourg Verlag, 1992), pp. 207–24

Lanza, Lidia, '*Ei autem qui de politia considerat…*': Aristotele nel pensiero politico medievale*, Textes et Études du Moyen Âge, 71 (Barcelona: FIDEM, 2013)

——, 'The "Scriptum super III–VIII libros Politicorum": Some Episodes of its Fortune until the Early Renaissance', in *Peter of Auvergne: University Master of the 13th Century*, ed. by Christoph Flüeler, Lidia Lanza, and Marco Toste, Scrinium Friburgense, 26 (Berlin: De Gruyter, 2015), pp. 255–319

Miethke, Jürgen, 'Einleitung', in Marsilius of Padua, *Defensor pacis, Der Verteidiger des Friedens*, trans. and commented by Horst Kusch (†), ed. with a new introduction by Jürgen Miethke (Darmstadt: Wissenschaftliche Buchgesellschaft, 2017), pp. xv–xciii

——, 'Praktische Bedürfnisse und die Rezeption der aristotelischen "Politik" im 13. und 14. Jahrhundert: Das Beispiel des Albertus Magnus', *Scripta mediaevalia: Revista de pensamiento medieval*, 5 (2012), 79–104

Moreno-Riaño, Gerson, and Cary J. Nederman, 'Marsilius of Padua's Principles of Secular Politics', in *A Companion to Marsilius of Padua*, ed. by Gerson Moreno-Riaño and Cary J. Nederman, Brill's Companions to the Christian Tradition, 31 (Leiden: Brill, 2012), pp. 117–38

Nederman, Cary J., *Community and Consent: The Secular Political Theory of Marsiglio of Padua's 'Defensor Pacis'* (Lanham, MD: Rowman & Littlefield, 1995)

——, 'The Meaning of "Aristotelianism" in Medieval Moral and Political Thought', *Journal of the History of Ideas*, 57.4 (1996), 563–85

Piaia, Gregorio, '"Aristotelicus magis quam christianus": Lo sfondo filosofico della "civitas" marsiliana', in *Europa e America nella storia della civiltà: Studi in onore di Aldo Stella*, ed. by Paolo Pecorari (Treviso: Antilia, 2003), pp. 53–66

Salvatelli, Luca, 'Suggestioni da una libraria cardinalizia di fine Duecento: I codici miniati scientifico filosofici di Gonsalvo Gudiel', in *Memoria e materia dell'opera d'arte: Proposte e riflessioni*, ed. by Elisa Anzellotti, Costanza Rapone, and Luca Salvatelli (Rome: Gangemi, 2015), pp. 65–75

Scholz, Richard, 'Einleitung', in Marsilius von Padua, *Defensor pacis*, ed. by Richard Scholz, Monumenta Germaniae Historica: Fontes iuris germanici antiqui in usum scholarum seperatim editi, 7.2 (Hanover: Hahn, 1933), pp. v–lxx

Schütrumpf, Ernst, *The Earliest Translations of Aristotle's Politics and the Creation of Political Terminology*, Morphomata Lectures Cologne, 8 (Paderborn: Fink, 2014)

Shogimen, Takashi, 'Medicine and the Body Politic in Marsilius of Padua's *Defensor pacis*', in *A Companion to Marsilius of Padua*, ed. by Gerson Moreno-Riaño and Cary J. Nederman, Brill's Companions to the Christian Tradition, 31 (Leiden: Brill, 2012), pp. 71–115

Syros, Vasileios, *Marsilius of Padua at the Intersection of Ancient and Medieval Traditions of Political Thought* (Toronto: University of Toronto Press, 2012)

——, 'The Sovereignty of the Multitude in the Works of Marsilius of Padua, Peter of Auvergne, and Some Other Aristotelian Commentators' in *The World of Marsilius of Padua*, ed. by Gerson Moreno-Riaño, Disputatio, 5 (Turnhout: Brepols, 2006), pp. 227–48

Toste, Marco, 'The Naturalness of Human Association in Medieval Political Thought Revisited', in *La nature comme source de la morale au Moyen Âge*, ed. by Maaike van der Lugt, Micrologus' Library, 58 (Florence: SISMEL–Edizioni del Galluzzo, 2014), pp. 113–88

——, 'An Original Way of Commenting on the Fifth Book of Aristotle's *Politics*: The *Questiones super I-VII libros Politicorum* of Peter of Auvergne', in *Peter of Auvergne: University Master of the 13th Century*, ed. by Christoph Flüeler, Lidia Lanza, and Marco Toste, Scrinium Friburgense, 26 (Berlin: De Gruyter, 2015), pp. 321–53

——, 'La socievolezza umana nel *Defensor Pacis* di Marsilio da Padova', *Philosophical Readings*, 12 (2020), 22–34

GERT-JAN VAN DE VOORDE

'What More Do You Want?'[*]

The Use of the Roman Trial of Jesus by Augustine and Marsilius of Padua

Introduction

> 'Well, let's say, by your life', the procurator replied. 'It's high time you swore by it, since it's hanging by a hair, I can tell you'.
> 'You don't think it was you who hung it, Hegemon?' the prisoner asked. 'If so, you are very mistaken'.
> Pilate gave a start and replied through his teeth:
> 'I can cut that hair'.
> 'In that, too, you are mistaken', the prisoner retorted, smiling brightly, and shielding himself from the sun with his hand. 'YOU must agree that surely only he who hung it can cut the hair?'[1]

The fragment above, taken from the famous Russian novel *The Master and Margarita* written by Mikhail Bulgakov in the late 1920s and 1930s, is a part of Bulgakov's reimagining of Christ's Roman trial before Pontius Pilate. The main narrative is occasionally interrupted by episodes from the story of the *Hegemon*. The quoted fragment resembles the exchange between Pilate and Christ in the nineteenth chapter of the Gospel of John:

> So, Pilate said to him, 'You will not speak to me? Do you not know that I have authority to release you and authority to crucify you?'
> Jesus answered him, 'You would have no authority over me at all unless it had been given you from above'.[2]

---

[*] I would like to thank David Lloyd Dusenbury for his advice and help during the writing process of this chapter.

[1] Bulgakov, *The Master and Margarita*, p. 39.

[2] John 19. 10–11. The Bible translation used, here and below, is the English Standard Version.

Gert-Jan Van de Voorde is a doctoral researcher at the University of St Andrews and the UGent, where he works on the project 'Lordship and the Rise of the State (1300–1600)', Languedoc case study.

Marsilius of Padua, ed. by Alessandro Mulieri, Serena Masolini, and Jenny Pelletier, Disputatio, 36 (Turnhout: Brepols, 2023), pp. 49–74

BREPOLS ❧ PUBLISHERS   10.1484/M.DISPUT-EB.5.132907

Bulgakov's story shows that the trial of Christ has long held a strong grip over the minds of artists and scholars. In Late Antiquity and throughout the Middle Ages Church Fathers such as Augustine, Lactantius, and Chrysostom, theologians such as Theophylact, Alcuin, and Giles of Rome, and political theorists such as Dante Alighieri and Marsilius of Padua all used the Roman trial of Christ to support their arguments.

In his *Defensor pacis* (1324) Marsilius aims to make universal points and therefore appeals to universally established authorities. One of these authorities is Augustine of Hippo, whose words Marsilius lifts from their theological context and fits into the political framework he proposes in the *Defensor pacis*. The Paduan doctor often cites Augustine in his work, but rarely directly. Instead, Marsilius quotes him through the filter of the *Catena aurea* of Thomas Aquinas,[3] who included many of Augustine's words in this work alongside those of other Church Fathers and theologians. Analysing Marsilius's use of Augustine is not unproblematic. First, Augustine did not have a concise political theory, and his views bearing political implications are scattered across a vast oeuvre.[4] Second, the Church Father's thought process was driven by the need to resolve external tensions, bringing his ideas into a recorded state of flux.[5] This makes a comparison of Augustine's thought as if it were unified or systematic with Marsilius's a complicated matter. Marsilius, on the other hand, only wrote a single large work that contains his controversial political theory. Besides the *Defensor pacis*, he wrote a handful of much shorter treatises in which he developed his ideas further.[6] The oeuvre of these two authors therefore appears to be strikingly different in scope, character, and aim. This is certainly true for the Augustinian writings regarding Jesus's trial before Pilate, which Marsilius cites.

The goal of this chapter is to analyse Marsilius's arguments in the *Defensor pacis* that are based on the Roman trial of Jesus. Marsilius develops two arguments based on three biblical verses (John 18. 36, and a combination of John 19. 11 and Romans 13. 1) and provides quotations from Augustine to support them. I assess whether Marsilius accurately represents Augustine's point of view. Further, I argue that while Marsilius's first argument was influenced by Augustine, the second argument draws instead on Bernard of Clairvaux.

---

3 Thomas Aquinas, *Catena Aurea*, trans. by Newman (henceforth, *Catena*), pp. 562–77.

4 Breyfogle, 'Toward a Contemporary Augustinian Understanding of Politics', p. 218.

5 Brown, 'St Augustine's Attitude to Religious Coercion', p. 107.

6 The first was the *Defensor minor*, in which he also incorporated a few earlier pamphlets, such as *De matrimonio* (Chapters 13–15) and *Forma dispensationis super affinitatem consanguinitatis* (Chapter 16). See the chronology in Marsilius of Padua, *Defensor minor*, ed. by Nederman, p. xxvii.

This chapter contains three sections. The first is a discussion of the debate between Daniel Mulcahy and Conal Condren that took place in the early seventies. It offers insights into the relation between Augustine and Marsilius. Especially useful is Condren's distinction between use and influence. Condren brought to the fore the fact that citing can be nothing more than claiming support from an authority, while one's ideas may descend from other sources. The second part of this study is the most substantial. It is divided into two sections that each discuss an argument that Marsilius makes based on the Roman trial of Jesus with supporting quotations from Augustine. In the first of these sections Marsilius uses John 18. 36, where Christ tells Pilate that his kingship is not from this earth. The verse also features prominently in Augustine's *In Iohannis evangelium tractatus* CXV, which reached Marsilius via the *Catena aurea*. With John 18. 36 Marsilius argues for Christ's voluntary rejection of temporal power. Within this subsection the Roman trial will be situated in the context of the second *dictio*, by means of a brief introduction. The second of these sections will deal with a combination of two verses, namely John 19. 11 and Romans 13. 1 where Paul informs his Roman audience that all power originates from God.[7] Marsilius discusses Christ's personal relationship with temporal power and maintains that Christ was bound by the decisions of legitimate rulers. This argument is accompanied by a quote from Augustine's *In Iohannis evangelium tractatus* CXVI. The chapter's last section contains an analysis of the influence of the issue of guilt in Augustine's and Marsilius's use of the trial and their attitude towards the Roman Empire. This is presented to better contextualize the findings of this chapter's second and third sections.

The main Augustinian sources that Marsilius uses are the *Tractatus* CXV and CXVI, which he consults through the *Catena*.[8] To better understand Augustine's thought, several of his works will be used such as *De trinitate Dei* and several homilies. For a better understanding of Marsilius's ideas and methods the *Defensor minor* will be used.

---

7 John 19. 11: 'respondit Iesus non haberes potestatem adversum me ullam nisi tibi esset datum desuper propterea qui tradidit me tibi maius peccatum habet' (Jesus answered, 'You would have no power over me if it were not given to you from above. Therefore, the one who handed me over to you is guilty of a greater sin').

8 For instance, the first argument based on Augustine's *Tractatus* CXV that Marsilius makes is taken from the third fragment cited in the *Catena aurea* and corresponds to the sixth point Augustine makes. *DP*, II, 4–5; cf. *Catena*, pp. 564–65; cf. Augustine, *In Johannis evangelium tractatus* (henceforth, *Io.ev.tr.*), CXV, 1. All abbreviations of and dates of works by Augustine are taken from Pollmann and Otten, eds, *The Oxford Guide to the Historical Reception of Augustine*, III, pp. xiii–xvi. References to *Io.ev.tr.* have been taken from the seventh volume of Nicene and Post-Nicene Fathers by Shaff. All other English translations of St Augustine's work have been taken from the series The Works of Saint Augustine: A Translation for the 21st Century (see Primary Sources for details), unless stated otherwise.

Marsilius's Use of Augustine

Status quaestionis

The relation between Augustine and Marsilius has been extensively researched.[9] This section will focus on the contested influence of the saint on the Paduan and the reasons why Marsilius employed Augustine in the way he did. Augustine is quoted often by Marsilius, primarily in the second *dictio*. This was noticed by Alan Gewirth, whose translation of the *Defensor pacis* was recently superseded by Annabel Brett's 2005 edition, which is used for all English translations from the *Defensor pacis* in this chapter.[10] Gewirth explained that since Augustine was the third most frequently cited authority, after Aristotle and the Bible, he was necessarily of great influence in the *Defensor pacis*. Despite this fact, he lamented: 'the importance of Augustinianism for Marsilius's political thought has received almost no recognition.'[11] Gewirth then pointed to a French authority on Marsilius, George de Lagarde, as an example of a scholar who ignored the possibility of Augustinian influence on the Paduan.[12]

The first to comment on Gewirth's claims (given that Lagarde had died before he could respond), was Daniel Mulcahy, who disagreed with Gewirth. Mulcahy first stressed the importance of the distribution of quotations from Augustine. Unlike Aristotle, Augustine was almost solely referenced in the second *dictio*. He was cited directly only once in the first *dictio*. Given the importance of *Dictio* I to Marsilius's thesis in the *Defensor pacis*, which Mulcahy — perhaps erroneously — interpreted as the main argument,[13] he concluded that Augustine's influence on the political thought of Marsilius was negligible.[14] Furthermore, Mulcahy argued that in the second *dictio* the Paduan often added biblical texts and cited a few of the patristic commentaries which Peter Lombard or Thomas Aquinas had collected.[15] The fourth chapter of the second *dictio* contains a clear

---

9 For example, the unpublished thesis, which I have been unable to access, Butts, 'The Political Doctrines of Augustine of Hippo and Marsilius of Padua'.

10 The Latin text added in the footnotes is taken from the Previté-Orton critical edition. I chose to use this version rather than Scholz, because Brett used Previté-Orton for her translation.

11 Gewirth, *Marsilius of Padua*, p. 37 n. 17.

12 Gewirth, *Marsilius of Padua*, p. 37.

13 Mulcahy, 'The Hands of Augustine', pp. 458–59.

14 Mulcahy also wrote that *Dictio* III contains no references to Augustine. He interprets this as proof that Augustine did not influence Marsilius, but Augustine's absence is probably more related to the purpose of the last *dictio*. It appears to be intended as a summary or a guidebook and was therefore stripped bare. Mulcahy, 'Marsilius of Padua's Use of St Augustine', p. 181; Brett, 'Introduction', p. xxxi.

15 Mulcahy, 'Marsilius of Padua's Use of St Augustine', p. 183.

example. Marsilius adds quotations from Augustine, Theophylact, and Chrysostom in an order identical to the *Catena*.[16] The two Augustinian works that Aquinas used (and Marsilius quoted) for exegesis of the trial of Jesus in the Gospel of John are *De consensu evangelistarum* (*c.* 400–405) and *In Johannis evangelium tractatus* (*c.* 406–420).[17] Augustine wrote these texts to defend the Gospels against pagans, or to make Scripture easier to understand, giving his compositions a theological focus.[18] This does not mean it is entirely devoid of political meaning, but Augustine never developed his own political thought in isolation from his theology.[19]

One of Mulcahy's weaknesses was his fixation on the first *dictio* and his interpretation of the second *dictio* as a mere patristic confirmation of points developed previously.[20] On the contrary, the two parts of the *Defensor pacis* do not fight the same battle in Marsilius's war against the papacy, the goal of which was a radical reform of the papacy.[21] The first *dictio* uses Aristotle to make a case against papal expansion into temporal matters, while the second *dictio* attempts to undermine the political aspirations of the papacy by appealing to the authorities who built the Church's theological foundations. Marsilius picked those Church Fathers who made statements that could be interpreted as favouring the conclusion he desired to argue.[22]

In his first reply to Mulcahy, Conal Condren argued that the final structure of the *Defensor* gives no indication of the order in which these three *dictiones* were created, nor does it suggest that the first *dictio* is necessarily the most important.[23] Furthermore, Marsilius's use of quotations and allusions to great authorities cannot be simply interpreted as equivalent to the modern scholarly use of citations. Marsilius was not a twentieth-century scholar. Instead, he was a fourteenth-century polemicist who sought to undermine the papacy in favour of the empire.[24] His attitude towards authorities discernible in the *Defensor pacis* and *Defensor minor* betrays a certain utilitarian mindset that is similar to what George Rosen sensed was

---

16 *DP*, II, 4.5–6.

17 Citations from the *cons.ev.* mostly came from Book III, Chapters 3, 6, 7, 8, 21, 22, 23. From *Io.ev.tr.*, treatises CXV to CXVI are particularly important.

18 The *cons.ev.* was intended to defend the Gospels against pagan critics, to clarify their historical validity, and to demonstrate the absence of contradictions between them, but the *Io.ev.tr.* is far more heterogeneous, consisting of both sermons and sermon-like texts of which the purpose remains unclear; cf. Pollmann and Otten, eds, *The Oxford Guide to the Historical Reception of Augustine*, III, pp. 261 and 439.

19 In fact, the literature is very quick to point this out, but one reference will suffice here. Weithman, 'Augustine's Political Philosophy', p. 234.

20 Mulcahy, 'The Hands of Augustine', pp. 458 and 466.

21 Setton, *The Papacy and the Levant*, p. 171 n. 42.

22 Mastnak, *Crusading Peace*, p. 197.

23 Condren, 'On Interpreting Marsilius' Use of St Augustine', pp. 218–19.

24 Condren, 'On Interpreting Marsilius' Use of St Augustine', p. 218.

Marsilius's utilitarian attitude towards medicine.[25] Thus Marsilius could not choose his authorities freely; rather he would have picked those sources he thought would create the greatest impact, sometimes regardless of the suitability of such sources. This is undoubtedly an important reason why Marsilius did not always use Augustinian quotations to prove something that Augustine would have claimed.[26] Marsilius did likewise with quotations from Aristotle, whom he cites repeatedly throughout the first *dictio*.[27]

Another point of contention raised by Mulcahy was the extensive use of medieval collections as a source for patristic and specifically Augustinian quotations in the *Defensor pacis*.[28] Marsilius's choice is understandable in light of the above discussion, since the Paduan required as much support from as many Church Fathers as he could muster. In his much smaller, and aptly named, *Defensor minor*, Marsilius wrote for a different audience — he wrote it at Ludwig's court — and therefore used his authorities differently. In this work, most references were taken from the *Sentences* by Peter Lombard, and Marsilius even confuses comments by Lombard with those of Ambrose. Augustine is again the most frequently cited Church Father, but he is cited directly on only three occasions.[29] The Paduan chose to refer nearly always to collections compiled by famous authors. In the *Defensor minor* they were Thomas Aquinas, Walafried Strabo, and Peter Lombard. Marsilius could expect their work to be known and appeal to most of his audience.

Ultimately, motivating a large audience to act against the papacy was Marsilius's intention, given that the third *dictio* of the *Defensor* is a call for such action. By using famous collections, Marsilius avoided including passages which were the special preserve of theologians, and which therefore would not have helped the Paduan's cause. Instead, he can venture to portray his conclusions as manifestly true, and throughout his work Marsilius shows a clear drive to portray his reasoning as evident. Strewn across all three *dictiones*, words such as *palam*, *evidenter*, *aperte*, *manifeste*, etc. announce the way in which Marsilius wishes his audience to think about his arguments.[30] Even the chapter title of *DP*, II, 4 contains

---

25 Rosen, 'The Historical Significance of Some Medical References', p. 356.

26 Mulcahy, 'The Hands of Augustine', p. 465.

27 Mulcahy, 'Marsilius of Padua's Use of St Augustine', p. 181.

28 Marsilius used mainly the *Collectanea* by Peter Lombard and the *Catena aurea* by Thomas Aquinas; cf. Mulcahy, 'Marsilius of Padua's Use of St Augustine', p. 181.

29 Most cases are either indirect references, often taken from the *Sentences* of Peter Lombard, or refer back to the discussion in the *Defensor pacis*. All references can be easily found in Nederman's notes and index to Marsilius of Padua, *Defensor minor*, ed. by Nederman, pp. 63–64 and 85.

30 A few examples of other words used can be found in the following subsections: *DP*, II, 4.12 and 5.9; *DP*, II, 9.2 and 22.18.

the word *evidenter*, and Marsilius adds later in the chapter that 'this is plain and undoubted, firstly, from the passage of the Gospels in John 18'.[31] This approach achieves two related things. On the one hand, Marsilius uses what Cary Nederman and Gerson Moreno-Riaño called the theme of 'good sense': 'Marsilius's task in all his works is [...] to assist his audience in recollecting, remembering, or identifying self-evident truths and conclusions that they already know'.[32] The authorities are omnipresent and quoted to assist Marsilius's argumentation, although he does not always consider them necessary:

> And although in fact this passage of the gospels very clearly contains and demonstrates our proposition more fully than the glosses of the saints, we have nevertheless quoted them for greater confirmation of our position, and so that we should not be said to be expounding Scripture with temerity.[33]

The above does not mean that Marsilius does not engage with his authorities: he does add clarifications and emendations to integrate the cited words into the framework of the *Defensor*. One example is the discussion of Origen's interpretation of Romans 13, which, according to Marsilius, is more accurate than Jerome's.[34] Marsilius intended his work to be clear, which can be tied to the observation that he appears to overlook or be unaware of paradoxes that were produced by conflicts between certain definitions or concepts. Joanna Scott suggested that these ideas were familiar to a medieval audience and did not necessarily result in a paradox from a medieval perspective.[35]

'Use' versus 'Influence'

The observations made above do not prove that Augustine was necessarily as important to Marsilius's thought as his use of the Church Father would suggest. Marsilius was certainly familiar first-hand with parts of Augustine's work, because he quotes directly from *De civitate Dei* in the first *dictio* and elsewhere. With these direct quotations Marsilius includes references, which he does not do elsewhere.[36] There remains, however, a

---

31 Cf. *DP*, II, 4.4, ed. by Previté-Orton: 'hoc autem primum apparet indubie per seriem evangelicam Iohannis XVIII'.

32 Moreno-Riaño and Nederman, 'Marsilius of Padua's Principles of Secular Politics', p. 121.

33 *DP*, II, 4.8, ed. by Previté-Orton: 'Et licet re vera series evangelica patentissime contineat et demonstret propositum nostrum aplius quam glossae sanctorum [...] eas tamen induximus ad maiorem propositi confirmationem, et ne temerarie Scripturam dicamur exponere'.

34 *DP*, II, 4.11.

35 Scott, 'Influence or Manipulation?', p. 63.

36 *DP*, I, 9.2.

difference between 'use' and 'influence'. As remarked above, Marsilius does not need to agree with everything Augustine wrote when he quotes him.[37] Augustine and Marsilius certainly had convergent ideas. But due to Marsilius's limited direct engagement with the work of Augustine, one cannot assume Marsilius got his ideas from studying Augustine. The waters are muddled, because the Paduan likely could have acquired Augustinian ideas via contemporary sources.

Marsilius was neither the first nor the only one to use the combination of John 19. 11 and Romans 13. 1 to make an argument accompanied by Augustinian quotations. An example of this combination of verses can be found in the work of an author who died less than a decade before Marsilius finished his *Defensor*. In many ways Giles of Rome was Marsilius's antithesis, yet both relied strongly — or gave the appearance of reliance — on Augustine in their work. Giles, who was a monk and theologian of the Augustinian order, cited directly from many of Augustine's works.[38] Given his position as an Augustinian theologian, Giles was better placed to be profoundly influenced by Augustine than was Marsilius.

When comparing the treatment of the argument regarding Romans 13. 1 and John 19. 11 by Giles and Marsilius in their respective works, it becomes evident that Giles engages with Augustine on a level that Marsilius does not. For instance, the number of first-hand quotations is low in the *Defensor*, because most quotations are taken from the *Catena* and are therefore second-hand. Consequently, one could agree with Mulcahy that despite having quoted the Church Father so frequently, the Paduan was not sufficiently familiar with Augustine to have experienced a direct influence.[39] Naturally, there is a certain degree of indirect influence, ideas Marsilius espouses without citing. For example, while Marsilius's thoughts on the formation of polities were based on his engagement with Aristotle,[40] the addition of views on the fall of man, humanity's frailty, and the establishment of communities were borrowed from Augustine.[41]

The last word regarding the issue of Augustinianism in the *Defensor* has certainly yet to be written. Nevertheless, the scholarly consensus zeroes in

---

37 Condren, 'On Interpreting Marsilius' Use of St Augustine', pp. 220–21.

38 John Eastman remarks that in *De renunciatione papae* Giles uses nine works by Augustine, most notably *De civitate*, *Confessiones*, and *De trinitate*; cf. Eastman, 'Giles of Rome and his Use of St Augustine', p. 131.

39 Mulcahy, 'Marsilius of Padua's Use of St Augustine', p. 184.

40 Scott, 'Influence or Manipulation?', p. 73.

41 Blythe, *Ideal Government and the Mixed Constitution*, p. 21; Syros, *Marsilius of Padua at the Intersection*, p. 29.

on use rather than influence,[42] while acknowledging that there are areas of Augustinian influence. As will become apparent in the following sections, this chapter will not deviate from that consensus. Marsilius did not foster a straightforward relationship with Augustine. The following remarks are important. Marsilius did not necessarily quote Augustine so frequently because they agreed; instead his choice of sources seems to be based on what he could expect his intended audience to know. By citing from collections, rather than the works themselves, he could assure himself that his audience would not only be familiar with the texts he cited, but if they were not that they would also be able to find the quotations he used, without him or his readership being necessarily aware of the complete context of said quotes. Lastly, Marsilius did navigate intellectual circles, such as the University of Paris, that relied on biblical verses and the opinions of Church Fathers to build arguments. Marsilius and Augustine may not be directly linked, but by virtue of the context in which Marsilius lived an indirect influence is unavoidable.[43]

John 18. 36: Christ's Voluntary Rejection of Temporal Power

The Trial in the Second Dictio

The two arguments that Marsilius built surrounding the trial of Christ before Pilate serve as case studies to assess the Augustinian influence or use in the Paduan's thought. These arguments bear a great but superficial resemblance to each other: both are based on the same biblical events and rely heavily on quotes from Augustine. However, Marsilius treats them as two fully distinct arguments since their purpose and underlying roots are very different. In the Gospel of John this episode of Christ's passion begins at verse 18. 28 and ends at verse 19. 16. Not all verses, however, are equally important, and Marsilius bases his arguments on only a few. The first of these verses is John 18. 36, in which Christ says that his kingdom is not of this earth. He offers the absence of servants fighting to ensure his liberation as proof. Marsilius uses 19. 11 in the first and second part of the *Defensor* in two different ways. As was noted in the previous section, the first *dictio* consisted of an analysis of Aristotle with the intention to prove that Aristotle's ideas lead to a legitimation of temporal domination over

---

42 This point can be made for many authorities Marsilius uses; for instance Condren states about Marsilius's use of Aristotle that 'reference to him [...] signifies no more than the propriety of using his name as a means of stamping legitimacy on the institutional arrangements of a given society'; cf. Condren, 'Democracy and the *Defensor Pacis*', p. 306.

43 Scott, 'Influence or Manipulation?', p. 62.

spiritual power. The second *dictio*, on the other hand, dealt with strengthening this position by undermining the theological basis for ecclesiastical supremacy, or fullness of power, over temporal powers.

Marsilius writes:

'My kingdom is not of this world', i.e., I did not come into this world to reign with temporal government or dominion, in the way that the kings of the world reign. [...] If I had come into the world to reign with worldly or coercive government, I would have servants of this government, sc. fighting men to coerce transgressors, like other kings; but I have no such servants.[44]

With these verses from John 18, the Paduan intends to argue that Christ excluded himself from having a part in the temporal government of the world. Chapters 4 and 5 are devoted to proving this thesis, and at the end of Chapter 5 Marsilius believes 'that Christ renounced principate or coercive jurisdiction over anyone in this world'.[45] Marsilius discusses the trial several times in the second *dictio*, but the first time is at the beginning of Chapter 4. To gain an insight into the importance of the argument it is necessary to first illuminate the structure of the second *dictio*. *DP*, II, 1.1 and *DP*, II, 2.1–8 are the introduction in which Marsilius states his intentions and defines three key terms, 'the Church', 'temporal', and 'spiritual'. This is followed by an overview of the arguments in favour of papal temporal power.[46] He cites the gift of the keys of heaven by Jesus to Peter, the power of binding and loosing, and among other claims he recounts the biblical episode in which Jesus drives demons into a herd of subsequently suicidal pigs.[47] From that, Marsilius recounts, one can state that Jesus owned all worldly matters, since he had the power to take possession of the pigs without consequence.[48] It is not surprising that most Augustinian citations from the first five chapters of this *dictio* are related to the temporal power of priests.[49]

DP, II, 4.1–13 and *DP*, II, 5.1–9 contain his first rebuttals to papal fullness of power. First Marsilius uses the Gospels, but in Chapter 5 he uses Acts and the Letters of Paul. In *DP*, II, 4, Marsilius explains his

---

44 *DP*, II, 4.4–5, ed. by Previté-Orton: '"Regnum meum non est de hoc mundo", id est, regnare non veni regimine seu dominio temporali quo modo regnat mundane reges. [...] Si venissem regnare in hunc mundum mundane regimine seu coactive, haberem ministros huius regiminis, decertatores scilicet ac transgressorum coactores, quemadmodum ceteri reges habent; sed tales ministros no habeo'.

45 *DP*, II, 5.9, ed. by Previté-Orton: 'quod quidem igitur principatum seu coactivam iurisdictionem cuiuscumque in hoc saeculo Christus abdicaverit'.

46 *DP*, II, 3.1–15.

47 Matthew 8. 31–32.

48 *DP*, II, 3.4.

49 Mulcahy, 'Marsilius of Padua's Use of St Augustine', p. 186.

'WHAT MORE DO YOU WANT?' 59

position and follows it up with his first argument: the position Christ took regarding coercive power in the trial before Pilate, which is based on John 18. 36. It is followed by other biblical passages, such as Jesus fleeing to avoid a coronation in John 6. 15,[50] and Luke 12. 13–14, in which Jesus refused to act as a secular judge,[51] before moving on to paying tribute to the emperor (Matthew 22. 21).[52] Then, Marsilius returns to the trial, with the intention to demonstrate that Pilate's jurisdiction even applies to Christ's person and bases this on John 19. 11 and Romans 13. 1. The chapter ends with Marsilius reminding his audience that the clergy should imitate Christ.[53] The trial in the Gospel of John thus takes an important place in the *Defensor*, since it provides the verses for the first theological argument. Marsilius believed this argument to be persuasive, because he repeats it near the end of and in several other places throughout the second *dictio* as well.[54]

Christ and Temporal Power in the Words of Augustine and Marsilius

The importance of John 18. 36 was lost on neither Marsilius nor Augustine.[55] Marsilius sees Pilate as a representative of temporal coercive authority, who was pitted against Christ. Christ is a king, but not of a temporal kingdom, and therefore had no coercive power. Augustine dedicated the first half of his *Tractatus* CXV to its explanation. As the only Augustinian source on this topic, it was included in the *Catena*, and subsequently in the *Defensor*.[56] Augustine's purpose in the first three sections of the *Tractatus* was to explain the political and eschatological meanings of John 18. 36.

Augustine focuses primarily on Christ's statement that his kingdom is not of this world.[57] Augustine concludes from this verse that although Christ had power, it was not of a nature that would interfere with temporal authority. Augustine remembers the Massacre of the Innocents by Herod the Elder, who by this slaughter hoped to safeguard his dynasty. Herod's fear was unnecessary because Christ would not interfere in such temporal matters. Hence Augustine rhetorically asks temporal authorities: What

---

50 *DP*, II, 4.7.

51 *DP*, II, 4.8.

52 *DP*, II, 4.9–11, 28.24.

53 *DP*, II, 4.13.

54 *DP*, II, 4.12.

55 John 18. 36: 'respondit Iesus regnum meum non est de mundo hoc si ex hoc mundo esset regnum meum ministri mei decertarent ut non traderer Iudaeis nunc autem meum regnum non est hinc' (Jesus answered, 'My kingdom is not of this world. If my kingdom were of this world, my servants would have been fighting, that I might not be delivered over to the Jews. But my kingdom is not from the world').

56 *Catena*, pp. 563–67.

57 *Io.ev.tr.*, CXV, 1–2.

more do you want?[58] The kingdom is no danger to any secular ruler because it is built on faith in Christ, which is followed by an eschatological conclusion:

> [Humanity is] created indeed by the true God but generated from Adam as a vitiated and condemned stock; and there are made into a kingdom no longer of the world, all from thence that have been regenerated in Christ.[59]

This conclusion appears in the *Defensor pacis* only in passing, since explaining the need for Christ's kingdom is not within Marsilius's scope. For Marsilius it suffices to report on the spiritual nature of the kingdom that Augustine described.[60] The *Defensor* does not contain the full argument, because the *Catena*, and consequently Marsilius also, omits the lesson Augustine draws from Herod. This means that Augustine's idea, that the fear of temporal rulers to lose power to Christ's kingdom will lead to unnecessary cruelty and suffering, is absent from the *Defensor*. In its place, Marsilius independently comes to a similar point when he states: 'For two coercive dominions not ranked in respect of each other and over the same multitude do hinder each other'.[61] Thus Marsilius strongly implies that if Christ's kingdom had been vested with coercive power, a war with temporal powers would have ensued, but this problem is avoided because 'as Augustine said, Christ had not come to hinder their dominion'.[62] Quoting Augustine, Marsilius can go even further: 'if you deny that you are a king, then what have you done to be handed over to me; as if it would not be surprising if someone who called himself a king should be handed over to a judge for punishment'.[63]

As Marsilius explains, Augustine does continue to state that if Jesus had claimed to be a temporal monarch 'he should thus deserve to be delivered unto the judge'.[64] For Marsilius this phrase clarifies that Jesus only claimed spiritual power and rejected temporal power. Augustine does note that this does not exclude interventions in the natural world, but

---

58 *Io.ev.tr.*, CXV, 1.

59 *Io.ev.tr.*, CXV, 2: 'De mundo est ergo quidquid hominum a vero quidem Deo creatum, sed ex Adam vitiate atqua damnata stirpe generatum est; factum est autem regnum non iam de mundo, quidquid inde in Christo regeneratum est'.

60 *DP*, II, 4.6.

61 *DP*, II, 4.5, ed. by Previté-Orton: 'Duo namque coactive domina non subinvicem posita ac respect eiusdem multitudinis se impediunt'.

62 *DP*, II, 4.5, ed. by Previté-Orton: 'Christus autem horum dominium non venerat impedire, ut dixit Augustinus'.

63 *DP*, II, 4.5, ed. by Previté-Orton: 'Si te regem negas, quid fecisti, ut tradereris mihi, quasi mirum non esset si puniendus iudici traderetur qui se diceret regem'.

64 *Io.ev.tr.*, CXV, 1: 'quaerendum ab illo esset quid aliud forte fecisset, unde tradi iudici dignus esset'.

this is not something Marsilius mentions.[65] The Paduan continues his argument to demonstrate that Christ rejected any temporal crown in a new paragraph, now no longer based on the biblical account of the trial. It is still accompanied by quotations from Augustine, Theophylact, and Chrysostom.[66]

In *DP*, II, 4.7, Marsilius continues his argument, again leaving the trial behind. He bases the argument on an episode recounted in John 6. 15, but Augustine's opinion on the nature of Christ's kingdom and who constitutes it, which Marsilius cites, is the same as in *Tractatus* CXV.[67] Marsilius appears to have been particularly interested in the Augustinian conceptualization of the kingdom of Christ. He chooses Augustine over the views of Chrysostom, whose ideas regarding the kingdom are also well represented in the *Catena*.[68] This choice might have been inspired by the fact that in the *Tractatus*, and subsequently in the *Catena* also, Augustine steers clear of mentioning a precise hierarchy; instead he appears to treat the two kingdoms as different and ideally non-overlapping. Chrysostom, however, did rank them, but Marsilius does not quote this.[69]

Chrysostom was a bad choice for Marsilius, but this raises the question of whether Augustine was a better choice. Augustine clearly states that the purpose of the trial was to allow Christ to teach and that Christ spoke the way he did because he knew it would be recorded in Scripture.[70] Although the *Catena* only contains fragments of the *Tractatus* CXV and Aquinas mixed up the order of the arguments that Augustine made, Marsilius appears to have grasped the contents of the *Tractatus*. Nevertheless, there are discrepancies between them. One manifests elsewhere as the absence of the four trial narratives in Augustine's work with the clearest political bent: *De civitate Dei*,[71] a work Marsilius was familiar with.[72] As a consequence John 18. 36, which forms the basis for the political considerations in the *Tractatus* CXV, especially 'hear me Jews and gentiles, [...] I do not hinder

---

65 Trainor, 'Augustine's Glorious City', p. 544; Rensberger, 'The Politics of John', p. 408.

66 *DP*, II, 4.6.

67 *DP*, II, 4.7; *Io.ev.tr.*, CXV, 2.

68 Augustine is cited six and Chrysostom seven times in the commentary on verses 18. 33–38; cf. *Catena*, pp. 563–67.

69 Cf. *DP*, II, 4.6 and *Catena*, 18, 10, pp. 68–69.

70 *Sermo 299E*, 2; *Io.ev.tr.*, CXV, 1; Augustine's statement regarding the recording in Scripture also appears in *Catena*, p. 564.

71 The citation lists show a gap where the trial is that repeats in each gospel, in Mark, for example, the trial runs from 27. 11 to 27. 24, but citations stop in 27. 3 (when Judas receives his blood money) and resume from 27. 34 on (when Jesus is fed vinegar). He also does not mention Romans 13. 1. Augustine, *The City of God*, II, p. 563.

72 He cites the work twice: *DP*, I, 19.7; II, 20.11.

your domination in this world. [...] What more do you want?',[73] does not appear in *De civitate*.

In fact, Augustine rarely discussed the trial, instead using a few quotations to prove different points.[74] The bishop despised Pilate, referring to him as swelling with arrogance, and even comparing him to the devil in his work *De diversis quaestionibus*.[75] Marsilius, on the other hand, shies away from any value judgements, because these would be detrimental to his argument. According to Augustine the temporal government is a necessary evil to suppress certain kinds of loves or desires that would pull people away from the city of God; thus he interprets government as an institution intent on forcibly curbing excesses that are the result of unchecked desires, which is a rather negative outlook.[76] Marsilius shares parts of this view on government, but with a far more positive stance.[77]

Marsilius also strives for a clear distinction between the powers, but this is expressed differently. For Augustine, a good Christian is a good servant of the state, he writes in his *Expositio quarundam propositionum ex epistola ad Romanos*, which he completed around 394/395:

> For we are both soul and body, and however long we exist in this temporal life, we use temporal things to support it. Thus, it behoves us in our temporal, physical aspect to be subject to the authorities, that is, to the men who administer human affairs in some office.[78]

Augustine is of the opinion that if the state attempts to interfere in religious matters, Christians can rebel.[79] Thus Augustine fears intrusions from temporal authorities, whereas Marsilius reacts against ecclesiastical intrusions in temporal matters. By means of an example Marsilius explains that papal influence in the worldly affairs of Italy were the cause of that peninsula's ruin.[80] Unlike Augustine, Marsilius advocates for secular intervention in religious affairs, in the sense that the Roman emperor should convene the council to replace the papacy as the supreme legislative

---

73 *DP*, II, 4.5, ed. by Previté-Orton: 'audite ergo, Iudaei et gentes; [...] Non impedio dominationem uestram in hoc mundo; [...] Quid uultis amplius?'; cf. *Io.ev.tr.*, CXV, 2.

74 See the end of 'John 19. 11 and Romans 13. 1: Christ's Personal Relationship with Secular Power' for a brief overview.

75 *div.qu.*, LXXIX, 5.

76 Weithman, 'Augustine's Political Philosophy', pp. 234–38, and 249.

77 *DP*, II, 6.9.

78 *Augustine on Romans*, trans. by Landes; *Exp.prop.Rm*, 64, 44.19: 'cum enim constemus ex anima et corpore et, quamdiu in hac uita temporali sumus, etiam rebus temporalibus ad subsidium degendae eius uitae utamur, oportet nos ex ea parte, quae ad hanc uitam pertinet, subditos esse potestatibus, id est, hominibus res humanas cum aliquo honore administrantibus'.

79 *Exp.prop.Rm*, 72.

80 *DP*, I, 19.12.

body of the Church.[81] Here Marsilius appealed to Augustine's principle of non-obedience, but with the Church and State reversed. For the Church, however, the solution is the same: a passive Church when it comes to temporal affairs, since, according to Marsilius, the Church has no coercive temporal power.

John 19. 11 and Romans 13. 1: Christ's Personal Relationship with Secular Power

John 19. 11 and Romans 13. 1 form the basis for the second argument Marsilius develops based on the trial. The combination of these verses appears in both the first and second *dictio*, but as this study focuses primarily on the second *dictio*, the argument in the first *dictio* is left for future study. For the previous argument Marsilius was arguably influenced by Augustine, but in this section Marsilius was inspired by a later theologian: Bernard of Clairvaux. Marsilius borrows from Bernard the idea that Pilate had legitimate power over Christ.

Augustine discusses the trial before Pilate in the *Tractatus* CXV and CXVI. In *Tractatus* CXVI, the bishop develops several arguments, including one that ties Romans 13. 1 to John 19. 10–11. Through the *Catena* this entire argument is copied into the second *dictio*. In this *Tractatus* the focus has shifted away from the political, and although Marsilius did not quote directly from the treatise, his clarification that Augustine has shifted to the authority of jurisdiction (*auctoritas iurisdictiones*),[82] or the authority to judge someone, is in accordance with the content of the treatise. Marsilius further clarifies that this jurisdiction applies to the person of Christ, which deviates from Augustine's words. As in *Tractatus* CXV, the Church Father uses these insights to address a theological question:

> Of such a sort, indeed, was the power which God had given to Pilate, that he should also be under the power of Caesar. Wherefore 'thou wouldest have', He says, 'no power against me', that is, even the little measure thou really hast, 'except' this very measure, whatever its amount, 'were given thee from above'. But knowing as I do its amount, for it is not so great as to render thee altogether independent, 'therefore he that delivered me unto thee hath the greater sin'.[83]

---

81 Nederman, *Lineages of European Political Thought*, pp. 170–71.

82 *DP*, II, 4.12.

83 *Io.ev.tr.*, CXVI, 5: 'Talem quippe Pilato Deus dederat potestatem, ut etiam esset sub Caesaris potestate. Quapropter non haberes, inquit adversum me potestatem ullam, id est, quantulamcumque habes, nisi hoc ipsum quidquid est, tibi esset datum desuper. Sed quoniam scio quantum sit, non enim tantum est, ut tibi omni modo liberum sit; propterea qui tradidit me tibi, maius peccatum habet'.

By appealing to the greater sin, Augustine delves into the issue of sin and guilt. But, while this prompted Giles of Rome to elaborate on the bishop's argument,[84] Marsilius does not explore the issue of guilt beyond what Augustine writes, as he was arguing for the legitimacy of Pilate's power over Christ's person. Therefore, he emphasizes that Pilate's power was given from above.[85] Overall, Marsilius's argument is more reminiscent of Bernard of Clairvaux's argument based on John 19. 11 and Romans 13. 1, than Augustine's in this *Tractatus*. Bernard is one of the few authorities Marsilius regularly cited directly, though he only cited two works by him, most often *De consideratione*.[86] For Marsilius's argument regarding the trial of Christ *De moribus et officio Episcoporum* — a letter written by Bernard to the archbishop of Sens, Henri Sanglier (1122–1142) — is important. In total it is referenced eight times in the *Defensor*, seven of these alongside the two Bible verses, or references to the argument based on the verses. The last remaining reference is accompanied by Romans 13. 1 only.[87] In his letter to Sanglier, Bernard urged him to better his conduct and not to disobey the pope any longer.[88] After Bernard reminded the archbishop of Romans 13. 1, which he represented as being foreshadowed by John 19. 11, he wrote:

> So go on, resist the Vicar of Christ, when Christ did not even resist his enemy; or say if you dare, that God does not recognise the ordination of his pontiff when Christ acknowledged that the authority of a Roman governor, even over his own person, had been given him from above.[89]

In *De moribus* Bernard takes the position that rebellion against authority is an act of rebellion against God, even if, as in the example of Christ and Pilate, that person was an enemy. One should note that this attitude aligns closely to Augustine's views on the same subject. A key similarity between Bernard's argument and Marsilius's is the emphasis put on Pilate's authority over Christ's person, which does not appear in Augustine's works. In *Tractatus* CXVI, which Marsilius partially cites, the emphasis falls on the issue of blame and guilt that emerges from John 19. 11. Augustine makes

---

84 Giles of Rome, *On Ecclesiastical Power*, pp. 153–55.

85 *DP*, II, 4.12.

86 *De consideratione* is cited twenty-two times in the *Defensor pacis*, all instances in the second *dictio*, but not all references are unique. In *DP*, II, 28.22 Marsilius cites *De consideratione* alongside a reference to the argument in *DP*, II, 4.3–5 based on John 18. 36.

87 *DP*, II, 4.12; II, 5.4; II, 5.9; II, 28.24; II, 30.5; cf. *DP*, II, 4.11.

88 Bernard of Clairvaux, *On Baptism and the Office of Bishops*, ed. by Stiegman, trans. by Newman, pp. 20–22.

89 Bernard of Clairvaux, *De moribus*, 80, ed. by Stiegman, trans. by Newman: 'Ite nunc ergo, resistite Christi Vicario, cum nec suo adversario Christus restiterit: aut dicite, si audetis, sui Praesulis Deum ordinationem nescire, cum Romani Praesidis potestatem Christus super se quoque fateatur fuisse coelitus ordinatam'.

the connection with Romans 13. 1, which justifies the following statement by Marsilius: 'Pilate's coercive judicial power over Christ's person was therefore from God, as Christ openly avowed, and Augustine expressed clearly and Bernard said openly to the Archbishop of Sens in one of his letters'.[90]

The question remains, however, what Augustine's perspective was regarding Pilate having power over Christ. Could the one who is the source of all power be voluntarily subject to a part of said power, as Bernard and Marsilius propose? There are reasons to suspect Augustine did not believe this. Throughout his extensive *corpus* Augustine combines John 19. 11 and Romans 13. 1 on a few occasions, usually applying Romans 13. 1 as a universal statement, and John 19. 11 as an example. This approach is echoed in Bernard's. Augustine developed the notion that God gives certain people power but does not determine how they use this power. An example of this appears in *De diversis quaestionibus ad octoginta tribus* (388–395) and *De spiritu et littera* (412/413). Augustine explained with another quote from Romans that 'God handed them over to the desires of their hearts'.[91] In these instances John 19. 11 is used as an example of what happens when Pilate, whom Augustine described as 'tumidus' or 'swelling with arrogance',[92] was given the power to act out an evil desire of his heart. The power given to a person with bad intent is, according to Augustine, intended to teach the Christian a valuable lesson.[93]

The Roman trial of Jesus was not a demonstration of the power of a worldly government per se, but a pre-emptive re-enactment of the persecutions that Christians would suffer in the following centuries. Augustine believed secular power was legitimate, since all power comes from God, even if the ruler is considered evil. Thus, he points out in *De civitate* that Julian the Apostate received his power from God, just like Constantine the Great, and both needed to be obeyed by good Christians.[94] Hence Pilate would have to be obeyed as well, a position which falls in line with Marsilius's arguments. Unless, and this will be discussed in the following section, secular power intended to interfere in matters of faith.[95] Would persecuting the son of God not be a grave interference of a secular government in matters of faith? Pilate's power was legitimate and divinely granted, but his use of it was free and, as Augustine points out in the sermon quoted above, inspired fear. Much of this is, of course, theoretical, and it is notable that

---

90 *DP*, II, 4.12: 'Fuit ergo iudicialis coactive Pilati supra Christi personam a Deo, sicut aperte Christus confessus est, et Augustinus palam expressit, et aperte dixit Bernardus ad archiepiscopum Senonensem epistola quadam'.

91 Romans 1. 24: 'tradidit illos Deus in desideria cordis eorum'.

92 *Sermo 299ᴱ*.

93 *div.qu.*, LXXIX, 4.

94 *civ.Dei*, V, 21.

95 *Exp.prop.Rm.*, 72.

Augustine does not immediately posit the inverse standpoint, namely that the ecclesiastical authorities would step out of line if they took on temporal roles. He did, however, posit just that in his *Tractatus* CXV: 'hear, all ye kingdoms of the earth: I interfere not with your government in this world, My kingdom is not of this world. [...] What more do you want?'[96] Again Augustine and Marsilius are aligned.

Legitimacy, Guilt, and the Perversion of Justice

Despite having developed two arguments based on the trial narrative, Marsilius pushed the person of Pontius Pilate into the background. Pilate was a problem for Marsilius, as this was the man who condemned Christ to the cross. Therefore, Marsilius opted to reduce Pilate to his secular legitimacy. Augustine, however, wrote openly about his dislike of Pilate. This explains why the question regarding the guilt of Christ's death features prominently in Augustine's work, but not in the *Defensor*. According to Augustine, both Pilate and the Jews are guilty but not to the same degree. The Church Father divided the guilt according to two criteria: the amount of power and the actions taken by the actors. Since God, who is the source of all power, had only indirectly given power to Pilate, the brunt of Roman blame fell on the emperor, who had power over the prefect. Pilate therefore received the smaller share. The Jews, however, were the guiltiest.[97]

The conclusion that the Paduan draws is simply a confirmation of Pilate's legitimacy. By doing so, he separates Christ's death from the trial. This was impossible for Augustine, who treated the trial and Christ's subsequent death as one chain of events. The trial was unjust, and the Jews are blamed for slaying the innocent.[98] Jewish guilt would return in other works in which Augustine analysed the trial of Jesus, such as other treatises on the Gospel of John and in a few sermons, for example, 223/C *De Nocte Sancta*.[99] In the Church Father's eyes the trial before Pilate was thus a perversion of justice, which fits with his opinion that justice was never fully realized by pagan society:

---

96 *Io.ev.tr.*, CXV, 2: 'audite, omnia regna terrena: Non impedio dominationem vestram in hoc mundo; Regnum meum non est de hoc mundo. [...] Quid vultis amplius?'

97 *DP*, II, 4.12; *Io.ev.tr.*, CXVI, 5.

98 *Io.ev.tr.*, CXV, 5.

99 The guilt for the murder of Christ befalls Pilate, while in *Tractatus* CXV the Jews are blamed, but at the same time Christ had the liberty to choose his death. Augustine explores how this affects the guilt of the involved parties; cf. *Sermo* 223/C *De Nocte Sancta*, in Augustine, *Predigten zum österlichen Triduum*, trans. by Drobner pp. 299–304.

Then he shows the use of definition in debate; and from these definitions of his own he gathers that a republic, or 'weal of the people', then exists only when it is well and justly governed, whether by a monarch, or an aristocracy, or by the whole people. But when the monarch is unjust, [...] then the republic is not only blemished [...], but by legitimate deduction from those definitions, it altogether ceases to be.[100]

None of these considerations feature in the *Defensor pacis*, as they would have counted against Marsilius's argument, though Marsilius would likely not have disagreed with Augustine's conclusion that a republic, in the sense of *res publica*, could only exist (or have permanent justice) if it were founded by Christ. This analysis indicates that Augustine's thoughts on the trial beyond the parts that Marsilius uses deviate strongly from the argument he constructs. From Marsilius's perspective an all-encompassing analysis of the trial including the issues of legitimacy, the perversion of justice, and the question of who was guilty would have overly complicated his argument or even refuted it. For the Paduan's argument to function only the issue of legitimacy is to be addressed. Thus, Marsilius states that Christ accepted the Roman state's legislative powers, which acts as a *pars pro toto* for all worldly government.[101] Marsilius also thinks Christ considered the normal court procedure to be valid even when it applied to him:

But according to the opinion of our adversaries, Christ should not have said what Theophylact says — viz. that Pilate should carry out an ordinary investigation about him — but rather that such an investigation did not apply to him; in that according to our adversaries he was not and did not want to be subject to Pilate as of right in coercive jurisdiction or judgement.[102]

Lastly, Augustine's thinking has been characterized as associative,[103] and his interest extends far beyond the political. This is apparent when investigating the wide range of topics to which Augustine applies John 18. 36 and 19. 11. This range is broader than the political and judicial use Marsilius

---

100 *civ.Dei*, II, 21: ' atque ex illis suis definitionibus colligit tunc esse rem publicam, id est rem populi, cum bene ac iuste geritur siue ab uno rege siue a paucis optimatibus siue ab uniuerso populo. Cum uero iniustus est rex [...] cui nomen usitatum non repperit, [...] sed sicut ratio ex illis definitionibus conexa docuisset'.

101 Although his use of the Roman Empire could also support an argument for the rule of a universal empire; cf. Nederman, *Lineages of European Political Thought*, p. 176.

102 *DP*, II. 4.5: 'Hoc autem, quod dicit Theophylactes, non debuisset dicere Christus, quod videlicet Pilatus inquisitionem de ipso faceret ordinariam, quinimo dicere debuisset hanc inquisitionem ad ipsum non pertinere, ex quo sibi secundum adversantium opinionem de iure subiectus non erat vel esse nolebat in iurisdictione sive iudicio coactivo'.

103 Lee and Dupont, 'Augustine's Two Cities Revisited', p. 83.

GERT-JAN VAN DE VOORDE

has for those two verses. The eschatological significance of the trial in *Epistula ad Simplicianum* and *Tractatus* CXV has been pointed out. *Contra Faustum* also interprets the trial as teaching martyrs,[104] but in *De ordine*, for instance, Augustine appeals to John 18. 36 to demonstrate a philosophical point. Christ informing Pilate that his kingdom is not of this world shows, according to the Church Father, that there is indeed another world, like the Platonists suggested.[105] From *De diversis quaestionibus* q. 74 a third use emerges: Augustine uses both the trial and Romans 13. 1, this time at the end of a discussion regarding the difference between the power of saints and the power of magicians to do miracles. The same reasoning also appears in *De trinitate*.[106] Augustine also used John 19. 11 to draw a parallel between Christ's suffering and Job's in his second exposition on Psalm 29.[107] This difference in scope is one of the clearest differences between Augustine and Marsilius.

Conclusions

The two arguments based on the Roman trial of Jesus that Marsilius develops in the *Defensor* are very different in nature and purpose. In the first argument Christ excludes himself from secular power, while in the second he validates the authority of that power even over him. While for both arguments Marsilius appealed to Augustine, the Paduan uses his sources differently. The first argument, the one based on John 18. 36, is first introduced by a discussion of the biblical account, which is followed by a strengthening of Marsilius's case with Church Fathers, in this case mainly Augustine, though authors such as Chrysostom and Theophylact are given minor roles. In the case of Chrysostom, who is quoted in the relevant section of the *Catena* more often than Augustine, this is due to the incompatibility of his thought with Marsilius's. In the *Catena*, but also in the *Tractatus* CXV (the source used by Aquinas) Augustine does not lay out a clear hierarchy between Church and State, unlike Chrysostom. Marsilius built his argument carefully, taking small parts of Augustine's text and rearranging them in an order that fits the *Defensor*. Augustine's arguments surrounding John 18. 36 were easily integrated in the *Defensor*. By inverting State and Church, Marsilius could use the arguments without many further alterations. The second argument, based on the combination of John 19. 11 and Romans 13. 1, appears in the two *dictiones*, but the version in the first *dictio* is more an appeal to different authorities than

---

104 *c.Faust*, 22, 20.
105 *De ordine*, I, 11.32.
106 *div.qu.*, LXXIX, 1–4; *Trin.*, III. 2.12.
107 *en. Ps.*, II, 29.7.

an argument and discusses the divine establishment of government, something Marsilius does not devote much attention to as he considers it unprovable.

In the second *dictio* the argument based on John and Romans is introduced similarly as the John 18. 36 argument. The use of authorities, however, is different. Augustine is quoted once, and although the quote is lengthy, the Church Father is not the primary authority. The Augustinian quote is taken from the *Catena*, which in turn cites the *Tractatus* CXVI, and although it does appear to tackle Christ's personal and voluntary subjection to Pilate's power, the issue that Augustine is considering is one of guilt. Necessity requires Marsilius to cite it, and he uses it to prove that Pilate's coercive power is of divine origin, although guilt is not something Marsilius can use in his arguments. Instead, Marsilius is more indebted to the argument based on the same verses Bernard of Clairvaux made in his letter to Sanglier, archbishop of Sens, which omits the issue of guilt entirely and does clearly state that Christ willingly bowed to Pilate's power because it was legitimate. Bernard does not reference Augustine, but his opinion aligns with Augustine's on this matter. Nevertheless, in its construction Marsilius's argument is very similar to Bernard's, though in an expanded form.

Marsilius, therefore, used Augustine's words in different ways depending on the nature of his arguments. Regarding the first argument Augustine arguably influenced Marsilius, but the case cannot be proven conclusively, as it is unclear whether Marsilius began by consulting the Church Fathers or by reasoning from the Bible, which the structure of his arguments suggests. Once, Marsilius states outright that he adds the arguments made by authorities so that he would not be accused of misusing Scripture.[108] This, however, cannot be applied to all arguments Marsilius deployed. Certainly not the argument based on John and Romans which is more akin to Bernard's argument. The positions espoused by Marsilius regarding the Roman trial of Christ appear like each other. Both are in favour of a separation between the Church and the State, with Christians serving the latter, rather than opposing it or rejecting its authority. Marsilius also appears to have understood what Augustine wrote in *Tractatus* CXV, despite not having consulted it directly, given the fitting remarks the Paduan made. They also agreed on the issue of ecclesiastical coercive temporal power. Augustine lived in a time where the emperor had that power, and the Bishop of Hippo appealed to that imperial power against the Donatists. By consequence it meant that the Church itself had none, which is a central argument of the *Defensor*. While making his John 18. 36 argument,

---

108 *DP*, II, 4.8.

Marsilius remarks that if Christ's kingdom had had coercive power, it would have hindered the legitimate temporal powers.

There are many differences between the two authors. One could put it bluntly that Augustine was a theologian whose political considerations served his theology, and Marsilius was a political strategist whose theological considerations underpinned his political theory. A last difference that inspired the different treatment of the trial in the work of Augustine and Marsilius is Augustine's dislike of Pilate and the trial, which alongside other considerations, made Augustine avoid using the trial narrative. Marsilius keeps the unpopular figure in the background, lest he undermine his own argument regarding the state.

Works Cited

Primary Sources

Augustine of Hippo, *The Answer to Faustus, a Manichean: Contra Faustum Manichaeum*, ed. by Boniface Ramsey, trans. by Roland J. Teske, The Works of Saint Augustine: A Translation for the 21st Century, 1.20 (New York: New City Press, 2007)

——, *Answer to the Pelagians*, ed. by John E. Rotelle, trans. by Roland J. Teske, The Works of Saint Augustine: A Translation for the 21st Century, 1.23 (New York: New City Press, 1997)

——, *Augustine on Romans: Propositions from the Epistle to the Romans, Unfinished Commentary on the Epistle to the Romans*, trans. by Paula Fredriksen Landes, Texts and Translations, Early Christian Literature Series, 23.6 (Chico: Scholars Press, 1982)

——, *The City of God (Books 1–10)*, ed. by Boniface Ramsey, trans. by William Babcock, The Works of Saint Augustine: A Translation for the 21st Century, 1.6 (New York: New City Press, 2012)

——, *The City of God (Books 11–22)*, ed. by Boniface Ramsey, trans. by William Babcock, The Works of Saint Augustine: A Translation for the 21st Century, 1.7 (New York: New City Press, 2013)

——, *Lectures or Tractates on the Gospel According to St John*, ed. by Philip Schaff, trans. by John Gibb, Nicene and Post-Nicene Fathers, 7 (Buffalo: T&T Clark, 1888)

——, *Predigten zum österlichen Triduum (Sermones 218–29/D): Einleitung, Text, Übersetzung und Anmerkungen*, trans. by Hubertus R. Drobner, Patrologia, 16 (Frankfurt am Main: P. Lang, 2006)

——, *Responses to Miscellaneous Questions*, ed. by Boniface Ramsey, trans. by Raymond Canning, The Works of Saint Augustine: A Translation for the 21st Century, 1.12 (New York: New City Press, 2008)

——, *Sermons 273–305A*, ed. by John E. Rotelle, trans. by Edmund Hill, The Works of Saint Augustine: A Translation for the 21st Century, 3.8 (New York: New City Press, 1990)

——, *Sermons 306–340A*, ed. by John E. Rotelle, trans. by Edmund Hill, The Works of Saint Augustine: A Translation for the 21st Century, 3.9 (New York: New City Press, 1990)

——, *The Trinity*, ed. by Edmund Hill, trans. by John E. Rotelle, The Works of Saint Augustine: A Translation for the 21st Century, 1.5 (New York: New City Press, 2015)

Bernard of Clairvaux, *On Baptism and the Office of Bishops, on the Conduct and Office of Bishops, on Baptism and Other Questions: Two Letter-Treatises*, ed. by Emero Stiegman, trans. by Martha G. Newman, Cistercian Fathers Series, 67 (Kalamazoo: Cistercian Publications, 2004)

Giles of Rome, *On Ecclesiastical Power: A Medieval Theory of World Government. A Critical Edition and Translation*, trans. by Robert Dyson, Records of Western Civilization (New York: Columbia University Press, 2004)

Marsilius of Padua, *The Defender of the Peace*, trans. by Annabel Brett, Cambridge Texts in the History of Political Thought (Cambridge: Cambridge University Press, 2005)

——, *Defensor minor*, in *Writings on the Empire: 'Defensor minor' and 'De translatione Imperii'*, ed. and trans. by Cary J. Nederman, Cambridge Texts in the History of Political Thought (Cambridge: Cambridge University Press, 1993), pp. 1–64

——, *The Defensor pacis of Marsilius of Padua*, ed. by Charles W. Previté-Orton (Cambridge: Cambridge University Press, 1928)

——, *De translatione Imperii*, in *Writings on the Empire: 'Defensor minor' and 'De translatione Imperii'*, ed. and trans. by Cary J. Nederman, Cambridge Texts in the History of Political Thought (Cambridge: Cambridge University Press, 1993), pp. 65–81

Thomas Aquinas, *Catena Aurea: Commentary on the Four Gospels Collected out of the Works of the Fathers*, IV: *Gospel of Saint John*, trans. by John Henry Newman (Oxford: John Henry Parker, 1841)

Secondary Works

Blythe, James M., *Ideal Government and the Mixed Constitution in the Middle Ages* (Princeton, NJ: Princeton University Press, 2016)

Brett, Annabel, 'Introduction', in Marsilius of Padua, *The Defender of the Peace*, trans. by Annabel Brett, Cambridge Texts in the History of Political Thought (Cambridge: Cambridge University Press, 2005), pp. xi–lxi

Breyfogle, Todd, 'Toward a Contemporary Augustinian Understanding of Politics', in *Augustine and Politics*, ed. by John Doody, Kevin L. Hugues, and Kim Paffenroth (Lamham: Lexington Books, 2005), pp. 218–35

Brown, Peter, 'St Augustine's Attitude to Religious Coercion', *Journal of Roman Studies*, 54 (1964), 107–16

Bulgakov, Mikhail, *The Master and Margarita*, trans. by Richard Pevear and Larissa Volokhonsky (New York: Penguin, 2001)

Butts, Mary Alice, 'The Political Doctrines of Augustine of Hippo and Marsilius of Padua: A Comparison' (unpublished doctoral dissertation, University of Toronto, 1974)

Condren, Conal, 'Democracy and the *Defensor Pacis*: On the English Language Tradition of Marsilian Interpretation', *Il Pensiero Politico*, 13 (1980), 301–16

————, 'On Interpreting Marsilius' Use of St Augustine', *Augustiniana*, 25 (1975), 217–22

Eastman, John, 'Giles of Rome and his Use of St Augustine in Defense of Papal Abdication', *Augustiniana*, 38.1 (1988), 129–39

Gewirth, Alan, *Marsilius of Padua: The Defender of Peace*, I: *Marsilius of Padua and Medieval Political Philosophy*, Records of Civilization, Sources and Studies, 46 (New York: Columbia University Press, 1951)

Lee, Gregory, and Anthony Dupont, 'Augustine's Two Cities Revisited: Contemporary Approaches to *De civitate Dei*', *Archiwum Historii Filozofii i Mysli Spolecznej*, 61 (2016), 79–105

Mastnak, Tomaž, *Crusading Peace: Christendom, the Muslim World, and Western Political Order* (Berkeley: University of California Press, 2002)

Moreno-Riaño, Gerson, and Cary J. Nederman, 'Marsilius of Padua's Principles of Secular Politics', in *A Companion to Marsilius of Padua*, ed. by Gerson Moreno-Riaño and Cary J. Nederman, Brill's Companions to the Christian Tradition, 31 (Leiden: Brill, 2011), pp. 117–38

Mulcahy, Daniel G., 'The Hands of Augustine, but the Voice of Marsilius', *Augustiniana*, 21 (1971), 457–66

————, 'Marsilius of Padua's Use of St Augustine', *Revue d'Etudes Augustiniennes et Patristiques*, 18.1–2 (1972), 180–90

Nederman, Cary J., *Lineages of European Political Thought: Explorations along the Medieval/Modern Divide from John of Salisbury to Hegel* (Washington, DC: Catholic University of America Press, 2009)

Pollmann, Karla, and Willemien Otten, eds, *The Oxford Guide to the Historical Reception of Augustine*, 3 vols (Oxford: Oxford University Press, 2013)

Rensberger, David, 'The Politics of John: The Trial of Jesus in the Fourth Gospel', *Journal of Biblical Literature*, 103.3 (1984), 395–411

Rosen, George, 'The Historical Significance of Some Medical References in the Defensor Pacis of Marsilius of Padua', *Sudhoffs Archiv für Geschichte der Medizin und der Naturwissenschaften*, 37.3–4 (1953), 350–56

Scott, Joanna Vecchiarelli, 'Influence or Manipulation? The Role of Augustinianism in the Defensor Pacis of Marsiglio of Padua', *Augustinian Studies*, 9 (1978), 59–79

Setton, Kenneth M., *The Papacy and the Levant (1204–1571), the Thirteenth and Fourteenth Centuries*, Memoirs of the American Philosophical Society, 144 (Philadelphia: American Philosophical Society, 1976)

Syros, Vasileios, *Marsilius of Padua at the Intersection of Ancient and Medieval Traditions of Political Thought* (Toronto: University of Toronto Press, 2012)

Trainor, Brian T., 'Augustine's Glorious City of God as Principle of the Political', *Heythrop Journal*, 51.4 (2010), 543–53

Weithman, Paul, 'Augustine's Political Philosophy', in *The Cambridge Companion to Augustine*, ed. by Eleonore Stump and Norman Kretzmann, Cambridge Companions to Philosophers (Cambridge: Cambridge University Press, 2001), pp. 234–52

MARCO TOSTE

The Early *Politics* Commentaries as the Missing Link between Marsilius and Aristotle

Introduction

Together with Giles of Rome's *De regimine principum* and Ptolemy of Lucca's continuation of Thomas Aquinas's *De regno*, the *Defensor pacis* is, of any throughout the Middle Ages, the work that quotes Aristotle's *Politics* most frequently — indeed, it is by far the most quoted work in *Dictio* I. However, while Giles follows the structure of the first three books of the *Politics* to such an extent that, in some parts, it comes closer to being regarded as a commentary on the *Politics*, and Ptolemy turns Book IV of the *De regno* into a sort of commentary on Book II of the *Politics*,[1] Marsilius does not stick to its structure. He uses its eight books in a much more ingenious way, quoting from and referring to different and unrelated parts of it to construct his arguments.

For this reason, scholars have long debated the relationship between *Dictio* I of the *Defensor pacis* and the *Politics*, analysing the extent to which Marsilius depends on the *Politics* — sometimes engaging in a subdiscussion on whether he should be labelled Aristotelian — and to what degree he transformed the ideas found in his source on account of both the historical context and the purposes he had in composing the *Defensor pacis*.[2] The major problem with this long-standing and still open scholarly debate is that it often fails to take into consideration one factor, that is,

---

1 On Giles's use of the *Politics*, see Lambertini, '*Philosophus videtur tangere tres rationes*'; Lanza, 'La *Politica* di Aristotele'. On Ptolemy's use, see Laurenti, 'Tommaso e Tolomeo da Lucca'.

2 This topic is the object of many studies, especially after the publication of Alan Gewirth's *Marsilius of Padua*. It is not necessary to pad this note with bibliography. For further studies

> **Marco Toste** is affiliated with the University of Coimbra (Instituto de Estudos Filosóficos). He has published extensively on medieval political thought with a focus on the reception of the *Politics*.

Marsilius of Padua, ed. by Alessandro Mulieri, Serena Masolini, and Jenny Pelletier, Disputatio, 36 (Turnhout: Brepols, 2023), pp. 75–102

BREPOLS ❧ PUBLISHERS   10.1484/M.DISPUT-EB.5.132908

whether Marsilius drew directly on the *Politics* or whether he occasionally also relied on medieval commentaries on this work and read Aristotle's text through the lens of its commentators. This is not of secondary importance, because, on the one hand, what scholars regard as innovative and hence significant in Marsilius — for instance, the secular framework of his theory in *Dictio* I — might in fact be taken from a commentary. On the other hand, if the interpretations of the *Politics* advanced by other medieval authors were of little account to Marsilius, it is difficult to understand why, to give but one example, he dedicated the longest chapter of *Dictio* I, that is, Chapter 16, not only to settling whether hereditary monarchy is preferable to an elective form of government but, more importantly, to determining what Aristotle's view on the subject was.[3] In other words, if we overlook that Marsilius on occasion wishes to clarify *what* the true interpretation of specific views of Aristotle in the *Politics* is, we are unable to explain why he engages in this kind of discussion.

The aim of this chapter is, therefore, to examine the relationship between *Dictio* I of the *Defensor pacis* and the early commentaries on the *Politics* and to provide further evidence demonstrating that Peter of Auvergne (or perhaps the Anonymous of Milan) is a major source for (as well as a key target of) *Dictio* I of the *Defensor pacis*.[4] The chapter is divided into three parts: in the first, I explain why Marsilius took medieval interpretations on the *Politics* into consideration; I also give an account of the historiographic picture of the relationship between Marsilius and the commentators. Next, I focus on two precise but distinct points: the qualifications required of the ruler advanced in Chapter 14 and the use of the organic analogy throughout *Dictio* I. Analysis of these two topics

---

on this topic, see the notes throughout this chapter. See also Roberto Lambertini's chapter in this volume and the bibliography quoted there.

3 This is a question intimately connected to the medieval reception of the *Politics* and not to any other context, such as Marsilius's contemporary Italian political setting. This question was suggested by an incidental remark found in *Politics* III, 15, 1286b22–27. It came to the fore thanks to Giles of Rome's *De regimine principum* (III, 2.5) and Peter of Auvergne's two commentaries on the *Politics*, where he deals with the question at length. It became so important in the early fourteenth-century scholasticism that it is also found, with arguments similar to those of Giles and Peter, in quodlibetal questions, for instance, by the Pseudo-Rigauld, John of Naples, and Henry of Germany. By contrast, the question is not found in Italian political works produced around the time when Marsilius wrote the *Defensor pacis*.

4 Peter of Auvergne is the author of two commentaries on the *Politics*: the *Scriptum super III–VIII libros Politicorum* (a literal commentary) and the *Questiones super I–VII libros Politicorum* (a commentary in question form). These two works have recently been the object of critical editions. In the introduction to the critical edition of the *Questiones*, I provide evidence to date it to sometime between late 1291 and 1296, and after the completion of the *Scriptum*. The commentary of the Milan commentator was probably produced at the turn of the fourteenth century and is highly influenced by Peter's *Questiones*. It is contained in the manuscript Milan, Biblioteca Ambrosiana, MS A.100.inf., fols 1ra–54vb.

will show that, for some of the specific views advanced by Marsilius, for example, the qualifications of a ruler, the commentaries on the *Politics* were indeed his main source — and not the *Politics*, much less the *Politics* alone — and that, in other cases, that is, at a more general level, the commentaries provided the intellectual equipment for Marsilius's ideas; this holds for the use of the organic analogy in different chapters of *Dictio* I. In fact, as will be argued, Marsilius's use of the organic analogy should not be traced back to medical literature. The study of these two topics, though very different from one another, permits a better understanding of the multifarious ways in which the medieval reception of the *Politics* influenced Marsilius.

Marsilius and the Medieval Interpretation of the *Politics*

Any fourteenth-century political author had a vast array of sources available that he could use to support his views, Aristotle being one among others. The fact that Marsilius chose to quote the *Politics* abundantly must be understood as deliberate, and this extends to his explication of the authentic views of Aristotle. Marsilius certainly did not view the *Defensor pacis* as a piece of scholarly erudition the main aim of which was to discuss Aristotle — if that were his purpose, he would have produced a commentary on the *Politics* in his capacity as master of arts. Instead, he conceived of the *Defensor pacis* as a work by which he could intervene in the political reality of his time. This being so, the fact that he illustrates his positions with Aristotelian passages and engages in discussions as to what the view of Aristotle was speaks volumes, for it suggests that he deemed it worth discussing interpretations of the *Politics* and, what is more, that the centre of gravity of *Dictio* I is the *Politics*. In fact, not only is the *Politics* (followed by the *Nicomachean Ethics*) the most quoted work in *Dictio* I,[5] but the interpretations of the *Politics* are the only ones Marsilius addresses there; nowhere does he bother to discuss interpretations of other works, including medical sources.

The significance of Marsilius's extensive use of the *Politics* is not actually altered whether we think that he simply intended to present his views as though they were Aristotelian — and in this case being faithful to Aristotle would have been irrelevant for Marsilius, and Aristotle would be just grist to his mill — or whether we presume that Marsilius presented what he thought was the most correct interpretation of Aristotle. For this reason, we can in some measure apply to Marsilius's use of Aristotle the

---

5 See the chapter by Lambertini in this volume.

distinction Conal Condren made with regard to the presence of Augustine in the *Defensor pacis*, that is, that the *use* of an author is distinct from *adherence* to his views.[6] The question that emerges is, therefore, why Marsilius decided to use Aristotle so extensively, even taking the trouble to discuss the interpretations that certain people (*quidam*) held regarding the *Politics*.

What would be the point of discussing in detail Aristotle's authentic opinion if it were not for the fact that, in that particular passage, Marsilius is presenting his views as genuinely Aristotelian and himself as a valid, if not *the* legitimate interpreter of Aristotle?[7] If his views were anti-Aristotelian or, say, Ciceronian, he would merely criticize Aristotle without taking into account his medieval interpreters.[8] This is not, however, what Marsilius does: for instance, in Chapter 16, he draws on different Aristotelian works to maintain that Aristotle himself identified an elective form of government as the best and criticizes unnamed authors who use Aristotle to argue the opposite. The same is seen in Chapter 13, where he discusses the participation of the masses in the law-making process and, using Aristotle as his main source, refutes the view according to which the masses should be excluded from said process altogether.[9] It must be underlined that the *Defensor pacis* is the only medieval political work which, while not a commentary on the *Politics*, discusses interpretations of the *Politics*. No other medieval or Renaissance political treatise, even those heavily reliant on the *Politics*, such as the works of Giles of Rome, Lauro Quirini, Lippo Brandolini, Tostado, and Rodrigo Sánchez de Arévalo, to mention but a few, discusses the interpretations of the commentators on the *Politics*. For this reason, the fact that Marsilius engages in such a discussion is highly significant.

---

6 Cf. Condren, 'On Interpreting Marsilius of Padua's Use of St Augustine'. In some cases, we can speak of influence of Aristotle over Marsilius, while in others of the use that Marsilius made of Aristotle.

7 To avoid any misunderstanding, 'Aristotelian' should not be confused with 'Aristotelianism'. The discussion of how we should understand 'political Aristotelianism' exceeds the scope of this chapter. I address this point in a monograph I am currently preparing.

8 The rejection of specific theories of Aristotle by medieval thinkers, including masters of arts in commentaries on Aristotelian works, was not uncommon. See, by way of example, Peter of Auvergne, *Questions on Aristotle's 'De Caelo'*, ed. by Galle, pp. 96*–97*. On the fact that medieval Aristotelians criticized Aristotle, see Bianchi, '*Aristotele fu un uomo e poté errare*'. Therefore, that Marsilius does not reject a single theory of Aristotle throughout *Dictio* I and, on top of that, discusses medieval interpretations of Aristotle's views tells us that he deliberately situated himself within an Aristotelian framework. What is more, since Marsilius engages in discussions with interpreters of the *Politics*, we cannot but conclude that he wishes to present *his* Aristotle as *the* true Aristotle. Perhaps a comparison with twentieth-century philosophy may be illuminating in this regard: only authors who saw themselves as Marxists took the trouble to discuss Kautsky, Gramsci, Lukács, or Althusser. For authors outside that current, such as Rawls, Nozick, and MacIntyre, to discuss what the 'authentic' view of Marx was (and the views of his interpreters) was irrelevant.

9 On this last point, see Toste, 'The Parts and the Whole'.

As to the question of why he discussed interpretations of the *Politics*, the answer is that Marsilius understood such interpretations to be overly 'monarchist' and 'elitist', that is, they presented Aristotle as having maintained that hereditary monarchy was the best form of government, as favouring the view that the ruler is above the law, and as having completely excluded the masses from the law-making process. This answer, while correct, is incomplete, however. Marsilius could have simply ignored these interpretations of the *Politics*, adapting the text to his own agenda. Rather, he took them into account because he was so influenced by the intellectual milieu at the University of Paris that, when composing the *Defensor pacis*, he could not but make use of the sources most used there.

As William Courtenay has argued,

> Despite a long historiography that links Marsilius and his *Defensor pacis* to Padua and political conditions in Italy, most of his education, teaching, and writing in the first three decades of the fourteenth century occurred at Paris. The core of his world was the University of Paris.[10]

At Paris, we may add, the *Politics* together with the *Nicomachean Ethics* constituted the core of the teaching of practical philosophy. Indeed, Marsilius turned more to the *Politics* in order to construct his argumentation in *Dictio* I than to Italy. As I have argued elsewhere, the source of Marsilius's understanding of the law-making process as one based on specific roles assigned to the multitude and a few wise men is most likely Peter of Auvergne's question-commentary on the *Politics*, not the *Politics* itself, nor the reality of Italian communal life.[11] The intellectual world of Marsilius was more centred in Paris than in Italy,[12] and it is this that explains his attention to the interpretations of the *Politics*, which were produced by his fellow masters of arts, who would have been some of his sparring-partners in *Dictio* I.[13]

In a previous article, I have demonstrated how the notions of tranquillity and peace, understood as political effects inherent to the *civitas* and stemming from the consensus reached by the body of citizens, or at least by its prevailing part, were elaborated on in the earliest

---

10 Courtenay, 'Marsilius of Padua at Paris', p. 70.

11 Toste, 'The Parts and the Whole'.

12 This does not exclude the point that the Italian political reality looms large in some of Marsilius's views. Indeed, his conception of the ruler is more suitable to an Italian *podestà* than to a French king.

13 I take this idea from Lidia Lanza's paper presented at the conference that originated this volume, though Lanza used this expression with respect to *Dictio* II and to Marsilius's use of contemporary theological works, such as *Sentences* commentaries produced at the Faculty of Theology of Paris while Marsilius was a student there. For Marsilius's reliance on theological works produced at Paris in *Dictio* II, see Lambertini, 'Marsilius and the Poverty Controversy'.

question-commentaries on the *Politics*, notably in Peter of Auvergne's questions. In the same article, I emphasized that Chapter 17 of *Dictio* I, on numerical unity, should be seen in connection with the final questions of Book VI of Peter's questions.[14] I have also brought Marsilius closer to Peter of Auvergne regarding the role of the will and consensus in political life.[15] In another article still, I have emphasized that Marsilius's views on the naturalness of human association, specifically Chapters 3–5 and 7 of *Dictio* I, are better understood if seen against the backdrop of the *Politics* commentaries.[16] There, I also provided evidence for Marsilius's use of Aquinas's commentary on the *Politics*.[17] I have more recently demonstrated that the question-commentary of Peter of Auvergne (as well as possibly that of the Anonymous of Milan) was, in all probability, the source of Chapters 12–13 of *Dictio* I, but that Marsilius's use of Peter was twofold: while he certainly took ideas from Peter, he also strongly opposed him. Peter is indeed Marsilius's main target in Chapter 13.[18]

Although my research was carried out over the past decade, it is part of a historiographic trend that compares the *Defensor pacis* with the earliest commentaries on the *Politics*, its aim being to highlight the similarities and also the differences between the two works. This path is less travelled than others in the scholarship on Marsilius. Even so, because it is a comparative approach based on textual evidence, it provides results essential to the understanding of the intellectual framework in which the *Defensor pacis* appeared.[19] In this sense, this approach effectively argues that *Dictio* I can only be fully understood against the backdrop of the reception of the *Politics* (even though *Dictio* I cannot be reduced to a mere paraphrasing of Aristotle).[20]

The scholar who initiated this approach was Ferdinand Cranz, who focused on the relationship between Peter of Auvergne's question-commentary on the *Politics* and the *Defensor pacis*. Cranz briefly examined the questions as to whether it is better to be ruled by the best man or by the best law (*Questiones* II, q. 22 = *DP*, I, 11), whether the multitude should have a share in power (*Questiones* III, qq. 15–17 = *DP*, I, 12–13), and whether it is better for the ruler to come to office by election or

---

14 Cf. Toste, 'An Original Way of Commenting', pp. 346–47 and 350–51.

15 Cf. Toste, 'The Naturalness of Human Association', pp. 165–68.

16 Cf. Toste, 'La socievolezza umana', pp. 24–31.

17 Cf. Toste, 'La socievolezza umana', pp. 25–26.

18 Cf. Toste, 'The Parts and the Whole'. On this topic, see also Syros, 'The Sovereignty of the Multitude'.

19 This has been acknowledged in Lambertini, '*À la recherche de l'ésprit laïque*', pp. 369–70.

20 On the reception of the *Politics* and its impact in medieval political thought, see, apart from the studies mentioned throughout this chapter, the overviews provided in Fioravanti, 'La *Politica* aristotelica'; Lambertini, 'Lo studio e la recezione'; and Lanza, 'I commenti medievali'.

through hereditary succession (*Questiones* III, q. 25 = *DP*, I, 16).[21] Following on from Cranz, Alan Gewirth studied more or less the same topics.[22] Some decades later, Christoph Flüeler concentrated on the question of election vs. hereditary succession.[23]

Analysis of this last question leaves no doubt that Marsilius was 'debating' with the previous interpreters of the *Politics*. Chapter 16 is the longest chapter of *Dictio* I and, perhaps more importantly, is arranged as a scholastic disputed question presenting arguments for and against his solution. Marsilius begins the chapter by stating that certain (*quidam*) authors have supported the view that the ruler's holding office by hereditary succession is preferable to election, and he then presents his opponents' arguments, eleven in total. Cranz maintained that Giles of Rome and the Anonymous of Milan were Marsilius's targets, whereas Flüeler demonstrated that the first six arguments along with the eleventh argument adduced by Marsilius find a correspondent in Peter's *Questiones*. To this, we can add that Peter is undoubtedly Marsilius's target in the tenth argument *contra*.[24]

Chapter 11 of *Dictio* I is also revealing in terms of how much Marsilius takes heed of the interpretations of the *Politics*, for he disputes and concurrently takes inspiration from them there. Even though Marsilius does not structure this chapter as a disputed question, in *DP*, I, 11.4–7, he clearly contests the views of Peter and Giles, who used *Politics*, III, 15 to argue, as though it were the view of Aristotle himself, that it is better to be ruled by an outstanding virtuous man than by the best law.[25] By contrast, in *DP*, I, 11.3, where Marsilius sets forth one of his most significant views, which he then develops in the successive chapters, namely that the law-making process cannot be undertaken by one man alone but, like the sciences, is a collective work improved over time through the work of different

---

21 Cf. Cranz, 'Aristotelianism in Medieval Political Theory', pp. 319–63.

22 Cf. Gewirth, *Marsilius of Padua, ad indicem*.

23 Cf. Flüeler, *Rezeption und Interpretation*, I, pp. 120–31. Roberto Lambertini can be added to this group of scholars, because, even though he has not produced a study comparing the two works, he has repeatedly subscribed to this approach. See, for instance, Lambertini, 'À la recherche de l'ésprit laïque'.

24 Compare the *Defensor pacis* with Peter's *Questiones*: 'Rursum, quo plures et in pluribus regionibus ac populis et pluri tempore perfeccior est modus assumendi monarcham; quoniam magis naturalis, magis perfectus, magis naturale autem quod in pluribus est. Natura namque rerum est, que pluribus et plurimo tempore inest, ut in 3° Celi et Mundi et 2° Physice eciam scriptum est' (*DP*, I, 16.9, ed. by Scholz, p. 99); Peter of Auvergne, *Questiones*, III, q. 25, ed. by Toste, pp. 568–69: 'Sed ad hoc dicendum quod hoc est contra naturam quod bonus generet malum, et ideo ut rarius contingit: natura enim est causa eorum que semper uel frequentius fiunt, ut dicitur 2° Phisicorum. Et ideo magis naturale est semper bonum succedere bono; minus autem naturale semper bonum eligere'. Strikingly, the two texts quote the same source.

25 That Marsilius is criticizing Peter is now a commonplace in scholarship. See, for instance, Annabel Brett's note in Marsilius of Padua, *The Defender of the Peace*, p. 57 n. 2.

generations, he quotes, among other texts of Aristotle, the *Politics* (several times), *Metaphysics,* and *Sophistical Refutations* in support of this view. Marsilius takes inspiration from *Politics*, II, 8, 1268b34–40, where Aristotle compares the improvement in laws through the ages to the progress achieved in the sciences. However, it was not only the *Politics* which was his source here, since the *Metaphysics* and the *Sophistical Refutations* are mentioned together in Giles's *De regimine* and in one question of Book II of Peter's *Questiones* precisely to argue (in Giles's case) that no man alone can discover everything, including in politics, or (in Peter's case) that, unlike in the sciences, laws should not always be changed when there is a better law, since laws, contrary to science, also take their binding force from custom (*consuetudo*).[26]

We can thus conclude that the relationship between Marsilius and the commentators is complex. On the one hand, Marsilius takes issue with views advanced by the commentators, whom he never names, and on those occasions, he strives to demonstrate that Aristotle himself maintained his own view. On the other hand, he also tacitly relies on commentaries in putting forward some of his views. This will be even more evident in the next section of this chapter.

The Qualifications of the Ruler

Chapter 14 of *Dictio* I is dedicated to defining the main qualifications that the ruler of a just political regime must have.[27] Throughout the chapter, Marsilius quotes the *Politics* fifteen times and the *Nicomachean Ethics* on five occasions. These two works are almost exclusively the only sources Marsilius quotes in this chapter; he also quotes Sallust's *Catiline* in *DP*, I, 14.3, but this serves to provide a historical example and it is, therefore,

---

26 Cf. Giles of Rome, *De regimine principum*, III, 1.6, p. 415: 'ut patet per Philosophum, 2 Metaphisicorum et circa finem Elenchorum, nullus sibi sufficit in inveniendo artem aliquam, sed oportet ad hoc iuvari per auxilium praecedentium tradentium notitiam aliquam de arte illa'; Peter of Auvergne, *Questiones*, II, q. 17, ed. by Toste, pp. 490, 492: 'sed in factiuis uidemus quod, que prius inuenta sunt, melioribus superuenientibus mutantur, ut patet in medicina et etiam in sutoria, ut 1° Metaphisice et 2° Elenchorum; ergo sic est in legislatiua [...]. Ad rationes dicendum quod in factiuis bene potest prius <inuenta> mutari, quia nichil est ibi propter quod per accidens, si debeat mutari, <timendum sit>, quod non oportet ibi timeri de inobedientia, que est uoluntatis; uoluntas autem ad factiua non pertinet. Iterum in speculatiuis potest aliquid mutari, quia scientia ibi fit non ex consuetudine, sicut mores in actiuis'. The same argument, albeit slightly different, is found in Question 17 of Book II of the Milan commentary (Milan, Biblioteca Ambrosiana, MS A.100.inf., fol. 18ʳᵃ). Also note that, commenting on *Politics*, II, 8, 1268b34–40, Albert the Great already quotes the *Sophistical Refutations*; cf. Albertus Magnus, *Politicorum Lib.* VIII, II, 6, ed. by Borgnet, p. 153.

27 *DP*, I, 14, ed. by Scholz, pp. 78–84.

THE EARLY *POLITICS* COMMENTARIES   83

not significant from a doctrinal point of view. The number of quotations from Aristotle's two works is an immediate sign that Marsilius framed this chapter in Aristotelian terms.

According to Marsilius, the qualifications of a ruler are (1) prudence, (2) moral virtues (especially justice and *epieikeia*), (3) love or goodwill (*amor seu benivolencia*) towards the political regime (*policia*), and (4) coercive power to punish disobedient citizens. Among all these qualifications, Marsilius emphasizes prudence and stresses that prudence and the moral virtues cannot be detached. Marsilius's obvious main source for this chapter is *Politics*, v, 9, 1309a33–35, which he only quotes explicitly at the beginning of the last paragraph of the chapter. In this passage of the *Politics*, Aristotle lists three qualifications, which in William of Moerbeke's Latin version are translated as *amor ad consistentem politiam, potentia*, and *virtus et iustitia*, that is, the justice proper to each political regime.[28] They correspond to the qualifications listed by Marsilius, except that Marsilius adds prudence. In fact, after quoting this passage from the *Politics*, Marsilius adds that virtue must be understood here as prudence,[29] which seems a novelty of his own. This is not, however, the case.

In his commentaries on the *Politics*, in the *Scriptum super III–VIII libros Politicorum* and in the *Questiones super I–VII libros Politicorum*, Peter of Auvergne names the three qualifications as *amor principatus* (in the *Scriptum*) or *amor politie* and *dilectio politie* (in the *Questiones*), *potentia*, and *virtus et iustitia*. In fact, it is Peter who first connects Aristotle's reference to virtue with prudence — and, like Marsilius, with the concept of prudence found in Book VI of the *Ethics* — and to such a great extent that he also connects the need for love or loyalty to the political regime with it.[30] This is even clearer in the *Questiones*, where Peter, commenting

---

28 Aristotle, *Politicorum libri octo*, ed. by Susemihl, p. 548.

29 *DP*, I, 14.8, ed. by Scholz, p. 84: 'tercio autem virtutem et iusticiam; per virtutem intelligens prudenciam, que omnium vinculum est et magistra virtutum'.

30 Peter of Auvergne, *Scriptum*, ed. by Lanza, pp. 315–16: 'dicit quod debentem perfecte principari principali principatu tria oportet habere. Primum est amor principatus: oportet enim, si perfecte debeat principari, quod diligat principatum. Et ratio huius est quia perfecte principans debet habere prudentiam, quia prudentia est recta ratio agibilium: princeps autem, cum habeat regere alios, oportet quod habeat rectam rationem de agibilibus, quare oportet quod habeat prudentiam perfectam. Sed prudentiam non potest habere, nisi habeat appetitum rectum ad finem; hoc autem non potest esse nisi diligat finem et ea que sunt ad finem, secundum quod huiusmodi. Principatus autem principium est eorum que ordinantur ad finem politie. Quare manifestum est quod bene principantem oportet habere amorem ad principatum et politiam. Secundo oportet quod habeat potentiam respectu operum principatus, que maxima sunt [...] alii autem sunt qui non de facili suadentur a ratione, sed sunt inobedientes et insolentes: et pro talibus indiget potentia coactiua; cohercere autem et punire non potest nisi potentiam habeat [...]. Tertio oportet quod habeat uirtutem [...]. Oportet enim principantem habere prudentiam; hoc autem non est nisi habeat appetitum rectum, sed rectitudo appetitus est per uirtutem moralem'.

on Book v, raises three questions inspired by *Politics*, v, 9, 1309a33–35, namely 'utrum ad recte principandum exigatur scientia in principe' (q. 11), 'utrum ad perfectionem principantis exigatur amor politie' (q. 12), and 'utrum potentia exigatur ad perfectionem principantis' (q. 13).[31]

In q. 11, Peter establishes that a ruler needs to possess practical science and therefore the principles of prudence in order to rule his subjects. Unlike Marsilius, however, Peter substantiates the need for prudence on teleological grounds: as the ruler moves his subjects towards an end, that is, the purpose towards which the political regime aims, the ruler needs to have the virtue of being able to deliberate about the right means of reaching an end — this virtue, according to the sixth book of the *Ethics*, is prudence.[32] Peter stresses the need for prudence even more in q. 12, on whether a ruler needs to have *amor politie* (this syntagm can be understood as meaning loyalty or devotion to the political regime). For Peter, since a ruler needs prudence to deliberate on the means of reaching an end, he also needs to have a correct desire for the end and, therefore, devotion (*dilectio*) to the end of the political regime. This is because unless one prizes (*diligit*) something, say, an end, one cannot desire it and choose the best means of reaching it. It is only by means of this devotion (*dilectio*) that a ruler can also care for the political regime. It is noteworthy that, like Marsilius, Peter insists here that prudence needs to be connected with the moral virtues, the role of which is to regulate the desire for the end.[33]

---

31 For an analysis of these questions, though from a different point of view than the one I have here, see Toste, 'Virtue and the City', pp. 95–98.

32 Peter of Auvergne, *Questiones*, v, q. 11, ed. by Toste, pp. 644–45: 'ad rationem principantis <oportet> habere eum scientiam aliquam necessarie, necessitate inquam ex suppositione, scilicet, si bene debet operari. Cuius ratio est quia mouens, si debet mouere, oportet habere principium, quia agens agit per principium agendi existens in ipso; sed principium per quod agit et mouet princeps est scientia, que est forma et ratio agendi [...]. Agibilia sunt quorum principium per se est prudentia et electio, cuius electionis necessario principium est consilium et ratio. Ergo oportet principantem habere scientiam aliquam ut bene agat. [...] Notandum autem ulterius quod ratio principantis, et eorum que sunt circa principatum, a fine accipitur et ex fine dependet; operatio autem principis est mouere et dirigere alios in finem politie; oportet ergo quod hec directio fiat per rationem supradictam ex fine, et ideo principantem oportet habere scientiam que est principium ordinandi aliqua in finem. Hec autem scientia est prudentia'. Because different political regimes pursue different ends, Peter argues that, in the case of unjust regimes, the ruler's prudence is only *secundum quid*; cf. Toste, 'Virtue and the City', pp. 95–98.

33 Peter of Auvergne, *Questiones*, v, q. 12, ed. by Toste, pp. 646–48: 'ad principantem in magno principatu exigitur dilectio politie. Cuius ratio est quia ad perfectionem principantis, si debet recte principari, exigitur perfectio prudentie; hec autem non est in non habente primum principium prudentie, quod est rectus appetitus finis; ergo ille rectus appetitus finis necessario exigetur ad perfectionem principantis. Rectus autem appetitus finis politie non est sine dilectione politie et consistentie eius, quia nullus recte bonum et finem illius appetit quod non diligit, sed potius uult malum illius quam bonum. Et ideo dilectio politie necessario principi est. Item, prudentia est recta ratio eorum que in finem et recta electio

THE EARLY *POLITICS* COMMENTARIES 85

Finally, in q. 13, he argues that a ruler needs to have coercive power (*potentia ciuilis*) to repress disobedient citizens, his opponents, and those who are arrogant. This qualification, Peter stresses, is not something a ruler may use in whatever way he so wishes, but rather must be 'regulated by reason', that is, prudence.[34] For this reason, while prudence and virtue are qualifications required of the ruler in an unqualified way, power is a qualification that belongs to a ruler only *ex consequenti*, that is, as a secondary qualification required insofar as lawbreakers must be punished.[35]

Peter provides a deeper and much more philosophically substantive account of the need for these attributes than Marsilius, and stresses the teleological aspect of these qualifications, something absent from the *Defensor pacis*. There can be no doubt, however, that Marsilius took inspiration from Peter or from a commentary influenced by him, for example, the Anonymous of Milan.[36]

It should be noted, however, that in some passages Marsilius's wording is closer to Peter's *Scriptum* than to the *Questiones*. For instance, in *DP*, I, 14.8, Marsilius writes that the ruler needs a limited number of armed man so that 'suas civiles sentencias in rebelles et inobedientes per coactivam potenciam exequi possit',[37] which finds a correspondent in Peter's

---

illorum secundum rationem sumptam ex fine. Non contingit autem bona eligere circa illud et illi quod non diligimus; et ideo, si finem debemus diligere, necessario eligemus ea que in finem et ea diligemus [...]. Item, qui non diligit politiam non curat eam, ut dicitur 2° huius: dilectio enim est una causarum sollicitudinis circa aliquid; sed non curare politiam est contra rationem principantis, que est dirigere in finem; ergo et cetera. Ex hoc autem sequitur quod necessario ad principantem rectum et simpliciter, qui utitur prudentia simpliciter, exigitur uirtus, que de necessitate connexa est prudentie, circa cuius finem appetitum rectificat uirtus et cui principium ministrat. Et ideo ad principantem exigitur et dilectio politie et uirtus, ad minus condependens prudentie tali, siue sit uirtus moralis seu alia'.

34 Peter of Auvergne, *Questiones*, V, q. 13, ed. by Toste, pp. 650–51: 'illud per quod insolentes compescuntur et aduersarii reprimuntur, illud est de perfectione et necessitate principantis inquantum huiusmodi; sed hoc est potentia; ergo et cetera [...]. Ad principatum autem maximum non exigitur per se et primo, sicut patet ex hoc quod aliquis ea posset uti ad principandum indifferenter; sed ad illum exigitur per se ratio prudentie et primo, ex consequenti autem potentia. Intendit enim legislator eos qui sub se sunt in finem politie ducere per leges et precepta et exercitationes; contingit tamen quod non omnes ei obediant; ideo, si debet eos dirigere in finem, de necessitate indiget potentia, et hoc propter inobedientiam ciuium et malignitatem insidiantium. Et sic necessaria est potentia ciuilis, sed tamen non quecumque potentia ciuilis nec quocumque modo accepta, sed solum commensurata et regulata ratione recta sumpta ex fine'.

35 Peter deals at great length with this distinction in the questions in Book III dedicated to the political role of the multitude; cf. Toste, 'The Parts and the Whole', pp. 216–18.

36 See questions 7–8 of Book V, contained in Milan, Biblioteca Ambrosiana, MS A.100.inf., fols 44ra–45vb. In these two questions, the anonymous commentator sticks to the *Questiones* as far as the topic covered here is concerned, and for this reason, it is not necessary to provide his text.

37 *DP*, I, 14.8, ed. by Scholz, p. 82.

86   MARCO TOSTE

sentence that some citizens 'sunt inobedientes et insolentes: et pro talibus [princeps] indiget potentia coactiua'.[38]

In any case, that Marsilius drew on Peter's interpretation is also evident in other specific passages. In *DP*, I, 14.3 and 5, Marsilius adds a further reason for why a ruler needs prudence: he must deliberate and pronounce judgement about particular cases and circumstances that are not determined by law.[39] Although Marsilius supports his claim by appealing to *Politics*, III, 6, 1282b3–6, where Aristotle states that the rulers ought to regulate matters undetermined by law, Aristotle does not, in fact, make any reference to prudence there. Once again, Marsilius's source is Peter. In this way, it is extremely telling that Marsilius ends *DP*, I, 14.4 with a reference to *Politics*, III, 9, 1287b19–23, where Aristotle asks whether it is preferable to be ruled by the best law or by the most virtuous man. A question with this title became topical at Paris, being found in important works of the late thirteenth century, including commentaries on the *Politics* and *Ethics*.[40] We can be positively sure, however, that Peter's *Questiones* is Marsilius's source here, since Peter is the only author who addresses this question by contending that prudence is the virtue that permits one to judge and deliberate on particular cases not covered by law.[41] The other authors addressing this question prior to the composition of the *Defensor pacis*, such as Giles of Rome, Giles of Orleans, Radulphus Brito, and James of Viterbo, speak of 'right reason' and none of them states that prudence is a proviso for deliberation on particular cases.[42]

Finally, in *DP*, I, 14.7, Marsilius includes the ruler's need for *epieikeia* in those cases in which the law is defective.[43] As Marsilius himself acknowledges, this virtue is discussed in *Ethics*, V, 10, and *epieikeia* was therefore dealt with in commentaries on that work. It is, however, significant that in the *Scriptum*, in his explanation of *Politics*, III, 9, 1287b23–24 — the passage cited by Marsilius at the end of *DP*, I, 14.4 — Peter remarks that a ruler ought to have *epieikeia*, for he must deliberate on particular cases

---

38 See note 30, above.

39 *DP*, I, 14.3 and 5, ed. by Scholz, pp. 79–81.

40 See the classic study Renna, 'Aristotle and the French Monarchy' and Toste, '*Nobiles, optimi viri, philosophi*', pp. 290–92.

41 Peter of Auvergne, *Questiones*, III, q. 22, ed. by Toste, p. 560: 'homo bonus per rationem rectam et prudentiam potest bene iudicare de omnibus, uniuersalibus et particularibus: potest enim applicare rationem ad x particulares casus; lex autem, cum sit propositio uniuersalis, hoc non potest, immo solum uniuersalia iudicat secundum rationem finis uniuersalis; particularia autem relinquit prudentie iudicis determinanda'.

42 Cf. Giles of Rome, *De regimine principum*, III, 2.30, pp. 531–34; Cranz, 'Aristotelianism in Medieval Political Theory', pp. 336–40 (where the question from Giles of Orleans's *Ethics* commentary is partially edited); James of Viterbo, *Disputatio quarta de quolibet*, Quodlibet IV, q. 30, ed. by Ypma, pp. 107–10; and Brito's question in his *Ethics* commentary edited in Radulphus Brito, *Le 'questiones'*, ed. by Costa, pp. 455–57.

43 *DP*, I, 14.7, ed. by Scholz, pp. 81–82.

not determined by law.[44] We cannot be positively certain that Marsilius sourced the idea from Peter, but this seems likely the case.

Chapter 14 of *Dictio* I is, therefore, a clear instance of Marsilius's reliance on the *Politics*, but through the lens of Peter of Auvergne (probably both of his commentaries). It is difficult to imagine that Marsilius would have emphasized the need for prudence so much in a chapter about the ruler's qualifications had he not read Peter of Auvergne, who, in both of his *Politics* commentaries, attaches a great weight to prudence. In this, Peter is completely distinct from Albert: for instance, commenting on *Politics*, v, 9, Albert does not mention prudence as one of the qualifications of the ruler.[45]

The Organic Analogy

Various scholars have studied the association that Marsilius makes between the heart of an animal and the main office (*principatus*) of the *civitas* and have suggested that Marsilius drew the organic analogy from works of medicine and from authors such as Galen, Avicenna, and Peter of Abano.[46] In this sense, the *Defensor pacis* would represent a new conception of the body politic and an intersection between the methodologies of medicine and political thought. In my view, it is fruitless, however, to seek out texts on medicine and 'underground influences' possibly exerted by authors whom Marsilius never quotes.[47] In fact, in the Middle Ages, knowledge of medical literature was not limited to students of the Faculty of Medicine,

---

44 Peter of Auvergne, *Scriptum*, ed. by Lanza, p. 126: 'ubi lex scripta deficit in aliquo casu particulari, dirigat, et hoc est per uirtutem que dicitur epieikes [*sic*]'.

45 Cf. Albertus Magnus, *Politicorum Lib. VIII*, v, 4, ed. by Borgnet, pp. 495–96.

46 See, for instance, Aichele, 'Heart and Soul of the State'; Shogimen, 'Medicine and the Body Politic'; Kaye, *A History of Balance*, pp. 299–344.

47 One might object that Marsilius does not explicitly quote the commentators on the *Politics*, either. This does not hold, however. Medieval scholastic authors quoted those authors by name who were recognized as part of the tradition and considered to be 'authorities', e.g., Aristotle, Avicenna, Averroes, Eustratius, Simplicius, Proclus, Maimonides, Augustine, Anselm, etc. They did not, however, name contemporary authors or fellow masters. They simply reproduced the ideas of such authors without mentioning them (for instance, Aquinas, a major source for the Aristotelian commentators of the Arts Faculty of Paris, was almost never mentioned by them; the major exception to this was Albert the Great, who was often mentioned by name). When they wished to criticize a contemporary author, they would simply state, 'quidam dicunt'. This only started to change in the 1330s, when they began to identify the authors that they opposed. For this reason, it would have been unusual for Marsilius to have mentioned Peter of Auvergne, while it would have been perfectly normal to have quoted Galen and Avicenna, if he had wanted to.

as theologians and masters of arts such as Marsilius were more or less familiar with that corpus as well.[48]

Marsilius compares the body politic with the animal body four times in *Dictio* I:

> (1) In *DP*, I, 2.3, where he refers to *Politics*, V, 3 and states that all the parts of the body must be proportionate to each other and that their activities are realized for the sake of the whole, this balance representing the animal's health. Likewise, the balance between the parts of the *civitas*, which are proportionate among themselves and work for the benefit of the whole, produce tranquillity in the *civitas*. Political tranquillity stands, therefore, to the *civitas* as health stands to the animal's well-being.
>
> (2) In *DP*, I, 15.5–6 and 13, where he cites *Politics*, V, 3 and VII, 8, the *On Animals* (*De animalibus*), and Galen to argue that the main office stands to the rest of the community as the heart to the animal's parts. This is arguably where the organic analogy plays the greatest role in Marsilius's argument in the whole of *Dictio* I. There, he makes the case that just as the heart is the first part of the animal to be formed, so that it has the capacity to preserve all the other parts of the animal because of the heat it generates, so too a ruler must be the first element instituted by the body politic, so that he assigns specific functions to different parts of the *civitas* and preserves it through his executive authority.
>
> (3) In *DP*, I, 17.8, drawing on the *Movement of Animals*, Marsilius states that, just as an animal cannot have a plurality of principles responsible for its motion, the political community as well must have one single main office to which all the others are subordinate.
>
> (4) In *DP*, I, 18.2, Marsilius argues that, just as the heart in an animal, the ruler regulates the other parts of the community.[49]

The first aspect that stands out from this list is that Marsilius cites Aristotle almost every time he compares the *civitas* with an animal. In the fourth instance, however, he does not mention any author. Galen is cited only once throughout *Dictio* I, and Avicenna, another major medical authority, is never mentioned. This is remarkable enough in and of itself, since Albert the Great and Peter of Auvergne quote Avicenna's *Canon of Medicine* in Book VII of their *Politics* commentaries.[50] One might ask why Marsilius does not quote medical literature more often, as he does make use of

---

48 This has been demonstrated in Ziegler, '*Ut dicunt medici*'; Lugt, *Le ver, le démon et la vierge*.

49 For these four passages, see *DP*, I, 2.3, ed. by Scholz, pp. 11–12; I, 15.5–6 and 13, pp. 87–89 and 93–94; I, 17.8, pp. 117; I, 18.2, pp. 121–22.

50 See, for instance, Peter of Auvergne, *Scriptum*, ed. by Lanza, pp. 575–76, with the *apparatus fontium*.

THE EARLY *POLITICS* COMMENTARIES   89

works on natural philosophy such as *On the Soul* and *On Generation and Corruption*, and even of the *Metaphysics*.[51]

However, the most important question is how original Marsilius is in drawing these analogies. Roberto Lambertini has already noted that the comparison between the heart and the ruler is found in several works produced before the *Defensor pacis* and influenced by the *Politics*, such as Aquinas's *De regno*, Giles of Rome's *De regimine*, and Peter's commentaries on the *Politics*.[52] Moreover, because the analogy between the city and the animal is found in Aristotle's *Movement of Animals* and, therefore, also in commentaries on this work — including that by Peter of Auvergne[53] — the analogy was known to any person such as Marsilius with an adequate knowledge of Aristotle. Indeed, Marsilius was a master at the Arts Faculty of Paris, where the curriculum was largely based on the *corpus Aristotelicum*, and he wrote the greater part of, if not all of, the *Defensor pacis* in Paris. This suggests that it was more likely that he took ideas from Aristotle that were *also* found in works on medicine.[54] To illustrate my point, it suffices to mention a passage from Peter's literal commentary on the *Politics* where he explains Aristotle's claim that quarrels among the notable men of the political community must be stopped at the outset. To elucidate this passage of the *Politics*, Peter states, first, that a small difference in the animal's heart causes a great difference in the other parts of the animal and, second, that a small difference in the semen produces a great difference in what results from it: whether it is cold or hot will produce a male or a female, respectively.[55] Should we conclude, therefore, that Peter of Auvergne was influenced by medical works when these ideas are easily found in Aristotle? There is no reason to assume so with respect to either Peter or Marsilius, both of whom were masters of arts.

---

51 We should not assume a priori that just because medieval sources identify Marsilius as a physician, that he *necessarily* had to quote medical sources. In his commentary on the *Economics*, Bartholomew of Varignana, a professor of medicine at the University of Bologna, drew on Giles of Rome's *De regimine principum* instead of medical works and did not deal with medical issues; cf. Lambertini, 'L'arte del governo della casa'.

52 Lambertini, 'Il cuore e l'anima della città'.

53 For the analogy in commentaries on the *Movement of Animals*, see Rossi, 'È da ritenere'.

54 In Toste, 'La socievolezza umana', I have demonstrated that Marsilius's views on the human body advanced in the opening chapters of the *Defensor pacis* are found in the *corpus Aristotelicum* and some of them in Peter's *Questiones* on the *Politics* too, which renders it pointless to seek for works of medicine as sources of Marsilius.

55 Peter of Auvergne, *Scriptum*, ed. by Lanza, p. 270: 'dissensio que accidit inter maiores et principantes est peccatum in principio [...]. Nam peccatum in principio proportionaliter se habet ad ea peccata que fiunt in partibus animalium principalibus: utrobique est in primis. Videmus autem quod, modica facta diuersitate in parte principali in animali, scilicet in corde, magna fit diuersitas in aliis partibus. Similiter, modica existente diuersitate in semine, fit magna diuersitas in eo quod fit ex semine, quia ex modica differentia calidi et frigidi in eo causatur differentia maris et femine'.

90   MARCO TOSTE

Medieval political works are full of analogies and metaphors.[56] The organic analogy is certainly found repeatedly in medieval political discourse,[57] and the same can be said of the comparison between a ruler and a physician,[58] along with that between peace in the *civitas* and a healthy body.[59] In terms of works produced at the Arts Faculty, it should come as no surprise that their arguments rather draw at times on works of natural philosophy and metaphysics, since this reflects the *curriculum studiorum* of the Arts Faculty of Paris. By way of example, a work such as the *On the Difference between the Spirit and the Soul* by Costa Ben Luca was part of the curriculum from 1255,[60] and arts students were well familiar, therefore, with the concept of *spiritus* as it was used in medical and philosophical literature. Thanks to the influence of Albert's works on natural philosophy, they were also familiar with the notion of *complexio* and used it, for instance, in commentaries on the *Politics*, like the one by the Anonymous of Baltimore, to argue that the law must be adapted to the citizens, since men in different regions have different *complexiones* and thus different intellectual abilities.[61]

It can thus be seen that Marsilius was far from being the only author who used medical or natural philosophy analogies in the context of political argumentation. This becomes absolutely clear when we consider Peter's commentaries on the *Politics*. Indeed, if there is a medieval work dealing with political matters in which the comparison between the *civitas* and the animal body is often reiterated, this work is the *Questiones super I–VII libros Politicorum*. Peter makes the comparison no fewer than fourteen times throughout this commentary, and these occurrences can be brought closer to Marsilius's views mentioned above.

By way of example, Peter uses the organic analogy in each of the set of four questions of Book VI of the *Questiones* dedicated to explaining that

---

56 See, for instance, Lambertini, 'Il cuore e l'anima della città', and Langeloh, '*Minorem probat per simile*'.

57 The literature is vast, but see principally Struve, *Die Entwicklung*.

58 See, for instance, Giles of Rome, *De regimine principum*, III, 1.13, p. 434; III, 2.17, p. 496; and III, 2.23, p. 549.

59 Giles of Rome, *De regimine principum*, II, 1.12, p. 254: 'Nam pax inter homines se habet quasi sanitas respectu humorum'; but see also II, 2.2, p. 290: 'Nam sicut sanitas corporis naturalis dependet ex sanitate omnium membrorum, et maxime ex sanitate cordis et membrorum principalium, eo quod cor et principalia membra habent influere in alia et rectificare ipsa, sic bonitas regni dependet ex bonitate omnium civium; maxime tamen dependet ex iis qui principantur et dominantur in regno'.

60 Cf. Lohr, 'The New Aristotle', p. 257.

61 Baltimore, Johns Hopkins University, Milton S. Eisenhower Library, MB MSB 18, fol. 3[vb]: 'unde alia lex debet statui in regione frigida et alia in regione calida, et secundum diuersas complexiones hominum'. See also Toste, 'The Naturalness of Human Association', pp. 140–41, 161–62, where it is demonstrated how Peter of Auvergne used the notion of *complexio* in his question on whether man is naturally a social and political being.

THE EARLY *POLITICS* COMMENTARIES   91

the *civitas* needs a plurality of offices hierarchically subordinate to one supreme public office — which was probably the source for Chapter 17 of *Dictio* I.[62] Moreover, within the initial set of questions of Book V, in which Peter emphasizes the need for tranquillity and peace in the political community, he raises a question as to whether unlikeness (*dissimilitudo*) is a cause of dissension. There, Peter asserts that, like an animal, the *civitas* needs different parts but only one leading element, namely the heart in the case of the animal while, in the *civitas*, it is the agreement of the citizenry on the end to be pursued by the political regime.[63] A similar view is found in questions 2 and 4 of Book II of the *Questiones*: while both the parts of an animal and the *civitas* are distinct with respect to each other and have different functions, all their activities are for the sake of the whole animal (and *civitas*) — the feet move according to the needs of the whole animal.[64]

That a ruler is equivalent to the animal's heart is stated by Peter in Book III, q. 26, on whether it is preferable for the *civitas* to be ruled by one or by many,[65] and in Book IV, q. 4, on whether the forms of government are distinguished in accordance with the distinction of the parts of the *civitas*.[66] In a similar way, in Book III, q. 16, on whether it is expedient

---

62 Cf. Toste, 'An Original Way of Commenting', pp. 346–47 and 350–51.

63 Peter of Auvergne, *Questiones*, V, q. 5, ed. by Toste, pp. 628–29: 'Dispositio autem diuersa diuersorum potest esse dupliciter: uel inter se et etiam in ordine ad fines diuersos, uel etiam potest esse diuersa dispositio diuersorum inter se solum, ita quod tamen sit unitas in ordine ad unum finem, sicut patet in partibus animalis, <ubi> est diuersa dispositio diuersorum membrorum, tamen est unitas in ordine ad finem uel ad unum principium, ut ad cor; sed diuersorum animalium est diuersa dispositio et inter se et in ordine ad principium uel finem illius principii. Similiter autem oportet estimare in ciuitate sicut in animali, sicut econuerso dicitur in De Motibus Animalium. Ergo et in ciuitate potest esse dissimilitudo: uel ita quod sit diuersa dispositio ciuium inter se et etiam in ordine ad finem diuersum, et ista diuersitas et dissimilitudo est causa seditionis; alia autem potest esse diuersitas inter ciues, que tamen stet cum unitate ordinis in unum finem, et ista dissimilitudo est de necessitate ciuitatis, quia ista dissimilitudo est unitas secundum proportionem, que necessario est in ciuitate'.

64 Peter of Auvergne, *Questiones*, II, q. 2, ed. by Toste, p. 456: 'Item, libro De Motibus Animalium dicitur quod estimandum est animal esse unum sicut ciuitatem esse unam. Accipiatur autem hoc econuerso hic: modo in animali optimum est ipsum animal esse unum ordine, salua tamen distinctione partium. Nam operatio partium in operationem totius ordinatur, quia pes ita ambulat sicut toti expedit, et auris ita audit. Sic etiam oportet esse ciuitatem unam ut, licet sint partes, operationes tamen singulorum partium in operationem totius ordinentur'; II, q. 4, ed. by Toste, p. 461: 'Item, ciuitatem oportet ymaginari sicut animal ordinatum; in illo autem sunt multe partes propriam habentes operationem, licet ultimo in unum finem ordinentur, et etiam habent distinctum nutrimentum; ergo similiter debet esse in ciuitate'.

65 Cf. Peter of Auvergne, *Questiones*, III, q. 26, ed. by Toste, p. 571. On this question, see Lambertini, 'La monarchia prima della *Monarchia*'.

66 Peter of Auvergne, *Questiones*, IV, q. 4, ed. by Toste, pp. 586–87: 'ordo enim est habitudo prioris et posterioris inuicem; et ubi est reperire prius et posterius, ibi est reperire primum, et ideo ubi est ordo oportet esse aliquid primum, sicut in animali uidemus: sed si

for the multitude to hold the highest office, Peter suggests that the few wise men 'set in motion' the multitude, just as the heart sets in motion the animal's parts.[67] Finally, in Book VII, q. 4, on whether the happiness of one man and of the whole *civitas* are the same, and q. 6, on whether happiness consists in the act of prudence that is ruling, Peter declares that the main activity and the highest good of the *civitas* consist in the activity of its main part — the ruler — just as the main activity and the good of an animal rely on its heart.[68] Peter's use of this analogy reveals a monarchical stance, since he identifies the happiness of the *civitas* with that of the ruler, a view that is mirrored in the *Metaphysics* commentary of John of Jandun,[69] but which is far removed from Marsilius's political conception.

The organic analogy runs throughout Peter's output and is even found in one of his quodlibetal questions where he deals with the topic of taxation. There, Peter states that, just as the animal's movement flows from the heart to the other members in accordance with a certain proportion and that, by contrast, the members must provide it with nutrients because they depend on the heart, likewise in the *civitas* the citizens must provide the ruler with what is necessary for the maintenance of the common good because the ruler moves and directs his subjects towards the end. Moreover, all this is done in accordance with a certain proportion, that is, that of distributive justice.[70]

Should we assume that Peter was a student of medicine or that he drew on medical literature? Not at all: the inspiration for all these ideas can be traced back to the *corpus Aristotelicum* and its medieval interpretation. Marsilius's claim that all the parts of the animal's body (and of the *civitas*) must be proportionate with respect to each other and that a

---

consideremus naturam animalis secundum corpus, tunc natura eius consistit in ordine ad aliquod primum, ut ad cor. Similiter in plantis et anime partibus hoc patet. Forma autem ciuitatis est politia uel ordo quidam habitantium ciuitatem uel principantium, et ideo oportet quod in ciuitate inueniatur aliqua pars prima, et ista est in qua inuenitur prima ratio ordinis et principium: hoc autem est ipse principans in ciuitate'.

67 Cf. Peter of Auvergne, *Questiones*, III, q. 16, ed. by Toste, p. 542. For this passage, see Toste, 'The Parts and the Whole', p. 217.

68 Peter of Auvergne, *Questiones*, VII, q. 4, ed. by Toste, p. 699: 'in ordinatis essentialiter, bonum et operatio totius est bonum et operatio partis principalis, sicut operatio animalis, ut est uidere, alia <est> ab operatione cordis, <sed operatio et bonum cordis, quod est eius pars principalis, est operatio> et bonum <totius> animalis. Sed principalis pars ciuitatis aliquando est unus ciuis; ergo eadem erit operatio totius ciuitatis et unius alicuius ciuis, scilicet principantis'; VII, q. 6, ed. by Toste, p. 707: 'quando aliquid est compositum ex aliquibus, tunc bonum totius consistit in actu partis principalioris, ut bonum animalis consistit in actu cordis uel anime, similiter bonum anime in bono intellectus; sed politia est aliquid compositum, cuius principalior pars est principans; ergo in actu principantis secundum perfectissimam prudentiam consistet felicitas ciuitatis'.

69 Cf. Lambertini, '*Felicitas politica* und *speculatio*'; Toste, '*Nobiles, optimi viri, philosophi*', pp. 299–300.

70 Cf. Brown, '*Cessante causa* and the Taxes of the Last Capetians', p. 586.

THE EARLY *POLITICS* COMMENTARIES   93

disproportionate increase in one of its parts jeopardizes the very life of the animal (and of the *civitas*) is found in *Politics*, V, 3, 1302b33–1303a1.

Peter is not the only commentator to employ the analogy extensively. The Milan commentator sometimes uses it in the same contexts as Peter, other times in contexts different from those in which Peter does. In the first question of Book V of the Anonymous of Milan's commentary, on whether peace is the purpose of the *civitas*, he states that peace and concord form the state in which every citizen is pleased about his condition with respect to the common good and abides by what is proportional with respect to the other citizens. When this does not happen, upheavals and sedition arise. Likewise, when an animal has its limbs in their proper place, it will experience well-being, but should a joint become dislocated, it will feel an intolerable pain.[71] This view is not very different from Marsilius's. Moreover, in the question on whether the multitude may hold the highest office, his answer is positive, though with a caveat: the multitude may hold the highest office provided one of its members alone commands and directs the others and never in a manner whereby all the members of the multitude would rule together at the same time. This point is illustrated with the case of the animal's movement, in which the animal does not move forward all at once, but rather each part moves another and so on.[72] In the same question, arguing that the ruler needs coercive power, the commentator notes that the ruler must be like the animal's heart, which commands the other parts of the body, and these obey it in order for the animal to move.[73]

Because Peter's commentaries on the *Politics* turned into the most authoritative interpretation thereof shortly after they were produced and because Peter had on many occasions the approach of a natural philosopher,[74] he contributed perhaps more than any other author of his time to the use of this kind of analogy. We should, of course, not forget that each author appropriates his sources as he so wishes and for his own

---

71 Milan, Biblioteca Ambrosiana, MS A.100.inf., fol. 40ra: 'illa autem pax uel concordia est quando quilibet statu suo contentus in ordine ad bonum commune non molestat alium in suo nec uult ipsum transgredi ultra proportionale. Sic etiam uidemus in animalibus quod, quando membra sunt in suis sitibus naturalibus, habet quietem; si autem unum membrum dislocetur et exeat locum debitum (*cod.*: tebitum), sentit dolorem intolerabilem. Ita etiam ciues qui sunt partes communicationis politice habitudines (*cod.*: habites) sui ordinis <uolentes> exire, turbationem et seditionem (*cod.*: seductionem) faciunt in politica.' See also Lanza, 'Guerra e pace in Aristotele', p. 197.

72 Cf. Toste, 'The Parts and the Whole', pp. 222–23.

73 Milan, Biblioteca Ambrosiana, MS A.100.inf., fol. 27rb: 'Vnde in ciuitate oportet talem principem esse, cui sint subditi obedientes et in <nullo> rebelles: sicut cor enim in animali precepit motum aliis membris et sunt organa obedientia cordi ut animal ex<e>quatur motum suum, sic (*cod.*: sicut) etiam princeps se habet in ciuitate et se habere debet'.

74 To give but one example, one of the longest questions of Peter's *Questiones* is for the greater part devoted to the topic of 'radical moisture' (*humidum radicale*), where Peter refutes one

94   MARCO TOSTE

purposes. That Marsilius did not employ the analogy quite exactly as his predecessors does not imply that he drew on other sources, such as medical literature. Quite the contrary, for we should not expect that Marsilius, or any other author drawing on the *Questiones*, simply reproduced what he found in his source. The influence of any given work is always more complex.

Conclusions

Roughly thirty years separate Peter's *Questiones* and Marsilius's *Defensor pacis*. Even so, one of the manuscripts containing the *Questiones* was copied in the early 1320s from a manuscript owned by Annibaldo di Ceccano, a master of arts at Paris between 1307 and 1322.[75] This is a sign that the *Questiones* was still attracting attention and was deemed worthy of being reproduced around the time Marsilius was writing the *Defensor pacis*. Moreover, Courtenay has conjectured that Marsilius was connected in Paris with and was perhaps the teacher of Niccolò di Ceccano, Annibaldo's brother. Courtenay labels the group that included men such as the Ceccano brothers, Marsilius, Johann Hake, and John of Jandun as the 'Ceccano network'.[76] As I have argued elsewhere, Jandun was possibly influenced by Peter's *Questiones* in the political views he advanced in his *Metaphysics* commentary (though with regard to ideas that were not shared by Marsilius).[77] It seems quite probable, therefore, that Marsilius had access to Peter's *Questiones*.

In the first two decades of the fourteenth century, Peter was still regarded as a major authority: his commentaries on the *Politics* (both the *Questiones* and the *Scriptum*), *Metaphysics*, *Movement of Animals*, and *On the Heavens* became the standard commentaries at the Arts Faculty of Paris; five of his commentaries circulated through the *pecia* system, meaning that he is surpassed in the number of works transmitted in this way only by Albert the Great, Aquinas, and Giles of Rome; he influenced younger masters of arts, such as Radulphus Brito (in more than one Aristotelian commentary), Bartholomew of Bruges, John of Jandun, John Dinsdale (outside Paris), and possibly Antonius Andreae; authors such as Duns Scotus and Peter Auriol discussed his views; and his *Quodlibeta* survive in seventeen manuscripts (almost all of them copied in the first

---

specific case in which for him the organic analogy is invalid. This question is also significant because Peter shows here that he has a good understanding of a theory found in Avicenna's *Canon of Medicine*. The same does not hold for the *Defensor pacis*.

75 Cf. Flüeler, *Rezeption und Interpretation*, I, p. 104.

76 Cf. Courtenay, 'Marsilius of Padua at Paris', pp. 66–67.

77 Cf. Toste, '*Nobiles, optimi viri, philosophi*', pp. 299–300 and 302–04.

decades of the fourteenth century).[78] All this suggests that, when Marsilius arrived in Paris, and even though Peter had left the university in 1302 (or in 1303), he regarded Peter as an authoritative figure, at least within the context of the Arts Faculty. Nothing would be more natural than, when writing a political work, he should look for and address the leading interpretation of the time in that field.

It can hardly be overstated that medieval Aristotelian commentators did not limit themselves to explaining their source text slavishly and that they often transformed Aristotle's views and adjusted some of the ideas to their medieval reality. The two cases studied here confirm this: they reinterpreted the passage in which Aristotle addresses the qualifications of a ruler, by justifying the need for prudence, and employed the organic analogy to explain Aristotle's political views (and in ways that Aristotle would never have imagined). In doing so, they shaped the reading of the *Politics*.

There are further aspects in which we can bring Marsilius closer to the *Politics* and its medieval commentary tradition. Three examples suffice. First, it was in the context of Book VII of the *Politics* that the priesthood came to be seen as a part of the *civitas* on a par with all the others,[79] which is one of the main theses of the *Defensor pacis*. Second, the *Politics* commentaries do not deal with natural law, since the reach of politics is positive law, an approach that resonates in *Dictio* I.[80] Third, Marsilius subscribes to the notion, formulated in the *Politics* commentaries, that laws that are unjust in an unqualified way still need to be obeyed.[81] In whatever way we wish to interpret the ideas expressed in *Dictio* I, we need to study them against the background of the commentary tradition on the *Politics*. Only in this way can we fully appreciate the relationship between *Dictio* I and its main source, namely the *Politics*.

This is in fact the aim of this chapter (and one might say of others of this kind): *not* simply to identify Marsilius's sources for the sake of erudition, but to demonstrate that the *Defensor pacis* would have been a completely different work without both the *Politics* and its medieval interpretations. The *Defensor pacis* is a work by a medieval master of arts; its first part should be studied bearing this in mind. As another medieval political author, whom Marsilius met in Munich, might say: it is useless to seek out more sources when fewer suffice. There is no need to evoke

---

78 For all these claims, see the introductory study to my edition of the *Questiones* and the bibliography quoted there.

79 On priesthood and its role in the *Politics* commentaries, see Toste, 'Nobiles, optimi viri, philosophi', pp. 302–04; Lanza, 'Luciferianae pravitatis imago', pp. 167–68.

80 Cf. Lambertini, 'À la recherche de l'ésprit laïque', p. 369. This is not to say that Marsilius's conception of law completely depends on the commentaries on the *Politics*.

81 Cf. Toste, '*Tantum pauper quantum diues*', p. 305.

additional medical literature when the sources used in teaching at the Arts
Faculty are enough to explain the outline and most of the ideas of *Dictio* I,
a text welded to the medieval reception of the *Politics* and yet, at the same
time, one of the most original texts of the late Middle Ages.

Works Cited

Manuscripts

Baltimore, Johns Hopkins University, Milton S. Eisenhower Library, MB MSB 18
Milan, Biblioteca Ambrosiana, MS A.100.inf.

Primary Sources

Albertus Magnus, *Politicorum Lib. VIII*, vol. VIII of *Opera omnia*, ed. by Auguste
  Borgnet (Paris: Vivès, 1891)
Aristotle, *Politicorum libri octo cum vetusta translatione Guillelmi de Moerbeka*, ed. by
  Franz Susemihl (Leipzig: Teubner, 1872)
Giles of Rome, *De regimine principum Libri III, per Fr. Hieronymum Samaritanium*
  (Rome: Bartholomaeus Zannettus, 1607)
James of Viterbo, *Disputatio quarta de quolibet*, ed. by Eelco Ypma, Cassiciacum.
  Supplementband, 5 (Würzburg: Augustinus-Verlag, 1975)
Marsilius of Padua, *The Defender of the Peace*, trans. by Annabel Brett, Cambridge
  Texts in the History of Political Thought (Cambridge: Cambridge University
  Press, 2005)
——, *Defensor pacis*, ed. by Richard Scholz, Monumenta Germaniae Historica:
  Fontes iuris germanici antiqui in usum scholarum separatim editi, 7.2
  (Hannover: Hahn, 1933)
Peter of Auvergne, *Questiones super I–VII libros Politicorum: A Critical Edition and
  Study*, ed. by Marco Toste, Ancient and Medieval Philosophy, Ser. 1, 61
  (Leuven: Leuven University Press, 2022)
——, *Questions on Aristotle's 'De Caelo': A Critical Edition with an Interpretative
  Essay*, ed. by Griet Galle, Ancient and Medieval Philosophy, Series 1, 29
  (Leuven: Leuven University Press, 2003)
——, *Scriptum super III–VIII libros Politicorum Aristotelis*, ed. by Lidia Lanza,
  Scrinium Friburgense, 50 (Wiesbaden: Reichert, 2021)
Radulphus Brito, *Le 'questiones' di Radulfo Brito sull''Etica Nicomachea':
  Introduzione e testo critico*, ed. by Iacopo Costa, Studia Artistarum, 17
  (Turnhout: Brepols, 2008)

Secondary Works

Aichele, Alexander, 'Heart and Soul of the State: Some Remarks Concerning
  Aristotelian Ontology and Medieval Theory of Medicine in Marsilius of
  Padua's *Defensor Pacis*', in *The World of Marsilius of Padua*, ed. by Gerson
  Moreno-Riaño, Disputatio, 5 (Turnhout: Brepols, 2006), pp. 163–86

Bianchi, Luca, '*Aristotele fu un uomo e poté errare*: Sulle origini medievali della critica al *principio di autorità*', in *Filosofia e teologia nel Trecento: Studi in ricordo di Eugenio Randi*, ed. by Luca Bianchi, Textes et Études du Moyen Âge, 1 (Louvain-la-Neuve: F.I.D.E.M., 1994), pp. 509–33; repr. in Luca Bianchi, *Studi sull'Aristotelismo del Rinascimento*, Subsidia Mediaevalia Patavina, 5 (Padua: Il Poligrafo, 2003), pp. 101–24

Brown, Elizabeth, '*Cessante causa* and the Taxes of the Last Capetians: The Political Applications of a Philosophical Maxim', in *Post Scripta: Essays on Medieval Law and the Emergence of the European State in Honor of Gaines Post*, ed. by Joseph R. Strayer and Donald E. Queller, Studia Gratiana, 15 (Rome: Libreria Ateneo Salesiano, 1972), pp. 565–87; repr. in Elizabeth Brown, *Politics and Institutions in Capetian France*, Collected Studies Series, 350 (Hampshire–Brookfield, VT: Aldershot 1991), item 2

Condren, Conal, 'On Interpreting Marsilius' Use of St Augustine', *Augustiniana*, 25 (1975), 217–22

Courtenay, William J., 'Marsilius of Padua at Paris', in *A Companion to Marsilius of Padua*, ed. by Gerson Moreno-Riaño and Cary J. Nederman, Brill's Companions to the Christian Tradition, 31 (Leiden: Brill, 2012), pp. 57–70

Cranz, Ferdinand E., 'Aristotelianism in Medieval Political Theory: A Study of the Reception of the *Politics*' (unpublished doctoral dissertation, Harvard University, 1938)

Gewirth, Alan, *Marsilius of Padua: The Defender of Peace*, 1: *Marsilius of Padua and Medieval Political Philosophy*, Records of Civilization, Sources and Studies, 46 (New York: Columbia University Press, 1951)

Fioravanti, Gianfranco, 'La *Politica* aristotelica nel Medioevo: Linee di una ricezione', *Rivista di storia della filosofia*, 52.1 (1997), 17–29; French Version: 'La réception de la *Politique* d'Aristote au Moyen Age tardif', in *Aspects de la pensée médiévale dans la philosophie politique moderne*, ed. by Yves-Charles Zarka, Fondements de la politique. Série essais (Paris: Presses Universitaires de France, 1999), pp. 9–24

Flüeler, Christoph, *Rezeption und Interpretation der aristotelischen 'Politica' im späten Mittelalter*, Bochumer Studien zur Philosophie, 19, 2 vols (Amsterdam: B. R. Grüner, 1992)

Kaye, Joel, *A History of Balance, 1250–1375: The Emergence of a New Model of Equilibrium and its Impact on Thought* (Cambridge: Cambridge University Press, 2014)

Lambertini, Roberto, 'À la recherche de l'ésprit laïque in the Late Middle Ages', in *The Medieval World*, ed. by Peter Linehan, Janet L. Nelson, and Marios Costambeys, 2nd edn (London: Routledge, 2018), pp. 368–84

———, 'L'arte del governo della casa: Note sul commento di Bartolomeo da Varignana agli *Oeconomica*', *Medioevo*, 17 (1991), 347–90

——, 'Il cuore e l'anima della città: Osservazioni a margine sull'uso di metafore organicistiche in testi politici bassomedievali', in *Anima e corpo nella cultura medievale: Atti del V convegno di studi della Società Italiana per lo Studio del Pensiero Medievale, Venezia, 25–28 settembre 1995*, ed. by Carla Casagrande and Silvana Vecchio, Millenio Medievale, 15 (Florence: SISMEL–Edizioni del Galluzzo, 1999), pp. 289–303

——, '*Felicitas politica* und *speculatio*: Die Idee der Philosophie in ihrem Verhältnis zur Politik nach Johannes von Jandun', in *Was ist Philosophie im Mittelalter? Akten des X. internationales Kongresses für mittelalterlichen Philosophie*, ed. by Jan A. Aertsen and Andreas Speer, Miscellanea Mediaevalia, 26 (Berlin: De Gruyter, 1998), pp. 984–90

——, 'Marsilius and the Poverty Controversy in *Dictio* II', in *A Companion to Marsilius of Padua*, ed. by Gerson Moreno-Riaño and Cary J. Nederman, Brill's Companions to the Christian Tradition, 31 (Leiden: Brill, 2012), pp. 229–63

——, 'La monarchia prima della *Monarchia*: Le ragioni del *regnum* nella ricezione medievale di Aristotele', in *Pour Dante: Dante et l'Apocalypse. Lectures humanistes de Dante*, ed. by Bruno Pinchard and Christian Trottmann, Le savoir de Mantice, 7 (Paris: Honoré Champion, 2001), pp. 39–75

——, '*Philosophus videtur tangere tres rationes*: Egidio Romano lettore ed interprete della *Politica* nel terzo libro del *De regimine principum*', *Documenti e studi sulla tradizione filosofica medievale*, 1 (1990), 277–325

——, 'Lo studio e la recezione della *Politica* tra XIII e XIV secolo', in *Il pensiero politico dell'età antica e medioevale*, ed. by Carlo Dolcini (Turin: UTET, 2000), pp. 145–73

Langeloh, Jacob, '*Minorem probat per simile*: Analogical Reasoning in the Commentaries on Aristotle's Politics by Albert the Great and Thomas Aquinas', in *Von Natur und Herrschaft: 'Natura' und 'Dominium' in der politischen Theorie des 13. und 14. Jahrhunderts*, ed. by Delphine Carron, Matthias Lutz-Bachmann, Anselm Spindler, and Marco Toste, Schwächediskurse und Ressourcenregime, 3 (Frankfurt: Campus Verlag, 2018), pp. 49–70

Lanza, Lidia, 'I commenti medievali alla *Politica* e la riflessione sullo stato in Francia (secoli XIII–XIV)', in Lidia Lanza, *'Ei autem qui de politia considerat...': Aristotele nel pensiero politico medievale*, Textes et Études du Moyen Âge, 71 (Barcelona: FIDEM, 2013), pp. 115–37

——, 'Guerra e pace in Aristotele: Alcune riflessioni sui commenti medievali alla *Politica*', in Lidia Lanza, *'Ei autem qui de politia considerat...': Aristotele nel pensiero politico medievale*, Textes et Études du Moyen Âge, 71 (Barcelona: FIDEM, 2013), pp. 181–203

————, 'Luciferianae pravitatis imago: Il tiranno tra alto e basso Medioevo', in Lidia Lanza, 'Ei autem qui de politia considerat...': Aristotele nel pensiero politico medievale, Textes et Études du Moyen Âge, 71 (Barcelona: FIDEM, 2013), pp. 139–80

————, 'La Politica di Aristotele e il De regimine principum di Egidio Romano', in Lidia Lanza, 'Ei autem qui de politia considerat...': Aristotele nel pensiero politico medievale, Textes et Études du Moyen Âge, 71 (Barcelona: FIDEM, 2013), 233–92

Laurenti, Maria Cristina, 'Tommaso e Tolomeo da Lucca commentatori di Aristotele', Sandalion: Quaderni di cultura classica, cristiana e medievale, 8–9 (1985–1986), 343–71

Lohr, Charles H., 'The New Aristotle and science in the Paris Arts Faculty (1255)', in L'enseignement des disciplines à la Faculté des Arts (Paris et Oxford, XIII–XV siècles), ed. by Olga Weijers and Louis Holtz, Studia Artistarum, 4 (Turnhout: Brepols, 1997), pp. 251–69

Lugt, Maaike van der, Le ver, le démon et la vierge: Les théories médiévales de la génération extraordinaire (Paris: Les Belles Lettres, 2004)

Renna, Thomas, 'Aristotle and the French Monarchy, 1260–1303', Viator, 9 (1978), 309–24

Rossi, Pietro B., 'È da ritenere che l'animale sia come una città ben governata da leggi: Note sulla ricorrente analogia fra civitas e corpo organico nel medioevo', Rivista di storia della filosofia, 71.4 (suppl.) (2016), 51–65

Shogimen, Takashi, 'Medicine and the Body Politic in Marsilius of Padua's Defensor pacis', in A Companion to Marsilius of Padua, ed. by Gerson Moreno-Riaño and Cary J. Nederman, Brill's Companions to the Christian Tradition, 31 (Leiden: Brill, 2012), pp. 71–115

Struve, Tilman, Die Entwicklung der organologischen Staatsauffassung im Mittelalter, Monographien zur Geschichte des Mittelalters, 16 (Stuttgart: Hiersemann, 1978)

Syros, Vasileos, 'The Sovereignty of the Multitude in the Works of Marsilius of Padua, Peter of Auvergne, and Some Other Aristotelian Commentators', in The World of Marsilius of Padua, ed. by Gerson Moreno-Riaño, Disputatio, 5 (Turnhout: Brepols, 2006), pp. 227–48

Toste, Marco, 'The Naturalness of Human Association in Medieval Political Thought Revisited', in La nature comme source de la morale au Moyen Âge, ed. by Maaike van der Lugt, Micrologus' Library, 58 (Firenze: SISMEL–Edizioni del Galluzzo, 2014), pp. 113–88

————, 'Nobiles, optimi viri, philosophi: The Role of the Philosopher in the Political Community at the Faculty of Arts in Paris in Late Thirteenth Century', in Itinéraires de la raison: Études de philosophie médiévale offertes à Maria Cândida Pacheco, ed. by José F. Meirinhos, Textes et Études du Moyen Âge, 32 (Louvain-la-Neuve: FIDEM, 2005), pp. 269–308

————, 'An Original Way of Commenting on the Fifth Book of Aristotle's *Politics*: The *Questiones super I–VII libros Politicorum* of Peter of Auvergne', in *Peter of Auvergne: University Master of the 13th Century*, ed. by Christoph Flüeler, Lidia Lanza, and Marco Toste, Scrinium Friburgense, 26 (Berlin: De Gruyter, 2015), pp. 321–53

————, 'The Parts and the Whole, the Few Wise Men and the Multitude: Consent and Collective Decision Making in Two Medieval Commentaries on Aristotle's *Politics*', *Storia del pensiero politico*, 9 (2020), 209–31

————, 'La socievolezza umana nel *Defensor pacis* di Marsilio da Padova', *Philosophical Readings*, 12 (2020), 22–34

————, '*Tantum pauper quantum diues, tantum ydiota quantum studiosus*: How Medieval Authors Made Sense of Democracy', in *Von Natur und Herrschaft. 'Natura' und 'Dominium' in der politischen Theorie des 13. und 14. Jahrhunderts*, ed. by Delphine Carron, Matthias Lutz-Bachmann, Anselm Spindler, and Marco Toste, Schwächediskurse und Ressourcenregime, 3 (Frankfurt: Campus Verlag, 2018), pp. 281–351

————, 'Virtue and the City: The Virtues of the Ruler and the Citizen in the Medieval Reception of Aristotle's *Politics*', in *Princely Virtues in the Middle Ages, 1200–1500*, ed. by István P. Bejczy and Cary J. Nederman, Disputatio, 9 (Turnhout: Brepols, 2007), pp. 73–98

Ziegler, Joseph, '*Ut dicunt medici*: Medical Knowledge and Theological Debates in the Second Half of the Thirteenth Century', *Bulletin of the History of Medicine*, 73 (1999), 208–37

IACOPO COSTA

Marsilius of Padua on Human Acts, Law, and the (Toothless) Law of Christ

Introduction

The aim of this chapter is to study the psychological foundations of Marsilius of Padua's conception of law and its coercive strength in light of *Defensor pacis* (hereafter *DP*), II, 8–9, as well as its consequences on what we can call Marsilius's Christology, that is to say Marsilius's conception of salvation as accomplished by Christ and the nature of the law that Christ is author and promulgator of. These two elements — that is, Christology and a conception of law — seem to be closely linked in Marsilius's thought. I will try to show that Marsilius is the author of a profoundly radical and innovative doctrine, especially when compared with other sources that remained consistent with a fairly broad consensus, such as certain views expressed by Thomas Aquinas in the second part of the *Summa theologiae*.

This aim requires, at least, two preliminary clarifications: first, *DP* can (and must) be read not only as a political treatise but also as a theological text. As we shall see, Marsilius does not hesitate to deal with topics that belong to theology, and shows great originality in this regard. Second, in order to give a correct interpretation of certain passages of *DP*, we have to take into account certain late thirteenth-century authors, especially Thomas Aquinas. The positions that I will examine in *DP* can indeed be considered radically anti-Thomistic, and Marsilius's Christology as conveying radical, heterodox aspects. I will proceed as follows. First, I will present the classification of human actions and laws proposed by Marsilius. This will help to identify some of his sources and define the relevant concepts for the rest of the present study. Second, I will study the relationship between divine law and human acts as conceived by Marsilius. Third, I will elucidate Thomas Aquinas's positions on the same issues as

Iacopo Costa is director of research at the CNRS and member of the Commissio Leonina. He is a specialist of moral philosophy and theology in the thirteenth and fourteenth centuries.

Marsilius of Padua, ed. by Alessandro Mulieri, Serena Masolini, and Jenny Pelletier, Disputatio, 36 (Turnhout: Brepols, 2023), pp. 103–122

BREPOLS ❧ PUBLISHERS   10.1484/M.DISPUT-EB.5.132909

well as the interest in comparing his to Marsilius's. Last, I will analyse exactly how Marsilius diverges from Aquinas. This analysis will show the originality of Marsilius and the novelty of his conception of the law.[1]

Actions, Laws, and Judges

First of all, we should recall the classification and definition of law proposed by Marsilius in *DP*, I, 10. The term 'law' (*lex*) has four meanings. (1) A law is any natural tendency to act in a certain way, thus the tendency of the flesh to sin is a law (as an example, Marsilius uses the famous verse from Paul, Romans 7. 23: 'But I see in my flesh another law, fighting against the law of my mind, and imprisoning me in the law of sin that dwells in my flesh').[2] (2) The dispositions of arts and techniques can be called law. In this sense, the rule by which an architect builds a house is a law. The fact that Marsilius refers here to *habitus operativi* indicates that he includes practical philosophy in general in this second sense of law.[3] (3) Religions are, or include, laws. In this sense, laws are admonitions or counsels (*monita*) regarding punishments or rewards in the afterlife.[4] (4) In a more proper sense, law is the universal science of political justice and injustice.[5]

In the last sense (4), 'law' can still be understood in two ways. (4.1) As the determination and definition of justice, utility, and their opposites, the law is thus identified with a science or doctrine ('iuris scientia vel doctrina').[6] (4.2) The law is the same science, but now endowed with coercive force, that is, the power to distribute punishments and rewards in the present life to those who violate or observe the rules established in that life. This last meaning — Marsilius adds — is the most proper meaning of the law.[7]

---

1 The following studies are relevant to the conception of the law in Marsilius's thought: Lewis, 'The "Positivism" of Marsiglio of Padua'; Ghisalberti, 'Sulla legge naturale'; Tierney, 'Marsilius on Rights'; Tierney, *Liberty and Law*; Brett, 'Political Right(s) and Human Freedom'. See also Dolcini, *Introduzione a Marsilio da Padova*.

2 *DP*, I, 10.3, ed. by Scholz, p. 48, ll. 25–30: 'Video autem aliam legem in membris meis, repugnantem legi mentis meae, et captivantem me in lege peccati, quae est in membris meis'; my translation.

3 *DP*, I, 10.3, ed. by Scholz, pp. 48–49, ll. 30–6.

4 *DP*, I, 10.3, ed. by Scholz, p. 49, ll. 6–24.

5 *DP*, I, 10.3, ed. by Scholz, p. 49, ll. 24–27: 'Quarto autem importat hoc nomen lex et famose magis scienciam seu doctrinam sive iudicium universale iustorum et conferencium civilium, et suorum oppositorum'.

6 *DP*, I, 10.4, ed. by Scholz, pp. 49–50, ll. 28–2.

7 *DP*, I, 10.4, ed. by Scholz, p. 50, ll. 3–7: 'Alio modo considerari potest, secundum quod de ipsius observacione datur preceptum coactivum per penam aut premium in presenti

On the basis of these definitions, we can observe two important details: First, religion is indeed a law, but it is not a law in the full sense of the term; this is true for the Christian religion as well as for other religions. To be sure, for Marsilius, the religion of Moses and the religion of Christ are the only true religions, but this does not mean that they are laws in the most proper sense of the word.[8] Second, Marsilius takes up, as a definition of law in the most proper sense (4.2), Aristotle's definition in *Nicomachean Ethics*, x:

> Moreover Aristotle's definition takes it [i.e. the law] in this way, when he said in *Ethics* x, 8: 'Law has coercive power, being speech [*sermo*] from a certain prudence [*prudentia*] and understanding [*intellectus*]'; a law, then, is a 'speech' (or a speech pronouncement [*oratio*]) 'from a certain' (sc. political) 'prudence and understanding', i.e., an ordinance [*ordinacio*] concerning the just and the beneficial and their opposites arrived at through political prudence, 'having coercive power', i.e., that a command has been given in respect of its observation which an individual is forced to observe, or that it has been enacted by way of such a command.[9]

Since Marsilius's intention is to understand how these different types of laws relate to human actions, he proposes a classification of human acts in *DP*, ii, 8.[10] To do this, he proceeds through a complex series of dichotomies, and the process takes into account both theological and Aristotelian sources (mainly drawn from Aristotle's *Nicomachean Ethics*). Marsilius's classification of human acts must be read and understood in light of the distinction between divine law and human law in particular.

Such a classification is supposed to clarify the classification of judges and judgements, and, namely, imperative judgements (*iudicium*

---

seculo distribuenda, sive secundum quod per modum talis precepti traditur; et hoc modo considerata propriissime lex vocatur et est'.

8 *DP*, i, 10.3, ed. by Scholz, p. 49, ll. 16–20: 'Hac eciam legis accepcione dicuntur leges omnes secte, ut que Machometi aut Persarorum, secundum se totas aut aliquas sui partes, licet ex hiis Mosaica et evangelica, Christiana scilicet, sole contineant veritatem'. On the relationship between religion and law, see Briguglia, 'I filosofi finsero e persuasero'; as well as Mulieri, 'Against Classical Republicanism'.

9 *DP*, i, 10.3, trans. by Brett, pp. 53–54; cf. ed. by Scholz, p. 50, ll. 7–16: 'Quam eciam sic sumptam [sc. legem] diffinit Aristoteles ultimo Ethicorum, 8° capitulo, cum dixit: *Lex autem coactivam habet potenciam sermo ens ab aliqua prudencia et intellectu; sermo* igitur seu oracio *ab aliqua prudencia seu intellectu*, politico scilicet, id est ordinacio de iustis et conferentibus et ipsorum oppositis per prudenciam politicam, *habens coactivam potenciam*, id est, de cuius observacione datur preceptum, quod quis cogitur observare, seu lata per modum talis precepti, lex est'; cf. Aristotle, *Nicomachean Ethics*, x, 1180a21–22.

10 *DP*, ii, 8, ed. by Scholz, p. 221, ll. 20–22: 'De divisione actuum humanorum, et qualiter referantur ad humanam legem et iudicem seculi huius'.

coactivum).[11] The idea of imperativeness (*coactio*) is indeed one of the theoretical cores of the chapters that are the subject of the present study.

Concerning human acts, Marsilius immediately introduces a fundamental distinction, between acts that realize the end of earthly life and those that realize the end of future life. We should understand that the former are those that are subject to human laws, while the latter are those that fall under divine law. Judgements and judges are classified following this distinction: an imperative judgement (or law) concerning the acts leading to the perfection of the present life (*sufficientia vitae mundanae*) is different from an imperative judgement concerning the acts leading to the perfection of the afterlife (*vita eterna*, or *gloria*). This means that the two main *genera* of acts — that is, the acts producing happiness or perfection in the present life and in the afterlife — are ruled by two different kinds of laws.[12] As I will show, Marsilius conceives of these two *genera* of laws as being strictly separate. This conception is, we might say, 'discontinuist' since it supposes a split between worldly/earthly jurisdiction and heavenly jurisdiction.[13]

Human acts that depend on knowledge and desire ('proveniencium per cognicionem et desiderium') are divided into two groups: (i) acts that are elicited without control of the rational soul (*mentis imperium*) and (ii) those that are elicited under such control.[14] The *imperium* (or *preceptum*) is of course a psychological stage of the action, which corresponds to the control, or the mastery, that the agent has over his own actions; this mastery is expressed by a judgement that prescribes whether or not to carry out a certain action. The first kind of acts are those acts (including acts of knowledge, desire, love, and pleasure)[15] that the intellect and the will do not deliberately command. Marsilius gives, as an example, the perceptions or affective motions (*cogniciones, affecciones*)[16] that one has while sleeping and those that are the result of perception and ordinary experience in relation to which the agent is passive and over which he does not have any mastery. The second kind of acts (*mentis imperia* or *precepta*) are

---

11 See the classification of judges in *DP*, II, 2.8, ed. by Scholz, pp. 150–52, ll. 26–7: 'judge' can be taken in three senses: the one who judges on any matter, the legal expert, and the one to whom it belongs to order. Only the third sense entails coercive power.

12 *DP*, II, 8.1, ed. by Scholz, pp. 221–22, ll. 23–4: 'Quoniam autem omne iudicium coactivum est de humanis actibus voluntariis secundum aliquam legem aut consuetudinem, et de hiis quidem vel in quantum ad finem huius seculi ordinabilibus, vite mundane scilicet sufficienciam, aut quantum ad finem venturi seculi, quem vitam seu gloriam vocamus eternam; ut amplius appareat distinctio iudicum seu iudicare debencium, et secundum quas leges, quo iudicio et qualiter, de ipsorum actuum differenciis aliqualiter disseramus'.

13 The radical strength of this position will appear in particular in the comparison with Aquinas's positions, which were, on the contrary, 'continuist'.

14 *DP*, II, 8.2, ed. by Scholz, p. 222, ll. 5–8.

15 *DP*, II, 8.2, ed. by Scholz, p. 222, ll. 8–9: 'cogniciones, desideria, dilecciones et delectaciones'.

16 *DP*, II, 8.2, ed. by Scholz, p. 222, ll. 8–13.

acts of knowledge, consent, and affective motions (*cogniciones, consensus, affecciones*) concerning the realization of the first acts.[17] For example, an act of desire caused by perception is an act of the first kind (e.g. seeing a desirable object); but the decision whether or not to satisfy the desire derives from an act of the second kind, which is a rational and deliberate act.

Marsilius is presenting here a rather simple model of human agency according to which a human act has two main stages: a first stage that lies outside the rational mastery of the agent and a second stage that is, on the contrary, rational, voluntary and as such has moral and juridical weight. The fundamental difference between acts (i) and (ii) lies in the fact that the former acts are not free, while the latter are free; that is, the former acts are not the result of deliberation and choice, and thus no guilt or merit can be ascribed to them, while the latter acts depend on us.[18]

Marsilius adds here a consideration that shows a rather refined view of psychological and moral dynamics as well as an accurate knowledge of Aristotle's ethics. Indeed, he does not assert that the first kind of acts are completely involuntary, but rather that they are not completely voluntary. And he explains this by affirming that voluntary acts can dispose the soul in such a way that the soul can feel more or less acute desires with regard to thoughts and sensations that occur without the subject's consent.[19] This is a clear reference to Book III of the *Nicomachean Ethics* (1114a31–b3). According to Aristotle, the fact that a person feels desire towards certain objects depends on the moral *habitus* of his or her soul: if this person is virtuous, an object of vice will be felt with repugnance; if he or she is vicious, the same object will be felt with desire. Since the subject is responsible for the acquisition of virtuous or vicious *habitus*, one can claim that the subject is in some way the master of the motions of the first type.[20]

Insistence on this point may also demonstrate that Marsilius knows and exploits intellectualist psychology.[21] According to Godfrey of Fontaines (*Quodlibet* XV, 22), one of the leaders of intellectualist

---

17 *DP*, II, 8.2, ed. by Scholz, p. 222, ll. 13–19.

18 *DP*, II, 8.3, ed. by Scholz, p. 222, ll. 20–31.

19 *DP*, II, 8.3, ed. by Scholz, p. 222, ll. 24–31: 'Et dixi primorum actuum non omnino potestatem in nobis, quoniam non est in potestate nostra totaliter horum eventum prohibere, quamvis per secundos actus, qui dicuntur imperia, et hiis consequentes sic animam disponere possimus, ut non facile sit factiva seu receptiva primorum, videlicet cum horum oppositos fuerit assuetus sibi quisque precipere diligere aut considerare'.

20 See Aquinas's commentary on this point: *Sententia Libri Ethicorum*, III, 13, Leonina edn, XLVII.1, p. 157, ll. 73–78: 'Et ideo dicit [Aristoteles] quod, cum homo aliqualiter sit causa sui habitus mali propter consuetudinem peccandi [...] consequens est quod ipse etiam sit sibi causa fantasiae consequentis talem habitum, id est apparitionis qua sibi videtur hoc esse secundum se bonum'.

21 Hoffmann, 'Intellectualism and Voluntarism', I, pp. 414–27.

theologians, we must admit that the first acts of desire are not completely within our power, since otherwise the distinction between venial and mortal sin would be impossible. Indeed, if we admit that every form of human desire depends on free will (as the voluntarist theologians thought) we would have to concede that someone is fully responsible even for those acts that are not completely subject to deliberation.[22]

To return to Marsilius's two kinds of human act, the second kind of acts, acts *imperati*, are either internal (ii[a], *immanentes*) or external (ii[b], *transeuntes*). The former (ii[a]) are acts of knowledge and desire, as well as habits (*cogniciones, affecciones, habitus*) of the higher part of the soul (to which Marsilius refers as the *mens*), and these acts affect no subject other than the *mens* and the psychic powers of the agent itself. Since they express moral dispositions of the agent, these acts have moral value. The latter (ii[b]) are the practical actualization of the former, which require the cooperation of the agent's bodily organs (*prosecuciones desideratorum, motus facti per organum*, and especially *per motum localem*).[23] The first level corresponds to the realization of the agent's internal will (X wants to perform action y); the second corresponds to the action itself (X performs y).[24] The external acts have a juridical value: indeed, they can be done either without inflicting any damage on the community (ii[b1]); or they do (ii[b2]).[25]

The following table summarizes this subdivision:

Actus humani:				
non imperati (i)	imperati (ii)			
	immanentes (ii[a])	transeuntes (ii[b])		
		sine iniuria (ii[b1])	cum iniuria (ii[b2])	

After classifying human acts, Marsilius studies their relation to different types of rules or laws (*regule, mensure, habitus*). Indeed, different acts are regulated by different rules, and these rules must regulate human actions both in relation to the perfection of worldly life (*vita huius seculi*) and

---

22 Godfrey of Fontaines, *Le Quodlibet* XV, 22, ed. by Lottin, p. 9: 'Si voluntas haberet dominium super primum actum volendi, tunc omnis complacentia vel consensus quantumcumque subitus in his quae de genere suo sunt circa materiam peccati mortalis, sicut est fornicatio vel furtum, esset peccatum mortale, nec in talibus nunquam esset veniale peccatum. Hoc autem falsum et erroneum secundum omnes'.

23 *DP*, II, 8.3, ed. by Scholz, p. 223, ll. 1–9.

24 The division between internal and external acts corresponds to Aquinas's division between *actus eliciti* and *actus imperati*: see Thomas Aquinas, *Summa Theologiae*, I II, q. 6 4, resp., Leonina edn, VI, p. 59a–b.

25 *DP*, II, 8.3, ed. by Scholz, p. 223, ll. 9–19.

in relation to the perfection of future life (*vita future seculi*).[26] In effect, Marsilius intends to study the relationship of both human and divine law to human acts.

In order to classify laws, Marsilius uses the fundamental concept of constraint (*coactio*). In a first case (r[a]), rules can regulate human actions without the distribution of punishments or rewards dispensed by a coercive power (*potentia coactiva*). These are the rules in ethics and technical disciplines or arts (*discipline operative vel factive*).[27] For example, within Aristotle's ethics, virtuous or vicious action is not always rewarded or punished. The person who acts in an intemperate manner is not punished. The same can be said for the arts: one does not punish the architect who builds an ugly temple. In a second case (r[b]), rules can regulate human actions by means of the distribution of punishments or rewards by a coercive power.[28] This second category of rules is divided into two sets: first (r[b1]), those rules that distribute earthly punishments and rewards are human and civil laws (*leges et humane consuetudines civiles*); second (r[b2]), those rules that distribute punishments and rewards in the afterlife are divine laws that are determined by the different religions (*secte*), among which only the Christian religion is true.[29]

Once again, let us visualize this classification by means of a table:

Leges:		
discipline operative vel factive (r[a])	*leges* (r[b])	
	pro vita presentis seculi: leges et humane consuetudines civiles (r[b1])	*pro vita futuri seculi: leges divine, secte* (r[b2])

It is necessary to note that this classification of law does not coincide precisely with the one Marsilius had developed in *DP*, i, 10 (discussed above). Specifically, Marsilius here does not take into account meaning (1) of 'law' as a natural tendency. Meaning (2) of 'law' corresponds to (r[a]), that is, to practical philosophy and technique. Meaning (3) corresponds to (r[b2]), that is to say, to religion. And meaning (4) corresponds to (r[b1]), the universal science of political justice and injustice, and we know from the classification of *DP*, i, 10 that this meaning includes both the science of

---

26 *DP*, ii, 8.4, ed. by Scholz, p. 223, ll. 19–24.

27 *DP*, ii, 8.4, ed. by Scholz, p. 223, ll. 24–29. The division between *discipline active* and *factive* comes from Book vi of the *Nicomachean Ethics* (1140a1–23) and *Metaphysics* vi (1025b18–25): the first are the practical sciences (ethics, politics, economics); the second are the arts (e.g. architecture or medicine). See Maierù, 'La scienza bizantina e latina'.

28 *DP*, ii, 8.4, ed. by Scholz, pp. 223–24, ll. 29–2.

29 *DP*, ii, 8.4, ed. by Scholz, p. 224, ll. 2–11.

law-making (4.1) and the dispositions governing their application in civil society (4.2).

Now we have to consider how this classification applies to the classification of human acts. Human laws (r^{b1}) only regulate the deliberate external acts (ii^{b1-2}),[30] which means that human laws do not concern involuntary acts (i) nor deliberate acts that are internal to the agent (ii^{a}), that is, those acts that have no practical realization and bodily performance, for instance a bad intention that remains unrealized (these acts fall under the 'jurisdiction' of moral philosophy, not of human law). The law of Christ partly applies to this kind of act, for it regulates all deliberate acts (ii^{a-b}), but regulates them only with a perspective of reward or punishment in the future life. It must therefore be understood that the law of Christ is more extensive as compared to human law, since it regulates both internal and external acts, whereas internal acts are beyond the reach of human law. Nevertheless, the law of Christ regulates both kinds of acts exclusively from the point of view of the rewards and punishments of the life after death.[31]

The conclusion that Marsilius wants to reach, emphasizing in particular Romans 13. 4,[32] is that all the clergy, at every level,[33] must be subject to human law and to secular judges. Marsilius's reasoning, which here takes on an ontological aspect, argues that if a judge passes judgement on a criminal priest (*sacerdos*), the fact that the person in question is a priest is only accidental to his being a criminal (*transgressor*). Similarly, if a physician judges the health of a musician, the fact that the ill person is a musician is an accident of being ill: 'what is *per se* is not removed or altered

---

30 *DP*, II, 8.5, ed. by Scholz, p. 224, ll. 12–17: 'Est igitur pro vita seu vivere sufficienti huius seculi posita regula humanorum actuum imperatorum transeuncium fieri possibilium ad commodum vel incommodum, ius aut iniuriam alterius a faciente, preceptiva et transgressorum coactiva supplicio sive pena pro statu presentis seculi tantum. Quam *legem humanam* communi nomine diximus'.

31 *DP*, II, 8.5, ed. by Scholz, p. 224, ll. 20–29: 'Pro vita seu vivere in hoc seculo, pro statu tamen futuri seculi tradita et posita est lex per Christum. Que siquidem lex regula est humanorum actuum imperatorum, et qui sunt in potestate nostra activa nostre mentis, tam immanencium quam transeuncium, secundum quod fieri possunt vel omitti, debite aut indebite in hoc seculo, pro statu tamen sive fine futuri seculi, coactiva et distributiva pene vel premii, et horum illativa in futuro seculo, non in isto, secundum merita vel demerita observatorum aut transgressorum illius in vita presenti'.

32 'Dei enim minister est tibi in bonum. Si autem malum feceris, time: non enim sine causa gladium portat. Dei enim minister est: vindex in iram ei qui malum agit'.

33 Marsilius refers to 'presbyteri seu episcopi et generaliter omnes templorum ministri communi nomine vocati clerici' (*DP*, II, 8.4, ed. by Scholz, p. 225, ll. 17–18), and a few lines below to the *sacerdos* (p. 226, ll. 10, 19).

by what is *per accidens*; otherwise, there would be infinite species of judges or physicians'.[34]

So, the question to be asked is: If human law regulates deliberate but only external human acts of the present life by the distribution of punishments and rewards in this life, and if the law of Christ regulates these same acts only by the distribution of punishments and rewards in the future life, what degree of power does the law of Christ really possess over the acts of the present life? Indeed, to take this reasoning to its extreme would mean removing any coercive power from the law of Christ over human acts performed in this life. This is the solution Marsilius chooses, which ultimately results in a radical separation of human and divine law.

Divine Law and Human Acts

In *DP*, II, 8, Marsilius considers three fundamental concepts: the law, the human act, and the judge. He also establishes that two kinds of judge exist: a human judge (which he refers to as *iustum animatum*, i.e. living justice, quoting Aristotle's *Nicomachean Ethics*, Book V)[35] and a supernatural judge (Christ). In *DP*, II, 9,[36] Marsilius insists on the difference between these two judges and between the nature of their judgements. This is where we can find what I call his discontinuist conception of Christ's law. Marsilius's position is grounded on two ideas: first, the law of Christ has no imperative strength in the earthly life; second (which is a consequence of the first), the law of Christ has the same force as counsels.

Here is the truly groundbreaking step in Marsilius's theory: his conception of divine law, especially evangelical law, abolishes the distinction between precepts (*praecepta*) and counsels (*consilia*), since, in his opinion, this law contains only counsels.[37]

That the law of Christ has no coercive power, that is, the power of a precept, in earthly life is clearly stated by Marsilius:

---

34 *DP*, II, 8.7, ed. by Scholz, p. 226, ll. 12–18: 'Esse enim sacerdotem vel non sacerdotem accidit transgressori per comparacionem ad iudicem, sicuti esse agricolam aut domificatorem, quemadmodum eciam sanabili aut egrotabili musicum aut non musicum esse in comparacione ad medicum. Non enim tollitur id quod est per se neque variatur per id quod accidit; alioquin essent infinite iudicum species atque medicorum'.

35 *DP*, II, 8.6, ed. by Scholz, p. 225, ll. 5–7. See Robert Grosseteste's translation of *Eth. Nic.* V, 1132a21–22: 'iudex enim vult esse velut iustum animatum' (*Aristoteles Latinus*, XXVI, 2.2, p. 234, l. 13).

36 *DP*, II, 9, ed. by Scholz, p. 231, ll. 6–9: 'De humanorum actuum relacione ad legem divinam et iudicem alterius seculi, Christum videlicet, qualiter eciam ad doctorem legis eiusdem, episcopum sive sacerdotem, in hoc seculo comparentur'.

37 See Mulieri, 'Against Classical Republicanism', pp. 243–44, where other radical, especially anti-Thomistic, aspects of Marsilius's thought are highlighted.

> But the coercive power of this judge [i.e. Christ] is not exercised upon anyone in this world to mete out penalty or punishment or reward to those who transgress or observe the law laid down directly by him, which we have often called the evangelical law.[38]

This radical thesis requires a reflection on the role of Christ and clerics with regard to human life and salvation. Marsilius's explanation is that Christ, in his mercy, gave man the possibility of deserving (*mereri*) and repenting (*penitere*) the sins he has committed until the last moment of his life.[39] The coercive power of Christ will not be exercised until after death through the punishments and rewards earned during one's earthly life. But what about the power of the clerics? Is it possible to admit that they hold some form of coercive power in the exercise of their functions towards the members of the Church? According to Marsilius, the earthly function of the cleric is that of teaching the divine law ('doctor est in hoc seculo divine legis'),[40] but this function has no coercive power over our acts in the present life.[41] The reason for this is a rather refined psychological consideration: in fact, the precepts of the divine law must make one deserve eternal life, but it is impossible to deserve anything by means of acts that one is obliged to perform, since merit consists precisely in the fact of acting freely and voluntarily.[42] The function of the cleric, as well as the function that Christ had during his earthly life, is more comparable to that of a physician than to that of a judge. The physician can diagnose, counsel, predict, and, of course, prescribe, but these do not have the binding force of human law; and Christ spoke of himself more as a doctor than as prince or as a judge,[43] a position that Marsilius confirms by the authority of Luke's

---

38 *DP*, II, 9.1, trans. by Brett, p. 221; cf. ed. by Scholz, p. 231, ll. 16–20: 'Verum huius iudici coactiva potestas in quemquam non exercetur in hoc seculo, ad penam seu supplicium aut premium distribuenda transgressoribus aut observatoribus legis late per ipsum immediate, quam evangelicam persepe diximus'.

39 *DP*, II, 9.1, ed. by Scholz, p. 231, ll. 20–23: 'Voluit enim ex sui misericordia Christus usque ad extremum cuiusque periodum concedere mereri et de commissis in ipsius legem penitere posse'.

40 *DP*, II, 9.1, ed. by Scholz, pp. 231–32, ll. 27–1.

41 *DP*, II, 9.2, ed. by Scholz, p. 232, ll. 3–5: 'non tamen habens coactivam potestatem in hoc seculo arcendi quemquam ad preceptorum secundum ipsam [i.e. legis divinae] observacionem'.

42 *DP*, II, 9.2, ed. by Scholz, p. 232, ll. 5–7: 'Frustra enim ad hec [sc. agenda, fugienda] quemquam cogeret, quoniam observatori talium coacto nihil ipsa proficerent ad eternam salutem'.

43 *DP*, II, 9.2, ed. by Scholz, p. 232, ll. 9–15: 'Ideoque iudex hic convenienter assimilatur medico, cui data est auctoritas docendi atque precipiendi et prognosticandi seu iudicandi de hiis que sunt utilia fieri vel omitti ad corporalem sanitatem consequendam et mortem aut egritudinem declinandam. Propter quod eciam Christus in statu et pro statu vite presentis vocavit se medicum, non principem aut iudicem'.

Gospel (5. 31: 'Those who are healthy do not need a physician, but those who are ill do').[44]

The status of the evangelical law is twofold depending on whether it is related to earthly life or to the afterlife. In the first case, since it lacks coercive strength, it only has the value of a theoretical or practical doctrine (*doctrina speculativa aut practica*).[45] The fact that Marsilius mentions these *doctrinae* is particularly instructive. Like the *Nicomachean Ethics* or *Metaphysics*, the Gospel is the source of certain and true knowledge, which is nevertheless devoid of coercive power. Indeed, Marsilius seems to think that Aristotle's ethics has no prescriptive character, just as his metaphysics does not impose any truth; in other words, these forms of knowledge do not require us to act or to believe. In the second case, the evangelical law is a law in the proper sense, since it is fully coercive.[46] Yet its coercive force is exercised only by the supernatural and thus supra-mundane judge, Christ, who distributes rewards and punishments in the afterlife. The consequence of this conception is that neither clerics nor Christ during his earthly life were ever endowed with coercive power.[47] Marsilius once again draws on medical language: 'A doctor, like a physician, is in the same or an analogous situation with regard to the judgement of men's bodily health, with no coercive power over anyone'.[48] With regard to the theory I have just outlined, two things should be noted: First, to my knowledge, Marsilius is the only author in the medieval context to have adopted this conception of law and of the relationship between human and evangelical law, namely that evangelical law is limited to counsel, excluding

---

44 *DP*, II, 9.2, ed. by Scholz, p. 232, ll. 16–22: 'Non egent medico qui sani sunt, sed qui male habent'; my translation.

45 *DP*, II, 9.3, ed. by Scholz, pp. 232–33, ll. 23–28: 'ut sic [sc. evangelica lex] racionem habet magis doctrine speculative aut operative vel utriusque, quantum ad diversas sui partes, quam levis dicte secundum propriam et ultimam significacionem' (pp. 232–33, ll. 23–1); 'Ideoque, ad statum hominis in hoc et pro hoc seculo comparata, debet dici doctrina, non lex' (p. 233, ll. 11–12).

46 *DP*, II, 9.3, ed. by Scholz, pp. 233–34, ll. 29–17: 'ut sic [sc. evangelica lex] nomen legis propriissime dicte sortitur, et qui secundum ipsam iudicabit tunc propriissime iudex' (p. 234, ll. 2–4).

47 *DP*, II, 9.3, ed. by Scholz, pp. 234, ll. 5–13: 'Sacerdos autem seu episcopus quicumque sit ille, quoniam secundum hanc disponit et regulat homines solummodo in statu vite presentis, licet ad futuram vitam, nec sibi secundum ipsam arcerem quemquam in hoc seculo concessum est ab illius immediato latore, Christo videlicet, idcirco nec proprie iudex dicitur [...] nec quemquam tali iudicio in hoc seculo pena reali aut personali potest nec debet arcere'. Cf. *DP*, II, 9.7, ed. by Scholz, p. 238, ll. 14–15: 'Christus non exercuit in hoc seculo iudiciariam potestatem, coactivam scilicet'.

48 *DP*, II, 9.3, trans. by Brett, p. 223, slightly modified; ed. by Scholz, p. 234, ll. 13–16: 'Quo eciam vel proporcionali modo doctor aliquis operativus, ut medicus, se habet ad iudicium sanitatis corporalis hominum absque coactiva cuiusquam potencia'.

114   IACOPO COSTA

any precept, and that as a consequence human law alone is imperative in this life. Moreover, Marsilius's view of the relationship between divine and human law challenges Aquinas's theory of law.

Aquinas on the New Law, Human Acts, Precepts, and Counsels

We will now see how the doctrine we have just presented squarely opposes the parallel position of Aquinas, especially in the sections of the *Prima secundae* of the *Summa theologiae* that deal with the law in general and the New Law (that is, Christ's law) in particular.[49] The need for this comparison arises from two considerations: first, Aquinas's treatise on the law was already authoritative when Marsilius composed the *DP*, which means that he could not have been ignorant of Aquinas's views on the subject; second, Marsilius closely draws on the concepts used by Aquinas, but he employs them to reach opposite conclusions. We can, therefore, legitimately see a critique of this part of Aquinas's moral theology in Marsilius's theory on the relation between law and human acts.

In q. 108 of the *Prima secundae*, Aquinas develops a detailed theory of the imperative force of the New Law, that is, the evangelical law, and its relation to both internal and external human acts. I will outline the four main theses corresponding to the four articles that constitute the question.

First thesis (108 1): the New Law is imperative in relation to exterior acts in the present life. Since the novelty of the New Law 'consists in the grace of the Holy Ghost that manifests itself through faith that acts through love',[50] it rules over the external acts by which grace is received by the faithful and over those by which the gift of grace in the faithful is manifested. The former are the sacraments, which allow the presence of grace in the soul of the faithful; the latter are the acts that are accomplished by the inspiration of grace. In the latter, a further distinction must be made: some of these acts are commanded by the New Law, such as the confession of faith (*confessio fidei*: Matthew 10. 32–33), while other acts expressing grace are not the object of a precept on the part of the New Law, but the faithful are free with regard to these acts.[51]

---

49 On Aquinas's conception of justice, see Hause, 'Aquinas on Aristotelian Justice'; Perkams, 'Aquinas's Interpretation'.

50 Thomas Aquinas, *Summa Theologiae*, I II, q. 108 1, resp., Leonina edn, VII, p. 283a–b: 'principalitas legis novae est gratia Spiritus Sancti, quae manifestatur in fide per dilectionem operantem'. Translations from Aquinas's *Summa* are mine.

51 Thomas Aquinas, *Summa Theologiae*, I II, q. 108 1, resp., Leonina edn, VII, pp. 283b–284a: 'Sic igitur exteriora opera dupliciter ad gratiam pertinere possunt. Uno modo, sicut inducentia aliqualiter ad gratiam. Et talia sunt opera sacramentorum [...]. Alia vero sunt opera exteriora quae ex instinctu gratiae producuntur. Et in his est quaedam differentia

Second thesis (108 2): the New Law adequately commands external human acts. On the one hand, it commands the sacraments, which allow for the acquisition of grace; on the other hand, it commands the moral precepts (*praecepta*), which allow its expression and were already contained in the Ancient Law (e.g. 'do not steal' or 'do not kill'). As far as the external execution of moral precepts is concerned, the New Law does not add anything to the Old Law. On the contrary, the New Law does not command the ceremonial and judicial precepts (*praecepta caerimonialia, iudicialia*) that were already adequately established in the Old Law.[52]

Third thesis (108 3): the New Law adequately commands internal human acts. Aquinas's position is based on the Augustinian interpretation of Christ's Sermon on the Mount.[53] In this sermon 'the interior motions of man are perfectly established'.[54] To understand this point, we need to make some further distinctions: these precepts of Christ's Sermon can concern either man as such or man in relation to his neighbour. In the first case, the precepts command the will to act and the intention of the end (*voluntas de agendis, intentio de fine*); in the second case, it commands the interior

---

attendenda. Quaedam enim habent necessariam convenientiam vel contrarietatem ad interiorem gratiam, quae in fide per dilectionem operante consistit. Et huiusmodi exteriora opera sunt praecepta vel prohibita in lege nova: sicut praecepta est confessio fidei, et prohibita negatio [...]. Alia vero sunt opera quae non habent necessariam contrarietatem vel convenientiam ad fidem per dilectionem operantem. Et talia opera non sunt in nova lege praecepta vel prohibita ex ipsa prima legis institutione; sed relicta sunt a legislatore, scilicet Christo, unicuique, secundum quod aliquis curam gerere debet. Et sic unicuique liberum est circa talia determinare quid sibi expediat facere vel vitare; et cuicumque praesidenti, circa talia ordinare suis subditis quid sit in talibus faciendum vel vitandum. Unde etiam quantum ad hoc dicitur lex Evangelii lex libertatis, nam lex vetus multa determinabat, et pauca relinquebat hominum libertati determinanda'.

52 Thomas Aquinas, *Summa Theologiae*, I II, q. 108 2, resp., Leonina edn, VII, pp. 284b–285a: 'lex nova in exterioribus illa solum praecipere debuit vel prohibere, per quae in gratiam introducimur, vel quae pertinent ad rectum gratiae usum ex necessitate. Et quia gratiam ex nobis consequi non possumus, sed per Christum solum, ideo sacramenta, per quae gratiam consequimur, ipse Dominus instituit per seipsum [...]. Rectus autem gratiae usus est per opera caritatis. Quae quidem secundum quod sunt de necessitate virtutis, pertinent ad praecepta moralia, quae etiam in veteri lege tradebantur. Unde quantum ad hoc, lex nova super veterem addere non debuit circa exteriora agenda [...]. Sic igitur lex nova nulla alia exteriora opera determinare debuit praecipiendo vel prohibendo, nisi sacramenta, et moralia praecepta quae de se pertinent ad rationem virtutis, puta non esse occidendum, non esse furandum, et alia huiusmodi'.

53 Augustine, *De sermone Domini in monte*, ed. by Mutzenbecher. On the importance of this text for Aquinas's moral theology, see Pinckaers, 'Le commentaire du Sermon sur la montagne'.

54 Thomas Aquinas, *Summa Theologiae*, I II, q. 108 3, resp., Leonina edn, VII, p. 286a: 'sermo quem Dominus in Monte proposuit, totam informationem Christianae vitae continet'.

motions towards our neighbour, such as humility in the judgement of the other person.[55]

Fourth thesis (108 4): in addition to precepts, the New Law contains counsels. 'The difference between counsel and precept is that the precept implies necessity, whereas counsel depends on the choice of whom it is given to'. As far as their content is concerned, precepts and counsels differ in this way: precepts command acts that are necessary for the salvation of the soul and for eternal beatitude; counsels encourage acts by which man can attain salvation and beatitude in a more secure manner.[56] There is a difference of degree between the acts of precept and the acts of counsel: one detaches oneself from the world by means of precepts such that he or she does not identify the end of his or her life with the goods of the world, without nevertheless excluding them or abandoning them completely. By contrast, one perfectly renounces the goods of the world by evangelical counsels.[57] Citing the traditional source of John (1 John 2. 16), Thomas states that the goods of the world fall into three categories: (1) wealth, which is the object of the desire of the eyes (*concupiscentia oculorum*); (2) pleasures of the flesh, which are the object of the desire of the flesh (*concupiscentia carnis*); (3) honours, which are the object of the pride of life (*superbia vitae*). These three disordered motions of the spirit (desire of the eyes, desire of the flesh, pride of life) are respectively counteracted by

---

55 Thomas Aquinas, *Summa Theologiae*, I II, q. 108 3, resp., Leonina edn, VII, p. 286a–b: 'Quantum autem ad seipsum, dupliciter; secundum duos interiores hominis motus circa agenda, qui sunt voluntas de agendis, et intentio de fine. Unde primo ordinat hominis voluntatem secundum diversa legis praecepta: ut scilicet abstineat aliquis non solum ab exterioribus operibus quae sunt secundum se mala, sed etiam ab interioribus, et ab occasionibus malorum. Deinde ordinat intentionem hominis, docens quod in bonis quae agimus, neque quaeramus humanam gloriam, neque mundanas divitias, quod est thesaurizare in terra. Consequenter autem ordinat interiorem hominis motum quoad proximum: ut scilicet eum non temerarie aut iniuste iudicemus, aut praesumptuose; neque tamen sic simus apud proximum remissi, ut eis sacra committamus, si sint indigni'.

56 Thomas Aquinas, *Summa Theologiae*, I II, q. 108 4, resp., Leonina edn, VII, p. 288a: 'haec est differentia inter consilium et praeceptum, quod praeceptum importat necessitatem, consilium autem in optione ponitur eius cui datur [...]. Oportet igitur quod praecepta novae legis intelligantur esse data de his quae sunt necessaria ad consequendum finem aeternae beatitudinis, in quem lex nova immediate introducit. Consilia vero oportet esse de illis per quae melius et expeditius potest homo consequi finem praedictum'.

57 Thomas Aquinas, *Summa Theologiae*, I II, q. 108 4, resp., Leonina edn, VII, p. 288a: 'Est autem homo constitutus inter res mundi huius et spiritualia bona, in quibus beatitudo aeterna consistit: ita quod quanto plus inhaeret uni eorum, tanto plus recedit ab altero, et e converso. Qui ergo totaliter inhaeret rebus huius mundi, ut in eis finem constituat, habens eas quasi rationes et regulas suorum operum, totaliter excidit a spiritualibus bonis. Et ideo huiusmodi inordinatio tollitur per praecepta. Sed quod homo totaliter ea quae sunt mundi abiiciat, non est necessarium ad perveniendum in finem praedictum: quia potest homo utens rebus huius mundi, dummodo in eis finem non constituat, ad beatitudinem aeternam pervenire. Sed expeditius perveniet totaliter bona huius mundi abdicando. Et ideo de hoc dantur consilia Evangelii'.

MARSILIUS OF PADUA ON HUMAN ACTS, LAW, AND LAW OF CHRIST   117

the counsels of poverty, chastity, and obedience.[58] This last point is particularly important in Aquinas's theology because, according to him, religious life is based principally on the advice and abandonment of worldly goods that respect for these three counsels implies. The specificity of religious life depends, so to speak, ontologically on counsels. It is easy to understand to what extent the distinction between evangelical precepts and counsels is central to Aquinas's ecclesiology.

We saw above that Marsilius justifies the assertion that evangelical law is not coercive on the grounds that it is impossible to merit or demerit through acts that one is forced to perform. One only deserves through free acts, and freedom does not tolerate coercion. In the same question 108 of the *Prima secundae*, Aquinas had already raised this issue, namely in objection 2: 'There is no freedom, if one is obliged to fulfil or abstain from certain external acts. Hence the New Law does not contain any precepts or prohibitions regarding external acts'.[59] The answer to this objection is interesting, since it mixes the definition of freedom of Aristotelian origin (*Metaphysics* I, 982b25–28) with the Christian idea that human freedom cannot be effectively exercised without the help of grace. According to Aquinas's reading of Aristotle, to be free means to be the cause of one's own acts (*causa sui*). But since grace belongs to the individual who receives it, grace acts as a principle internal to the individual and not as an external and constraining principle, since then it would negate the individual's freedom.[60] And then Aquinas adds:

---

58 Thomas Aquinas, *Summa Theologiae*, I II, q. 108 4, resp., Leonina edn, VII, p. 288a: 'Bona autem huius mundi, quae pertinent ad usum humanae vitae, in tribus consistunt: scilicet in divitiis exteriorum bonorum, quae pertinent ad concupiscentiam oculorum; in deliciis carnis, quae pertinent ad concupiscentiam carnis; et in honoribus, quae pertinent ad superbiam vitae; sicut patet I Ioan. II [16]. Haec autem tria totaliter derelinquere, secundum quod possibile est, pertinet ad consilia Evangelica. In quibus etiam tribus fundatur omnis religio, quae statum perfectionis profitetur: nam divitiae abdicantur per paupertatem; deliciae carnis per perpetuam castitatem; superbia vitae per obedientiae servitutem'.

59 Thomas Aquinas, *Summa Theologiae*, I II, q. 108 1, arg. 2, Leonina edn, VII, p. 283a: 'lex nova est *lex spiritus*, ut dicitur Rom. VIII [2]. Sed *ubi Spiritus Domini, ibi libertas*, ut dicitur II ad Cor. III [17]. Non est autem libertas ubi homo obligatur ad aliqua exteriora opera facienda vel vitanda. Ergo lex nova non continet aliqua praecepta vel prohibitiones exteriorum actuum'.

60 Thomas Aquinas, *Summa Theologiae*, I II, q. 108 1, ad 2m, Leonina edn, VII, p. 284a–b: 'secundum Philosophum, in I Metaphys., liber est qui sui causa est. Ille ergo libere aliquid agit qui ex seipso agit. Quod autem homo agit ex habitu suae naturae convenienti, ex seipso agit: quia habitus inclinat in modum naturae. Si vero habitus esset naturae repugnans, homo non ageret secundum quod est ipse, sed secundum aliquam corruptionem sibi supervenientem. Quia igitur gratia Spiritus Sancti est sicut interior habitus nobis infusus inclinans nos ad recte operandum, facit nos libere operari ea quae conveniunt gratiae, et vitare ea quae gratiae repugnant'.

The New Law is said to be a law of liberty in two ways. Firstly, because it obliges to perform or avoid only those acts which are necessary for salvation or which prevent it, acts which are subject to the precept or prohibition of the law. Secondly, since it makes us respect these precepts or prohibitions in a free manner, insofar as we fulfill them by the impulse of grace. For these two reasons, the New Law is said to be the law of perfect liberty, James I [25].[61]

According to Aquinas, the New Law is a law of freedom in both an extrinsic and an intrinsic sense. First, its strength is limited to precepts; second, its strength does not come from a principle that denies freedom; on the contrary, it comes from a principle that safeguards freedom and makes it more powerful.

Comparing Marsilius and Aquinas

I will now try to show what is the novelty of Marsilius's position on law and precepts, and why it is possible to see it as a radically anti-Thomistic and heterodox theory of power.

Marsilius's strategy is to try to minimize the earthly power of divine law as much as possible. Thus, divine law is mainly applied to two types of acts: deliberate internal and external acts. Compared to deliberate internal acts, the power of divine law has the same force as practical or theoretical philosophy. With respect to external acts, its power has the same force as counsels. There is no doubt that, according to Aquinas, clerics have the right to exercise coercive power in the present life. A particularly significant passage is found in the *Disputed Question on Brotherly Correction*. Here Aquinas uses the Aristotelian definition of law as being endowed with coercive power, taken from Book x of *Nicomachean Ethics*, and employs the example of the physician, two elements that are found together in Marsilius. But he concludes, contrary to Marsilius, that both the cleric and the physician can use coercive power:

> There are two ways of correcting an offender. The first is by simply admonishing him; this is brotherly correction, and it has a place only among those people among whom it is accepted that they agree to such admonition of their own free will. The second sort of correction uses

---

61 Thomas Aquinas, *Summa Theologiae*, I II, q. 108 1, ad 2m, Leonina edn, VII, p. 284b: 'Sic igitur lex nova dicitur lex libertatis dupliciter. Uno modo, quia non arctat nos ad facienda vel vitanda aliqua, nisi quae de se sunt vel necessaria vel repugnantia saluti, quae cadunt sub praecepto vel prohibitione legis. Secundo, quia huiusmodi etiam praecepta vel prohibitiones facit nos libere implere, inquantum ex interiori instinctu gratiae ea implemus. Et propter haec duo lex nova dicitur *lex perfectae libertatis*, Iac. I [25]'.

compulsion by inflicting a punishment, as Aristotle says [*Nicomachean Ethics*, x, 1180a5–12]. This sort belongs to superiors [*prelatos*], who ought to make an effort to free from the danger of sin even those who are scornful, just as a doctor makes an effort to heal someone who is mad, even by binding or beating him.[62]

It is not true, according to Aquinas, that the physician limits himself to advising or diagnosing: he may well use force when treating someone who is mentally ill. In the same way, clerics may have recourse to constraint when there is a question of keeping a faithful person away from sin.

Let us add that the simple concept of non-binding law is incoherent according to Aquinas. In the famous treatise *de lege* of the second part of the *Summa*, Aquinas repeatedly insists that the law (the law in general, and therefore any law) is a law precisely because it obligates: 'law [*lex*] is said from binding [*a ligando*], since it obligates to act',[63] he states at the beginning of the question on the essence of law (*de essentia legis*).

It is this idea that Marsilius openly contradicts, asserting that the New Law is not coercive in the earthly life. But Marsilius's position also ends up falling back on what we could call a theology of individual grace and freedom. Indeed, any theology inspired by Augustine must admit that human beings, in order to act well and deserve eternal life, must act in grace and can act freely just to the extent that divine grace inspires and informs them. And grace comes, of course, from the New Law. Without grace, it is impossible to deserve eternal life. But grace is absent from Marsilius's theory: a human being can act well or badly, following or not following human law; a human judge will be in charge of rewarding or punishing that person. In the same way, a human being can act rightly or wrongly, following or not following evangelical counsels; the judge of the afterlife, Christ, will be in charge of rewarding or punishing that person.

The two dimensions appear to be radically separated. This is the reason why I described the conception of the two laws — human and evangelical — in Marsilius's thought as 'discontinuist'. By contrast, according to

---

62 Thomas Aquinas, *Quaestio disputata de correctione fraterna*: 'duplex est correctio delinquentis: una quidem per simplicem ammonitionem, et hec est fraterna correctio et non habet locum nisi in illis de quibus presumitur quod propria uoluntate ammonitioni consentiant; alia uero est correctio habens uim coactiuam per inflictionem penarum, ut Philosophus dicit in X Ethicorum, et talis correctio pertinet ad prelatos, qui etiam contempnentes a periculo peccati studere debent ut liberent, sicut medicus furiosum studet sanare ligando et uerberando eum'. I quote, with the kind permission of Father Adriano Oliva, the Latin text of the critical Leonine edition now under revision in view of publication; the English translation here quoted is in Thomas Aquinas, *Disputed Questions*, trans. by Atkins, p. 201.

63 Thomas Aquinas, *Summa Theologiae*, I II, q. 90 1, resp., Leonina edn, VII, p. 149a: 'lex quaedam regula est et mensura actuum, secundum quam inducitur aliquis ad agendum, vel ab agendo retrahitur: dicitur enim lex a ligando, quia obligat ad agendum'.

Aquinas, the moral quality of human acts is ensured by divine grace, both in relation to the present life and in relation to the future life, the grace that makes it possible to act well in the present life and to deserve the reward of the future life. According to Aquinas, better described as a 'continuist', a theory of civil justice cannot be separated from a theory of supernatural justice while Marsilius's theory of law attempts to demolish the very foundations of this idea.

Conclusions

The analysis conducted here has sufficiently shown that Marsilius is the author of a profoundly innovative and radical conception of the law. The idea that the law of Christ is not imperative is probably one of the most revolutionary ideas that a medieval author put forward. Texts such as those we have analysed show that the *Defensor pacis* is much more than a treatise on political theory. On the contrary, it is a text that proposes a radical rethinking of the relationship between sacred and human law, and in so doing, its author has challenged the foundations of the world in which he lived.

Works Cited

Primary Sources

Augustine of Hippo, *De sermone Domini in monte*, ed. by Almut Mutzenbecher, Corpus Christianorum Series Latina, 35 (Turnhout: Brepols, 1967)

Godfrey of Fontaines, *Le Quodlibet XV et trois Questions ordinaires de Godefroid de Fontaines*, ed. by Odon Lottin, Les philosophes belges: Textes et études, 14 (Louvain: Éditions de l'Institut Supérieur de Philosophie, 1937)

Marsilius of Padua, *The Defender of the Peace*, trans. by Annabel Brett, Cambridge Texts in the History of Political Thought (Cambridge: Cambridge University Press, 2005)

——, *Defensor pacis*, ed. by Richard Scholz, Monumenta Germaniae Historica: Fontes iuris germanici antiqui in usum scholarum separatim editi, 7.2 (Hannover: Hahn, 1933)

Thomas Aquinas, *Disputed Questions on the Virtues*, ed. by E. Margaret Atkins and Thomas Williams, trans. by E. Margaret Atkins, Cambridge Texts in the History of Philosophy (Cambridge: Cambridge University Press, 2005)

——, *Sententia Libri Ethicorum*, in *Opera omnia iussu Leonis XIII P. M. edita*, vol. XLVII, 2 vols (Rome: Ad Sanctae Sabinae, 1969)

——, *Summa Theologiae, Prima secundae*, in *Opera omnia iussu impensaque Leonis XIII P. M. edita*, vols VI–VII: (Rome: Ex Typographia Polyglotta, 1891–1892)

Secondary Works

Brett, Annabel, 'Political Right(s) and Human Freedom in Marsilius of Padua', in *Transformations in Medieval and Early-Modern Rights Discourse*, ed. by Virpi Mäkinen and Petter Korkman, The New Synthese Historical Library, 59 (Dordrecht: Springer, 2006), pp. 95–116

Briguglia, Gianluca, 'I filosofi finsero e persuasero: Osservazioni sulla funzione civile della religione pagana in Marsilio da Padova', *Rivista di filosofia Neo-Scolastica*, 113 (2021): 725–42 (online first, 2020, doi:)10.26350/001050_000162

Dolcini, Carlo, *Introduzione a Marsilio da Padova*, I filosofi, 63 (Rome: Editori Laterza, 1995)

Ghisalberti, Alessandro, 'Sulla legge naturale in Ockham e in Marsilio', *Medioevo*, 5 (1979), 303–15

Hause, Jeffrey, 'Aquinas on Aristotelian Justice: Defender, Destroyer, Subverter or Surveyor?', in *Aquinas and the 'Nicomachean Ethics'*, ed. by Tobias Hoffmann, Jörn Müller, and Matthias Perkams (Cambridge: Cambridge University Press, 2013), pp. 146–64

Hoffmann, Tobias, 'Intellectualism and Voluntarism', in *The Cambridge History of Medieval Philosophy*, ed. by Robert Pasnau and Christina Van Dyke, 2 vols (Cambridge: Cambridge University Press, 2010), I, pp. 414–27

Lewis, Ewart, 'The "Positivism" of Marsiglio of Padua', *Speculum*, 38 (1963), 541–82

Maierù, Alfonso, 'La scienza bizantina e latina: La nascita di una scienza europea. La struttura del sapere', available at <https://www.treccani.it/enciclopedia/la-scienza-bizantina-e-latina-la-nascita-di-una-scienza-europea-la-struttura-del-sapere_%28Storia-della-Scienza%29/> [accessed 11 September 2021]

Mulieri, Alessandro, 'Against Classical Republicanism: The Averroist Foundations of Marsilius of Padua's Political Thought', *History of Political Thought*, 40.2 (2019), 218–45

Perkams, Matthias, 'Aquinas's Interpretation of the Aristotelian Virtue of Justice and his Doctrine of Natural Law', in *Virtue Ethics in the Middle Ages: Commentaries on Aristotle's 'Nicomachean Ethics', 1200–1500*, ed. by István P. Bejczy, Brill's Studies in Intellectual History, 160 (Leiden: Brill, 2007), pp. 131–50

Pinckaers, Servais, 'Le commentaire du Sermon sur la montagne par saint Augustin et la morale de saint Thomas', *Revue d'éthique et de théologie morale*, 253.1 (2009), 9–28

Tierney, Brian, *Liberty and Law: The Idea of Permissive Natural Law, 1100–1800*, Studies in Medieval and Early Modern Canon Law, 12 (Washington, DC: Catholic University of America Press, 2014)

——, 'Marsilius on Rights', *Journal of the History of Ideas*, 52.1 (1991), 3–17

ALESSANDRO MULIERI

Marsilius of Padua and Collective Prudence

Introduction

In Chapter 10 of the first *dictio* of his *Defensor pacis* (1324), Marsilius of Padua draws on Aristotle's *Nicomachean Ethics* (henceforth *NE*) to argue that human law is 'a "speech" (or a pronouncement) "from a certain" (sc. political) "prudence and understanding", i.e., an ordinance concerning the just and the beneficial and their opposites arrived at through political prudence, "having coercive power".[1] Marsilius explains this conception of prudence in the subsequent Chapter 11, where he provides a theory of collective experience that forms the very basis of his notion. As he writes:

> One man alone — and not even, perhaps, all the men of one era — could discover or keep note of all civil actions defined in law. On the contrary, what was said on the subject by the initial discoverers, and even by all the men of the same era who took note of them, amounted to a modest and imperfect thing, which was later supplemented by the contributions of posterity. And familiar experience is enough to see this, in the addition and subtraction and total change to the contrary which has sometimes been made in the laws, depending on different eras and on different times within the same era [...]. And this is confirmed by reason, since acts of legislation need prudence (as was

---

1 For the English translation, I rely on Marsilius of Padua, *The Defender of the Peace*, ed. and trans. by Brett. If needed, I will also quote from the Scholz edition of the Latin text. For this passage, see *DP*, I, 10.4, trans. by Brett, p. 53.

Alessandro Mulieri is a Global Marie Skłodowska-Curie Fellow at Ca' Foscari University of Venice and University of Pennsylvania, and an affiliated researcher of the Institute of Philosophy at KU Leuven. He specializes in the late medieval and early modern history of political thought and in contemporary political theory.

Marsilius of Padua, ed. by Alessandro Mulieri, Serena Masolini, and Jenny Pelletier, Disputatio, 36 (Turnhout: Brepols, 2023), pp. 123–146

BREPOLS ❧ PUBLISHERS   10.1484/M.DISPUT-EB.5.132910

plain earlier from the description of law), but prudence needs long experience, and this in turn needs a great deal of time.[2]

This chapter offers a detailed analysis of the meaning, function, and sources of collective prudence in the *Defensor pacis* (henceforth *DP* or *Defensor*). In so doing, it aims to address a topic to which very few studies have been devoted so far. The serious lack of engagement with Marsilius's theory of collective prudence is surprising if we consider the absolutely crucial role that it plays in the *Defensor*. At the same time, however, Marsilius scholars are hardly to blame for this neglect, given the scarce presence of collective prudence in Marsilius's contemporary ethical and political debate. This is probably also the reason why so few studies have been devoted to this topic.[3]

There is little doubt that the origins of several of the ideas from which Marsilius draws to describe collective prudence are Aristotelian, as Marsilius's own exposition of this theory is filled with direct references to Aristotle's texts. However, bits and pieces of Marsilius's theory can also be found in Averroes (in Chapter 11 of the first *dictio*, in fact, we can see the only direct reference to Averroes in the whole *DP*)[4] and in at least three authors that Marsilius does not explicitly mention in his text: Peter of Abano[5] (Marsilius's teacher in Padua or Paris), Peter of Auvergne (who continued Aquinas's unfinished commentary on Aristotle's *Politics* and authored some *Questiones* on the same text), and, as I will try to show, Thomas Aquinas himself. Reconstructing Marsilius's idea of collective prudence and its relation to these authors allows us to shed light on two problems that are crucial in the scholarly literature on Marsilius.

---

2 *DP*, I, 11.3, trans. by Brett, p. 58: ed. by Scholz, pp. 54–55, 'Quoniam unus solus homo, nec fortasse omnes unius etatis homines invenire aut retinere possent omnes actus civiles determinatos in lege. Quinimo, quod de ipsis dixerunt inventores primi et omnes eciam eiusdem etatis homines, talium observatores, fuit res modica et imperfecta, que postmodum ex addicione posteriorum complementum suscepit. Quod quidem vivere satis experiencia nota per addicionem et subtraccionem ac totaliter in contrarium mutacionem quandoque factam in legibus, secundum diversas etates et secundum diversa tempora eiusdem etatis [...] Et confirmatur id racione, quoniam legislaciones indigent prudencia, ut pridem ex descripcione legis apparuit, prudencia vero longa eget experiencia, hec autem temporis multitudine'.

3 Two exceptions are Mulieri, 'Marsilius of Padua and Peter of Abano', and Syros, 'The Sovereignty of the Multitude'. A fascinating possibility is that the roots of Marsilius's idea are to be found in the reflection on the plural nature of philosophy in Jewish-Arabic sources, which were translated into Latin. See de Libera, *Penser au Moyen Age*, pp. 320–21.

4 This new finding allows us to determine the likely source of the only two Averroes quotations in the *Defensor pacis*. For the debate on Marsilius's Averroism, see at least Piaia, '"Averroïsme politique"' and Mulieri, 'Against Classical Republicanism', especially nn. 2 and 6, which provide compelling accounts of this debate.

5 Mulieri, 'Marsilius of Padua and Peter of Abano'. Marsilius is also mentioned in Peter of Abano's will. See Pesenti, 'Per la tradizione del testamento di Pietro d'Abano'.

The first problem is the complex relationship between Marsilius's collective prudence and Aristotle's thought. Indeed, if very few studies have focused on Marsilius's theory of collective prudence in itself, little has also been written on how the Aristotelian problem of prudence, as a dianoetic virtue or a disposition of the soul that comes in many kinds, evolves in Marsilius of Padua in comparison with other late medieval Aristotelians.[6] Comparing Marsilius to Aristotle on collective prudence, then, can also help better elucidate one of the most controversial themes in the Marsilian scholarship: his relation to Aristotelianism in general.[7] This is a topic that continues to spark divisions among interpreters of Marsilius and overlaps with other important discussions, such as Marsilius's relationship with Augustinianism, Cicero, Averroism, and other traditions.[8]

The second problem is concerned with how Marsilius's theory of collective prudence can be compared to that of other authors who, while also drawing on this same theory, give it a different function. It is likely that the source of Marsilius's idea of collective prudence lies in the thought of one of his teachers in Padua and/or Paris, Peter of Abano,[9] as Marsilius elaborates on the latter's theory of astrological science but shifts its focus to the legal and political domains. In addition to this source, traces of ideas similar to Marsilius's application of the notion of collective prudence in the *Defensor* can be found in Peter of Auvergne's *Questiones* on Aristotle's *Politics*, a likely source for Marsilius's *Defensor*, and, partially, in Dante Alighieri's *Monarchy*, which is not a source of the *DP*.[10] Above all, this theory can be found in one of the texts that generally served, alongside others, as the model for ethical and political elaborations of prudence and law in early fourteenth-century Paris: Thomas Aquinas's *Summa theologiae*. By comparing Marsilius's take on collective prudence to Aquinas's quite limited use of a similar theory of collective experience in the context of

---

6 Important exceptions can be seen in Lambertini, 'Political Prudence in Some Medieval Commentaries', and Toste, 'Virtue and the City'. They both mention Marsilius among several authors who dealt with prudence. For more on prudence in general, see also Celano, *Aristotle's Ethics and Medieval Philosophy* who, however, does not mention Marsilius.

7 On the nature of political Aristotelianism in the Middle Ages, see especially Nederman, 'The Meaning of "Aristotelianism"' and Briguglia, *Il pensiero politico medievale*, pp. 91–96. On the reception of political Aristotelianism, see Flüeler, *Rezeption und Interpretation* and Fioravanti, 'La *Politica* aristotelica', among others.

8 As an example of these debates, see at least Nederman, 'Nature, Sin and the Origins of Society'.

9 Mulieri, 'Marsilius of Padua and Peter of Abano'.

10 For more on Peter of Auvergne's *Questiones* — which had been unedited so far but whose edition by Marco Toste was just published in 2022, when this volume was already at the proofs stage — and their relationship with Marsilius's *Defensor*, see at least Toste, 'The Parts and the Whole'; Syros, 'The Sovereignty of the Multitude'. On this theory in Dante Alighieri, see Brenet, 'Multitude et *bene esse* chez Averroès et Dante'.

changing laws (*mutatio legum*), we can highlight the considerable originality of Marsilius's use of this theory.[11]

In the following, I will tackle both these questions in three different
steps. First, I will briefly describe Marsilius's collective prudence as the
ground of human laws by focusing on the three crucial notions that
Marsilius draws on to elaborate this theory: law, experience, and prudence.
Second, I will highlight the extensive and complex debt of Marsilius's
theory to Aristotle's texts, showing Marsilius's strategic employment of
the Aristotelian sources in the pages where he addresses the problem of
collective prudence. Third, I will compare Marsilius's theory to Aquinas on
the change of laws as a self-cumulative form of knowledge across several
generations. This will allow me to explore the different normative implications that the collective nature of law-changing plays in both thinkers and
eventually highlight the originality of Marsilius's exposition of collective
prudence in his system as well as in relation to the problem of natural law.
The chapter concludes with some thoughts on how this Marsilian theory
can be situated within Aristotelianism and Thomism.

Exposition of Marsilius's Theory

Before analysing how Marsilius conceptualizes collective prudence, it is
important to briefly examine the meanings of the three key concepts
that Marsilius uses to present this theory: law, experience, and prudence.
Marsilius's idea of collective prudence aims to provide a solid foundation
for one particular understanding of law: human law. In Chapter 10, which
precedes the chapter in which he elaborates collective prudence, Marsilius
reports four different meanings of law.[12] He first reports two basic meanings of law that are not treated in depth in Chapter 10: they are law as
'a disposition of the soul'[13] and as a rule that governs a work of art. He
then briefly discusses a third notion of *lex*, which is used as a synonym for
religion, arguing that according to this meaning, law indicates a 'rule containing admonitions for those human acts that result from an imperative,
insofar as they are ordered towards glory or punishment in the world to
come.'[14] Finally, in its fourth meaning, Marsilius defines law as 'a science or
doctrine or universal judgment of matters of civil justice and benefit, and

---

11 For an example of a text that stresses the importance of Aquinas's *Summa theologiae* for
understanding the developments of late medieval ethical and political thought, especially in
Marsilius's context, see *Anonymi Artium Magistri Questiones*, ed. by Costa, who proves how
many commentaries on the *NE* between the end of the thirteenth and the beginning of the
fourteenth centuries engaged extensively with the *Summa theologiae*.

12 *DP*, I, 10, trans. by Brett, pp. 51–54.

13 *DP*, I, 10.3, trans. by Brett, p. 51.

14 *DP*, I, 10.3, trans. by Brett, p. 52.

of their opposites'.[15] This fourth definition of *lex* can refer to two different meanings. It can mean 'a science or doctrine of right' — and here it is conceptualized in terms of its content — or it can be seen as a rule that must be effectively enforced: and here the law is conceptualized in terms of how it is implemented. Marsilius couples these two different meanings together because he argues that in order for a norm to be considered a 'perfect law', it should unite justice with coercive power.[16] We will see that Marsilius's discussion of human law in this section will have to be related to his very original position on natural right in the second *dictio* of the *Defensor*. Indeed, this is probably Marsilius's most original contribution to the problem of collective prudence. I will return to this point in the third section.

For now, it is important to emphasize that Marsilius's discussion of human law, or the fourth definition of a perfect law that unites justice with coercive power in Chapter 10, leads him to discuss its foundations and origins in the subsequent Chapter 11 of the first *dictio*. The key idea that leads him to conceptualize the origins of human law in Chapter 11 is that, since any interpretation of a judge or a ruler in specific cases is subjective and biased, there must be a way to ensure that laws are always impartial and objective. This begs the question of how to guarantee the impartiality of the law. For Marsilius, the best way to do this is to ground human law in a specific idea of prudence. In so doing, Marsilius reinstates Aristotle's claim that law derives from political prudence, an idea that can be found in other Aristotelian commentators to the *NE* in late medieval political thought as well.[17] In Chapter 11, he then complements this claim by saying that 'acts of legislation need prudence (as was plain earlier from the description of law)', and then adds that since 'prudence needs long experience', this 'in turn needs a great deal of time'.[18]

Experience occupies a special status in Marsilius's *DP*. This is hardly surprising given his training as a physician, which included medicine and natural philosophy. The notion of experience bears three main meanings in the *DP*. The first is very basic and identifies experience with observation, meaning the empirical verification of something through human senses. In these cases, Marsilius uses phrases such as everyone's 'sense-experience' or 'the experience of the senses' and calls upon experience to verify certain claims that he presents in crucial parts of the *DP*.[19] The second occurrence

---

15 *DP*, I, 10.3, trans. by Brett, p. 52; ed. by Scholz, pp. 49–50: 'iuris sciencia vel doctrina'.

16 For more on this, see Lewis, 'The "Positivism" of Marsiglio of Padua'; Tierney, 'Marsilius on Rights'; and Tierney, *Liberty and Law*.

17 See Lambertini, '"Est autem et politica et prudencia, idem quidem habitus"'.

18 *DP*, I, 11.3, trans. by Brett, p. 58.

19 *DP*, I, 17.9, I, 4.3, and I, 11.6, trans. by Brett, pp. 119, 19, and 62. On this, see Brett, 'Introduction', p. xix.

of experience treats it as a crucial factor in the growth of human communities. Likewise, this meaning is coupled with reason because it indicates all the arts and sciences that are needed to fulfil the two main goals of political life, namely living and living well (*vivere* and *bene vivere*). Marsilius often frames this second formulation of his notion of experience as the 'mistress of the disciplines' (*magistra rerum*), in many passages of *DP*.[20] In its third meaning, which is more prominently ethical and political, Marsilius follows Aristotle and couples experience with prudence, as in the passage from *DP* I, 10, which we mentioned above. This is aimed at following the Aristotelian idea that prudence is a dianoetic virtue that requires training and therefore presupposes extensive practice and experience. It is also this meaning that is most relevant for Marsilius's discussion in Chapter 11. Here, Marsilius presents an idea of collective experience that forms the basis of the idea of prudence that will ground human laws and guarantee their being impartial.

'Prudence' is the third term that is obviously relevant for the present analysis and the most difficult to disentangle in any depth. In fact, the very topic of prudence in the *DP* deserves an analysis of its own. Ever since the earliest translations of the *NE* in the early thirteenth century by Robert Grosseteste, the status of prudence had been the centre of a heated debate.[21] The discussion on the *species prudentiae* aimed to clarify the complex status of the very Aristotelian idea of *phronesis*, which was discussed actively in the medieval commentaries on the *NE*.[22] Indeed, in the *NE*, Aristotle defines prudence as an intellectual or dianoetic virtue that plays an intermediary role between the practical intellect and the desiderative part of the soul, and allows a particular action to be subsumed under a universal principle of the intellect. He also thinks of *phronesis* in the *NE* as an intellectual virtue that guides moral action. In this sense, *phronesis* plays an intermediary role between the practical intellect and the moral virtues in order to specify the right mean. The act by which a universal principle of the intellect can subsume a particular moral action allows us to see rather easily why Aristotle, and Marsilius with him, claims that prudence is the result of experience. This is linked with Aristotle's idea that it is necessary to establish a relationship with the empirical world to perfect prudence. However, Aristotle's characterization of prudence in the *NE* is not limited to its strict definition as a dianoetic virtue. In fact, scholastic commentators extensively discussed a passage of *NE*, VI, 8 on the relationship between prudence and politics where Aristotle claims that there are other types of prudence, that is, in domestic, legislative,

---

20 For example, in *DP*, II, 18.2, trans. by Brett, p. 353.

21 For example, see Celano, *Aristotle's Ethics and Medieval Philosophy* and Lambertini, 'Political Prudence in Some Medieval Commentaries'.

22 On this, see especially Lambertini, 'Political Prudence in Some Medieval Commentaries'.

and political environments, that do not seem to completely overlap with prudence as an intellectual virtue.[23] This discussion became rather detailed in the Paris university debates of the first decades of the fourteenth century at the exact time when Marsilius is reported to have been there (he held the office of rector in 1312–1313 and is said to have left the city in 1324 or 1325).[24] Besides, as we will see immediately below, Aristotle refers to the 'prudence of the many' in a passage from Book III of the *Politics*. Some commentators of this latter text, especially Peter of Auvergne, discussed this collective notion of prudence.[25]

Marsilius's definition of human law as deriving from political prudence broadly reflects these discussions.[26] However, his characterization of the idea of political prudence as something from which human law derives is different from the way other Aristotelians, and in fact Aristotle as well, talk about political prudence. In Chapter 11, the Paduan goes beyond Aristotle's conception of prudence in the *NE*, as he claims that the experience needed to perfect prudence is not that of an individual, but of a particular collective nature. For Marsilius, this experience results from the knowledge of several human beings belonging to one generation plus the addition of several subsequent generations of human beings. In other words, in Marsilius we find an idea of political prudence which is collective and trans-historical. It is worth emphasizing that there are no traces of this conception of collective prudence in the several commentaries on the *Nicomachean Ethics* written after 1277 and in the first three decades of the fourteenth century, when Marsilius was at the University of Paris.[27] Nor can we find traces of this same theory in the *quaestiones quodlibetales*, which were a genre that included a lively discussion of the *species prudentiae*.[28] Marsilius could find traces of this theory in the work of Peter of Auvergne, but the latter's discussion of this theme is brief and generic and, moreover, never employs a trans-generational idea of prudence as a systematic normative foundation of human law. Therefore, it seems that in the *Defensor* we find a fully developed theory of collective prudence that has no equal examples in late medieval ethical and political thought. Marsilius draws on Aristotle's claims in the *NE* that prudence always

---

23 See Aristotle, *NE*, VI, 1141b23–1142a11 and Lambertini's detailed discussion of the analysis of this passage in late medieval authors in Lambertini, '"Est autem et politica et prudencia, idem quidem habitus"'.

24 Godthardt, 'The Life of Marsilius of Padua'.

25 Syros, 'The Sovereignty of the Multitude', pp. 231–34. For more on Auvergne as a thinker, see Flüeler, Lanza, and Toste, eds, *Peter of Auvergne*.

26 See Toste, 'Virtue and the City'.

27 Due to this absence, it is not surprising that no discussion of the topic can be found in major studies on late medieval ethical political thought. See Celano, *Aristotle's Ethics and Medieval Philosophy*, and *Anonymi Artium Magistri Questiones*, ed. by Costa.

28 Lambertini, 'Political Prudence in Some Medieval Commentaries'.

requires experience, and he firmly grounds this notion of prudence in a certain idea of experience, which is collective.

The three notions that have been discussed in this section are closely bound to each other in Marsilius's treatment. Marsilius's reasoning is that human law, or law according to its fourth meaning, presupposes an idea of collective prudence that is built on collective and trans-generational experience. It is in this context that we have to understand Marsilius's claim in Chapter 11 according to which the experience needed to acquire prudence comes from the addition of several people over time. This short analysis of the uses of law, experience, and prudence in Marsilius's *Defensor* raises two important questions: First, how does Marsilius connect the three notions, that is, law, experience, and prudence, that we have analysed so far? Second, in making this connection, how does Marsilius draw on Aristotle's authority to present his theory of collective prudence?

Marsilius's Debt to Aristotle

In Chapter 11 of the first *dictio*, the Paduan *magister* provides two different arguments that link law, experience, and prudence, as we analysed in the previous section. The first is that political and legal judgement should not be based on personal interest or bias but instead on laws that are objective and impartial. The second, which aims to provide a justification for the first, is that the impartiality of laws depends on the accumulation of the experience of several subsequent generations of human beings plus the human beings who belong to a single generation. Marsilius grounds both of these claims in Aristotle's ideas.

Starting with the first argument, Marsilius draws extensively on Aristotle's *Politics* and *Rhetoric* to confirm his claim that political judgement must be based on impartial laws. In several passages of these works, Aristotle stresses the importance of impartial laws vis-à-vis decisions that are based only on the will of individual judges. For example, in Book I of the *Rhetoric*, Aristotle says that laws should determine everything in political matters and leave as little as possible to the decisions of individual judges because laws guarantee impartiality that no single man or judgement can provide.[29] Similarly, in Book IV of the *Politics*,[30] Aristotle says that it is better for princes to only be masters of a few things that are not regulated by the law. In reporting these passages, Marsilius reinstates Aristotle's ideas

---

29 These ideas can be found, for example, in Aristotle, *Rhetoric*, I, 1354a and 1354b. In *DP*, trans. by Brett, pp. 57–58, Marsilius mentions passages I, 1354b4–11; I, 1354b1–2; I, 1354a31–32.

30 Aristotle, *Politics*, IV, 1292a32–33, and Book V of *Politics*, 1313a20–23, mentioned respectively in *DP*, trans. by Brett, *DP*, I, 11.5–6, pp. 61 and 63.

on the impartiality of the law and unites this claim with the idea that without impartial laws there would in fact be no polity.[31]

In another passage of the *Politics*, from Book v,[32] Aristotle talks about the different causes of sedition in a polity, enumerating tyranny as one of the main causes of its destruction. Marsilius draws on this passage and communicates the risk that in a polity, men can only rely on the arbitrary will of the prince and not on the law. This allows the Paduan to show the importance of making decisions in the polity that depend on impartial laws in order to avoid 'perverse' ideas that can lead to the self-destruction of the polity.[33] If rulers and princes do not comply with the law and base their decisions on their will, the risk is tyranny. Here, the argument about the necessity to base judgements on laws that are impartial and not on judges' personal interests is linked to the very main theme of the *Defensor*, namely Marsilius's critique of the perverted opinion of the plenitude of power. Tyranny or disregard for the impartiality of the law might lead to such individual biased judgements as, for example, the plenitude of power, and eventually cause the destruction of the polity.

Marsilius also reports a passage from *Politics*, Book III,[34] where Aristotle advances his idea, which he also discusses at length in other parts of this work, on the superiority of the multitude over the single person or the few, as far as important political decisions are concerned. Aristotle does so by proposing an organicist comparison concerning the qualitative superiority of more organs to one. Here, the physician Marsilius draws on Aristotle's words to define the law as an eye made of several eyes,[35] thereby explicitly linking the claim that the law should be made by the many with the idea that prudence is the cumulative experience of several human beings. Once again, Peter of Auvergne discusses this passage from Aristotle and proceeds to attach some significance to the notion of collective prudence in particular circumstances.[36]

In fact, we saw that the latter, that is, the idea that experience and prudence must be collective and trans-historical, is Marsilius's second main idea in Chapter 11 of the first *dictio*. To support this argument, Marsilius draws on Aristotelian ideas that were widespread among his contemporaries. Mostly, however, he borrows them from Peter of Abano who presents a similar idea of collective experience to the one Marsilius

---

31 *DP*, I, 11.4 and I, 11.7, trans. by Brett, pp. 61 and 63. It is worth mentioning that, both in his *Continuatio* and in his *Questiones*, Peter of Auvergne discusses these problems of the objectivity and impartiality of the laws. See Blythe, *Ideal Government and the Mixed Constitution*, pp. 77–91.

32 Aristotle, *Politics*, v, 1312b38–1313a5.

33 *DP*, I, 11.5–6, trans. by Brett, p. 62.

34 Aristotle, *Politics*, III, 16, 1287b26–29.

35 *DP*, I, 11.3, trans. by Brett, p. 60.

36 *DP*, trans. by Brett, p. 77 n. 9.

discusses in the *Defensor*. In the *Lucidator*, Peter of Abano draws on Aristotle's and Averroes's ideas that sciences, both speculative and practical, need the collective accumulation of knowledge over subsequent generations to explain the functioning of the science of the stars (*scientia stellarum*). As I have shown elsewhere, Marsilius takes up this same idea and applies it to the science of law-making.[37] He translates Peter of Abano's reflections on science to the political realm. By shifting Peter's argument to the domain of law-making, Marsilius substantially reinstates the same quotations from Aristotle's *Metaphysics* and the *Sophistical Refutations*, as well as from Averroes's commentary to the *Metaphysics*, that we can find in Peter of Abano's *Lucidator*. However, he also adds his own contributions to these quotations.

For example, in *Metaphysics*, Book II,[38] Aristotle deals with the problem of the search for truth in philosophy and argues that one single man cannot fully and adequately grasp it. A considerable grasp of the truth can only come about through the union of all the single contributions of several men taken together. Marsilius first complements this quotation with one from Averroes's commentary on the *Metaphysics* and another from Aristotle's *Sophistical Refutations*, both of which are texts quoted by Peter of Abano. Like the latter, Marsilius takes Aristotle in Book II of the *Sophistical Refutations* to say that 'arts in their greater part [...] are not brought to completion except by the aid given by a forerunner to a successor'.[39] He applies this claim to rhetoric and to the other arts, and then complements the Aristotelian text by asserting that the only exception to this is logic, an art that does not need to develop by a continuous accumulation of knowledge as it is already complete in itself.

The Paduan thinker then proceeds to further analyse Aristotle's quotation from the *Metaphysics* where Aristotle gives an example from music and writes that Timotheus, a known poet and musician who lived between the sixth and fifth centuries BCE and composed many melodies, would not have existed without Frini, who was his master.[40] Marsilius handles these passages by either selectively emphasizing some parts of them or by partly modifying what they mean. First, he applies Aristotle's discourse on philosophical truth to the science of law-making and ascribes to the latter an eminently ethical character because of the strong link that he emphasizes between science and prudence. Second, in order to support his idea that prudence should come from the accumulation of experience over several subsequent generations, he stresses the Aristotelian idea that the arts, and music in this particular case, are based on the accumulation

---

37 Mulieri, 'Marsilius of Padua and Peter of Abano'.

38 Aristotle, *Metaphysics*, II, 993b2 and 15–16.

39 Aristotle, *Sophistical Refutations*, 183b26 ff.

40 Aristotle, *Metaphysics*, II, 993b2.

of the knowledge of subsequent practitioners, something which Aristotle does not at all link with prudence. Therefore, without Frini there would be no Timotheus. In order to remain more faithful to the text, Marsilius describes Aristotle's comparison with the arts but then integrates it with Averroes's commentary on the same text.[41] According to Averroes, the example of Timotheus is meant to confirm that all theoretical and practical arts cannot be perfected without the help of what subsequent practitioners add to the previous ones.[42] Here, Marsilius appears to agree with Averroes by coupling the speculative with the practical arts, something implicit but not fully developed in Aristotle's original text.

There is no equivalent to Marsilius's systematic development of the theory of collective prudence from the *Defensor* in any text of Aristotle. In fact, even when Aristotle hints in his *Politics* at the prudence (*phronesis*) of the masses in electing certain magistracies,[43] he never presents a comprehensive and extensive discussion of what would characterize prudence as a collective enterprise. This is because, as we already said, Aristotle mainly describes prudence as a dianoetic virtue that pertains to a single moral agent. Only in the *Politics* and unsystematically does he refer to it as a collective form of knowledge. Marsilius's instrumental use of Aristotelian sources leads him to gather several Aristotelian ideas and passages and to unify them so as to find support for his claims that experience and prudence must be collective and trans-historical. This instrumental use of Aristotle is also reflected in Marsilius's treatment of the main text in which Aristotle presents his own theory of prudence, the *NE*. Something notable in Chapter 11 of the first *dictio* of the *Defensor* is the absence or omission of any detailed reference to the discussion of prudence as a virtue of the individual in the *Nicomachean Ethics*. This cannot be due to Marsilius's ignorance of the discussion of the *species prudentiae* that we mentioned in the previous section because, in other parts of the *Defensor*, the Paduan

---

41 *DP*, I, 11.3, trans. by Brett, pp. 59–60. Aristotle's discussion can be found in *Metaphysics*, II, 993b10–30. An analysis of this passage and of the theory of knowledge as cumulative across several subsequent generations can be found not only in Ibn Rushd but also in Latin commentators, e.g. Albert, Thomas, and Dante Alighieri. See Brenet, 'Multitude et *bene esse* chez Averroès et Dante', p. 366 n. 24. I will come back to this point later in the essay.

42 Averroes, *Aristotelis Metaphysicorum libri XIII*, II, 1, in *Aristotelis opera cum Averrois commentariis*, VIII, fol. 28ᵛ, quoted in *DP*, trans. by Brett, p. 59 n. 9.

43 In fact, the interpreters who focus on this passage of Aristotle's *Politics* pay little attention to the collective theory of prudence, as they prefer to translate it or discuss it as the more generic idea of 'collective wisdom'. See Waldron, 'The Wisdom of the Multitude', and Cammack, 'Aristotle on the Virtue of the Multitude'. Unsurprisingly, Peter of Auvergne's discussion of collective prudence is equally brief and unsystematic both in his *Continuatio* and in his *Questiones*, which were most likely two sources, among others, for Marsilius's *Defensor*. See Blythe, *Ideal Government and the Mixed Constitution*, pp. 77–91.

physician proves that he is aware of this debate[44] and, as we have seen, isolates an eminently political idea of prudence that he explicitly links to the law. Marsilius's low-profile discussion of the *NE* in a chapter where prudence has a crucial role could be due to his awareness that the idea of collective prudence is not crucial in Aristotle's *NE*.

In fact, as for the other quotations from Aristotelian texts, Marsilius's references to the *NE* in Chapter 11 of the first *dictio* are simply aimed at providing further arguments to defend a theory of collective prudence that is barely mentioned in Aristotle. These passages are from Books VI and VIII of the *NE*.[45] In one, which echoes what we already explained in the previous paragraph, Aristotle writes that the young cannot be considered wise, even if they are experts in some disciplines, because wisdom requires experience and experience needs time. Here, Aristotle mentions the word *phronesis*.[46] However, when Marsilius employs this word as *prudentia*, he provides no hint to the fact that, when making this claim, Aristotle obviously means to refer to prudence as a dianoetic virtue that pertains to the action of the single moral agent, not to a collective form of knowledge, which is the way Marsilius discusses prudence in this passage.

In the second passage, Aristotle talks about the importance of friendship and says that two men who walk together have a better capacity to think and act.[47] This is something that Aristotle says, but without at all focusing on the problem of the formations of truth and science. Marsilius comments on this quotation from Aristotle by writing that if the latter's claim applies to two people, it must also apply to several men, considering one generation of them and many subsequent generations.[48] This instrumental interpretation of Aristotle's words is also present when Marsilius handles another quotation of Aristotle from Book V of the *NE*,[49] where the Greek philosopher argues that men can become only rulers according to reason and uses this latter term as a synonym for law. Marsilius comments on Aristotle's words by saying that a lack of compliance with this Aristotelian rule can lead to a 'perverted affection', which is another name for how Marsilius refers to the plenitude of power in Book I of *DP*, as a perverse opinion (*opinio perversa*).[50] Here, once again, Marsilius shows just how strong the bond is between his usage of Aristotelian language and his main political purpose, which is that of contrasting the idea of the plenitude of power. In these three cases, Marsilius uses these quotations, in

---

44 For example, in a chapter where Marsilius discusses the prudence of the prince as a virtue in the traditional Aristotelian sense; see *DP*, I, 14, trans. by Brett, pp. 81–87.

45 *NE*, VI, 9, 1142a12–16, and VIII, 1, 1155a15–16.

46 *DP*, I, 11.3, trans. by Brett, p. 59.

47 Aristotle, *NE*, VIII, 1155a15–16, mentioned in *DP*, trans. by Brett, p. 60.

48 *DP*, I, 11.3, trans. by Brett, p. 59.

49 Aristotle, *NE*, V, 1134a35.

50 *DP*, I, 11.4, trans. by Brett, p. 61.

which Aristotle refers respectively to individual prudence and the theory of friendship, to advance his (Marsilius's) theory of collective prudence, which in itself is not an idea that can be found in any of these three passages from the *NE*.

An analysis of the Aristotelian passages from which Marsilius draws in Chapter 11 of the first *dictio* of the *Defensor* allows us to highlight a pattern in the way that the Paduan *magister* relies on Aristotle to present his theory of collective prudence. In his handling of the Aristotelian sources, Marsilius seems to follow a common logic in his reasoning that is based on three different steps. First, Marsilius starts from ideas that he finds in previous traditions or authors — in this case, Peter of Abano, Averroes, and, partly, Peter of Auvergne — and reinterprets them to present his original theory of collective prudence. Second, Marsilius draws on passages from Aristotle's texts and interprets them instrumentally to further support his notion of collective prudence. Some of these passages are already present in Peter of Abano (the *Metaphysics*, the *Sophistical Refutations*, or Averroes's commentary), and Marsilius either edits them or emphasizes those parts that are most helpful for his view. In other Aristotelian passages that he mentions from the *Politics*, the *Rhetoric*, and, above all, the *NE*, Marsilius emphasizes those elements that, while only being implicit or even missing, can better serve the purpose of legitimizing the ideas that he himself wants to uphold. He complements these passages, especially those from the *NE*, with others that give a more precisely legal and political dimension to the Aristotelian idea that science comes from the accumulation of knowledge of several generations of human beings. Third, his usage of Aristotle's text, and of Averroes's, Peter of Abano's, and Peter of Auvergne's ideas, to expose collective prudence aims to sustain a specific normative purpose, which is different from Aristotle's and from all the other sources that draw on these Aristotelian passages.

Marsilius and Aquinas

As Marsilius uses collective prudence to ground the legitimacy of human law, we might claim that this idea helps him establish the grounds of justice upon which the whole theory of the legislator as the people or the *universitas civium* is based. The importance of collective prudence in the Marsilian system as a whole cannot be fully understood without relating it to his position on natural right.[51] In the second *dictio* of the *DP*, Marsilius draws on Aristotle's discussion of this matter in the *NE* to present two different accounts of natural law. In one account, law is something 'upon

---

51 I have already done this in Mulieri, 'Marsilius of Padua and Peter of Abano', pp. 279–81.

which almost all agree as something honest that should be observed',[52] whereas in the second natural law is a 'dictate of right reason' that is placed under divine law. While Marsilius rejects the former, because he considers it equivocal insofar as 'natural' here is a synonym for 'conventional', he considers the second to be the valid meaning of 'natural' law because, as he maintains, it provides a standard for distinguishing right from wrong, and also sets an extra-juridical criterion for assessing human conduct via its foundation in divine law.[53] However, while this standard has a certain importance in ruling the moral behaviour of people in the present life, transgressions against it can only be punished in the afterlife. Therefore, Marsilius's second conception of natural law has little or no importance in determining the making of human laws. Marsilius does not deny the moral importance of natural law in guiding human behaviour and for establishing a moral or extra-juridical criterion of behaviour. However, he clearly dismisses the relevance of this given the role of natural law in the formation of just human laws.[54]

It is in light of this position on natural law that we can better understand the importance of Marsilius's theory of collective prudence for his overall political system. Marsilius uses this theory as the foundation of human law in order to find an alternative ground to natural law. His innovative use of this theory can be better seen when it is opposed to another important view on the link between natural and human law, namely that of Thomas Aquinas. In the *Summa theologiae* (henceforth *ST*), Aquinas mentions a theory of the accumulation of knowledge that bears some resemblance to Marsilius's. In *ST* I–II, q. 97, art. 1, Aquinas devotes an entire paragraph to talking about changes of law and tackles the question of the conditions under which laws change.[55] According to Aquinas, laws can be justified on two bases: 'on the part of reason' and 'on the part of men whose actions are regulated by the law'.[56] Laws that change 'on the part of reason' do so because, in Aquinas's words,

---

52 *DP*, II, 12.7, trans. by Brett, p. 253.

53 For more on this, see Tierney, 'Marsilius on Rights' and Brett, 'Political Right(s) and Human Freedom'.

54 Marsilius's view shows a certain degree of dependence on Ibn Rushd's view on this same subject. In his commentary on the *NE*, which was available in Latin at the time, Ibn Rushd highlights Aristotle's definition of natural right as a ubiquitous convention, referring to natural right as 'natural legal justice' (*ius naturale legale*) (Averroes, in *Moralia Nicomachia Expositio*, V, 7, in *Aristotelis opera cum Averrois commentariis*, III, fols 73^r–74^v). I will deal with this topic in depth in a specific study that I am preparing.

55 I have suggested this comparison in Mulieri, 'Marsilius of Padua and Peter of Abano', p. 283 n. 18, but is not further analysed here.

56 *ST*, I–II, q. 97, a. 1, co; Eng. trans. Thomas Aquinas, *Selected Political Writings*, trans. by Dawson, pp. 142–43.

it would seem natural for human reason to proceed by stages from the imperfect to the more perfect. So, we see in speculative science that those who first began to philosophize arrived at an incomplete system which their successors later elaborated into something more perfect. It is the same also in practical affairs. For those who first set themselves to consider what was useful to the common well-being of man, not being able to solve the entire problem themselves, established certain regulations which were imperfect and deficient in many respects; and these regulations were later modified by their successors to retain those which were the least defective from the point of view of the public interest.[57]

Although he does not use the word 'prudence' in this passage, Aquinas here clearly draws on a similar idea as the one that we discussed in Marsilius. Also, from the reading of it, Aquinas's Aristotelian sources are likely to be the same as some of Marsilius's, that is, Aristotle's *Metaphysics* and *Sophistical Refutations*. In fact, as we anticipated in the previous section, this is confirmed by the fact that Albert the Great and Thomas Aquinas mention this theory of the accumulation of knowledge in their commentaries on Aristotle's *Metaphysics*.[58] However, they hardly give a political connotation to this doctrine or extensively discuss its implications for law-making. Moreover, there are a number of important differences between Aquinas's handling of this theory and Marsilius's notion of collective prudence.

The first is that in this passage (but in the other works where he talks about this topic as well), Aquinas does not use the words 'experience' or 'prudence' that, as we have seen, are so important in Marsilius's political thought. Therefore, to be precise, Aquinas, unlike Marsilius, does not have a theory of collective prudence, but he mentions the Aristotelian idea that to change laws requires knowledge that is accumulated in one generation as well as across many subsequent generations. The second is that for Aquinas, law-making is not a science in itself and is not identified with political prudence. While Marsilius quite often uses the very same word for law as a synonym for 'prudence' (or 'science'), Aquinas has a very clear idea of the difference between the disposition of the soul as science and the other dispositions of the soul such as, for example, prudence.

A third important difference between Marsilius's and Aquinas's handling of their similar ideas on the collective transgenerational nature of law-making is that, following the previous point, whereas the latter maintains that there is a clear distinction between speculative and practical sciences, the former does not think of them as different. In fact, Aquinas

---

57 *ST*, I–II, q. 97, a. 1, co; Thomas Aquinas, *Selected Political Writings*, trans. by Dawson, p. 143.
58 For more on this, see Brenet, 'Multitude et *bene esse* chez Averroès et Dante', pp. 364–66.

presents this theory not to suggest that speculative and practical sciences have the same epistemological status, but only to claim that there is a parallel between the way that speculative sciences and the knowledge required to change laws progress over time. Marsilius's suggestion that the prudence or science necessary for having laws must be accumulated over time is not simply based on a parallel with the progressive nature of knowledge in the speculative sciences, but substantively identifies speculative sciences with such a practical activity as law-making. In fact, Marsilius claims that speculative and practical sciences share a similar criterion of apodictic certainty and, following Peter of Abano (and possibly other authors in the context of the fourteenth century),[59] claims that they are all part of the same idea of science. For him, the science of law-making thus works exactly like the self-cumulative idea of knowledge that, drawing on Aristotle, he ascribes to metaphysics.

The fourth and main point of difference between Aquinas and Marsilius, however, pertains to the role played by the idea of self-cumulative knowledge as the basis of law-making in their broader argumentation. In Aquinas, this theory plays a quite limited role. Aquinas does not fully develop its function in his system and exclusively relates his ideas on this topic to the specific question of the mutation of the laws. In Chapter 11, Marsilius also mentions the importance that self-cumulative knowledge has for the change of laws.[60] However, the two Marsilian ideas — (1) that collective prudence is the foundation of human laws and (2) that natural law does not have any role in the legitimization of human laws — have no place in Aquinas. Indeed, for Aquinas, natural law can be defined as nothing other than the rational creature's participation in eternal law,[61] meaning it is directly related to divine Providence. Moreover, Aquinas unequivocally states that 'the essential characteristic of human law is that it derived from natural law',[62] because if there is an absolute criterion of justice that can applied to any law, this must certainly be rooted in a rule of reason that is identified with the law of nature. Aquinas also takes a further step in his discussion of the problem of human law. He claims that human law *qua* law depends on its being derived from natural law and, when it does not, it is just a perversion of natural law and, in fact, human laws are not even really laws at all. As he explains in II–II, q. 95, art. 1:

---

59 On this, see Mulieri, 'Marsilius of Padua and Peter of Abano'.

60 *DP*, I, 11.2 and I, 11.3, trans. by Brett, p. 58. Here in the Latin text, Marsilius uses the phrase *mutatio legum* like Aquinas; see *DP*, ed. by Scholz, p. 54: 'mutacionem [...] factam in legibus'.

61 See *ST*, I–II, q. 91, a. 1, ad. 3; Thomas Aquinas, *Selected Political Writings*, trans. by Dawson, pp. 114–15.

62 *ST*, I–II, q. 95, a. 4, co; Thomas Aquinas, *Selected Political Writings*, trans. by Dawson, p. 131.

in human affairs a thing is said to be just when it accords aright with the rule of reason: and, as we have already seen, the first rule of reason is the natural law. Thus all humanly enacted laws are in accord with reason to the extent that they derive from the natural law. And if a human law is at variance in any particular with the natural law, it is no longer legal, but rather a corruption of law.[63]

Marsilius clearly rejects these two claims of Aquinas. First, as we saw, even if he attests to the moral importance of natural law as the dictate of right reason, he does not think that this notion of natural law bears any relevance in the determination of the content of human laws. In Chapter 12 of the first *dictio* of DP, Marsilius claims that the legislator is the primary and proper 'efficient cause' of the laws and defines it as:

> the people or the universal body of the citizens or else its prevailing part, when, by means of an election or will expressed in speech in a general assembly of the citizens, it commands or determines, subject to temporary penalty of punishment, that something should be done or omitted in respect of human civil acts.[64]

This legislator is not simply the author of the laws but also provides their content and, therefore, a normative foundation to human laws as perfect and coercive rules that regulate human action. In fact, to ground the idea of *lex perfecta* that we presented above, Marsilius draws on the idea of collective prudence also described above in this chapter. This theory of collective prudence is transgenerational, but Marsilius also extends it to the action of the many in the present. Therefore, he sees the prudence of the many not only as an accumulation of knowledge over time but also as the accumulation of knowledge that can be accomplished in a single generation of human beings who form the legislator in the present.[65]

The idea of collective prudence is not simply related to a particular aspect of law-making, contrary to Aquinas who links its equivalent as collective knowledge to the necessity of the mutability of laws. Rather, it constitutes the very foundation of human laws in the *Defensor*. In fact, in Marsilius's theory of law, collective prudence plays the same

---

63 *ST*, I–II, q. 95, a. 4, co; Thomas Aquinas, *Selected Political Writings*, trans. by Dawson, p. 129.

64 *DP*, I, 12.3, trans. by Brett, p. 66; ed. by Scholz, p. 63, 'Nos autem dicamus [...] legislatorem seu causam legis effectivam primam et propriam esse populum seu civium universitatem aut eius valenciorem partem, per suam eleccionem seu voluntatem in generali civium congregacione per sermonem expressam precipientem seu determinantem aliquid fieri vel omitti circa civiles actus humanos sub pena vel supplicio temporali'.

65 We also find a reflection on the wisdom of the multitude in Peter of Auvergne and Dante Alighieri. In 'Multitude et *bene esse* chez Averroès et Dante', p. 365, Brenet says that, while the theory of accumulation over time is quite common among Latin commentators, the idea of knowledge *simul* is novel in Dante Alighieri. Certainly, this idea of collective prudence in the present is *in nuce* in Aristotle and Peter of Auvergne and is fully developed in Marsilius.

role that natural law does in Thomas Aquinas for grounding human laws. This is the key difference between Marsilius's theory of collective prudence and Aquinas's idea of the *mutatio legum* as the accumulation of trans-generational knowledge. Marsilius uses collective prudence with a specific normative goal, which is that of countering the papal theory of the *plenitudo potestatis*.[66] For Marsilius, collective prudence is a foundational political principle that replaces the idea of natural law. On the contrary, for Aquinas, the self-cumulative idea of knowledge necessary in law-making is solely concerned with the problem of changing laws and is meant to clarify how this process works. I think that this is precisely why this theory is so crucial in Marsilius. While natural law is the very foundation of human law in Aquinas, for Marsilius this lies in his theory of collective prudence.

This opposition between Marsilius and Aquinas, however, should not be interpreted along the lines of the old debate that polarizes the orthodox Thomas against a heterodox Marsilius.[67] First, insofar as Marsilius ascribes a crucial role to the idea of collective prudence in his political theory, this is unlikely to have been for eminently philosophical reasons. Aquinas's thoughts on how self-cumulative knowledge is necessary for changing laws are contained in a theological text. And, while Aquinas tackles the question for scholarly or pedagogical purposes,[68] Marsilius primarily deals with a political problem in the *Defensor*, a text which he is writing for a broader audience that addresses whomever wants to read the treatise, not simply theologians, students, or university professors.[69] This might be why Marsilius places centre-stage what can be considered a secondary idea in the scholarly milieu of this contemporary ethical and political debate, that is, the notion of collective prudence, in drawing his conception of law that, in turn, is so important for structuring his ideological attack against the plenitude of power.

Moreover, the function and perception of most of Aquinas's ideas in Marsilius's time and, more generally, after the condemnation of 1277 and at the beginning of the fourteenth century, was different from the way these same ideas were perceived a few generations earlier (and when Aquinas was still alive) in the thirteenth century. In the earlier

---

66 For more on the generic character of the legislator, see Nederman, *Community and Consent*; and Condren, 'Democracy and the *Defensor Pacis*'.

67 To see how this applies to the problem of Averroism in Marsilius of Padua, see Piaia, '"Averroïsme politique"'.

68 On the pedagogical function of the *Summa*, see Johnson, 'Aquinas's *Summa theologiae* as Pedagogy'.

69 As Marsilius says in Chapter 3 of the third *dictio* of the *Defensor pacis*. See *DP*, III, 3, trans. by Brett, p. 557: 'Both prince and subject, the primary elements of any civil order, can understand by this treatise what they must do in order to preserve the peace and their own liberty'. On the public dimension of Marsilius's ideas, see Godthardt, 'The Philosopher as Political Actor'.

period, Aquinas's thought was perceived as potentially subversive, especially by Franciscans and other theologians at Paris University (for example, Bonaventure), who were worried about the proliferation of new Aristotelian philosophical ideas through the mediation of Islamic and Jewish sources in the world of the Latin university.[70] Marsilius wrote one generation after this period in a context in which Thomism had shifted to being part of the mainstream ideas discussed in the milieu of the Parisian university, which was now challenged from several different standpoints, that is, Scotus, Averroism, Ockham, etc. It is in this context that we can better understand the tendency, as detected by some studies on authors who worked on ethical and political matters at the University of Paris in those decades, to de-theologize Aquinas's work between the end of the thirteenth century and the beginning of the fourteenth century. The so-called Averroist commentaries on the *NE* from the end of the thirteenth and the beginning of the fourteenth century have been described as examples of this trend.[71] It is within this context, then — and not within a presumed simplistic opposition between orthodox Thomism and heterodox Aristotelianism — that we should consider Marsilius's use of the theory of collective prudence in the *Defensor*. In this sense, and only in this qualified sense, Marsilius's theory makes him an anti-Thomist thinker.

Conclusions

Three different concluding thoughts can be drawn based on the analysis presented in this chapter. The first is concerned with the very originality of Marsilius's idea of collective prudence within late medieval political thought. Marsilius's theory of collective prudence seems to be a *unicum* with respect to the lively debate on prudence that took place in the University of Paris at the beginning of the fourteenth century when Marsilius was there. To formulate this theory, Marsilius re-adapts the ideas of science and experience that were discussed in the debate over Aristotelian natural philosophy in Padua, where he had been trained before going to Paris. More specifically, Marsilius draws on Peter of Abano's theory of astrological science and applies it to an eminently political problem, that is, the science of law-making. Marsilius shifts a debate that figured prominently in the history of science to one which can be fully considered a part of the history of political thought.

Second, Marsilius links the collective idea of prudence found in Peter of Abano to the Aristotelian idea that judgements must be based on impartial laws. On the one hand, in the *Defensor*, he reports the same Aristotelian

---

70 For more on this, see Bianchi, *Il vescovo e i filosofi*.
71 *Anonymi Artium Magistri Questiones*, ed. by Costa.

quotations as well as a quotation from Averroes, which Peter of Abano had already mentioned in the *Lucidator*. On the other hand, however, Marsilius expands upon these quotations and integrates them with others from Aristotle's ethical and political texts, especially the *NE*, the *Politics*, and the *Rhetoric*. His reliance on these texts shows an instrumental use of Aristotle's reflection to further support the claims that the judgements and decisions of any ruler should be based on the law and not on individual desires or biases that can lead to perverse and seditious judgements. The idea of collective prudence, then, is instrumental in justifying this claim about the impartiality of laws.

The third and most important point is that the very originality of Marsilius's theory of collective prudence not only lies in the fact that he uses this theory in the *Defensor* as a *unicum* in an ethical and political text. Rather, such originality lies more in the function that Marsilius ascribes to this theory in his 1324 work. As the comparison has shown, whereas Aquinas employs a self-cumulative idea of law-making to explain the mechanisms necessary for changing human laws, Marsilius draws on a theory of collective prudence (and experience) to provide the main foundation of human laws. In so doing, he ascribes to the theory of collective prudence a function that other authors, including Aquinas, had ascribed to natural law. The reasons for Marsilius's choice might be entirely political. As natural law had such a strong role in grounding many ideas in support of the plenitude of power, Marsilius might have found it appealing to give it up and substitute it with a fully secular idea of knowledge that could do without natural law at all. This is why he devotes so much attention to a theory, that is, collective prudence, which neither Aristotle nor his colleagues at the University of Paris who had dealt with ethical and political matters had systematically employed in their reflections. For Marsilius, collective prudence is thus a political weapon with which to fight the perverse opinion of the plenitude of power. What originated as a theoretical problem of natural philosophy became an ideological tool that aimed to address a pressing political problem.

Works Cited

Primary Sources

Anonymi Artium Magistri Questiones super Librum Ethicorum Aristotelis (Paris, BnF, lat. 14698), ed. by Iacopo Costa, Studia artistarum: Études sur la faculté des arts dans les universités médiévales, 23 (Turnhout: Brepols, 2010)

Averroes, Aristotelis opera cum Averrois commentariis, vol. III (Venice: apud Iunctas, 1562)

———, Aristotelis opera cum Averrois commentariis, vol. VIII (Venice: apud Iunctas, 1562; repr. Frankfurt a.M.: Minerva, 1962)

Marsilius of Padua, The Defender of the Peace, trans. by Annabel Brett, Cambridge Texts in the History of Political Thought (Cambridge: Cambridge University Press, 2005)

———, Defensor pacis, ed. by Richard Scholz, Monumenta Germaniae Historica: Fontes iuris germanici antiqui in usum scholarum separatim editi, 7.2 (Hannover: Hahn, 1933)

Thomas Aquinas, Selected Political Writings, ed. by Alessandro P. d'Entrèves, trans. by John H. Dawson (Oxford: Basil Blackwell & Mott, 1974)

Secondary Works

Bianchi, Luca, Il vescovo e i filosofi: La condanna parigina del 1277 e l'evoluzione dell'aristotelismo scolastico (Macerata: Pierluigi Lubrina, 1990)

Blythe, James M., Ideal Government and the Mixed Constitution in the Middle Ages (Princeton, NJ: Princeton University Press, 2014)

Brenet, Jean-Baptiste, 'Multitude et bene esse chez Averroès et Dante: Retour sur la Monarchie I, 3', in Dante et l'averroisme, ed. by Alain de Libera, Jean-Baptiste Brenet, and Irène Rosier-Catach, Docet omnia (Paris: Les Belles Lettres, 2019), pp. 357–83

Brett, Annabel, 'Introduction', in Marsilius of Padua, The Defender of the Peace, trans. by Annabel Brett, Cambridge Texts in the History of Political Thought (Cambridge: Cambridge University Press, 2005), pp. xi–lxi

———, 'Political Right(s) and Human Freedom in Marsilius of Padua', in Transformations in Medieval and Early-Modern Rights Discourse, ed. by Virpi Mäkinen and Petter Korkman, The New Synthese Historical Library, 59 (Dordrecht: Springer, 2006), pp. 95–116

Briguglia, Gianluca, Il pensiero politico medievale, Piccola biblioteca Einaudi: Mappe, 68 (Turin: Einaudi, 2018), pp. 91–96

Cammack, Daniela, 'Aristotle on the Virtue of the Multitude', Political Theory, 41.2 (2013), 175–202

Celano, Anthony, Aristotle's Ethics and Medieval Philosophy: Moral Goodness and Practical Wisdom (Cambridge: Cambridge University Press, 2016)

Condren, Conal, 'Democracy and the *Defensor Pacis*: On the English Language Tradition of Marsilian Interpretation', *Il Pensiero Politico*, 13 (1980), 301–06

Fioravanti, Gianfranco, 'La *Politica* aristotelica nel Medioevo: Linee di una ricezione', *Rivista di storia della filosofia*, 52.1 (1997), 17–29

Flüeler, Cristoph, *Rezeption und Interpretation der aristotelischen 'Politica' im späten Mittelalter*, Bochumer Studien zur Philosophie, 19, 2 vols (Amsterdam: B. R. Grüner, 1992)

Flüeler, Christoph, Lidia Lanza, and Marco Toste, eds, *Peter of Auvergne: University Master of the 13th Century*, Scrinium Friburgense, 26 (Berlin: De Gruyter, 2015)

Godthardt, Frank, 'The Life of Marsilius of Padua', in *A Companion to Marsilius of Padua*, ed. by Gerson Moreno-Riaño and Cary J. Nederman, Brill's Companions to the Christian Tradition, 31 (Leiden: Brill, 2012), pp. 13–55

——, 'The Philosopher as Political Actor — Marsilius of Padua at the Court of Ludwig the Bavarian: The Sources Revisited', in *The World of Marsilius of Padua*, ed. by Gerson Moreno-Riaño, Disputatio, 5 (Turnhout: Brepols, 2006), pp. 29–46

Johnson, Mark F., 'Aquinas's *Summa theologiae* as Pedagogy', in *Medieval Education*, ed. by Ronald B. Begley and Joseph W. Koterski, Fordham Series in Medieval Studies, 4 (New York: Fordham University Press, 2005), pp. 133–42

Lambertini, Roberto, '"Est autem et politica et prudencia, idem quidem habitus": Appunti sul rapporto tra *prudentia* e politica in alcuni interpreti medievali del VI libro dell'Etica Nicomachea (da Alberto Magno e Buridano)', *Etica & Politica*, 2 (2002), <http://hdl.handle.net/10077/5492>

——, 'Political Prudence in Some Medieval Commentaries on the Sixth Book of the *Nicomachean Ethics*', in *Virtue Ethics in the Middle Ages: Commentaries on Aristotle's 'Nicomachean Ethics', 1200–1500*, ed. by István P. Bejczy, Brill's Studies in Intellectual History, 160 (Leiden: Brill, 2007), pp. 223–46

Lewis, Ewart, 'The "Positivism" of Marsiglio of Padua', *Speculum*, 38 (1963), 541–82

Libera, Alain de, *Penser au Moyen Age*, Chemins de pensée (Paris: Le Seuil, 1991)

Mulieri, Alessandro, 'Against Classical Republicanism: The Averroist Foundations of Marsilius of Padua's Political Thought', *History of Political Thought*, 40.2 (2019), 218–45

——, 'Marsilius of Padua and Peter of Abano: The Scientific Foundations of Law-Making in *Defensor Pacis*', *British Journal for the History of Philosophy*, 26.2, (2018), 276–96

Nederman, Cary J., *Community and Consent: The Secular Political Theory of Marsiglio of Padua's 'Defensor Pacis'* (Lanham, MD: Rowman & Littlefield, 1995)

——, 'The Meaning of "Aristotelianism" in Medieval Moral and Political Thought', *Journal of the History of Ideas*, 57.4 (1996), 563–85

———, 'Nature, Sin and the Origins of Society: The Ciceronian Tradition in Medieval Political Thought', *Journal of the History of Ideas*, 49.1 (1988), 3–26

Pesenti, Tiziana, 'Per la tradizione del testamento di Pietro d'Abano', *Medioevo*, 6 (1980), 533–42

Piaia, Gregorio, '"Averroïsme politique": Anatomie d'un mythe historiographique', in *Orientalische Kultur und europäisches Mittelalter*, ed. by Albert Zimmermann and Ingrid Craemer-Ruegenberg, comp. by Gudrun Vuillemin-Diem, Miscellanea Mediaevalia, 17 (Berlin: De Gruyter, 1985), pp. 288–300

Syros, Vasileos, 'The Sovereignty of the Multitude in the Works of Marsilius of Padua, Peter of Auvergne, and Some Other Aristotelian Commentators', in *The World of Marsilius of Padua*, ed. by Gerson Moreno-Riaño, Disputatio, 5 (Turnhout: Brepols, 2006), pp. 227–48

Tierney, Brian, *Liberty and Law: The Idea of Permissive Natural Law, 1100–1800*, Studies in Medieval and Early Modern Canon Law, 12 (Washington, DC: Catholic University of America Press, 2014)

———, 'Marsilius on Rights', *Journal of the History of Ideas*, 52.1 (1991), 3–17

Toste, Marco, 'The Parts and the Whole, the Few Wise Men and the Multitude: Consent and Collective Decision Making in Two Medieval Commentaries on Aristotle's *Politics*', *Storia del pensiero politico*, 9.2 (2020), 209–32

———, 'Virtue and the City: The Virtues of the Ruler and the Citizen in the Medieval Reception of Aristotle's *Politics*', in *Princely Virtues in the Middle Ages, 1200–1500*, ed. by István P. Bejczy and Cary J. Nederman, Disputatio, 9 (Turnhout: Brepols, 2007), pp. 73–98

Waldron, Jeremy, 'The Wisdom of the Multitude: Some Reflections on Book 3, Chapter 11 of Aristotle's *Politics*', *Political Theory*, 23.4 (1995), 563–84

PART 2

Marsilius's Thought and his
Contemporaries

JUHANA TOIVANEN

The Social and Political Functions of Emotions in Marsilius of Padua's *Defensor pacis* (and *Defensor minor*)[*]

Introduction

Medieval authors defined human beings as rational animals, but they did not think that rationality is the only guide to human behaviour. Emotions have an equally important role to play, and to understand the social and political dimension of human life, the dynamic between rationality and emotions must be taken into account. Arguably, this also applies to Marsilius of Padua's famous political theory, which he presents in his major political works, *Defensor pacis* and *Defensor minor*.

The present chapter discusses the social and political functions of emotions in Marsilius's political works from two perspectives. First, it focuses on the role of emotions in the emergence of social and political institutions. When medieval authors explained the idea that human beings are political animals by nature, they combined elements from the Ciceronian and Aristotelian traditions and focused on a natural inclination to live with others.[1] This social inclination was in many cases thought to include an emotional aspect: humans *desire* to live with others. Second, the chapter analyses the role that emotions play within existing political communities. Mutual love keeps communities together, while harmful emotions pose a threat for their proper functioning and existence. In addition, emotions guide human behaviour — for better or worse — and they can be used to steer that behaviour in the desired direction. This is one reason why

---

[*] This research has been funded by the Academy of Finland.

[1] Nederman, 'Nature, Sin and the Origins of Society'; Blažek, *Die mittelalterliche Rezeption*, pp. 315–32; Toivanen, *The Political Animal in Medieval Philosophy*, pp. 56–123; Toste, 'The Naturalness of Human Association', pp. 121–56.

Juhana Toivanen, DSocSc (2009), is a Senior Lecturer in Philosophy at the University of Jyväskylä, Finland.

Marsilius of Padua, ed. by Alessandro Mulieri, Serena Masolini, and Jenny Pelletier, Disputatio, 36 (Turnhout: Brepols, 2023), pp. 149–178

BREPOLS ❧ PUBLISHERS   10.1484/M.DISPUT-EB.5.132911

the lawgiver aims to promote virtuous behaviour that entails avoiding excessive emotional reactions, and an efficient way of guiding the subjects towards this aim is to incite fear and foster moderate positive emotions in them. Emotions clearly have an important political function.

I explore to what extent Marsilius of Padua elaborates on these two functions of emotions in his political works. Although he does not provide a detailed and systematic treatment of the role of emotions in his political theory, it is clear that they are not absent from his theory. On many occasions he shows a keen understanding of the complex psychological mechanisms that are at play in the political reality. Analysing this aspect of his thought allows us to have a more thorough grasp of the sophisticated relation between human psychology and social and political life.

The chapter proceeds as follows. I begin with a brief analysis of Marsilius's conception of emotions: he does not provide a theory of emotions, but some of his remarks, as well as the way he uses emotion terms like 'anger', 'desire', and 'fear', give us an indication of how his view relates to medieval theories of emotions in general. The next section focuses on the role of emotions as the *explanans* of the emergence of organized forms of human social life. I argue that although emotions are not the most important element, they play a role in Marsilius's view of the origins of the political community. The final two sections elaborate on the sociopolitical functions that emotions have within the political community. The main claims, respectively, are that Marsilius attributes a political function to emotions by suggesting that they can be used to control the external behaviour of citizens and that laws can be considered to be rational means aiming to eradicate the harmful effect of emotions from the community. Overall, the present chapter analyses the social and political functions of emotions and thus sheds light on the relation between human psychology and social life in Marsilius's political philosophy.

Inklings of Marsilius's Conception of Emotions

As already mentioned, Marsilius does not provide a full-fledged theory of emotions, at least not in his political works. Neither of his two *Defences* (*Defensor pacis* and *Defensor minor*) aims to present a detailed exposition of human psychology, and Marsilius is not interested in elaborating on the theoretical side of emotions, mainly because it is not directly relevant for reaching the goals that he sets himself in these two works.

Something can be said of his conception nevertheless. The first noticeable feature is how generously he uses terms that might be taken as instances of singular emotions. He writes about carnal lust (*concupiscen-*

tia carnalis), desire (*desiderium, appetitus*),[2] shunning/avoidance (*declinatio, refugium*), joy (*gaudium*), enjoyment/pleasure (*delectatio, voluptas*), sadness (*tristitia*), love (*amor, dilectio*), friendliness (*amicitia*), hatred (*odium*), jealousy (*zelus*), and pity (*misericordia*); and about ambition/cupidity (*ambitio, cupiditas*), sluggishness (*segnitia*), hope (*spes*), despair (*desperatio*), arrogance (*superbia*), desire for power (*desiderio principatus/appetitus dominandi*), contempt (*contemptus*), desire for vengeance (*appetitus vindictae*), humility (*humilitas*), reverence (*reverentia*), bravery (*audacia, temeritas*), penitence (*paenitentia*), impatience (*impatientia*), fear (*timor, terror*), and magnanimity (*magnanimitas*).[3]

Although several of these terms were commonly used to refer to virtues rather than to emotions,[4] there are reasons to include them in the list. First, in the Aristotelian framework, being virtuous means not only that one chooses the right course of action but also that one is in an emotional state that is appropriate to the situation; virtues are, as Aristotle famously writes, 'concerned with pleasures and pains' and 'with passions and actions, in which the excess is a form of failure, and so is defect, while the intermediate is praised and is a form of success'.[5] Thus, even if humility and the like count as virtues, many medieval authors think that they are, or at least are related to, dispositions of the sensory part of the soul (in particular, of powers that are responsible for emotions, i.e. the concupiscible and irascible powers), and they make it liable to be regulated by reason. One's virtuous character reveals itself in emotional reactions.[6]

However, there is also another reason for considering these terms as related to the emotional life of humans: there are precedents for doing so. Many of the terms in the previous list, which is gathered from *Defensor*

---

2 Marsilius often uses *desiderium* and *appetitus* as general terms in contrast to cognitive operations, and as such they may refer also to acts of the will. See e.g. *DP*, I, 7.3, ed. by Scholz, p. 36; and I, 18.3, ed. by Scholz, p. 122. When referring to *DP*, I include the page numbers of Marsilius of Padua, *The Defender of the Peace*, ed. and trans. by Brett in parenthesis; here pp. 38–39 and p. 124.

3 Admittedly, some of these are mentioned only a few times and (as already mentioned) none of them plays any significant theoretical role as such. Moreover, it is not always clear that these refer to acts of the sensitive part of the soul; for instance, when Marsilius argues that the will may be corrupted by affections such as love or hate, it remains unclear whether they are emotional affections that influence the will from outside, or are affections of the will itself: 'Per unius solius hominis voluntatem, quam prece aut precio, amore vel odio aut alia quavis affectione sinistra leviter et quasi cotidie videmus perverti' (*DP*, II, 28.17, ed. by Scholz, p. 548 (trans. by Brett, p. 499)).

4 Also Marsilius uses some of these terms (esp. *dilectio* and *spes*) when he writes about virtues (*DP*, II, 13.13–22, ed. by Scholz, pp. 282–87 (trans. by Brett, pp. 269–74)).

5 Aristotle, *Nicomachean Ethics*, II, 3, 1104b9–10; and II, 6, 1106b25–27, trans. by Ross and Brown.

6 For discussion, see Boquet and Nagy, *Sensible moyen âge*, pp. 214–15 and pp. 220–21. Note that there were authors who attributed virtues to the intellectual part of the soul, i.e. the will; see e.g. Kent, *Virtues of the Will*.

pacis, were commonly used in discussions concerning human emotions, and it is close to what we find in John of la Rochelle's (d. 1245) influential *Summa de anima* — more so than, for instance, the lists of emotions presented by Albert the Great or Thomas Aquinas, which are rather brief in comparison. The first set of terms (from carnal lust to pity) corresponds to John's concupiscible emotions, while the rest (from ambition to magnanimity) belong to the irascible power of the soul. Most emotions in both groups come in pairs in which one is a positive and the other negative.[7] I emphasize that by comparing these two authors I do not suggest that Marsilius would have been directly influenced by John's work. What the comparison shows is that Marsilius was well-marinated in the medieval terminology that pertained to the emotional/affectional aspect of human psychology, in which the distinction between virtues and emotions was occasionally blurred.[8]

From a more theoretical point of view, the general term that Marsilius uses when he talks about emotions is *affectio* (with an occasional *passio* here and there), which is not entirely coextensive with modern 'emotion'.[9] Although he never properly defines the term *affectio* or explains in detail what kinds of affective states there are, Annabel Brett has pointed out that he follows Cicero's definition from *De inventione*: '*Affectio* is a temporary change of the mind or body as a result of some cause; such as joy, cupidity, fear, irritation, disease, weakness and other things found in the same category'.[10] He also approaches emotions from the point of view of medical theories of his time (especially Peter of Abano's, who was his teacher),[11]

---

7 John of la Rochelle's list of emotions can be found in Knuuttila, 'Medieval Theories of the Passions of the Soul', pp. 67–69, who draws on John of la Rochelle, *Summa de anima*, ed. by Bougerol, II, 107, pp. 256–62. See also Boquet and Nagy, *Sensible moyen âge*, pp. 216–18. In comparison to John, Marsilius does not mention disgust (*fastidium*) or pain (*dolor*); and he adds friendliness (*amicitia*) and cupidity (*cupiditas*). Moreover, the terms used by these two authors are not always exactly the same. For instance, Jean's *abhominatio, invidia, ira*, and *paupertas spiritus* correspond to Marsilius's *declinatio/refugium, zelus, appetitus vindicate*, and *segnitia*, respectively.

8 For thirteenth- and fourteenth-century theories of emotions, see Boquet and Nagy, *Sensible moyen âge*, pp. 187–224; Knuuttila, *Emotions*, pp. 177–286; Cohen-Hanegbi, *Caring for the Living Soul*, pp. 1–67; and the contributions in Pickavé and Shapiro, eds, *Emotions and Cognitive Life*.

9 Of the relevance and fluidity of medieval terminology, see Cohen-Hanegbi, *Caring for the Living Soul*, pp. 22–27.

10 Cicero, *De inventione*, trans. by Hubbell, modified, I, 25.36, pp. 72–73: 'Affectio est animi aut corporis ex tempore aliqua de causa commutatio, ut laetitia, cupiditas, metus, molestia, morbus, debilitas et alia, quae in eodem genere reperiuntur'. See also Brett, 'Introduction', p. xli.

11 See e.g. Mulieri, 'Marsilius of Padua and Peter of Abano'; Shogimen, 'Medicine and the Body Politic'; Kaye, *A History of Balance*, p. 309.

THE SOCIAL AND POLITICAL FUNCTIONS OF EMOTIONS   153

according to which emotions are one of the so-called 'six non-naturals',[12] that is, circumstances that influence the natural balance of the human body and make it healthy or sick — air, food and drink, rest and exercise, sleep and waking, excretions and retentions, and mental affections. Generally speaking, the term *affectio* refers to various involuntary movements of the soul/body composite, which are directly or indirectly caused by external things, including states that we would classify as emotions.

It seems safe to say that Marsilius accepts the philosophical (Aristotelian/Avicennan) theory, according to which emotions can be classified more specifically as acts of the appetitive powers of the sensory part of the soul.[13] This can be seen when he distinguishes bodily changes that result from natural causes without any cognitive operation from changes that require cognition:

> Of human actions and their passions, some are the result of natural causes without our cognition [...]. There are other actions and passions, however, which come from us or occur within us as a result of our cognitive and appetitive powers. [...] Such are the thoughts and desires or affections of men.[14]

As Simo Knuuttila has pointed out, medieval theories of emotions are compositional in the sense that emotions involve (1) a cognitive component in the form of an estimative act concerning the harmfulness or

---

12 See Marsilius of Padua, *The Defender of the Peace*, ed. and trans. by Brett, p. 25 n. 8. For the concept of 'non-naturals', see Robert, 'Le corps d'après', pp. 197–200; Jarcho, 'Galen's Six Non-Naturals'; Niebyl, 'The Non-Naturals'. Peter of Abano writes: 'Notandum est quod ira, tristitia, timor, gaudium, etc. appellantur ab Aristotele passiones animae; et a medicis autem accidentia animae. Quas et ipsi unam de sex rebus non naturalibus posuerunt. Haec autem causantur propter motum caloris interius vel exterius factum vel utrobique, ita quod vere simul moveantur nunc intus, nunc quidem extra. Et si moventur extra, aut erit subito, et sic est ira (ipsa enim secundum Haly, 5° Theo, est exitus caloris ad exteriora semel subito factus. Aut movent paulative et sic est gaudium, nisi fuerit perniciosum. Si vero ad interiora sit motus, similiter aut fit subito et sic est timor, aut paulative et tunc est tristitia. Si vero utroque modo, sic est angustia vel sollicitudo seu verecundia; in talibus enim inest nunc spes, nunc desperatio, et ideo calor cito movetur fatigatus modo intra, modo extra, etc.' (Peter of Abano, *Expositio*, II, problem 31). Marsilius knew this work: see Mulieri, 'Marsilius of Padua and Peter of Abano', p. 278; Shogimen, 'Medicine and the Body Politic', p. 71.

13 It may be worth noting that the philosophical and medical models are not necessarily incompatible with each other but rather two perspectives to the same phenomenon. At least this is how Avicenna thinks when he discusses the internal senses in his *Canon medicinae*, which Marsilius would have known through his medical studies (Kaye, *A History of Balance*, p. 317). See Avicenna, *The Canon of Medicine*, ed. by Bakhtiar, trans. by Gruner and Shah, 8.1, 557, pp. 163–64.

14 *DP*, I, 5.4, ed. by Scholz, p. 22: 'Accionum autem humanarum et suarum passionum quedam proveniunt a causis naturalibus preter cognicionem [...]. Alie vero sunt acciones et passiones a nobis vel in nobis per virtutes nostras cognoscentes et appetentes. [...] ut sunt cogitaciones et hominum desideria seu affecciones'; trans. by Brett, pp. 24–25, modified.

usefulness of the object; (2) an affective component, which is a pleasant or unpleasant feeling about the object and includes a physiological aspect (such as boiling of the blood around the heart); and (3) a causal component that stimulates a behaviour typical for the emotion.[15] Marsilius's view seems to follow this structure, but since (as already mentioned) he does not provide a detailed theoretical analysis of emotions, this reconstruction remains somewhat hypothetical. However, there is one particularly interesting passage in the *Defensor pacis* which not only supports it but further seems to allude to a theory that is rooted in the ancient Stoic view. As is well known, the Stoics recommended complete extirpation of emotions (*apátheia*). Yet, since they could not deny that even the most virtuous persons show signs of emotional reaction, some of them suggested a theory that proved to be quite influential: before emotions proper, there are so-called first movements or pre-passions (*propátheiai*), which are involuntary impulses that emerge naturally and cannot be prevented. These first movements are followed by acceptance or rejection, which are under the agent's control. Even virtuous philosophers may experience the first movement of fear and display external signs of it (becoming pale, sweating), but they do not assent to the appearance that the frightening thing is something evil.[16] Echoing this theory, Marsilius argues:

> Of human actions that proceed from thought and desire, some proceed apart from the command of the mind, and some as a result of the command of the human mind. Among the first are thoughts, desires, delights and pleasures which come from us and in us without a command or precept on the part of the intellect or the appetite being made with regard to them: such are the thoughts and affections we find ourselves with when we are woken from sleep, or which have been otherwise produced in us without a command of our mind. But these are followed by certain thoughts, assents and affections towards either continuing the previous acts or questioning and detaining some

15 Knuuttila, 'Medieval Theories of the Passions of the Soul', p. 50. For what it is worth, Peter of Abano mentions the physiological element: 'Ira est inflammatio caliditatis circa cor, qua quis fortis et audax apparet. Timor etiam est infrigidatio exteriorum et caloris contractio ad partes inferiores sub corde' (*Expositio*, X, problem 61); and 'Universaliter omne quod est contra naturam ingerit dolorem quoad corpus magis et tristitiam quoad animam, sicut patet primo *De anima*; licet enim operatio non sit nisi coniuncti, tamen quaedam passiones primo insunt corpori et per corpus animae, ut dolor et aegritudo, quaedam econverso, ut tristitia et ratio' (*Expositio*, V, problem 19). While Peter is interested in the material aspect of emotions, Marsilius places stronger emphasis on their psychological, cognitive, moral, and social dimensions.

16 Knuuttila, *Emotions*, pp. 62–67; Inwood and Donini, 'Stoic Ethics', pp. 703–05; Brennan, 'Stoic Moral Philosophy', p. 275; Sorabji, *Emotion and Peace of Mind*, pp. 343–417. In addition, the Stoics accepted that virtuous people have positive emotion-like attitudes, *eupátheai* (Brennan, 'Stoic Moral Philosophy', p. 270).

THE SOCIAL AND POLITICAL FUNCTIONS OF EMOTIONS   155

of them [...]. These are and are called 'commands of the mind' or 'precepts', firstly because they happen or are elicited as a result of our command, and also because certain others, like pursuit or avoidance, are elicited by them. The difference between these 'commanded' and 'non-commanded' acts stems from what we said before: that we do not have full freedom or control over non-commanded acts as to whether they happen or not, whereas according to the Christian religion, power over commanded acts lies in us. And of the first kind of acts I said that the power is not fully in us because it is not in our power wholly to prevent their occurrence; even though by the second kind of acts (which are called commands), and those that follow upon them, we can dispose our soul in such a way that it does not easily produce or accommodate the first kind: viz. when a person has accustomed himself to command, love, or think upon their opposites.[17]

It would be too much to say that this is a Stoic description of the mechanism of emotions, first, because the idea of pre-passions was only one aspect of the Stoic theory of emotions, and second, because it is unlikely that Marsilius was drawing directly from Stoic sources.[18] The aforementioned ideas were common currency in early medieval theological literature, and consequently they were repeatedly used in twelfth- and thirteenth-century discussions on sin. Marsilius is just repeating some of the basic assumptions of these debates, where theologians negotiated the borderline between sinful and excusable movements of the soul. They made fine-grained distinctions into different stages of emotions, but the basic idea is that the initial states of harmful and blameworthy emotions

---

17 *DP*, II, 8.2–3, ed. by Scholz, p. 222: 'Actuum humanorum, provenientium per cognitionem et desiderium, quidam proveniunt absque mentis imperio, alii vero per humane mentis imperium. Primorum quidem sunt cognitiones, desideria, dilectiones et delectationes a nobis et in nobis evenientes absque imperio seu precepto intellectus aut appetitus de ipsis facto; quales sunt cognitiones et affectiones ad quas eximus, dum excitamur a sompno, vel aliter facte in nobis absque nostre mentis imperio. Hiis autem assequuntur cognitiones, consensus et affectiones alique de prioribus actibus continuandis aut quibusdam inquirendis et comprehendis [...]; et hee sunt et dicuntur mentis imperia seu precepta, tum quia nostro imperio fiunt seu eliciuntur, aut ipsis alia quedam, veluti prosecutiones et fuge. Est autem imperatorum actuum et non imperatorum differentia, ex eo quod pridem diximus, quoniam non imperatorum actuum non omnino est in nobis libertas seu imperium, ut fiant aut non. Imperatorum vero secundum Christianam religionem potestas in nobis est. Et dixi primorum actuum non omnino potestatem in nobis, quoniam non est in potestate nostra totaliter horum eventum prohibere, quamvis per secundos actus, qui dicunt imperia, et hiis consequentes sic animam disponere possimus, ut non facile sit factiva seu receptiva primorum, videlicet cum horum opposites fuerit assuetus sibi quisque precipere diligere aut considerare'; trans. by Brett, pp. 213–14, modified.

18 It is not impossible, however, since the idea of pre-passions could be found in Cicero and especially Seneca (Knuuttila, *Emotions*, pp. 63–67). On the influence of Stoicism on medieval thought, see e.g. Ebbesen, 'Where Were the Stoics?'.

are due to the inherited weakness caused by the original sin, and unless these pre-passions are immediately defeated, they will count as additional sins. The situation is even worse if one *accepts* the first movement and decides to cherish the emotion or, in the worst case, follows the emotional impulse and allows it to turn into action. In medieval terminology, as used by Marsilius in the quotation above, this is to give assent (*consensus*) to the involuntary movement of the appetitive power(s) of the soul, and possibly also to the external (transitive) action.[19]

The main point that Marsilius's text conveys is that the non-commanded first movements are not under our direct control. It is possible to habituate oneself to focus on their opposites in such a way that they do not arise as easily — here Marsilius's text recalls the cognitive therapy that was developed in early Christian sources and monastic literature[20] — but basically we are not in a position to prevent them completely. By contrast, it is within our power to assent to them or try to reject them, because our will is free. Likewise, we have the freedom to assent or not to assent to the action suggested by these emotions.

Apart from the passage quoted above, pre-passions do not play an important role in Marsilius's work, and he does not seem to be interested in the theological question of whether they count as sins. The reason for this is rather obvious: they cannot be controlled, and thus they do not have the same kind of political significance as emotions that are assented to do. The *Defensor pacis* is a political work, and from a political point of view it suffices that people behave peacefully. Thus, instead of pre-passions, Marsilius focuses on the voluntary control of one's actions and attitudes in the face of occurrent emotions because that control is directly relevant for their social and political role. In particular, he wants to (1) clarify the scope of law, both human and divine, by pointing out that only those external acts that are under our direct control are subject to laws; and (2) make room for a division of labour between political power and the sacerdotal part of the community. His general point is that even when pre-passions and emotions are sinful, the lawgiver and judges should not worry about them. Insofar as they do not affect the external action of individual human beings, they belong to the scope of religion. We shall return to this theme below.

---

19 For discussion, see Knuuttila, 'Medieval Theories of the Passions of the Soul', pp. 53–54; Knuuttila, *Emotions*, pp. 178–95; and Boquet and Nagy, *Sensible moyen âge*, pp. 189–94. The terms *consensus* and *delectatio* in the quotation are particularly important: consent is the freely given acceptance of *delectatio* that some authors (e.g. Anselm of Canterbury) identified with the Stoic *propassio* or with the continuing enjoyment thereof (Knuuttila, *Emotions*, pp. 179–80).

20 Knuuttila, *Emotions*, pp. 111–76; Boquet and Nagy, *Sensible moyen âge*, pp. 21–149. One strategy used in this therapy was to ward off an emerging pre-passion by thinking about something else than the object of the passion.

Emotions and Origins of Social Life

Emotions play a central role at critical stages of Marsilius's political theory. His conception of the origins of social/political life and the emergence of the political community is a case in point. This topic has been widely discussed in scholarly literature,[21] and in this context I can only briefly elaborate on certain aspects of his theory, which are relevant for understanding the function that emotions have in it.

As is well known, Marsilius incorporates both Aristotelian and Ciceronian elements into his theory of the origins of the political community. At the beginning of the first part of *Defensor pacis*, he explains the development of the political community from more basic types of communities — from the association between a man and woman to a household, to a village, and finally to a full-fledged political community. This reconstruction is rather similar to Aristotle's genetic argument for the naturalness of the city state, except that Marsilius emphasizes that the perfection of human institutions, just like the perfection of sciences, requires time and the accumulated experience of many generations.[22]

A slightly different position is defended in *Dictio* II, which lays out a view concerning the origins of the political community that is largely based on Cicero's *De inventione*:[23]

> So it is highly reasonable that a convocation and congregation of the faithful was possible in the ways mentioned above. For it is just as when men gathered together in the beginning to form a political community and to ordain the law, and their prevailing part agreed on those things that are necessary for a sufficient life; and yet they were not called by any individual man or men who had coercive authority over the rest. Rather it happened at the persuasion or encouragement of wise and resourceful men, whom nature produced with a greater inclination for this than the others: these then both made progress of themselves with their own efforts, and directed others (in succession or at the same time) towards the form of the perfect community. And men easily obeyed those who persuaded them, being naturally inclined to this perfect form.[24]

---

21 One may begin with, e.g., Nederman, *Community and Consent*, pp. 29–48; Briguglia, *Marsilio da Padova*, pp. 63–84; Coleman, *A History of Political Thought*, pp. 143–46.

22 Mulieri, 'Marsilius of Padua and Peter of Abano'.

23 Nederman, 'Nature, Sin and the Origins of Society', p. 22.

24 *DP*, II, 22.15, ed. by Scholz, pp. 433–44: 'Secundum itaque iam dictos modos convocationem et congregationem fidelium fuisse possibilem, racionabile valde. Sicut enim ad civilem communitatem et legem ordinandam convenerunt homines a principio, ipsorum valenciori parte concordante in hiis que sunt ad vite sufficienciam, non quidem vocati per singularem hominem aut per plures aliquos habentes auctoritatem coactivam in reliquos,

There are certain tensions between these two accounts.[25] At the outset, it seems that the political community either is a result of a natural development (à la Aristotle), or emerges from a common decision (à la Cicero); it cannot be both. However, as Marco Toste has shown, this tension can be partially mitigated by focusing on the earlier commentary tradition on Aristotle's *Politics*. Toste points out that medieval commentators defended an interpretation according to which the political community is based on a natural inclination but nevertheless is established by human action — it is both natural and voluntary. Marsilius may have been influenced by this interpretation, which would explain why he did not see any problem in bringing the two ancient conceptions together.[26] This way of conceptualizing the origins of the political community does not necessarily remove the tension completely, since gradual development and contractual emergence are different historical narratives, but the details of this problematic are not highly relevant for my purposes here.

What is relevant is that Marsilius appeals to the idea that the political community stems from a natural inclination to live with other people and that this inclination includes an emotional aspect, even though the inclination alone does not explain the existence of the community without conscious decision and persuasion.[27] The concept of *inclinatio* is used in the Ciceronian account in *Dictio* II (as the passage quoted above shows) and it is mentioned in *Defensor minor*, when Marsilius discusses the relation between man and woman,[28] but it plays a central role also in *Dictio* I, Chapter 4, where he draws on Aristotle's so-called teleological argument concerning the final cause of the political community. Marsilius begins the chapter by arguing that the political community comes to be for the sake

---

sed suasione seu exortacione prudentum et facundorum virorum, quos natura inter alios produxit inclinatos ad hoc, ex se postmodum proficientes suis exerciciis et alios dirigentes successive vel simul ad formam communitatis perfecte, ad quam eciam homines naturaliter inclinati obtemperaverunt suadentibus facile'; trans. by Brett, p. 402, slightly modified.

25 For instance, Annabel Brett points out that the section in *Dictio* II resembles Cicero, and 'is somewhat at odds with the genesis described in I 3–5' (Marsilius of Padua, *The Defender of the Peace*, ed. and trans. by Brett, p. 402 n. 19). Likewise, Nederman ('Nature, Sin and the Origins of Society', p. 22) argues that the contractual model presented here is in conflict with Aristotle's naturalistic account.

26 Toste, 'The Naturalness of Human Association', pp. 121–56. See also Toivanen, 'Extending the Limits of Nature'.

27 The hero of Cicero's story is not only a wise man (philosopher) but also an orator: he needs to convince people of the usefulness of the political community (Cicero, *De inventione*, 1.2, trans. by Hubbell, pp. 4–7). Cicero does not say explicitly that persuasion requires arousing emotions in the audience, but according to Aristotle's *Rhetorics*, to which Marsilius refers several times in *DP*, this is a key strategy of a rhetorician (see *Rh.*, II, 1–11).

28 Marsilius of Padua, *Defensor minor*, 13, 2, ed. by Jeudy and Quillet, p. 262. When referring to *Defensor minor*, I include the page numbers of Marsilius of Padua, *Writings on the Empire*, ed. and trans. by Nederman in parenthesis; here p. 43.

THE SOCIAL AND POLITICAL FUNCTIONS OF EMOTIONS   159

of life but that its final cause is a good life, that is, having the possibility for partaking in activities related to practical and theoretical sciences.[29] The remainder of the chapter focuses on the first function, the sufficient life, and Marsilius takes up the inclination (or impulse) with a quote from *Politics*:

> But on the subject of living and living well or the good life in its first mode, sc. the worldly, and those things that are necessary for it, the glorious philosophers grasped almost the entire matter by demonstration. From this they concluded the necessity, for securing it, of the political community, without which this sufficient living cannot be obtained. The most excellent of them, Aristotle, said in *Politics* I, chapter 1, that all men are borne to it, and according to a natural impulse for the sake of this.[30]

And again, in *DP*, I, 13.2:

> From what we earlier laid down as the foundation of almost everything that would be demonstrated in this book, viz. that all men desire the sufficient life and reject its opposite, we concluded through demonstration, in chapter 4 of this discourse, that they engage in political community because through it they can attain this sufficiency, and without it not at all. For this reason, too, Aristotle says in *Politics* I, chapter 1: 'By nature therefore there exists in all men an impulse towards such a community', sc. political.[31]

Let us focus on the latter quotation, which can be taken to suggest that the inclination has an emotional dimension. The key element in the text is the desire for a sufficient life and avoidance of 'its opposite', a life of scarcity and deficiency; the political community is a necessary means for fulfilling this desire. The Latin word that Marsilius uses for desire is

---

29 *DP*, I, 4.1, ed. by Scholz, p. 16 (trans. by Brett, p. 18). See e.g. Briguglia, *Marsilio da Padova*, pp. 76–84; Syros, *Marsilius of Padua at the Intersection*, pp. 46–47.

30 *DP*, I, 4.3, ed. by Scholz, pp. 17–18: 'De vivere autem et bene vivere seu bona vita secundum primum modum, mundanum scilicet, ac de hiis que propter ipsum necessaria sunt, comprehenderunt per demonstracionem philosophi gloriosi rem quasi completam. Unde propter ipsum consequendum concluserunt ipsi necessitatem civilis communitatis, sine qua vivere hoc sufficiens obtineri non potest. Quorum eciam eximius Aristoteles 1° sue Politice, cap. 1° dixit: *Omnes <homines> ferri ad ipsam, et secundum nature impetum propter hoc*'; trans. by Brett, p. 19, slightly modified.

31 *DP*, I, 13.2, ed. by Scholz, p. 39: 'Ex supposito nobis in prioribus, quasi omnium in hoc libro demonstrandorum principio, videlicet: *Omnes homines appetere sufficienciam vite et oppositum declinare*, per demonstrationem conclusimus ipsorum communicacionem civilem 4° huius, quoniam per ipsam sufficienciam hanc adipisci possunt, et preter eam minime; propter quod eciam Aristoteles 1° Politice, capitulo 1° inquit: *Natura quidem igitur in omnibus impetus est ad talem communitatem*, civilem scilicet'; trans. by Brett, p. 74, slightly modified.

appetitus, which in itself does not tell much, as it is a general term that can refer to phenomena as diverse as the downward movement of heavy things towards the centre of the earth and the inclination of the rational will towards the good.[32] But in this particular context it seems clear that Marsilius has in mind a more specific kind of desire, one that emerges in the appetitive powers of the sensitive soul. Following Cicero's *De officiis,* he argues:

> Let us then lay this down as the fundamental principle of everything that we must demonstrate, a principle naturally held and believed and freely conceded by all: sc. that all men not deficient or otherwise impeded naturally desire a sufficient life, and by the same token shun and avoid those things that are harmful to them. Indeed, this principle is not only granted for man, but also for every kind of animal.[33]

The desire for self-preservation is common to human beings and non-rational animals. In the case of animals it manifests itself in the form of emotions. Animals are able to judge if a thing is beneficial or harmful to them, and the judgement is followed by a corresponding emotion that motivates and initiates an action that is conducive to achieving the desired aim: life.[34] For human beings, the situation is somewhat different because they are rational beings, and thus the desire to preserve one's life can lead to rational considerations of how to avoid death and acquire material necessities. Presumably this is what happens when human beings are convinced that establishing a political community is the best means of achieving their desired aim and they decide to do so. But even if the desire to preserve one's life may entail rational considerations, its core is a desire that we share with other animals; and as such it either is an emotion or at least includes emotions (such as desire and fear).

Thus, the concept of *inclinatio* is rooted in the biological nature of human beings, as natural needs explain the motivation for setting up a political community. Humans are born naked and without the ability to take care of and defend themselves, and because the arts that are

---

32 See e.g. Thomas Aquinas, *Summa theologiae,* I, 80.1.

33 *DP,* I, 4.2, ed. by Scholz, pp. 16–17: 'Hoc ergo statuamus tamquam demonstrandorum omnium principium naturaliter habitum, creditum et ab omnibus sponte concessum: omnes scilicet homines non orbatos aut aliter impeditos naturaliter sufficientem vitam appetere, huic quoque nociva refugere et declinare; quod eciam nec solum de homine confessum est, verum de omni animalium genere'; trans. by Brett, pp. 18–19. Marsilius refers to Cicero, *De officiis,* I, 4.11.

34 Although Marsilius does not refer to the Avicennan estimative power, this analysis of animal action was so generally accepted that there is little doubt that he would have accepted it. Interestingly, Syros (*Marsilius of Padua at the Intersection,* p. 28) connects the desire to self-preservation with Stoic *oikeiosis*; this seems correct, although it should be noted that the idea that all animals seek to preserve their life was by no means exclusive to Stoicism.

THE SOCIAL AND POLITICAL FUNCTIONS OF EMOTIONS 161

necessary to compensate for this lack of natural gifts require collaboration and specialization, it was natural and necessary to come together in an organized political community.[35] This is how the natural inclination must be understood: it makes us seek for the things that keep us alive and avoid the contrary. The way in which the inclination does this is psychologically manifested as various kinds of emotions.

Marsilius does not write much about the positive emotions that human beings have towards social life. He focuses on the negative, the avoidance of harm. But the transition from non-political to political life is motivated also by the good that the community provides, and the desire of this good is not an impartial, detached attitude; their own well-being is at stake, and in this respect the motivation is emotion-based, or at least emotion-laden. This does not exclude the possibility that rational considerations play an important role as well. In many cases fulfilling an emotional drive requires reasoning:

> And therefore one should take note that if man is to live and live well, his actions must be done and done well, and not just his actions, but his passions too: 'well', i.e. in the appropriate temper. And because we do not receive from nature entirely perfectly the means with which to achieve this tempering, man needed to go beyond natural causes and use his reason to create those things needed to complete the production and preservation of his actions and passions of both body and soul.[36]

The term 'passions' refers to various ways in which human beings are at the mercy of natural changes — that is, the six non-naturals such as

---

35 *DP*, I, 4.3, ed. by Scholz, pp. 17–18 (trans. by Brett, pp. 19–20). Marsilius's explanation of the human condition has a medical tone, but the main point is made also by Avicenna, Thomas Aquinas (in *De regno*), and Giles of Rome (Rosier-Catach, 'Communauté politique', pp. 232–35) and ultimately it stems from Aristotle's 'for the sake of life' (Toivanen, *The Political Animal in Medieval Philosophy*, pp. 57–109). Cf. *DP*, I, 4.5: sufficient life is the aim of the community. Alan Gewirth has claimed that Marsilius sees the function of the political community in secular terms, discards Aristotle's good life (moral and theological ends), and focuses on the role of the community as the provider of life (biological and economic needs); see Gewirth, *Marsilius of Padua*, pp. 50–53; see also Shogimen, 'Medicine and the Body Politic', p. 112; Briguglia, *Marsilio da Padova*, pp. 77–84; Kaye, *A History of Balance*, p. 311. The same view is endorsed by Nederman, 'The Meaning of "Aristotelianism"', p. 583.

36 *DP*, I, 5.3, ed. by Scholz, pp. 21–22: 'Et propterea oportet attendere, quod si debeat homo vivere et bene vivere, necesse est, ut ipsius acciones fiant et bene fiant, nec solum acciones, verum eciam passiones, bene inquam, id est in temperamento convenienti. Et quoniam ea quibus hec temperamenta complentur, non accipimus a natura omniquaque perfecte, necessarium fuit homini ultra causas naturales per racionem aliqua formare, quibus compleatur efficiencia et conservacio suarum accionum et passionum secundum corpus et animam'; trans. by Brett, p. 24, slightly modified. See also *DP*, I, 5.5, ed. by Scholz, p. 22 (trans. by Brett, p. 25).

climate, hunger, and emotions. In order to live and live well, these must be done 'in the appropriate temper', which means that human beings must find ways to balance the effects of constant changes that their bodies undergo. As it turns out, the means that Marsilius mentions here are the different offices of the political community (agriculture, manufacturing, military, priesthood, etc.),[37] and thus this passage is simply a more detailed explanation of the same fundamental idea that we have already seen: humans establish the political community so as to ward off and control the impact of natural causes that constantly threaten their lives. Establishing the political community means inventing various professions that help in this process, and the purpose of the division of labour is to meet the natural needs of humans.

Marsilius draws from Augustinian political philosophy and emphasizes that these offices and professions result from original sin. One of the main effects of the Fall was the emergence of needs that cannot be satisfied easily, and this made the political community a necessity.[38] Marsilius does not think that original sin has an epistemological impact (humans can *know* how to live well and invent efficient ways to counterbalance the non-naturals),[39] but he thinks that the rational control of one's emotions is lost due to it. Every human being is corrupted and 'it is a fact that every soul has this, i.e., affection that is sometimes malign', and 'it is God alone [...] who is not moved by any perverse affection'.[40] Without original sin and the corruption of human nature there would have been no need for human institutions.[41]

Despite appearances, this view is not necessarily in tension with the aforementioned idea that the social and political life is based on a natural inclination. Supposing that our natural inclination is not towards political

---

37 Marsilius gives a list of these offices in *DP*, I, 5.1, ed. by Scholz, p. 20 (trans. by Brett, pp. 22–23).

38 *DP*, I, 6.1–2, ed. by Scholz, pp. 28–29 (trans. by Brett, pp. 31–32); Brett, 'Introduction', p. xxviii. On Marsilius's conception of the political implications of the original sin, see Briguglia, *Marsilio da Padova*, pp. 89–93. For Augustine, see Deane, *The Political and Social Ideas*, pp. 39–77, and the contributions in Dougherty, ed., *Augustine's Political Thought*. The relation between Augustine and Marsilius has been discussed, e.g., in Mulcahy, 'The Hands of Augustine', and Scott, 'Influence or Manipulation?'.

39 Moreno-Riaño and Nederman, 'Marsilius of Padua's Principles of Secular Politics', pp. 129–31.

40 Respectively, *DP*, I, 11.6, ed. by Scholz, p. 59: 'Omnem animam contingit habere hanc, id est, affectionem quandoque sinistram'; trans. by Brett, p. 62, modified; and *DP*, II, 6.9, ed. by Scholz, pp. 206–07: 'Quoniam solus Deus est [...] qui affectione perversa neque movetur'; trans. by Brett, p. 200.

41 *DP*, I, 6.1, ed. by Scholz, pp. 28–29 (trans. by Brett, p. 31). Human beings would have lived an apolitical life in the Paradise. See Brett, 'Introduction', p. xxviii; Briguglia, *Marsilio da Padova*, pp. 90–93. On emotions before the original sin, see Casagrande and Vecchio, 'Les passions avant et après la chute'.

THE SOCIAL AND POLITICAL FUNCTIONS OF EMOTIONS   163

institutions and social life as such but rather equal to an emotionally loaded drive for self-preservation, there is no need to think that it would not have existed in the Paradise before the Fall. Original sin led to a situation where our needs are not easily satisfied anymore — the human body lost its integrity and nature became harsh[42] — and for this reason it was necessary to establish political institutions to preserve human life. The inclination is there all the time, but the effects of sin made the political community necessary, and although the latter is a remedy for the effects of sin, it can nevertheless be based on the original inclination.

In sum, Marsilius sees an intrinsic connection between emotions and the emergence of the political community, as he emphasizes natural needs and desire for self-preservation as the fundamental factors that make us social. The political community is a means for satisfying these needs and the desire to live.[43] We may rationally understand that living with others is the only way to stay alive in the long run, but our attitude towards the means for a desired goal is not emotionally detached, a result of impartial rational considerations. We are emotionally motivated to accept the result of this rational consideration.

Functions of Emotions in Social Life

In addition to playing a central role in Marsilius's account for the existence of the political community, emotions have various functions in the social life of human beings. One starting point for unravelling this aspect of Marsilius's thought is the idea that emotions have harmful consequences for individuals and their societies. They are a source of trouble insofar as they lead to unreasonable and vicious action, and therefore they need to be controlled.[44] Alas, most people are not able to do that — this was considered, to use a modern expression, a sociological and statistical fact.

The obvious remedy for this situation is that the human legislator must forbid certain kinds of actions. Jurisdiction functions as an externalized control for those who cannot control themselves, so to speak. And this is where things become interesting. As we have seen, Marsilius distinguishes actions and emotions to which we assent (and which are therefore under our control) from involuntary movements of the appetitive powers(s) of

---

42 Brett, 'Political Philosophy'; Deane, *The Political and Social Ideas*, pp. 13–153; Weithman, 'Augustine's Political Philosophy'; and the contributions in Briguglia and Rosier-Catach, eds, *Adam, la nature humaine, avant et après*.

43 Kempshall, *The Common Good*, pp. 354–58; and the references in note 35 above.

44 Marsilius applies this idea to the pope in *DP*, II, 21.12, ed. by Scholz, pp. 415–16 (trans. by Brett, p. 387).

the soul, which are beyond our direct control.[45] Further, he divides the former into what he calls 'immanent' and 'transitive' actions:

> There are other actions and passions, however, which come from us or occur within us as a result of our cognitive and appetitive powers. Some of these are called 'immanent', i.e. because they do not cross over into a subject different from the agent nor are they performed by means of an external organ or limb moved in respect of place. Such are the thoughts and desires or affections of men. Whereas others are and are called 'transitive', because in one or other of the said ways they are in contrast with those just mentioned.[46]

Marsilius's core idea is that our thoughts, inclinations, and emotions are immanent insofar as they do not turn into action. One may feel, say, anger but keep it to himself without letting it show in his external behaviour. The very same anger that may remain immanent may also become transitive, if the agent assents not only to the emotion itself but also to the external behaviour that the emotion suggests — he does not try to calm down but rages and curses the object of his anger. This means that instead of making a division between inner mental life and external action, Marsilius focuses on the difference between (1) inner mental life that remains internal and does not turn into action, and (2) inner mental life that turns into action.[47]

Laws and political control pertain only to transitive actions; they do not directly control our inner mental life, although it can be influenced indirectly. We may have all kinds of ideas, thoughts, intentions, and emotions, but as long as we do not act on them, we cannot be punished or rewarded. Only when these internal feelings turn into external action may they be considered from the point of view of legal framework.[48]

Immanent actions belong to the domain of the sacerdotal part of the political community.[49] The main function of religion is to help people

---

45 *DP*, II, 8.2–3, ed. by Scholz, p. 222 (trans. by Brett, pp. 213–14); quoted above, at note 17.

46 *DP*, I, 5.4, ed. by Scholz, p. 22: 'Alie vero sunt acciones et passiones a nobis vel in nobis per virtutes nostras cognoscentes et appetentes. Quarum quedam vocantur immanentes, ut quia non transeunt in aliud subiectum a faciente, nec exercentur per aliquod exteriorum organorum seu membrorum motorum secundum locum, ut sunt cogitationes et hominum desideria seu affecciones. Alie vero sunt et dicuntur transeuntes, quia modo altero vel utroque predictorum opposite se habent immediate predictis'; trans. by Brett, pp. 24–25, modified. For discussion, see e.g. Briguglia, *Marsilio da Padova*, pp. 80–81.

47 See e.g. *DP*, I, 5.7, ed. by Scholz, pp. 23–24 (trans. by Brett, p. 26).

48 *DP*, I, 5.7, ed. by Scholz, pp. 23–24 (trans. by Brett, p. 26); I, 5.10–11, ed. by Scholz, pp. 25–27 (trans. by Brett, pp. 27–29); II, 8.3–5, ed. by Scholz, pp. 222–24 (trans. by Brett, pp. 214–15). For discussion, see e.g. Coleman, *A History of Political Thought*, pp. 147–48; Syros, *Marsilius of Padua at the Intersection*, pp. 56–57.

49 For a systematic analysis of Marsilius's conception of the relation between spiritual and temporal powers, see Koch, 'Marsilius of Padua on Church and State'.

THE SOCIAL AND POLITICAL FUNCTIONS OF EMOTIONS 165

follow the divine law, and this happens by perfecting their actions and passions, both immanent and transitive:

> Under this function [scil. the priestly] it is appropriate to include all those disciplines invented by human ingenuity, theoretical as much as practical, which temper those human acts (both immanent and transitive) which result from desire and cognition, and by which man becomes well-disposed in his soul for the status of this present world as well as of that to come.[50]

Although their final aim is to prepare human beings for the afterlife by making them virtuous, the sacerdotal part of the community also curbs transitive acts. In other words, religious practices and sermons aim at influencing the thoughts and emotions of individual human beings both when they remain internal to them and when they are liable to turn into external action — to make them think in the right way, to suppress their anger, *and* to act in a civilized manner.

The division of labour between the sacerdotal and judicial parts is not based on the immanent/transitive division, because both parts are concerned with the way human beings behave by virtue of their external actions. The main difference between the two parts lies in the respective means that they have their disposal. The judicial part uses coercive power and punishes transitive actions, while the sacerdotal part convinces people, teaches them, calms them down, and so forth.[51] Given that both transitive and immanent actions stem from inner mental life (suppressed anger is immanent, while anger that turns into a violent outburst is a part of the transitive action), there is also another difference. The sacerdotal part influences mental life directly and external action indirectly by influencing the mental life, whereas the human legislator and judicial system directly influence external action only. This is what Marsilius means when he places immanent actions outside the scope of human law.

How does religion control immanent and transitive actions and passions? I suppose there are many possible ways of doing this,[52] but Marsilius

---

50 *DP*, I, 6.9, ed. by Scholz, pp. 32–33: 'In hoc autem officium convenienter veniunt omnes discipline humano ingenio adinvente, tam speculative quam active, humanorum actuum moderative tam immanentium quam transeuntium, ab appetitu et cognitione provenientium, quibus bene disponitur homo secundum animam pro statu tam presentis seculi, quam venituri'; trans. by Brett, p. 35. See also *DP*, I, 6.1, ed. by Scholz, pp. 28–29 (trans. by Brett, p. 31).

51 As a matter of fact, Marsilius is quite vague about the exact way these parts, especially the sacerdotal, influence human beings.

52 Briguglia, *Marsilio da Padova*, p. 94, suggests that 'in questo senso specifico di funzione moderatrice delle azioni e dei desideri umani, il sacerdozio si trova alleato con tutte le discipline umane, speculative e pratiche, che condividono questo compito e che sorgono dalle capacità umane e dall'insegnamento dei filosofi'.

166   JUHANA TOIVANEN

emphasizes one of them in a particularly strong manner: religion fights fire with fire. It arouses fear of eternal punishment and hope for future reward, and thereby affects the behaviour of citizens. Speaking of pagan religions, Marsilius famously writes:

> For even if the various philosophers who invented these religions or followings may not have perceived or believed in the resurrection of men and the life that is called eternal, they nevertheless developed and encouraged the fiction of its existence, including the delights and afflictions it contained in relation to the nature of human deeds in this mortal life, in order thereby to induce in men a reverence and fear of God and a desire to avoid the vices and cultivate the virtues. For there are certain acts that a legislator cannot regulate by human law [...]. And out of terror of all this men avoided acting wrongly, were aroused to virtuous deeds of piety and mercy, and became well-framed with regard to themselves and to others. Because of this, many disputes and injuries within communities came to an end. And also as a result the peace or tranquillity of cities, and the sufficient life of human beings for the status of this present world, was preserved with less difficulty.[53]

As many commentators have noted, the fear of eternal punishment and hope for future reward affect the behaviour of citizens in such a way that peace becomes more likely.[54] Although the previous quote is about pagan religions, and Marsilius does not explicitly say that the same mechanism also works in Christian communities, we may suppose that it does. Vicious and harmful actions (but also sinful thoughts) are avoided because their consequences in the afterlife are believed to be detrimental. Emotions

---

53 *DP*, I, 5.11, ed. by Scholz, pp. 26–27: 'Nam licet philosophorum aliqui, talium legum sive secretarum adinventores, non senserint aut crediderint hominum resurreccionem et illam vitam que vocatur eterna, ipsam tamen esse finxerunt et persuaserunt, et in ipsa delectaciones et tristicias, secundum qualitates humanorum operum in hac vita mortali, ut ex hoc inducerent hominibus Dei reverenciam et timorem, desiderium fugiendi vicia et colendi virtutes. Sunt enim actus quidam, quos legislator humana lege regulare non potest [...]. Ex quorum terrore fugiebant homines perverse agere, ad studiosa quoque operum pietatis et misericordie excitabantur, ad seipsos atque alios disponere bene. Cessabantque propter hec in communitatibus multe contenciones et iniurie. Unde pax eciam seu tranquillitas civitatum et vita hominum sufficiens pro statu presentis seculi difficile minus servabatur'; trans. by Brett, pp. 28–29.

54 'For Marsilius, fear of eternal punishment enables citizens to observe those measures which are necessary for civil *pax et tranquillitas*' (Kempshall, *The Common Good*, p. 357). Shogimen argues that the role of the Church in society is utilitarian, as it enables good life by inducing virtuous behaviour (Shogimen, 'Medicine and the Body Politic', p. 97). See also Coleman, *A History of Political Thought*, p. 148; Briguglia, *Marsilio da Padova*, pp. 84–86. In *DP*, I, 16.21, ed. by Scholz, pp. 109–10 (trans. by Brett, p. 111), Marsilius explains that virtuous men refrain from stirring up sedition if they 'have hope' (*sperantes*) that one day they may be elected rulers, even when they see that their rulers are less virtuous than them.

THE SOCIAL AND POLITICAL FUNCTIONS OF EMOTIONS   167

are aroused in order to incite good behaviour, which means that religion has political significance. It enables and justifies the use of emotions as a political tool. It should be noted, however, that this is not the only way (Christian) religion affects human behaviour: instruction and education are at least equally important tools, and Marsilius also seems to accept the idea that religion should focus on inciting hope and love instead of fear.[55]

We find a detailed explanation of how the fear of future punishment is supposed to work in Marsilius's *Defensor minor*, where he deals with the usefulness of confession (which is not necessary for salvation):

> For priests proclaim and denounce in full view of the church the sins which men are committing or plan to commit, and either they do not repent of them, but, persisting in doing or planning such acts, they are made liable to eternal damnation, or, repenting or regaining their senses about what they have done or plan to do, the sinners repent of the commission of sin and are absolved from the already mentioned eternal damnation. They examine themselves and grieve before God, and they are deterred from planning to commit other such acts by the fear of future punishment that has been aroused in them by priests.[56]

The main aim is to help the sinner to avoid eternal punishment in the afterlife, but given that many sins have harmful societal effects, there are also political reasons to make people avoid them. The fear of eternal punishment is an extremely powerful tool for this. Although not all sins are based on emotional impulses, some clearly are, and in their case the emotion of fear is set against other emotions that easily lead to strife and other social problems.

The reason why I emphasize the role of emotions and their control by other emotions is that the same mechanism also applies in the case of secular political power. As I already mentioned, religion influences mental life directly and external action indirectly, while the legal part punishes external action directly. However, it can also have an indirect effect on our

---

55 See *DP*, II, 4.13, ed. by Scholz, p. 175 (trans. by Brett, p. 173), where Marsilius quotes approvingly from Aquinas's *Catena aurea* to this effect.

56 Marsilius of Padua, *Defensor minor*, 5, 12, ed. by Jeudy and Quillet, p. 200: 'Nam pronuntiantibus et denuntiantibus sacerdotibus in faciem ecclesiae peccata, quibus homines committentes aut committere proponentes, neque de ipsis poenitentes, sed persistentes in ipsis factis aut propositis obligantur ad damnationem aeternam et poenitentes aut resipiscentes tam factis quam fieri propositis, ab aeterna iam dicta damnatione solvuntur, poenitet peccatoris de peccatis commissis; recognoscunt atque tristantur coram Deo, et revocantur a proposito talia ulterius committendi metu poenae futurae sibi per sacerdotes incussae'; trans. by Nederman, p. 14; see also Marsilius of Padua, *Defensor minor*, 5, 13, ed. Jeudy and Quillet, p. 204: 'Ut propter terrorem seu timorem revocentur peccatores a peccatis commissis aut etiam committendis' (trans. by Nederman, p. 16: 'On account of their terror and fear sinners may be recalled from sins committed or yet to be committed').

mental life. We can see this if we consider briefly how laws are supposed to regulate human behaviour. In principle, there are two possibilities, which are not mutually exclusive. First, punishments that civil law prescribes for the commission of crimes enter the decision-making process of individual citizens and alter their estimations of the profitability of a given course of action. Simply put, a certain action, say robbing a bank, may seem like a good idea to someone for the simple reason that it would make him rich. However, if the human legislator has determined that such a crime will be punished severely, the situation is different. The person weighs the pros and cons of robbing the bank, and the prospect of punishment alters the balance.

Second, laws influence individual citizens by inciting fear. In this case the wannabe robber refrains from robbing the bank because he *is afraid* of the punishment that the law prescribes for this crime. The difference with the first case is that unlike in the impartial weighing of pros and cons, here the process is based on an emotional attitude or reaction.[57] However, it may be argued (and with good reason) that the difference between these cases is blurry or perhaps merely semantic because practical reasoning involves emotions; the reason why the cons look like cons is that they are emotionally appalling.

And this is also what Marsilius recognizes. Admittedly, he thinks that the main function of laws and the judicial part of the political community is to take care of retributive justice and to redress the balance of the community once it has been violated by criminal activity,[58] but on at least one occasion he writes about the preventive function of law:

> If they [viz. powerful members of the community who have been brought to justice by the prince] nevertheless conceive such hatred [of him] along with a desire for vengeance, because of their ignorance, malice, or both, they will still not dare break out into active vengeance through fear of the legislator and the next prince, for they will worry — plausibly — that they will be punished again by him just as they were by his predecessor.[59]

---

57 This is what Marsilius suggests in *Defensor minor*, 13, 7, ed. by Jeudy and Quillet, p. 274 (trans. by Nederman, p. 47), where he points out that humans should fear an eternal more than a temporal punishment.

58 See e.g. *DP*, I, 15.11–12, ed. by Scholz, p. 93 (trans. by Brett, pp. 95–96).

59 *DP*, I, 16.22, ed. by Scholz, p. 110: 'Quod si tamen id cum appetitu vindicte conceperint, propter ipsorum ignoranciam, maliciam aut utramque, ad vindictam non audebunt prorumpere metu legislatoris et reliqui principantis, a quo velut a predecessore rursum puniri verisimiliter dubitabunt'; trans. by Brett, p. 112. Marsilius is discussing the reasons why elective monarchy is better than hereditary monarchy. See also Marsilius of Padua, *Defensor minor*, 1, 4, ed. by Jeudy and Quillet, p. 174 (trans. by Nederman, p. 2); and *DP*, II, 5.4, ed. by Scholz, pp. 185–87 (trans. by Brett, pp. 182–83).

Hatred of the ruler and a desire for vengeance are kept at bay by the emotion of fear. Thus, even if laws do not pertain to immanent acts, it is obvious that they evoke emotions and are intended to do so. Punishments are given for external actions; but if law incites enough fear, there will be no need for punishment in the first place. Emotions are used to counter other emotions in secular legislation as well: those individuals who cannot control their own emotions can be regulated by arousing other emotions in them.

To put it in another way, arousing fear of punishment or desire for reward is a way of encouraging the subject to keep their vicious actions and passions immanent and refrain from making them transitive. The main responsibility for moderating immanent acts falls on the sacerdotal part of the community, but civil laws also aim at keeping immanent acts immanent, that is, keeping them in the domain of the sacerdotal part. Given that transitive actions stem from immanent ones — immanent actions become transitive once the agent consents to the external action suggested by them — controlling and influencing the latter is an effective way to control the former.

Reducing the Effects of Emotions

One important aspect of Marsilius's conception of the societal role of emotions is their harmfulness at the level of decision-making. An Aristotelian virtuous person knows what is the right course of action in a given situation (she is practically wise), but she also has a steady inclination to act in accordance with right reason — her emotional reaction is appropriate to the situation at hand. Marsilius is highly sceptical about the possibility that most people ever become virtuous in this sense. Civil law does not even aim to make humans virtuous, and the influence of religion on the immanent actions and passions also seems to be rather limited. Following the general lines of Augustinian pessimism concerning fallen human nature, Marsilius emphasizes that every human being is flawed:

> Someone will put forward an objection about the best man, that he has no ignorance or perverted affection. Let us say, though, that this is a very rare occurrence — and even then, not in a way equal to the law. We argued this point earlier on the basis of Aristotle, from reason and the experience of the senses, since it is a fact that every soul has this, i.e. affection that is sometimes malign. [...] No one, however virtuous, can lack perverted passion and ignorance in the same way as the law.[60]

---

60 *DP*, I, 11.6, ed. by Scholz, pp. 59–60: 'Obiciet autem aliquis de optimo viro, quod careat ignorancia et affeccione perversa. Nos autem dicamus rarissime id contingere, nec tamen

This pessimism is most clearly visible when Marsilius discusses the pope and clergy. The idea that human beings too easily fall prey to harmful emotions is a recurrent theme in *Dictio* II, where Marsilius argues why the Church should not have any political and coercive power,[61] but the same pessimism applies to holders of secular political power. Marsilius thinks that they should be emotionless — or at least not haunted by harmful and too strong emotions that shadow the proper use of the reason — because emotions are ultimately selfish and self-centred. Alas, rulers are human. Becoming virtuous is as difficult for them as it is for their subjects:

> However, because the prince, being human, has an intellect and a desire which can take on different forms — such as a false conception or a perverted desire or both — it is possible for him, if he follows them, to do things contrary to what is laid down by law.[62]

Harmful emotions are likely to take control over the rulers, which is the principal reason why the civil law should be above them, as the passage in *DP* I, 11.6 (quoted above) shows. In the same vein, judges ought not to have strong emotions concerning the cases they judge. But they do:

> For a judgement to be completely good there is required, on the part of judges, both a righteous affection and a true cognisance of the matters to be judged, the opposites of which corrupt civil judgements. For a perverted affection on the part of the judge, like hate or love or avarice, corrupts his desire. [...] 'That has the advantage' i.e. is superior for the purposes of judging 'which entirely lacks the element of passion' i.e. the affection that can corrupt a judgement 'over that to which it is innate. Now therefore this' viz. passion or affection 'is not inherent in the law; but every human soul necessarily has it' — and he said 'every', not excepting anyone, however virtuous.[63]

---

equaliter ipsi legi, ut pridem induximus ab Aristotele, a racione et sensata experiencia, quoniam omnem animam contingit habere hanc, id est affeccionem quandoque sinistram. [...] Neminem certe quantumcumque studiosum sic posse carere passione perversa et ignorancia, quemadmodum lex'; trans. by Brett, pp. 62–63, modified.

61 The harmful emotions of the pope as a source of great evils are mentioned repeatedly in *Dictio* II; see e.g. *DP*, II, 21.12, ed. by Scholz, pp. 415–16 (trans. by Brett, p. 387).

62 *DP*, I, 18.3, ed. by Scholz, p. 122: 'Verum quia principans homo existens habet intellectum et appetitum, potentes recipere formas alias, ut falsam extimacionem aut perversum desiderium vel utrumque, secundum quas contingit ipsum agere contraria eorum, que lege determinata sunt'; trans. by Brett, p. 124. Shogimen, 'Medicine and the Body Politic', pp. 109–10, points out that Marsilius acknowledges here the limits of medical metaphors and argues that unlike the heart, which cannot be inclined to an action that is contrary to its nature, the ruler is a complex human being and thus fallible.

63 *DP*, I, 11.1–2, ed. by Scholz, pp. 52–53: 'Ad iudicii complementum in bonitate requiritur affeccio recta iudicum et iudicandorum vera cognitio, quorum opposita civilia corrumpunt iudicia. Nam perversa iudicantis affeccio, ut odii vel amoris aut avaricie, desiderium iudicantis pervertit. [...] *Valencius autem*, id est prestancius ad iudicandum, *cui non adest,*

Marsilius also quotes approvingly the first book of Aristotle's *Rhetoric*:

> But a prefect and a judge make their judgements concerning things already present and defined, to which love and hate and personal convenience are often annexed, so that they cannot sufficiently discern the truth, but attend their judgement to what is disagreeable or pleasant to them personally.[64]

Marsilius's solution to this problematic situation is simple: law should prevail over individual decisions. Law is rational and it is not influenced by emotion:

> Aristotle said that 'Because law is intelligence without appetite' [*Pol.*, III, 16, 1287a34] — as if to say that the law is intelligence or cognisance without appetite, i.e. without any kind of affection.[65]

Law is rational, and while judges and princes are liable to be affected by their emotions, law itself is not. It is a result of long 'evolution', as it is gradually improved by several generations, and this process apparently removes any self-centred partiality from it. Ruling in accordance to law is better than ruling without (or above) law precisely because it is a rational principle, a reason without emotions.[66] Marsilius is somewhat pessimistic about the ability of individuals to control their harmful emotional drives. Yet, at the same time, he is rather optimistic about group decisions and especially of the human ability to develop well-functioning societies over time.[67] He writes:

---

quod passionale omnino, id est affeccio que iudicium pervertere potest, *quam cui connaturale. Legi quidem igitur hoc non inest*, passio videlicet sive affectio; *humanam autem animam necesse hoc habere omnem*; et dixit *omnem*, non excipiendo quemquam quantumcumque studiosum'; trans. by Brett, pp. 56–57.

64 *DP*, I, 11.2, ed. by Scholz, p. 54: 'Prefectus autem et iudex iam de presentibus et determinatis iudicant, ad quod et amare iam et odire et proprium commodum annexa sunt saepe, ut non adhuc possint videre sufficienter verum, sed attendere in iudicio proprium delectabile aut triste'; trans. by Brett, p. 58; *Rh.*, I, 1, 1354b4–11.

65 *DP*, I, 11.4, ed. by Scholz, p. 58: 'Cum dixit: *Propter quod sine appetitu intellectus lex est*; quasi dicat legem intellectum seu cognitionem esse absque appetitu, id est affeccione aliqua'; trans. by Brett, p. 61, slightly modified. See *Pol.*, III, 16, 1287a30–34; III, 15, 1286a17–19; *Rh.*, I, 1, 1354a31–32.

66 Law is an expression of human reason, which Marsilius sees in a very optimistic light (Moreno-Riaño and Nederman, 'Marsilius of Padua's Principles of Secular Politics', pp. 130–31; Coleman, *A History of Political Thought*, p. 152; Nederman, *Community and Consent*, p. 40, and pp. 73–94). He establishes a close analogy between the human body and the political community and, as Kaye has argued, sees human law as an instrument for maintaining the proper balance in the community (*A History of Balance*, pp. 299–344, esp. pp. 322–23). Emotions are one of the six non-naturals that threaten the balance of the human body; if the analogy holds, they can also be seen as threatening the balance of the body politic.

67 Mulieri, 'Marsilius of Padua and Peter of Abano', pp. 281–84.

> For citizens in the plural are neither wicked nor undiscerning, at least in respect of most individuals and most of the time: all or most are of sound mind and reason and of an upright desire for the polity and what is necessary for its survival.[68]

This combination of pessimism concerning individuals and optimism concerning groups applies to both the secular government and the Church.[69] The tension between these two perspectives is radical; one might ask how is it possible that wicked individuals, who generally lack the necessary self-control for good and virtuous behaviour, turn into a reasonable group that makes good decisions. Marsilius does not tell us how exactly the joint decision-making and evolution of law is supposed to work — he does not give us a political theory in that sense.[70] However, he is quite traditional in his belief in human weakness, not only in a biological but also in a moral sense, and he places his trust in institutions, which are above individuals and enable them to live according to reason in a way that would not be possible for them alone.[71]

Humans may be able to *know* what is right, but without the help of (and regulation exercised by) political institutions, it is difficult for them to *do* what is right, because they are liable to be controlled by their emotions. Perhaps one could say that law represents what humans would have been without original sin; after sin we still have reason (and Marsilius places much trust in our reason), but our ability to live in accordance with reason is hampered by harmful emotions. Law is institutionalized reason; its point is to get rid of the harmful effects of emotions in the social sphere.

Conclusions

Marsilius does not offer a systematic analysis of the role of emotions in social and political life, but the emotional dimension of human life nevertheless has an important role in his political theory. We have seen how the natural inclination to establish political (and other) communities is based on the desire for self-preservation, which also manifests itself

---

68 *DP*, I, 13.3, ed. by Scholz, p. 72: 'Nam civium pluralitas neque prava neque indiscreta est quantum ad pluralitatem suppositorum, et in pluri tempore; omnes enim aut plurimi sane mentis et racionis sunt et recti appetitus ad policiam et que necessaria sunt propter eius permanenciam'; trans. by Brett, p. 75.

69 *DP*, II, 6.13, ed. by Scholz, p. 214 (trans. by Brett, p. 206); *DP*, II, 28.17, ed. by Scholz, p. 548 (trans. by Brett, p. 499).

70 See, however, Mulieri, 'Marsilius of Padua and Peter of Abano'.

71 When writing about voluntary poverty, Marsilius claims that giving up possessions reduces harmful emotions (see e.g. *DP*, II, 13.23–24, ed. by Scholz, pp. 287–89 (trans. by Brett, pp. 274–76)). This means that he recognizes that institutional(ized) practices can help control emotions and thus have a positive societal role.

in the form of emotions. Moreover, Marsilius ascribes explanatory and political functions to emotions within already existing community. The human tendency to assent to emotional impulses without checking them with reason causes societal trouble and turmoil, but emotions can be used to counter this tendency and thus exert political control over subjects. The human condition also explains why Marsilius gives a prominent role to laws, which can be seen as embodied rationality that is free of emotional influences: individual human frailty can be overcome by institutional means.

When Marsilius writes about emotions, his aim is not to discuss their societal functions from a theoretical perspective. But if we connect the dots, a rather coherent picture emerges. Investigating Marsilius's theory from the point of view of emotions highlights several nuances of his political philosophy in an interesting way. The same approach might apply to other medieval political theories as well; but that is a more general question that needs to be answered elsewhere.

Works Cited

Primary Sources

Aristotle, *Nicomachean Ethics*, trans. by David Ross and Lesley Brown (Oxford: Oxford University Press, 2009)

Avicenna, *The Canon of Medicine (al-Qānūn fī'l-tibb)*, ed. by Lāla Bakhtiar, trans. by O. Cameron Gruner and Mazar H. Shah, Great Books of the Islamic World (Chicago: KAZI, 1999)

Cicero, *De inventione*, in *Cicero in Twenty-Eight Volumes*, ii: *De inventione, De optimo genere oratorum, Topica*, trans. by H. M. Hubbell (Cambridge, MA: Harvard University Press, 1949)

John of la Rochelle, *Summa de anima*, ed. by Jacques Guy Bougerol, Textes philosophiques du Moyen Age, 19 (Paris: Vrin, 1995)

Marsilius of Padua, *The Defender of the Peace*, trans. by Annabel Brett, Cambridge Texts in the History of Political Thought (Cambridge: Cambridge University Press, 2005)

——, *Defensor minor*, in *Oeuvres mineures: Defensor minor, De translatione imperii*, ed. by Colette Jeudy and Jeannine Quillet, Sources d'histoire médiévale (Paris: Éditions du Centre National de la Recherche Scientifique, 1979), pp. 173–311

——, *Defensor pacis*, ed. by Richard Scholz, Monumenta Germaniae Historica: Fontes iuris germanici antiqui in usum scholarum separatim editi, 7.2 (Hannover: Hahn, 1933)

——, *Writings on the Empire: 'Defensor minor' and 'De translatione Imperii'*, ed. and trans. by Cary J. Nederman, Cambridge Texts in the History of Political Thought (Cambridge: Cambridge University Press, 1993)

Peter of Abano, *Expositio problematum Aristotelis* (Venice: Joannes Herbort, 1482)

Thomas Aquinas, *Summa Theologiae*, in *Opera omnia iussu impensaque Leonis XIII P. M. edita*, vols iv–xii (Rome: Ex Typographia Polyglotta, 1888–1906)

Secondary Works

Blažek, Pavel, *Die mittelalterliche Rezeption der aristotelischen Philosophie der Ehe von Robert Grosseteste bis Bartholomäus von Brügge (1246/1247–1309)*, Studies in Medieval and Reformation Traditions, 117 (Leiden: Brill, 2007)

Boquet, Damien, and Piroska Nagy, *Sensible moyen âge: Une histoire de émotions dans l'Occident medieval* (Paris: Éditions du Seuil, 2015)

Brennan, Tad, 'Stoic Moral Philosophy', in *The Cambridge Companion to the Stoics*, ed. by Brad Inwood (Cambridge: Cambridge University Press, 2003), pp. 257–94

Brett, Annabel, 'Introduction', in Marsilius of Padua, *The Defender of the Peace*, trans. by Annabel Brett, Cambridge Texts in the History of Political Thought (Cambridge: Cambridge University Press, 2005), pp. xi–lxi

———, 'Political Philosophy', in *The Cambridge Companion to Medieval Philosophy*, ed. by Arthur S. McGrade (Cambridge: Cambridge University Press, 2003), pp. 276–99

Briguglia, Gianluca, *Marsilio da Padova*, Pensatori, 31 (Rome: Carocci editore, 2013)

———, and Irène Rosier-Catach, eds, *Adam, la nature humaine, avant et après: Épistemologie de la chute* (Paris: Publications de la Sorbonne, 2016)

Casagrande, Carla, and Silviana Vecchio, 'Les passions avant et après la chute: Modèle thomasien et tradition augustinienne', in *Adam, la nature humaine, avant et après: Épistemologie de la chute*, ed. by Gianluca Briguglia and Irène Rosier-Catach (Paris: Publications de la Sorbonne, 2016), pp. 153–71

Cohen-Hanegbi, Naama, *Caring for the Living Soul: Emotions, Medicine and Penitence in the Late Medieval Mediterranean*, The Medieval Mediterranean, 110 (Leiden: Brill, 2017)

Coleman, Janet, *A History of Political Thought*, II: *From the Middle Ages to the Renaissance* (Oxford: Blackwell, 2000)

Deane, Herbert, *The Political and Social Ideas of St Augustine* (New York: Columbia University Press, 1963)

Dougherty, Richard J., ed., *Augustine's Political Thought* (Rochester: University of Rochester Press, 2019)

Ebbesen, Sten, 'Where Were the Stoics in the Late Middle Ages?', in *Stoicism: Traditions and Transformations*, ed. by Steven K. Strange and Jack Zupko (Cambridge: Cambridge University Press, 2004), pp. 108–31

Gewirth, Alan, *Marsilius of Padua: The Defender of Peace*, I: *Marsilius of Padua and Medieval Political Philosophy*, Records of Civilization, Sources and Studies, 46 (New York: Columbia University Press, 1951)

Inwood, Brad, and Pierluigi Donini, 'Stoic Ethics', in *The Cambridge History of Hellenistic Philosophy*, ed. by Keimpe Algra and others (Cambridge: Cambridge University Press, 1999), pp. 675–738

Jarcho, Saul, 'Galen's Six Non-Naturals: A Bibliographic Note and Translation', *Bulletin of the History of Medicine*, 44 (1970), 372–77

Kaye, Joel, *A History of Balance, 1250–1375: The Emergence of a New Model of Equilibrium and its Impact on Thought* (Cambridge: Cambridge University Press, 2014)

Kempshall, Matthew S., *The Common Good in Late Medieval Thought* (Oxford: Clarendon Press, 1999)

Kent, Bonnie, *Virtues of the Will: The Transformation of Ethics in the Late Thirteenth Century* (Washington, DC: Catholic University of America Press, 1995)

Knuuttila, Simo, *Emotions in Ancient and Medieval Philosophy* (Oxford: Clarendon Press, 2004)

———, 'Medieval Theories of the Passions of the Soul', in *Emotions and Choice from Boethius to Descartes*, ed. by Henrik Lagerlund and Mikko Yrjönsuuri, Studies in the History of Philosophy of Mind, 1 (Dordrecht: Kluwer, 2002), pp. 49–83

Koch, Bettina, 'Marsilius of Padua on Church and State', in *A Companion to Marsilius of Padua*, ed. by Gerson Moreno-Riaño and Cary J. Nederman, Brill's Companions to the Christian Tradition, 31 (Leiden: Brill, 2012), pp. 139–79

Moreno-Riaño, Gerson, and Cary J. Nederman, 'Marsilius of Padua's Principles of Secular Politics', in *A Companion to Marsilius of Padua*, ed. by Gerson Moreno-Riaño and Cary J. Nederman, Brill's Companions to the Christian Tradition, 31 (Leiden: Brill, 2012), pp. 117–38

Mulcahy, Daniel G., 'The Hands of Augustine but the Voice of Marsilius', *Augustiniana*, 21 (1971), 457–66

Mulieri, Alessandro, 'Marsilius of Padua and Peter of Abano: The Scientific Foundations of Law-Making in Defensor Pacis', *British Journal for the History of Philosophy*, 26.2 (2018), 276–96

Nederman, Cary J., *Community and Consent: The Secular Political Theory of Marsiglio of Padua's 'Defensor Pacis'* (London: Rowman & Littlefield, 1995)

——, 'The Meaning of "Aristotelianism" in Medieval Moral and Political Thought', *Journal of the History of Ideas*, 57.4 (1996), 563–85

——, 'Nature, Sin and the Origins of Society: The Ciceronian Tradition in Medieval Political Thought', *Journal of the History of Ideas*, 49.1 (1988), 3–26

Niebyl, Peter H., 'The Non-Naturals', *Bulletin of the History of Medicine*, 45 (1971), 486–92

Pickavé, Martin, and Lisa Shapiro, eds, *Emotions and Cognitive Life in Medieval and Early Modern Philosophy* (Oxford: Oxford University Press, 2012)

Robert, Aurélien, 'Le corps d'après: La Chute entre théologie et médecine (XIIe– XIVe siècle)', in *Adam, la nature humaine, avant et après: Épistemologie de la chute*, ed. by Gianluca Briguglia and Irène Rosier-Catch (Paris: Publications de la Sorbonne, 2016), pp. 173–204

Rosier-Catch, Irène, 'Communauté politique et communauté linguistique', in *La légitimité implicite*, vol. I, ed. by Jean-Philippe Genet (Rome: École française de Rome, 2015), pp. 225–43

Scott, Joanna Vecchiarelli, 'Influence or Manipulation? The Role of Augustinianism in the Defensor Pacis of Marsiglio of Padua', *Augustinian Studies*, 9 (1978), 59–79

Shogimen, Takashi, 'Medicine and the Body Politic in Marsilius of Padua's Defensor Pacis', in *A Companion to Marsilius of Padua*, ed. by Gerson Moreno-Riaño and Cary J. Nederman, Brill's Companion to the Christian Tradition, 31 (Leiden: Brill, 2012), pp. 71–115

Sorabji, Richard, *Emotion and Peace of Mind: From Stoic Agitation to Christian Temptation* (Oxford: Oxford University Press, 2000)

Syros, Vasileios, *Marsilius of Padua at the Intersection of Ancient and Medieval Traditions of Political Thought* (Toronto: University of Toronto Press, 2012)

Toivanen, Juhana, 'Extending the Limits of Nature: Political Animals, Artefacts, and Social Institutions', *Philosophical Readings*, 12 (2020), 35–44

——, *The Political Animal in Medieval Philosophy: A Philosophical Study of the Commentary Tradition, c. 1260–c. 1410*, Studien und Texte zur Geistesgeschichte des Mittelalters, 129 (Leiden: Brill, 2021)

Toste, Marco, 'The Naturalness of Human Association in Medieval Political Thought Revisited', in *La nature comme source de la morale au Moyen Âge*, ed. by Maaike van der Lugt, Micrologus' Library, 58 (Florence: SISMEL–Edizioni del Galluzzo, 2014), pp. 113–88

Weithman, Paul, 'Augustine's Political Philosophy', in *The Cambridge Companion to Augustine*, ed. by Eleonore Stump and Norman Kretzmann, Cambridge Companions to Philosophers (Cambridge: Cambridge University Press, 2001), pp. 234–52

FERDINAND DEANINI

The Good Life and the Perfect Life in the *Defensor pacis*

Introduction

The concept of the good life is central to Marsilius of Padua's *Defensor pacis*. It underpins his entire political theory, as any city is ultimately founded for the sake of 'living and living well'. Human beings become citizens in order to live better, and the citizen strives to perfect the city to fully attain the good life. At the same time, the *Defensor* also includes the idea that to be a perfect follower of Christ it is necessary to reject all worldly property and power completely. The true *imitatio Christi* consists in supreme poverty. Marsilius argues at great length that supreme poverty is possible in this life and that the Church as a whole should also follow this principle of supreme poverty.

This position is grounded in the ongoing controversy surrounding the Franciscan order and its concept of apostolic poverty, a controversy that had troubled the Church for decades.[1] But in the *Defensor pacis* apostolic poverty also attains a different meaning because it is presented in the context of a political theory that privileges political peace and the unhindered development of the city, including the increase of property. Marsilius thus presents us with two accounts of human perfection: on the one hand, the perfection of the citizen who maintains the peace to build the perfect city, desiring to 'live and live well', and on the other hand, the *perfectus*, who, in imitating Christ, rejects all the wealth of this world and, in this way, also the promises of the city.

---

1 Regarding the influence of the poverty controversy on Marsilius, see Tierney, 'Marsilius on Rights', p. 7; Brett, 'Political Right(s) and Human Freedom'; Lambertini, 'Marsilius and the Poverty Controversy'.

> **Ferdinand Deanini** is a PhD student in Philosophy at the LMU Munich. His main research interests are in natural theology and political philosophy, especially in the works of Marsilius of Padua, Thomas Hobbes, and Leo Strauss.

Marsilius of Padua, ed. by Alessandro Mulieri, Serena Masolini, and Jenny Pelletier, Disputatio, 36 (Turnhout: Brepols, 2023), pp. 179–196

BREPOLS ❦ PUBLISHERS   10.1484/M.DISPUT-EB.5.132912

The present chapter intends to confront these two ways of life and seeks to answer the question of how Marsilius tries to reconcile their seemingly incongruent demands. In the first part of this chapter, I will sketch his understanding of the civic life and its basis in the desire for living well. In the second part, I will discuss the *perfecti* and the virtue of their supreme poverty. Finally, in the third part, I intend to show how Marsilius tries to integrate the *perfecti* into the city.

The Civil Life

The Aristotelian idea of the city as the means of human survival and happiness is fundamental to Marsilius's argument. All human beings naturally desire to 'live and live well',[2] to lead a sufficient life (*sufficienter vivere*) in this world.[3] Human beings are naturally weak, having no claws or other bodily weapons, and thus require tools to provide for themselves (*DP*, I, 4.3). To produce these tools and to overcome their natural weakness generally, human beings have to cooperate. To this end, the first social units were founded to secure survival. But while primitive associations are able to provide the means for life as such, human beings desire more. They want to live a good life, a life that can fulfil all their desires, 'sc. having leisure for the liberal activities that result from the virtues both of the practical and of the theoretical soul'.[4] The attainment of this satisfaction is the final cause of the city.

The good life is thus naturally dependent on the perfect city, that is, a city developed enough to provide for all human needs. Only the fully developed city can — through cooperation between its citizens and their specialization into different functions — satisfy all human needs completely. This description of humankind as necessarily directed towards the perfect city is entirely in accordance with Aristotle's arguments in Book I of the *Politics*.[5]

But in his description of the city, Marsilius emphasizes the economic aspect of politics more: the fulfilment of human needs through prosperity

---

2 *DP*, I, 4.1, trans. by Brett, p. 18: 'Now in saying, "having come about for the sake of living, but existing for the sake of living well", Aristotle signifies its final and perfect cause, for those who live a civil life do not just live [...] but live well, sc. having leisure for the liberal activities that result from the virtues both of the practical and of the theoretical soul'.

3 *DP*, I, 4.5, trans. by Brett, p. 21: 'Men gathered together in order to live the sufficient life'.

4 *DP*, I, 4.1, trans. by Brett, p. 18; ed. by Scholz, p. 16: 'scilicet operibus liberalibus, qualia sunt virtutum tam practice, quam speculative anime'.

5 See Aristotle, *Politics*, I, 1252b28–1253a18. On Marsilius's relationship to the Aristotelian tradition in general, see Quillet, 'L'aristotélisme de Marsile de Padoue'; Syros, *Die Rezeption der aristotelischen politischen Philosophie*; Syros, 'Did the Physician from Padua Meet the Rabbi from Cordoba?', pp. 52–56; Mulieri, 'Against Classical Republicanism'.

THE GOOD LIFE AND THE PERFECT LIFE IN THE *DEFENSOR PACIS*   181

and the acquisition of goods.[6] He stresses peace as the precondition for a well-ordered city, beginning the *Defensor* by citing Cassiodorus: 'Every realm must desire tranquillity, under which peoples prosper and the profit of the nations is safeguarded'.[7] Not conquest, but prosperity through peace is the basis of a successful city. Peace gives human beings the ability to fulfil their needs and — when necessary — to develop techniques to produce the desired effects. Agriculture and mechanics are discovered to provide for material well-being (*DP*, I, 5.4–6). While some things may be available naturally, to acquire other things and capabilities 'man needed to go beyond natural causes'.[8] The citizens have to invest work and thought into developing their city so it can fulfil all their needs.[9] Roads and bridges must be constructed, buildings have to be maintained, and the harvest must be stored to provide for times of scarcity (*DP*, I, 5.9). It requires forethought and prudent judgement to understand both the needs of the city and how to satisfy them. Accordingly, when discussing the virtues necessary for a good ruler, Marsilius specifically singles out justice and prudence as the two most important virtues for good government (*DP*, I, 14.3, 14.7).[10] Citing a passage from the *Politics* where Aristotle points out virtue and justice as necessary for a good ruler, Marsilius interprets virtue here as specifically meaning prudence.[11]

Marsilius's particular emphasis on the fulfilment of needs as the basis of the city can also be seen in his argument for the participation of all citizens in law-making (*DP*, I, 12). There he argues against the position that the many do not have the capacity to recognize good laws by referring to their natural self-interest. While the lower classes may not have the same knowledge as the few well-educated citizens, they still share the same natural drive for attaining the good life. Marsilius grants that there may be some people of a *natura orbata* (stunted nature) who cannot recognize their own good, but for the vast majority care for their own good will always remain true and allow them to judge laws correctly in this regard.[12] All human beings are interested in a government that fulfils their desires

---

6 See Gewirth, *Marsilius of Padua*, pp. 89–91.

7 *DP*, I, 1.1, trans. by Brett, p. 3; ed. by Scholz, p. 1: 'Omni quippe regno desiderabilis debet esse tranquilitas, in qua et populi proficiunt, et utilitas gencium custoditur'.

8 *DP*, I, 5.3, trans. by Brett, p. 24; ed. by Scholz, pp. 21–22: 'necessarium fuit homini ultra causas naturales per racionem aliqua formare, quibus compleatur efficiencia et conservacio suarum accionum et passionum secundum corpus et animam'.

9 *DP*, I, 5.5, trans. by Brett, p. 25: 'Different kinds of arts were discovered [...] and men of different functions were instituted to practise them, in order to remedy human need'.

10 On prudence in late medieval thought in general, see Toste, 'Virtue and the City'; Lambertini, 'Political Prudence in Some Medieval Commentaries'.

11 *DP*, I, 14.10, trans. by Brett, p. 86: '"And thirdly, virtue and justice"; by virtue understanding prudence, which is the bond and the mistress of all the virtues'.

12 *DP*, I, 12.5. See also *DP*, I, 12.8; *DP*, I, 13.2.

prudently and justly. All human beings — or at least most of them — are good enough to participate in politics.

Overall, the *Defensor pacis* considers the concern of the citizens for their own good as a necessary and justified part of politics and human life in general. This does not preclude limits to material interests or to radical economic individualism. Marsilius understands the concern for the good in this world as a communal, necessarily collective effort that requires the cooperation of the different parts that form a city.[13] But the human desire for the good life as such — and the acquisition of property connected with it — are justified insofar as they are a fundamental part of human nature. Material needs and human self-interest in general may have moral limits, but they are not in themselves immoral or unreasonable. On the contrary, they are fundamental for the good life that is possible in this world.

But the good life of the city is not the only way of life available to human beings. Marsilius distinguishes two modes of life: 'Modes [...] of this same living and living well that is appropriate for man: one temporal and worldly, but also another, which is customarily called eternal or heavenly'.[14] Marsilius continues: 'Philosophers could not convincingly demonstrate the second mode, that is the sempiternal, nor was it among things that are self-evident'.[15] The philosophers, we come to understand, base their doctrines entirely on what is evident in this world and as such only passed on rules for the good life in this — our — world. The philosophers did not and could not give any recommendations about the sempiternal life.[16] As we shall see later, Marsilius will lightly revise this supposed philosophical reluctance to address the hope for an eternal life at a later moment in his argument.

We can identify the *vivere sempiternum* here as the heavenly life of the Christian faithful after death. But we can also understand it as an initial reference to the life of supreme poverty, the apostolic life, which Marsilius will describe in greater detail in the second part of the *Defensor*. Marsilius makes a clear distinction between a worldly mode of life, the *modus mundanus*, which finds its fulfilment in the city, and the eternal life, the *modus eternus*, which is made possible through God's grace (*DP*, I, 6.1–6). These two modes of life correspond to the general distinction, emphasized by Marsilius throughout the entire *Defensor pacis*, between our

---

13 See Nederman, *Community and Consent*, pp. 53–55.

14 *DP*, I, 4.3, trans. by Brett, p. 19; ed. by Scholz, p. 17: 'Vivere autem ipsum et bene vivere [...] est in duplici modo, quoddam temporale sive mundanum, aliud vero eternum sive celeste vocari solitum'.

15 *DP*, I, 4.3, trans. by Brett, p. 19; ed. by Scholz, p. 17: 'Quodque istud secundum vivere, sempiternum scilicet, non potuit philosophorum universitas per demonstracionem convincere, nec fuit de rebus manifestis per se'.

16 *DP*, I, 4.3, trans. by Brett, p. 19: The philosophers 'did not trouble themselves to pass on whatever might be in order to it'.

THE GOOD LIFE AND THE PERFECT LIFE IN THE *DEFENSOR PACIS*   183

world as ruled by human laws and the coercive power enforcing them, and the divine law given by Jesus Christ for the promised world to come. While both these worlds follow their own sets of rules, they ultimately form a continuum.

From this perspective, the coexistence of the two modes of the good life may seem unproblematic. First, there is the good civic life in this world, its outlines circumscribed by political philosophy, and then there will be the good eternal life, governed by Jesus Christ. But this harmony is called into question when we compare the life of the citizen to the life of supreme poverty, that is, the way of life that is most in line with the teaching of Christ. This life of supreme poverty is to be lived in our world, but it demands a way of life that seems to be at odds with the citizen's way of life.

The Apostolic Life

In *Dictio* II of the *Defensor* Marsilius describes the apostolic way of life — a life of 'supreme poverty' (*paupertas suprema*) — and argues both for the possibility of supreme poverty and for the duty of all priests to practise it. The starting point for his argument is the example of Jesus and the apostles, who taught and observed the highest form of poverty and humility (*DP*, II, 12.1). Only by emulating this humility can a Christian become 'perfect' (*perfectus*) in his imitation of Christ.[17]

The apostolic way of life, as Marsilius describes it, has two important aspects. The first aspect is a vow to renounce all property and the comforts that come with it. To truly imitate Christ, to become perfect, one may not own anything nor claim lordship over anything, and one must divorce oneself from all the desires of this world: 'It is a vow […] by which he wills, for the sake of Christ, to be deprived of […] all power, disposition, and handling or use of them superfluous to what is sufficient for him at the present moment'.[18]

The second aspect is that the *perfecti* must reject all political power, which is connected to the renunciation of all lordship. 'My kingdom is not of this world' — Marsilius opposes all clerical rule with these famous words of Jesus.[19] As Christ relinquishes his rule of this — our — world, so must those who are following in his footsteps give up the possibility of any worldly rule. Absolute poverty in imitation of Christ is

---

17 For Marsilius's definition of the terms 'supreme poverty' and '*perfectus*', see *DP*, II, 13.22.

18 *DP*, II, 13.22, trans. by Brett, p. 273; ed. by Scholz, p. 286: 'Votum inquam eciam, quo propter Christum, tam in proprio quam eciam in communi, privari vult et carere omni potestate, habitu et contractacione vel usu ipsorum superfluo in quanto et quali presenti sufficiencie'.

19 *DP*, II, 4.4; John 18. 36.

an all-encompassing way of life. It is a full rejection not only of political power, but also of the comforts of life. The *perfecti* are not supposed to marry, to swear oaths, or to participate in most other aspects of society. They exist on the fringes of the city, if not completely outside of it. As such, the *perfecti* reject the good life in this world, even though they do not reject life as such.

Marsilius grants that supreme poverty does not entail a complete rejection of material goods. The *perfecti* are allowed to make use of things like food and clothing, as long as they do so solely to satisfy their basic needs. The argument for this concession is interesting for our comparison of the civil and apostolic life. While in *Dictio* I, Marsilius holds that the desire to acquire property and the material means of a sufficient life are necessitated by human nature, his arguments now are very different. He makes his case by referring to divine law, which forbids man to harm himself (*DP*, II, 13.5; *DP*, II, 13.23). It is a duty even for those living in supreme poverty to maintain their body by using the means provided to them. Basic needs have to be satisfied even in complete poverty, and the *perfecti* may not deny themselves in this regard. But they should only care for the present moment, not prudently prepare for future eventualities, which would make their desires unlimited and absolute poverty impossible (*DP*, II, 13.22).

The civil life as presented in *Dictio* I is legitimated by human nature, which provides its direction and limits. The apostolic life, by contrast, is regulated by divine law and the model of Christ. It is not rooted in human nature. One could even argue that it is contrary to human nature as that nature is outlined in *Dictio* I. If the desire for the good life is so fundamental that human beings will necessarily congregate in cities, how can some people willingly give up all the benefits of that life? The demands of the apostolic life appear otherworldly, no longer rooted in the laws and necessities of this world. Coming back to Marsilius's distinction between the *modus mundanus* and the *modus eternus*, one could argue that the apostolic life is already an example of the latter, a mode of life that follows the divine laws for the world to come, while still being lived in this world.

Marsilius's arguments for supreme poverty are neither new nor particularly unique. The concept that the true *imitatio Christi* demanded supreme poverty had become increasingly prominent during the thirteenth century, especially due to the Franciscan movement. The question of poverty had led to an ongoing conflict between the Franciscans and the Church.[20] But it is important to recognize the connection between the defence of apostolic poverty and the critique of papal power and priestly power in general. It is obvious that the argument for supreme poverty as a

---

20 On the poverty controversy see note 1, above, and more generally Mäkinen, *Property Rights*.

THE GOOD LIFE AND THE PERFECT LIFE IN THE *DEFENSOR PACIS*   185

precondition of the priestly office grants Marsilius a powerful weapon in his fight against papal power. Not only would the renunciation of all wealth weaken ecclesiastical power, but the example of Jesus Christ as lawgiver only for the world to come denies the papal claim for power in this world at its very source.

Furthermore, the context of Marsilius's argument for apostolic poverty is peculiar. The *Defensor pacis* is not simply a defence of the Franciscan way of life, but presents first and foremost a political theory that is concerned with building a good city for the non-perfect. It is written as a defence of *civil* peace, not of supreme poverty, even though it contains a defence of the latter. And in this context supreme poverty becomes deeply problematic. As we have seen, the apostolic life exists by its very nature on the fringes of the city, if not wholly outside of it. It denies, to some degree at least, the needs that lead to the founding and development of the city and thus calls the necessity of political life into question. From this perspective, the apostolic life seems apolitical, if not anti-political. Indeed, Marsilius explicitly says that the evangelical law does not give guidance to uphold a proper life in this world and that without a human law 'scandal and contention would arise among men'.[21] While the evangelical law gives directions to the believer as an individual, allowing him to follow Christ's example properly and to become a *perfectus*,[22] it does not provide a law for the city.

What then is the relationship between the *perfecti* and all other believers, who do not practice complete poverty, and who are called in the Bible, as Marsilius points out, *infirmi* (the weak) (*DP*, II, 13.37)? Could this inferiority not be understood as an indictment of the civil life? And how can the 'weak' citizens understand their own life as sufficient, as the good life, when they fall short of living up to the standard of Christ?

A first answer is provided by the distinction between actions that are necessary for salvation and actions that are not necessary but that may be performed by someone who goes beyond what is strictly necessary for salvation. The perfection of supreme poverty is not a demand placed on all believers. While the apostolic way of life is characterized as more meritorious, it is not required for salvation. It is purely an act of supererogation, freely undertaken and without any expectation of benefit.[23]

---

21 *DP*, II, 9.12, trans. by Brett, p. 230; ed. by Scholz, p. 243: 'sine quibus eciam propter defectum iusticie contingeret ex hominum scandalo seu contencione ipsorum pugna et separacio ac humane vite mundane insufficiencia'.

22 *DP*, II, 9.12, trans. by Brett, p. 230: 'But let us say for our part that we are adequately directed by the evangelical law in what we should do or avoid in the present life, but this is nevertheless for the status of the world to come'.

23 *DP*, II, 13.37. See also the constant emphasis on the self-imposed, voluntary character of supreme poverty: *DP*, II, 13.14–25.

While the life of apostolic poverty is not a demand placed upon all the faithful, it is the model for the priestly life.[24] Christian priests commit themselves to following in the footsteps of Jesus and to imitating his way of life. Their authority derives from the unbroken succession of priests stretching back to the apostles, and ultimately to Christ himself (*DP*, I, 19.5; *DP*, II, 15.2). To continue this tradition fully, priests are expected to practice the life of the apostles, that is, supreme poverty. Not all *perfecti* are priests, but all priests should practice supreme poverty. Apostolic poverty remains a *supererogatum* in regard to Christian believers as a whole but attains the status of a duty — or at least a quasi-duty — for Christian priests.[25] This allows Marsilius to both maintain the 'good life', and with it economic success and property, as the standard of good politics, and to criticize priests for wanting to 'live well' themselves. While becoming a priest is a call that only a few will follow, those that do so are bound to a life in accordance with *paupertas suprema*.

But, as successors to the apostles, priests are also assigned to teach Christian doctrine. This distinguishes them as a subgroup from the *perfecti* as a whole, for whom such an obligation is not explicitly mentioned. The teaching of the Bible provides a connection to the good city, because, as Marsilius argues, it prepares the souls of the citizens for both this life and the life to come.[26] But from this perspective the city would only serve as the means for attaining the good life in the world to come, and it would not be intrinsically good as the precondition for the good life in this world. The evangelical office of teaching and preaching thus only provides a preliminary answer to the question of priests' relationship to other human beings. The duty to spread the holy word is an office that is not directed at others *qua* citizens, but *qua* human beings. For the political role of the *perfecti*, and more specifically of the perfect priests as part of a city, we have to look elsewhere.

---

24 See the identification of the Church and the perfect in *DP*, II, 14.12. See also the subordination of all temporal goods of the Church to the legislator: *DP*, II, 17.16–19; *DP*, II, 21.14. Only what is 'not superfluous to what is sufficient for poor ministers of the gospel' should be exempt from taxation. 'For let priests be content with their food and clothing' (*DP*, II, 21.14, trans. by Brett, p. 389).

25 Marsilius avoids a full commitment to a life of perfect poverty as a necessary precondition of the priesthood. This is in line with his argument for the right of the legislator to freely institute and depose all ministers of the Church (*DP*, II, 17.8–15). This avoids the possibility of someone claiming priestly authority solely based on the holiness of his way of life. The adequacy of any candidate for priesthood should be considered by the legislator, advised by 'doctors of divine law and other honest men' (*DP*, II, 17.14, trans. by Brett, p. 346), but there remains no room for a delegitimization of the final decision based on the imperfect life of the chosen candidate.

26 *DP*, I, 6.9, trans. by Brett, p. 35: 'By which man becomes well-disposed [...] for the status of this present world as well as of that to come'.

The Good Life and the Perfect Life in the *Defensor Pacis* 187

The Civil Priesthood

How should the *perfecti* relate to the city? A first hint at an answer can be found at the end of Chapter 13 of *Dictio* II. There, after discussing the demands of supreme poverty, Marsilius poses the question of how any human being can be so perfect as to truly deny themselves all temporal things beyond the bare necessities. Does human nature even allow for the life of the *perfecti* to be possible? Marsilius continues an exhortation: 'I say that Christ can, and any others who are willing, even if there be few such individuals; [...] And you tell me, I ask: How many voluntary martyrs are there in these times, how many heroic men, how many Catos, Scipios and Fabricii?'.[27]

The comparison to figures from the ancient Roman Republic is surprising. One would rather expect the invocation of Christian saints and martyrs, perhaps even of prominent apostles as exemplars of supreme poverty. Instead, Marsilius chooses to present several pagan politicians as examples and combines this with a direct exhortation to the reader, which in itself is rare in the *Defensor*. One might think that Marsilius here merely wants to show off his erudition, but the list of personalities is chosen with care: Scipio, the model of the wise statesman; Fabricius, famous for his austerity; and finally, Cato, a name almost synonymous with moral severity, and furthermore in the case of the younger Cato, also the name of a martyr, although a martyr of the Roman Republic.

One might say that these pagan *viri heroici* represent the counterpoint to Christ. While Jesus Christ is the model of the apostolic life, he, as both man and God, stands beyond what is humanly possible, more perfect than any of the *perfecti*. Fabricius, Scipio, and Cato, by contrast, represent a heroism that is purely grounded in this world. Indeed, the shift from Jesus Christ as the highest example of otherworldliness, bound by nothing in this world, to the exhortation to be more like the great heroes of the Roman Republic immediately afterwards, seems baffling and inappropriate (*DP*, II, 13.38–39).

But Scipio, the central figure of the three virtuous Romans, may indicate that the connection between Christian perfection and civic heroism is less arbitrary than it seems at first glance. The likely source for the idea of Scipio as one of the great heroes of Rome was Cicero's *Somnium Scipionis*. While the bulk of Cicero's *Republic* was unavailable in the fourteenth century, only to be rediscovered long after the Middle Ages, the *Somnium* had survived and was widely circulated, often as an appendix to Macrobius's

---

27 *DP*, II, 13.39, trans. by Brett, p. 286; ed. by Scholz, p. 300: 'Dico, quod Christus et alii quicumque volentes, quamvis tales pauci sint [...]. Et dic mihi tu, queso, quot sint martyres voluntarii temporibus hiis? Quot viri heroici? Quot Catones, Scipiones atque Fabricii?'.

Commentary on the *Somnium Scipionis*.[28] Considering its popularity, it is quite likely that Marsilius was familiar with both these texts and may have expected that some of the more erudite readers of his work would have been as well.

On the basis of the *Somnium*, the connection between the supreme poverty of Christ and the virtue of the great Roman statesmen appears far less puzzling. As Scipio Africanus explains to his descendant of the same name, selfless service to one's country is the noblest of all activities and will help the soul realize its true immortal state by leading it away from any connection to bodily existence.[29] Civic excellence appears here strikingly similar to supreme poverty as a form of self-denial that divorces the soul from the bonds of the material and helps in its path to immortality.

By calling upon the greatest examples of Roman political virtue, Marsilius shifts the reader's attention towards the question of the human life in this world, that is, the life in the city. It provides a connection to the civil role of the priests as it is described in *Dictio* I of the *Defensor pacis*. There, while treating the different parts and offices of the city, Marsilius also discusses the role of the priests. The treatment of the priests as a part of the city in the *Defensor* is far more extensive than Aristotle's, whom Marsilius otherwise constantly refers to in his discussion of the parts of the city.[30] In the *Politics*, priests are enumerated among the many offices necessary in the *polis*, but there is no deeper discussion of their specific role.[31] It is unsurprising that Marsilius has a stronger interest in the role of the priest than Aristotle does, because the *Defensor* deals with the problem of priestly power and the *potestas indirecta* of the pope. This makes the intended role of the priesthood in the city a much more pertinent question.

---

28 Macrobius, *Kommentar zum Somnium Scipionis*, ed. by Heberlein.

29 Cicero, *De re publica*, VI. 29. Marsilius gives no hint which of the two famous Scipios is specifically meant in II, 13.38. But considering how much the *Somnium Scipionis* itself blurs the difference between their achievements, abilities, and personalities, it is not inappropriate to assume that Marsilius effectively treats them as one person.

30 *DP*, I, 5.5–9. It is indeed striking that Marsilius here refers to Aristotle every time he discusses a specific part of the city, but only mentions that 'all peoples have agreed' on the necessity of an organized priesthood (*DP*, I, 5.10, trans. by Brett, p. 28), only naming Pythagoras and Hesiod among the ancients who 'paid attention to an entirely different reason for handing down divine religions' (*DP*, I, 5.11, trans. by Brett, p. 28). Only at the end of his discussion of the priestly part does Marsilius return to Aristotle (*DP*, I, 5.13). One might understand this omission as a tacit critique of Aristotle's insufficient attention to the problematic role of the priesthood in the city. This would be in line with Marsilius's earlier statement in the beginning of the book that Aristotle had described all forms of political strife, except one 'which Aristotle could not perceive' and that Marsilius now sets out to expose in his book (*DP*, I, 1.7, trans. by Brett, p. 9; see also *DP*, I, 19.3–13). While Aristotle is constantly presented by Marsilius as his highest philosophical authority, the *Defensor pacis* itself is written to amend the Aristotelian political teaching in one important regard, viz. the increased importance and independence of the priesthood in a Christian world.

31 Aristotle, *Politics* IV, 1299a18–20. See also *DP*, I, 19.12.

THE GOOD LIFE AND THE PERFECT LIFE IN THE *DEFENSOR PACIS*   189

Marsilius distinguishes two different aspects of the priesthood. On the one hand, he assigns a general role to the priestly part of the city that applies to all cities, and which includes pre-Christian, pagan priests. On the other hand, he assigns them a particular role that includes the *causa finalis* of the Christian priestly office, namely the teaching of Christian doctrine. For our discussion, it is the first understanding of the priestly role that is of particular interest. According to Marsilius, pagan priests were tasked with handling holy things and performing religious rites (*DP*, I, 5.12). This was due to the idea, common to all people, that such acts were necessary to prepare souls for the world to come, where they expected to be punished or rewarded. Thus, the existence of the priestly office is at first explained by the popular belief in a life after death, a belief that appears to be natural to all men, or at least, if not to all individual human beings, to all peoples (*populi*). On this view, even the pagan priesthood would not have existed for the well-being of the city, like the other offices, but rather for something that lies beyond the city, in the afterlife.

But Marsilius provides a second reason for the existence of the priestly part, which is more closely connected to the needs of the city. The pagan priests also served as the teachers of moral rules, supplementing the laws of the city by promising punishments and rewards in the future world (*DP*, I, 5.11–12). Even acts not known to anyone but God would thus be subject to reward and punishment, assuring the adherence of the citizens to the laws even when there is no immediate benefit in this world. For this reason, Marsilius continues, philosophers like Hesiod and Pythagoras invented religions to provide guidance.[32] From this perspective, the office of the priest is purposefully implemented for the good in this world, the good of the city.

> As a result the peace or tranquility of cities, and the sufficient life [...] was preserved with less difficulty — which was precisely what those sages had intended as their end in the exposition of such religions.[33]

While the philosophers did not give a philosophical, rational guide for attaining eternal life beyond this world, as Marsilius had stated earlier (*DP*, I, 4.3), they nonetheless still invented religions to answer the question of a life after death, promising the citizens punishments and rewards for their deeds. In this way, philosophers fulfilled the political need for religion,

---

32 On similar ideas in Siger of Brabant and John of Jandun, see Bianchi, 'Nulla lex est vera, licet *possit esse utilis*', pp. 334–43. See also for parallels in Arabic and Jewish thought Syros, 'Did the Physician from Padua Meet the Rabbi from Cordoba?', pp. 61–63.

33 *DP*, I, 5.11, trans. by Brett, p. 29; ed. by Scholz, p. 27: 'Unde pax eciam seu tranquilitas civitatum et vita hominum sufficiens pro statu presentis seculi difficile minus servabatur, quod exposicione talium legum sive sectarum sapientes illi finaliter intendebant'.

even though they could not provide a rational basis for any belief in an eternal life.

Marsilius, of course, makes a strong distinction between the pagan priesthood and the new priesthood of the Christian era. The true goal, the *causa finalis*, of the priestly office comes into view only through Christianity, which now provides the true teaching to prepare citizens for the world to come.[34] As such, the priestly part of the city is perfected by biblical revelation, as it now can completely fulfil its function after all. But this does not render obsolete the aspect of a more general moral teaching that had been the more important element of the pagan priesthood.

As Marsilius says at the end of his chapter on the final cause of the priestly office and its office of general education:

> Under this function (i.e. education of men) it is appropriate to include all those disciplines invented by human ingenuity [...] which temper those human acts [...] which result from desire and cognition, and by which man becomes well-disposed in his soul for the status of this present world as well as of that to come. And we possess almost all of these handed down to us by the admirable Philosopher and all the other glorious men.[35]

Christian priests, just like pagan ones, have the office to educate morally the citizens *pro statu presenti seculi*, and that education is based on the precepts handed down by philosophers. Christian revelation itself is purely concerned with teaching what is necessary for salvation in the world to come.[36] It is the duty of Christian priests to teach the instructions revealed by Christ, but 'it is appropriate to include all those disciplines invented by human ingenuity' in this act of teaching so 'man becomes well-disposed in his soul for the status of this present world as well as

---

34 *DP*, I, 6.8, trans. by Brett, p. 35: 'The end, therefore, of the priestly part is the instruction and education of men on the subject of those things which [...] it is necessary to believe, do, or omit in order to attain eternal salvation and avoid eternal misery'.

35 *DP*, I, 6.9, trans. by Brett, p. 35; ed. by Scholz, pp. 32–33: 'In hoc autem officium convenienter veniunt omnes discipline humano ingenio adinvente, tam speculative quam active, humanorum actuum moderative [...], ab appetitu et cognocione proveniencium, quibus bene disponitur homo secundum animam pro statu tam presentis seculi, quam venturi. Has etenim quasi omnes habemus ex tradicione admirabilis philosophi et reliquorum gloriosorum virorum'.

36 See *DP*, I, 6.4–8, especially 6.7. In contrast, the law revealed to Moses is described by Marsilius as concerning both the present world and the world to come (*DP*, I, 6.3). See also *DP*, II, 9.12, trans. by Brett, p. 230: 'Therefore the evangelical law could not be an adequate measure of human acts for the end of the present world. For it does not contain any standards that would make such acts commensurate in the proportion men want — and licitly — for the status of this present life, but rather it supposes that such standards are or should be contained in human laws'.

THE GOOD LIFE AND THE PERFECT LIFE IN THE *DEFENSOR PACIS*   191

of that to come'.[37] This pedagogical aspect of the priestly office takes on a particular importance when we reconsider Marsilius's argument for the multitude as the final legislator. There he allows for the possibility of individuals having a *natura orbata* (*DP*, I, 12.5; stunted nature) who may not want to live in accordance with public tranquillity and peace (*DP*, I, 13.2). While it may seem that Marsilius has full confidence in the perpetual prevalence of 'non-deficient' people,[38] one could also say that a conception of political power that tries to invest legislation into the hands of the whole citizenry has a particularly strong need for an institution that provides an appropriate education to all citizens. In this way, the concept of the *universitas civium* as legislator may even be said to compel Marsilius's focus on the priesthood as a civic institution for moral education.

To sum up Marsilius's position, we can say that Christian priests still fulfil the same political function as their pagan predecessors. They form a natural part of the city. But how is their status as *perfecti* related to their civic function? We might expect to find the main difference between Christian and pagan priests here. The pagan priests were drawn from that group of citizens who had some particular civic merit: 'For they did not institute any kind of people as priests, but rather certain virtuous and approved citizens who had been of military or judicial or councillor office.'[39] They were recruited from the most politically active and accomplished citizens, far from the apolitical existence of those who practised supreme poverty. Marsilius continues: 'I mean citizens who had given up worldly business and were now excused from civil burdens and offices because of their age'.[40] This kind of person seemed most fitting for priestly duty, because they were 'distanced now from the passions, and whose words would carry more weight on account of their age and the gravity of their manners'.[41] Having moved beyond the immediate needs of politics and the ambition for personal advancement, they can serve as models for the good civic life.[42]

---

37 *DP*, I, 6.9, trans. by Brett, p. 35; ed. by Scholz, pp. 32–33: 'In hoc autem officium convenienter veniunt omnes discipline humano ingenio adinvente, [...] quibus bene disponitur homo secundum animam pro statu tam presentis seculi, quam venturi'.

38 *DP*, I, 13.2, trans. by Brett, p. 74: 'As to why it should be impossible, this is clear: because it would be for nature to be at fault or deficient as to the most part'.

39 *DP*, I, 5.13, trans. by Brett, p. 30; ed. by Scholz, p. 27: 'Nam sacerdotes instituebant non quoscumque, sed cives aliquos studiosos et approbatos, qui fuerant ex officio militari, iudicario vel consiliativo'.

40 *DP*, I, 5.13, trans. by Brett, p. 30; ed. by Scholz, pp. 27–28: 'cives inquam, qui secularia negocia abdicaverant, excusati iam a muneribus et officiis civilibus propter etatem'.

41 *DP*, I, 5.13, trans. by Brett, p. 30; ed. by Scholz, p. 28: 'separatis a passionibus, et quorum dictis propter etatem et morum gravitatem amplius credebatur'.

42 See also *DP*, II, 22.14.

This leads us back to the peculiar passage in *Dictio* I, where Marsilius appeals to Scipio, Fabricius, and Cato as role models for the apostolic life. All these men were active politicians, holding offices in Rome, but they also distinguished themselves as austere and dispassionate, which gave them a particular authority. The comparison of the Christian *perfecti* with these heroic Romans points to the similarity in their relationship to the city as a whole. While the *perfecti* practise a way of life that leads them beyond the city and makes them disinterested in it as the means to the good life in this world, they also gain a certain kind of authority from their austere way of living. Their distance from the passions is not only a Christian virtue, but also gives them a particular moral authority as models of temperance and fortitude, the true civic virtues of the Roman Republic. Like the older citizens who were chosen for the pagan priesthood due to their detachment from day-to-day involvement, they have given up on the business of the world, making them suitable for fulfilling the duties of the priestly part of the city. It is the stark contrast between their way of life and the civil quest for the good life that makes them stand out as moral examples. The heroic austerity of the *perfecti* reminds the citizens that their civic duties will require of them to sacrifice their own immediate good for the good of the city.

One might say that in this way Marsilius reintroduces an element of sacrifice and self-denial that was largely absent from his description of the political community in *Dictio* I of the *Defensor*. The promise of an afterlife both justifies a heroic sacrifice for the city and provides deterrence against a purely exploitative relationship to the city, as bad deeds will be punished in the world to come even if one might escape prosecution in this world. Seen from this purely utilitarian perspective, the veracity of a religion seems irrelevant. It can provide its this-worldly benefits just so long as it is generally believed, irrespective of whether the religious content is true or not. This is the case even for Christianity. The revealed, evangelical law, which is taught by the Christian priests, may replace the religious inventions of the philosophers, but it still fulfils the same political function. While Marsilius does profess Christianity as the true religion, because it alone truly holds its promise of a life after this world, its civic function does not hinge on this difference.[43] The Christian priesthood serves to teach morality just as the pagan priests of old did. They are not — and should not be — lawgivers or rulers, instituting a new, specifically Christian political order in this world.

This puts Christian priests not only in a subservient position regarding the city, but also in a relationship — and maybe even competition — with the philosophers who are the original lawgivers to have used religion as

---

43 Gewirth, *Marsilius of Padua*, pp. 83–84. See also Mulieri, 'Against Classical Republicanism'.

a political tool for the preservation of the law (*DP*, I, 5.11). It is indeed notable that Marsilius here at first casts the philosophers in the role of legislator, even though he later argues for the entire citizen body, the *universitas civium*, as the ultimate source of legislation (*DP*, I, 12.5). The invention of a religion as a quasi-law that can regulate those acts that 'a legislator cannot regulate by human law' seems exclusive to philosophers as lawgivers.[44] It is the only 'legislative' function that the citizen body seems incapable of fulfilling and that requires either philosophical invention or divine revelation.

This raises the question of the general relationship between the philosophers and those who practise supreme poverty as a way of life, that is, the priests and the *perfecti* in general. This question is difficult to answer, as Marsilius reveals little about his understanding of any specific way of life of a philosopher in contrast to a citizen or a priest. But it seems clear that in his view the philosophers are more aligned with the city than are the *perfecti*. The city provides the leisure necessary for philosophy: 'For those who live a civil life do not just live [...], but live well, sc. having leisure for the liberal activities that result from the virtues both of the practical and of the theoretical soul'.[45] Unlike the life of supreme poverty, the philosophical life presupposes the city. The philosophers would, therefore, be far more immediately concerned with good government and maintaining the peace than would the priesthood.[46]

The *perfecti* on the other hand remain distant to the concerns of the city. While Marsilius does provide a political role for the priests among them, the *perfecti* as a whole lack any real connection to the city. The trajectory of a life of supreme poverty remains directed towards something entirely beyond the city. Within the constraints of his specifically Christian conception of religious perfection, Marsilius cannot fully reintegrate the most fervent adherents of the Christian teaching into the city. It remains an accommodation of two ultimately disconnected ways of life.

---

44 *DP*, I, 5.11, trans. by Brett, p. 29; ed. by Scholz, p. 26: 'quos legislator humana lege regulare non potest'.

45 *DP*, I, 4.1, trans. by Brett, p. 18; ed. by Scholz, p. 16: 'Viventes civiliter non solum vivunt [...] sed bene vivunt, vacantes scilicet operibus liberalibus, qualia sunt virtutum tam practice, quam speculative anime'.

46 Torraco, *Priests as Physicians of Souls* argues for a somewhat similar position by emphasizing the political role of the Christian priests as moral 'physicians'. But Torraco conflates priests and philosophers, something that is intentionally avoided here. It seems questionable to identify both groups, considering that Marsilius clearly distinguishes between philosophers or the learned and priests (e.g. *DP*, I, 4.3, *DP*, II, 20.13). For a deeper discussion of the relationship between politics and philosophy in Marsilius, see also Mulieri, 'The Political Thinker as a Civil Physician'.

Conclusions

We have seen that the *perfecti* have a mixed status regarding the city. They are not really citizens, insofar as they do not share the basic goals of the city, that is, the perfection of the city and the prosperity that comes with it. They are, as *perfecti*, not directed towards 'living and living well' in this world. But as priests they are put into service to the city by teaching the divine law and as such fulfil a purpose that is not specific to Christianity, but is rather a necessary element of all fully developed cities.

Their motivation, though, which would lead them to want to fulfil the function of the priestly part, remains hard to grasp. They are required to teach moral virtue in the city, but their interest lies beyond the limits of the city. They are not merely distanced from their passions by age, but the passions represent a weakness that ought to be eradicated. While Marsilius can show the necessity of the priestly part in the city, he cannot provide a fully convincing argument for why the *perfecti* should engage in civic activity. Their willingness to do so thus appears to depend on a kind of supererogation, or, in worldly terms, on heroism, an imitation not only of Jesus, but also, and maybe more importantly, of the citizen-martyr Cato.

Works Cited

Primary Sources

Aristotle, *Politics*, ed. by H. Rackham, Loeb Classical Library, 264 (Cambridge, MA: Harvard University Press, 1959)

Cicero, *De re publica*, ed. by Konrat Ziegler, vol. XXXIX of *M. Tulli Ciceronis Scripta quae manserunt omnia*, Bibliotheca scriptorum Graecorum et Romanorum Teubneriana (Berlin: De Gruyter, 1969)

Macrobius, *Kommentar zum Somnium Scipionis*, ed. by Friedrich Heberlein, Bibliothek der lateinischen Literatur der Spätantike, 1 (Stuttgart: Franz Steiner Verlag, 2019)

Marsilius of Padua, *The Defender of the Peace*, trans. by Annabel Brett, Cambridge Texts in the History of Political Thought (Cambridge: Cambridge University Press, 2005)

——, *Defensor pacis*, ed. by Richard Scholz, Monumenta Germaniae Historica: Fontes iuris germanici antiqui in usum scholarum separatim editi, 7.2 (Hannover: Hahn, 1933)

Secondary Works

Bianchi, Luca, '*Nulla lex est vera, licet possit esse utilis*: Averroes' 'Errors' and the Emergence of Subversive Ideas about Religion in the Latin West', in *Irrtum-Error-Erreur*, ed. by Andreas Speer and Maxime Mauriège, Miscellanea Mediaevalia, 40 (Berlin: De Gruyter, 2018), pp. 325–48

Brett, Annabel, 'Political Right(s) and Human Freedom in Marsilius of Padua', in *Transformations in Medieval and Early-Modern Rights Discourse*, ed. by Virpi Mäkinen and Petter Korkman, The New Synthese Historical Library, 59 (Dordrecht: Springer, 2006), pp. 95–116

Gewirth, Alan, *Marsilius of Padua: The Defender of Peace*, I: *Marsilius of Padua and Medieval Political Philosophy*, Records of Civilization, Sources and Studies, 46 (New York: Columbia University Press, 1951)

Lambertini, Roberto, 'Marsilius and the Poverty Controversy in *Dictio* II', in *A Companion to Marsilius of Padua*, ed. by Gerson Moreno-Riaño and Cary J. Nederman, Brill's Companions to the Christian Tradition, 31 (Leiden: Brill, 2012), pp. 229–63

——, 'Political Prudence in Some Medieval Commentaries on the Sixth Book of the *Nicomachean Ethics*', in *Virtue Ethics in the Middle Ages: Commentaries on Aristotle's 'Nicomachean Ethics', 1200–1500*, ed. by István P. Bejczy, Brill's Studies in Intellectual History, 160 (Leiden: Brill, 2007), pp. 223–46

Mäkinen, Virpi, *Property Rights in the Late Medieval Discussion on Franciscan Property*, Recherches de théologie et philosophie medievales. Bibliotheca, 3 (Leuven: Peeters, 2001)

Mulieri, Alessandro, 'Against Classical Republicanism: The Averroist Foundations of Marsilius of Padua's Political Thought', *History of Political Thought*, 40.2 (2019), 218–45

——, 'The Political Thinker as a Civil Physician: Some Thoughts on Marsilius of Padua and Machiavelli beyond Leo Strauss' al-Fârâbî', *Early Science and Medicine*, 25 (2020), 22–45

Nederman, Cary J., *Community and Consent: The Secular Political Theory of Marsiglio of Padua's 'Defensor Pacis'* (London: Rowman & Littlefield, 1995), pp. 29–48

Quillet, Jeannine, 'L'aristotélisme de Marsile de Padoue et ses rapports avec l'averroisme', *Medioevo*, 5–6 (1979–1980), 81–142

Syros, Vasileios, 'Did the Physician from Padua Meet the Rabbi from Cordoba? Marsilius of Padua and Maimonides on the Political Utility of Religion', in *Revue des Études Juives*, 170 (2011), 51–71

——, *Die Rezeption der aristotelischen politischen Philosophie bei Marsilius von Padua: Eine Untersuchung zur ersten Diktion des 'Defensor pacis'*, Studies in Medieval and Reformation Traditions, 134 (Leiden: Brill, 2007)

Tierney, Brian, 'Marsilius on Rights', *Journal of the History of Ideas*, 52.1 (1991), 3–17

Torraco, Stephen, *Priests as Physicians of Souls in Marsilius of Padua's Defensor Pacis* (Lewiston, NY: Edwin Mellen, 1992)

Toste, Marco, 'Virtue and the City: The Virtues of the Ruler and the Citizen in the Medieval Reception of Aristotle's *Politics*', in *Princely Virtues in the Middle Ages, 1200–1500*, ed. by István P. Bejczy and Cary J. Nederman, Disputatio, 9 (Turnhout: Brepols, 2007), pp. 73–98

GIANLUCA BRIGUGLIA

Ghibelline Marsilius[*]

Remarks on Marsilius of Padua's Ghibelline Politico-Institutional Theory

1.

There is no doubt that Marsilius of Padua was politically engaged on the Ghibelline front well before he drafted the *Defensor pacis* — or at least, its final version.[1] Before delving into the details, it is important to note that we are not interested here in Marsilius of Padua's stance vis-à-vis the actual political struggle of his time. Rather, our question is that of trying to understand whether it makes sense to speak of Marsilius's Ghibellinism (or of Ghibellinism and Guelphism as a set of ideas) from the perspective of political theory — that is, not from the viewpoint of the specific political position endorsed by Marsilius, but from that of the political system he conceived — a point which is often overlooked in the literature.

My hypothesis is that, from a theoretical point of view, a Ghibelline (or Guelph) political system must present, or at least hint at, a twofold level of power: that of autonomy and self-government and that of a higher status and a set of specific functions of the empire (or papacy).

Let's proceed in a step-by-step fashion. We have already mentioned that there is no doubt concerning Marsilius's commitment to the Ghibelline alliance, at least at a certain stage of his life. We also know that Marsilius took part in the political events of 1317–1318, when Pope John XXII

---

[*] This chapter was translated into English by Serena Masolini and revised by Alessandro Mulieri.

[1] On the presence of different sections in the *Defensor pacis* that correspond to different phases of composition, cf. Collodo, 'Scienze della natura e ricerca politica'. For instance, the first part, which is structured in a more orderly way from the theoretical point of view, might have been conceived as a *Liber de pace et tranquillitate reipubblice* in Padua, after 1315 (thus, almost one decade before the final draft of the *Defensor*).

> **Gianluca Briguglia** is Professor of History of Political Thought at Ca' Foscari University of Venice. He has published extensively on medieval political philosophy.

Marsilius of Padua, ed. by Alessandro Mulieri, Serena Masolini, and Jenny Pelletier, Disputatio, 36 (Turnhout: Brepols, 2023), pp. 197–214

BREPOLS ❧ PUBLISHERS   10.1484/M.DISPUT-EB.5.132913

sent his legates, Bertrand de la Tour and Bernard Gui, to Lombardy in an attempt to break up the alliance of the Ghibelline cities and propel the imperial vicars who ruled those cities into crisis.[2] Robert of Anjou, an ally of the pope, was appointed imperial vicar of the entire Italian peninsula. According to the pope, the strategy of splitting up the alliance would have divested power from the vicars who had been nominated by Henry VII and reconfirmed or directly nominated by Ludwig of Bavaria. One should not forget, however, that in most cases the imperial vicars reflected the politics of the Italian cities themselves and of their own internal dynamics and were not blindly imposed from above by the emperor. As we shall see, the case of Matteo Visconti is telling, as he renounced the vicariate due to strong papal pressure but, nonetheless, continued to govern Milan because the system of self-government in the city and its respective institutions granted him the leadership. A strong Ghibelline league was soon established by Visconti, who had already been excommunicated, as well as by the powerful Cangrande della Scala of Verona and Frederick of Aragon, king of Sicily and an enemy of the Anjou House of Naples, both of whom were loyal allies of the pope and beneficiaries of his foreign policy. In March 1319, the ambassadors of the Ghibelline league offered command to Charles, count of La Marche and future king of France. Charles of La Marche did not accept the proposal, but evidence attests to the presence of our Marsilius of Padua among the ambassadors.

Furthermore, a letter by Albertino Mussato, which is difficult to date, mentions Marsilius's contacts with Cangrande della Scala, leader of the Ghibelline league, and Matteo Visconti — therein referred to as the 'Hound' and the 'Viper' — which would likely have distracted Marsilius from being able to concentrate on his studies at that time.[3]

Thus, there is little reason to doubt Marsilius's sympathy for the Ghibelline cause, even though many events in his biography remain unknown. Setting aside the theoretical and philosophical aspects of the *Defensor pacis*, Marsilius's remarks about Italian affairs in this work explicitly give a Ghibelline reading of political events. It suffices to consider how Marsilius traced the events relating to the excommunication of Matteo Visconti (and of his network of eight hundred Lombard supporters), and the role of Bertrand du Pouget in the military campaign against the Ghibellines.[4]

---

2 For a summary of the events and the philosophical and political conceptualization of Marsilius's Ghibellinism, see Briguglia, *Marsilio da Padova*, pp. 36–50. For an analysis of the documents, their contextualization, and the (not so easily decodable) role of Marsilius, the best starting point remains the classic study, Pincin, *Marsilio*. On Marsilius's biography, see Godthardt, *Marsilius von Padua und der Romzug Ludwigs des Bayern*. For a recent consideration on the Ghibelline positioning of Marsilius, see Piaia, 'Non solo Aristotele'.

3 Mussato, *Epistola ad magistrum Marsilium phisicum Paduanum*, p. 62.

4 See, for instance, *DP*, II, 26.17–18. One should also consider the possible references to Cangrande della Scala in the prologue of the *Defensor pacis*, regarding which Piaia, 'The

But, beyond Marsilius's actual endorsement of the Ghibelline front, are we allowed to consider the *Defensor pacis* an example of a political philosophy of Ghibellinism — that is, as a philosophical interpretation of the political events that amounts to a theory of Ghibellinism itself? In other words, we know that Marsilius was a Ghibelline, but was he also a political theorist of Ghibellinism? Is Ghibellinism (or Guelphism) a possible (additional, not exclusive) hermeneutical key to understanding his theoretical system (and that of other thinkers of the time)? To answer these questions, it is necessary to make certain distinctions and to discuss key examples.

2.

The first consideration, which is historical in nature, relates to the political practice of medieval cities. From the perspective of the actual political struggle, the divergence between Guelphs and Ghibellines was not a fixed gap that hinged on irreconcilable and static differences. Rather, it consisted in a system of networks and interests — which could be subject to rapid change and organized political positioning within the Italian cities (where there existed families of different political orientation, which were always based on interests) — as well as foreign policy. The families, parties, or cities that supported the emperor or the pope during the thirteenth and fourteenth centuries acted on the basis of well-considered choices, which were founded on a sort of *Realpolitik* and on heterogeneous antagonisms that took into account a multiplicity of factors and variants. Moreover, Guelphism and Ghibellinism were not consistent ideologies across different times, in different moments, and in different areas, and did not evoke the same political projects in the minds of their proponents.

In some historical periods, as in Marsilius's time, factions were clearly determined and clashes were resolved through armed conflict. But this should not mislead one to underestimate the historical interdependence between the Guelph and Ghibelline factions.[5] Although one should not deny the existence of consistent political traditions, belonging to one

---

Shadow of Antenor', believes that the Marsilian emphasis should be read as a result of his Antenorid origin. In this study Piaia presents a somewhat different opinion compared to the one he defended in Piaia, '"Anthenorides ego quidam"', where those same references were understood as an elevation of Marsilius's tone, so as to emphasize his own possible role in support of Emperor Ludwig of Bavaria.

5 A recent study uses the expression of 'fake enmity'; cf. Grillo, *La falsa inimicizia*. As a prime example in Marsilius's times, see Grillo's study on the temporary shift of Milan to the Guelph front and the geopolitical and trading consequences that derived from it, with the ousting of Matteo Visconti in 1302 and his return in 1310, which determined the definitive Ghibelline stance of the city; cf. Grillo, *Milano guelfa*.

faction or to another was so blurred that Pope Gregory X himself was a Ghibelline and not a Guelph, since Gregory tried to diminish Charles I of Anjou's influence, and Charles himself was a champion of the Guelph party.

In this respect, Guelphism and Ghibellinism can also be understood as driving factors of political creativity, which introduced dynamism into the institutional framework. They provided a conceptual and ideological ethos that might well have promoted a theorical discussion on the manifold layers of political action at local, regional, and international levels.

Besides these political and institutional entanglements, one should consider the social complexity and difference of status within the two groups. In the first half of the twelfth century, the labels of 'Guelphs' and 'Ghibellines' referred to political players who belonged to the knightly class, which was a minority (albeit an essential one) of multi-tiered Italian civil society. Starting from the mid-twelfth century, however, the division into factions not only concerned the nobility, but extended to many other members of the social base, including notaries, craftsmen, manufacturers, and financial investors.[6]

Belonging to one front or another did not necessarily translate into simple ideological devotion to the politics of the emperor or to that of the pope, as if the matter at stake was to support one universal power over the other. On the contrary, this framework contributed to calling into question the power of the two universal institutions, each of which sought to have a full sovereignty but did not in fact have it. During this long historical period, not only did the so-called universal powers not overshadow local powers, but they in fact strongly needed local support.

Thus, it is interesting to analyse this multiplicity of political levels and interests at play in the work of certain influential thinkers of the time who belonged either to the Guelph or to the Ghibelline front.

3.

In this regard, the case of the Florentine Brunetto Latini — an author who precedes Marsilius of Padua by two generations — is rather helpful. Recently, scholars have reconsidered the political project that Brunetto

---

6 On the distinction between Guelph and Ghibellines, see, at least, Ferente, *Gli ultimi guelfi*; Raveggi, *L'Italia dei guelfi e dei ghibellini*; Mucciarelli, *Magnati e popolani*; Bruni, *La città divisa*; Ferente, 'Guelphs! Factions, Liberty and Sovereignty'; Artifoni, 'Guelfi e ghibellini'. On the political meaning of the social organization of the Italian *comuni*, see Vigueur, *Cavalieri e cittadini*; on the pervasiveness of the 'myth of the nobility', see Castelnuovo, *Être noble dans la cité*.

proposes in the *Tresor, Tesoretto,* and in his Ciceronian translations in light of new ideas and perspectives.[7]

Following certain useful suggestions proposed by Quentin Skinner and by others before him, scholars have often approached Brunetto's works — as is also evidenced in the case of the *Defensor pacis,* although according to different historiographical perspectives — by focusing on his 'republicanism'. However, less emphasis has been placed on the specific nature of Brunetto's republicanism,[8] which was above all 'Guelph' republicanism, and turned not only to Florence but also to the Angevin reorganization of Italy as models. Indeed, Brunetto composed his works while in exile, following the defeat at Montaperti in 1260, which marked the end of the popular government of Florence. And it is not a rash statement to say that a good part of Brunetto Latini's intellectual effort was aimed first at the preparation for his return to Florence, with the hope of overthrowing the Ghibelline government that had ruled the city for those years,[9] and then at building new institutions on different bases.[10]

Brunetto Latini was aware that a new government of the so-called 'Primo Popolo', with those characteristics, was impossible at that stage. He also knew that, within the new institutions, the popular element would have to be connected to the Guelph nobility in an even more structured way (and perhaps that it would also have to include elements of the Ghibelline component on a new basis).[11] Since 1263, the Guelph front was led by Charles of Anjou, son and brother of French kings, the future king of Sicily, and duke of Provence, as well as future *podestà* of free cities, including Florence — an expression at the highest possible level not only of papal politics (at least at that time), but above all of the purest nobility and aristocracy.[12]

In short, Brunetto's vision does not simply fit within a system that can be described as solely republican (if we understand 'republicanism'

---

7 For some examples of the different trends in the literature, see Milani, 'Brunetto volgarizzatore'; Briguglia, 'Brunetto Latini'; Briguglia, '"Io, Burnetto Latini"'; Nederman, 'Commercial Society and Republican Government'; Artifoni, 'Preistorie del bene comune'; Artifoni, 'I governi di "popolo" e le istituzioni comunali'.

8 Among the few studies that focus on this point, see Nederman, 'Commercial Society and Republican Government'.

9 For more on the six years of Ghibelline rule in Florence (1260–1266), for which little documentation is available, see Faini, 'I sei anni dimenticati'.

10 Cf. Briguglia, *Il pensiero politico medievale,* esp. pp. 34–54.

11 More generally, we should perhaps recognize that various elements of chivalric culture played a role in city politics as well. In this regard, see Castelnuovo, *Être noble dans la cité;* Sposato, 'Reforming the Chivalric Elite'; Milani, 'La guerra e la giustizia'.

12 For more on the possible dedication of *Tesoretto* — composed almost certainly after the return to Florence — to Charles of Anjou, I refer to Briguglia, '"Io, Burnetto Latini"', which also includes a summary of the essential bibliography on this topic.

merely according to Skinner's perspective),[13] as this would seem a bit anachronistic. Rather, we must understand it as an overall 'hybrid' reorganization of the Italian situation.[14] This context was that of a system that was meant to be unitary, but which was also a complex network of interests, institutions, bodies, and structures of power, both economic and financial, as well as different governmental traditions. And although this system was organized into fields, factions, and alliances, and indeed for this very reason, one cannot forget that the political players always had in mind the level of city self-government, with its distinct institutions and practices. And in the same way, there was a higher system, which in Brunetto's case was broadly speaking identified with the pope, and that nonetheless was concretely led by the Angevins, which represented a second level of power that did not contradict the first.

We must not be too philosophically demanding when studying Brunetto's analysis, as he was also a pragmatic intellectual and a man of great cultural and political sensitivity. Here, it is enough to note that his work as a whole does not theorize the twofold level of institutional powers that we mentioned earlier, but he seems to take it for granted as something natural and implicit. Brunetto oriented his focus more towards the operational tools of politics, implying that his oeuvre was intended for pedagogical purposes for the leading class.[15] His work represents the building of a political culture that centres around self-government. In this sense, even here, 'Guelph', just like 'Ghibelline', did not mean taking sides uncritically and ideologically for either the pope or the emperor.

If we are not philosophically too demanding with Brunetto Latini, we should perhaps be with another author who belonged to a very different philosophical and theological background, namely, the Florentine Dominican Remigio dei Girolami, whose father was a member of the Council of Elders during the very first phase of the so-called 'Governo di Popolo'. Remigio's political thought was permeated with Aristotelianism, combined with a clear Guelph faith and a love for the Florentine Commune. For Remigio, the proper space for political sociality was precisely the *comune*:

---

13 It is almost superfluous to cite a classic book as important and influential as Skinner's *Foundations of Modern Political Thought*, which developed a particular notion of 'republicanism' and opened up historiographical but also ideological pathways of great interest. It is not possible to deepen the perimeter of this category here, nor the criticisms it has received, especially for the medieval period. For different and more fluid interpretations of medieval and humanistic 'republicanism', it is, however, useful to see, among the most recent studies, Nederman, 'Post-Republicanism and Quasi-Cosmopolitanism'; Pedullà, 'Humanist Republicanism'; Coleman, *A History of Political Thought*.

14 On the 'hybrid' system, Zorzi, 'L'Italia dell'età di Federico II a quella di Carlo d'Angiò'.

15 See the studies by Artifoni, including, for instance, 'I governi di "popolo" e le istituzioni comunali'.

the common good was the good of the commune.[16] His writings are a defence of Florentine self-government, and in the background one can see that he was aware of two existing levels of power that had to be coordinated: power at the local level and the universal power of the Church. This coordination should not be understood as the former overlapping the latter. While the Church represented a higher and thus universal institution, the pope was nevertheless not entitled to intervene on just any issue whatsoever and could not crush the self-government of the communes.[17] Indeed, the Guelph Remigio placed limits on those papal claims that he understood to be irrational, such as having a temporal or ownership power over civil institutions. In short, in Remigio's view universal powers existed and were necessary, but it was much better if the pope and the emperor remained in their respective places, without mutual interference and without trying to exercise those powers in an overly intrusive way.

In this regard, if we read these authors as we read Giles of Rome, who endorsed an uncompromising and absolute theocratic position that was papalist and hierocratic to the highest degree, we would risk not properly understanding the peculiarity of their positions and the novelty of their points of view. This new point of view was provided by, for instance, the Dominican Ptolemy of Lucca, who perhaps more than any other author absorbed the tensions of the Italian politics of his time and reconsidered them from a Guelph perspective in a philosophically relevant manner.[18] Scholars have even regarded Ptolemy of Lucca's view as an example of republicanism — although this may look strange at first glance, if we consider that Ptolemy theorized the advent of a *monarchia Christi*, which was represented by the papacy. However, the attention that Ptolemy paid to the level and role of cities is undeniable, and in particular to the historical role of Rome and of the Roman Republic.

According to Ptolemy, the Romans were so wise that, without even knowing it, they imitated the regime that human beings would have given themselves in the state of innocence. The history of the Roman Republic is filled with characters, such as Atilius Regulus, Marcus Curtius, Fabricius, Brutus, Torquatus, and many others, who were extraordinary in their virtue and abilities. This Roman excellence, however, created a kind of paradox: the extraordinary characteristics of the Roman people, that is, of the republican tradition, allowed the city to become a universal

---

16 This point has been stressed several times by Panella, the most profound expert on Remigio's thought. See, for instance, Panella, 'Per lo studio di fra Remigio de' Girolami' and Panella, *Dal bene comune.*

17 See, for instance, Remigio dei Girolami, *Contra falsos ecclesiae professores*, ed. by Tamburini.

18 For more on Ptolemy of Lucca, see at least Carron, '*Unde dominium exordium habuit*'; Carron, 'Le pouvoir politique avant et après le péché originel'; Blythe, *The Life and Works of Tolomeo Fiadoni.*

empire that would assume *dominium* over the whole world. There is no empire without a republic — one could sum up — and there is no great republican virtue without, consequently, the rise of universal imperial domination. In Ptolemy's vision, the dream of the Roman Republic, its 'political' regime, and the mission of imperial Rome are welded together and seem to reinforce each other. Moreover, Ptolemy claims, the history of the Roman Empire must be considered as part of the broader history of humanity in which different empires succeed one another until the advent of the monarchy of Christ — a notion that is at once eschatological, historical, and political — of which the Roman Church is the custodian and caretaker. The wholeness of Roman history and its actual Christian meaning are then symbolized by the figure of the pope, who represents the vicar of Christ. In short, the three 'Romes' that fought against each other during the time of Ptolemy of Lucca — the Roman Republic of the free cities, the imperial Rome of the Germanic peoples, and the Christian Rome of the pope — are reabsorbed in a multilayered vision of power and in a historical path that transfigures their original meaning.

Ptolemy of Lucca was, therefore, not simply a 'papalist' author, as Giles of Rome in the *De ecclesiastica potestate* could be, but a thinker who gave shape to a Guelph theoretical discourse: his thought combines the twofold levels of power and government that characterized Italy at the time. In this sense, one can certainly use the notion of republicanism, provided that one avoids excessive schematizations and anachronism when interpreting Ptolemy's thought. In the Roman Republic, Ptolemy identified a model for cities and communes that granted them freedom and autonomy. He also lamented the fact that there were free cities in his own time that had collapsed into tyrannies. Based on these ideas, we can consider Ptolemy to have been a republican.[19] Nonetheless, Ptolemy acknowledged the existence of a superior power, that is, that of the pope, who brings order and embodies the history of a city and of a particular *respublica*, namely, the Roman one.

Let us make one last very brief example, so as to outline a different case, namely, that of Dante's *Monarchy*. The precise political stance of the White Guelph Dante — who perhaps joined the circle of the Tuscan Ghibellines in the hopes of acquiring a prominent position in that circle after the exile — is a matter for an open and interesting discussion.[20] However, Dante's most important political treatise does not provide a

---

19 See the fluid categorization by Hankins, 'Exclusivist Republicanism and the Non-Monarchical Republic', as well as, in addition to the studies quoted in the previous note, Carron, 'Ptolemy of Lucca', and Blythe, '"Civic Humanism" and Medieval Political Thought'.

20 The debate on Dante's political positioning — considered in the light of the complex evolution of his thought — has been recently reproposed by Fenzi, *Dante ghibellino*, which collects an updated version of some previous studies. Fenzi sees in Dante a Ghibelline

specific or focused account of the experience of self-government in the cities of central and northern Italy. His political Aristotelianism — though, to avoid interpretative ambiguities, it would perhaps be better to speak of post-Aristotelianism with respect to all of these authors[21] — was complicated by his juridical thought, which provided him with a foundation for profoundly rethinking the relations between politics and the development of peoples and of humanity as a whole. Dante was specifically interested in the exclusive role of the empire and the emperor, that is, his civil and salvific function, which does not include divisions or mechanisms for power-sharing. Dante dedicated most of his focus to the 'monarchy', to the role of the people of Rome, and to the mission of the empire. In short, Dante was perhaps politically Ghibelline, but only at a certain phase of his life, yet he was not a thinker of Ghibellinism — and certainly not of Guelphism. Rather, he was an author who aligned himself with the imperial side — which, from the point of view of political theory and according to the hypothesis we proposed at the beginning of this chapter, is not exactly the same thing.[22]

4.

One final consideration — this time of an institutional nature — can help us further understand one of the theoretical points of focus in Marsilius of Padua's thought. I am here referring to the use of an office that was not new, but rather reinstated in a broad and strategic way during the political conflicts of Marsilius's times, namely, the imperial vicariate. Henry VII had already made extensive use of this function, but the office became more commonplace with Ludwig of Bavaria. The emperor would appoint an imperial vicar to a specific commune as a representative of its rights. While many cities in northern Italy were autonomous and independent, by right they were bound to the empire. And the emperors — who were 'Roman' emperors (although they almost always had a Germanic origin) — were ideologically connected to Italy, which still represented the historical seat of their empire. In Marsilius's time, which was that of Emperor Ludwig of Bavaria, the function of imperial vicar was often held by someone who had a prominent role within the city; that is, someone whom the institutions

---

'moment', especially in the drafting of the *De vulgari eloquentia* and in the *Convivio*, also in consideration of Dante's biography. Tavoni, 'L'idea imperiale nel *De vulgari eloquentia*', emphasizes instead how Dante showed an 'imperial' attitude even in earlier times.

21 For this expression, see Briguglia, *Il pensiero politico medievale*, pp. 91–96.

22 In this sense, Dante is ideologically more similar to imperial authors such as Engelbert of Admont (author of the *De ortu, progressu et fine Romani imperii*) or Leopold of Bebenburg (author of the *De juribus regni et imperii Romanorum*), despite the differences in their settings and the outcomes of their positions.

of the city's self-government had already elevated to the rank of city elite. In this way, the vicar had often (albeit not always) a double legitimacy: a legitimacy from above, because the investiture came from the empire, and one from below, because the specific person had already been chosen by the local institutions.

Therefore, the vicar was not exclusively an imperial agent, even though he could assert his imperial investiture against local powers. He was also not an exclusive representative of the local political parties who had appointed him, even if he could occasionally enforce the city's choices against the emperor. This double investiture created an unstable equilibrium, which allowed for the preservation of the prerogatives of the communes as well as the advantages brought about by the emperor (primarily of an economic kind, because the office was bought at a high price). Furthermore, the two levels of power were united in a single person or, better, in the block of powers and interests which that person (and his group) represented.

In turn, whoever was appointed to the office of vicar held the enormous advantage of possessing a juridical authority that substantially changed his stature and role in city institutions and in the city's mechanisms of control. These years — not only for the office of the imperial vicar, but also in a broader sense for a series of other juridical and social transformations — have been defined as the period in which the *signorie di popolo* were built.[23]

This, however, is a paradox only if we see it through a contemporary lens, or if we follow the historiographic trend of drawing a sharp distinction between *comune* and *signoria*.[24] There was certainly a considerable development of *signorie* in Italy during Marsilius's times, but these processes were not as evident to the eyes of the protagonists, nor were they understood as instantaneous, irreversible, or univocal. In the age of Marsilius, this dialectic remained rather ambivalent and open. It did not necessarily appear as an irremediable gap between city liberties and government of the *signori*, but rather as determining a multiplicity of governmental options.

In this sense, the abovementioned case of Matteo Visconti is quite telling and interesting. Visconti assumed the title of imperial vicar of Milan when he was appointed by Henry VII in 1311. The office could not be passed on to his heirs, and in order to obtain it, he paid fifty thousand gold florins to the emperor. Visconti also had to pay twenty-five thousand

---

23 See Rao, *Signori di popolo*.

24 For more on the rise of the *signorie*, see Vallerani, ed., *Tecniche di potere nel tardo medioevo*; Zorzi, ed., *Tiranni e tirannide*; and Zorzi, *Le signorie cittadine in Italia*. For literature on the relationship between *comune* and *signoria*, the stakes involved, and for a more articulated reading of the long historiographical debate on this topic, see Vallerani, '"La democrazia che ha per ventre la tirannia"'.

gold florins a year, in four instalments, by way of tax collection in the city. The emperor could have dismissed him at will, but in that case, he would have had to return the money. In 1313, however, Visconti asked the institutions of the city to confer upon him the title of *dominus generalis*. Being forced by papal pressure to step down from his position as vicar in 1317, he was confirmed as the ruler of Milan by the city itself. Over time, Matteo Visconti reconfigured certain institutional arrangements by placing them more under the jurisdiction of a *signoria*, excluding the 'people' from the city council, and therefore weakening certain interests of the city corporations as well as reducing the members of the council. With this, he opened the door to a new political era.

In short, the political struggles of Marsilius's time were the product of ongoing transformations, but they cannot be understood as a simple clash between two great hegemonic designs — that is, that of the papacy and that of the empire — for the two great universal powers were not the only protagonists at work.

5.

What implications can we draw from these premises and reflections on Marsilius of Padua's political, philosophical, and institutional project? Marsilius was the political philosopher who, more than any other, understood the political struggles as well as the profound and ambiguous institutional transformations of his day and managed to reflect all of them in a Ghibelline political theory. If one reads the *Defensor pacis* in light of the twofold levels of power that characterized Italian politics of the fourteenth century — in a long trend that began in the previous century with different phases and characteristics depending on the historical and geographical context but that took shape in a new way during the years of Marsilius — this work can be understood as a theoretical and militant interpretation of a possible Ghibelline order in Italy, with all the analytical premises and the conceptual consequences that this entails.

According to this perspective, the gap between 'republican' interpretations and imperial interpretations should be revised and reinterpreted in a way that is more respectful of the historical and conceptual context. Likewise, this perspective prevents one from upholding an 'absolutist' understanding of the *signorie* — which in those years had not yet acquired a complete form — and offers an image of this form of government that is more flexible and avoids teleological readings or a posteriori considerations. We must then remark upon the multiplicity and plurality of levels of power that structured the Italian political experience in those decades and that Marsilius transformed into a complete political theory.

Anyone who has read the *Defensor pacis* knows that in the first *dictio* Marsilius clearly illustrates the level of self-government, with its rules, the functioning of its councils, its legislative power, and the role of the people — that is, of the actual people in the cities. In identifying this fundamental and incoercible level of self-government, a Ghibelline and a Guelph would tend to agree. Marsilius of Padua based this first level of participation and institutional construction on a complex political anthropology, which is in large part Aristotelian (however permeated with Augustinian, Ciceronian, and Christian themes, as well as political practice) and allowed him to understand the many tensions of social life philosophically.

In the second *dictio*, Marsilius instead bends his theory to a broader vision, in which the uncovering of papal ideology and its claims to power is also central. This unmasking then allows him to build a new ecclesiology, which he understands as a return to the origins of the Christian community and which, in turn, involves reshaping all powers.

This is where the second aspect of the specifically Ghibelline dimension of Marsilius's political thought appears. It is here that he establishes the power of the empire as a last resort, and likewise radically reshapes and in some respects even erases any possible papal influence. What is perhaps rather surprising in Marsilius's work is the transparency with which the role of the emperor absorbs certain functions of the Christian *ecclesia* — for example, the power of summoning the general council — and how this radically redefines politics and religion.

However, this does not eliminate the importance of the experience of the communes — that is, the role of citizens in public life — and in some respects, even raises the issue of consent (which, of course, does not at all coincide with the modern idea of democracy). These two levels are not incompatible, as it is not impossible to reconcile the consent and will of the citizens with the assumption of political responsibility and lordship of some individuals or families. According to Marsilius, this vision was instead incompatible with Roman ecclesiology, which nourished the Guelph project and which for him consisted simply of a papist ideology.

In this sense, Marsilius was neither simply a republican author nor a simple imperial author, but above all a political philosopher of Ghibellinism — which, as should now be clear, includes both an imperial and a 'republican' level. This image of a strictly 'medieval' Marsilius of Padua may be disappointing. Nonetheless, this is an understanding of the figure of Marsilius that opens up intellectual pathways that lead to some foundational aspects of modernity, albeit in a rather non-linear way.

Another question — which is of great interest, but with which we will not deal here — is that of how this worldview, that is, that of the Ghibellines and the Guelphs, which is so very different from ours and which produced specifically medieval political thought, and a political horizon which is not our own, has given rise to treatises full of ideas (not only those of Marsilius, but also those of Ptolemy, Brunetto, Dante, and many others) that have profoundly influenced the modern period. Nor should we forget that that world — let's venture to call it that philosophico-political *episteme* — is in turn also the active result of stratifications from various eras, of re-actualizations of previous theories, or of systems, or of shreds of readapted arguments, that interact with new needs, new problems, and new ideas. And, it is that world that creates — as a further stratification that also loses itself — the substratum on which modernity will be built. But once modernity arose (assuming that we can speak of a single modernity), we became in danger of forgetting the entire historical world that produced it or helped it to emerge, leaving it up to historians to partially reconstruct it.

Works Cited

Primary Sources

Brunetto Latini, *Tresor*, ed. by Pietro G. Beltrami (Turin: Einaudi, 2007)

——, *Tesoretto*, in Brunetto Latini, *Poesie*, ed. by Stefano Carrai (Turin, Einaudi, 2016), pp. 3–155

Dante Alighieri, *Monarchia*, ed. by Prue Shaw, Le Opere di Dante Alighieri, 5 (Florence: Le Lettere, 2009)

Giles of Rome, *De ecclesiastica potestate*, in *Giles of Rome's On Ecclesiastical Power: A Medieval Theory of World Government*, ed. by Robert W. Dyson (New York: Columbia University Press, 2004)

Marsilius of Padua, *Defensor pacis*, ed. by Richard Scholz, Monumenta Germaniae Historica: Fontes iuris germanici antiqui in usum scholarum separatim editi, 7.2 (Hannover: Hahn, 1933)

Mussato, Albertino, *Epistola ad magistrum Marsilium phisicum Paduanum*, in Jürgen Miethke, 'Die Briefgedichte des Albertino Mussato an Marsilius von Padua', *Pensiero politico medievale*, 6 (2008), 49–65 (pp. 62–64)

Ptolemy of Lucca, *De regimine principum*, in Thomas Aquinas, *Opuscula Omnia necnon Opera Minora*, I: *Opuscula Philosophica*, ed. by Joannes Perrier (Paris: P. Lethielleux, 1949), pp. 221–445

Remigio dei Girolami, *Contra falsos ecclesiae professores*, ed. by Filippo Tamburini, Utrumque ius, 6 (Rome: Libreria Editrice della Pontificia Università Lateranense, 1981)

——, *De bono comuni*, in Remigio dei Girolami, *Dal bene comune al bene del comune: I trattati politici*, ed. by Emilio Panella, with an introduction by Francesco Bruni (Florence: Nerbini, 2014), pp. 146–221

——, *De bono pacis*, in Remigio dei Girolami, *Dal bene comune al bene del comune: I trattati politici*, ed. by Emilio Panella, with an introduction by Francesco Bruni (Florence: Nerbini, 2014), pp. 222–47

Secondary Works

Artifoni, Enrico, 'I governi di "popolo" e le istituzioni comunali nella seconda metà del secolo XIII', *Reti Medievali*, 4 (2003), < [last accessed 12 June 2022]10.6092/1593-2214/283>

——, 'Guelfi e ghibellini', in *Enciclopedia del medioevo* (Milan: Garzanti, 2007), pp. 833–35

——, 'Preistorie del bene comune: Tre prospettive sulla cultura retorica e didattica del Duecento', in *Il bene comune: Forme di governo e gerarchie sociali nel basso medioevo*, Convegni, 48 (Spoleto: Fondazione Centro italiano di studi sull'alto Medioevo, 2012), pp. 63–87

Blythe, James M., '"Civic Humanism" and Medieval Political Thought', in *Renaissance Civic Humanism: Reappraisals and Reflections*, ed. James Hankins, Ideas in Context, 57 (Cambridge: Cambridge University Press, 2000), pp. 30–74

——, *The Life and Works of Tolomeo Fiadoni (Ptolemy of Lucca)*, Disputatio, 16 (Turnhout: Brepols, 2009)

Briguglia, Gianluca, 'Brunetto Latini: Italian (Political) Theory?', *Rivista di filosofia Neo-Scolastica*, 1 (suppl.) (2021), 41–56

——, '"Io, Burnetto Latini": Considerazioni su cultura e identità politica di Brunetto Latini e il *Tesoretto*', *Philosophical Readings*, 10 (2018), 176–85

——, *Marsilio da Padova*, Pensatori, 31 (Rome: Carocci, 2013)

——, *Il pensiero politico medievale*, Piccola biblioteca Einaudi: Mappe, 68 (Turin: Einaudi, 2018), pp. 91–96

Bruni, Francesco, *La città divisa: Le parti e il bene comune da Dante a Guicciardini* (Bologna: Il mulino, 2003)

Carron, Delphine, 'Le pouvoir politique avant et après le péché originel chez Ptolémée de Lucques († 1327)', in *Adam, la nature humaine, avant et après: Épistémologie de la chute*, ed. by Gianluca Briguglia and Irène Rosier-Catach, Panthéon Sorbonne, 39 (Paris: Publications de la Sorbonne, 2016), pp. 231–53

——, 'Ptolemy of Lucca: One of the First Medieval Theorists of Republicanism? Some Observations on the Relevance of Associating a Medieval Thinker with the Republican Tradition', *Quaestiones Medii Aevi Novae*, 20 (2015), 65–92

——, '*Unde dominium exordium habuit*: Origine et légitimation du pouvoir politique chez Ptolémée de Lucques', in *Legitimation of Political Power in Medieval Thought*, ed. by Celia López Alcalde, Josep Puig Montada, and Pedro Roche Arnas, Rencontres de philosophie médiévale, 17 (Turnhout: Brepols, 2018), pp. 101–18

Castelnuovo, Guido, *Être noble dans la cité: Les noblesses italiennes en quête d'identité (XIIIᵉ–XVᵉ siècle)*, Bibliothèque d'Histoire Médiévale, 12 (Paris: Classiques Garnier, 2014)

Coleman, Janet, *A History of Political Thought*, II: *From the Middle Ages to the Renaissance* (Oxford: Oxford University Press, 2000)

Collodo, Silvana, 'Scienze della natura e ricerca politica: La civitas terrena nel *Defensor pacis* di Marsilio da Padova', in *Filosofia naturale e scienze dell'esperienza fra medioevo e umanesimo: Studi su Marsilio da Padova, Leon Battista Alberti, Michele Savonarola*, ed. by Silvana Collodo and Remy Simonetti, Contributi alla storia dell'Università di Padova, 47 (Treviso: Antilia, 2012), pp. 15–240

Faini, Enrico, 'I sei anni dimenticati: Spunti per una riconsiderazione del governo ghibellino di Firenze, 1260–1266', in *Tra storia e letteratura: Il parlamento di Empoli del 1260. Atti della giornata di studio in occasione del 750° anniversario*, ed. by Vanna Arrighi and Giuliano Pinto, Biblioteca storica toscana, 67 (Florence: Olschki, 2012), pp. 29–49

Fenzi, Enrico, *Dante ghibellino* (Napoli: La scuola di Pitagora editrice, 2019)

Ferente, Serena, 'Guelphs! Factions, Liberty and Sovereignty: Inquiries about the Quattrocento', *History of Political Thought*, 28.4 (2007), 571–98

——, *Gli ultimi guelfi: Linguaggi e identità politiche in Italia nella seconda metà del Quattrocento*, La storia: Temi, 33 (Rome: Viella, 2013)

Godthardt, Frank, *Marsilius von Padua und der Romzug Ludwigs des Bayern: Politische Theorie und politisches Handeln*, Nova Mediaevalia: Quellen und Studien zum europäischen Mittelalter, 6 (Göttingen: V&R Unipress, 2017)

Grillo, Paolo, *La falsa inimicizia: Guelfi e ghibellini nell'Italia del Duecento*, Aculei, 34 (Rome: Salerno, 2018)

——, *Milano guelfa (1302–1310)*, Italia comunale e signorile, 2 (Rome: Viella, 2013)

Hankins, James, 'Exclusivist Republicanism and the Non-Monarchical Republic', *Political Theory*, 38.4 (2010), 452–82

Milani, Giuliano, 'Brunetto volgarizzatore: Il maestro e i Fiorentini in alcuni studi recenti', in *Toscana bilingue (1260 ca.–1430 ca.): Per una storia sociale del tradurre medievale*, ed. by Sara Bischetti, Michele Lodone, Cristiano Lorenzi, and Antonio Montefusco (Berlin: de Gruyter, 2021), pp. 125–49

——, 'La guerra e la giustizia: Brunetto Latini e l'esclusione politica', *Arzanà*, 16–17 (2013), 37–51

Mucciarelli, Roberta, *Magnati e popolani: Un conflitto nell'Italia dei Comuni (secoli XIII–XIV)*, ([Milan]: Bruno Mondadori, 2009)

Nederman, Cary J., 'Commercial Society and Republican Government in the Latin Middle Ages: The Economic Dimensions of Brunetto Latini's Republicanism', *Political Theory*, 31.5 (2003), 644–63

——, 'Post-Republicanism and Quasi-Cosmopolitanism in Marsiglio of Padua's *Defensor pacis*', in *Al di là del Repubblicanesimo: Modernità politica e origini dello Stato*, ed. by Guido Cappelli, with the assistance of Giovanni De Vita, Quaderni della ricerca, 5 (Naples: UniorPress, 2020), pp. 131–46

Panella, Emilio, *Dal bene comune al bene del comune: I trattati politici* (Florence: Nerbini, 2014)

——, 'Per lo studio di fra Remigio de' Girolami († 1319)', *Memorie Domenicane*, 10 (1979), 1–313

Pedullà, Gabriele, 'Humanist Republicanism: Towards a New Paradigm', *History of Political Thought*, 41.1 (2020), 43–95

Piaia, Gregorio, '"Anthenorides ego quidam": Chiose al prologo del *Defensor pacis*', in Gregorio Piaia, *Marsilio e dintorni: Contributi alla storia delle idee*, Miscellanea erudita, 61 (Padua: Antenore, 1999), pp. 37–53

——, 'Non solo Aristotele: La legittimazione del potere politico in Marsilio da Padova', in *Legitimation of Political Power in Medieval Thought*, ed. by Celia López Alcalde, Josep Puig Montada, and Pedro Roche Arnas, Rencontres de philosophie médiévale, 17 (Turnhout: Brepols, 2018), pp. 281–94

——, 'The Shadow of Antenor: On the Relationship between the *Defensor pacis* and the Institutions of the City of Padua', in *Politische Reflexion in der Welt des späten Mittelalters / Political Thought in the Age of Scholasticism: Essays in Honour of Jürgen Miethke*, ed. by Martin Kaufhold, Studies in Medieval and Reformation Traditions, 103 (Leiden: Brill, 2004), pp. 193–207

Pincin, Carlo, *Marsilio*, Pubblicazioni dell'Istituto di scienze politiche dell'Università di Torino, 17 (Turin: Giappichelli, 1967)

Rao, Riccardo, *Signori di popolo: Signoria cittadina e società comunale nell'Italia nord-occidentale 1275–1350*, Storia, 412 (Milan: Franco Angeli, 2011)

Raveggi, Sergio, *L'Italia dei guelfi e dei ghibellini* (Milan: Bruno Mondadori, 2009)

Skinner, Quentin, *The Foundations of Modern Political Thought*, 2 vols (Cambridge: Cambridge University Press, 1978)

Sposato, Peter W., 'Reforming the Chivalric Elite in Thirteenth-Century Florence: The Evidence of Brunetto Latini's *Il Tesoretto*', Viator, 46 (2015), 203–27

Tavoni, Mirko, 'L'idea imperiale nel *De vulgari eloquentia*', in *Enrico II e Pisa a 700 anni dalla morte dell'imperatore e dalla Monarchia (1313–2013)*, ed. by Giuseppe Petralia and Marco Santagata (Ravenna: Longo, 2016), pp. 203–11

Vallerani, Massimo, '"La democrazia che ha per ventre la tirannia": Il comune e la democrazia nella storiografia tra Ottocento e Novecento', *Storia del pensiero politico*, 8.3 (2019), 367–92

——, ed., *Tecniche di potere nel tardo medioevo: Regimi comunali e signorie in Italia* (Rome: Viella, 2010)

Vigueur, Jean-Claude, *Cavalieri e cittadini: Guerra, conflitti e società nell'Italia comunale* (Bologna: Il mulino, [2004])

Zorzi, Andrea, 'L'Italia dell'età di Federico II a quella di Carlo d'Angiò: Qualche appunto', in *Tra storia e letteratura: Il parlamento di Empoli del 1260. Atti della giornata di studio in occasione del 750° anniversario*, ed. by Vanna Arrighi and Giuliano Pinto, Biblioteca storica toscana, 67 (Florence: Olschki, 2012), pp. 9–27

——, *Le signorie cittadine in Italia (secoli XIII–XV)* (Milan: Bruno Mondadori, 2010)

——, ed., *Tiranni e tirannide nel Trecento italiano* (Rome: Viella, 2013)

CHARLES F. BRIGGS

Defenders of the Peace[*]

The Political Thought of Marsilius's Italian Dominican Contemporaries

In his dedication of the *Defensor pacis* to Emperor Ludwig IV, Marsilius credits this 'minister of God' with 'the desire to extirpate heresies, to support and safeguard the catholic truth and every other discipline of study, to excise vice and further the study of the virtues, to put an end to quarrels and to spread and nourish peace and tranquillity everywhere'.[1] However accurately, or not, these words may have reflected Ludwig's actual intentions, it is striking how closely they accord with the job description of Marsilius's contemporaries in the Dominican order. Although there is no reason to assume that Marsilius was taking aim at the Order of Preachers in this particular passage, elsewhere in the *Defensor pacis* he expresses his disapproval of the popes for having exempted the mendicant orders from episcopal jurisdiction. He goes on to target the Dominicans more pointedly, when he accuses his chief historical source for *Dictio* II, Martinus Polonus, O.P., of 'justifying as best he can the said usurpations of the Roman pontiffs and obfuscating the rights of princes and the human legislator', and warns against trusting 'Martin on this matter [of whether or not the emperor has the power to choose a pope], since he together with his order was a participant in this usurpation'.[2] For its part, the Order of Preachers was hardly likely to be anything but officially hostile towards Marsilius's condemnations of papal *plenitudo potestatis* and clerical

---

[*] Thanks to George Dameron, Cary Nederman, Patrick Nold, and the participants of the Dartmouth medieval seminar for helpful suggestions, and to Walter Simons for making available useful pre-publication material. Special thanks to Roberto Lambertini for encouraging me to pursue this project.

1 *DP*, I, 1.6, trans. by Brett, p. 8.

2 *DP*, II, 24.13 and II, 25.8, trans. by Brett, pp. 426, 438.

> **Charles F. Briggs** is a senior lecturer in the Department of History at the University of Vermont. He is a specialist in late medieval political thought and particularly in the work of Giles of Rome.

Marsilius of Padua, ed. by Alessandro Mulieri, Serena Masolini, and Jenny Pelletier, Disputatio, 36 (Turnhout: Brepols, 2023), pp. 215–252

privilege, as well as his political opposition to John XXII, given that pope's friendly relations with the order and support for the canonization of Thomas Aquinas in 1323, the year preceding Marsilius's completion of his magnum opus.[3]

When indeed members of the order went on record with what they thought of Marsilius's chief political claim that 'within the confines of the Holy Roman Empire' the '*pars principans* or *principatus* of each province had to be subordinate to the single *pars principans* of the faithful human legislator, the emperor', they, with the notable exception of the pro-Capetian John of Paris, unfailingly contested it.[4] This position had already been adumbrated in the first decade of the fourteenth century by the strong support of Ptolemy of Lucca (Tolomeo Fiadoni da Lucca) for papal universal sovereignty in *Determinatio compendiosa de iurisdictione imperii* (*c.* 1277–1281/*c.* 1300) and Book III of his *De regimine principum*, and Remigio de' Girolami's less direct suggestion of the same in *De bono comuni*.[5] Writing in 1316/1317 in response to the dogmatically pro-papal position of his fellow friar Giovanni Regina da Napoli, the Paris Dominican Pierre de la Palud provided further ammunition to John of Paris's challenge to papal temporal sovereignty over France while at the same time confirming that same sovereignty over the empire.[6] At Avignon *c.* 1325, a Dominican chaplain to Cardinal Luca Fieschi, Dondino da Pavia, dedicated to John XXII a 'Dialogue on the Power of the Supreme Pontiff.'[7] And, in the aftermath of the publication of Dante's *Monarchia* and Marsilius's treatise, both Guido Vernani da Rimini, in his treatises *De potestate summi pontificis* (1327) and *De reprobatione Monarchiae compositae a Dante* (*c.* 1329), and Galvano Fiamma da Milano, in a disputed question 'Utrum papa Romanus sit dominus in temporalibus et spiritualibus in toto orbe

---

3 On the latter, see Vauchez, *Sainthood in the Later Middle Ages*, pp. 74–75, and Gerulaitis, 'The Canonization of Saint Thomas Aquinas', pp. 37, 40–42.

4 For this summation of Marsilius's political programme, see Garnett, *Marsilius of Padua and 'the Truth of History'*, pp. 163–64. Although in *De potestate regia et papali* John of Paris denied any temporal jurisdiction to the pope, he also, in Chapter 21, takes care to strictly limit and even question the jurisdiction of the emperors: John of Paris, *On Royal and Papal Power*, trans. by Watt, pp. 220–28.

5 Ptolemy of Lucca, *De regimine principum*, III, x and III, xvi–xix, trans. by Blythe, pp. 173–77, 193–204; Yun, 'Ptolemy of Lucca'. For the dating of *Determinatio compendiosa*, see Blythe, 'Aristotle's *Politics* and Ptolemy of Lucca', pp. 106–07. Remigio de' Girolami, *De bono comuni*, ed. by Panella, p. 124: 'Quanto bonum est comunius tanto est magis amandum, scilicet bonum civitatis magis quam bonum unius civis et bonum provincie que multas continet civitates magis quam bonum unius civitatis. Unde et per consequens bonum regni magis amandum est quam bonum unius provincie et bonum universalis ecclesie magis quam bonum unius regni'.

6 Dunbabin, 'Hervé de Nédellec, Pierre de la Palud'.

7 Nold, 'John XXII and History', pp. 18–24; Kaeppeli, *Scriptores Ordinis Praedicatorum*, I, p. 337.

terrarum' (Whether the Roman pope should have universal lordship in temporal and spiritual things, *c.* 1338), sought to demolish arguments made in defence of the pro-imperialist position, including those of Dante and Marsilius.[8]

Despite being on opposing sides of the question of papal vs. imperial sovereignty, however, Marsilius and his Italian Dominican adversaries shared much in common. They were inhabitants and products of the same intellectual/textual, socio-economic, and political environment: the cities of Italy's centre-north of the late thirteenth and early fourteenth centuries and Europe's *studia generalia*.[9] They also were responding to the same social and political problems. Both Marsilius and the Dominicans discussed in this chapter deplored the factional, violent politics that plagued their cities. They also were in agreement that 'the greatest of all human goods, viz. the sufficiency of this life' could not be achieved 'without peace and tranquillity'.[10] Where they differed was in their conceptualizations of the root source of the problem and in their prescriptions for the problem's solution. Marsilius's answer was undoubtedly more original and, at least to our modern sensibilities, more compelling. Yet the political thought and political solutions discussed in this chapter represent a point of view that likely was more widely shared and carried greater weight among not only the prelates of the Church against whom Marsilius railed but also the lay elites of the cities that the Paduan hoped to free from the destructive interference of those same prelates.

During the five decades that coincided with Marsilius's adult life, several of his fellow Italians in the Order of Preachers wrote works of political counsel for their lay compatriots in order to remedy and improve civic life in the peninsula. These include five authors of works that more or less conform to the genre of 'mirrors of princes', as well as a number of writers of an assortment of treatises, manuals, chronicles, and sermons bearing on political rule and civil peace. The mirrors' authors were Jacopo da Cessole (*Libellus de moribus super ludo scaccorum, c.* 1300); Ptolemy of Lucca, who, *c.* 1303, 'completed' his confrère Thomas Aquinas's *De regno* (*c.* 1271–1273) under the title *De regimine principum*; Enrico da Rimini (*De quattuor virtutibus cardinalibus ad cives Venetos*, 1300–1310); Guido Vernani da Rimini, who wrote his *Liber de virtutibus quae ad vitam verae militiae requiruntur* (*c.* 1324–*c.* 1334) for the Malatesta lords of Rimini (almost certainly the brothers Galeotto and Malatesta III Malatesta, nicknamed 'Guastafamiglia'); and, lastly, the Florentine Luca Mannelli, who in early

---

8 Matteini, *Il più antico oppositore politico di Dante*; Creytens, 'Une question disputée de Galvano Fiamma'.

9 On this, see Piron and Coccia, 'Poésie, sciences et politique', and the chapters in Bartuschat, Brilli, and Carron, eds, *The Dominicans and the Making of Florentine Cultural Identity*.

10 *DP*, I, 1.1, trans. by Brett, p. 3.

1344 or shortly before dedicated his *Compendium moralis philosophie* to the bibliophile and poet Bruzio Visconti, bastard son of Luchino Visconti of Milan.

Among the Dominican authors of other works with political content, the best known to modern-day scholars is Remigio de' Girolami of Florence, who in addition to his treatises *De iustitia* (unfinished, *c.* 1295), *De bono comuni* (1301–1302), and *De bono pacis* (1304), delivered several sermons on such themes as civil peace and the qualities of a good ruler.[11] While Remigio was penning his treatises on the common good and peace, another friar at his convent of Santa Maria Novella, Bartolomeo da San Concordio, prepared the *Documenta antiquorum*, a compilation of moral precepts and political advice drawn mostly from biblical wisdom literature, the Fathers of the Church, Aristotle, and Roman classical authors. Bartolomeo almost immediately translated this work into the Tuscan dialect (under the title *Ammaestramenti degli antichi* (Instructions of the Ancients)) perhaps for presentation to the banker and leading Black Guelf Geri Spini.[12] In 1346, Luca Mannelli reflected on political questions in a sermon he delivered at the papal Curia of Clement VI on the subject of princely rule (Inc. 'Factus est principatus super humerum eius etc., Ysaie IX° capitulo' (Isaiah 9. 6)).[13] Whereas Luca holds up Christ as the model of perfect princely rule, several of his contemporaries composed sermons praising the virtues of recently deceased earthly rulers. Thus, Remigio de' Girolami wrote memorial sermons for the Capetian kings Philip IV and his son Louis X, and between them the Neapolitan friars Federico Franconi and Giovanni Regina engaged in a veritable cottage industry of eulogizing defunct Angevin princes, including Kings Charles II and Robert, as well as John of Durazzo and Philip of Taranto. Back in Tuscany, Giovanni da San Gimignano prepared a collection of model sermons memorializing temporal rulers.[14] In Milan, Galvano Fiamma heaped praise on the virtuous characters and deeds of his Visconti patrons, not in sermons but rather

---

11 Remigio de' Girolami, *Tractatus de iustitia*, ed. by Capitani, pp. 125–28; *Tractatus de bono comuni*, ed. by Panella, pp. 123–68; *Tractatus de bono pacis*, ed. by Panella, pp. 169–83; *Sermones de pace*, ed. by Panella, pp. 187–98; *Sermo de domino Carolo*, ed. by Panella, pp. 41–42.

12 Segre, 'Bartolomeo da San Concordio'. Bartolomeo also translated Sallust's *Jugurthan War* and *Catiline's Conspiracy* into Italian, wrote commentaries on Vergil and the tragedies of Seneca, and compiled the vast *Summa de casibus conscientiae*. On the problematic ascription of Bartolomeo's dedication of the *Ammaestramenti*, see Conte, 'Gli "Ammaestramenti degli antichi"', pp. 183–86.

13 Beattie, 'The Sermon as *Speculum Principi*'.

14 D'Avray, *Death and the Prince*.

in his chronicle *De rebus gestis ab Azone, Luchino et Johanne Vicecomitibus* (early 1340s).[15]

It strikes us as significant that so many works doling out political advice or treating political themes can be ascribed to members of the Order of Preachers in Italy during this period of just over four decades. Why might this be? No doubt this profusion of texts can be set in the more general context of the mendicant preoccupation with composing mirrors of princes, beginning with a cluster of works directed at King Louis IX and other members of the Capetian family in the decades just after 1250, and then being taken up with alacrity by several Franciscans connected to the Iberian monarchies.[16] Likewise, as Jean-Philippe Genet has indicated, it was the Dominicans Vincent of Beauvais, Guillaume Peyraut, and Thomas Aquinas who played an especially important role in establishing what he calls the '*tractatus* didactico-moral' format of the kind of mirror of princes that held sway in the later Middle Ages.[17] So part of the answer to this question is that our Dominicans were just doing what mendicants did, and that Dominicans had taken a precocious leading role in developing the mirrors of princes genre. But this does not really explain why Thomas Aquinas was the sole Italian Dominican writing political advice prior to *c.* 1300, or why after the mid-1340s their impressive output of political writing stops.[18] Nor does it account for the lack of writings of this kind from the other mendicant orders in Italy during the same period when the Dominicans were so active. During the first decades of the fourteenth century the Augustinians Giles of Rome, Giacomo da Viterbo, and Agostino d'Ancona made signal contributions to the theory of papal sovereignty, but when it came to other kinds of writing of a political nature members of the order seem to have been content to compile abridged versions

---

15 Boucheron, 'Paroles de paix et seigneurs de guerre' and Boucheron, 'Tout est monument'; Green, 'Galvano Fiamma, Azzone Visconti'.

16 The mirrors destined for members of the Capetian dynasty were Vincent of Beauvais, O.P., *De eruditione filiorum nobilium* (1250/1254–1260) and *De morali principis institutione* (1263); Guibert de Tournai, O.F.M., *Eruditio regum et principum* (1259); Giles of Rome, O.E.S.A., *De regimine principum* (*c.* 1279); Durand de Champagne, O.F.M., *De informatione principum* (1297–1305) and *Speculum dominarum* (*c.* 1300). In Lyon *c.* 1265, Guillaume Peyraut, O.P. wrote *De eruditione principum*, which he addressed to 'some prince'. The Iberian mirrors were Juan Gil de Zamora, O.F.M., *De preconiis Hispanie* (1279/1280 for Prince Sancho [IV] of Castile); the Franciscan mirror, perhaps by Juan García de Castrojeriz, *Glosa Castellana al Regimiento de Principes* (1340s, for Prince Pedro [I] of Castile); Álvaro Pelayo, O.F.M., *Speculum regum* (1344, for Alfonso XI of Castile); Pere of Aragon, O.F.M., *Tractatus de vita, moribus et regimine principum* (*c.* 1355, for Pere IV of Aragon); Francesc Eiximenis, O.F.M. (1383, for the city council of Valencia). For more on this, see Briggs and Nederman, 'Western Medieval *Specula, c.* 1150–*c.* 1450'.

17 Genet, 'L'évolution du genre des Miroirs des princes', p. 537.

18 The answer to the question of why this output stops in the mid-fourteenth century will not be attempted here, but I intend to do so in a future study.

of Giles's *De regimine principum*.[19] Like their counterparts in the other mendicant orders, the Franciscans Guglielmo da Sarzano and Andrea da Perugia threw themselves into the polemical battle over papal and imperial power, lending their pens to the cause of Robert of Naples and John XXII against the threats posed by Emperors Henry VII and Ludwig IV along with, in the case of Ludwig, the polemical supporters of the imperial cause Marsilius and William of Ockham.[20] But when it came to works of political advice or instruction, the sole Minorite contributor of the first half of the fourteenth century is Paolino da Venezia, who *c.* 1315 compiled a brief adaptation of Giles's *De regimine principum* destined for the Venetian duke of Crete (probably Marino Badoer).[21]

It will be argued here that this efflorescence of Dominican political writing in Italy during the first half of the Trecento was the product of a complex dialectic between the Dominicans' distinctive pastoral mission and educational programme on the one hand and, on the other, the divisive, conflictual, and highly fluid social and political conditions that members of the order confronted in the *Italia comunale* of the late thirteenth and early fourteenth centuries. Dedicated to a mission of preaching correct doctrine and good morals and encouraging the same through the confessor's art, they developed a programme of education designed to hone their rhetorical skills while teaching them to be prudent judges of the differentiated circumstances and impacts of sinful actions as well as persuasive purveyors of moral remedies for sinful impulses. A key curricular component of this education was a moral philosophy that was largely Aristotelian in form and content but inflected through the writings of the order's doctor Thomas Aquinas. Witnesses to the factional discord and turbulent, contested politics of communal life and intercommunal relations, and themselves products of those same communes, born to and raised in citizen families, the Dominicans of the early Trecento saw the fate of their order, of their cities, and of the Church as being inextricably intertwined; they also believed they had both the expertise and the obligation to help impose the conditions necessary for peace in the form of 'the tranquillity of order'.[22] One way they did this was by creating a literature of political counsel and instruction that put a premium on inculcating the civic virtues and strengthening the bonds of love, friendship, and concord.

---

19 Bartolomeo da Urbino prepared an abridgement sometime in the second quarter of the fourteenth century and Leonino da Padova made his abridgment sometime in the latter half of the century: Briggs, *Giles of Rome's 'De regimine principum'*, p. 15.

20 Kelly, *The New Solomon*, pp. 37–39, 82, 111–12; Lambertini, 'Governo ideale e riflessione politica', pp. 263–66.

21 This is his *De regimine rectoris*: Evangelisti, 'I *pauperes Christi* e i linguaggi dominativi'. In the 1390s Andrea de Pace, O.F.M. wrote the mirror *Viridarium principum* for Count Nicolò Peralta of Sicily: Toste, '*Unicuique suum*', pp. 26–31.

22 Augustine, *De civitate Dei*, XIX, 13.

Mendicants and Cities before 1300

Already by the mid-thirteenth century the mendicant orders were playing an integral part in several aspects of the religious, social, administrative, and political life of the cities of northern and central Italy. This was, as Augustine Thompson has pointed out, partly because they located their convents and churches in the new *borghi* of growing cities, that is, in the most demographically and commercially dynamic parts of town that were the strongholds of that 'class that dominated the later communes', the *popolo*. Over time the 'friars sponsored confraternities and established "chapters" of their third orders, which drew people away from their neighbourhood cappelle and the earlier religious associations of the commune', and city governments began to allot alms and various tax exemptions to mendicant establishments.[23] Likewise, the friars' reputation for virtuous living, superior learning, and skill as preachers and pastors ingratiated them with an increasingly literate and devotionally engaged citizenry looking for efficacious confessors, and with reforming prelates like Archbishop Federigo Visconti of Pisa (r. 1254–1277), 'who used them as a stick to beat the other clergy' of his diocese whose sexual laxity and ignorance undercut their ability to function as priests.[24]

Although Archbishop Visconti respected all the mendicant orders, he especially admired the intellectual qualities of the Preachers. This was owing in part no doubt to his having studied theology at the Dominicans' convent of Saint-Jacques at Paris. But it may also have had something to do with the Dominicans' rigorous and questioning attitude towards knowledge: 'like Aquinas, Federigo saw knowledge as something no longer to be merely prayed and waited for as a gift from God. It cost time and diligence.'[25] Visconti's attitude towards knowledge was part of what Alexander Murray has characterized as his 'ethical humanism'.[26] Perhaps one could extend this notion of ethical humanism to Aquinas's and many of his fellow Dominicans' openness to Aristotle's moral philosophy, and their willingness to apply what they learned to their own moral theology. Thomas and his confrères Albert the Great and William of Moerbeke seized on Aristotle's moral philosophical corpus with enthusiasm. Moerbeke retranslated the *Nicomachean Ethics* in the 1250s and translated the *Politics c.* 1260, with Albert and Thomas preparing between them several treatments of the

---

23 Thompson, *Cities of God*, pp. 422–24.
24 For this, see the chapters on 'Counselling in Medieval Confession', and 'Archbishop and Mendicants in Thirteenth-Century Pisa', in Murray, *Conscience and Authority*, pp. 87–103, 107–62. Quote on p. 153.
25 Murray, *Conscience and Authority*, p. 126.
26 Murray, *Conscience and Authority*, p. 121.

Ethics and *Politics* and of moral philosophy more generally.[27] Perhaps even more crucial to the key role moral philosophy was to play in the order's educational curriculum was Thomas's decision to include an extensive treatment of it in his *Summa theologiae*.[28] There is evidence that by the first decade of the 1300s at the latest the Dominicans had followed their doctor's lead and incorporated the teaching of moral philosophy into the curriculum of their *studia generalia*, and in 1314 this practice was made official at the Dominicans' general chapter and extended to the theology course of the order's provincial *studia*.[29]

This interest in Aristotelian-Thomist moral philosophy on the part of the Order of Preachers quickly manifested itself in a plethora of teaching texts. A commentary on the *Politics*, no longer extant, by one Giovanni Guerrisco da Viterbo is attested from the years on either side of 1300.[30] Sometime after 1307 and before his death in 1319, Remigio de' Girolami was lecturing on the *Ethics* at Florence.[31] Corrado d'Ascoli, Dominican lector at Bologna in 1313, produced a *Compendium Ethicorum*, and *c.* 1316, Galvano Fiamma compiled a *Tractatus yconomicus* during his stint of lecturing on the *Ethics, Politics, Economics,* and *Rhetoric* at his convent of San Eustorgio, Milan.[32] More productive still was Guido Vernani, who between 1312 and 1324 compiled a *Lectura super Ethicam* and *Sententiae* on the *Rhetoric* and the *Politics* in connection with his teaching duties at the order's Bologna *studium*. After 1324 Guido abbreviated and simplified his work on the *Ethics* either for a lay readership or for his fellow friars.[33] In the 1330s, Emiliano da Spoleto, lector at the convents of Narni and Arezzo, was responsible for a collection of alphabetically arranged extracts from the *Ethics*. The Dominicans were also open to using Giles of

---

27 Albert treated moral philosophy in his commentary on Lombard's *Sentences*, and compiled two commentaries and a set of *quaestiones* on the *Ethics* and a *Politics* commentary. Thomas discussed moral philosophy in his *Sentences* commentary and in a *quaestio disputata* on the cardinal virtues, and prepared a commentary and *tabula alphabetica* on the *Ethics* and a partial *Politics* commentary, later completed by the secular master Peter of Auvergne: Wieland, 'The Reception and Interpretation of Aristotle's *Ethics*'; Dunbabin, 'The Reception and Interpretation of Aristotle's *Politics*'; Houser, *The Cardinal Virtues*, pp. 56–82, 128–205.

28 The likelihood that Thomas wrote the *Summa theologiae* for the immediate purpose of preparing students destined to teach theology in the convent schools of the order's Roman province has been plausibly argued by Johnson, 'Aquinas's *Summa theologiae* as Pedagogy'.

29 Mulchahey, 'First the Bow is Bent in Study'; Mulchahey, 'Education in Dante's Florence Revisited', p. 155.

30 Flüeler, *Rezeption und Interpretation*, II, p. 96.

31 Mulchahey, 'Education in Dante's Florence Revisited', pp. 152–55.

32 Kaeppeli, *Scriptores Ordinis Praedicatorum*, I, pp. 6–10 (Corrado d'Ascoli), II, pp. 273–74 (Galvano Fiamma).

33 A lay readership is argued for by Dunbabin, 'Guido Vernani of Rimini's Commentary on Aristotle's "Politics"'. For the attribution to a fraternal audience, see Cova, *Il 'Liber de virtutibus' di Guido Vernani da Rimini*, pp. 59–60.

Rome's heavily Aristotelian and Thomist *De regimine principum* as an aid to studying moral philosophy, and two members of the order, Bartolomeo da San Concordio and Bartolomeo Capodilista prepared abbreviations of that work (the former fortified with numerous annotations from a wide assortment of authorities) in association with their teaching at the order's *studia* in Tuscany and at Padua.[34]

The embrace by the Dominican *studia* of moral philosophy with a strongly Aristotelian stamp contrasts with the Franciscans' reception. True, it was that close associate of the Franciscans Robert Grosseteste who, in 1246–1247, prepared the first complete Latin translation of the *Ethics*, with an eye towards helping those friars with the 'practical difficulties in the moral life' that they encountered when hearing confessions.[35] Also Grosseteste's Franciscan fellow Englishman Roger Bacon incorporated a discussion of moral philosophy into his *Opus maius* (1267). Yet the attitude of the Franciscans towards moral philosophy prior to the end of the thirteenth century was more that of Bonaventure, who adopted a critical and limiting stance with regard to Aristotle's brand of philosophical ethics.[36] Even Bacon drew his moral philosophy almost entirely from the Roman authors Seneca, Cicero, Valerius Maximus, and Sallust, and from the Pseudo-Aristotelian work of Arabic origin, *Secretum secretorum*, rather than from Aristotle himself.[37]

Franciscan interest in Aristotle's moral philosophy had certainly grown by the end of the thirteenth century. Johan von Erfurt, lector at Erfurt and Magdeburg in the 1270s–1309, compiled a *Tabula totius philosophiae moralis*, and Johannes de Fonte, lector at Montpellier, compiled the *Parvi flores*, a compilation of brief propositions drawn from all Aristotle's translated works, including his moral philosophy, *c.* 1300. Also, if one can trust the sole testimony of the sixteenth-century antiquary John Bale, one Robert de Cruce, O.F.M. compiled a commentary on the *Ethics* in the late 1200s. Later, Gerald Odon (Guiral Ot, *c.* 1290–1349) compiled what became the Franciscans' standard *Ethics* commentary, probably while studying theology at Paris in 1326–1329; and sometime after 1330 and before his death in 1361, Pietro dell'Aquila compiled a paraphrase of the *Ethics*.[38] Evidence of serious engagement with Aristotle's *Politics* specifically in Franciscan education is more limited. One of the very earliest extant manuscripts containing Peter of Auvergne's commentary was acquired

---

34 Briggs, 'Moral Philosophy and Dominican Education'; Lapidge, Nocentini, and Santi, eds, *Compendium Auctorum Latinorum Medii Aevi*, p. 709.

35 Murray, *Conscience and Authority*, pp. 98–99.

36 Speer, 'Veritas Morum'.

37 Bacon, *Opus Majus*, ed. by Bridges, pp. 223–404.

38 Lohr, 'Medieval Latin Aristotle Commentaries', (24), 164–65; (26), 195–96; and (28), 346; Hamesse, 'Les manuscrits des "Parvi flores"'; Sharpe, *A Handlist of the Latin Writers*, p. 533. Cova, *Il 'Liber de virtutibus' di Guido Vernani da Rimini*, pp. 41–42.

c. 1300 by the Cambridge Franciscan Walter de Bosevile.[39] Other than this, however, the abbreviated commentary, surviving in a single manuscript, of Raimundus Acgerii, a friar from Mende in the south of France who was active in the fourteenth century, is all that survives of a Minorite teaching text dedicated to this work prior to the late 1400s commentary of Pedro de Castrovol of Leon.[40]

This more limited output of Franciscan moral philosophical teaching texts, compared with that of the Dominicans, should not be read as a sign of the order's disinterest in moral philosophy per se, but rather its more critical and independent stance vis-à-vis Aristotelian doctrine. Two moral philosophical problems in particular engaged late thirteenth- and early fourteenth-century Franciscans, these being the relationship between the virtues and the will, and the proper relationship to and use of wealth. As far as the first problem was concerned, the Franciscans tended to reject the eudaemonistic Aristotelian teaching of the Dominicans (and Giles of Rome) which stressed the necessary connection between a cultivated virtuous *habitus* and the attainment of happiness in this life (both individually and in the *polis*), and opted instead for a more libertarian voluntarist position.[41] It was when dealing with the second problem, however, that the Franciscans found themselves tackling matters related to the economy (prices and value, contracts, exchange, usury, restitution) and thus to certain political questions involving virtue, civil justice, and the common good. In addition to these economic concerns showing up in some Franciscan *quodlibeta* debated at this time, including those by a friar of the Florentine convent Petrus de Trabibus (*c.* 1295–1296), Peter of John Olivi composed, at Narbonne, the most important and original treatment of the economy and civil life, *De contractibus* (1293–1295).[42]

At this point certain patterns make themselves evident. First of all, during the five decades spanning the 1290s to the 1340s Italian Dominicans composed an astonishing number of both moral philosophy teaching texts and works of political instruction. Secondly, this textual output contrasts sharply with that of Italian Franciscans, in both the number and kinds of texts produced; and this contrast is probably at least partly the result of the two orders' distinctly different attitudes towards and approaches to

---

39 Peter of Auvergne, *Scriptum super III–VIII libros Politicorum*, pp. xviii–xix.

40 Florence, Biblioteca Medicea Laurenziana, MS San Marco 452 (20), fols 49^r–75^v: Flüeler, *Rezeption und Interpretation*, II, pp. 43–45. As Andrea Tabarroni points out, 'Questa relativa infertilità dei francescani nell'ambito della produzione di commenti alla *Politica* appare tanto più degna di nota se confrontata con la dovizia di attestazioni che si possono invece rinvenire in ambito domenicano': Tabarroni, 'Francescanesimo e riflessione politica sino ad Ockham', p. 211.

41 Kent, 'The Good Will'.

42 Piron, 'Franciscan *Quodlibeta*'; Piron, 'Marchands et confesseurs'; Todeschini, 'Participer au Bien Commun'; Lambertini, 'L'usura tra Santa Croce e Santa Maria Novella'.

moral philosophy. And thirdly, four Dominicans, Remigio de' Girolami, Bartolomeo da San Concordio, Guido Vernani, and Galvano Fiamma, were responsible for authoring texts associated with teaching moral philosophy as well as works of political advice and instruction for a broader, lay audience. Viewed purely from the point of view of pastoral theology, the Dominicans' keen interest in Aristotle's moral philosophy had a very practical goal: the Stagirite's sophisticated treatment of the passions and the nature of the virtues was tailor-made for assisting the preacher-confessor in stimulating the penitent's self-examination and contrition by means of preaching, and then navigating with the penitent the complex issues involved in counselling them and assigning proper penance, since 'it was here in the confessional [...] that the friar's education came into its own, in [...] the battle to discover, and develop, an informed conscience in the layman'.[43] But in the sociopolitical context of medieval Europe, where 'preachers and the act of preaching were embedded in political society, and political society was embedded in Christianity', and in an Italy where 'the communes were simultaneously religious and political entities', a properly informed conscience not only fostered the 'inner peace' necessary for individual salvation but also the 'external peace' manifested in 'the tranquillity of the social order and the common good'.[44] The communes of the later thirteenth and early fourteenth centuries, riven by faction, discord, and violence, and confronted by fundamental questions of how to determine political legitimacy, were certainly crying out for tranquillity.

These social and political problems prompted several creative responses. Perhaps the most spectacular but ephemeral of these were the popular peace movements that manifested themselves from time to time, like the Alleluia of 1233, the flagellants of 1260, the Battuti of 1310, and the Colombini, led by the Dominican Venturino of Bergamo, of 1335.[45] These were brief punctuations in a more continuous process of peacemaking encouraged by clerical and civic authorities and instrumentalized by public ritual, the preaching of the friars, and the 'steady refinement of a model of infra-judicial justice which involved both the courts and various extra-judicial members who operated hand-in-hand'.[46] The promoters of peace, order, and legitimacy also engaged on the ideological front, using words and images to theorize and propagate the values and rationales of these ends, all the while serving the varied interests both of themselves and those on whose behalf they laboured. Armed with the intellectual tools of their various literate professions, several Italians began in the middle

---

43 Murray, *Conscience and Authority*, p. 159.
44 Thompson, *Cities of God*, p. 3; Rupp, '"Love justice, you who judge the Earth"', p. 252; Jansen, *Peace and Penance*, p. 211.
45 Jansen, *Peace and Penance*, pp. 38–48.
46 Palmer, 'Peace Movements', p. 112; Jansen, *Peace and Penance*.

decades of the thirteenth century to pioneer what has aptly been called an 'Italian tradition of practical political literature'.[47] Many, including most notably Giovanni da Viterbo, Albertano da Brescia, and Brunetto Latini, were laymen trained in the law and notarial arts and were also personally engaged in the business of governing.

Thomas Aquinas and Giles of Rome

Another promoter of peace was Thomas Aquinas, who in *De regno*, as Jeremy Catto has argued, brought to bear his academic learning and personal political experience, both at the University of Paris and in Italy, on the problems of tyranny and strife that grew out of the Guelf/Ghibelline conflict of the 1250s and 1260s. For although Thomas dedicated his unfinished mirror of princes to the king of Cyprus (either Hugh II or Hugh III), there is good reason to think that he addressed it less to a king than to 'the politically conscious section of the community' in Italy.[48] This is in part because he repeatedly alludes to aspects of contemporary political and social reality in Italy. Problems specific to communal polities are acknowledged, including their tendency towards being troubled by internal dissension which in turn leads to the seizure of power by a lord or tyrant, and the opportunities for dissension, vice, and sedition created by excessive reliance on the commerce of merchants.[49] Likewise Thomas repeatedly associates tyranny with imperial rule and suggests that it is licit to depose or place limitations on the power of elected monarchs (read German emperors?) who tyrannize.[50] Finally, his unequivocal assertion of papal supremacy, 'it is necessary that all kings of the Christian people be subject' to 'the highest priest, the successor of Peter, the Vicar of Christ, the Roman Pontiff', can plausibly be read as a reference to the righteous assertion of the pope's lordship over both the defeated (in 1266 and 1268 at Benevento and Tagliacozzo) Hohenstaufen and the newly ascendant Angevins in Thomas's native kingdom of Sicily.[51]

But it is at the more fundamental level of its approach, sources, and subject matter that *De regno* exhibits the productive and innovative

---

47 Catto, 'Ideas and Experience', p. 20.
48 Catto, 'Ideas and Experience', p. 13. Although Thomas's authorship has not been (and likely cannot be) definitely proven, I ascribe to the current scholarly consensus that attributes *De regno* to Thomas. I also accept Flüeler's dating of the work to 1271–1273, and therefore the dedication of the work to King Hugh III: Flüeler, *Rezeption und Interpretation*, I, pp. 23–29. See also Blythe, *The Life and Works of Tolomeo Fiadoni*, pp. 157–69.
49 Thomas Aquinas, *De regno*, I, 3.5; I, 5.2; I, 6.3; and II, 3.3–6, trans. by Blythe, pp. 66–67, 71, 73, 111–12.
50 Thomas Aquinas, *De regno*, I, 7.7, trans. by Blythe, pp. 75–76.
51 Thomas Aquinas, *De regno*, I, 15.10, trans. by Blythe, p. 100.

interaction of Thomas's political experience, scholarly pursuits, and Dominican pastoral instincts. This becomes evident when *De regno* is compared with the mirrors written by Thomas's French Dominican and Franciscan contemporaries. All of the latter present an essentially negative, 'Augustinian' explanation of the origins of power in society, tend to reduce politics to religion, and assume that government is, purely and simply, an outgrowth and function of royal lordship.[52] They also avoid the new Aristotelian (and Pseudo-Aristotelian) moral philosophy and subordinate pagan classical material to biblical, patristic, and Christian monastic authorities.[53] Contrastingly, when Thomas read Aristotle's *Ethics* and *Politics*, and the Roman authors Sallust, Cicero, and Valerius Maximus, he realized that these ancient writers offered him the conceptual tools and the historical precedents to make sense of his complicated political and social world. Crucial to his thinking is Aristotle's idea that humans are naturally social and political beings and that the communities formed of their association are prior to any form of government. Moreover, the proper purpose of human life is living well, and to live well requires a community large enough (either a city or realm) to provide the variety of material and social goods sufficient to the good life, a shared desire for the common good enacted through the life of virtue, and a government to help direct the community in its pursuit of living well. An important consequence of this is that a government's legitimacy is not predicated on its form, that is, on whether it is a government of one, few, or many, but on its mode, with legitimate governments (kingship, aristocracy, polity) seeking to secure the common good and illegitimate ones (tyranny, oligarchy, democracy) intent on the private good of the ruler or ruling group.

Nonetheless, among the three legitimate forms of government, kingship is best suited to promoting and preserving the common good. This is because Thomas equates the common good with peace, and for him peace is 'the tranquillity of order', and order requires that a multiplicity be reduced to a unity: 'the good and well-being of a multitude joined in society is that its unity should be preserved, and this is called peace. If this is taken away, the utility of social life perishes. [...] Therefore, a rector of a multitude ought especially to attend to this, so as to procure the unity of peace'.[54] But for many, or indeed a few, to govern the multitude, 'a certain unity [...] would be required', and 'many could not pull a ship in one direction unless they are united in some way. But many are said to be

---

52 For this characterization, see Casagrande, 'Le roi, les anges et la paix', p. 153; Verweij, 'Princely Virtues or Virtues for Princes?', p. 55; and Catto, 'Ideas and Experience', pp. 7–8.

53 Briggs and Nederman, 'Western Medieval *Specula, c.* 1150–*c.* 1450', pp. 170–76.

54 Thomas Aquinas, *De regno*, I, 3.1, trans. by Blythe, p. 65.

228   CHARLES F. BRIGGS

united to the degree that they approach to one. So it is better for one to govern than many, who only approach to one'.[55]

Governments, however, can only promote and preserve unity in the multitude; they cannot generate it, nor can they impose it. Rather unity arises among the members of a community on account of the fact that they share in common a desire for living well, which Thomas, referring to *Ethics*, VIII, 1, calls 'friendship' (*amicitia*): 'Among all worldly things there is nothing which seems worthy of being preferred to friendship. It is this which unites the virtuous and conserves and promotes virtue. It is this which all need to transact any of their affairs'.[56] And when the ruler participates with and directs the many in the virtuous life and towards the common good he becomes their friend, 'since the subjects feel that they receive many benefits from this zeal and since the kings demonstrate that they love their subjects'. Unified by this love, 'the kingdom of good kings is stable'.[57] Conversely, the tenure of illegitimate governments, and of tyrants most especially, cannot be stable or long-lasting, because their devotion to their own private good means their relationship with the multitude is founded on fear rather than friendship, and on coercion rather than virtue.[58]

However, while 'a virtuous life is the end of human congregation' in earthly terms, that same life of virtue is only a means towards reaching our ultimate end, which is 'heavenly beatitude'. Government, then, is responsible for ensuring 'the good life of the multitude to make it suitable for attaining heavenly beatitude'. But that beatitude cannot be reached through human virtue alone; it needs the help of divine virtue, 'and to lead to that end will not pertain to human government, but to divine', that is, to Jesus Christ, and thus 'to priests, and especially to the highest priest [...] the Roman Pontiff.[59] It has already been noted that Thomas deduces from this that all Christian kings must be subject to the pope, and that his position will be adopted by subsequent Italian Dominican writers on the subject of papal power. But Thomas's teachings on government had other implications for the political thought of his successors. By saying that the human community rather than the government is the foundation of civil society and that a government's legitimacy and utility are a function of the degree to which it encourages and protects human flourishing, he leaves the door open to a certain flexibility regarding both the form of government (albeit expressing a preference for monarchy) and the optimal size of the state, since he equates city and realm. Moreover, in, on the

---

55 Thomas Aquinas, *De regno*, I, 3.3, trans. by Blythe, p. 66.
56 Thomas Aquinas, *De regno*, I, 11.3, trans. by Blythe, p. 88.
57 Thomas Aquinas, *De regno*, I, 11.4–5, trans. by Blythe, p. 89.
58 Thomas Aquinas, *De regno*, I, 4.5–8; I, 11.5–8, trans. by Blythe, pp. 68–70, 89–90.
59 Thomas Aquinas, *De regno*, I, 15.8–10; I, 16.2, trans. by Blythe, pp. 99–101.

one hand, accepting Aristotle's definition of human flourishing as the pursuit in common of the life of virtue and, on the other, distinguishing the happiness achieved in this life from eternal beatitude, he can grant a certain validity and autonomy to civil society, to the secular civic virtues, and to 'political' friendship, while at the same time subordinating them to ecclesiastical oversight and the theological virtues, love (*caritas*) being chief among them, given its relation to friendship.[60] Finally, his avid use of Aristotelian concepts and paradigms and of examples and precepts drawn from the Roman *auctores* helps establish the framework of an ethical humanist political discourse among the Dominicans and those influenced by them.

In the decades following his death in 1274, a number of Thomas's students set themselves the task of working out and applying the implications of their teacher's political thought. The first to do so was not a Dominican, but rather Giles of Rome, who in *De regimine principum* (*c.* 1279) expands considerably upon *De regno*'s unfinished Aristotelian ethico-political project by synthesizing (and often modifying the intention of) the Stagirite's moral philosophical doctrine and that found in Thomas's *De regno* and *Summa theologiae*, as well as his *Ethics* and *Politics* commentaries.[61] The Augustinian friar's mirror of princes quickly joined his Dominican master's works to become the most important ancillary texts for the study of moral philosophy at the universities and in the *studia* of the religious orders.[62] Having dedicated his work to the heir to the throne of France Philip the Fair, it is hardly surprising that Giles reinforced considerably Thomas's arguments in favour of kingship as the best form of government. He does, however, acknowledge that in those states where the whole people rules, as 'is common in the cities of Italy' ('Communiter enim in civitatibus Italiae dominantur multi'), good government can exist as long as the *gubernatio populi* aims at the common good of all, whether poor, middling, or rich, 'according to their estate'.[63]

Dominicans and Politics in Florence c. 1300

Securing the common good of city republics was very much on the mind of two other former students of Thomas, Ptolemy of Lucca and Remigio de' Girolami.[64] In addition to playing an active role in the administration

---

60 For the term 'political friendship', see Reichberg, 'Human Nature, Peace, and War', p. 33.

61 The extensive scholarship is efficiently summarized in Lambertini, 'Political Thought'.

62 Briggs, 'Life, Works, and Legacy'.

63 Giles of Rome, *De reg. princ.*, III, 2.2.

64 Remigio studied theology at Paris during Thomas's second regency of 1269–1272: Gentili, 'Girolami, Remigio de''. Ptolemy's relationship with Thomas can be securely dated back to

of the Dominicans' Roman province, both friars occupied positions of authority in the convents of their native cities, with Ptolemy being named prior of San Romano in 1285 and Remigio serving as lector at Santa Maria Novella from *c.* 1275. From these vantage points they could not help but engage in communal politics. This was especially the case with Remigio, whose membership in a prominent (mostly White) Guelf family gave him strong personal reasons for trying to quell the factionalism and violence that plagued his city. The worsening relations between Blacks and Whites in Florence may well have been the reason why Ptolemy was brought in as prior of Santa Maria Novella in July 1300, probably 'to guarantee as much as possible the neutrality of the Dominicans' there.[65] Over the course of Ptolemy's two-year tenure at Florence not only did the city's politics go from bad to worse with the taking of power by the Whites and their subsequent overthrow and exile by the Blacks, but the conflict over jurisdiction that broke out in 1301 between Philip IV and Boniface VIII imperilled the unity of the entire Church. Faced with what must have seemed at the time like existential threats to the peace and order of both State and Church, and no doubt in frequent consultation with one another, Ptolemy and Remigio composed *De regimine principum* and *De bono comuni*.

To be sure, the two works differ in tone, purpose, and scope. *De regimine principum* presents itself as a continuation of Thomas's *De regno*, and proceeds in the same calm, systematic, exhaustive way to examine and compare different forms of political constitution. By contrast, *De bono comuni* is a much more focused work that sets out to prove one thing, 'that the common good is preferable to the individual private good' ('quod bonum comune preferendum sit bono privato proprio'),[66] and that specifically addresses the deplorable state of current Florentine politics.[67] And yet the two treatises also share much in common. To begin with, both are republican in their assumptions and sympathies. Viewed in strictly constitutional terms, Ptolemy appears to be alone in this, since unlike Remigio (and in contrast to Thomas), he explicitly argues in favour of republican regimes 'for wise and virtuous persons' who 'have a virile spirit, a bold heart, and a confidence in their intelligence'. He goes on to say that such peoples, who are especially common in Italy, 'cannot be ruled other than by political [that is, republican] rule, using the common name

---

1272, when he helped Thomas establish the order's new theological *studium* at Naples and served as his confessor: Schmugge, 'Fiadoni, Bartolomeo'.

65 Schmugge, 'Fiadoni, Bartolomeo'.

66 Remigio de' Girolami, *De bono comuni*, ed. by Panella, p. 123.

67 For the pointed references to Florentine politics, see Remigio de' Girolami, *De bono comuni*, ed. by Panella, pp. 138, 148–50.

here to extend also to aristocratic rule'.[68] And yet while Remigio makes no explicit claims in favour of republican constitutions, a republican ethos infuses *De bono comuni* as well as his other political treatises, if what is meant by republican is that which pertains to the *res publica*, that is, to the common or commune.[69] In *De bono comuni* Remigio appropriates Augustine's fourfold 'order of love' (*ordo caritatis*), explicating it as love of 'one that is above us — namely God — another that is ourself, a third that is beside us — namely our neighbour — a fourth that is beneath us — namely our body'. He then inserts a fifth element, the *comune*, which 'seems to relate to the neighbour':

> And it can be said that the common/commune applies in some way both to us and our neighbour insofar as we and our neighbour are both parts of it. And in another way it [the common/commune] applies to God insofar as God, to be sure, is the common and total good of all.[70]

If citizens put their love of God first and then love themselves only in relation to their *comune*/neighbours, then all will be in concord with one another and there will be peace, which for Remigio is identical to the *bonum comune*.[71]

Moreover, in the context of life in the commune, Remigio, following Thomas, equates love (*caritas/amor*) and friendship (*amicitia*). Love/ friendship can only flourish, however, where citizens (both rulers and ruled) are virtuous, since only then will they have the capacity for

---

68 Ptolemy of Lucca, *De regimine principum*, II, 9.4 and IV, 8.4, trans. by Blythe, pp. 124, 238.

69 The generally agreed-upon meaning of *res publica* in late medieval Europe conforms to that in Cicero, *De re publica*, I, 25, ed. and trans. by Keyes, pp. 64–65: 'Well, then, a commonwealth [*res publica*] is the property of a people. But a people is not any collection of human beings brought together in any sort of way, but an assemblage of people in large numbers associated in an agreement with respect to justice and a partnership for the common good'.

70 Remigio de' Girolami, *De bono comuni*, ed. by Panella, p. 161: 'Secundum beatum Augustinum in I libro *De doctrina christiana* "quatuor sunt diligenda: unum quod supra nos est — scilicet Deus — alterum quod nos sumus, tertium quod iuxta nos est — scilicet proximus –, quartum quod infra nos" scilicet corpus proprium. [...] Sed inter ista quatuor, comune nonnisi ad proximum pertinere videtur, quem sine dubio post nos diligere debemus. Et dicendum quod comune ex aliqua ratione pertinet ad nos et proximum in quantum et nos et proximus sumus partes eius. Ex alia autem ratione pertinet ad Deum in quantum scilicet Deus est comune et totale bonum omnium'. See also the discussion of this passage in Mineo, 'Cose in comune e bene comune', pp. 41–44. On the double meaning of *comune*, and on the synonymy of *civitas* and *bonum commune*, see, respectively, Rubinstein, 'Marsilius of Padua and Italian Political Thought', pp. 54–55, and Mineo, 'Cose in comune e bene comune', pp. 60–61.

71 Remigio de' Girolami, *De bono comuni*, ed. by Panella, p. 124: 'Item *Eccli*. 4 [.33] dicitur "Usque ad mortem certa pro iustitia", per quam scilicet bonum comune multitudinis, quod est pax, acquiritur et conservatur'.

friendship while also being worthy of it.[72] His list of virtues includes the intellectual virtues of wisdom and prudence, and the moral virtues of mildness, liberality, courage, justice, mercy, 'and such like'.[73] But even more productive and worthy of love is the *city* populated by those virtuous citizens, 'because, indeed, in the city the intellectual, moral, and even theological virtues are more abundant than in a single citizen on his own [...] and also because that same citizen can be made more virtuous in every way, in human terms, when coupled together with a city than when he exists alone by himself'.[74] Ptolemy makes a similar connection between virtue, friendship, and the city. Listing the moral virtues 'such as temperance, fortitude, prudence, and justice', he asserts that these virtues, which 'are included under practical action [...], are ordered towards another person and therefore require the multitude of persons from which a city is constituted'. Likewise, the speculative virtues, because they are inculcated through teaching, 'presuppose the multitude of persons from which the city is constituted'. Friendship, which Ptolemy identifies as a virtue of the will, 'principally requires a community and does not exist without it'. Moreover, the city too needs friendship, since 'if friendship thrives and concord is nurtured there, the city displays a certain harmony and pleasantness of spirit'.[75] Given that, after God, the city together with its community is the most worthy object of its citizens' love, both friars stress that the most perfect expression of that love is *amor patriae*, the willingness to undergo hardships and, if need be, sacrifice oneself in order to preserve and protect it.[76]

If, then, citizens properly order the objects of their love and practise a life of virtue, the human community will achieve its proper end, a state of peace and harmony, which Ptolemy calls political felicity (*felicitas politica*) and Remigio, blessedness (*beatitudo*).[77] Ptolemy goes even further to assert, following his teacher Thomas, that this earthly felicity, although imperfect, is nonetheless an important precondition for achieving the

---

72 Remigio de' Girolami, *De bono comuni*, ed. by Panella, p. 144: 'Est autem amicitia proprie loquendo quando aliquis amat aliquem propter virtutem quam habet'.

73 Remigio de' Girolami, *De bono comuni*, ed. by Panella, p. 144: 'Virtus existens in aliquo homine, sive sit virtus intellectualis ut sapientia et prudentia, sive sit virtus moralis ut mansuetudo liberalitas fortitudo iustitia misericordia et huiusmodi'.

74 Remigio de' Girolami, *De bono comuni*, ed. by Panella, p. 145: 'Quia scilicet in civitate plus habundat et virtus intellectualis et moralis sive etiam theologica quam in uno cive per se [...] et iterum quia ipse civis magis potest fieri modis omnibus virtuosus, humaniter loquendo, comparatus ad civitatem quam in se ipso solus existens'.

75 Ptolemy of Lucca, *De regimine principum*, IV, 3.2–4; IV, 3.9–10, trans. by Blythe, pp. 222–24.

76 Ptolemy of Lucca, *De regimine principum*, III, 34.3–5, trans. by Blythe, pp. 154–56; Remigio de' Girolami, *De bono comuni*, ed. by Panella, pp. 125–26, 141; Remigio de' Girolami, *De bono pacis*, ed. by Panella, p. 170.

77 Ptolemy of Lucca, *De regimine principum*, IV, 23.1, trans. by Blythe, p. 272; Remigio de' Girolami, *De bono comuni*, ed. by Panella, p. 140.

DEFENDERS OF THE PEACE   233

'remote' end, 'which is God himself', that is, 'eternal beatitude, which consists of the vision of God'.[78] An important corollary of their acknowledgement of the naturalness and validity of political life and civic virtue is these authors' frequent and enthusiastic use of pagan Greek and Roman philosophers and historians. Because they were pagans their lessons applied strictly to happiness in this life rather than the next. Nonetheless, what they had to say was crucially relevant because their polities looked very much like those of contemporary Italy. 'I have mentioned these things', says Ptolemy, 'to show that the government of the Greeks in the time of Aristotle was quite similar to our own'.[79] The philosophers, Aristotle chief among them, followed by his Roman counterparts Cicero and Seneca (and Pseudo-Cicero and Pseudo-Seneca), speak authoritatively on virtue, friendship, and the structures and ends of political life. Likewise, the historians Sallust and Valerius Maximus recount the tales of virtuous heroes of ancient Greece and Republican Rome like Damon and Pythias, Cato, Fabricius, Marcus Curtius, and Marcus Regulus. The lessons of the ancients demonstrated 'the acts of a virtuous government, from which comes the perfect and happy polity' and recounted how 'very often they exposed themselves to death for the republic, that is, for the common good'.[80] So also did they teach by negative examples. Tyrannizing villains condemned by Thomas and Ptolemy like Dionysius of Syracuse and Nero were the ancient manifestations of the factious Florentines chastised by Remigio who, perverted by pride, put love of self before that of God and neighbour, and valued their own good over the common good.[81]

In *De regimine principum*, and in *De bono comuni* and *De bono pacis*, Ptolemy and Remigio constructed a practically orientated political theory to address contemporary political problems. Although it seems likely they wrote these works with an immediate audience of their confrères and fellow clergy primarily in mind, their message nonetheless was swiftly amplified and disseminated outside the walls of Santa Maria Novella.[82] This was certainly the case with the political doctrine found in Remigio's

---

78 Ptolemy of Lucca, *De regimine principum*, III, 3.4 and III, 3.7, trans. by Blythe, pp. 152–53. For Thomas, see Reichberg, 'Human Nature, Peace, and War', pp. 38–39.

79 Ptolemy of Lucca, *De regimine principum*, IV, 19.6, trans. by Blythe, p. 266. Shortly before this he says of ancient Chalcedon, with its governing counsel of five men 'chosen from the wealthy', and '104 honoured ones called the Gerousia', that 'today the cities of Italy and especially of Tuscany observe this mode': IV, 19.4.

80 Ptolemy of Lucca, *De regimine principum*, IV, 23.5, trans. by Blythe, p. 274; Remigio de' Girolami, *De bono comuni*, p. 128.

81 Remigio de' Girolami, *De bono communi*, ed. by Panella, p. 123.

82 On Remigio, see Jansen, *Peace and Penance*, pp. 68–69. Although in the concluding paragraph of *De regimine principum*, Ptolemy gives the impression he is writing for an academic audience, his modern English translator writes, 'Ptolemy's formulations [...] had considerable impact on contemporary and future writers': Ptolemy of Lucca, *De regimine principum*, trans. by Blythe, pp. 45, 288.

treatises, since he incorporated many of the same ideas in sermons he delivered on multiple occasions to mixed audiences on the themes of peace, justice, and the character and duties of rulers.[83] Moreover, during these same years two of Ptolemy's and Remigio's fellow friars at Santa Maria Novella, the Pisans Giordano da Rivalto and Bartolomeo da San Concordio, were incorporating elements of a similar ethico-political programme in products aimed at a broader, lay audience. In a series of popularizing sermons preached *in volgare*, Giordano connects his mentor Remigio's political teachings on concord and peace, the common good, and privileging the city as 'the place par excellence of human political life' to exhortations to root out the sins of pride and selfishness and to practise the sacrament of penance, beginning with contrition and concluding by renouncing vengeance against one's enemies.[84] In his *Documenta antiquorum*, Bartolomeo compiled a guide for living a virtuous life in concert with one's fellow citizens.[85] Gathering together hundreds of passages drawn from numerous Christian and ancient pagan authorities, Bartolomeo organized these into four *trattati*, on 'the natural disposition of the body', the virtues, the vices, and 'future things'.[86]

Several features of this massive project of compilation stand out. The first is the astonishing variety and number of quotations assembled, and especially the breadth and depth of Bartolomeo's familiarity with classical sources (he was famed in his order for having an intellect and memory 'like a living library').[87] Secondly, there is the 'elegance, fluidity, and expressive richness' of his Italian.[88] What is most striking for the purposes of this chapter, however, is how closely the elements of his programme of instruction express the ideas found in the works of his fellow friars. For instance, he concludes his first *trattato* with a series of teachings on a citizen's 'natural inclination towards the *patria*' and follows this in the second *trattato* with not only a detailed examination of the virtues as practised by the individual but also a careful exploration of different aspects of human association, including companionship, speech, giving

---

83 Jansen, *Peace and Penance*, pp. 67–86; Carron, 'Influences et interactions entre Santa Maria Novella et la Commune de Florence'.

84 Iannella, 'La paix dans la prédication de Giordano de Pise'.

85 I consulted two editions of the *Ammaestramenti degli antichi/Documenta antiquorum*. Citations from Bartolomeo's Italian version from the edition of Pier Giuseppe Colombi have been compared with the Latin in the Latin/Italian facing-page edition of Vincenzio Nannucci. All page references are to the Colombi edition.

86 Bartolomeo further divided the text into forty *distinzioni*, each of which is subdivided into from two to as many as twelve chapters.

87 This according to one of Bartolomeo's former students at Santa Caterina, Pisa, Domenico da Peccioli: Bonaini, ed., 'Chronica antiqua conventus Sanctae Catharinae de Pisis', p. 522. See also Vecchio, '*Quasi armarium scripturarum*'.

88 Segre, 'Bartolomeo da San Concordio'.

and receiving benefits, friendship, forbearance of slights and pardoning of enemies, and agreeableness (*giocondità*) in relaxation and play.[89] Moreover, when discussing the vices, he singles out pride as being both 'the worst and first of the vices' and the vice associated with the 'love of one's own excellence'.[90] He concludes the final *trattato* with an extended treatment of government ('Di dignità e suggezione').[91] If, as mentioned earlier, Bartolomeo dedicated his translation to one of the leaders of the Black faction, Geri Spini, then no doubt this was done in part as a gesture of amity towards a wealthy and influential patron. But it also seems likely that Bartolomeo's gift was intended as a contribution to the peace-making efforts of his fellow friars during those first fraught years of the fourteenth century in Florence.[92]

Jacopo da Cessole and Enrico da Rimini

At roughly the same time as Bartolomeo and his Tuscan colleagues were turning Santa Maria Novella into a veritable workshop of moral-political advice literature, Jacopo da Cessole in Genoa and Enrico da Rimini in Venice made their own contributions to this genre. Jacopo's *Libellus de moribus hominum et de officiis nobilium ac populi super ludo scaccorum* (Booklet on the Game of Chess Concerning the Character of Men and the Duties of Nobles and People) can in some ways be seen as the counterpart to Bartolomeo's *Ammaestramenti* in that it too examines the role and place of the virtues in political society, addresses both preachers and the laity, and relies heavily on classical sources. Likely composed around 1300, the *Libellus de moribus* allegorizes the game of chess, in which the board symbolizes an idealized city, each of whose pieces represents a different segment of society, and where the social order is respected by distinguishing the 'noble' pieces (king, queen, knights, judges, royal lieutenants) from the pawns, which signify the various professions and occupations of the *popolo*.[93] To each piece Jacopo assigns some combination of the civic virtues and illustrates these by way of copious *exempla* and the occasional maxim, almost all drawn from classical sources, Valerius Maximus chief among them.[94] Thanks in large part to its utility for preachers and to the 'honour and pleasure' that its ludic conceit and entertaining stories

---

89 Bartolomeo da San Concordio, *Ammaestramenti degli antichi*, ed. by Colombi, pp. 39–161.

90 Bartolomeo da San Concordio, *Ammaestramenti degli antichi*, ed. by Colombi, pp. 202–05.

91 Bartolomeo da San Concordio, *Ammaestramenti degli antichi*, ed. by Colombi, pp. 270–84.

92 Conte, 'Gli "Ammaestramenti degli antichi"', pp. 186–87; see also Conte, 'Il lessico politico negli *Ammaestramenti degli antichi*'.

93 Labriola, '"Allegoria del buon governo"', p. 56.

94 Jacopo likely accessed virtually all his material second-hand, through Vincent of Beauvais, John of Salisbury, and John of Wales: Kalning, 'Virtues and Exempla'.

conveyed to lay readers, Jacopo's 'allegoria del buon governo' achieved immediate and long-lasting popularity. And yet, as Ada Labriola has argued, this allegory of good government articulates the clear political message that if each social group performs its proper role 'with virtue and honesty' and 'mutually complement each other', then 'order and harmony' will flourish in the cities.[95]

Virtue, order, and harmony in urban society are also the key political values expressed by Enrico da Rimini in *De quattuor virtutibus cardinalibus ad cives Venetos*. Enrico first appears in the historical record in 1304, during a visit to the papal curia working on behalf of Venice, where he was prior of SS Giovanni e Paolo. Four years later he served as papal envoy to the king of Serbia and, shortly thereafter, as a representative of Venice during negotiations with Pope Clement V's nuncios regarding the two parties' conflicting claims to lordship over Ferrara.[96] Perhaps these experiences inspired him to write *De quattuor virtutibus*, a voluminous treatise on the four cardinal virtues that relies heavily on the teaching of Thomas Aquinas and is richly stocked with borrowings of *dicta* and *exempla* from Christian sources, including the Bible and the Latin Fathers, Boethius, Chrysostom, chronicles and saints lives, Bernard of Clairvaux, John of Salisbury, and Peter Comestor, as well as the classical *auctores*, especially Aristotle's *Ethics* and *Politics*, Cicero, Seneca (and the Pseudo-Senecan *Formula vitae honestae* of Martin of Braga), Valerius Maximus, Vegetius, Ovid, and Sallust.

What has repeatedly drawn the attention of readers to Enrico's treatise, from the Venetian chronicler Lorenzo de' Monaci (*c.* 1420) to the modern-day scholars James Blythe and Maurizio Viroli, is that it contains the earliest recorded description of Venice's mixed constitution.[97] Enrico praises this government in which the doge is a kind of elective monarch, and the councils (of six, forty, and four hundred) are collectively the aristocratic and popular elements.[98] Thanks to their constitution, and to their notable virtuousness:

> the Venetian people enjoys so much peace and security, that no one is ever driven out by reason of party, newcomers and fugitives remain in safety, no one oppresses another, no one invades another's home, everything is secure. Here murders or bloodshed are never or rarely

---

95 Labriola, '"Allegoria del buon governo"', pp. 55–56.
96 Casagrande, 'Enrico da Rimini'.
97 Robey and Law, 'The Venetian Myth and the "De Republica Veneta"'; Blythe, *Ideal Government*, pp. 282–83; Viroli, *From Politics to Reason of State*, pp. 39–41.
98 Enrico is being rather disingenuous here about the popular element in Venice's government. It is almost certain he wrote his treatise within a decade of the beginning, in 1297, of the series of reforms known as the *serrata* which limited government participation to adult male members of the republic's aristocratic families.

DEFENDERS OF THE PEACE   237

heard of. Said people, rejoicing in the greatest liberty, does not suffer being subjected to other men.[99]

Yet if Venice looks a bit like the perfect Aristotelian polity, Enrico constantly reminds the reader that it is nonetheless a Christian one. Like Thomas and Ptolemy, then, he argues that while the good political life is both natural and desirable, it should rightly be conducted in preparation for the ultimate end of eternal bliss. Necessary to achieving these ends, of course, are the virtues, both civic (or cardinal) and divine. Enrico organizes his treatise into four lengthy *tractatus*, devoted in turn to prudence, justice, fortitude, and temperance. At the same time, he takes great care to point out that these virtues need the help of the three divine virtues of faith, hope, and love, because 'the aforesaid four virtues of the soul perfect only in the civil life, whereas for the construction of the spiritual life they do not suffice'.[100]

Just as he does with the virtues and with the ends of the political life, Enrico touches on many of the same themes as his fellow Dominicans. Here again we see the interest in establishing concord and harmony in the city, the need to place the common good before the singular good, and to love God and neighbour, the latter defined as both fellow citizen and *patria*. Even more so than in Jacopo's *Libellus de moribus*, however, *De quattuor virtutibus* evinces a concern, verging on obsession, with the subject of order. One is repeatedly instructed on the hierarchy of ends in the life of a Christian citizen. The practical intellect is ordered to political felicity, the speculative intellect to eternal blessedness.[101] *Fortitudo* strengthens the spirits of men who fight to preserve and protect the *patria*, but 'just as many men make one body which is the people or city, for the defence of which individual citizens ought to expose themselves to death [...], we many are also one in Christ', so 'if one may die defending the temporal republic, how much more ought one to do so for the celestial republic which is God?'[102] Enrico repeatedly stresses the importance of maintaining the social order. In the household wives are subject to husbands, children

---

99 Enrico da Rimini, *De quattuor virtutibus cardinalibus*, tract. 2, c. 3, pt. 16, fol. 48ᵛ: 'Hec autem venetorum gens tanta pace et securitate fruitur, quod nullus unquam inde intuitu partis expellitur, advenientes et profugi in tuto servant, nullus alterius oppressor, nullus alieni habitaculi est invasor. Secura sunt omnia. Homicidia vel humani sanguinis effusiones, aut nunquam aut raro audiuntur. Nulli hominum subdi patitur dicta gens summa gaudens libertate'.

100 Enrico da Rimini, *De quattuor virtutibus cardinalibus*, prologue, fol. 12ʳ⁻ᵛ: 'He sunt quatuor columne angulares que predictas quatuor virtutes anime perficiunt solum in vita civili, unde [fol. 12ᵛ] ad constructuram vite spiritualis non sufficiunt'.

101 Enrico da Rimini, *De quattuor virtutibus cardinalibus*, tract. 1, c. 2, pt. 3, fol. 15ᵛ.

102 Enrico da Rimini, *De quattuor virtutibus cardinalibus*, tract. 3, c. 1. pt. 3, fol. 72ᵛ: 'Sicut enim multi homines faciunt unum corpus quod est populus vel civitas, pro cuius defensione singuli cives morti se debent exponere [...] multi unum corpus sumus in Christo [...].

to fathers, slaves to masters. The prudence of state officials (*magistratus*) is different from that of ordinary citizens, which is different from that of resident foreigners. Citizens are directed to show their love for one another by sharing benefits and duties, but they are instructed to be faithful to the ruler (*princeps*) even to the point of being willing to die for him just as they would for their city, 'since he represents the *patria*'.[103] Assuming that by *princeps* Enrico means any kind of legitimate regime,[104] it is tempting to think that here Enrico anticipates the idea, later expressed by Marsilius, Bartolo da Sassoferrato, and Baldo degli Ubaldi, and by Ambrogio Lorenzetti's frescos in the Sala dei Nove in Siena's Palazzo Pubblico, that a state's government is a kind of fictive person.[105]

Disorder and its causes also haunt Enrico's political vision. The strongest bulwark against this is justice.[106] He stipulates that without justice being served, the state is nothing more than a den of thieves.[107] Likewise, where distributive justice is absent and citizens are thereby denied the 'honours, dignities, and offices' due them, according to their 'diverse conditions and merits', the entire political order (*totus ordo policie*) is corrupted. Coercive justice is also essential so that malefactors can be punished and the ordered unity of the multitude and the common peace are not destroyed and broken to pieces.[108] As if to underline the importance of justice for the well-ordered polity, Enrico fortifies his discussion with what amounts to a manual on legal practice whose thirty-five sections examine the character and duties of judges and lawyers and offer instructions for accusers and defendants, in both civil and ecclesiastical courts. Disorder, however, also sneaks in by the countless paths of uncorrected vice. The domicile is a fertile zone for eruptions of dissension, should intemperate wives and intrusive, grasping in-laws not be properly looked after and governed by husbands.[109] Conviviality too requires constant regulation, with drunkenness being especially dangerous on account of its potential

---

Et ideo si licet pro defensione reipublice temporalis mortem subire et vitam corporis contemnere, multomagis oportet pro republica celesti que Deus est'.

103 Enrico da Rimini, *De quattuor virtutibus cardinalibus*, tract. 2, c. 4, pt. 11, fol. 46ᵛ: 'Debet enim quilibet ciuis se morti exponere pro tutela sui principis, sicut et pro defensione civitatis, cum ipse personam patrie gerat'.

104 He consistently refers to legitimate regimes as *principatus* and, as discussed above, prefers a mixed constitution.

105 Mineo, 'Cose in comune e bene comune', pp. 44–49, 60–63, and Mineo, 'Liberté et communauté en Italie'; Ryan, 'Bartolus of Sassoferrato and Free Cities'.

106 Enrico da Rimini, *De quattuor virtutibus cardinalibus*, tract. 2, c. 3, pt. 3, fol. 39ᵛ: 'Apparet quantus est fructus iusticie in conservatione reipublice in tuitione et gubernatione omnium subditorum et in custodia ordinata cuiuslibet multitudinis'.

107 Augustine, *De civitate Dei*, IV, 4.

108 Enrico da Rimini, *De quattuor virtutibus cardinalibus*, tract. 2. c. 3, pts. 1–3, fols 38ᵛ–39ᵛ.

109 Enrico da Rimini, *De quattuor virtutibus cardinalibus*, tract. 1, c. 5, pts. 3–8, fols 22ᵛ–24ᵛ, and tract. 4, c. 3, pt. 33, fol. 131ᵛ.

to ignite quarrels and violence and thus 'disrupt social life'.[110] Moreover, in keeping with Enrico's theme of virtue in this present life being the necessary precondition for both political peace and heavenly blessedness, there is a shift in the middle of the *tractatus* on fortitude to a more penitential mode in the form of a lengthy discussion of the many remedies for moral weakness and of the fruits which come of moral rectitude in the face of temptation. The penitential mode continues throughout the *tractatus* on temperance, where this virtue is regarded for the most part as a bridle on the sins of gluttony, drunkenness, and lust, and on the proper uses of leisure, clothing, and women's makeup.

Like his Tuscan contemporaries, Enrico was fond of quoting Augustine's assertion that peace is the tranquillity of order.[111] Yet whereas for Remigio and his confrères at Santa Maria Novella civil peace was the prize they desperately sought in the face of Florence's political faction and violence, for Enrico the aristocratic republic of Venice was the living example of such a peace.

Preachers and Signori

Over the course of the next few decades the removal of the papacy to Avignon and the Italian pretensions of Emperors Henry VII and Ludwig IV introduced new instabilities into Italian politics that foregrounded the problems of papal–imperial relations and signorial takeovers of government. By the time Guido Vernani da Rimini and Luca Mannelli came to write their treatises of political advice the targets of their counsel were not citizens but rather *signori*. Guido dedicated his *Liber de virtutibus* to 'the noble and magnificent lords of Malatesta', who undoubtedly were the brothers Galeotto and Malatesta III Malatesta of Rimini. The text's modern editor, Luciano Cova, rightly cautions against dating this work any more specifically than after June 1323, the time of Thomas Aquinas's canonization, since Guido repeatedly refers to Thomas as *beatus*.[112] It seems likely, however, that he wrote it after returning from several years of teaching at Bologna to his home convent of San Cataldo, Rimini, in 1324 and before the Malatesta brothers officially took control of Rimini's government a decade later. Heavily reliant on both Thomas's *Ethics* commentary and *Summa theologiae*, and adorned with numerous borrowings from the *Politics* and *Rhetoric*, several of Augustine's works, the Bible, and Valerius Maximus, the *Liber de virtutibus* teaches the same lessons

---

110 Enrico da Rimini, *De quattuor virtutibus cardinalibus*, tract. 4, c. 2, pt. 24, fols 125ᵛ–126ʳ.

111 See, for example, Enrico da Rimini, *De quattuor virtutibus cardinalibus*, tract. 1, c. 5, pt. 31, fol. 34ʳ and tract. 2, c. 3, pt. 1, fol. 38ᵛ.

112 Guido Vernani, *Liber de virtutibus*, ed. by Cova, pp. 99–100, 197, 242, 248.

that have become familiar to us from other Dominican works of political advice.[113] Here, however, stress is laid on the role of princes as protectors and defenders of 'the peaceful state of the republic' ('pacificum rei publice statum protegant et defendant').[114] So, Guido says, the acquisition of political beatitude requires riches and honours since they are prerequisites for works of liberality, magnificence, temperance, and magnanimity.[115] The magnanimous man confronts dangers on behalf of great things, like justice, liberty of the *patria*, and religion, but he also should guard against being too familiar with the multitude, lest he appear servile.[116] Guido lavishes attention on justice and prudence, the cardinal virtues most associated with rulership and the maintenance of peace and the common good.[117] So too is he especially concerned with the subject of friendship and its adjuncts benevolence, beneficence, and concord, since these relationships bind all the people of the city, high and low, rich and poor, familiar and unfamiliar together in harmony and peace.[118]

Although informed by the same political goals of civil peace and the common good as the earlier Dominican works surveyed above, the signorial identity of the addressees of the *Liber de virtutibus* makes it a true mirror of princes. But Guido makes it quite clear beginning in the prologue and throughout the remainder of the work that the duty of these 'Christian princes' is first and foremost to the welfare of the republic (*bonus rei publice status*). And while he addresses the Malatesta respectfully, Guido speaks with the voice of learned authority, explaining that in the *Liber de virtutibus*, 'we will proceed insofar as we can in a plain style, so that those reading this may easily and clearly understand what is being said and fulfil the tasks that are required of the life of true knighthood.'[119] But if one gets the sense that Guido is speaking *to* power, Luca Mannelli's *Compendium moralis philosophie* gives one the impression that its author is speaking *for* power.

Born in the mid-1290s to a wealthy Florentine family of bankers with Ghibelline sympathies, Luca entered the order at Santa Maria Novella when still a young boy and thus likely received at least part of his schooling there from Remigio de' Girolami. Having gained a reputation for his high level of learning, excellent character, and ready memory, he served as lector in several of the important convents of the Dominicans' Roman province, as well as being named prior of the convent of San Domenico,

---

113 Guido Vernani, *Liber de virtutibus*, ed. by Cova, pp. 78–98.
114 Guido Vernani, *Liber de virtutibus*, ed. by Cova, p. 187.
115 Guido Vernani, *Liber de virtutibus*, ed. by Cova, p. 196.
116 Guido Vernani, *Liber de virtutibus*, ed. by Cova, pp. 230–32.
117 Guido Vernani, *Liber de virtutibus*, ed. by Cova, pp. 245–67.
118 Guido Vernani, *Liber de virtutibus*, ed. by Cova, pp. 277–93.
119 Guido Vernani, *Liber de virtutibus*, ed. by Cova, p. 188.

Pistoia, in 1331 and preacher general in the Roman province in 1332.[120] Luca also seems to have had a talent for making connections with the influential and well-connected. In 1344 he accompanied the patrician (and Dominican) bishop of Florence Angelo Acciaiuoli on a legation to Avignon and managed to remain at the Curia for the next fourteen years. There he became a member of the household of Petrarch's patron, the powerful Roman Cardinal Giovanni Colonna, and was named successively to three bishoprics, the first two of which he administered *in absentia*. He seems to have owed his second and third episcopates, at Osimo (1347) and Fano (1358), to the friendship between his family and the Malatesta; indeed, his election to each office came shortly after those towns fell under Malatesta control.

While at Avignon, Luca's intellectual gifts were employed by Clement VI, who *c.* 1349 commissioned him to compile a vast alphabetically arranged 'encyclopaedia of the concepts present in the works of Seneca'.[121] Pope Clement likely called on Luca's services because of the Florentine Dominican's demonstrated familiarity with and interest in Antiquity. Sometime before 1344 Luca had compiled an *Expositio Valerii Maximi, Factorum ac dictorum memorabilium libri IX.*[122] Luca's classicism is also very much on display in the *Compendium moralis philosophie*, with its copious quotations from Cicero's *Tusculan Disputations* and *De officiis*, as well as from Seneca, Macrobius, Vergil, Juvenal, Valerius, Sallust, and Quintilian. He also relies heavily on Aristotle's *Ethics* and *Politics*, Thomas's *Summa theologiae*, the Bible, several patristic authors, and Isidore of Seville and Boethius.

In terms of sources, then, the *Compendium* is a typical early Trecento Italian Dominican political text. The same can be said for its arrangement into three books, examining, respectively, the basic elements of moral philosophy, the civic virtues, and friendship. And yet the text and accompanying illustration found in the sole existing copy of the Latin original (now Paris, Bibliothèque nationale de France, MS lat. 6467) seems to betray a new, and altogether more deferential, if not subservient, attitude on the part of its author. In the prologue Luca repeatedly lavishes fulsome praise on his dedicatee Bruzio Visconti. Lord Bruzio not only surpasses all others in his nobility and the glory of his forebears, but has also been endowed by nature with a superbly keen wit, tenacious memory, and fluent tongue. And Luca, instead of claiming to speak with authority, adopts a pose of servile powerlessness. Should anyone accuse him of writing out of

---

120 Kaeppeli, 'Luca Mannelli', p. 238.
121 Cinelli, 'Mannelli, Luca'; Kaeppeli, 'Luca Mannelli', pp. 238–44.
122 Di Stefano, 'La diffusion de Valère Maxime'.

242   CHARLES F. BRIGGS

arrogance, the fault is not his because he has simply done as Bruzio has commanded.[123] Moreover,

> should anyone want to censure this work, let him know that I copied whatever is in it from Aristotle's *Ethics*, Cicero's *De officiis* and *Tusculan Disputations*, and the *prima* and *secunda secundae* of Thomas's [*Summa theologiae*]; I gathered together little from my own thoughts beyond arranging the narrative order. And on this account he who attempts to misrepresent these opinions offends not me but rather the aforementioned authors.[124]

In vain does one looks for any mention of peace, concord, harmony, love, the common good, the republic, or even the city in the nearly four manuscript pages of the prologue. What one finds instead is a language of *cultivation*, whether in terms of culture (philosophical wisdom and refined pleasure) or of character (virtue). But this cultivation is presented as something entirely personal, leading to an individual's *felicitas*, while virtue is undifferentiated (always *virtus*, never *iustitia*, *fortitudo*, etc.) and, again, personal. Certainly, all these terms and concepts appear in the *Compendium*'s three books (how could they not?), but they are so neutrally presented, so banalized in the endless strings of quotations, as to become mere *information*, rather than exhortation or reasoned instruction.

What might account for Luca having compiled 'this compendium, which both materially and in terms of literary merit is a mediocre work', and for having done so at the command of a prince known not only for his literary accomplishments but also for his cruelty and perversity?[125] Part of the answer may lie in the manuscript's exquisite opening-page illustration, which was executed by an artist in Bologna, perhaps Andrea da Bologna or a member of his workshop.[126] In the historiated initial Luca presents his work to Bruzio. In the centre of the base of the page Bruzio appears again enthroned, holding a sword in his right hand and open book in his left, and trampling underfoot a horned devil, labelled 'Superbia'. Three pagan philosophers — designated as Valerius (Maximus), Seneca, and

---

123 Luca Mannelli, *Compendium moralis philosophie*, Paris, BnF, MS lat. 6467, fol. 2ᵛ: 'Sic vero mihi ad arrogantiam asseribatur [*sic for* ascribatur?] quod scribo, possem causam reprehensionis in uobis referre nisi insipiens factus sum sapientium usurpans officium vos domine coegistis'.

124 Luca Mannelli, *Compendium moralis philosophie*, Paris, BnF, MS lat. 6467, fol. 2ᵛ: 'Sed aliam excusationem affero, quia quicumque hoc opus culpare uoluerit cognoscat quod que in hoc opere expressi ab Aristotele ex libro ethicorum, a Tullio ex libro de officiis et Tusculanis questionibus, a Thoma ex prima et secunda secunde, collegi pauca de meis cogitationibus preter formam procedenti subiungens. Et ideo non me sed supradictos auctores ledit qui has sententias deprauare conatur'.

125 Dorez, ed., *La Canzone delle virtù e delle scienze*, p. 19.

126 Pellegrin, *La bibliothèque des Visconti et des Sforza*, p. 27.

Aristotle — stand to his right (on the left side of the page), while on his left stand Saints Thomas Aquinas, Ambrose, and Augustine. Milan appears in the centre of the top of the page, accompanied to its immediate left and right by the heraldic symbols of the Visconti. Representations of the twelve Lombard cities subject to Milan's overlordship appear in roundels running down each side of the page. The figure of Bruzio at the base of the page suggests a personification of Justice subduing Pride, and this would accord well with the teaching of Bartolomeo da San Concordio, who identified pride as the sin most dangerous to the republic, and of Enrico da Rimini's and Guido Vernani's privileging of justice as a virtue of principal importance for rulers.

And yet here trampled Pride (and Bruzio's sword) may also have suggested to the book's dedicatee the recent subjection of the Lombard cities, symbolized in the frontispiece, to Visconti rule. There is broad agreement among scholars that the *Compendium* and BnF, MS lat. 6467 were both executed in the early 1340s, and were completed before Luca was named to his first bishopric on 28 May 1344. During the very same time the co-*signori* of Milan, Bruzio's father Luchino and uncle Giovanni, archbishop of Milan, were patronizing the design and construction of an elaborate tomb for the former *signore*, their nephew and Bruzio's cousin, Azzone (r. 1329–1339). Symbolized on this monument were the same cities depicted in MS lat. 6467, offering themselves in subjection to the patron saint of Milan, Ambrose.[127] Moreover, both the tomb project and the *Compendium* date to a brief period of warming relations between the Visconti and the papacy, and to a time of especially close alliance between the Order of Preachers and rulers of Milan, an alliance that had been initiated and fostered in large part by Galvano Fiamma, who served as confessor to both Luchino and Bruzio, and almoner and scribe to Archbishop Giovanni.[128] Perhaps, too, Luca's services to Bruzio were part of an effort on the part of his bishop and confrère Angelo Acciaiuoli to make diplomatic overtures to the Visconti during the bishop's bid to remove the Angevin-allied Gauthier de Brienne from his brief *signoria* over Florence in 1343. This might also explain why the bishop brought Luca with him when he went to Avignon in March 1344 for the purpose of justifying this ouster to Pope Clement. Simply put, he invited Luca because the latter had demonstrated his command of the brand of Dominican political thinking that had served the order, and arguably the Italian cities, so well over the course of so many turbulent decades.

---

127 The subject cities represented in Paris, BnF, MS lat. 6467 are Piacenza, Parma, Bergamo, Novara, Asti, Lodi, Brescia, Cremona, Como, Vercelli, Bobbio, and Crema. The same, with the exception of Parma and Crema, are depicted on Azzone's tomb.

128 Boucheron, 'Tout est monument', pp. 314–16. See also Green, 'Galvano Fiamma, Azzone Visconti' and Creytens, 'Une question disputée de Galvano Fiamma', pp. 107–08.

Conclusion: *The Defender of the Peace* or Defenders of the Peace?

Trying to account for the classicizing and Aristotelian ideology of princely magnificence and magnanimity advocated by Galvano Fiamma on behalf of the Visconti, Louis Green suggested in an article published in 1990 that it might 'be explained by the influence on him of the scholastic tradition exemplified by such masters of his order as John of Paris who had, earlier in the century, upheld secular power; or by Marsiglio of Padua whom Galvano may have met in 1327 during the latter's visit to Milan in the retinue of Ludwig of Bavaria'.[129] I hope this chapter has shown that the principal influences on Galvano were in fact much closer to home, being embedded in the moral philosophical and penitential, commune-centred ideology that dominated the political discourse within the convents and *studia* of the Dominican order in north and central Italy during the late thirteenth and first half of the fourteenth century. This discourse had since the time of Thomas Aquinas proved itself adaptable to many kinds of civic polity, from communes ruled by the *popolo*, to aristocratic republics, to *signorie*. In doing so it participated in and contributed to many of the cultural currents active during these decades, including early civic humanism and the rise of vernacular learned and literary culture. It also formed a distinct branch of Italian political thinking which, like those associated with the jurists and with Marsilius of Padua, was dedicated to securing peace and the common good in cities, and to theorizing what constituted legitimate and stable political authority. In common with the jurists and Marsilius, these Dominicans were creatures of the communes, born to citizen families and actively engaged in the political life of their *patriae*. But they were also members of a religious order charged with the pastoral mission of instilling the orthodox faith of the universal Church and the morally upright behaviour of the people of the city of God. They saw these two realms, political and religious, as being inextricably intertwined and interdependent, and they saw themselves as being uniquely qualified to do the work of guiding their fellow Christian citizens on the path of earthly and heavenly peace.

Recently E. Igor Mineo has identified the writings of Remigio de' Girolami and Marsilius of Padua as being indicative of two principal streams of civic political thought in early fourteenth-century Italy. For Remigio (and, I believe, for the other writers considered here) 'the whole, the community, is anterior to its parts, and these, its individual *cives*, exist only within it'. In contrast, for Marsilius, 'the totality is an artificial entity, the fruit of the desire of the parts to live well'. And yet while these

---

129 Green, 'Galvano Fiamma, Azzone Visconti', p. 111.

two streams of thought are diametrically opposed, they both spring from the same desire for peace and horror of political violence, and from the same 'idealization of peace'.[130] Had Marsilius, in *Defensor pacis*, limited his discussion of the causes of political intranquillity and discord to Aristotle's 'notice in Book v of his civil science, which we have called the *Politics*' (whose subject, according to Aristotle, is 'how dissensions and revolutions arise' in polities), it is likely his Dominican contemporaries would have taken no exception to it. But when he went on to place the principal blame for the intranquillity of his contemporary Italy on 'the certain unusual cause [...] which took its occasion from an effect produced by the divine cause outside all its habitual activity in things, and which [...] neither Aristotle nor any other philosopher of his time or before was able to perceive'[131] — that is, on the popes and the priesthood — this they could not abide. How could they, after all, these priests who had taken it upon themselves to be not only defenders of the papacy's *plenitudo potestatis* but also defenders of the peace, giving expert political advice to citizens and princes?

---

130 Mineo, 'Cose in comune e bene comune', p. 47.
131 *DP*, I, 19.3, trans. by Brett, pp. 128–29; Aristotle, *Politics*, v, 2, 1302a16.

Works Cited

Manuscripts

Florence, Biblioteca Medicea Laurenziana, MS San Marco 452 (20)
Paris, Bibliothèque nationale de France, MS fonds latin 6467: Luca Mannelli,
  Compendium moralis philosophie

Primary Sources

Bacon, Roger, *Opus Majus*, pt. 7: *The 'Opus Majus' of Roger Bacon*, vol. II, ed. by
  John Henry Bridges (London: Williams and Norgate, 1900)
Bartolomeo da San Concordio, *Ammaestramenti degli antichi*, ed. by Pier Giuseppe
  Colombi (Siena: Edizioni Cantagalli, 1963)
———, *Ammaestramenti degli antichi latini e toscani*, ed. by Vincenzio Nannucci
  (Florence: Ricordi e Compagno, 1840)
Cicero, *De re publica*, ed. and trans. by Clinton W. Keyes (Cambridge, MA:
  Harvard University Press, 1928)
Enrico da Rimini, *De quattuor virtutibus cardinalibus* (Strasbourg, 1472–1475)
Giles of Rome, *De regimine principum libri III* (Rome, 1607; repr. Aalen: Scientia
  Verlag, 1967)
Guido Vernani, *Il 'Liber de virtutibus' di Guido Vernani da Rimini: Una rivisitazione
  trecentesca dell'etica tomista*, ed. by Luciano Cova (Turnhout: Brepols, 2011)
John of Paris, *On Royal and Papal Power*, trans. by John A. Watt (Toronto:
  Pontifical Institute of Mediaeval Studies, 1971)
Marsilius of Padua, *The Defender of the Peace*, trans. by Annabel Brett, Cambridge
  Texts in the History of Political Thought (Cambridge: Cambridge University
  Press, 2005)
Peter of Auvergne, *Scriptum super III–VIII libros Politicorum Aristotelis*, ed. by Lidia
  Lanza, Scrinium Friburgense, 50 (Wiesbaden: Reichert Verlag, 2021)
Ptolemy of Lucca, *De regimine principum*, in *On the Government of Rulers/De
  regimine principum: Ptolemy of Lucca with Portions Attributed to Thomas
  Aquinas*, trans. by James M. Blythe, Middle Ages series (Philadelphia:
  University of Pennsylvania Press, 1997), pp. 112–288
Remigio de' Girolami, *De bono comuni*, in Emilio Panella, 'Dal bene comune al
  bene del comune: I trattati politici di Remigio dei Girolami nella Firenze dei
  bianchi-neri', in 'Politica e vita religiosa a Firenze tra '300 e '500', special issue,
  Memorie Domenicane, n.s., 16 (1985), 1–198 (pp. 123–68)
———, *De bono pacis*, in Emilio Panella, 'Dal bene comune al bene del comune:
  I trattati politici di Remigio dei Girolami nella Firenze dei bianchi-neri', in
  'Politica e vita religiosa a Firenze tra '300 e '500', special issue, *Memorie
  Domenicane*, n.s., 16 (1985), 1–198 (pp. 169–83)

———, *Tractatus de iustitia*, in Ovidio Capitani, 'L'incompiuto "tractatus de iustitia" di fra Remigio de' Girolami († 1319)', *Bullettino dell'istituto storico italiano per il Medio Evo*, 72 (1960), 91–134

Thomas Aquinas, *De regno*, in *On the Government of Rulers/De regimine principum: Ptolemy of Lucca with Portions Attributed to Thomas Aquinas*, trans. by James M. Blythe, Middle Ages series (Philadelphia: University of Pennsylvania Press, 1997), pp. 60–112

Secondary Works

Avray, David d', *Death and the Prince: Memorial Preaching before 1350* (Oxford: Clarendon Press, 1994)

Bartuschat, Johannes, Elisa Brilli, and Delphine Carron, eds, *The Dominicans and the Making of Florentine Cultural Identity (13th–14th Centuries)* (Florence: Florence University Press, 2020)

Beattie, Blake, 'The Sermon as *Speculum Principis*: A Curial Sermon by Luca Mannelli, O.P.', *Medieval Sermon Studies*, 42 (1998), 26–51

Blythe, James M., 'Aristotle's *Politics* and Ptolemy of Lucca', *Vivarium*, 40.1 (2002), 103–36

———, *Ideal Government and the Mixed Constitution in the Middle Ages* (Princeton, NJ: Princeton University Press, 1992)

———, *The Life and Works of Tolomeo Fiadoni (Ptolemy of Lucca)*, Disputatio, 16 (Turnhout: Brepols, 2009)

Bonaini, F., ed., 'Chronica antiqua conventus Sanctae Catharinae de Pisis', *Archivio Storico Italiano*, Ser. 1, 6 (1845), 399–593

Boucheron, Patrick, 'Paroles de paix et seigneurs de guerre en Italie dans le premier tiers du XIVe siècle: Quelques problèmes iconographiques', in *Paroles de paix en temps de guerre*, ed. by Sylvie Caucanas, Rémy Cazals, and Nicolas Offenstadt (Toulouse: Privat, 2006), pp. 165–79

———, 'Tout est monument: Le mausolée d'Azzone Visconti à San Gottardo in Corte de Milan (1342–1346)', in *Liber largitorius: Études d'histoire médiévale offertes à Pierre Toubert par ses élèves*, ed. by Dominique Barthélemy and Jean-Marie Martin (Geneva: Droz, 2003), pp. 303–26

Briggs, Charles F., *Giles of Rome's 'De regimine principum': Reading and Writing Politics at Court and University, c. 1275–c. 1525* (Cambridge: Cambridge University Press, 1999)

———, 'Life, Works, and Legacy', in *A Companion to Giles of Rome*, ed. by Charles F. Briggs and Peter S. Eardley (Leiden: Brill, 2016), pp. 6–33

———, 'Moral Philosophy and Dominican Education: Bartolomeo da San Concordio's *Compendium moralis philosophiae*', in *Medieval Education*, ed. by Ronald B. Begley and Joseph W. Koterski, Fordham Series in Medieval Studies, 4 (New York: Fordham University Press, 2005), pp. 182–96

Briggs, Charles F., and Cary J. Nederman, 'Western Medieval *Specula, c.* 1150–*c.* 1450', in *A Critical Companion to the 'Mirrors for Princes' Literature*, ed. by Noëlle-Laetitia Perret and Stéphane Péquignot (Leiden: Brill, 2023), pp. 160–96

Carron, Delphine, 'Influences et interactions entre Santa Maria Novella et la Commune de Florence : Une étude de cas. Les sermons de Remigio de' Girolami (1295–1301)', in *The Dominicans and the Making of Florentine Cultural Identity (13th–14th Centuries)*, ed. by Johannes Bartuschat, Elisa Brilli, and Delphine Carron (Florence: Florence University Press, 2020), pp. 53–68

Casagrande, Carla, 'Enrico da Rimini', in *Dizionaria Biografico degli Italiani*, 42 (1993), <https://www.treccani.it/enciclopedia/enrico-da-rimini_%28Dizionario-Biografico%29/>

———, 'Le roi, les anges et la paix chez le franciscain Guibert de Tournai', in *Prêcher la paix et discipliner la société: Italie, France, Angleterre (xiiie–xve siècles)*, ed. by Rosa Maria Dessì (Turnhout: Brepols, 2005), pp. 141–53

Catto, Jeremy, 'Ideas and Experience in the Political Thought of Aquinas', *Past & Present*, 71 (May 1976), 3–21

Cinelli, Luciano, 'Mannelli, Luca', in *Dizionario Biografico degli Italiani*, 69 (2007), <https://www.treccani.it/enciclopedia/luca-mannelli_(Dizionario-Biografico)>

Conte, Maria, 'Gli "Ammaestramenti degli antichi" di Bartolomeo da San Concordio: Prime osservazioni in vista dell'edizione critica', in *The Dominicans and the Making of Florentine Cultural Identity (13th–14th Centuries)*, ed. by Johannes Bartuschat, Elisa Brilli, and Delphine Carron (Florence: Florence University Press, 2020), pp. 157–91

———, 'Il lessico politico negli *Ammaestramenti degli antichi* di Bartolomeo da San Concordio', *Archivum Fratrum Praedicatorum*, n.s., 3 (2018), 7–36

Cova, Luciano, *Il 'Liber de virtutibus' di Guido Vernani da Rimini: Una rivisitazione trecentesca dell'etica tomista* (Turnhout: Brepols, 2011)

Creytens, Raymond, 'Une question disputée de Galvano Fiamma O.P. sur le pouvoir temporel du pape', *Archivum Fratrum Praedicatorum*, 15 (1945), 102–33

Dorez, Leone, ed., *La Canzone delle virtù e delle scienze di Bartolomeo di Bartoli da Bologna* (Bergamo: Istituto italiano d'arti grafiche editore, 1904)

Dunbabin, Jean, 'Guido Vernani of Rimini's Commentary on Aristotle's "Politics"', *Traditio*, 44 (1988), 373–88

———, 'Hervé de Nédellec, Pierre de la Palud and France's Place in Christendom', in *Political Thought and the Realities of Power in the Middle Ages*, ed. by Joseph Canning and Otto Gerhard Oexle, Veröffentlichungen des Max-Planck-Instituts für Geschichte, 147 (Göttingen: Vandenhoeck & Ruprecht, 1998), pp. 159–72

———, 'The Reception and Interpretation of Aristotle's *Politics*', in *The Cambridge History of Later Medieval Philosophy*, ed. by Norman Ketzmann, Anthony Kenny, and Jan Pinborg (Cambridge: Cambridge University Press, 1982), pp. 723–28

Evangelisti, Paolo, 'I *pauperes Christi* e i linguaggi dominativi: I francescani come protagonisti della costruzione della testualità politica e dell'organizzazione del consenso nel bassomedioevo (Gilbert de Tournai, Paolino da Venezia, Francesc Eiximenis)', in *La propaganda politica nel basso medioevo: Atti del XXXVIII Convegno storico internazionale, Todi, 14–17 ottobre 2001* (Spoleto: Centro italiano di studi sull'alto medioevo, 2002), pp. 315–92

Flüeler, Christoph, *Rezeption und Interpretation der Aristotelischen 'Politica' im späten Mittelalter*, Bochumer Studien zur Philosophie, 19, 2 vols (Amsterdam: B. R. Grüner, 1992)

Garnett, George, *Marsilius of Padua and 'the Truth of History'* (Oxford: Oxford University Press, 2006)

Genet, Jean-Philippe, 'L'évolution du genre des Miroirs des princes en Occident au Moyen Âge', in *Religion et mentalités au Moyen Âge: Mélanges en l'honneur d'Hervé Martin*, ed. by Sophie Cassagnes-Brouquet (Rennes: Presses universitaires de Rennes, 2003), pp. 531–41

Gentili, Sonia, 'Girolami, Remigio de'', in *Dizionario Biografico degli Italiani*, 56 (2001), <https://www.treccani.it/enciclopedia/remigio-de-girolami_(Dizionario-Biografico)>

Gerulaitis, Leonardas V., 'The Canonization of Saint Thomas Aquinas', *Vivarium*, 5.1 (1967), 25–46

Green, Louis, 'Galvano Fiamma, Azzone Visconti and the Revival of the Classical Theory of Magnificence', *Journal of the Warburg and Courtauld Institutes*, 53 (1990), 98–113

Hamesse, Jacqueline, 'Les manuscrits des "Parvi flores": Une nouvelle liste de témoins', *Scriptorium*, 48 (1994), 299–332

Houser, R. E., *The Cardinal Virtues: Aquinas, Albert, and Philip the Chancellor* (Toronto: Pontifical Institute of Mediaeval Studies, 2004)

Iannella, Cecilia, 'La paix dans la prédication de Giordano de Pise (ves 1260–1310)', in *Prêcher la paix et discipliner la société: Italie, France, Angleterre (XIIIe–XVe siècles)*, ed. by Rosa Maria Dessì (Turnhout: Brepols, 2005), pp. 367–82

Jansen, Katherine L., *Peace and Penance in Late Medieval Italy* (Princeton, NJ: Princeton University Press, 2018)

Johnson, Mark F., 'Aquinas's *Summa theologiae* as Pedagogy', in *Medieval Education*, ed. by Ronald B. Begley and Joseph W. Koterski, Fordham Series in Medieval Studies, 4 (New York: Fordham University Press, 2005), pp. 133–42

Kaeppeli, Thomas, 'Luca Mannelli (d. 1362) e la sua tabulatio et expositio Senecae', *Archivum Fratrum Praedicatorum*, 18 (1948), 237–64

———, *Scriptores Ordinis Praedicatorum Medii Aevi*, 4 vols (Rome: Ad S. Sabinae, 1970–1993)

Kalning, Pamela, 'Virtues and Exempla in John of Wales and Jacobus de Cessolis', in *Princely Virtues in the Middle Ages, 1200–1500*, ed. by István P. Bejczy and Cary J. Nederman, Disputatio, 9 (Turnhout: Brepols, 2007), pp. 139–76

Kelly, Samantha, *The New Solomon: Robert of Naples (1309–1343) and Fourteenth-Century Kingship* (Leiden: Brill, 2003)

Kent, Bonnie, 'The Good Will According to Gerald Odonis, Duns Scotus, and William of Ockham', *Franciscan Studies*, 46 (1986), 119–39

Labriola, Ada, '"Allegoria del buon governo" nel *Libro del gioco degli scacchi* di Jacopo da Cessole', *Paragone (Arte)*, 65.114–15 (2014), 54–65

Lambertini, Roberto, 'Governo ideale e riflessione politica dei frati mendicanti nella prima metà del Trecento', in *Etica e politica: Le teorie dei frati mendicanti nel due e trecento* (Spoleto: Centro italiano di studi sull'alto medioevo, 1999), pp. 233–77

——, 'Political Thought', in *A Companion to Giles of Rome*, ed. by Charles F. Briggs and Peter S. Eardley (Leiden: Brill, 2016), pp. 254–74

——, 'L'usura tra Santa Croce e Santa Maria Novella: Pietro de Trabibus e Remigio de' Girolami a confronto', in *The Dominicans and the Making of Florentine Cultural Identity (13th–14th Centuries)*, ed. by Johannes Bartuschat, Elisa Brilli, and Delphine Carron (Florence: Florence University Press, 2020), pp. 193–205

Lapidge, Michael, Silvia Nocentini, and Francesco Santi, eds, *Compendium Auctorum Latinorum Medii Aevi*, vol. I, fasc. 6 (Florence: SISMEL, 2003)

Lohr, Charles H., 'Medieval Latin Aristotle Commentaries: Authors G–I', *Traditio*, 24 (1968), 149–245; 'Jacobus–Johannes Juff', *Traditio*, 26 (1970), 135–216; and 'Narcissus–Richardus', *Traditio*, 28 (1972), 281–396

Matteini, Nevio, *Il più antico oppositore politico di Dante: Guido Vernani da Rimini. Testo critico del 'De reprobatione Monarchiae'* (Padua: Casa Editrice Dott. Antonio Milani, 1958)

Mineo, E. Igor, 'Cose in comune e bene comune: L'ideologia della comunità in Italia nel tardo medioevo', in *The Languages of Political Society: Western Europe, 14th–17th Centuries*, ed. by Andrea Gamberini, Jean-Philippe Genet, and Andrea Zorzi (Rome: Viella, 2011), pp. 39–67

——, 'Liberté et communauté en Italie (milieu XIIIe–début XVe siècle)', in *La République dans tous ses états: Pour une histoire intellectuelle de la république en Europe*, ed. by Claudia Moatti and Michèle Riot-Sarcey (Paris: Payot, 2009), pp. 215–50

Mulchahey, M. Michèle, 'Education in Dante's Florence Revisited: Remigio de' Girolami and the Schools of Santa Maria Novella', in *Medieval Education*, ed. by Ronald B. Begley and Joseph W. Koterski, Fordham Series in Medieval Studies, 4 (New York: Fordham University Press, 2005), pp. 143–81

——, *'First the Bow is Bent in Study': Dominican Education before 1350* (Toronto: Pontifical Institute of Mediaeval Studies, 1998)

Murray, Alexander, *Conscience and Authority in the Medieval Church* (Oxford: Oxford University Press, 2015)

Nold, Patrick, 'John XXII and History', in *Papst Johannes XXII: Konzepte und Verfahren seines Pontifikats*, ed. by Hans-Joachim Schmidt and Martin Rohde, Scrinium Friburgense, 32 (Berlin: De Gruyter, 2014), pp. 17–40

Palmer, James A., 'Peace Movements: Peace in the Communes', in *A Cultural History of Peace*, II: *In the Medieval Age*, ed. by Walter Simons (London: Bloomsbury Academic, 2020), pp. 101–18

Pellegrin, Elisabeth, *La bibliothèque des Visconti et des Sforza, ducs de Milan. Supplement* (Florence: Leo S. Olschki, 1969)

Piron, Sylvain, 'Franciscan *Quodlibeta* in Southern *Studia* and at Paris, 1280–1300', in *Theological Quodlibeta in the Middle Ages: The Thirteenth Century*, ed. by Christopher Schabel (Leiden: Brill, 2006), pp. 403–38

——, 'Marchands et confesseurs: Le *Traité des contrats* d'Olivi dans son contexte (Narbonne, fin XIIIe–début XIVe siècle)', in *L'argent au Moyen Âge: Actes des congrès de la Société des historiens médiévistes de l'enseignement supérieur public, 1997* (Paris: Publications de la Sorbonne, 1998), pp. 289–308

Piron, Sylvain, and Emanuele Coccia, 'Poésie, sciences et politique: Une génération d'intellectuels italiens (1290–1330)', *Revue de Synthèse*, 129.4 (2008), 551–86

Reichberg, Gregory M., 'Human Nature, Peace, and War', in *A Cultural History of Peace*, II: *In the Medieval Age*, ed. by Walter Simons (London: Bloomsbury Academic, 2020), pp. 33–49

Robey, David, and John Law, 'The Venetian Myth and the "De Republica Veneta" of Pier Paolo Vergerio', *Rinascimento*, Ser. 2, 15 (1975), 3–59

Rubinstein, Nicolai, 'Marsilius of Padua and Italian Political Thought of his Time', in *Europe in the Late Middle Ages*, ed. by J. R. Hale, J. R. L. Highfield, and B. Smalley (London: Faber and Faber, 1965), pp. 44–75

Rupp, Teresa, '"Love justice, you who judge the Earth": Remigio dei Girolami's Sermons to the Florentine Priors, 1295', in *Preaching and Political Society from Late Antiquity to the End of the Middle Ages*, ed. by Franco Morenzoni (Turnhout: Brepols, 2013), pp. 251–63

Ryan, Magnus, 'Bartolus of Sassoferrato and Free Cities', *Transactions of the Royal Historical Society*, 10 (2000), 65–89

Schmugge, Ludwig, 'Fiadoni, Bartolomeo', in *Dizionario biografico degli Italiani*, 47 (1997), <https://www.treccani.it/enciclopedia/bartolomeo-fiadoni_(Dizionario-Biografico)>

Segre, Cesare, 'Bartolomeo da San Concordio', in *Dizionario Biografico degli Italiani*, 6 (1964), <https://www.treccani.it/enciclopedia/bartolomeo-da-san-concordio_(Dizionario-Biografico)>

Sharpe, Richard, *A Handlist of the Latin Writers of Great Britain and Ireland before 1540* (Turnhout: Brepols, 1997)

Speer, Andreas, '*Veritas Morum*: Practical Truth and Practical Science according to Bonaventure', in *Les philosophies morales et politiques au Moyen Âge*, vol. I, ed. by B. Carlos Bazán, Eduardo Andújar, and Léonard G. Sbrocchi (Ottawa: Legas, 1995), pp. 581–90

Stefano, Giuseppe di, 'La diffusion de Valère Maxime au XIVe s.: Du nouveau sur le comment de Frater Lucas', in *Genèse et débuts du Grand Schisme d'Occident*, ed. by Jean Favier (Paris: Éditions du Centre national de la recherche scientifique, 1980), pp. 269–75

Tabarroni, Andrea, 'Francescanesimo e riflessione politica sino ad Ockham', in *Etica e politica: Le teorie dei frati mendicanti nel due e trecento* (Spoleto: Centro italiano di studi sull'alto medioevo, 1999), pp. 205–30

Thompson, Augustine, *Cities of God: The Religion of the Italian Communes 1125–1325* (University Park: Pennsylvania State University Press, 2005)

Todeschini, Giacomo, 'Participer au Bien Commun: La notion franciscaine d'appartenance à la *civitas*', in *De Bono Communi: The Discourse and Practice of the Common Good in the European City (13th–16th c.)*, ed. by Elodie Lecuppre-Desjardin and Anne-Laure van Bruaene (Turnhout: Brepols, 2010), pp. 225–35

Toste, Marco, '*Unicuique suum*: The Restitution to John of Wales, OFM of Parts of Some Mirrors for Princes Circulating in Late Medieval Portugal', *Franciscan Studies*, 73 (2015), 1–58

Vauchez, André, *Sainthood in the Later Middle Ages*, trans. by Jean Birrell (Cambridge: Cambridge University Press, 1997)

Vecchio, Silvana, '*Quasi armarium scripturarum*: Bartolomeo da San Concordio come biblioteca vivente', *Doctor Virtualis: Rivista online di storia della filosofia medievale*, 11 (2012), 25–43

Verweij, Michiel, 'Princely Virtues or Virtues for Princes? William Peraldus and his *De eruditione principum*', in *Princely Virtues in the Middle Ages, 1200–1500*, ed. by István P. Bejczy and Cary J. Nederman, Disputatio, 9 (Turnhout: Brepols, 2007), pp. 51–71

Viroli, Maurizio, *From Politics to Reason of State: The Acquisition and Transformation of the Language of Politics 1250–1600* (Cambridge: Cambridge University Press, 1992)

Wieland, Georg, 'The Reception and Interpretation of Aristotle's *Ethics*', in *The Cambridge History of Later Medieval Philosophy*, ed. by Norman Ketzmann, Anthony Kenny, and Jan Pinborg (Cambridge: Cambridge University Press, 1982), pp. 660–62

Yun, Bee, 'Ptolemy of Lucca — A Pioneer of Civic Republicanism? A Reassessment', *History of Political Thought*, 29.3 (2008), 417–39

JACOB LANGELOH

How History Happens[*]

Contingency and Finality in the Political Philosophy
of Marsilius of Padua, with a View on John Quidort
of Paris and Dante Alighieri

Introduction: Contingency and Finality

To answer the question 'what should I do', one ought to consider how much time one has, what one's goals are, and how free one is. Therefore, most eschatological claims pose a moral challenge. If one is convinced that the apocalypse or the end of days is close, one generally assumes that events will follow a pattern that has been foretold. Individual planning, then, would make little sense, and temporal goals might have to give way to eternal ones. That such thinking can challenge moral conventions and undermine the rules of society is not just a theoretical point; it has repeatedly manifested itself in history. Different ideological or political groups would often identify the head of an opposing group as the Antichrist or a precursor to the Antichrist to galvanize the members of one's own group. We see this, for example, in Pope Gregory IX's propaganda against Frederick II.[1] Or in movements such as the Anabaptists' rebellion at Münster, which led to the death of thousands while seeking to secure salvation.

The Christian faith possesses a very detailed description of how the apocalypse will unfold. Any Christian political philosophy, therefore, faces

---

[*] I want to thank the editors of this volume as well as my colleagues Hanna-Myriam Häger, Michelle Thompson, and Shevek K. Selbert for their precious feedback.

[1] See the letter by Gregory IX from 1 July 1239, where he identifies Frederick with the beast of the apocalypse, *Epistolae saeculi XIII e regestis pontificum Romanorum selectae*, ed. by Rodenberg, p. 646.

> **Jacob Langeloh** received an MA (2009) and a PhD (2015) from Freie Universität Berlin. His research focuses on medieval political theory, especially *Exempla* and historical argumentation, the *Begriffsgeschichte* of musical performance concepts, and most recently the engagement of Latin scholastics with Islam and the Qur'an in the later Middle Ages. He is currently affiliated with the University of Copenhagen.

Marsilius of Padua, ed. by Alessandro Mulieri, Serena Masolini, and Jenny Pelletier, Disputatio, 36 (Turnhout: Brepols, 2023), pp. 253–284

254   JACOB LANGELOH

a dilemma: How can the expectation of the apocalypse be reconciled with establishing a stable political system? What is the role and the possibility of everyday morality and virtuous human action?

These questions are especially urgent when looking at the dominant political philosophy of the later Middle Ages, Aristotelianism.[2] Generally speaking, Aristotelian political philosophy is about shaping what is contingent.[3] This is neatly captured in Thomas Aquinas's principal statement of *De regno ad regem Cypri*: 'in any field where something is directed towards a final goal, and where it can happen that one proceeds in this way or another, one needs someone or something providing guidance so that one attains the due end by direct means'.[4] Political communities try to direct things to go one way and *not* another by choosing the best course of action. If contingency is defined as the possibility for things to go this way or that, then political communities are a tool for dealing with the contingent on the most significant level,[5] since they allow a person to 'live well' and through communal effort to become a good person too.[6]

Any kind of prophecy, particularly about the apocalypse, will challenge this approach to human behaviour and community-building. For Christianity, how the end of days will unfold could be read in the Book of

---

2 Nederman, 'The Meaning of "Aristotelianism"' argues convincingly that one should differentiate between different kinds of Aristotelianism but that despite some differences they share the same footing. For a list of scholarship regarding the meaning of political Aristotelianism, especially in relation to Marsilius, see Briguglia, *Marsile de Padoue*, p. 61, n. 1.

3 Modern research has rather frequently focused on the question of contingency in the sciences, as e.g., Omodeo and Garau, eds, *Contingency and Natural Order*. Maier, 'Notwendigkeit, Kontingenz und Zufall', p. 219, remarks that it was deemed obvious that human action was free and therefore contingent. One major source for the medieval discussion of the contingent was Aristotle's *De interpretatione* 9; cf. Knuuttila, 'Medieval Theories of Future Contingents'.

4 Thomas Aquinas, *De regno*, I, 1, Leonina edn, p. 449: 'In omnibus autem quae ad finem aliquem ordinantur, in quibus contingit sic et aliter procedere, opus est aliquo dirigente, per quod directe debitum perveniatur ad finem'. Translations are my own unless specified otherwise. Thomas Aquinas, *On Kingship*, trans. by Eschmann and Phelan, p. 3: 'In all things which are ordered towards an end, wherein this or that course may be adopted, some directive principle is needed through which the due end may be reached by the most direct route'.

5 Albert the Great also appears to view politics as the art of dealing with the contingent when he defines the object of political science according to Aristotle and his commentator Averroes. Albertus Magnus, *Super ethica*, I, 2, ed. by Kübel, p. 12: 'Unde concludit, quod cum non possit reduci ad uniformitatem, amabile, idest desiderabile, est de talibus, scilicet civilibus, quantum ad conclusiones, et ex talibus, quantum ad principia dicentes. Ostendit modum: grosse per sensibilia exempla et proverbia vulgaria, quibus multum utitur, et figuraliter per argumentationes imperfectas et de his quae ut frequentius, quia Commentator distinguit triplex contingens, scilicet rarum, quod committitur fortunae, et ad utrumlibet, de quo est consilium, et ut in pluribus, quae cadunt in artem, sicut sunt etiam naturalia'.

6 For this overlap of politics and ethics, cf. Bertelloni, 'Die Rolle der Natur', pp. 692–95.

Daniel 7–11 and in the Revelation of John. There was a constant temptation to interpret contemporary events as corresponding to the allegories contained in these prophecies. The main difficulty was to identify current events with the preordained narratives described in Scripture. If they were matched up successfully, current events could be read as manifestations of types and figures (*typi et figurae*) that had been prophesied a long time ago and could not be influenced by humans.

If prophecy reveals the 'outcome of things with unshakable truth',[7] then politics faces a difficult question. If the outcome is already known, why would it matter whether and how we form political communities or act morally? This potential conflict between Aristotelian political philosophy, which teaches us how to shape history according to human needs, and eschatology, which assumes history will unfold in a predetermined way, was a problem for Christianity ever since Aristotle's *Politics* was translated into Latin in the 1260s,[8] but it was especially prominent in some of the earliest interpretations of the newly discovered Aristotle.

In this chapter, I will try to answer the question of how Marsilius of Padua positioned himself on the spectrum between contingency and finality. As a backdrop, I will first outline the positions that two earlier authors took regarding contingency and finality, namely John Quidort of Paris and Dante Alighieri. Like Marsilius, they defended a worldly ruler against the claims of the papacy with the help of Aristotelian philosophy.[9] Their solutions demonstrate that there is no necessary connection between political contingency and apocalyptic finality — one could be interested in the apocalypse but see contemporary events as entirely contingent (John), and one could see finality in the current events without identifying them with the finality of the apocalypse (Dante).

Turning to Marsilius, I first outline some general impressions when situating him on the spectrum between contingency and finality. The main part of this section will consist in a consideration of a publication by George Garnett. Contrary to nearly all previous interpretations of Marsilius, Garnett claimed that Marsilius regarded history, and especially the conflict of his times, as 'providentially ordained'.[10] While I agree that Marsilius sees a certain truth in history, I reject Garnett's claim that

---

7 Petrus Lombardus, *Prologus Commentarii*, ed. by Migne, col. 58: 'Est igitur prophetia inspiratio vel revelatio divina rerum eventus immobili veritate denuntians'. Peter is paraphrasing Cassiodorus's definition from the *Expositio psalmorum* here while substituting 'inspiratio' for 'aspiratio'.

8 For the context of the translation and its early reception, see Flüeler, *Rezeption und Interpretation*.

9 For an article comparing their points of view as to whether an empire is necessary, see Koch, 'Against Empire?'.

10 Garnett, *Marsilius of Padua and 'the Truth of History'*, p. 48, with frequent other mentions; the argumentation reaches its peak on pp. 157–59.

Marsilius saw his own era as immediately leading up to the apocalypse.[11] To make my case, I discuss Garnett's arguments and key passages of the *Defensor pacis* in detail. Based on this material, I conclude that Marsilius had a knack for teleological narration but ultimately took a rather contingent view on the political events of his day. What can be concluded, however, is that an awareness of the workings of history played an important role in the political philosophy of all three authors that I discuss here.

Defending Contingency and Finding Finality: John Quidort of Paris and Dante Alighieri

John Quidort of Paris

John Quidort of Paris is most renowned for his work *De potestate regia et papali* (*c.* 1300),[12] in which he defended the French king, Philip IV 'the Fair', in his conflict with Boniface VIII. This conflict began with a dispute about whether it was legitimate to tax the clergy but then led to a more general question about how the powers (*potestates*) in this world, the secular and the spiritual, relate to each other. John Quidort of Paris finds himself arguing against the longer treatises of Giles of Rome and James of Viterbo,[13] but battles were also fought through papal bulls and shorter anonymous works.[14]

What stance does John take towards history in his most famous work, *De potestate regia et papali*? To answer this question, it helps to consider his main goal. He did not intend to create an entirely new of way of thinking about politics but rather to undercut the force of papal arguments threatening Philip the Fair. John's main goal, therefore, can be described as a defensive one. As I have tried to show elsewhere, he mostly attempts to disarm opposing arguments and tends to argue that things are far more complex than the other side lets on. This also applies to history. He frequently consults several sources on historical precedent and tries to

---

11 For a more precise characterization of Garnett's point, see 'Garnett's Challenge' below.

12 Two editions exist with a French and German translation respectively: Leclercq, *Jean de Paris et l'ecclésiologie du XIIIᵉ siècle*, pp. 171–260, and John Quidort of Paris, *De potestate regia*, ed. by Bleienstein. The first is especially valuable in pointing out the various borrowings that John Quidort makes, a fact that Bleienstein sadly neither expands upon nor makes explicit enough.

13 Giles of Rome, *On Ecclesiastical Power*, ed. and trans. by Dyson; James of Viterbo, *De regimine Christiano*, ed. by Dyson.

14 Editions and translations: *Quaestio de Potestate Papae (Rex Pacificus)*, ed. and trans. by Dyson, and *Three Royalist Tracts*, ed. by Dyson.

give the best reconstruction of events that have happened.[15] However, he also expresses doubt about the extent to which history can be understood as a model for the present.[16] If singular historical events were taken as indicative of general laws, John asks, would we not lapse into absurdity?

Consistent with this goal of constructing history as something complex and unpredictable, John presents many factors that contributed to the current power struggle between Philip IV and Boniface VIII as entirely contingent. Here, he imitates Thomas Aquinas, whose work *De regno* John had liberally borrowed from to compose his own treatise.[17] As indicated above, Aquinas frequently uses the word *contingit* to depict things that can happen but are not necessary. Another example occurs in the prologue of his work, where Thomas names the institution of just government as the primary goal of a political community. He continues that one is more likely to find a single 'rotten egg' amidst a multitude of governing persons than with one single person who is not part of that multitude, thereby expressing a contingent view of political processes: 'It happens more frequently that one person of a group deviates from striving towards the common good, than that a single person does'.[18] Aquinas sees this as a possible and likely development but not a necessary one. John expands the use of the word into questions of faith that are beyond Thomas's focus. As John writes in the very beginning of his own work, clearly targeting the papalists' position, sometimes it occurs that in trying to avoid one mistake, one lapses into another.[19] Later he remarks that, 'ever since Christ's corporal presence was removed, it sometimes happens in questions regarding faith that the Church is divided by the differences of opinion'.[20] While Thomas used the small word *contingit* to paint the success and failure of the state as a contingent matter that can be influenced, John Quidort marked

---

15 A good example is the deposition of the king of the Franks, Childerich. For a more thorough discussion, see Langeloh, *Erzählte Argumente*, p. 264.

16 See Langeloh, *Erzählte Argumente*, pp. 265–66, and John Quidort of Paris, *De potestate regia*, ed. by Bleienstein, p. 150.

17 Cf. Leclercq, *Jean de Paris et l'ecclésiologie du XIIIᵉ siècle*, pp. 35–36.

18 Thomas Aquinas, *De regno*, I, 5, Leonina edn, p. 454: 'Plerumque enim contingit ut ex pluribus aliquis ab intentione communis boni deficiat, quam quod unus tantum'.

19 John Quidort of Paris, *De potestate regia*, ed. by Bleienstein, p. 69: 'Interdum contingit quod vitare volens aliquem errorem dilabitur in errorem contrarium'. The two poles of opposition that John cautions avoiding are the Waldensians, who did not ascribe any authority to the pope and the Church, and King Herod, who thought Christ had come to claim worldly rule. John then classifies the claims of Boniface VIII to *dominium in temporalibus* as a type of 'Herodianism'. See Piaia, 'L'"Errore di Erode"', especially pp. 174–76.

20 John Quidort of Paris, *De potestate regia*, ed. by Bleienstein, p. 81: 'Nam post corporalem substractionem praesentiae corporalis christi contingit interdum circa ea quae fidei sunt quaestiones moveri in quibus per diversitatem sententiarum divideretur ecclesia quae ad sui unitatem requirit fidei unitatem nisi per unius sententiam unitas servaretur'.

the rise of tensions between State and Church as a historical development that was accidental but not unusual.

As mentioned earlier, contingency can be challenged by finality. It is therefore instructive to consider if a staunch defender of the separation between the secular and sacred realms like John Quidort thought that his current times could be interpreted according to some historical-prophetic scheme. Clearly, John Quidort was invested in this topic.[21] He wrote two works, the *De adventu Christi*,[22] which remains unedited, and the *Tractatus de Antichristo*,[23] which I will use as a point of reference here. The *Tractatus* was compiled in 1300 and responded to a contemporary debate, namely to the work *De Tempore Adventus Antichristi* by Arnold of Villanova.[24] Arnold had claimed to be able to predict the advent of the Antichrist very precisely, which lead to the condemnation of his work by the Faculty of Theology at Paris. Arnold's text was refuted by multiple works, among them John Quidort's tract. Without going into much detail in this debate, we can note two points: first, John refused to superimpose the apocalyptic structure onto his own time, and second, he used similar methods to call into question the political prophecies of his time, which he did in his *Tractatus de Antichristo*,[25] and to question universal papal authority in *De potestate*.

John takes great care to avoid what has fittingly been called 'Political Prophecy'.[26] In this mode of prophecy, one appears to be talking about the future but is actually referring to the present while leaving sufficient clues for listeners to realize that this is what one is doing. John not only refuses to do this, he also tries to disperse the arguments offered by anyone who claimed to be able to prophesize in this mode, for example, King Edward the Confessor, Hildegard von Bingen, and Joachim of Fiore.[27] One of his arguments against their prophecies is that they are too general to be accurately applied to present circumstances.[28] Addressing Joachim of

---

21 Milne-Tavendale, 'John of Paris and the Apocalypse', p. 121, calls it a 'certain preoccupation'.

22 Grabmann, 'Studien zu Johannes Quidort von Paris O. Pr.', pp. 21–23.

23 John Quidort of Paris, *Tractatus de antichristo*, ed. by Clark.

24 For the context, see John Quidort of Paris, *Tractatus de antichristo*, ed. by Clark, pp. 7–10, and Milne-Tavendale, 'John of Paris and the Apocalypse', pp. 122–23.

25 Milne-Tavendale, 'John of Paris and the Apocalypse', p. 129.

26 Milne-Tavendale, 'John of Paris and the Apocalypse', p. 129. On the complex and various ways in which prophecy was understood in the later Middle Ages, see FitzGerald, *Inspiration and Authority*. For the question of political prophecy, see e.g., the works by Reeves, *The Influence of Prophecy* and Coote, *Prophecy and Public Affairs*.

27 John Quidort of Paris, *Tractatus de antichristo*, ed. by Clark, pp. 37–42.

28 Milne-Tavendale, 'John of Paris and the Apocalypse', p. 135, writes in regard to Hildegard von Bingen: 'John uses very generalized statements to disengage the prophecy from the political and historical narratives with which it was associated, clearly stating that it is difficult to define what Hildegard meant by "womanish time"'. See John Quidort of Paris, *Tractatus de antichristo*, ed. by Clark, pp. 38–39.

Fiore, he writes: 'Even though the prophecy has become true in parts, [...] the rest remains unclear, since it is questionable what the names signify and whether all other things to come will happen simultaneously, or separately, or with how much distance.'[29]

To summarize, John's stance towards prophecy mimics his stance towards historical precedent in the conflict between king and pope. In both instances, he argues against putting too much weight on history. In the first case, he regards the conflict of his time as an unfortunate but not uncommon and thus normal historical development. In the second case, he calls out existing prophecies for being too vague and questions their potential to predict future developments. Through both means, he directly or indirectly defends the freedom of the political community to determine its own destiny.

Dante Alighieri

It is tempting to view Dante Alighieri and his treatise *De Monarchia* as a close companion to John Quidort of Paris and Marsilius of Padua. After all, all three attempted to defend a secular monarch from papal claims to power. However, Dante expounded a view on contingency that is very different from his two colleagues.

This difference is especially noticeable in the second book of *De Monarchia*. Dante's goal in Book II is to make the theoretical framework he developed in Book I correspond to historical reality. In Book I, he had named peace as the major factor in helping humanity reach its proper fulfilment, which consists in actualizing all possibilities of human understanding.[30] Only a monarch, a single ruler over all the world, can guarantee peace, so a monarch is necessary for humanity's fulfilment. In the cadenza of Book I, Dante merges this abstract requirement with the real-world event of the *Pax Augusta*. The *Pax Augusta* was supposedly achieved at the moment when Emperor Augustus was able to close the doors of the Temple of Janus to declare the end of all hostilities within the Roman Empire.[31] Dante's conclusion is that whatever was possible can happen again, but one

---

29 John Quidort of Paris, *Tractatus de antichristo*, ed. by Clark, p. 42: 'Hec autem prophetia licet sit verificata in parte [...] tamen quantum ad residuum est obscura quia dubium est quid significent nomina et utrum vel alia omnia simul, vel distanter, vel in quanta distancia sint futura'.

30 Dante Alighieri, *Monarchia*, I, 4.5 and I, 4.1, ed. and trans. by Imbach and Flüeler, pp. 72 and 70, respectively.

31 Cf. *Res Gestae Divi Augusti*, 13. As Goldsworthy, *Pax romana*, p. 169, notes, the symbolic act could at most be applied to the end of the civil war, as Rome was still 'almost permanently at war somewhere in the world'. The declaration of peace reached its symbolic peak in the dedication of the *ara pacis augusti* in 9 BC; see most recently Cornwell, *Pax and the Politics of Peace*.

must find the right person or institution to do it. In Book II, Dante tries to prove that the most promising and most deserving candidate to establish universal peace again is the Roman Empire that still existed in his day.

Book II of the *Monarchia* has a clear structure. Each single argument can be reconstructed as a syllogism — sometimes long, sometimes brief — that has distinctive components. The major premise is usually a very general statement. The minor premise, however, conforms to Dante's specific goal in this book, that is, to prove that the Roman emperor is the legitimate monarch by history. Since his goal is to make a historical point, the minor premises are usually historical in nature. The general shape of any one of his arguments, therefore, is this: (premise 1) If the historical state is such and such, then so-and-so; (premise 2) the state of the Roman Empire was such-and-such; (conclusion) therefore so-and-so applies to the Roman Empire. If Dante's general point is to be confirmed, the historical coincidences have to match one another.

Now, all of these minor premises, which become true through historical events, could have occurred through chance; they are contingent. However, Dante now chooses a different argumentative route. It is not only contingency, determination, or virtue that enabled the Roman Empire to meet the criteria of the minor premises, but God's explicit will also plays a role. One such case is described in Chapter 8 of Book II of *De Monarchia*. Dante claims that God sometimes expresses his will through athletic competitions.[32] And so, if we were to imagine that the various people of the world were racing for the prize of the Monarchy, the rule of the entire world, then when one people wins, God clearly approves of their success. Of course, Dante's argument is based on hindsight, as we know of course that the Romans managed to establish an empire (which is the condition expressed in the minor premise). However, their victory was not straightforward. As Dante tells us, Alexander the Great almost reached the finish line, insofar as he had sent a messenger to the Romans to demand their surrender. However, Alexander died before he was able to conquer the Romans. Why? Because God, who was not an entirely fair referee, took him out of the game. Dante exclaims:

> 'O the depth of riches both of the wisdom and knowledge of God', who will not pause in amazement before thee? For thou, when Alexander strove to entangle the feet of his Roman rival in the course, didst snatch him from the contest, lest his rashness wax more great.[33]

---

32 Dante Alighieri, *Monarchia*, II, 8.1, ed. and trans. by Imbach and Flüeler, p. 154.

33 Dante Alighieri, *Monarchia*, II, 8.10, ed. and trans. by Imbach and Flüeler, p. 158: '"O altitudo divitiarum scientie et sapientie Dei", quis hic te non obstupescere poterit? Nam conantem Alexandrum prepredire in cursu coathletam romanum tu, ne sua temeritas prodiret ulterius, de certamine rapuisti'; Dante Alighieri, *De Monarchia*, ed. and trans. by Henry, p. 114.

In this sense, Dante attributes a great degree of divine intervention in the events of the world and his scope is as universal as possible: God, his artful tool nature, and history proceed together and there is no reason to separate them from each other. Here, he displays a striking contrast to John Quidort of Paris, who was very reluctant to draw any such conclusions from historical events. Dante, on the other hand, does not hesitate to connect the Roman Empire's fortunes with God's own blessing, which is mediated through the workings of nature, the *ars dei*.[34]

To summarize, Dante uses the concepts of Aristotle's *Politics*, but he downplays contingency and imbues history with a sense of teleology and finality. This finality, however, is quite different from the Christian one that leads towards the apocalypse. The goal of complete intellectual expression can be achieved in life on earth already. Since this is apparently also God's intention, contingency is abolished to some degree since God, if necessary, heavily involves himself in worldly events. Of course, this argument is susceptible to reality checks, which critics as early as Guido Vernani (*c.* 1280–1344) were quick to exploit.[35] We know that the human world is divided, peoples go to war against each other. Is that what God intended? If one people conquer another, which people is God favouring? These fairly significant objections aside, Dante's text offers a radically different perspective on the relation between contingency and finality. While John Quidort saw mostly contingency in the history of the world, Dante sees purpose. History does lead towards a culmination point, and God himself is involved in shaping it. However, the culmination point is not identical with the end of days and the apocalypse, but remains on the worldly side of things.

Marsilius of Padua and the Apocalypse

Marsilius's Philosophy – Classically Contingent?

With the two examples of John of Paris and Dante Alighieri, I hope to have shown that it was possible to adopt different positions regarding contingency and finality within the tension between Christian prophecy and Aristotelian political philosophy. Now, I would like to consider if and how Marsilius of Padua positioned himself somewhere on this spectrum.

---

34 Dante Alighieri, *Monarchia*, I, 3.2, ed. and trans. by Imbach and Flüeler, p. 66.
35 On Vernani's opposition to Dante, cf. Kaeppeli, 'Der Dantegegner Guido Vernani', Matteini, *Il più antico oppositore politico di Dante*, and Cheneval, *Die Rezeption der Monarchia Dantes*.

The basis of Marsilius's Aristotelian political philosophy often appears very conventional.[36] Human beings need to come together to compensate for their natural disadvantages by using their skills to create a good life: 'those who live a civil life do not just live [...] but live well'.[37] To attain the good life, one has to cultivate one's actions.[38] There are some actions that are largely passive — receiving nutrition, for example — and there are active ones. For example, one should institute a police force to prevent excesses in those things that man does actively.[39] All of these statements go very well with the basic assumption of Aristotelian political philosophy that politics is a field that needs to be, and can be, actively shaped by human communities.

When determining where Marsilius advances beyond standard views, some commentators have found innovative elements in his focus on positive law.[40] Others have identified giving the *universitas civium* or even just the *valentior pars* the right to pass laws as the most radical and influential part of his political theory.[41] The good laws that Marsilius wants to focus on are not the ones that God himself gave, but the laws that result immediately from human will.[42] In this sense, Marsilius's focus appears to fall on assuring that the laws passed by citizens are the best possible laws.

While this kind of state might sound like a guaranteed success, Marsilius admits to some contingency on the side of the ruling class. Since rulers are also human beings, it can happen that a ruler acts contrary to what has been ruled by the law.[43] It is up to the legislator, which for Marsilius is the 'prevailing part' of the people,[44] to restrain such a ruler, and this depends on the circumstances of his actions, which are contingent.

---

36 See the discussion of innovation vs. conventionality in Moreno-Riaño and Nederman, 'Marsilius of Padua's Principles of Secular Politics', p. 120. See also the analysis of Marsilius's reception of Aristotle in Syros, *Die Rezeption der aristotelischen politischen Philosophie*, esp. the summary on pp. 281–84.

37 *DP*, I, 4.3, ed. by Scholz, p. 18 and p. 16: 'viventes civiliter non solum vivunt [...] sed bene vivunt'; trans. by Brett, p. 18. Cf. also the summary at *DP*, I, 4.5, ed. by Scholz, p. 19.

38 *DP*, I, 5.3, ed. by Scholz, p. 21: 'Et propterea oportet attendere, quod si debeat homo vivere et bene vivere, necesse est, ut ipsius acciones fiant et bene fiant'.

39 *DP*, I, 5.7, ed. by Scholz, pp. 23–24.

40 According to *DP*, I, 10.5, ed. by Scholz, p. 51, as pointed out by Miethke, *Politiktheorie im Mittelalter*, pp. 216–17, and Moreno-Riaño and Nederman, 'Marsilius of Padua's Principles of Secular Politics', p. 119.

41 *DP*, I, 12.3, ed. by Scholz, p. 63; *DP*, I, 12.5, ed. by Scholz, pp. 65–66. See the research history in Briguglia, *Marsile de Padoue*, pp. 8–20.

42 *DP*, I, 12.1, ed. by Scholz, p. 62: 'que immediate proveniunt ex arbitrio humane mentis'.

43 *DP*, I, 18.3, ed. by Scholz, p. 122: 'contingit ipsum agere contraria eorum, que lege determinata sunt'.

44 This translation of 'valentior pars' as 'prevailing part' is from *DP*, trans. by Brett, pp. 66–67.

His transgressions can be severe or mild, frequent or seldom, contrary to explicit law or not, and the law-giver is supposed to act accordingly.[45]

These few statements surely cannot convey the whole range of thought on the theoretical part of the *Defensor pacis*, *Dictio* I. But I would claim that they illustrate the central role that contingency plays within Marsilius's political theory. His position seems closely related to John of Paris's: within the realm of the political, human beings strive towards a certain goal. The path to fulfilling this goal is not straightforward, mistakes can happen, and abuse must be prevented. But if one acts virtuously, one's contingent actions can lead to a well-ordered state that allows for living and living well. On this reading, Marsilius strikes me as holding a view of the political community in which the contingency of human action is recognized and accommodated.

Garnett's Challenge

The assumption that Marsilius was a classical political theorist describing contingent matters has been challenged by George Garnett in his book *Marsilius of Padua and 'the Truth of History'*. With some simplification, Garnett's goals in his complex and richly sourced book can be narrowed down to two, which correspond to the two main sections of his work.

First, he attempts to rectify an imbalance by pitting himself against almost the entirety of previous Anglophone research on Marsilius. He accuses previous researchers of focusing exclusively on *Dictio* I of the *Defensor pacis*.[46] According to Garnett, these scholars have mischaracterized Marsilius as a precursor to modern republican theory and along the way have 'substituted their own modern words (and therefore thoughts) for Marsilius's, in the mistaken belief that he somehow transcended his age', leading to an 'unhistorical misrepresentation'.[47] The introduction, which is, in fact, a chapter of almost fifty pages, tries to rectify this situation by drawing attention to the fact that most of Marsilius's early readers consider the second *dictio* to be the most offensive part of the *Defensor pacis*. Garnett summarizes:

> Whatever their sympathies, fourteenth-century readers of Marsilius were and remained unanimous about what was the most noteworthy in his book [sc. *Dictio* II and the attack on the papacy]. It is a pity that many modern historians have tended to ignore this evidence.[48]

---

45 *DP*, I, 18.4–7, ed. by Scholz, pp. 123–25.
46 Garnett, *Marsilius of Padua and 'the Truth of History'*, pp. 3–8 and passim.
47 Garnett, *Marsilius of Padua and 'the Truth of History'*, p. 3.
48 Garnett, *Marsilius of Padua and 'the Truth of History'*, p. 45.

The undifferentiated blame that Garnett heaps on earlier scholars is somewhat problematic. To begin with, Garnett makes it sound as if historical reception should be the only perspective according to which a work should be situated by modern commentators. Obviously, this assumption can be contested.[49] Moreover, he later seems to shirk from this full-blown accusation by inserting qualifiers. Garnett states that historians 'tended' towards ignoring the evidence instead of doing so outright, and instead of blatantly substituting their own words for Marsilius's, they allegedly did so 'subtly'.[50]

In this chapter, I will not comment further on Garnett's criticism of previous research and the responses it generated. Instead, I will be concerned with the second goal of Garnett's work. As a consequence of his critique of previous research, Garnett presents a wide-ranging investigation of *Dictio* II. Through this, he argues, an entirely different perspective on the contents and the objectives of the *Defensor pacis* emerges:

> As I shall try to show, he [Marsilius] came to see the conflict as final in a different sense [from the one of today's research]. In his view, it was the apocalyptic consummation of a struggle which had been developing not just since the pontificate of Gregory VII, but over the preceding millennium. Indeed, it presaged the imminent conclusion of that providential process which had begun with the Fall of man.[51]

Quite innovatively, Garnett proposes that Marsilius wrote his book under the assumption that his work and the events of his time were the last stage in a divinely ordained apocalyptic process. By writing the *Defensor pacis*, Marsilius would thus have entered the realm of political prophecy. This claim has frequently been questioned in reviews and comments on Garnett's work, but to my knowledge, there has been no attempt to prove or refute it.[52] Joseph Canning wrote: 'Can Garnett be right that Marsilius was indeed proposing a providentially-willed but flawed historical process? This is the most striking claim of his book.'[53] Jürgen Miethke commented: 'However, it appears highly questionable to the reviewer, if it is legitimate to call the entire picture of history as developed by Marsilius "providen-

---

49 See, for example, Moreno-Riaño and Nederman, 'Introduction', pp. 10–11, who conclude: 'Marsilius was not imprisoned by the historicism of today that would relegate ideas to isolated and disconnected poles of existence. Marsilius was and is a part of a long lineage of great thinkers who believe their works are relevant not only for their contemporaries but also for posterity'.

50 Garnett, *Marsilius of Padua and 'the Truth of History'*, p. 3.

51 Garnett, *Marsilius of Padua and 'the Truth of History'*, p. 47.

52 See e.g. the balanced view in Briguglia, *Marsile de Padoue*, p. 111, and Briguglia, 'The Minor Marsilius', p. 286 n. 68.

53 Canning, '*Marsilius of Padua and "the Truth of History"*', p. 160.

HOW HISTORY HAPPENS   265

tially ordained" and even to ascribe an apocalyptical view of the present to him'.[54]

Given the heightened interest that this interpretation has received, I think it necessary to address it more directly. To do so, I will initially sketch how Garnett arrives at his conclusion. Then I will offer criticism on three levels. First, I will comment on some general features of the *Defensor pacis* that make Garnett's hypothesis unlikely. Second, I want to comment on how Garnett utilizes Marsilius's text in order to make his argument. As I will show, he often quotes Marsilius selectively and omits explaining how these quotations are tied to the argumentative framework in which they appear in Marsilius's text. My contention will be that one of these imprecise references stands at the core of Garnett's argument, linking the development of the secular state to salvation history. Finally, I will comment on one specific passage in the first chapter of the first *dictio*. I think it is this passage that captures precisely how Marsilius imagines the connection between God's foreknowledge and the current crisis that Marsilius is writing about. Garnett begins his chapter on Marsilius's conception of history by quoting this very passage and offering his own translation of it. I will show that the passage in question should be translated and interpreted differently. In the end, I maintain that Marsilius saw the crisis of his times as a dramatic but still contingent event and, therefore, not as part of a preordained plan.

Two Processes of Preordained History

In the second part of his book on Marsilius, George Garnett offers, as the title states, a reconstruction of what Marsilius understood as the 'truth of history'. Marsilius mentions historical facts at various points throughout the *Defensor pacis* but always in the context of some argument. Garnett arranges these statements chronologically and thereby reconstructs a history that Marsilius could have written had he bothered to arrange the facts that he is referring to in their temporal order. Garnett's approach has the great advantage of showing how deeply interwoven politics, history, and, in a sense, storytelling are in Marsilius's work. This 'true history' reaches all the way from Rome to the present, and from the inception of the Church to its current state of perversion in the first quarter of the fourteenth century.

In this history, according to Garnett, Marsilius sketches two great developments. Marsilius's account of the historical development of the secular state describes how it gradually becomes better over time, thus

---

54 Miethke, 'G. Garnett': 'Es ist dem Rez. freilich höchst fraglich, ob es erlaubt ist, das Gesamtbild der Geschichte, wie es Marsilius entwickelt, als durchwegs "providentially ordained" zu bezeichnen und ihm sogar eine apokalyptische Gegenwartsbestimmung zuzuschreiben' (my translation).

avoiding the impression that the *civitas* at its inception is instantly the best *civitas*.[55] The Church takes the opposite route. Its gradual decline from good to bad is the main cause for contemporary strife and, as Marsilius famously tells us, could not have been foreseen by Aristotle.[56] Sometime after the fall from grace that happened with the donation of Constantine, the Church poisoned the human ear with its claim to *plenitudo potestatis* and a lust for temporal possessions.[57]

Now, these stories of, on the one hand, gradual perfection and, on the other hand, steady decline into ever-increasing depravity are, in my view, indeed written into the *Defensor pacis*, and it is very helpful to have them pointed out. They also correspond nicely with Marsilius's attempt to rewrite the process of the *translatio imperii* in his work on that topic.[58] Both Marsilius's attempts to justify the empire and his historical narrative might have been challenged by the standard view that he found in Landulphus Colonna's work.[59] According to this view, all *translationes* were performed by the pope, so Marsilius had to rewrite it and make the *populus romanus* the driving force instead. One can therefore claim with Garnett that Marsilius's understanding of history is characterized by teleological processes and thereby by finality, which becomes apparent both in the *Defensor pacis* and in *De translatione imperii*. However, Garnett's analysis does not stop here. He also claims that Marsilius sees both processes as divinely ordained and that their clash, with Louis IV's victory over Pope John XXII, constitutes the beginning of the end:

> For Marsilius, the resulting apocalyptic crisis could have only one outcome: the reversal of the second fall of the Roman Empire and, ultimately, the wiping out of the effects of original sin. [...] Louis' victory in his conflict with John XXII — which was providentially inevitable — would mean that man could at last be perfected, in both temporal and spiritual terms. It would mark the apotheosis of human history and, by implication, herald the Last Judgement.[60]

It is this specific claim that many interpreters have found problematic and that I want to investigate in the remainder of this chapter. The positions of John Quidort of Paris and Dante Alighieri that I outlined above will serve as a useful backdrop for my discussion.

---

55 Garnett, *Marsilius of Padua and 'the Truth of History'*, pp. 59–66.
56 *DP*, I, 1.3, ed. by Scholz, p. 5.
57 Garnett, *Marsilius of Padua and 'the Truth of History'*, pp. 125–45.
58 Edited in Marsilius of Padua, *Œuvres mineures*, ed. by Jeudy and Quillet.
59 Landulphus Colonna, *De translatione imperii*.
60 Garnett, *Marsilius of Padua and 'the Truth of History'*, p. 157.

Apocalyptical Allusions in the Defensor pacis and Comparing it to Other Apocalyptic Narratives

If Marsilius was considering the conflict of his times as the beginning of the end of days described in the Bible, it would give his teleological narrative much more meaning, and it would also make him special as compared to the two cases I considered earlier. As we saw with Dante, there can be historical processes that are providentially influenced but do not nevertheless lead to Judgement Day. Similarly, as John Quidort of Paris reveals, one can be a political Aristotelian and have an opinion on the arrival of Judgement Day, and yet still refuse to impose this vision onto the present political situation.

If Marsilius was indeed a theorist of the imminent apocalypse, some aspects of his work might appear puzzling: Why did he even bother with political theory? Why would he stress the importance of good laws, the decisions of the majority, and living well in peace as the objectives of a community if everything was about to end? Why would he use medical metaphors to describe current political events? Such metaphors usually deal with contingent alterations of stability and try to recreate a healthy balance. Why bother, if one imagines the current historical process as the end of all balance and stability?[61]

Now, one can argue that there are clear apocalyptic allusions in the *Defensor pacis*. Marsilius's reinterpretation of the statue from Nebuchadnezzar's dream (Daniel 2) can be read this way. Normally, the gold, silver, brass, iron, and iron-and-clay parts of the statue are thought to represent a succession of four *regna* and the stone as Christ who will end worldly governance forever. Similar to the *Translatio imperii*, Marsilius also finds a spirited deviation from the standard interpretation. He interprets the parts of the statue as symbolizing the material greed and preposterous ambitions of the Church and the stone as Louis IV who smashes it.[62] Would this be a clear sign that Louis inherits the duty to initiate the apocalypse, as Garnett interprets it? Absolutely not. First, Garnett admits that the use of this image is more metaphorical here than prophetical. And second, we can ask: What happens after the statue is smashed (metaphorically speaking)? The emperor has the duty to fix all the problems caused by the Church while allowing it to continue. The emperor does not destroy the Church, he restores it. This becomes especially clear in the final point of Marsilius's analysis of the image. Marsilius's suggestion as to what one should do with

---

61 This question is also expressed in Nederman, 'Marsilius of Padua and "the Truth of History"', p. 343, raising the point that 'Garnett does not pause to ask why Marsiglio [...] sought to emphasize in such detail the wholly naturalistic (although not always entirely Aristotelian) foundations of earthly human community'.

62 *DP*, II, 24.17, ed. by Scholz, pp. 465–66.

268 JACOB LANGELOH

the Church's gold and silver does not sound like the apocalypse. Rather, it sounds like how one's treats an unruly teenager whose weekly allowance needs to be cut:

> And lastly he shall curb the silver and the gold, i.e., the avarice and rapacity of the Roman pontiff and the upper members of the Roman curia; he shall concede them the use of temporal goods with the moderation that is due.[63]

With maintaining the importance of a well-governed state and choosing to restore the Church rather than completely reform it, Marsilius clearly deviates from the apocalyptic narratives of his time. On the other hand, there are also some similarities. The leader of the Apostolics around 1300, Fra Dolcino, denounced the Church as being led by the Antichrist and hoped that Frederick III of Sicily would put Pope Boniface VIII and his followers to the sword. The pope-Antichrist would then be replaced by a truly pious pope.[64] Similar to Marsilius, Fra Dolcino attributes an important role to worldly rulers. And he, too, outlines four historical ages. The first comprised the Fathers of the Old Testament; the second began with Christ and lasted until Constantine accepted Christianity as the religion of the Roman Empire. In the third stage, religion went into decline and necessitated a return to the apostolic life. The restoration of the apostolic life would in turn herald the beginning of the fourth stage.[65]

In Marsilius's historical narrative there are some structural similarities to Fra Dolcino's vision but also differences. First, Fra Dolcino divides history into four ages. Reading Garnett's reconstruction, it might seem that Marsilius follows the same pattern, as Garnett divides the story into essentially the same four stages. However, this division is not Marsilius's own, but rather the form that Garnett imposes onto Marsilius's narrative. So, this is rather the effect of Garnett's reconstruction of Marsilius's scattered historical remarks into apocalyptic form than Marsilius himself. Second, both Fra Dolcino and Marsilius make various predictions concerning the future. However, Dolcino's apocalyptic statements are far more precise. They attach to specific historical circumstances, and they are bold, backed

---

63 *DP*, trans. by Brett, p. 431.

64 Carozzi, *Apocalypse et salut*, p. 137. It should be noted that Fra Dolcino's letters to his disciples are only transmitted through Bernard Gui's recording of them (*Historia fratris Dulcini*, ed. by Segarizzi), who does not leave his judgement in doubt. Despite the Apostolics' protestations that they want to revive the apostolic life, Gui counters that their acts give them away. Bernard Gui, *Historia fratris Dulcini*, ed. by Segarizzi, p. 17: 'Erat tamen revera vita ipsorum infecta interius et exterius abhominabiliter impudica et doctrina in suis occultis conventiculis tam heretica quam insana' (However, in reality their life was rotten from the inside and outside, horribly shameless; and the teaching in their small hidden convents was as heretical as it was insane).

65 Bernard Gui, *Historia fratris Dulcini*, ed. by Segarizzi, pp. 20–21.

up with scriptural evidence and by a plenitude of numerological specula-tions.[66] Third, it was common among the apocalyptic writers of Marsilius's age to decry the pope as the Antichrist. Marsilius, on the other hand, never refers to the pope as the Antichrist. He attributes a role to the Devil in the downfall of the Church, but frames this as one of the Devil's regular destructive works, not as a sign of the coming of the Antichrist.[67] Finally, Dolcino's work calls for radical change. The Church is to be cleansed and then ruled by the most pious pope, while Christians in general shall revert to the apostolic life. Marsilius, on the other hand, calls for a restoration of the political order after which both State and Church can fulfil their attributed purpose.

In conclusion, three main differences emerge between Marsilius and Fra Dolcino. Marsilius does not attempt to impose the apocalypse onto precise historical events; rather, he remains vague and allegorical. He does not call for a total upheaval of the current Church, but rather suggests a peaceful restoration that would enable priests to serve their appropriate function. And finally, he proposes solutions for the current crisis that are based on Aristotelian political philosophy and where the common good shall be promoted through good laws, not through divine favour.

Reconsidering the Evidence: Where and How Does Marsilius, Supposedly, Reveal Himself as an Apocalypticist?

In order for Garnett's argument to be convincing, one needs a clear under-standing of what he thinks Marsilius is arguing for. In the roadmap for the second part of his book, which Garnett lays out at the end of the first, sev-eral very evocative terms are used. As quoted earlier, Garnett speaks of an 'apocalyptic consummation', and of the 'the imminent conclusion of that providential process which had begun with the Fall of man'.[68] According to Garnett, Marsilius is describing the course of 'providential history'.[69] Gar-nett naturally arrives at this conclusion by interpreting passages from the *Defensor pacis*, occasionally supplemented with passages from Marsilius's shorter works, the *Defensor minor* and the *De translatione imperii*. When tracing this evidence back to the *Defensor pacis*, I have the impression that Garnett often quotes selected parts of larger arguments, thereby distorting the overall picture. I want to raise three instances. The first two illustrate a loss of context through selective quotation. The third is similar but carries even more weight. This passage stands at the core of Garnett's argument

---

66 Bernard Gui, *Historia fratris Dulcini*, ed. by Segarizzi, pp. 21–22.
67 See e.g. *DP*, II, 25.7, ed. by Scholz, p. 473 and II, 26.19, p. 517.
68 Garnett, *Marsilius of Padua and 'the Truth of History'*, p. 47.
69 Garnett, *Marsilius of Padua and 'the Truth of History'*, p. 52 and passim.

270   JACOB LANGELOH

that Marsilius identifies the gradual process of the perfection of the secular state with a divinely ordained providential process.

The first example may appear minor, but it is significant as the starting point of the narrative as Garnett presents it. When beginning to map out the 'historical tradition' that connects Marsilius to his adversaries,[70] Garnett quotes several passages that establish the role of Christ in the world: 'Christ had become "true man, being at the same time God", for a specific purpose "to redeem the sin of our first parents and, consequently, the Fall of the whole human race"'.[71] Certainly, Marsilius quotes this most common item of faith and also adds other parts of the apostolic creed, such as that Christ suffered under Pontius Pilate and was resurrected on the third day. But what sounds like the beginning of the historical narrative according to Garnett is merely an explanatory piece of information for Marsilius. Marsilius here wants to explain how the Church, which is causing problems, came into existence by reminding readers that Christ came to earth and 'gathered to himself for the salvation of the human race certain co-workers in the ministry of teaching the truth, who are called the apostles'.[72] The focus of this passage, thus, is clearly not on Christ himself and his role, but rather on the institution of ministers who were ordered to aid the purpose of salvation.

In the second passage that Garnett quotes, Marsilius comments on the way in which rulers are instituted by God.[73] Marsilius writes that only very rarely does God institute a ruler directly. Garnett continues the thought: 'In every other instance of the appointment of a ruler, God's providence worked through the rational decisions of men'.[74] But what does the work of 'God's providence' actually mean in terms of appointing a ruler? Should one think that God has a plan in mind for which worldly rulers are to be appointed at each point of time? If one reads further, Marsilius clearly opposes the thought that this constitutes a direct act of God. He writes that normally the election of principates 'results immediately from the human mind, even if from God as the remote cause'. Marsilius then admits that God 'grants all earthly principates', but 'in most cases and almost everywhere he establishes these principates through the medium of human minds, to which he granted the freedom to establish them in this way'.[75] The key word, here, is freedom. God grants human beings the freedom to choose their rulers, and thus God indirectly grants

---

70 Garnett, *Marsilius of Padua and 'the Truth of History'*, pp. 52–53.
71 Garnett, *Marsilius of Padua and 'the Truth of History'*, p. 53, who is quoting *DP*, I, 19.4, ed. by Scholz, p. 128.
72 *DP*, I, 19.4, trans. by Brett, p. 129.
73 *DP*, I, 9.2.
74 Garnett, *Marsilius of Padua and 'the Truth of History'*, p. 55.
75 *DP*, I, 9.2, trans. by Brett, p. 44; ed. by Scholz, p. 40.

the principates themselves. If God intervened directly in these decisions, freedom would be endangered. Still, God is named as a *causa remota*. If God is thought of as the cause of all things, of course all singular human decisions result from this cause *in a remote sense*. However, the immediate cause can still be found, as Marsilius writes, in the decisions of the 'human mind'. Also, again, the context of this passage in Marsilius is essential. He is highlighting the absence of God's direct intervention in the choice of leaders to make it impossible to portray the choice of any contemporary leader, including the pope, as such. It appears to me that Garnett seeks to magnify God's influence on the choice of worldly leaders at the expense of the text itself and the argument that Marsilius is actually proposing.

The third example is one that, to my mind, stands at the centre of Garnett's argument.[76] The topic is the change that Christ's incarnation brought to the world. As the previous two examples have shown, Marsilius is intent on differentiating the current state *after* Christ's incarnation from any other previous state. The old, Mosaic law that was in force until Christ's birth was concerned with both secular and sacral matters. Christ disentangled these strands from each other, but Christ still (in Garnett's translation) 'substituted precepts which were and would be given in human laws and He commanded every soul to observe them [...] at least in those precepts which were not opposed to the law of eternal salvation'.[77] From this, Garnett draws the conclusion: 'In other words, Christ had encompassed all present and future human law within the divine providential scheme, while distinguishing it from the New Law'.[78] If this were true, any human law after Christ would be inextricably bound to God's plan for the world.

This conclusion, however, misreads the passage in question and is actually the opposite of what Marsilius writes. Marsilius's main question in this passage is whether priests should have any coercive power under the New Law. He repeats several times that Christ did not leave any such laws, contrary to the Mosaic law that was in force previously. The sentence that Garnett half-quotes, reads in full (in Annabel Brett's translation):

> But Christ in the evangelical law did not give commands of this nature [i.e. resembling the Ten Commandments], but presupposed that they had been or should have been given in human laws; and he commanded that every human soul should observe those laws and obey princes in accordance with them, at least in those matters which did not oppose the law of eternal salvation.[79]

---

76 The passage is from *DP*, I, 9.2 and is later taken up in II, 9.9.

77 *DP*, II, 9.9, as translated in Garnett, *Marsilius of Padua and 'the Truth of History'*, p. 55.

78 Garnett, *Marsilius of Padua and 'the Truth of History'*, p. 55.

79 *DP*, II, 9.9, trans. by Brett, p. 228; ed. by Scholz, p. 240: 'Verum huiusmodi precepta in evangelica lege non tradidit Christus, sed tradita vel tradenda supposuit in humanis legibus,

In other words, Marsilius stresses that Christ did not involve himself in human law. While some secular instruction was contained in the Ten Commandments that had been in force before Christ, any secular commands would be given in the human law after the Incarnation. Garnett, on the other hand, makes it sound as if Christ laid the groundwork by 'substituting precepts'. In order to make this quotation work, Garnett omits the first part, stating clearly: 'Christ [...] did not give commands of this nature', which runs contrary to any substitution of precepts. He also interprets the verb 'supposuit' in the literal sense of 'substituting' instead of 'presupposing'. While this may be possible in a vacuum, the object of 'supposuit' should be, based on proximity, 'tradita vel tradenda'. As Brett correctly translates, he did not 'substitute precepts', but 'presupposed' that they 'had been or should have been given'. In short, when Marsilius clearly writes that Christ did not want to meddle in human laws, Garnett claims the opposite. If this interpretation was unclear, then the following scriptural authority that Marsilius cites should provide clarity. He attaches the canonical 'Render unto Caesar the things which are Caesar's' (Matthew 22. 20), which is generally used to defend the autonomy of human law-giving.

To summarize the third example, Garnett here interprets a passage where Marsilius explicitly denies that Christ is involved in human law-giving as an indication that Christ 'had encompassed all present and future human law within the divine providential scheme'. I believe that this very passage stands at the core of Garnett's argument for making Marsilius apocalyptic. Garnett refers back to it later in his explanation, basically reinforcing the earlier message:

> Christ, when He framed the evangelical law, took into account what human law was in His own time and what it would be in the future. [...] [The role of human law] had been permanently transformed by the New Law which Christ had proclaimed. That transformed role was providentially ordained.[80]

The interpretation of this half-sentence is the basis upon which the argument rests that ever since Christ, human law and salvation have been inextricably linked. As I have argued, I believe that this interpretation is mistaken and misconstrues the passage in question.

With these three examples, I hope to have shown that Garnett's interpretation of Marsilius's historical thinking as apocalyptic and providential relies at least in these cases on quoting selectively, out of context, and on ignoring the overall composition of the text. If considered more closely,

---

quas observari et principantibus secundum eas omnem animam humanam obedire precepit, in hiis saltem que non adversarentur legi salutis eterne'.

80 Garnett, *Marsilius of Padua and 'the Truth of History'*, p. 77.

these passages rather suggest the opposite: that God does not mingle with earthly processes. In addition, Garnett does not seem to provide even a working definition of what 'providential history' or 'providentiality' even mean. The matter is far from straightforward, and the question of how God's ultimate plan, the end of days (the apocalypse), and human freedom can be reconciled has been one of the defining challenges of Christian theology. If Marsilius is to be placed in this context, it should at least be mentioned how one understands this network of conflicting theological tenets.

A Crucial Passage on the Causality of History: DP, I, 1.3

Marsilius's conception of history as reconstructed by George Garnett sketched two processes: a process of perfection in secular rule and a process of perversion in the Church. While the previous examples were concerned with how Garnett tries to link the process of perfection to God's preordained plan, the question remains in which way Marsilius, according to Garnett, also sees the downfall of the Church as preordained. There is one passage of Marsilius's text that appears opaque at first, but that, upon closer inspection, clarifies this relationship. It is telling that this passage has been translated very differently in the English translations of Brett, Alan Gewirth, and Garnett himself.

I am referring to a passage from *Dictio* I (I, 1.3) that is later repeated almost verbatim in *Dictio* I, 19.3. Here, Marsilius refers to an *opinio perversa*. With this term, he is referring to the Church's claim to possess *plenitudo potestatis*, the right to govern both the secular and the spiritual realm. It might appear that the origins of this claim are somehow connected to a divine cause in this sentence:

> Est enim hec et fuit opinio perversa quedam in posteris explicanda nobis, occasionaliter autem sumpta, ex effectu mirabili post Aristotelis tempora dudum a suprema causa producto, preter inferioris nature possibilitatem et causarum solitam accionem in rebus.[81]

The differences between the three English translations are very revealing:

> For it was and is a certain perverted opinion to be unfolded by us below, actually adopted opportunistically by some, following from a miraculous effect produced by the supreme cause long after Aristotle's time; an effect beyond the possibility of lower nature and the usual action of causes in things. (Garnett, *Marsilius of Padua and 'the Truth of History'*, p. 49).

---

81 *DP*, I, 1.3, ed. by Scholz, p. 5.

> For this is, and was, a certain perverted opinion, which we shall unfold in what follows; assumed by way of occasion from a miraculous effect produced by the supreme cause long after the time of Aristotle, beyond the possibilities of inferior nature and the usual action of causes in things. (*DP*, I, 1.3, trans. by Brett, p. 15).
>
> For it was and is a certain perverted opinion (to be exposed by us below), which came to be adopted as an aftermath of the miraculous effect produced by the supreme cause long after Aristotle's time; an effect beyond the power of the lower nature and the usual action of causes in things. (*DP*, I, 1.3, trans. by Gewirth, p. 5).

In a note to her translation, Brett tells us, rather accurately, that this is 'a difficult sentence in the Latin'.[82] The place where the translations differ the most, and what I would consider the core behind these differences, is the interpretation of the term *occasionaliter sumpta* and how it is linked to the rest of the sentence. One has the choice of interpreting the *occasionaliter autem sumpta* as a separate clause, which then forces the translator to insert another verb form to connect the *opinio* to the *effectus mirabilis*.[83] Garnett chose this way by inserting that the *opinio* was 'following from' that miraculous effect. The second possibility is to attach the *occasionaliter* phrase to the rest of the sentence. Brett picks 'assumed by way of occasion from a miraculous effect'; Gewirth gives it as 'came to be adopted as an aftermath of the miraculous effect', where the 'came to be adopted' expresses the *sumpta* and the 'aftermath' supposedly the *occasionaliter*. In that sense, Garnett's translation offers the highest amount of interpretation, followed by Gewirth's, while Brett's retains more of the opacity of the original.[84] The passive phrases in Gewirth and Brett do not specify, though, who 'adopted' or 'assumed' the opinion. Garnett, again, offers more specificity by interpreting it as 'adopted [...] by some'. Marsilius's Latin here clearly presents a challenge that cannot be solved by philology alone, but rather requires interpretation.

Given the difficulties in translating and interpreting this passage, one should hesitate to use it as a central piece of evidence regarding Marsilius's overall intention. Yet, Garnett's explanation might still be plausible. As he interprets it, the passage tells us that certain opportunists adopted a 'perverted opinion', which consists in claiming superiority for the pope over the emperor in all matters, including worldly ones. What Marsilius would be decrying, then, would be how there was a 'deliberate perversion

---

82 *DP*, trans. by Brett, p. 6 n. 13.

83 I take this 'miraculous effect' to mean the incarnation of Christ, as is made explicit by Piaia, 'Forme della laicità', p. 1726, and the 'supreme cause' as God.

84 See Brett, 'Issues in Translating the *Defensor Pacis*', p. 92 and passim for a discussion of this fine line and the observation that Marsilius's 'Latin is often opaque and imprecise' (p. 93).

of the true interpretation [...] of Christian history',[85] which had been, as Garnett's translation says, 'adopted opportunistically by some'.

I do not think this is what the passage means. I would like to offer an alternative interpretation that focuses on the adverb *occasionaliter*. What the passage from Marsilius seems to imply at the very least is that there is a certain 'perverted opinion' which is in some way *from* or *out of the miraculous effect produced by the supreme cause*. I want to argue that the *occasionaliter* specifies *in what way* this perverted opinion is connected to the supreme cause (God) and its miraculous effect (Christ's birth). In my view, Marsilius tries to clarify that the 'pernicious opinion' did not originate directly from the 'miraculous effect', but rather did so in an oblique and unintended way.

In scholastic works, the word *occasionaliter* is frequently used to address problems of causality. Some actions might allow certain effects the occasion to arise, even though they are not the direct cause of these effects, nor are the effects intended when the action is performed. If I leave my window open and someone comes in and steals my belongings, I did not cause this theft. However, I provided the occasion for the theft to take place, since without the open window it would presumably not have happened. This appears to be the understanding of Thomas Aquinas when he discusses the severity of the sin of vilification (*contumelia*).[86] Thomas's original question is how serious of a sin detraction (*detractio*) is. In the third article, he compares it to other sins, namely adultery and vilification. For him, a sin is more severe the more it affects human society. Accordingly, the problem with adultery is not bodily contact per se, but the disruption of orderly procreation. In the same vein, the wrongness of *contumelia* depends on how much enmity (*inimicitia*) it sows in the

---

85 Garnett, *Marsilius of Padua and 'the Truth of History'*, p. 51.

86 The passage that I will be commenting on is from Thomas Aquinas, *Summa theologiae* II–II, q. 73 a. 3 ad 2: 'Contumelia tamen non est gravius peccatum quam adulterium, non enim gravitas adulterii pensatur ex coniunctione corporum, sed ex deordinatione generationis humanae. Contumeliosus autem non sufficienter causat inimicitiam in alio, sed occasionaliter tantum dividit unitos, inquantum scilicet per hoc quod mala alterius promit, alios, quantum in se est, ab eius amicitia separat, licet ad hoc per eius verba non cogantur. Sic etiam et detractor occasionaliter est homicida, inquantum scilicet per sua verba dat alteri occasionem ut proximum odiat vel contemnat'. I am adopting the English terminology from the translation by Freddoso, p. 496: 'However, vilification is not a more serious sin than adultery, since the seriousness of adultery is calculated not on the basis of the conjoining of the bodies, but on the basis of the disordering of human generation. Now the vilifier is not a sufficient cause of enmity in another individual; instead, he divides those who are united only as an occasional cause (*occasionaliter*), viz., insofar as, by presenting someone's bad points, he separates others, to the extent that it is within his power, from friendship with that individual — even though they are not forced to this by his words. In the same way, a detractor is a murderer as an occasional cause, viz., insofar as by his words he provides someone else with an occasion to hate or disdain his neighbor'.

community. Thomas responds that *contumelia* is not a 'sufficient' cause of *inimicitia* ('non sufficienter causat inimicitiam in alio'). Although learning about the flaws of one's friends might give occasion to rethink one's friendship ('occasionaliter tantum dividit unitos'), one still is not forced to act ('licet ad hoc per eius verba non cogantur'). In that sense, vilification does not cause enmity, but it can lead to it.

This use of *occasionaliter* is very typical for Thomas Aquinas. The *Index Thomisticus* lists eighty-one occurrences in sixty-four places.[87] Not surprisingly, the need to distinguish between consequences that follow *directe*, or according to the intention of the agent, from those that are *occasionaliter, per accidens*, or *praeter intentionem* arises most in discussions of sin. In his commentary on Paul's letter *Ad Romanos*, for example, Aquinas clarifies that sin does not directly occur because of the law that is given but 'on occasion', since without the law, one could not have recognized the sin.[88] Without being able to pursue this adverb further, I think the difference is also nicely shown in the reductio ad absurdum by Jan Hus in his polemic *Contra Iohannem Stokes*.[89] Hus points out that if one counted indirect causation as a reason to interdict reading certain works, then Holy Scripture would have to be banned. After all, heretics used it and Jews also relied on it to argue against Christianity. With this argument, Hus clearly distinguishes between direct and indirect, unintended causation.

In the aforementioned passage, Marsilius understands the source of the current conflict, the Church, in similar terms. If I were to adapt Brett's translation in a manner that supports my interpretation, it would read: 'For this is, and was, a certain perverted opinion, which we shall unfold in what follows; which, understood in an accidental way, came from the miraculous effect produced by the supreme cause long after the time of Aristotle, beyond the possibilities of inferior nature and the usual action of causes in things'. The *sumpta* would mean that a term has to be 'taken' or 'understood' in a certain way.[90] Marsilius uses it similarly when he

---

87 See <https://www.corpusthomisticum.org/it/index.age> [accessed 8 August 2020].

88 Thomas Aquinas, *Super Rom.*, cap. 7, l. 2. 'Et hoc est quod dicit *sed peccatum, ut appareat peccatum*, id est ex hoc apparet esse peccatum per legis bonum id est per mandatum legis: quia ex hoc ipsum bonum est, quod facit cognitionem peccati. Et hoc occasionaliter in quantum manifestat peccatum. Non autem sic intelligitur peccatum per legem operatum esse mortem, quasi sine lege mors non fuisset'.

89 Hus, *Contra Iohannem Stokes*, ed. by Eršil, p. 58: 'Item pari evidencia Scriptura sacra non esset legenda. Patet consequencia, quia a Scriptura sacra occasionaliter graviores heretici, ut Sabellius et Arrius, inciderunt in heresim, ymo hodie Iudei sunt pertinaces heretici et non aliunde nisi a Scriptura sacra, quam continue student et legunt, sed male intelligunt et oppositum pertinaciter dogmatisant etc'.

90 Thomas Aquinas can also serve as a model here. He writes in *Super Sent.* about *similitudo* taken in the common meaning. Cf. Thomas Aquinas, II *Super Sent.*, d. 16, q. 1, a. 4, ad 1: 'Ad primum ergo dicendum, quod similitudo communiter sumpta, non dividitur contra imaginem; sed similitudo deficiens a ratione imaginis, sicut proprium contra definitionem'.

is concerned with different modes of law.[91] Here, *sumpta* also refers to picking out one of two possible meanings, or 'taking something in a certain way'. *Sic sumpta*, thus, serves the same function and is used synonymously as the phrases *sic accepta* or *hoc modo considerata* that also occur in this passage to distinguish the two ways of looking at the law.

Why would Marsilius be so insistent that the 'perverted opinion' originated in an accidental or occasional way? The argument would be similar to the one Jan Hus makes regarding Scripture, only that it is concerned with Christ's sacrifice and the Church that Christ instituted. Founding the Church was necessary to steer man towards salvation. This divine institution (which, therefore, could not have been foreseen by Aristotle) can result in effects that are not intended per se, but become possible through it. A pope abusing his power was not intended when creating the Church, but without the institution of the Church, a pope would have lacked the opportunity to abuse his power. This is precisely what *occasionaliter* means. Within any form of causality there is contingent room for events that are not directly intended.

Now, what weight does Garnett actually put on this passage? He admits himself in a note that 'the "perverted opinion" cannot be a consequence of the "miraculous effect"'. However, in the main text, he seems to lump the two together, writing: 'In the first discourse Marsilius attempted to investigate this singular cause and its pernicious effects by certain methods devised by the human intellect'.[92] The phrase 'this singular cause and its pernicious effects' seems like a rhetorical sleight-of-hand to make the reader think that the decline of the Church was, in fact, directly caused by the singular, miraculous cause of Christ's birth. Yet, if my reading of 'occasionaliter sumpta' is correct, then this passage means the opposite of what George Garnett implies. Garnett seems to suggest that the decline of the Church resulted from the 'miraculous effect' and was thus preordained. But, no! The *occasionaliter* makes clear that, while the pernicious opinion did 'follow from' the 'miraculous effect', it did so in a fashion entirely unintended. In this sense, one should not conclude that it was preordained. It was a contingent effect of God's institution of the Church within his salutary plan, but not part of God's intention. And in that case, it also appears highly unlikely that Marsilius ascribes it any apocalyptic function.

---

91 *DP*, I, 10.4, ed. by Scholz, p. 50: 'Alio modo considerari potest, secundum quod de ipsius observacione datur preceptum coavtivum per penam aut premium in presenti seculo distribuenda, sive secundum quod per modum talis precepti traditur; et hoc modo considerata propriissime lex vocatur et est. Quam eciam sic sumptam diffinit Aristoteles ultimo Ethicorum'; trans. by Brett, p. 53: 'In a second way, it can be considered inasmuch as it is handed down by way of such a command. And considered in this way, it is most properly called, and most properly is, law. Moreover, Aristotle's definition *takes it in this way*' (my emphasis).

92 Garnett, *Marsilius of Padua and 'the Truth of History'*, p. 49 n. 2.

Conclusions

In this article, I have tried to flesh out some implications of contingency and finality in the political thought of the early fourteenth century. There is a general tension between these two terms. Aristotelian political philosophy presupposes a realm of contingency, in which man can commit virtuous deeds. With its preordained patterns, the apocalypse follows other rules. The first two writers I addressed coped with this tension in different ways. John Quidort of Paris was very true to himself when he, on the one hand, saw his contemporary conflict as a contingent one and was sceptical of the normative force of history in this context and, on the other hand, diffused arguments that claimed to be able to predict the end of days with precision. Dante Alighieri chose another solution by combining Aristotelian political philosophy with a preordained course of history. God even interfered in order to guarantee the rise of the Roman Empire, but this teleology too does not lead to Judgement Day.

In the main part of this chapter, I addressed whether Marsilius of Padua can be considered an apocalyptic thinker. Although preliminary evidence suggested he cannot, I discussed George Garnett's controversial hypothesis at length. I conclude that Marsilius is a gifted storyteller. He artfully modifies pre-existing prophecies. He gives us long, tension-filled arcs of the rise of the worldly state and the decline of the Church, something that George Garnett's book has beautifully illustrated. But do these narratives lead to the apocalypse? To my mind, no. I have made this point on three levels. First, the general thrust of Marsilius's argument seems to lead towards a peaceful restoration of a good, stable state, which sets him apart from other chiliasts of his time. Second, as I have illustrated, Garnett's argument rests on a one-sided reading of some passages of Marsilius's work. Third, I think that the use of the adverb *occasionaliter* by Marsilius clearly displays how he views the decline of the Church. He does not see it as a direct consequence of the first cause, and neither as a preordained process.

As a result, Marsilius's relation to contingency and finality seems to fall in the middle between Dante and John of Paris. As Dante, and unlike John, he sees a direction in history that led towards the decline of the Church and towards the restoration of both Church and empire through Louis IV. However, unlike Dante, he does not see a direct godly intervention, but God's causal role in this process is merely 'occasional', as I have pointed out last. What unites the three of them is their insistence that understanding historical processes and precedent is vital for understanding contemporary strife.

Despite not being focused on the apocalypse, Marsilius was later, as Thomas Izbicki has pointed out, at least in one instance associated with figures from that tradition. Henry VIII had demanded from 1534 on that his officials swear the 'Oath of Supremacy' and thereby declare exclusive loyalty to the English Crown, which marked a clear break with the Catholic Church. The apologists defending this move saw Marsilius on their side and grouped him with those who defended the true Church against the whore of Babylon, which was identified with the papacy.[93] If my interpretation is correct, Marsilius would not have seen himself in these terms. His ideal was to establish peace on earth. He viewed the disturbances of his time as a deeply disturbing but still contingent matter.

---

93 Izbicki, 'The Reception of Marsilius', pp. 323–24.

Works Cited

Primary Sources

Albertus Magnus, *Super ethica*, ed. by Wilfried Kübel, Alberti Magni Opera Omnia, 7 (Münster: Aschendorff, 1968–1972)

Alighieri, Dante, *The De Monarchia of Dante Alighieri*, ed. and trans. by Aurelia Henry (Boston: Houghton, Mifflin, 1904)

——, *Monarchia: Studienausgabe Lateinisch/Deutsch*, ed. and trans. by Ruedi Imbach and Christoph Flüeler (Stuttgart: Reclam, 1989)

Bernard Gui, *Historia fratris Dulcini (Fra Stefano Dolcino) Heresiarche di Anonimo sincrono e De secta illorum qui se dicunt esse de ordine Apostolorum di Bernardo Gui [Bernardus Guidonis]*, ed. by Arnaldo Segarizzi, Rerum Italicarum scriptores, 9.5 (Città di Castello: Lapi, 1907)

Epistolae saeculi XIII e regestis pontificum Romanorum selectae, ed. by Karl Rodenberg, Monumenta Germaniae Historica: Epistolae, 3 (Munich: Monumenta Germaniae Historica, 1883; repr. 1982)

Giles of Rome, *On Ecclesiastical Power: A Medieval Theory of World Government. A Critical Edition and Translation*, ed. and trans. by Robert Dyson, Records of Western Civilization (New York: Columbia University Press, 2004)

Hus, Jan, *Contra Iohannem Stokes*, in *Magistri Iohannis Hus Polemica*, ed. by Jaroslav Eršil, Corpus Christianorum Continuatio Mediaevalis, 238 (Turnhout: Brepols, 2010), pp. 57–70

James of Viterbo, *De regimine Christiano: A Critical Edition and Translation*, ed. by Robert W. Dyson, Brill's Texts and Sources in Intellectual History, 6 (Leiden: Brill, 2009)

John Quidort of Paris, *De potestate regia et papali*, ed. by Fritz Bleienstein as *Johannes Quidort von Paris über königliche und päpstliche Gewalt*, Frankfurter Studien zur Wissenschaft von der Politik, 4 (Stuttgart: Klett, 1968)

——, *The 'Tractatus de antichristo' of John of Paris: A Critical Edition, Translation, and Commentary*, ed. by Sara Beth Peters Clark (Ann Arbor, MI: University Microfilms International, 1981)

Landulphus Colonna, *De translatione imperii*, in *Monarchiae S. Romani Imperii, Sive Tractatuum De Iurisdictione Imperiali Seu Regia, & Pontificia seu Sacerdotali; deq[ue] potestate Imperatoris ac Papae, cum distinctione utriusque Regiminis, Politici & Ecclesiastici, [...] Tomus Secundus*, ed. by Melchior Goldast (Frankfurt: Biermann, 1614), II, pp. 88–95

Marsilius of Padua, *The Defender of the Peace*, trans. by Annabel Brett, Cambridge Texts in the History of Political Thought (Cambridge: Cambridge University Press, 2005)

——, *Marsilius of Padua: The Defender of Peace*, II: *The Defensor Pacis*, trans. by Alan Gewirth (New York: Columbia University Press, 1951; repr. 2000)

————, *Defensor pacis*, ed. by Richard Scholz, Monumenta Germaniae Historica: Fontes iuris germanici antiqui in usum scholarum separatim editi, 7.2 (Hannover: Hahn, 1933)

————, *Œuvres mineures: Defensor minor; De translatione imperii*, ed. with French trans. by Colette Jeudy and Jeannine Quillet, Sources d'histoire médiévale (Paris: Éditions du CNRS, 1979)

Petrus Lombardus, *Commentarium in Psalmos*, ed. by Jacques-Paul Migne, Patrologiae cursus completus: series Latina, 191 (Paris: Garnier 1854), cols 55–1296

Quaestio de Potestate Papae (Rex Pacificus) = An Enquiry into the Power of the Pope: A Critical Edition and Translation, ed. and trans. by Robert W. Dyson, Texts and Studies in Religion (Lewiston: Edwin Mellen, 1999)

Thomas Aquinas, *De regno ad regem Cypri*, in *Opera omnia iussu Leonis XIII P. M. edita*, vol. xlii (Rome: Editori di San Tommaso, 1979)

————, *New English Translation of St Thomas Aquinas's Summa Theologiae (Summa Theologica)*, trans. by Alfred J. Freddoso, <https://www3.nd.edu/~afreddos/summa-translation/TOC.htm> (accessed 30 June 2021)

————, *On Kingship, to the King of Cyprus*, ed. and trans. by Ignatius T. Eschmann and Gerald B. Phelan (Toronto: Pontifical Institute of Mediaeval Studies, 1949)

Three Royalist Tracts, 1296–1302: Antequam essent clerici; Disputatio inter Clericum et Militem; Quaestio in utramque partem, ed. by Robert W. Dyson, Primary Sources in Political Thought (Bristol: Thoemmes, 1999)

Secondary Works

Bertelloni, Francisco, 'Die Rolle der Natur in den "Commentarii in libros politicorum Aristotelis" des Albertus Magnus', in *Mensch und Natur im Mittelalter*, ed. by Albert Zimmermann and Andreas Speer, vol. ii, Miscellanea Mediaevalia, 21 (Berlin: De Gruyter, 1992), pp. 682–700

Brett, Annabel, 'Issues in Translating the *Defensor Pacis*', in *The World of Marsilius of Padua*, ed. by Gerson Moreno-Riaño, Disputatio, 5 (Turnhout: Brepols, 2006), pp. 91–108

Briguglia, Gianluca, *Marsile de Padoue*, trans. by Delphine Carron-Faivre, Savoirs anciens et médiévaux, 3 (Paris: Classique Garnier, 2014)

————, 'The Minor Marsilius: The Other Works of Marsilius of Padua', in *A Companion to Marsilius of Padua*, ed. by Gerson Moreno-Riaño and Cary J. Nederman, Brill's Companions to the Christian Tradition, 31 (Leiden: Brill, 2012), pp. 265–303

Canning, Joseph, '*Marsilius of Padua and "the Truth of History"*, by George Garnett' (review), *English Historical Review*, 125.512 (2010), 158–61

Carozzi, Claude, *Apocalypse et salut dans le christianisme ancien et medieval*, Collection historique (Paris: Aubier, 1999)

Cheneval, Francis, *Die Rezeption der Monarchia Dantes bis zur Editio Princeps im Jahre 1559: Metamorphosen eines philosophischen Werkes: Mit einer kritischen Edition von Guido Vernanis Tractatus de potestate summi pontificis*, Humanistische Bibliothek. Reihe 1. Abhandlungen, 47 (München: W. Fink, 1995)

Coote, Lesley A., *Prophecy and Public Affairs in Later Medieval England* (Woodbridge: Boydell & Brewer, 2000)

Cornwell, Hannah, *Pax and the Politics of Peace: Republic to Principate*, Oxford Classical Monographs (Oxford: Oxford University Press, 2017)

FitzGerald, Brian, *Inspiration and Authority in the Middle Ages: Prophets and their Critics from Scholasticism to Humanism*, Oxford Historical Monographs (Oxford: Oxford University Press, 2017)

Flüeler, Christoph, *Rezeption und Interpretation der aristotelischen 'Politica' im späten Mittelalter*, Bochumer Studien zur Philosophie, 19, 2 vols (Amsterdam: B. R. Grüner, 1992)

Garnett, George, *Marsilius of Padua and 'the Truth of History'* (Oxford: Oxford University Press, 2006)

Goldsworthy, Adrian K., *Pax romana: War, Peace, and Conquest in the Roman World* (London: Weidenfeld & Nicolson, 2016)

Grabmann, Martin, 'Studien zu Johannes Quidort von Paris O. Pr.', *Sitzungsberichte der Bayerischen Akademie der Wissenschaften. Philosophisch-Historische Klasse*, 3 (1922), 1–60

Izbicki, Thomas M, 'The Reception of Marsilius', in *A Companion to Marsilius of Padua*, ed. by Gerson Moreno-Riaño and Cary J. Nederman, Brill's Companions to the Christian Tradition, 31 (Leiden: Brill, 2012), pp. 305–34

Kaeppeli, Thomas, 'Der Dantegegner Guido Vernani O.P. von Rimini', *Quellen und Forschungen aus italienischen Archiven und Bibliotheken*, 28 (1937/1938), 107–46

Knuuttila, Simo, 'Medieval Theories of Future Contingents', in *The Stanford Encyclopedia of Philosophy*, ed. by Edward N. Zalta (Summer 2020 Edition), <https://plato.stanford.edu/archives/sum2020/entries/medieval-futcont/> [accessed 30 June 2021]

Koch, Bettina, 'Against Empire? John of Paris's Defence of Territorial Secular Power Considered in the Context of Dante's and Marsilius of Padua's Political Theories', in *John of Paris*, ed. by Chris Jones, Disputatio, 23 (Turnhout: Brepols, 2015), pp. 49–74

Langeloh, Jacob, *Erzählte Argumente: Exempla und historische Argumentation in politischen Traktaten c. 1265–1325*, Studien und Texte zur Geistesgeschichte des Mittelalters, 123 (Leiden: Brill, 2017)

Leclercq, Jean, *Jean de Paris et l'ecclésiologie du XIIIᵉ siècle*, L'Église et L'État au Moyen Âge, 5 (Paris: Vrin, 1942)

Maier, Anneliese, 'Notwendigkeit, Kontingenz und Zufall', in *Die Vorläufer Galileis im 14. Jahrhundert: Studien zur Naturphilosophie d. Spätscholastik*, XXII: *Storia e letteratura* (Rome: Ed. di Storia e Letteratura, 1949), pp. 219–50

Matteini, Nevio, *Il più antico oppositore politico di Dante: Guido Vernani da Rimini. Texto critico del 'De reprobatione monarchiae'*, Il pensiero medioevale: Collana di storia della filosofia, 6 (Padua: CEDAM, 1958)

Miethke, Jürgen, 'G. Garnett: Marsilius of Padua and the "Truth of History"', *Francia-Recensio: Mittelalter–Moyen Âge (500–1500)*, no. 4 (2008), <https://.net///recensio/2008-4/MA/garnett_miethke> [accessed 6 April 2023]

——, *Politiktheorie im Mittelalter: Von Thomas von Aquin bis Wilhelm von Ockham* (Tübingen: Mohr Siebeck, 2008)

Milne-Tavendale, Anna, 'John of Paris and the Apocalypse: The Boundaries of Dominican Scholastic Identity', in *John of Paris*, ed. by Chris Jones, Disputatio, 23 (Turnhout: Brepols, 2015), pp. 119–49

Moreno-Riaño, Gerson, and Cary J. Nederman, 'Introduction', in *A Companion to Marsilius of Padua*, ed. by Gerson Moreno-Riaño and Cary J. Nederman, Brill's Companions to the Christian Tradition, 31 (Leiden: Brill, 2012), pp. 1–11

——, 'Marsilius of Padua's Principles of Secular Politics', in *A Companion to Marsilius of Padua*, ed. by Gerson Moreno-Riaño and Cary J. Nederman, Brill's Companions to the Christian Tradition, 31 (Leiden: Brill, 2012), pp. 117–38

Nederman, Cary J., '*Marsilius of Padua and "the Truth of History" by George Garnett* (review)', *Catholic Historical Review*, 94.2 (2008), 342–43

——, 'The Meaning of "Aristotelianism" in Medieval Moral and Political Thought', *Journal of the History of Ideas*, 57.4 (1996), 563–85

Omodeo, Pietro D., and Rodolfo Garau, eds, *Contingency and Natural Order in Early Modern Science*, Boston Studies in the Philosophy and History of Science (Cham: Springer, 2019)

Piaia, Gregorio, 'L'"Errore di Erode" e La Via Media in Giovanni da Parigi', *Revista da Faculdade de Ciências Sociais e Humanas (Lisboa)*, 7 (1994), 169–84

——, 'Forme della laicità fra tardo medioevo e prima età moderna: Marsilio da Padova e Paolo Sarpi', *Revista Portuguesa de Filosofia*, 75.3 (2019), 1721–38

Reeves, Marjorie, *The Influence of Prophecy in the Later Middle Ages: A Study in Joachimism* (Oxford: Clarendon Press, 1969)

Syros, Vasileios, *Die Rezeption der aristotelischen politischen Philosophie bei Marsilius von Padua: Eine Untersuchung zur ersten Diktion des 'Defensor Pacis'*, Studies in Medieval and Reformation Tradition, 134 (Leiden: Brill, 2007)

DAVID LLOYD DUSENBURY

'The Great Refusal'

Pilate and Jesus in the Political Theologies of Dante, Valla, and Marsilius

This contribution begins to retrace the Augustinian tradition of Pilate's guilt in Latin Christian thought — and the political legacy of this tradition in texts by Dante Alighieri, Lorenzo Valla, and Marsilius of Padua. It will be claimed, here, that the Augustinian interpretation of the Roman trial of Jesus — in which Jesus renounces temporal 'kingship', and Pilate nevertheless convicts him as a 'king' — structures late medieval theories of 'secular' power in ways that have not been recognized. This tradition of Passion-interpretation is a hitherto unnoticed element in Marsilius of Padua's radical denunciations of the 'papal monarchy' in Europe.

Introduction

Behind the Augustinian tradition of Passion-interpretation in which Marsilius figures is a sophisticated Christian tradition in which the 'pagan' judge who interrogated Jesus on the morning of his death is guiltless.[1] One writer at the court of Constantine, Firmianus Lactantius, depicts Pontius Pilate, the Roman prefect of Judaea (c. 26–36 CE), as a functionary who merely questioned Jesus before 'the Judaeans [...] killed him'.[2] Lactantius's pro-Roman, anti-Judaean reading of the Passion culminates in a graphic

---

1 The bulk of this contribution is taken from Dusenbury, *The Innocence of Pontius Pilate*, chs 15–16. Material from the book is reprinted by permission of C. Hurst and Oxford University Press.

2 Lactantius, *Div. Inst.*, IV, 18.4. The edition used is *Institutions Divines, Livre 4*, ed. by Monat; and the translation is *The Divine Institutes, Books I–VII*, trans. by McDonald. Note, however, that premodern texts have been compared to the originals — here and below — and often modified.

David Lloyd Dusenbury is a Senior Fellow at the Danube Institute, and a Visiting Professor at Eötvös Loránd University.

Marsilius of Padua, ed. by Alessandro Mulieri, Serena Masolini, and Jenny Pelletier, Disputatio, 36 (Turnhout: Brepols, 2023), pp. 285–320

BREPOLS ❧ PUBLISHERS   10.1484/M.DISPUT-EB.5.132916

claim, for which there is no backing in the canonical Gospels, that 'the Judaeans hoisted Jesus up between two criminals'.[3] The lamentable history of Christian anti-Semitism in Europe is tied to this false claim.

And what, on Lactantius's telling, is Pilate's role in Jesus's death? It is emphatically not judicial. There is no Roman judgement of Jesus in Lactantius's *Divine Institutes*, where we read that Pilate 'did not himself utter a sentence'. This remains a crucial line in Passion exegesis — to the present day.[4] But if Pilate never judges him, how is it that Jesus comes to be crucified? Lactantius writes only that Pilate 'handed Jesus over to the Judaeans'.[5] He then writes that, 'in Tiberius' fifteenth year, in the consulship of the two Gemini [...] the Judaeans fastened Christ to the cross (*Iudaei Christum cruci adfixerunt*)'.[6] The same can be read in Lactantius's polemical chronicle, *On the Deaths of the Persecutors*, where he claims that 'in the latter days of the Emperor Tiberius, in the consulship of the two Gemini [...] Jesus Christ was crucified by the Judaeans (*Iesus Christus a Iudaeis cruciatus est*)'.[7]

It is the African philosopher-bishop Augustine who most forcefully refutes this Christian slander that Judaeans (or in modern terms, Jews) are 'Christ-killers'.[8] The figures of 'Judaeans' and 'Judaism' are fraught in Augustine's corpus,[9] yet it is not a coincidence that Augustine, for whom Pilate is guilty, asserts that Christian laws offer protection to late antique Judaeans.[10] Nor is it a coincidence that the myth of Judaean blood-guilt is dismissed in the medieval European Church precisely where Augustine's influence is the strongest.[11] But what, on Augustine's telling, is the role of Pilate in the world-historical death of Jesus?

According to Augustine, the Passion is — in a formal, juridical sense — a Roman affair. It ends on a Roman cross, and it begins with a Roman arrest. This is theologically and politically consequential. For, in Augustine's *Homilies on the Gospel of John* — from which Thomas Aquinas draws heavily in his *Catena aurea*, and from which Marsilius quotes a number of times in his *Defensor pacis* — he stresses that John's mention of a 'cohort'

---

3 Lactantius, *Div. Inst.*, IV, 18.6–9.
4 Dusenbury, 'The Judgment of Pontius Pilate'.
5 Lactantius, *Div. Inst.*, IV, 18.6.
6 Lactantius, *Div. Inst.*, IV, 10.
7 Lactantius, *Mort. pers.*, 2. The edition used is *Liber de Mortibus persecutorum*, ed. by Migne; and the translation is in *The Minor Works*, trans. by McDonald.
8 Dusenbury, *The Innocence of Pontius Pilate*, ch. 12.
9 Fredriksen, *Augustine and the Jews*; Cohen, 'Revisiting Augustine's Doctrine of Jewish Witness'; Lee, 'Israel between the Two Cities'.
10 Stroumsa, 'From Anti-Judaism to Antisemitism in Early Christianity?', p. 22; Stroumsa, *The Making of the Abrahamic Religions*, pp. 111–12.
11 Cohen, *The Friars and the Jews*, pp. 14–15, 19–22; Cohen, 'The Jews as the Killers of Christ'.

coming out to seize Jesus signals that he must have been taken by Roman troops on the night before his death. This is Augustine:

> The cohort was not of Judaeans (*non Iudaeorum*), but of [Roman] troops. Therefore, let the cohort be understood to have been received [by the Judaeans] from the governor [Pilate], as though for arresting a criminal, so that, since the order of legitimate jurisdiction was observed [...] no one might dare to resist those making the arrest.[12]

It is imperative to note the care with which Augustine states that 'the order of legitimate jurisdiction was observed' ('servato ordine legitimae potestatis') on the night before Jesus's death.[13] This stress on the legal validity of the proceedings is distinctive in the patristic corpus and will become a guiding intuition in later, legally attuned reconstructions of Jesus's Passion — the exemplary case being Dante's *Monarchia*, which we will read in the coming pages.

First, however, the question of Pilate's judgement must be elucidated: Augustine prepares his recognition of Pilate's guilt when his commentary moves from Jesus's high-priestly interrogations to what he calls 'the things done concerning the Lord before the governor, Pontius Pilate'.[14] Augustine notes — a rare thing, in the patristic corpus — that Pilate is, for Jesus and his Judaean accusers, 'a foreign judge' ('alienigenae iudicis').[15] But who, more precisely, is this 'foreign judge'? 'Pilate was a Roman', says Augustine, 'and the Romans had sent him to Judaea as governor'.[16] This means that, for Augustine — and he is correct — the sentence under which Jesus dies is a Roman sentence.

It bears repeating: the Passion is *legally*, for Augustine — unlike for many patristic commentators — *a thoroughly Roman affair*. On Augustine's reading, Jesus is arrested by the Romans;[17] the Judaeans formally deny before Pilate their legal right 'to put anyone to death';[18] and it is Pilate, a 'Roman judge' (*iudex Romanus*), who ultimately sentences Jesus to death.[19] Paul Winter is justified to conclude, in his 'Marginal Notes on the Trial of Jesus', that Augustine reads the Johannine trial narrative 'more carefully' than other early Christian writers.[20]

---

12 Augustine, *Tract.*, 112.2. The edition used is *In Iohannis Evangelium tractatus CXXIV*, ed. by Willems; and the translation is *Homilies on the Gospel of John*, trans. by Gibb and Innes, ed. by Schaff.
13 Augustine, *Tract.*, 112.2.
14 Augustine, *Tract.*, 113.6.
15 Augustine, *Tract.*, 114.2.
16 Augustine, *Tract.*, 114.5.
17 Augustine, *Tract.*, 112.2.
18 Augustine, *Tract.*, 114.4.
19 Augustine, *Tract.*, 114.5.
20 Winter, 'Marginal Notes on the Trial of Jesus, II', p. 242 n. 98.

In contrast to much of the Christian tradition, Augustine accepts that it is the Roman *imperium* which tortures, condemns, and kills Jesus. In his *Harmony of the Gospels*, Augustine recounts the ugly things which were 'done to the Lord' — in his words — 'by Pilate'.[21] And later in this *Harmony*, Augustine assigns the crucifixion to '*John's* narrative of what was done by Pilate'.[22] He concludes his reading of the Roman trial in *Homilies on the Gospel of John* in this way: 'Pilate, seated on his dais, judged and condemned Jesus' ('iudicante atque damnante Pilato pro tribunali').[23]

Augustine holds (*contra* Lactantius) that Jesus is killed 'by the judgement and power of the governor' ('judicio ac potestate praesidis').[24] What is more, he denies that there is any juridical uncertainty in the canonical Passion narratives: only Roman troops could have crucified Jesus.[25] This of course means that the Christian myth of a Judaean crucifixion could only be — for the Bishop of Hippo — a myth. 'It is clear', he concludes in *Homily* 118, that Roman troops 'obeyed the governor in crucifying Jesus'.[26]

It is in light of this recognition of Pilate's guilt, and of Augustine's striking interpretation of Jesus's words to Pilate, 'My kingdom is not of this world' (John 18. 36) — which become, in the African bishop's gloss: 'I obstruct not your dominion in this world'[27] — that we can now sketch the drama of Pilate and Jesus in the political theologies of Dante, Valla, and Marsilius.

The Pilate Trial in Dante Alighieri's Political Theology

'*I Beheld the Shade*'

It is strange that Pilate is not one of the moody, all-too-human dead that we meet in Dante's *Inferno*. In Canto III, a swooning Dante and a cold-blooded Vergil are at the gates of hell. They have not yet descended in. This is the undecided ground where the newly dead idle before they come to the place of torment. Here, the lost are past all hope, but they have not yet been driven down the coils of the damned. And it is here that Dante sees one of the most mysterious figures in his epic.

---

21 Augustine, *Cons. Ev.*, III, 8.32: 'per Pilatum gesta de Domino'. The edition used is *De Consensu Evangelistarum*, ed. by Weihrich; and the translation is *The Harmony of the Gospels*, trans. by Salmond, ed. by Schaff.

22 Augustine, *Cons. Ev.*, III, 8.35: 'Haec narravit Ioannes per Pilatum gesta'.

23 Augustine, *Tract.*, 117.1.

24 Augustine, *Tract.*, 116.9.

25 Augustine, *Tract.*, 116.9.

26 Augustine, *Tract.*, 118.2: 'unde apparet quatuor fuisse milites qui in eo crucifigendo praesidi paruerunt'.

27 Augustine, *Tract.*, 115.2.

This figure is not unknown to Dante, and that is part of the mystery. Dante knows who it is that he catches sight of, and he tells us that he knows. But he does not tell us who it is. This is what we read:

> I would not have thought
> death had undone so many. When more than one
> I recognized had passed, I beheld the shade
> of him who made the great refusal, impelled
> by cowardice.[28]

Who is the coward? He is disowned by the powers of heaven and hell, but he is not unpunished. He is 'galled by wasps and flies' and confined to a dead zone where the lost await their doom.[29] This must in some coded way symbolize his life (though Dante says, obscurely, that this man belonged to a 'dreary guild' of those who were 'never alive').[30] And what is 'the great refusal' ('il gran rifiuto')?[31] If we knew that, we would know who had thus refused. But Dante tells us nothing more.

Early Theories of the Great Refusal

The commentary tradition on this scene is intricate and conflicted. One of Dante's sons, Jacopo Alighieri, was the first to comment on *Inferno* III. According to Jacopo, the one who made the great refusal must be Celestine V — a pope who abdicated in the year 1294 (with Dante composing most of the *Inferno* between 1306 and 1308).[32] Papal abdication is an apocalyptically rare thing. Celestine V's renunciation of Peter's See struck most of his contemporaries — and, it seems, Dante — as a monstrosity.

But one of Dante's other sons, Pietro Alighieri, rejects the Celestine theory in his *Comment on Dante's Poem the Commedia*. For Pietro, the one who made the great refusal must be Diocletian — a Roman emperor who abdicated in the year 305.[33] The symmetry is clear: Celestine renounced the highest office in the Roman Church, and Diocletian renounced the

---

28 Dante, *Inferno*, III, 56–60; here and below, the edition and translation used are *The Inferno of Dante: A New Verse Translation*, trans. by Pinsky, pp. 20–21 (typography lightly modified). Consult Singleton, *Inferno*, II: *Commentary*, pp. 47–52.

29 Dante, *Inferno*, III, 66.

30 Dante, *Inferno*, III, 61–69. For more on this: Colish, 'Sanza'nfamia e sanza lodo'.

31 Dante, *Inferno*, III, 60.

32 Jacopo Alighieri, *Chiose alla Cantica dell'Inferno*, ed. by Piccini, ad loc. (Dante, *Inferno*, III, 58–60). The Celestine reading is upheld by Natalino Sapegno in the apparatus of *La Divina Commedia*, I: *Inferno*, pp. 39–40. For the *Inferno*'s dates of composition: Santagata, *Dante*, p. 219.

33 Pietro Alighieri, *Comentum super poema Comedie Dantis*, ed. by Chiamenti, ad loc. (Dante, *Inferno*, III, 34–60). Note that I am citing, here, the third edition of Pietro's *Comment*.

highest office in the Roman Empire. For Dante's sons, and for most fourteenth-century Europeans, no greater renunciations could be imagined.

Other early commentators on the *Inferno*, such as Guglielmo Maramauro,[34] Benvenuto da Imola,[35] and the novelist Giovanni Boccaccio,[36] thought Dante must have had in mind the biblical patriarch Isaac's son Esau who sold his birthright for a cup of 'red pottage' in the Book of Genesis.[37] None of these conjectures is thoroughly convincing, to my mind. But the renunciation of Isaac's blessing (Esau), Caesar's power (Diocletian), and Peter's authority (Celestine) are the early and recurring ones. They have a sort of canonical status in Dante commentaries until the late nineteenth century.[38]

A Renaissance Platonist Reads the Great Refusal

The most sophisticated reading of *Inferno* III 60, where Dante sees the one 'who made the great refusal', may have been written circa 1480 by a Renaissance Platonist, Cristoforo Landino, in his *Comment on the Commedia*. It is 'not without reason', Landino begins, that the poet decides to give no name here.[39] The lack of a name is not a lack of meaning. On the contrary, it contributes to the meaning of this stanza. Landino's question then becomes: If Dante is silent for a reason, what is his reason?

Landino reads Dante like a philosopher. He notes that Dante not only refuses to tell us *who* he sees, but *why* he is silent. The mystery of *il gran rifiuto* is not a sign that Dante's interpreters have failed, but that Dante has succeeded. The poet has constructed a mystery at *Inferno* III 60; it is a sign of his artistry that a mystery remains.

The new question, of course, is: Why the mystery? And Landino is not dogmatic in this regard. He gives three reasons why *Inferno* III 60 might omit a name:

---

34 Maramauro, *Expositione sopra l''Inferno'*, ad loc. (Dante, *Inferno*, III, 58–60).

35 Benvenuto da Imola, *Comentum super Dantis Aldigherij Comoediam*, ed. by Lacaita, ad loc. (Dante, *Inferno*, III, 58–60).

36 Boccaccio, *Esposizioni sopra la comedia di Dante*, ed. by Branca, ad loc. (Dante, *Inferno*, III, 58–60). Note that Boccaccio is not only one of the first commentators on the *Commedia*, but Dante's first biographer: Falkeid, *The Avignon Papacy Contested*, 52–54.

37 Genesis 25. 29–34 (Authorized Version).

38 See the commentary of Baldassare Lombardi, in which the only possibility other than Celestine, Diocletian, and Esau, is a Florentine known to Dante, such as Torrigiano de' Cerchi: Lombardi, *La Divina Commedia*, ad loc. (Dante, *Inferno*, III, 59–60).

39 Landino, *Comento sopra la Comedia*, ad loc. (Dante, *Inferno*, III, 58–60).

'THE GREAT REFUSAL' 291

1 Perhaps Dante prefers not to name a man who held high office and lived a holy life — read Pope Celestine — but who Dante felt had been degraded by his time in government.

2 Perhaps Dante gives no name here, *not* because he is thinking of a Celestine (or a Diocletian), but because he is referring to someone 'forgettable' or 'inglorious' (*sanza fama*): a Florentine non-entity.[40]

3 Or perhaps Dante wants to leave the question open — by which Landino means, to put it in perpetuity 'before the judgement of his hearers'.[41]

Landino concludes that the vagueness of the kind that Dante sees at *Inferno* III 60 'creates doubt'.[42] Perhaps that is Dante's intention.

A Nineteenth-Century Theory

A book printed in New York in the late nineteenth century seems to be the first to suggest that the blurred-out rogue who is glimpsed at *Inferno* III 60 is Jesus's Roman judge.[43] This is a neat conjecture, since it places Pilate — who is never named in the *Inferno* — in Dante's hell-cantos. On a moment's reflection, however, the placement is confusing. For the shade Dante sees in *Inferno* III — the one 'who made the great refusal' — is not in hell itself.[44] He is merely in hell's vestibule.[45] This may be why, for more than five hundred years after Dante wrote the *Inferno*, no one seems to have thought Pilate is the one Dante 'beheld' under a cloud of wasps in the *terra nullius* at the outskirts of hell.[46]

A Twentieth-Century Reception

By the turn of the twentieth century, the Pilate-conjecture had crossed the Atlantic. It soon became — and still seems to be — *de rigeur* in

---

40 Vieri de' Cerchi and Giano della Bella have been proposed: Singleton, *Inferno*, II: *Commentary*, p. 59.

41 Landino, *Comento sopra la Comedia*, ad loc. (Dante, *Inferno*, III, 58–60).

42 I say, 'concludes', not because this line about doubt is placed at the end of Landino's comment, but rather, because it seems to me to capture his point: Landino, *Comento sopra la Comedia*, ad loc. (Dante, *Inferno*, III, 58–60).

43 Schaff, *Literature and Poetry*, p. 380. This is not meant to impugn Philip Schaff, who wrote an irenic *History of the Christian Church* (eight volumes) and edited a collection of *Early Church Fathers* (thirty-eight volumes) which I have consulted hundreds of times.

44 Dante, *Inferno*, III, 58–60.

45 For 'vestibule of Hell' and a concise reception-history of *Inferno*, III, 60 (in which the Pilate-conjecture gets no more than a mention): Singleton, *Inferno*, II: *Commentary*, pp. 47–52.

46 Dante, *Inferno*, III, 59.

certain Italian circles.[47] In 1902 a symbolist poet, Giovanni Pascoli, wrote an essay for the avant-garde magazine *Il Marzocco*, 'Who Is "the One Who Made the Great Refusal"'. For Pascoli, it is Pilate.[48] And more than a century later noted cultural philosopher Giorgio Agamben still calls this 'Pascoli's hypothesis'.[49] It may not be a coincidence that many of Italy's twentieth-century *litterati* concluded that Pilate is the coward that Dante recognizes in *Inferno* III.[50]

It may be the Italian reception of a late nineteenth-century poet's interpretation of *Inferno* III 60 — 'Pascoli's hypothesis' — which primes a twentieth-century revival, in Italy, of a patristic misinterpretation of the Roman trial of Jesus.[51] And it may be Pascoli's hypothesis, too, which is responsible for a twentieth-century failure to see the significance of Pilate in Dante's political theory. It is one of the tasks of the present contribution to show that a 'great refusal' is critical for understanding the early history of European secularity in ways that seem to have gone unnoticed — not only in Dante's corpus, but in Marsilius's texts. But this *gran rifiuto* is not Pilate's. Quite the contrary.

Giovanni Rosadi on Pilate's Refusal

The idea that Pilate refuses to judge Jesus is nothing new. One of Constantine's courtiers, mentioned earlier, insisted in the early fourth century that Pilate 'did not himself utter a sentence' after he interrogated Jesus. Instead, on Lactantius's telling, the Roman prefect 'handed Jesus over to the Judaeans' to be crucified.[52] And Agamben's twenty-first-century reprise of Lactantius's reading could hardly be more precise.[53] In *Pilate and Jesus*, Agamben writes that Pilate 'did not pronounce his sentence', but 'simply "handed over" the accused to the Sanhedrin'.[54] But is this ancient theory of Pilate's refusal to pass judgement linked to the modern Italian theory that Pilate is the coward in *Inferno* III 60?

---

47 It is perplexing to me that the Pilate-conjecture is called 'the most credible' ('il più attendibile'), after Celestine V, in the commentary of Bosco and Reggio, eds, *La Divina Commedia. Inferno*, pp. 34–35. Like Landino, Bosco and Reggio are non-dogmatic, and they say that the Pilate-conjecture is not convincing. But to my mind, it is *far less* credible than all the others (Celestine, Diocletian, Esau), for reasons that will be stated in a moment.

48 Pascoli, 'Chi sia "colui che fece il gran rifiuto"'. Before this: Barbarani, *Due chiose dantesche*; cited by Penna, 'Pilato, Ponzio'.

49 Agamben, *Pilato e Gesù*, p. 68; Agamben, *Pilate and Jesus*, p. 50.

50 Though it is rejected by Natalino Sapegno in his apparatus: Sapegno, *La Divina Commedia*, I: *Inferno*, pp. 39–40.

51 Agamben, *Pilato e Gesù*, p. 68; Agamben, *Pilate and Jesus*, p. 50.

52 Lactantius, *Div. Inst.*, IV, 18.6.

53 Dusenbury, 'The Judgment of Pontius Pilate', pp. 358–64.

54 Agamben, *Pilate and Jesus*, p. 47.

The link is conspicuous in Pascoli's 1902 essay on *il gran rifiuto*, and it enters the 'critical' literature on Jesus's trial a couple of years later in Giovanni Rosadi's book, *The Trial of Jesus*. Rosadi is certainly thinking of Dante when he writes of 'the cowardice' of Pilate's 'refusal to act' during Jesus's Roman trial.[55] What is this 'refusal to act'? 'Pilate refused to choose', Rosadi writes in 1904, 'and his refusal was great'.[56] No cultured Italian could fail to hear Dante's words, *il gran rifiuto*, in Rosadi's words, 'his refusal was great'. Rosadi's Pilate is — like Pascoli's Pilate — Dante's coward.[57]

'There was in fact no sentence', writes Rosadi, 'the prisoner was merely handed over'. His recollection of Lactantius, like Agamben's in this century, could hardly be more exact. For Rosadi then adds, as a corollary: 'Jesus [...] was not condemned, but He was slain'.[58] What could this mean? Rosadi seems to have held that Pilate only uttered an 'inarticulate command which was to have the fatal power of a condemnation'.[59] And he is not the only modern commentator for whom Jesus's trial is concluded by Pilate's 'inarticulate command', whatever that might be. A nod? A glance? A gesture?

'I See the New Pilate'

Is 'Pascoli's hypothesis' — by which I mean, a twentieth-century revival of Lactantius's fourth-century Pilate-interpretation — one possible interpretation of Dante's lines in *Inferno* III?[60] It is not. The falsity of 'Pascoli's hypothesis' is first signalled by the fact that, though Pilate is never named in the *Inferno*, he is named in Dante's *Purgatorio* (most *cantos* of which appear to have been written between 1309 and 1315).[61] It is to that passage we now turn.

In *Purgatorio* XX, Dante portrays a 'new Pilate' (*novo Pilato*) who has nothing like the physiognomy of a coward, and nothing like the bearing of a man who, per *Inferno* III 64, never lived.[62] This is Dante, in the only lines of the *Commedia* where Pilate is named:

I see [...]
Christ imprisoned in His vicar.
I see him being mocked a second time;

---

55 Rosadi, *The Trial of Jesus*, p. 260.
56 Rosadi, *The Trial of Jesus*, pp. 222–24.
57 It must be said that Rosadi denies Pilate's *moral* innocence: Rosadi, *The Trial of Jesus*, p. 260.
58 Rosadi, *The Trial of Jesus*, p. 294 (translation modified).
59 Rosadi, *The Trial of Jesus*, p. 300.
60 Agamben, *Pilato e Gesù*, p. 68; Agamben, *Pilate and Jesus*, p. 50.
61 Santagata, *Dante*, pp. 219, 225.
62 Dante, *Purgatorio*, XX, 91 (new Pilate); Dante, *Inferno*, III, 64 (never lived).

I see the vinegar and the gall renewed,
and between living thieves I see them kill Him.
I see the new Pilate, so cruel
that this is not enough, without consent sail
his greedy sails into the Temple.[63]

Commentators have determined that this scene is a late medieval 'Passion' play in which the 'new Pilate' is King Philip IV of France (aka Philip the Fair), and 'Christ' is Pope Boniface VIII, who issued the ultra-papalist bull *Unam sanctam* in 1302, and died shortly after being brutalized and imprisoned by Philip's troops in 1303.[64]

Much could be said about Boniface VIII in Dante's political imaginary; the poet dubs him 'Prince of new Pharisees' in *Inferno* XXVII.[65] Or, about the reception of Boniface VIII's novel canonistic definition of 'secular persons' (*saecularium personarum*).[66] But the only thing that matters at present is how Dante imagines Pilate in this symbol-rich sketch of the 'Passion' of Boniface VIII. Is the *Purgatorio*'s Pilate a figure of cowardice and indecision? Is he a gutless, contourless figure? On the contrary. The one Dante calls a 'new Pilate' is 'so cruel' ('sì crudele') that he cannot rest until he, like Pompey in 63 BCE or Titus in 70 CE, profanes the *sanctum sanctorum* of the Temple.[67] Pilate's ravenousness in this scene, the fact that his cruel deeds are 'not enough' ('nol sazia'),[68] plainly refers to the tercet in which Christ — in the person of his vicar, Boniface VIII — is 'mocked', is given 'the vinegar and the gall' to drink, and is finally left to die 'between living thieves'.

In short: Christ is tortured, here, and crucified 'a second time' ('un'altra volta').[69] And who is responsible for this terrible scene? The one whose cruelty is not sated by it: Dante's Pilate.

There is no need to press this further. Despite what some modern commentators have said, Dante's lines on Pilate in *Purgatorio* XX terminate the modern hypothesis that Jesus's judge is the one who made 'the great refusal' in *Inferno* III.[70] The Pilate of Pascoli and Rosadi in the early

---

63 Dante, *Purgatorio*, XX, 86–93; here and below, the edition and translation used are Dante Alighieri, *Purgatorio: A New Verse Translation*, trans. by Merwin. Consult Singleton, *Purgatorio*, II: *Commentary*, pp. 486–89.

64 Falkeid, *The Avignon Papacy Contested*, pp. 26–27, 73. For the influence of this conflict on political theory: Briguglia, *La questione del potere*.

65 Dante, *Inferno*, XXVII, 85; Artinian, 'Dante's Parody of Boniface VIII'.

66 Cited by Strätz, 'Säkularisation, Säkularisierung', p. 799 n. 58: 'Liber sextus decretalium D. Bonifacii Papae VIII [...]. *i. Saeculares, i. saecularium personarum*'.

67 Dante, *Purgatorio*, XX, 91–93.

68 Dante, *Purgatorio*, XX, 92.

69 Dante, *Purgatorio*, XX, 88–90.

70 Dante, *Inferno*, III, 60.

twentieth century, and of Agamben in this century — which is to say, the Pilate who 'did not himself utter a sentence' — is not Dante's Pilate.[71]

In *Purgatorio* XX, Pilate seizes Christ, tortures him, and kills him. This suggests that Dante's image of Pilate is not influenced by Lactantius, who exculpates Pilate, but by Augustine, who inculpates Pilate in his much-read *Homilies on the Gospel of John*.[72] And the Bishop of Hippo seems to have informed Dante's image of Pilate not only in the *Commedia*, but in his treatise on political theology, *Monarchia*, which he seemingly wrote before completing the *Purgatorio*.[73]

'That Unique Census of the Human Race'

The modern hypothesis that Pilate is the one who made 'the great refusal' in *Inferno* III reflects a catastrophic misinterpretation of Dante's corpus. Two things are meant by this. First, in Dante's *Monarchia* — as will be shown in the coming pages — it is of world-redeeming significance that Pilate judged Jesus. To interpret *Inferno* III 60 in the modern Italian way is to mistake Dante's political theology *in toto*.[74] Second, and perhaps more interesting, Dante believes that a great refusal is made during Jesus's Roman trial; but it is not made by Pilate. For Dante, it is Jesus who makes the great refusal. And this refusal is not cowardly. We can begin by turning to *Monarchia* II.

Dante's question in *Monarchia* II is 'whether the Roman people took on empire by right'.[75] Having argued for the legitimacy of the Roman Empire on what he calls 'rational principles' for much of Book II, Dante formulates a couple of arguments 'from the principles of the Christian faith' in the book's final chapters.[76] In Chapter 10, he reasons from the circumstances of Jesus's birth — and this is where we will begin to read.

The Gospel of Luke narrates, Dante writes, that 'Christ chose to be born of his Virgin Mother under an edict emanating from Roman authority', by which he means the census that structures the birth-narrative in Luke (but not in Matthew). This means, Dante reasons, that 'Christ chose' to be 'enrolled as a man in that unique census of the human race'. And that means, he goes on, that 'the Son of God [...] acknowledged the

---

71 Lactantius, *Div. Inst.*, IV, 18.6.

72 Consult Dusenbury, *The Innocence of Pontius Pilate*, chs 6 and 13.

73 Santagata, *Dante*, pp. 261–75, 284–95.

74 Recent Italian correctives are Di Fonzo, 'La legittimazione dell'Impero e del Popolo romano presso Dante'; and Cecotti, 'La legittima validità dell'impero'. It seems necessary to register a 'volte-face' in Dante's politics between his composition of *Inferno* and *Purgatorio*: Santagata, *Dante*, p. 284.

75 Dante, *Monarchia*, II, 16.16. The edition used is *Monarchia*, ed. by Chiesa and Tabarroni; and the translation is *Monarchy*, ed. and trans. by Shaw.

76 Dante, *Monarchia*, II, 10.1.

validity of that edict'. A citation from Aristotle's *Nicomachean Ethics* proves, for Dante, that the recognition of a law by compliance in act is 'more effective' than a mere verbal recognition.[77] The circumstances of Jesus's birth therefore prove, for Dante, that 'the jurisdiction of the authority which promulgated' the Roman census — namely, that of the Roman Empire — 'is legitimate'.[78]

The timing of Christ's birth demonstrates concretely that Christ assented to the Roman edict. But it is unjust to assent to an unjust law. And since it is absurd to think — or rather, since it is absurd for a believer to think[79] — that Christ assented unjustly, the Roman edict must be just.[80] This is how Dante reasons from the circumstances of Jesus's birth to the legitimacy of the Roman Empire — and its European successor, the Holy Roman Empire.[81]

'To Pilate to Be Judged'

Far more intriguing in this context is Dante's reasoning in the next chapter of *Monarchia* II from the circumstances of Jesus's *death* to the legitimacy of the Roman Empire.[82] Just as the Roman edict in Luke is a hinge on which Dante's earlier argument turns, so here he fixes on a single dominical saying in John. Dante writes here that 'Christ himself, suffering punishment in his own person, says in John: "It is finished"'.[83] These are Jesus's last words in the crucifixion scene in John, and they naturally force us to ask: What is finished?

Quoting the New Testament letter of Ephesians, Dante infers that what is finished must be our 'redemption by [Christ's] blood' and the 'remission of [our] sins in accordance with the riches of his glory'.[84] Dante is sure that this redemption could not have been secured unless our sins had been 'punished in Christ' (a theological claim);[85] and that '"punishment" is not simply "a penalty imposed on one who does wrong", but "a penalty imposed on the wrongdoer *by one who has the legal authority* to punish

---

77 Dante, *Monarchia*, II, 10.6.

78 Dante, *Monarchia*, II, 10.8.

79 Dante, *Monarchia*, II, 10.5; trans. by Shaw, p. 59: 'If someone is a believer, he allows that this is false; if he does not allow it, he is not a believer, and if he is not a believer, this argument is not for him'.

80 Dante, *Monarchia*, II, 10.9–10.

81 For the influence of Peter of Spain on Dante's reasoning here: Falkeid, *The Avignon Papacy Contested*, pp. 35–36.

82 For the sources of Dante's arguments: Cecotti, 'La legittima validità dell'impero', pp. 401–07.

83 Dante, *Monarchia*, II, 11.3.

84 Dante, *Monarchia*, II, 11.3.

85 Dante, *Monarchia*, II, 11.1.

'THE GREAT REFUSAL' 297

him"' (a legal claim, perhaps taken from Justinian's *Institutes*).[86] This is crucial. For what this means is that, in Dante's mind, the redemption of humankind is legally and theologically unthinkable unless Jesus was *punished*, which is to say, made to suffer — though innocent — *by a legitimate judge.*

Who is Jesus's judge, according to Dante? Pontius Pilate. And of necessity, Dante has no use for a Roman judge who refuses to judge Christ. Nothing less than the redemption of the world hangs on the fact that, as Dante writes, the sufferings of Christ were inflicted 'by an authorized judge' ('sub ordinario iudice').[87] To deny this is, for Dante, to undermine the Christian faith. 'This is why Herod', he suggests (referring to a scene which is unique to the Gospel of Luke), 'sent Christ back to Pilate to be judged (*ad iudicandum*)'.[88] Why? Because Herod Antipas was a mere client-ruler of Galilee. But Tiberius Caesar, 'whose representative Pilate was, [had] jurisdiction over the whole of mankind (*supra totum humanum genus*)'.[89] Only a verdict by Pilate could inflict on Christ a punishment by 'the legitimate empire of the world' ('de iure orbis imperium');[90] and only a punishment by that world-empire, Dante reasons, could exact the redemption of humankind by Christ's blood. When Jesus says, in the death-scene of the Gospel of John, 'It is finished', what Dante believes is finished is *the exaction of a suffering imposed by Jesus's Roman judge.*

The judgement of Pilate is, therefore, no slight question in Dante's political theology. Pilate's judgement is a moment without which — it is not hyperbolic to say — Dante's world-picture becomes incomprehensible. For he believes that first-century Rome held the right to avenge the first humans' sin in paradise, as Beatrice reveals to Dante in the *Paradiso*. It is given to the Roman Empire, she says, through Pilate's sentence of death, to exact the divinely ordained 'vengeance of the ancient sin' ('la vendetta del peccato antico'): the crucifixion of Jesus.[91]

Because of this it is not possible to read Pilate into *Inferno* III, with the Italian modernists. When Dante sees 'the shade of him who made the great refusal', he cannot be referring to Pilate.[92] This is certain because of what Dante writes not only in *Purgatorio* XX, but in *Monarchia* II. For Dante

---

86 Dante, *Monarchia*, II, 11.4 (my emphasis).
87 Dante, *Monarchia*, II, 11.4.
88 Dante, *Monarchia*, II, 11.6.
89 Dante, *Monarchia*, II, 11.5.
90 Dante, *Monarchia*, II, 11.7.
91 Dante, *Paradiso*, VI, 82–93, here 93. I owe this to Falkeid, *The Avignon Papacy Contested*, pp. 33–34. The divine vengeance taken by Rome, in Jerusalem, at the crucifixion, is then divinely avenged by Rome, in Jerusalem, with the destruction of the Temple by Titus in 70 CE. For Dante's derivation of the last idea from the writings of Paulus Orosius (one of Augustine's protégés): Singleton, *Paradiso*, II: *Commentary*, pp. 123–24.
92 Dante, *Inferno*, III, 58–60.

believes that Christ is led before Pilate 'to be judged' ('ad iudicandum').[93] And Dante believes, in an acutely theorized way, that Pilate did judge Jesus. It is only because Pilate did *not* refuse to judge Jesus that Christ has 'freed us', as Dante writes in *Monarchia* III, 'from the power of darkness with his blood'.[94] We can now turn to *Monarchia* III.

'Christ Renounced the Kingdom'

There is, for Dante, a 'great refusal' during the Roman trial of Jesus. He articulates it in *Monarchia* III, where his new question is whether the Roman Church — by which he means the papal monarchy of late medieval Europe — holds 'the power to confer authority on the Roman prince': by which he means the Germano-Roman emperors of late medieval Europe.[95]

It is arresting that Dante says in *Monarchia* III that 'not only all [...] Africans, but also the greater part of those who live in Europe find the idea [of a universal papal monarchy] abhorrent'.[96] If it is the Roman Church which legitimizes the Roman Empire, Dante reasons here, it is certainly not by 'the consent of all men' living in late medieval Africa and Europe.[97] But Dante has a stronger argument in *Monarchia* III that 'the authority of the Empire does not derive from the authority of the Supreme Pontiff' — in other words, that the Holy Roman Empire is not legitimated by the Roman Church.[98] Further, this is an argument which harmonizes nicely with Dante's reading of the Roman trial of Jesus in *Monarchia* II.

In *Monarchia* II, Dante's reading of the Pilate trial is centred on Pilate; but in Book III, it is centred on Jesus. What Pilate accomplishes in *Monarchia* II is the punishment of Christ by his utterance of a formally valid Roman condemnation. What Jesus accomplishes in *Monarchia* III is the renunciation of what Dante calls 'the power to confer authority on the kingdom of our mortality'.[99] And what Dante calls 'the kingdom of our mortality' is, *sensu latissimo*, what late moderns call 'secularity'.[100] Thus Ernst Kantorowicz can write — after making the requisite caveats — that, in the pages of *Monarchia*, 'Dante distinguished between a "human" perfection and a "Christian" perfection — two profoundly different aspects of man's possible felicity'; and that 'the autonomous rights of human society [...] were so powerfully emphasized that indeed it is admissible to

---

93 Dante, *Monarchia*, II, 11.6.
94 Dante, *Monarchia*, III, 1.3.
95 Dante, *Monarchia*, III, 14.1.
96 Dante, *Monarchia*, III, 14.7.
97 Dante, *Monarchia*, III, 14.1.
98 Dante, *Monarchia*, III, 16.1.
99 Dante, *Monarchia*, III, 15.1.
100 Consult Dusenbury, *The Innocence of Pontius Pilate*, ch. 11.

say [with Étienne Gilson] that Dante has "abruptly and utterly shattered" the concept of the undisputed unity of the temporal and the spiritual".[101]

However that may be, Dante's reasoning about Christ's renunciation of secular power is clear. It seems to me to recollect Augustine's reading of the Roman trial of Jesus, which is also centred on the trial narrative in John. Dante cogently states that 'the "form" of the church is simply the life of Christ'. The *vita Christi* is the 'exemplar for the church militant, especially for the pastors, and above all for the Supreme Pastor' — that is, the pope.[102] The question then becomes, what is the testimony of the *vita Christi* with regards to 'the kingdom of our mortality' ('regnum nostre mortalitas')?[103] Dante writes this in *Monarchia* III:

> Christ renounced (*abnegavit*) the kingdom of this world (*huius mundi regnum*) in the presence of Pilate, saying [in John]: 'My kingdom is not of this world; if my kingdom were of this world, then my servants would fight, that I should not be delivered to the Jews; but now my kingdom is not from hence'. Which is not to be understood to mean that Christ, who is God, is not Lord of this kingdom [...] but that, as the exemplar for the church (*exemplar ecclesie*), he had no concern for this kingdom. [...] From this we deduce that the power to confer authority on the kingdom of this world is against the nature of the church (*contra naturam ecclesie*).[104]

In Dante's *Monarchia*, it is not a coward, but God, who makes the great refusal. It is not Pilate who refuses to judge, but Christ who refuses — in this world (*huius mundi*) and for the present time — *to judge his judge*. Because Pilate judges Jesus in *Monarchia* II humankind is redeemed. And because Jesus in *Monarchia* III refuses to judge Pilate — in this world (*huius mundi*) and for the present time — the Church is born. For Dante, it is because 'Christ renounced the kingdom of this world' that there is a kingdom *in* this world which is not *of* this world — namely, the Church.[105]

Dante believes that he has 'sufficiently proved', by means of this Augustinian — which is to say, African[106] — reading of the Pilate trial in John, that 'the authority of the Empire (*auctoritatem imperii*) in no way derives from the Church (*ab ecclesia* [...] *dependere*)'.[107] Dante states very clearly that the Roman Church and its head (the pope) are to be concerned with 'happiness in the *eternal* life'.[108] By way of contrast, the Roman Empire

---

101 Kantorowicz, *The King's Two Bodies*, p. 464.
102 Dante, *Monarchia*, III, 15.3.
103 Dante, *Monarchia*, III, 15.1.
104 Dante, *Monarchia*, III, 15.5–9.
105 Dante, *Monarchia*, III, 15.5.
106 Compare Dusenbury, *The Innocence of Pontius Pilate*, chs 1, 13, and 14.
107 Dante, *Monarchia*, III, 15.10.
108 Dante, *Monarchia*, III, 16.7.

and its head ('who is called the Roman prince'),[109] are to be concerned with 'happiness in *this* life'.[110] Referencing a celebrated formula by the late antique African pope Gelasius I (r. 492–496), we could say that, for Dante, the pope is the highest instance of 'the sacred authority of the priests' ('auctoritas sacra pontificum'), and the emperor is the highest instance of 'the royal power' ('regalis potestas').[111]

It is a real trial — the Roman trial of Jesus — which legitimizes, for Dante, a formal demarcation between the power of emperors and the authority of prelates. And it is a great refusal, by Jesus, of 'the kingdom of this world in the presence of Pilate' which legitimizes the power of emperors to realize a political order which conduces to 'happiness in *this* life'.[112]

'That Man Who Weakened your Empire'

There is an acute difficulty with this configuration, however, and Dante is keenly aware of it in the early fourteenth century.[113] For most of Dante's contemporaries (though not for Dante himself), the drama of Jesus's renunciation of secular power in the first century is cancelled out by a counter-drama set in the fourth century. The source of this counter-drama is a portmanteau of fifth- and eighth-century forgeries which came to be called, in the eleventh and twelfth centuries, the *Donation of Constantine*.[114] In this concocted 'donation', Constantine I gives to Pope Sylvester I (r. 314–335), in thanks for a divine act of healing, the Lateran palace, the city of Rome, and many of his territories, powers, and insignias. In short, in the pages of this *Donation*, the pope is made the *de jure* head of Rome and the Western Empire, though he is not given Constantinople or the Eastern Empire.[115]

Thus, when Dante writes to fourteenth-century 'Romans' in the last sentences of *Monarchia* II that it would have been better if 'that man who weakened your empire had never been born', he is cursing — from our distance, improbably — the man who Christianized the Roman Empire.[116] Dante seems to fleetingly concede in *Monarchia* that Constantine had

---

109 Dante, *Monarchia*, III, 16.11.

110 Dante, *Monarchia*, III, 16.7.

111 Gelasius I, *Epist.* 12.2, in *The Letters*, ed. by Neil and Allen, p. 74 (translation modified). For more on this: Dusenbury, *The Innocence of Pontius Pilate*, ch. 14.

112 Dante, *Monarchia*, III, 15.5–9 and III, 16.7.

113 Park, 'Dante and the Donation of Constantine'.

114 Park, 'Dante and the Donation of Constantine', pp. 68–70; Fried, *The 'Donation of Constantine'*.

115 Park, 'Dante and the Donation of Constantine', p. 67; Whalen, *Dominion of God*, pp. 18–26.

116 Dante, *Monarchia*, II, 11.8. Dante's tercets on the *Donation of Constantine* were written in the same period: Dante, *Paradiso*, VI, 1–9; Falkeid, *The Avignon Papacy Contested*, pp. 33–34.

'legitimately', in the *Donation*, 'handed over into the church's guardianship those things of the empire's which he did hand over'.[117] Yet there are many indications that Dante regarded the *Donation* as being, in Unn Falkeid's words, 'a weak, suspect document' which most convincingly demonstrated 'the greed of the church'.[118] In *Inferno* XIX, for instance, Dante calls the *Donation of Constantine* the mother of immense wickedness ('di quanto mal fu matre').[119] Of how much wickedness, we could ask. In *Paradiso* XX, Dante laments that Constantine's gift had led *the world* to ruination ('che sia'l mondo indi distrutto').[120] Of course, this is hyperbolic. The *Donation of Constantine* is one of premodern Europe's world-altering documents, even if it did not destroy 'the world'.[121] Its exposure as a fake is world-altering, too. Roughly 130 years after Dante wrote *Monarchia*, Lorenzo Valla demonstrates the spuriousness of the *Donation*.[122] And in the pages of Valla's exposé, as in Dante's *Monarchia*, the Roman trial of Jesus is decisive.[123]

The Pilate Trial in Lorenzo Valla's Political Theology

Medieval political theology is shaped by a 'great refusal' that Constantine was thought to have made in his *Donation* to a fourth-century pope, Sylvester. And early modern political theology is marked — perhaps inaugurated — by Lorenzo Valla's demonstration that the *Donation* is a fake.[124] It is immensely symbolic that Valla's exposé, written in 1440, went to press for the first time in the epochal year 1517 — the year to which Martin Luther's continent-shaping protest is dated.[125]

Luther himself read Valla's critique not much later, in February 1520, and it is Valla who seems to have convinced the Saxon monk-militant that

---

117 Dante, *Monarchia*, III, 13.7.
118 Falkeid, *The Avignon Papacy Contested*, pp. 42–43. Compare Benfell, *The Biblical Dante*, pp. 101, 181–88.
119 Dante, *Inferno*, XIX, 115–17; Park, 'Dante and the Donation of Constantine', p. 72.
120 Dante, *Paradiso*, XX, 55–60; Park, 'Dante and the Donation of Constantine', pp. 73–74.
121 The political history of the *Donation*'s reception is not limited to Europe: Wieczynski, 'The Donation of Constantine'.
122 The novelty of Valla's text is debated: Linde, 'Lorenzo Valla and the Authenticity of Sacred Texts', pp. 38–39.
123 I am grateful to Paul Richard Blum for insisting that I read Valla, and for providing me with the relevant texts. Among his many pages on Valla are Blum, *Philosophy of Religion*, pp. 77–94.
124 For 'modern' traits in the thought of Reginald Pecock, who concurrently — and differently — exposed the *Donation*: Levine, 'Reginald Pecock and Lorenzo Valla'.
125 For the date of composition (and Nicholas of Cusa's influence on Valla's text): Fubini, 'Humanism and Truth', pp. 82–83; and Linde, 'Lorenzo Valla and the Authenticity of Sacred Texts', pp. 36–38. For the 1517 first edition: Whitford, 'The Papal Antichrist', pp. 28 n. 5, 40.

the Roman pontiff was the Antichrist warned of in II Thessalonians.[126] 'I have here at my disposal [Ulrich von Hutten's] edition of Lorenzo Valla's *Confutation of the Donation of Constantine*', Luther writes in a 1520 letter to a confidant, the Bavarian humanist Georg Spalatin. 'I am greatly tormented', Luther tells Spalatin, '[and] I do not even doubt that the pope is properly the Antichrist'.[127] Within months, in his polemic *On the Papacy at Rome*, Luther can ask: 'Why then does the Roman See so furiously desire the whole world [...] as if it were the Antichrist?' By the summer of 1520 in Luther's new, billowing circles, this question is rhetorical.[128]

Of course, a chasm separates Valla's reading of the *Donation* from Luther's feverish end-times reading of Valla. The point is this. It is only because the *Donation of Constantine* is spurious — as revealed by Valla in the fifteenth century — that Christ's 'great refusal' ceases to be cancelled out, in sixteenth-century political theology and ultimately in Protestant politics, by Constantine's 'great refusal'.

Late modern historians tend to see the force and significance of Valla's text *On the Forged and Mendacious Donation of Constantine* in his epoch-inaugurating philological reasoning, which also led him to conclude that the Apostles' Creed is not the apostles' work (as the medieval Church held) and that the apostle Paul's correspondence with the philosopher Seneca (much loved by medieval Christians) is a later concoction.[129] Without diminishing the rigour and ingenuity of Valla's text-critical *tour de force*, it is worth remembering that much of his reasoning on the spurious *Donation* is theological, albeit in a highly rhetorical register.

Valla once wrote to a friend, Giovanni Tortelli, that his work on the *Donation* is 'concerned with canon law and theology but opposed to all canon lawyers and theologians'.[130] Nevertheless, Valla's text could not have survived, or influenced early modern political or literary culture, if it had truly been opposed to *all* theologians. On closer inspection, it proves not to be. Indeed, on the crucial question of Jesus's renunciation of secular power Valla echoes not only Dante, and the Augustinian tradition that structures this contribution, but Marsilius (on whom, more in a moment).[131]

The part of Valla's text that concerns us is a fictional reply by Sylvester I to a fictional donation by Constantine I, which would have conferred on

---

126 Whitford, 'The Papal Antichrist', pp. 28, 36–37, 40.
127 Cited by Whitford, 'The Papal Antichrist', p. 40 (Whitford's translation).
128 Cited by Whitford, 'The Papal Antichrist', p. 41 (Whitford's translation).
129 Bentley, *Humanists and Holy Writ*, pp. 46–47.
130 Cited in Bowersock's introduction to Valla, *On the Donation of Constantine*, trans. by Bowersock, p. viii (translation modified).
131 For Dante's and Marsilius' critiques of the *Donation of Constantine*, with Marsilius — like Valla — citing the Roman trial of Jesus: Falkeid, *The Avignon Papacy Contested*, pp. 42–44 (Dante), 62 (Marsilius).

the Roman pontiff the secular powers, fiscs, and holdings of the Western Roman Empire. Valla is certain on historical grounds that the *Donation* is fake. He reasons, for instance, that Constantine would have been assassinated if he had tried to alienate the powers and territories of imperial Rome. This is a convincing historical objection.[132]

Yet Valla is certain, too, on theological grounds that the *Donation* must be a fake. For, it is not only absurd that a fourth-century emperor would have 'donated' the empire to a pope. It is absurd that a fourth-century pope would have *accepted* the empire, because — Valla argues — temporal dominion conflicts with the early Christian idea of the pontificate. It is this second argument of Valla's that interests us, since it suggests that Dante had refuted the *Donation of Constantine* on a priori theological grounds in *Monarchia* before Valla demolished it on a posteriori philological grounds. The real trial of Jesus exposes the donation of Constantine as a fake: Valla concurs with Dante.[133]

To begin with, Valla's pope states his concern that 'secular affairs' ('secularium negotiorum') will corrupt the priesthood.[134] The terminology could remind us of Pope Gelasius's text *On the Bond of an Anathema*, where Christ divides the offices of pontiff and emperor so as to shelter his ministers from the cares and temptations of 'secular affairs' ('negotiis saecularibus').[135] It is after this conceivable echo of Gelasius that Valla's papal speech crescendos. 'Tell me', the humanist's half-imagined pope says to his half-imagined emperor, 'do you want to make me a king or rather a Caesar — a ruler of kings?' Valla's pope presses on:

> When the Lord Jesus Christ, God and man, king and priest, acknowledged that he was a king (*se regem affirmaret*), listen to what he said: 'My kingdom', he said, 'is not of this world. For if my kingdom were of this world, my ministers would assuredly fight back'. [...] When he said these things, did he not declare that a secular kingdom (*regnum seculare*) had nothing to do with him? [...] Therefore I have no need of your donation, by which I would assume a task that it would be as wrong for me to bear as it is impossible.[136]

Valla then lets his half-fictional fourth-century pope reformulate Jesus's *gran rifiuto*. This is Valla's Sylvester, admonishing his Constantine:

---

132 Valla, *Don. Const.*, 20. Note that both text and translation cited in this contribution are Valla, *On the Donation of Constantine*, trans. by Bowersock.

133 The same could be said of Marsilius of Padua's *Defensor pacis* — a point I owe to the descriptions in Falkeid, *The Avignon Papacy Contested*, pp. 62–64.

134 Valla, *Don. Const.*, 22.

135 Gelasius I, *Tom.* (no textual divisions); in consultation of Benson, 'The Gelasian Doctrine', p. 16; Ziegler, 'Pope Gelasius I and his Teaching', pp. 434–35.

136 Valla, *Don. Const.*, 24–25.

Caesar — allow me to say this without offence — do not play the devil for me, you who tell Christ, namely me, to accept kingdoms of the world (*regna mundi*) that are given by you. I prefer to despise (*spernere*) them than to possess them. [...] Even if you should offer it a thousand times, I would never accept.[137]

The genre of this scene could perhaps be called historical romance. But Valla is playing here — like Dante and his 'new Pilate' — with a historical drama that controlled the European imaginary for at least a thousand years. Valla's late antique pope is staying true to the Passion — meaning, here, to Christ's renunciation of temporal power — and in that way he reveals the corruption (to Valla's mind) of the papal monarchy and its defenders. This is a far cry, however, from Luther's papal 'Antichrist'. It is only necessary to recall that Valla is writing as a future secretary at the court of Pope Nicholas V (r. 1447–1455).[138] When Valla insists that it is impossible for a pope to imitate Christ if he does not 'despise' secular rule, he is not hostile to the Renaissance papacy per se.

We will not hear of *il gran rifiuto* 'a thousand times' in the coming pages, but Jesus's renunciation of 'kingdoms of the world' in Pilate's tribunal is a drama that recurs in a succession of canonical philosophical texts, at structurally critical moments, in late medieval and early modern Europe.[139] The first indications of this can be found in the oeuvre of one of Dante's contemporaries — and, perhaps, acquaintances.

The Pilate Trial in Marsilius of Padua's Political Theology

Marsilius of Padua's Radical Chic

One of the first rectors of the University of Paris, Marsilius of Padua, is commonly seen as the first architectonic theorist of secularity.[140] Like most premodern political theorists, Marsilius's theory is dramatic. A sacred drama structures his theory of human and divine law, coercion and jurisdiction, in his incendiary *Defensor pacis* and 'slanderous little book',

---

137 Valla, *Don. Const.*, 26.
138 Bentley, *Humanists and Holy Writ*, p. 57; Linde, 'Lorenzo Valla and the Authenticity of Sacred Texts', pp. 59–60.
139 Dusenbury, *The Innocence of Pontius Pilate*, chs 16–19.
140 One of Unn Falkeid's clarifications is germane here: 'This does not mean, however, that [Marsilius] reckoned on a society of nonbelievers. He accepted that the citizens of his perfect state would be Christians. Nonetheless, he presented a political structure where God was placed in the background as a remote rather than a direct cause'. See Falkeid, *The Avignon Papacy Contested*, pp. 57–58.

Defensor minor.[141] In light of the foregoing pages, it is intriguing that Dante and Marsilius may have met in the decade in which the poet wrote *Monarchia*. For as Unn Falkeid reminds us, they 'were both at Verona [...] during the second decade of the fourteenth century, both under the patronage of Cangrande della Scala' — then Lord of Verona — 'and both were staunch defenders of the Holy Roman Empire'.[142] Both, too, were reprobated by popes and condemned by cities.[143]

Marsilius is a salient actor in a brash, scarring conflict between the Roman Church and Holy Roman Empire in the early fourteenth century. A son of the Church but a fierce partisan of the empire, Marsilius belongs — like Dante — to the Ghibelline (imperial) faction of certain north Italian cities. Because of this, a papal bull from 1327 thunders that Marsilius — then sheltering in the Tyrolean city of Trent — is a 'son of perdition'.[144] And it should not be forgotten that Marsilius's books were banned in the vast Tridentine blocs of early modern Europe, as were Dante's (as Boccaccio tells us) and Valla's. They were listed for centuries on the Roman Curia's *Index of Prohibited Books*.[145]

The drama of Marsilius's life as a court philosopher of Ludwig of Bavaria is informed by his reading of Europe's Ur-drama: the Passion. It is Marsilius's interpretation of the Roman trial of Jesus, in defence of which he often cites Augustine's *Homilies on the Gospel of John*, that permits him to condemn, in 'orthodox' terms, the political and juridical order of late medieval Europe — and more concretely, the political theology of the late medieval 'papal monarchy'.[146]

It is because Marsilius reads the Pilate trial in an Augustinian vein — not only like Dante, but like the English Franciscan and radical nominalist

---

141 From a condemnation issued in June 1331 by the city of Milan of the 'erroneous beliefs' held by Marsilius and of the 'slanderous' little books (*libelli*) that he circulated: Godthardt, 'The Life of Marsilius of Padua', pp. 30–31, here p. 31: 'The *libelli* referred to in the bull were probably "pamphlets", i.e., short propaganda texts. Perhaps Marsilius' tract *De translatio Imperii* was one of these shorter texts composed in Milan'. Marsilius wrote *Defensor minor* much later than the Milan condemnation: Godthardt, 'The Life of Marsilius of Padua', p. 55; Nederman, 'From *Defensor pacis* to *Defensor minor*', p. 313.

142 Falkeid, *The Avignon Papacy Contested*, p. 53.

143 Godthardt, 'The Life of Marsilius of Padua', pp. 16–19; Falkeid, *The Avignon Papacy Contested*, pp. 53–54.

144 Pope John XXII's bull *Quia iuxta doctrinam* in fact calls out 'two worthless men, sons of perdition [...] one of whom lets himself be called Marsilius of Padua and the other John of Jandun'. Cited by Godthardt, 'The Life of Marsilius of Padua', pp. 25–28.

145 Falkeid, *The Avignon Papacy Contested*, pp. 52–54; Izbicki, 'The Reception of Marsilius', p. 309.

146 Morris, *The Papal Monarchy*.

William of Ockham[147] — that he can theorize the late medieval popes' holding of 'supreme coercive jurisdiction' as a drama of *usurpation*.[148] Marsilius is sure that the papal monarchy's fullness of power (*plenitudo potestatis*) is not full of grace.

'Outrageous and Dangerous'

For Marsilius, the continental tremors of late medieval European history — the tectonic shifts and abrasions of Church and empire that ultimately break out in the Protestant revolutions and wars of religion — force us to revisit the Roman trial of Jesus. Marsilius cites the Pilate trial once in his *Defensor minor* and scrutinizes it closely in a decisive chapter of *Dictio* II in *Defensor pacis*, which is 'by far the longest' of the treatise's three *dictiones*.[149] For him, papal usurpation is just that, a 'usurpation', rather than a legitimate rule or domination of Europe because of its place in sacred history.

It is no coincidence that the *homines novi* of early modern political philosophy are Protestants; we could think of Thomas Hobbes and Samuel Pufendorf. But here, we can ask what significance the Pilate trial had for a medieval 'Protestant' such as Marsilius. This crude descriptor is not only inspired by Marsilius's excommunication in April 1327 (a couple of years before a papal legate burned copies of Dante's *Monarchia*),[150] and by Marsilius's condemnation for heresy in October 1327 (in a bull that damns *Defensor pacis* as 'outrageous and dangerous'),[151] but by his early modern reception. For centuries, Marsilius is cited — like Dante — by partisans of both Reformation *and* Counter-Reformation as a Protestant *avant la lettre*.[152] One sign of Marsilius's radical chic is that Henry VIII's viceregent, Thomas Cromwell, who dissolved hundreds of English monasteries, commissioned a translation of Marsilius's book, *The Defence of Peace*,

---

147 William of Ockham, *De Imperatorum et Pontificum Potestate*, XXVII, 565–701. The edition used is *Opera Politica IV*, ed. by Offler; and the translation is William of Ockham, *On the Power of Emperors and Popes*, trans. by Brett.

148 Marsilius, *Def. pac.* (henceforth, *DP*), II, 1.3: 'suprema [...] coactiva jurisdictio'. The edition used is Marsilius of Padua, *Defensor pacis*, ed. by Scholz; and the translation is Marsilius of Padua, *The Defender of the Peace*, ed. and trans. by Brett.

149 Falkeid, *The Avignon Papacy Contested*, p. 62.

150 Corbett, *Dante's Christian Ethics*, pp. 48–49. A study of *Monarchia*'s notoriety is Cassell, *The 'Monarchia' Controversy*. And for 'Protestant' fore-echoes in Dante, as in the breath-taking lines at Dante, *Paradiso*, IX, 133–38: Falkeid, *The Avignon Papacy Contested*, p. 48.

151 Godthardt, 'The Life of Marsilius of Padua', pp. 32–34.

152 For several illuminating proofs of the Dante–Marsilius reception (or more precisely, citation) by sixteenth-century English Protestants: Boswell, 'Dante's Fame in England', pp. 237–39, 242. A far more thorough study of Marsilius's depiction in Reformation-era texts is Piaia, *Marsilio da Padova nella Riforma e nella Controriforma*. I am grateful to the editors of the present volume for bringing Piaia's important book to my attention.

in 1535.[153] And it is striking that the English translator of *The Defence of Peace*, William Marshall, also put Valla's demolition of the *Donation of Constantine* into English, as *A Treatise of the Donation Given unto Sylvester Pope of Rome*, in 1534.[154]

Jesus's Roman trial is of fundamental importance for Marsilius, as for Dante and Valla. The claim could even be hazarded that neither the structure nor the conceptual architecture of Marsilius's *Defensor pacis* or *Defensor minor* can be reconstructed without close attention to the Roman trial of Jesus. It is strange, then, that the Pilate trial has not (yet) been thematized in the literature on Marsilius.[155]

'Authority in This Age'

The Pilate trial is not salient in Marsilius's *Defensor minor*. Jesus's words to Pilate are only quoted once in this brief text, in a chapter in which Marsilius asserts the supremacy of divine law over human decrees.[156] It is in this setting that Marsilius writes that 'Christ *willed himself to lack* authority in this world-age in so far as he was human, in as much as he said [to Pilate]: "My kingdom is not of this world"'.[157]

At first glance the drama that Marsilius evokes here is the same that we reconstructed in Dante's and Valla's texts. Jesus is standing before Pilate, confessing that his 'kingdom is not of this world'. The dramatis personae are Jesus and Pilate, and the kingdom in question is Jesus's kingdom — the kingdom that is *not* of this world. But this rushed interpretation of Marsilius's words is flawed. The drama that Marsilius conjures up here is a *metaphysical* one — and it is this *metaphysical drama* which underlies Marsilius's political theory in a far more elaborate form than we find in Dante or Valla. For, notice that Pilate is a supernumerary in Marsilius's narration of the scene (which, *nota bene*, precedes the narration in John of Pilate's judgement). It is only Christ who acts, at this moment in his

---

153 Izbicki, 'The Reception of Marsilius', pp. 309–10. For Henry's world-historical dissolution of monasteries: Knowles, *The Religious Orders in England*; Knowles, *Bare Ruined Choirs*; and for a recent micro-history: Moorhouse, *The Last Office*. I am grateful to Arnold Hunt for these references, and for a state-of-the-art letter on the 'long process' of dissolution in April 2020.

154 Lockwood, 'Marsilius of Padua', p. 90.

155 I wish to thank two Marsilius scholars, Jürgen Miethke and Gianluca Briguglia, for confirming this in conversations at the University of Leuven in September 2018. It is indicative that a fine essay on Marsilius's political theology contains no mention of the Pilate trial: Koch, 'Marsilius of Padua on Church and State'.

156 For more on Marsilius's legal theory consult, for instance, Canning, *Ideas of Power*, pp. 81–106.

157 Marsilius, *Def. min.*, 13, 9. The edition used is Marsilius of Padua, *Œuvres mineures*, ed. by Jeudy and Quillet; and the translation is Marsilius of Padua, *Writings on the Empire*, ed. and trans. by Nederman.

trial. And notice that, on Marsilius's telling, the kingdom in question is the kingdom *of* this world — and only obliquely a kingdom which is *not* of this world. We can read Marsilius's sentence again, more analytically. 'Christ willed himself to lack authority in this world-age in so far as he was human', he writes, 'in as much as he said: "My kingdom is not of this world"'.[158]

To repeat, it is only Christ who acts in this sentence — by *willing*, and only incidentally by testifying before Pilate. And Christ's act of willing concerns '*this* world-age' — and only indirectly, the kingdom which is '*not* of this world'. Note, especially, Marsilius's terminology. Rendered literally, what Marsilius writes is that 'Christ willed himself to lack authority in *this age* (*hoc saeculo*)', because he said, 'My kingdom is not of *this world* (*hoc mundo*)'.[159] Marsilius's term *hoc saeculum* is, here, a precise counterpart to Jesus's phrase *hoc mundum* in (the relevant Latin versions of) John 18. It is impossible to reconstruct Marsilius's thought without clarifying his notion of the *saeculum* — the mundane, human order. What, then, is the sublime drama hidden in this epitomic sentence by Marsilius?

'Christ *willed himself to lack* authority in this world-age', we read. And this willing, this divine renunciation of coercive power, by Christ, 'in so far as he was human' ('inquantum homo'), is the dramatic act which shapes the structure of Marsilius's *Defensor minor* — and more clearly, of his *Defensor pacis*. This is a vast argument, of course, which we can only begin to justify in the coming pages.

'Transgressors in This World-Age'

The paragraph of the *Defensor minor* in which this sentence appears becomes much clearer once we have noticed exactly what Marsilius says in the line that has just been quoted. In the paragraph that comes before it, we notice that Marsilius asserts that the author of divine law, the Christians' God, 'has decided to be a judge of transgressors on the basis of this law' — divine law — 'only, and to restrain them by means of punishment in the future world-age *only*, and not in the present one (*in futuro saeculo* [...] *non in isto*)'.[160] Here, the jurisdiction of human law, and the punishment of transgressors of human law, is constituted by *a divine limitation of the divine jurisdiction*. The dramatic logic of this sentence is identical to the one we just analysed. And this dramatic logic is further elucidated by a formulation one paragraph before, where Marsilius states:

---

158 Marsilius, *Def. min.*, 13.9: 'tali auctoritate Christus in hoc saeculo carere voluit, in persona propria inquantum homo, dum dixit: "Regnum meum non est de hoc mundo"'.

159 Marsilius, *Def. min.*, 13.9.

160 Marsilius, *Def. min.*, 13.8 (my emphasis).

According to divine law, there is a coercive judge (*iudex [...] coactivus*), about whom Saint James said in his letter: 'There is one lawgiver and one judge (*Unus est legislator et iudex*), he who can condemn and deliver', namely Christ.[161]

This last clarification, 'namely Christ' ('Christus videlicet'), is Marsilius's gloss on the verse from James 4 that he cites here.[162] The one lawgiver, the one judge, is Christ. And it is this assertion which lies behind Marsilius's claim that 'Christ *willed himself to lack* authority in this world-age'.[163] For a kingdom in which the one lawgiver is *not* the sole lawgiver, and a jurisdiction in which the one judge is *not* the sole judge, could only be constituted by a decision of that lawgiver and judge to *cede jurisdiction*. And this — precisely this, for Marsilius — is what occurs in Christ's appearance before Pilate.

Before we move from the *Defensor minor* to *Defensor pacis*, note that Marsilius cites the same line from James 4, 'There is one lawgiver and one judge', in the first paragraphs of the *Defensor minor*.[164] There, Marsilius asserts that divine laws are 'coercive precepts' for 'transgressors in this world-age (*hoc saeculo*)', but that divine laws carry punishments 'to be carried out in the future rather than the present world-age (*in futuro saeculo, non in isto*)'.[165] His terminology, from the first paragraphs of the *Defensor minor*, is that of the *saeculum* (this *saeculum*, a future *saeculum*). And from the first paragraphs of the *Defensor minor*, Marsilius is clearing a space for human coercive power — which is to say, for human jurisdiction — by insisting upon a divine limitation of divine coercive power to a future world-age (*saeculum futurum*).

The *saeculum* is written into Marsilius's definition of human law. Marsilius formulates 'human law' as a 'coercive precept [...] on account of the pursuit of immediate ends *in the present world-age* and under threat of punishment to be inflicted upon transgressors *in that realm alone*'.[166] This definition depends, for its logical articulation — and indeed, for its political force in late medieval Europe — on the *dictum* concerning 'this world' in Jesus's reply to Pilate. Thus, though it is only cited once in Marsilius's *Defensor minor*, the Pilate trial is of fundamental importance from the first sentences of the work, where we read that human 'coercive precepts' — which is to say, human laws — only impinge on 'transgressors

---

161 Marsilius, *Def. min.*, 13.7.
162 James 4. 12.
163 Marsilius, *Def. min.*, 13.9.
164 Marsilius, *Def. min.*, 1.2.
165 Marsilius, *Def. min.*, 1.2; Marsilius of Padua, *Œuvres mineures*, ed. by Jeudy and Quillet, p. 172.
166 Marsilius, *Def. min.*, 13.6.

in this world-age.[167] Christ's dramatic renunciation of secular jurisdiction in the Pilate trial is structurally decisive before it is cited in the *Defensor minor*, precisely because Christ is the 'one lawgiver and one judge' in that epitomic text.

'Caesar's Viceregent Pontius Pilate'

The Roman trial's structural significance is far more visible in Marsilius's *Defensor pacis*. In the first paragraphs of *Defensor pacis* he quotes from the Pilate trial in John 18, where Jesus says: 'For this reason I have come into the world, that I should bear witness unto the truth'.[168] That is Jesus's gloss, in John 18. 37, on his statement in John 18. 36 that his 'kingdom is not of this world' (a gloss that will be decisive centuries later for Samuel Pufendorf's reading of the Pilate trial). There is an echo, then, of the Pilate trial in the first pages of *Defensor pacis* I — an echo that late modern readers are likely to miss, but that Marsilius's first readers were not.

It may not be a coincidence that Pilate is named in the last pages of *Defensor pacis* I, where Marsilius states that Christ is 'one individual who [is] simultaneously God and man', and who 'suffered and died [...] under Caesar's viceregent Pontius Pilate'.[169] It is between his echo of John 18 in *Defensor pacis* I, Chapter 1, and his mention of Pilate in *Defensor pacis* I, Chapter 19, that *Dictio* I of Marsilius's iconic text could, perhaps, be fruitfully reread. But these textual data are far too negligible to suggest a new reading of *Defensor pacis* I.

Or they would be, if they were not structurally integrated — in *Defensor pacis*, as in the *Defensor minor* — with Marsilius's claim that Christ is the 'one lawgiver and one judge' (James 4. 12). That, we recall, is an assertion that necessitates — and, within Marsilius's system, derives from — the sacred drama of Christ's renunciation of coercive power in secular affairs in the *Defensor minor*. And at the end of *Defensor pacis* I, the assertion of Christ's lordship takes a rather shocking form. Marsilius veers perilously close to the justificatory logic of papal 'fullness of power' in the last paragraphs of *Dictio* I.[170]

Marsilius's opponents, the defenders of universal papal monarchy, hold that Christ is 'king of kings and lord of lords, of all persons and things universally (*universorum omnium personarum et rerum*)'. 'And this is true', Marsilius concedes. His only objection is that the inference that his opponents want to make 'does not follow from this at all, as will become

---

167 Marsilius, *Def. min.*, 1.2.
168 *DP*, I, 1.5.
169 *DP*, I, 19.4.
170 *DP*, I, 19.9.

'THE GREAT REFUSAL'   311

clear [...] in what follows'.[171] The task of *Defensor pacis* II is to demonstrate
that the real *plenitudo potestatis* of Christ, far from justifying the *plenitudo
potestatis* of the Bishop of Rome, invalidates the papal claim as a sign of
what Marsilius calls, several pages on, 'perverse desire for government'.[172]

The political jurisdiction — meaning, the coercive power in secular
affairs — claimed by theorists of papal supremacy is, for Marsilius, a
usurpation. This is the continental drama in which Marsilius intervenes.
He seeks to demonstrate that the Roman pontiff is a usurper of the Roman
emperor's office. Yet Marsilius believes — or, what comes to the same in
this context, he insists that he believes — that the one the Roman pontiff
serves *is* possessed of *plenitudo potestatis*. The only way, then, in which
the pretenders to that power — namely, popes — can be shown to be
usurpers, is if the rightful claimant to that power — namely, Christ —
had renounced it for himself ('in persona propria inquantum homo' is the
salient caveat that we will recall from the *Defensor minor*), and forbade it to
his successors.[173]

Precisely this is what occurs in Marsilius's reading of the Roman trial
of Jesus in *Defensor pacis* II, Chapter 4. It is Jesus's renunciation of coercive
power in John — and less dramatically in the other Gospels — that dele-
gitimizes papal claims to temporal jurisdiction. And Marsilius indicates, as
early as *Defensor pacis* I, Chapter 1, that in this — Marsilius's most urgent
task — Aristotle's philosophy is an imperfect authority. This is because,
as he writes, 'Aristotle could not perceive' late medieval Europe's 'singular
cause of strife' — meaning, the medieval popes' claims to temporal jurisdiction, which compel Marsilius to write his treatise.[174] To be sure, in the
last sentences of *Defensor pacis* I, Marsilius mines Aristotle's *Politics* for
a claim that the office of priest 'is to be kept apart from political governments'.[175] But that line of Aristotle's, commented on by many generations
of European scholastics, would nevertheless be inert against the soaring,
Scripture-buttressed claims of the papal monarchy if it were not for the
sacred drama of John 18. Which is why Marsilius writes *Defensor pacis* II.

'Jurisdiction in This World-Age'

Marsilius's difficulty — and the centrality, for him, of the Pilate trial — is
most sharply stated in *Defensor pacis* II, Chapter 4:

---

171 *DP*, I, 19.9.
172 *DP*, I, 19.12: 'perversa [...] affeccio principatus'.
173 Marsilius, *Def. min.*, 13.9.
174 *DP*, I, 1.7.
175 *DP*, I, 19.12.

All Christian faithful are certain that Christ, who was true God and true man, was able to confer, not just upon the apostles but upon anyone else, coercive authority or jurisdiction in this world-age (*in hoc saeculo*) over all princes or principates of this world-age and over all individual persons; and perhaps even greater authority than this (*et hac ampliorem fortasse*), for example of creating beings, of destroying and restoring heaven and earth and all that are therein.[176]

There is some satirical bite in this suggestion (however doctrinally rooted) that the papacy's claims to universal jurisdiction are, set in a certain light, incredibly modest. A bold pope might hope for the right, not merely to rule this world-age, but to *make* worlds by fiat!

No matter. This is a sharp statement of the situation — the *dramatic situation* — that we observed in Marsilius's *Defensor minor*. There is one judge and one lawgiver: Christ. Because Christ (as true God) is the creator, his divine jurisdiction is — by rights — the world. The only conceivable limitation on the divine jurisdiction would be a *self-limitation*. Such a self-limitation, such a *renunciation* of coercive power in this world-age, would — in an instant — cede legitimacy to a 'secular' human jurisdiction (the concern of *Defensor pacis* I), and decide the illegitimacy of the papal claims to human jurisdiction (the concern of *Defensor pacis* II).

'Subject to the Powers of this World-Age'

Christ's renunciation of coercive power in this world-age is what Marsilius sees in the action of John 18 — or, more accurately, this renunciation is *half* of what Marsilius sees in that action. For *Defensor pacis* II, Chapter 4 — where Marsilius interprets the Pilate trial — has two parts (and a proem).[177] In both parts, he reflects on the scene in the Gospel of John where Jesus converses with Pilate. And he reads in this scene a demonstration that Christ 'excluded himself and wanted to exclude himself' from all 'government, judgement, or worldly coercive power (*coactiva potestate mundana*)'.[178] The sphere of human jurisdiction that Marsilius delineates in *Defensor pacis* I is the sphere of jurisdiction from which Christ, here in *Defensor pacis* II, 'excluded himself'. And what is more, it is this act of divine self-exclusion which reveals the papal claims to be those of a usurper.

Late in the chapter,[179] Marsilius reads in the Roman trial of Jesus a demonstration that it was Christ's 'will that he should be subject to the

---

176 *DP*, II, 4.2.
177 *DP*, II, 4.1–3.
178 *DP*, II, 4.13.
179 *DP*, II, 4.8–13.

princes and the powers of this world-age (*seculi potestatibus*) in coercive jurisdiction'.[180] Christ's subjection to human jurisdiction, which reveals and confirms the self-limitation of divine jurisdiction, is most decisively proved for Marsilius by the fact that 'a sentence of death was passed upon Christ'. By whom? The sentence under which Jesus dies is uttered by 'Pilate sitting in his tribunal'. And who crucified Christ? 'By his authority', Marsilius writes — that is, by the Roman prefect's — 'the sentence was executed'.[181] This means that for Marsilius — as for Augustine and, much later, Dante — Jesus's judge and killers were Romans, not Judaeans.

It is Pilate's sentence of death — denied by Lactantius, asserted by Augustine — that Marsilius anticipates when he writes in the last pages of *Defensor pacis* I that Christ 'suffered and died [...] under Caesar's viceregent'.[182] The judicial sentence that ends the *political* drama of Christ's life on earth (but not the mystical or theological drama) is no less critical for Marsilius in *Defensor pacis* II than for Dante in *Monarchia* II. For both iconic Ghibellines, who were read and cited in early modern Europe as Protestants *avant la lettre*, it is Jesus's great refusal during the Pilate trial that constitutes the secular.[183]

'Christ willed himself to lack authority in this world-age (*in hoc saeculo*)', is Marsilius's epochal line.[184] This is the renunciation drama that invites Europe's first master-thinker of the secular to delineate a space of pure (though not absolute) human jurisdiction. Pilate's death sentence functions as a sign, in Marsilius's texts, of a divine will to withdraw from temporal jurisdiction. The legitimacy of secularity (*Defensor pacis* I) and the illegitimacy of papal monarchy (*Defensor pacis* II) can both be traced to Marsilius's reading of the Roman trial of Jesus. One of the most critical chapters of *Defensor pacis*, on this reconstruction, would be that in which Marsilius's 'one lawgiver and one judge' ('unus legislator et iudex') — the mystic head of the Roman Church — wills to let an officer of the Roman Empire take his natural life.[185]

But though Marsilius frequently cites Augustine's *Homilies on the Gospel of John*, it is not certain he had read them. One probable line of transmission for Augustine's interpretation of the Pilate trial seems to be a patristic (and Byzantine) commentary on John edited by Thomas Aquinas, the *Catena aurea*. Augustine's commentary on the Pilate trial is salient in this text composed by the revered Dominican master.[186] A comprehensive

---

180 *DP*, II, 4.13.
181 *DP*, II, 4.12.
182 *DP*, I, 19.4.
183 Izbicki, 'The Reception of Marsilius', pp. 314–32; Cheneval, 'La réception de la "Monarchie"', pp. 261–64.
184 Marsilius, *Def. min.*, 13.9.
185 *DP*, II, 4.
186 Thomas Aquinas, *Cat. aur.* In Ioannem, 18–19.

examination of Marsilius's citations of Augustine in *Defensor pacis* and Aquinas's in *Catena aurea* has not yet been made. But regardless of Aquinas's own legal theories, he may have had a hand in the creation of one of the fourteenth century's most radical texts — by putting the African bishop's exegesis into the hands of Marsilius. Aquinas may have a significant place in the history of secularity, that is to say, not for anything that he wrote but for something he copied.[187]

Conclusions

The present contribution argues that if Jesus had not made his 'great refusal' before Pilate — as formulated by Augustine and received in a certain vein of Augustinian tradition — there is reason to believe that the secular could not have been theorized, or progressively actualized, in late medieval and early modern Europe. In seeking to reconstruct Marsilius's theory of divine and human jurisdiction — and thus, of the zones of medieval life which could legitimately be controlled by the Roman Church or the Holy Roman Empire — it is necessary to read him in light of certain biblical scenes (such as Jesus's Roman trial) and patristic interpretations (as transmitted by, for instance, Aquinas's *Catena aurea*). It is illuminating, too, to compare Marsilius's biblical tropes and patristic citations to those found in, or echoed by, other figures such as Dante and Valla. For, however disruptive Marsilius's *Defensor pacis* and *Defensor minor* may have been, he nevertheless belongs to a tradition. Late modern historians of thought should not forget to seek, in Marsilius's iconoclastic late medieval texts, 'canonical' precedents in the homilies and commentaries of Late Antiquity — in the first instance, those of Augustine.

---

187 I nevertheless agree with Unn Falkeid that Dante's *Monarchia* and Marsilius's *Defensor pacis* must be read in light of 'the Gelasian theory of the two swords, later echoed in the Thomistic idea of the twofold goal and the twofold happiness of man': Falkeid, *The Avignon Papacy Contested*, p. 52.

Works Cited

Primary Sources

Alighieri, Dante, *The Inferno of Dante: A New Verse Translation*, Italian with trans. by Robert Pinsky, annot. by Nicole Pinsky (New York: Farrar, Straus and Giroux, 1994)

——, *Monarchia*, ed. by Paolo Chiesa and Andrea Tabarroni with Diego Ellero (Rome: Salerno Editrice, 2013)

——, *Monarchy*, ed. and trans. by Prue Shaw (Cambridge: Cambridge University Press, 1996)

——, *Purgatorio: A New Verse Translation*, trans. by William S. Merwin (New York: Knopf, 2001)

Alighieri, Jacopo, *Chiose alla Cantica dell'Inferno di Dante Alighieri scritte da Jacopo Alighieri*, ed. by G. Piccini (Florence: Bemporad, 1915)

Alighieri, Pietro, *Comentum super poema Comedie Dantis: A Critical Edition of the Third and Final Draft of Pietro Alighieri's 'Commentary on Dante's "Divine Comedy"'*, ed. by Massimiliano Chiamenti, Medieval & Renaissance Texts & Studies, 247 (Tempe: Arizona Center for Medieval and Renaissance Studies, 2002)

Augustine, *De Consensu Evangelistarum*, ed. by Franz Weihrich, Corpus scriptorum ecclesiasticorum Latinorum, 43; Sancti Aureli Augustini Opera, 4 (Vienna: F. Tempsky, 1904)

——, *The Harmony of the Gospels*, trans. by S. D. F. Salmond, ed. by Philip Schaff (Edinburgh: T&T Clark, 1886)

——, *Homilies on the Gospel of John*, trans. by J. Gibb and J. Innes, ed. by P. Schaff (Edinburgh: T&T Clark, 1873)

——, *In Iohannis Evangelium tractatus CXXIV*, ed. by Radbodus Willems, Corpus christianorum. Series latina, 36; Aurelii Augustini Opera, 8 (Turnhout: Brepols, 1954)

Benvenuto da Imola, *Comentum super Dantis Aldigherij Comoediam*, ed. by Giacomo Filippo Lacaita, 5 vols (Florence: Barbera, 1887)

Boccaccio, Giovanni, *Esposizioni sopra la comedia di Dante*, vol. VI of *Tutte le opere di Giovanni Boccaccio*, ed. by Vittore Branca (Milan: Mondadori, 1965; archived online by Dartmouth College)

Gelasius I, *The Letters of Gelasius I (492–496): Pastor and Micro-Manager of the Church of Rome*, ed. by Bronwen Neil and Pauline Allen, Adnotationes: Commentaries on Early Christian and Patristic Texts, 1 (Turnhout: Brepols, 2014)

Lactantius, *The Divine Institutes, Books I–VII*, trans. by Mary Francis McDonald (Washington, DC: Catholic University of America Press, 1964)

————, *Institutions Divines, Livre 4*, ed. with French trans. and comm. by Pierre Monat, Sources chrétiennes, 377 (Paris: Éditions du Cerf, 1992)

————, *Liber de Mortibus persecutorum*, ed. by J.-P. Migne, Patrologiae cursus completes. Series Latina, 7 (Paris: Garnier, 1844), cols 157–76

————, *The Minor Works*, trans. by Mary Francis McDonald (Washington, DC: Catholic University of America Press, 1965)

Landino, Cristoforo, *Comento sopra la Comedia* (Florence, 1481); online at Dartmouth Dante Project, <https://dante.dartmouth.edu/biblio.php?comm_id=14815>

Marsilius of Padua, *The Defender of the Peace*, trans. by Annabel Brett, Cambridge Texts in the History of Political Thought (Cambridge: Cambridge University Press, 2005)

————, *Defensor pacis*, ed. by Richard Scholz, Monumenta Germaniae Historica: Fontes iuris germanici antiqui in usum scholarum separatim editi, 7.2 (Hannover: Hahn, 1933)

————, *Œuvres mineures: Defensor minor; De translatione imperii*, ed. with French trans. by Colette Jeudy and Jeannine Quillet, Sources d'histoire médiévale (Paris: Éditions du CNRS, 1979)

————, *Writings on the Empire: 'Defensor minor' and 'De translatione Imperii'*, ed. and trans. by Cary J. Nederman, Cambridge Texts in the History of Political Thought (Cambridge: Cambridge University Press, 1993)

Valla, Lorenzo, *On the Donation of Constantine*, trans. by Glenn W. Bowersock (Cambridge, MA: Harvard University Press, 2007)

William of Ockham, *On the Power of Emperors and Popes*, trans. by Annabel S. Brett (Bristol: Thoemmes Press, 1998)

————, *Opera Politica IV*, ed. by Hilary S. Offler (Oxford: Oxford University Press, 1997)

Secondary Works

Agamben, Giorgio, *Pilato e Gesù: Nuova versione accresciuta* (Rome: Nottetempo, 2014); Engl. trans.: *Pilate and Jesus*, trans. by Adam Kotsko (Stanford: Stanford University Press, 2015)

Artinian, Robert, 'Dante's Parody of Boniface VIII', *Dante Studies*, 85 (1967), 71–74

Barbarani, Emilio, *Due chiose dantesche* (Verona: Nozze Ciresola-Ronconi, 1897)

Benfell, V. Stanley, *The Biblical Dante* (Toronto: University of Toronto Press, 2011)

Benson, Robert L., 'The Gelasian Doctrine: Uses and Transformations', in *La notion d'autorité au Moyen Age: Islam, Byzance, Occident*, ed. by George Makdisi (Paris: Presses Universitaires de France, 1982), pp. 13–44

Bentley, Jerry H., *Humanists and Holy Writ: New Testament Scholarship in the Renaissance* (Princeton, NJ: Princeton University Press, 1983)

Blum, Paul Richard, *Philosophy of Religion in the Renaissance* (New York: Routledge, 2010)

Bosco, Umberto, and Giovanni Reggio, eds, *La Divina Commedia. Inferno* (Florence: Le Monnier, 1979)

Boswell, Jackson Campbell, 'Dante's Fame in England: 1536–1586', *Dante Studies*, 111 (1993), 235–43

Briguglia, Gianluca, *La questione del potere: Teologi e teoria politica nella disputa tra Bonifacio VIII e Filippo il Bello* (Milan: Franco Angeli, 2009)

Canning, Joseph, *Ideas of Power in the Late Middle Ages, 1296–1417* (Cambridge: Cambridge University Press, 2011)

Cassell, Anthony K., *The 'Monarchia' Controversy: An Historical Study with Accompanying Translations of Dante Alighieri's 'Monarchia', Guido Vernani's 'Refutation of the "Monarchia" Composed by Dante', and Pope John XXII's Bull 'Si fratrum'* (Washington, DC: Catholic University of America Press, 2004)

Cecotti, Samuele, 'La legittima validità dell'impero: Analisi degli argomenti sviluppati secondo la semantica della validità nel secondo libro della *Monarchia* di Dante condotta a partire dalla confutazione fattane da fra' Guido Vernani da Rimini nel suo *De Reprobatione monarchiae*', *Divus Thomas*, 115.1 (2012), 390–412

Cheneval, Francis, 'La réception de la "Monarchie" de Dante ou Les métamorphoses d'une œuvre philosophique', *Vivarium*, 34.2 (1996), 254–67

Cohen, Jeremy, *The Friars and the Jews: The Evolution of Medieval Anti-Semitism* (Ithaca, NY: Cornell University Press, 1982)

——, 'The Jews as the Killers of Christ in the Latin Tradition, from Augustine to the Friars', *Traditio*, 39 (1983), 1–37

——, 'Revisiting Augustine's Doctrine of Jewish Witness', *Journal of Religion*, 89 (2009), 564–78

Colish, Marcia, '*Sanza'nfamia e sanza lodo*: Moral Neutrality from Alan of Lille to Dante', in *Alain de Lille, le Docteur Universel*, ed. by Jean-Luc Solère, Anca Vasiliu, and Alain Galonnier (Turnhout: Brepols, 2015), pp. 263–73

Corbett, George, *Dante's Christian Ethics: Purgatory and its Moral Contexts* (Cambridge: Cambridge University Press, 2020)

Di Fonzo, Claudia, 'La legittimazione dell'Impero e del Popolo romano presso Dante', *Dante*, 6 (2009), 39–64

Dusenbury, David Lloyd, *The Innocence of Pontius Pilate: How the Roman Trial of Jesus Shaped History* (London: C. Hurst; New York: Oxford University Press, 2021)

——, 'The Judgment of Pontius Pilate: A Critique of Giorgio Agamben', *Journal of Law and Religion*, 32.2 (2017), 340–65

Falkeid, Unn, *The Avignon Papacy Contested: An Intellectual History from Dante to Catherine of Siena* (Cambridge, MA: Harvard University Press, 2017)

Fredriksen, Paula, *Augustine and the Jews: A Christian Defense of Jews and Judaism* (New Haven: Yale University Press, 2008)

Fried, Johannes, *The 'Donation of Constantine' and 'Constitutum Constantini': The Misinterpretation of a Fiction and its Original Meaning* (Berlin: De Gruyter, 2007)

Fubini, Riccardo, 'Humanism and Truth: Valla Writes against the Donation of Constantine', *Journal of the History of Ideas*, 57.1 (1996), 79–86

Godthardt, Frank, 'The Life of Marsilius of Padua', in *A Companion to Marsilius of Padua*, ed. by Gerson Moreno-Riaño and Cary J. Nederman, Brill's Companions to the Christian Tradition, 31 (Leiden: Brill, 2012), pp. 13–55

Izbicki, Thomas M., 'The Reception of Marsilius', in *A Companion to Marsilius of Padua*, ed. by Gerson Moreno-Riaño and Cary J. Nederman, Brill's Companions to the Christian Tradition, 31 (Leiden: Brill, 2012), pp. 305–34

Kantorowicz, Ernst H., *The King's Two Bodies: A Study in Medieval Political Theology* (Princeton, NJ: Princeton University Press, 2016)

Knowles, David, *Bare Ruined Choirs: The Dissolution of the English Monasteries* (Cambridge: Cambridge University Press, 1976)

——, *The Religious Orders in England*, III: *The Tudor Age* (Cambridge: Cambridge University Press, 1959

Koch, Bettina, 'Marsilius of Padua on Church and State', in *A Companion to Marsilius of Padua*, ed. by Gerson Moreno-Riaño and Cary J. Nederman, Brill's Companions to the Christian Tradition, 31 (Leiden: Brill, 2012), pp. 139–79

Lee, Gregory W., 'Israel between the Two Cities: Augustine's Theology of the Jews and Judaism', *Journal of Early Christian Studies*, 24 (2016), 523–51

Levine, Joseph M., 'Reginald Pecock and Lorenzo Valla on the *Donation of Constantine*', *Studies in the Renaissance*, 20 (1973), 118–43

Linde, J. Cornelia, 'Lorenzo Valla and the Authenticity of Sacred Texts', *Humanistica Lovaniensia*, 60 (2011), 35–63

Lockwood, Shelley, 'Marsilius of Padua and the Case for the Royal Ecclesiastical Supremacy', *Transactions of the Royal Historical Society*, 1 (1991), 89–119

Lombardi, Baldassare, *La Divina Commedia, novamente corretta, spiegata e difesa* (Rome: Antonio Fulgoni, 1791–1792)

Maramauro, Guglielmo, *Expositione sopra l'"Inferno" di Dante Alighieri*, ed. by Giacomo Pisoni and Saverio Bellomo (Padua: Antenore, 1998)

Moorhouse, Geoffrey, *The Last Office: 1539 and the Dissolution of a Monastery* (London: Phoenix, 2008)

Morris, Colin, *The Papal Monarchy: The Western Church from 1050 to 1250* (Oxford: Oxford University Press, 1991)

Nederman, Cary J., 'From *Defensor pacis* to *Defensor minor*: The Problem of Empire in Marsiglio of Padua', *History of Political Thought*, 16.3 (1995), 313–29

Park, Dabney G., 'Dante and the Donation of Constantine', *Dante Studies*, 130 (2012), 67–161

Pascoli, Giovanni, 'Chi sia "colui che fece il gran rifiuto"', *Il Marzocco*, 6 (27 July 1902); repr. in *Prose*, vol. II (Milan, 1952), pp. 1469–87

Penna, Angelo, 'Pilato, Ponzio', in *Enciclopedia Dantesca*, ed. by Umberto Bosco (Rome: Istituto dell'Enciclopedia Italiana, 1973)

Piaia, Gregorio, *Marsilio de Padova nella Riforma e nella Controriforma: Fortuna ed interpretazione*, Pubblicazioni dell'Istituto di storia della filosofia e del Centro per ricerche di filosofia medioevale, Università di Padova, n.s., 24 (Padua: Antenore, 1977)

Rosadi, Giovanni, *The Trial of Jesus*, trans. by Emil Reich (New York: Dodd, Mead, 1905)

Santagata, Marco, *Dante: The Story of his Life*, trans. by Richard Dixon (Cambridge, MA: Belknap Press, 2016)

Sapegno, Natalino, *La Divina Commedia*, I: *Inferno* (Florence: La Nuova Italia, 1980)

Schaff, Philip, *Literature and Poetry: Studies on the English Language; the Poetry of the Bible; the Dies Iræ; the Stabat Mater* [...] *Dante Alighieri; the Divina Commedia* (New York: Charles Scribner's Sons, 1890)

Singleton, Charles S., *Dante Alighieri, The Divine Comedy, Inferno*, II: *Commentary* (Princeton, NJ: Princeton University Press, 1977)

——, *Dante Alighieri, The Divine Comedy. Paradiso*, II: *Commentary* (Princeton, NJ: Princeton University Press, 1975)

——, *Dante Alighieri, The Divine Comedy. Purgatorio*, II: *Commentary* (Princeton, NJ: Princeton University Press, 1973)

Strätz, Hans-Wolfgang, 'Säkularisation, Säkularisierung, II. Der kanonistische und staatskirchenrechtliche Begriff', in *Geschichtliche Grundbegriffe: Historisches Lexikon zur politisch-sozialen Sprache in Deutschland*, ed. by Otto Brunner, Werner Conze, and Reinhart Koselleck, vol. V (Stuttgart: Klett-Cotta, 1984), pp. 792–809

Stroumsa, Guy G., 'From Anti-Judaism to Antisemitism in Early Christianity?', in *Contra Iudaeos: Ancient and Medieval Polemics between Christians and Jews*, ed. by Ora Limor and Guy G. Stroumsa (Tübingen: Mohr Siebeck, 1996), pp. 1–26

——, *The Making of the Abrahamic Religions in Late Antiquity* (Oxford: Oxford University Press, 2015)

Whalen, Brett Edward, *Dominion of God: Christendom and Apocalypse in the Middle Ages* (Cambridge, MA: Harvard University Press, 2009)

Whitford, David M., 'The Papal Antichrist: Martin Luther and the Underappreciated Influence of Lorenzo Valla', *Renaissance Quarterly*, 61.1 (2008), 26–52

Wieczynski, Joseph L., 'The Donation of Constantine in Medieval Russia', *Catholic Historical Review*, 55.2 (1969), 159–72

Winter, Paul, 'Marginal Notes on the Trial of Jesus, II', *Zeitschrift für die neutestamentliche Wissenschaft und die Kunde der älteren Kirche*, 50 (1959), 221–51

Ziegler, Aloysius K., 'Pope Gelasius I and his Teaching on the Relation of Church and State', *Catholic Historical Review*, 27.4 (1942), 412–37

PART 3

The Marsilian Moment

SERENA MASOLINI

Between Venice and Sant'Elmo[*]

Tommaso Campanella, Marsilius of Padua, and a 'Modern Theologian'

Introduction

The study of the influence of an author such as Marsilius of Padua in the early modern period can be approached from a variety of perspectives. One way would be to track down his doctrinal influence, establishing a set of theories that can be defined as 'typically' belonging to him, looking for similar ideas in later authors, and finally suggesting possible links based on those similarities.[1] Another method would be to examine the circulation of texts and offer hypotheses as to how they were accessed and referred to by his readers. A third possible perspective might consist in not considering (or, at least, not exclusively) the impact of Marsilius's own texts and theories, but rather the legacy of the image attached to his name — that is, the role that his *auctoritas* (or anti-*auctoritas*) played in the writings of those who referred to him, regardless of whether or not they had any direct access to his oeuvre.[2] The presence of Marsilius in the works

---

[*] I am grateful to Luca Burzelli, Jean-Paul De Lucca, Brian Garcia, Gregorio Piaia, Eleonora Rai, the co-editors, and the anonymous reviewer for their constructive comments; to Pete Bibby, for his careful revision of the English. Throughout the article, quotations from modern editions are reported in the original orthography, introducing, however, the *u/v* distinction. Biblical translations into English are taken from the Revised Standard Version. Unless otherwise stated, the remaining English translations are mine.

[1] The perspective based on the 'coincidenze fra le idee' — followed by Giacchi, 'Osservazioni sulla fortuna delle idee di Marsilio', here p. 170 — has been explicitly rejected by Piaia, *Marsilio da Padova nella Riforma e nella Controriforma*, p. 2.

[2] The primary reference for the study of Marsilius's heritage in early modern Europe remains Piaia, *Marsilio da Padova nella Riforma e nella Controriforma*, which combines these two historiographical perspectives. For further literature on this matter, see Condren, 'Democracy and the *Defensor Pacis*'; Simonetta, *Marsilio in Inghilterra*; Simonetta, *Dal*

Serena Masolini is a postdoctoral researcher at the Department of Philosophy, History, and Art Studies of the University of Helsinki, and an affiliated researcher of the Institute of Philosophy at KU Leuven.

Marsilius of Padua, ed. by Alessandro Mulieri, Serena Masolini, and Jenny Pelletier, Disputatio, 36 (Turnhout: Brepols, 2023), pp. 323–358

BREPOLS ❦ PUBLISHERS
10.1484/M.DISPUT-EB.5.132917

of the Calabrian Dominican Tommaso Campanella (1568–1639) should certainly be examined from this third perspective.[3]

It is unlikely that Campanella either read directly or had a detailed knowledge of the *Defensor pacis*.[4] Nevertheless, he referred to Marsilius at several points of his philosophical and theological works by summoning him as an antithetical role model, alongside other authors whom he regarded as similarly deplorable for either their Aristotelianism or their anticurialism. As Gregorio Piaia has shown in his monograph on the reception of Marsilius during the Reformation and Counter-Reformation, this twofold interpretation of Marsilius — Aristotelian or 'papalist bogey'[5] — was quite usual among sixteenth- and seventeenth-century authors. Campanella's originality, however, consists in having combined these two aspects, displaying how they could be read as two sides of the same coin. This is why Campanella's has been defined as the 'most wide-ranging contribution that a Counter-Reformation writer could provide to the "interpretation" of the Paduan'.[6]

Building on Piaia's findings, and in light of Vittorio Frajese and Paolo Ponzio's studies on the sources of Campanella's Italian and Latin versions of the *Monarchy of the Messiah* (*La monarchia del Messia* and *Monarchia Messiae*),[7] this chapter focuses on one of the contexts in which Campanella made use of the anti-*auctoritas* of Marsilius — namely, the pamphlet war which emerged from the conflict that pitted Pope Paul V against the

---

Difensore della pace al Leviatano; Izbicki, 'The Reception of Marsilius', as well as the studies cited by Piaia in his contribution to this volume.

3 The main contribution on Campanella's attitude towards Marsilius of Padua is Piaia, 'La "presenza" di Marsilio da Padova in Tommaso Campanella', which was later incorporated into Piaia, *Marsilio da Padova nella Riforma e nella Controriforma*, pp. 350–63. In the 1990s and early 2000s this topic was indirectly addressed in essays coming from the field of Campanellian studies — namely, Vittorio Frajese's and Paolo Ponzio's works on the Italian and Latin versions of Campanella's *Monarchy of the Messiah*; cf. Frajese, 'La "Monarchia del Messia" di Tommaso Campanella'; Frajese, 'Introduzione'; Frajese, *Profezia e machiavellismo*, pp. 118–56; and Ponzio, 'Introduction'. These studies, however, deal with Marsilius of Padua's presence only in passing and focus mostly on Campanella's direct targets from the recent past (such as Domingo de Soto and Diego de Covarrubias) and the present (Giovanni Marsilio and Robert Bellarmine). This chapter tries to combine the approaches and results of these two lines of research which, to my knowledge, have not hitherto crossed paths. I will thus take into consideration, on the one hand, Campanella's understanding of and way of referring to the figure of Marsilius and, on the other, his engagement in the discussions with his contemporary interlocutors, so as to further examine the role of Marsilius's anti-*auctoritas* therein.

4 Piaia, *Marsilio da Padova nella Riforma e nella Controriforma*, p. 358.

5 I borrow this fitting expression from Izbicki, 'The Reception of Marsilius', p. 305.

6 Piaia, *Marsilio da Padova nella Riforma e nella Controriforma*, pp. 362–63.

7 See note 3, above. Henceforth, I will refer to this work by using the Italian title, unless I refer specifically to the later Latin version. In notes and textual references, I will use *MDM* for *La monarchia del Messia* and *MM* for *Monarchia Messiae*.

Republic of Venice and lead to the Venetian Interdict (1606–1607). Its aim is to show how Campanella used Marsilius of Padua as an anti-*auctoritas* to reinforce his stance against his direct polemical targets and to express, by way of opposition, his own system of knowledge and theologico-political vision, inspired by the ideal of the *unum ovile et unus pastor*.[8] Campanella's ways of referring to Marsilius in *La monarchia del Messia* will be put into dialogue with the voices of two other players in the pamphlet war. The first — referred to in the original Italian as a *teologo moderno* (or, in the later Latin *Monarchia Messiae*, a *theologus quidam*) — is Giovanni Marsilio, a former Jesuit from Naples, who had authored an anonymous pamphlet in support of Venetian rights and had been accused by the supporters of the pope for expounding the heretical theories of the Paduan. The second is Cardinal Robert Bellarmine (1542–1621), one of the defenders (albeit a controversial one) of the papal position. Indeed, although Giovanni Marsilio was the primary polemical target of *La monarchia del Messia*, Campanella's view contrasted also with the theoretical framework of one part of the Thomistic tradition of his day, a part exemplified by those members of the Tridentine and post-Tridentine Catholic Church who rejected the theory of the direct power of the pope *in temporalibus*: Domingo de Soto (1494–1560), Diego de Covarrubias (1512–1577), and Cardinal Bellarmine himself.

In the first section, I provide an overview of the references to Marsilius of Padua — portrayed as a champion of Aristotelianism and anticurialism — found in Campanella's works. The next section will consider the way in which Campanella referred to Marsilius in the context of the Venetian Interdict, comparing his position to that of Giovanni Marsilio and Robert Bellarmine. In particular, it will analyse the three references included in *La monarchia del Messia*, concerning (1) the nature of the Petrine primacy and papal power *in temporalibus*, (2) the exegesis of the Gospel passages on the tribute to Caesar (Matthew 22. 15–22; Mark 12. 13–17; Luke 20. 20–26) and the temple tax (Matthew 17. 24–27), discussed in relation to the issue of clerical exemption, and (3) the figure of Melchizedek as a model for the papal office. The final section will offer some considerations on Campanella's criticisms of the theory of indirect papal power in temporal matters, Bellarmine's interpretation of Aquinas, and Aristotle's lack of political perspective.

---

8 For literature on Campanella's theologico-political thought, see the aforementioned studies by Frajese cited at note 3; Headley, *Tommaso Campanella*; and the introductions and notes to the edition of the Italian and Latin versions of the *City of the Sun* by Tornitore. Among the most recent publications, see Panichi, *Il volto fragile del potere* and Ricci, *Campanella*.

On the Trail of Marsilius

From Piaia's study,[9] one learns that Campanella mentions the name and opinions of Marsilius alongside the following philosophers and theologians in these works:

- *De gentilismo non retinendo*
  Aristotle, Theophrastus, Alexander or Aphrodisias, Themistius, Averroes, John of Jandun, Pietro Pomponazzi, Walter Burley, Antonio Bernardi della Mirandola, Cesare Cremonini, Simon Porzio, Niccolò Machiavelli, the 'secta politicorum et libertinorum', Lutherans, Calvinists, Puritans
- *Antiveneti*
  Waldensians, John Wyclif, Marin Luther, Jan Hus, 'un teologo venduto' (*Giovanni Marsilio? Paolo Sarpi?)
- *Monarchia del Messia / Monarchia Messiae*
  Waldensians, John Wyclif, Martin Luther, Jan Hus, 'un teologo moderno/Pseudo-teologo/theologus quidam' (*Giovanni Marsilio!), Dante Alighieri, Diego Covarrubias, Domingo de Soto, the 'heretici ultramontani'
- *Quod reminiscetur*
  Arnaldus of Brescia, Paolo Sarpi

Within this list, one can distinguish three main groups of characters whom Campanella considered reprehensible from a philosophical, political, or theological point of view.

The first group consists of authors belonging to the Aristotelian and Averroistic tradition.[10] A reference to Marsilius is found in the first article of the *De gentilismo non retinendo* (1609), where Campanella discusses 'whether it is convenient for a Christian philosopher to forge a new philosophy after that of the Gentiles, and how'. While presenting his criticism of Peripatetic philosophy, Campanella offers some remarks

---

9 Piaia, *Marsilio da Padova nella Riforma e nella Controriforma*, pp. 350–63.

10 Piaia hypothesizes that Campanella might have found inspiration for the juxtaposition Aristotle/Averroes–Marsilius either in the works of the Dutch theologian Albertus Pighius (1490–1542), who had defined Marsilius as 'homo Aristotelicum magis quam Christianus', or by extending to Marsilius the Aristotelian-Averroistic philosophical orientation — known by Campanella through the works of Augustinus Niphus — of John of Jandun, whose name appeared with Marsilius in Pope John XXII's bull *Licet iuxta doctrina* as a co-author of the *Defensor pacis*; cf. Piaia, *Marsilio da Padova nella Riforma e nella Controriforma*, pp. 358–59. Among the many studies on Campanella's conflicting attitude towards Aristotle, see Firpo, 'Campanella contro Aristotele'; Headley, *Tommaso Campanella*, pp. 145–79. For the discussion on the historiographical category of 'political Averroism' applied to Marsilius, see at least Piaia, '"Averroïsme politique"'; Piaia, 'Dalla *Politica* di Aristotele all'"averroismo politico"'; Mulieri, 'Against Classical Republicanism', and Mulieri's contribution to the present volume.

on the ineffectiveness of past attempts at reconciling Aristotle with the Christian religion. He reports how Thomas Aquinas, Albert the Great, and others tried to provide a benevolent interpretation of Aristotle ('in bonum sensum Aristotelem vertere') and disputed those of his theories which were in open opposition with the Christian faith. According to many, however, the outcome of this hermeneutical operation was that either Aquinas and Albert did not really understand the Stagirite or they offered a distorted reading of his texts ('non intellexisse vel torsisse').[11] The name of Marsilius of Padua is included among a group of authors ranging from the late thirteenth to the early seventeenth century — John of Jandun (1280–1328), Walter Burley (1275–1344), Pietro Pomponazzi (1462–1525), Antonio Bernardi della Mirandola (1502–1565), and Cesare Cremonini (1550–1631) — who rejected Aquinas's reading of Aristotle and followed instead the teaching of those whom they believed to be Aristotle's true interpreters: Theophrastus, Themistius, Alexander of Aphrodisias, and Averroes. It is from these doubts ('suspiciones') against Aquinas's position and out of the Aristotelian and Averroistic tradition that, according to Campanella's narrative, Machiavellianism sprouted — 'roots of evils, who transformed religion into *ragion di stato* and invaded courts of kings and civic governments'.[12] Resorting to the authority of Aquinas is no longer helpful, Campanella adds; on the contrary, it causes even more harm, as is shown in the case of heretical schools, 'politicians',

---

11 Campanella, *De gentilismo non retinendo*, p. 8.

12 Campanella, *De gentilismo non retinendo*, p. 8. The Campanella-Machiavelli relationship is one of most investigated topoi in Campanellian scholarship. If Machiavelli represented the arch-enemy of Campanella's political vision, it is nonetheless true that Campanella held some ideas that can be found also in Machiavelli, such as the utility of religion for the stability of a political community. Historiographical considerations concerning Campanella's possible 'hidden Machiavellianism' are also based on the fact that Campanella, in his own life, resorted to dissimulation or behaviour that could be seen as opportunistic. One example is the way in which Campanella endured the '*veglia* torture', faking insanity to escape capital punishment after having been arrested and charged for heresy and for having led an insurrection in Calabria against the Spanish government. Another example is the ambivalent attitude he showed towards the Spanish and French monarchies. In different phases of his life, Campanella appealed to one or the other as potential agents for the reunion of the world under a universal monarchy, which should have been ultimately led by the pope. A possible reading of this controversial issue is that Campanella's goal was the realization of the universal theocratic monarchy, and thus every means would be allowed — including his own messianic role in the Calabrian *congiura* against the Spanish, as well as his apparently contradictory support of Spain and later of France. On these points, see, for instance, Frajese, 'Cultura machiavellica e profezia messianica'; Frajese, *Profezia e machiavellismo*, pp. 58–83; as well as Headley, *Tommaso Campanella*, pp. 180–96; Ernst, 'La mauvaise raison d'Etat' and Ernst, 'Introduzione'; Caye, 'Campanella critique de Machiavel'; Addante, 'Campanella e Machiavelli'. For the biography of Campanella, see note 26, below.

libertines, or princes inspired by Machiavelli who reject papal decrees.[13] For this reason, Campanella advocates the necessity of a new philosophy which will eradicate old doctrinal systems.[14]

Later in the text, Campanella reaffirms that Aristotle, Averroes, Alexander of Aphrodisias, and their followers were the sources through which Machiavelli learned that religion is the *ars regnandi*, that laws are impostures devised by clever men, and that God does not look after human affairs. According to Campanella, it is within this tradition that one should understand the cases of the schismatics, the Ghibellines, the supporters of the emperor — such as Marsilius of Padua, Pomponazzi, and Simon Porzio — and others who promoted religious dissidence in Europe.[15]

From these passages of the *De gentilismo non retinendo*, one can make the following observations: (1) Campanella points out a problem, occurring during his own day, with the use of Aquinas's authority;[16] (2) he traces a line that goes from Aristotle–Averroes, through Marsilius, to Machiavelli, and accuses Aristotelianism of being the root of the doctrine supporting an opportunistic use of religion in politics; (3) he declares the need (and advent) of a *nova philosophia* that is going to supersede the aforementioned system of knowledge and vision of politics.

The second group — found in the *De gentilismo non retinendo*, *Antiveneti*, *La monarchia del Messia*, and *Quod reminiscetur* — is composed of characters who were considered dangerous from the theologico-political and ecclesiological perspective: heretics (Arnaldus of Brescia, Waldensians, John Wycliff, and Jan Hus), reformed theologians (Martin Luther, Lutherans, Calvinists, and Puritans), and a layman who challenged the principle of the pontiff's *plenitudo potestatis* in temporal matters: Dante Alighieri, whose *Monarchia* was among the books listed in the *Index*

---

13 Campanella, *De gentilismo non retinendo*, pp. 8–9: 'cum remedium St Thomae et aliorum hoc tempore non prosit, imo malitiosis obsit & astutis, ut haereticorum scholae, & Politicorum, & libertinorum ostendunt: Item Principum, adversantium decretis Papae praxis ostendit aulas Machiavellizare'.

14 Campanella, *De gentilismo non retinendo*, p. 9: 'propterea expedit novam Philosophiam struere, & dogmata prava evertere'. For a general introduction on Campanella's 'new philosophy', see Ernst, *Tommaso Campanella*; and Ponzio, *Tommaso Campanella*.

15 Campanella, *De gentilismo non retinendo*, pp. 20–21: 'A quo enim Machiavellus didicit Religionem esse artem regnandi, & leges imposturas astutorum, Deum humana non curare, nisi ab Aristotele, Averr., Alexandro Aphrodis. & horum sequacibus, ex quibus prodiere nuper pravi consultores schismatum Ghibellini & Imperiales, ut Marsilius Paduanus, Pomponatius, Simon Portius, & alii qui Venetis, & Hispanis, Germanis, & Gallis, Anglis, & Danis consuluerunt apostasiam pro dominatu amplificando [...] Adde Calvinistas, Lutheristas, & Puritanos'.

16 It is not clear whether, in the text quoted at note 13, Campanella is simply maintaining that Aquinas's authority per se during his time was not helpful and might rather have been harmful, or whether he claims that heretics, Machiavellians, and libertines made use of Aquinas's authority, and they did so in a distorted way.

Librorum Prohibitorum in Campanella's times.[17] Referring to Marsilius in association with medieval heretics and reformed theologians (but also Dante) constituted a topos among the authors of the Counter-Reformation.[18] To these common references, Campanella adds two authors of his day who played an important role in the discussions surrounding the Venetian Interdict: the Servite Paolo Sarpi (1552–1623),[19] and a 'modern theologian', that is, Giovanni Marsilio.

Finally, one can identify a third group, comprising two figures whose connection with Marsilius appears less evident. The last two names mentioned by Campanella in reference to the heretic Paduan are indeed those of two well-respected doctors of the Tridentine Church, professors at the 'School of Salamanca': the Dominican Domingo de Soto and one of his pupils, Diego Covarrubias.

The following section examines these second and third types of association in the writings Campanella composed on the occasion of the Venetian Interdict, the *Antiveneti* and *La monarchia del Messia*, analysing them in the light of the polemical context from which they emerged.

Against Marsilius and the *Novus Marsilius*

The *casus belli* of the quarrel that occurred from 1605 to 1607 between Pope Paul V and the Republic of Venice was a pair of actions taken by the Venetian government against ecclesiastical prerogatives in terms of civil jurisdiction: the first was the proclamation of two laws which stated that the building of churches and the alienation of ecclesiastical properties should be approved by the senate; the second was the refusal to hand over two clergymen accused of common crimes to the ecclesiastical authorities. In April 1606, the pope issued an interdict against Venice, which lasted one year, until the differences were smoothed over by the diplomatic intervention of Henry IV, king of France. This jurisdictional conflict produced a *battaglia di scritture* which again put into the spotlight the long-standing

---

17 Dante's *Monarchia* was inserted in the list in 1585 but had already been criticized by Friar Guido Vernani a few years after the death of its author, and then censored by Cardinal Bertrand du Pouget in 1328; cf. Cassell, *The 'Monarchia' Controversy*.

18 Piaia, *Marsilio da Padova nella Riforma e nella Controriforma*, p. 346.

19 Campanella refers to Paolo Sarpi, alongside Marsilius and Arnaldus of Brescia 'et alii huius farina' who disregarded the papal rights and were associated with schismatic rulers (cf. *Quod reminiscetur*, pp. 59–60). On Sarpi's contribution to the interdict, see Oakley, 'Complexities of Context'; Tutino, *Empire of Souls*, pp. 88–101; as well as the literature cited in note 20, below. For the relationship Campanella–Sarpi, see Firpo, 'Non Paolo Sarpi, ma Tommaso Campanella' and Pirillo, '"Questo buon monaco non ha inteso il Macchiavello"'. For the relationship Sarpi–Marsilius, see Piaia, *Marsilio da Padova nella Riforma e nella Controriforma*, pp. 396–403.

issue concerning the extent of papal power in temporal matters and the rights of secular rulers over the members and goods of the Church.[20]

The figure of Marsilius of Padua played a large part in the pamphlet war, at least from the pens of the papalists. The defenders of the papal position employed the memory of the heretic and heresiarch Marsilius as a weapon to be used against the pro-Venetian writers, accused of taking inspiration from his anticlerical doctrines.[21] This was the case with Giovanni Marsilio, who was blamed by several theologians — both for the tone of his first pamphlet and for his curious homonymy with the Paduan — of representing a *novus Marsilius de Neapoli*, or with less solemnity, a *Marsilietto Napolitano*.[22]

Giovanni's writing, published anonymously in May 1606, is entitled *Risposta d'un dottore in theologia ad una lettera scrittagli da un Reverendo suo Amico*.[23] It consists of eight propositions defining the limits of the *potestas papalis in temporalibus*, asserting the purely spiritual character of the ecclesiastical institution, and defending the right of the secular rulers to make laws concerning Church property. The first proposition (i) claims that the power which belongs to the secular rulers — including that of the pontiff over the *Patrimonium Sancti Petri* — is granted to them directly by God. The establishment of *dominium* occurred *de iure gentium*, either by election, heritage, donation, or war; thus, those who are in a position of power through these means 'have, with no exception, the authority by God of commanding, making laws, demanding tributes, judging, punishing their subjects'.[24] As the Levites under their High Priest Aron obeyed Moses in temporal matters, so too are the members of the clergy subject to their secular rulers. The second proposition (ii) argues that Christ while on this earth neither had nor exercised temporal power; indeed, he paid the tribute to Caesar, recognized Pilate as his rightful judge, and told him that his kingdom was not of this world. Since Christ did not exercise the authority of a secular prince, even more so did Christ not grant it to his vicar, the pope (iii). The fourth proposition (iv) asserts that the metaphor of the keys of the kingdom of heaven is purely spiritual, and that the papal

---

20 On the history of events and debates around the interdict, see Bouwsma, *Venice and the Defense of Republican Liberty*, esp. pp. 339–482, as well as Pirri, *L'Interdetto di Venezia del 1606 e i gesuiti*; Cozzi, *Paolo Sarpi tra Venezia e l'Europa*; Frajese, *Sarpi scettico*; and, recently, Tutino, *Empire of Souls*, pp. 81–116.

21 Piaia, *Marsilio da Padova nella Riforma e nella Controriforma*, pp. 374–403.

22 Benzoni, 'I teologi minori dell'interdetto', pp. 79–81. Puns on the homonymy can be found, for example, in Gregorio Servanzi, Antonio Possevino, Jacob Gretser, and in Francisco Peña, author of a pamphlet entitled *Assertio regni Christi, Pontificiae auctoritatis et ecclesiasticae immunitatis, adversus Novum Marsilium*; cf. Piaia, *Marsilio da Padova nella Riforma e nella Controriforma*, pp. 377–78, and Tutino, *Empire of Souls*, pp. 100–101.

23 For the dating, see Frajese, 'Introduzione', p. 6.

24 Giovanni Marsilio, *Risposta d'un dottore*, p. [A3r].

capacity to excommunicate is conditional on sin. The fifth proposition (v) maintains that the exemption of ecclesiastic goods and members of the clergy from secular jurisdiction is *de iure humano* and not *iure divino*. Based on these claims, Giovanni was able to conclude that the prince of Venice would not recognize any superior in temporal affairs and would have the right of both issuing laws concerning ecclesiastical property and the punishment of clergymen (vi). Thus, Venice could not be considered guilty, and the pope's sentence of interdict was void (vii–viii).

The proximity of Giovanni's position to that expressed by Marsilius of Padua in the second *dictio* of the *Defensor pacis*, condemned by Pope John XXII in his bull *Licet iuxta doctrina*, did not go unnoticed by his contemporaries. The pamphlet gained wide attention and was among the main polemical targets of the papal supporters in the quarrel — including Cardinal Robert Bellarmine, who engaged with Giovanni in a 'war of letters',[25] and Tommaso Campanella.

Campanella was informed of the Venetian Interdict — and probably was able to read Giovanni's pamphlet — in late August 1606 while he was incarcerated in Castel Sant'Elmo in Naples.[26] In a letter dated September 1606, addressed to the pope and aimed at pleading his case, Campanella writes that 'from the barber and the soldiers' he had heard that the Venetians had been hit by papal interdict.[27] He thus displayed to the pope his vision for a universal revolution ('riforma universale'), which had to start from the Church itself, and to be extended to the whole *societas christiana*. This revolution should have been founded on the recognition of the direct power of the pope *in spiritualibus et temporalibus*, on the

---

25 Bellarmine, *Risposta a due libretti*, which was, in its turn, contested by Giovanni in the *Difesa di Giovanni Marsilio a favore della Risposta dell'otto Propositioni*. After this first exchange, Bellarmine composed the *Risposta alla difesa delle otto propositioni*, which was followed by Giovanni's *Essame sopra tutte quelle scritture*. Some notes on the Bellarmine–Giovanni quarrel can be found in Piaia, *Marsilio da Padova nella Riforma e nella Controriforma*, pp. 390–94; and Bouwsma, *Venice and the Defense of Republican Liberty*, chs 7 and 8 (passim).

26 Frajese, 'Campanella a Sant'Elmo nell'estate 1606'. In 1606, Campanella had already spent seven years in prison under the accusation of having participated in the Calabrian conspiracy. For Campanella's biography, see Amabile, *Fra Tommaso Campanella, la sua congiura*; Amabile, *Fra Tommaso Campanella ne' castelli di Napoli*; Firpo, *I processi di Tommaso Campanella*; Ernst, *Tommaso Campanella*; and Ernst, ed., *Tommaso Campanella e la congiura di Calabria*.

27 Campanella, *Lettere*, no. 13, ed. by Ernst, pp. 64–75. Campanella had previously mentioned his awareness of the Venetian situation ('il negozio Venezia') in two letters addressed to the Cardinals Odoardo Farnese and Cinzio Aldobrandini on 30 August 1606 (no. 11, p. 43 and no. 12, p. 62). See also the post-scriptum, probably composed at the beginning of September, to the letter to the pope dated 13 August (no. 9, pp. 32–33), where Campanella claims that 'li Veneziani, facendo risposte e libri, saran la propria ruina'. Here Campanella may be referring to the 'grammar war' between Giovanni and the papal supporters — maybe Bellarmine himself.

abolition of civil law in favour of canon law, as well as the establishment of a common assembly (*conseglio commune*) gathering both cardinals and the ambassadors of secular rulers so that they could all deliberate together with the pope in matters of state.[28]

As his own contribution to the *guerra grammaticale*, Campanella composed two works in which he incorporated the contingent discussions on Venetian rights and clerical exemption within his broader theologico-political vision and prophetic horizon. In October, he had already completed the *Antiveneti*, while the manuscript of *La monarchia del Messia* was ready in March 1607; the Latin *Monarchia Messiae*, which included a few changes, would be published nearly thirty years later.[29]

The *Antiveneti* signalled a shift in Campanella's attitude towards Venice.[30] In a sonnet composed in 1601, he had described Venice as a 'new Noah's ark' which stood amid the waves during the flood: an 'intact virgin' and 'fertile mother', 'untouched by discord and servitude', which generated capable and learned men ('eroi chi ponno e sanno').[31] Campanella had praised Venice as a 'clock of princes and wise school' ('de' prencipi orologio e saggia scuola' — i.e. endowed with political wisdom), which 'carries alone the burden of freedom' ('di libertà portando il pondo, sola').[32] Besides being commended for its form of government and cultural prosperity, Venice was described as an ally of Rome and a skilful political agent in foreign affairs, which had to manage a difficult balance between the Italian peninsula, the northern countries, and the Mediterranean (with the Turk's menace). The Venice of the interdict is the reverse image of the one portrayed in the sonnet, as displayed in the palinode he included in the *Antiveneti*.[33] The ark of Noah has now become the boat of Charon,

---

28 Campanella, *Lettere*, no. 13, ed. by Ernst, pp. 68–71.

29 On the genesis and dating of *La monarchia del Messia*, see Frajese, 'La "Monarchia del Messia" di Tommaso Campanella'. On the history of the publication of the *Monarchia Messiae*, see Ponzio, 'Introduction', as well as De Mattei, *Il pensiero politico italiano*, I, pp. 211–29. By spring 1607 Campanella had also completed the *Ateismo trionfato* against the 'politici e macchiavellisti, chi son la peste di questo secolo e di tal monarchia [i.e. the universal Christian monarchy], fondando la ragion di stato sull'amor parziale' (Campanella, *Lettere*, no. 11, ed. by Ernst, p. 50).

30 An account of the main references to Venice in Campanella's works can be found in Plouchart-Cohn, 'Venezia'. See also Fournel, *La cité du soleil et les territoires des hommes*, pp. 275–81. In later works, Campanella's attitude towards Venice would become more positive. See, for instance, Campanella's *Dialogo tra un Veneziano, Spagnolo e Francese*, in which the Venetian character is a wise advisor and plays a central role in the discussion (cf. Plouchart-Cohn, 'Il "Dialogo tra un veneziano, spagnolo e francese"'). Campanella would return to the theme of the necessity of an alliance between Venice and Rome in the *Discorso terzo a Venezia* and *Avvertimenti a Venezia* of 1636 (cf. Ernst, 'Ancora sugli ultimi scritti politici di Campanella: I', pp. 135–37, 149–53, and pt. II).

31 Campanella, *Le Poesie*, no. 38, vv. 1–8, ed. by Giancotti, p. 135.

32 Campanella, *Le Poesie*, no. 38, vv. 9–14, ed. by Giancotti, p. 136.

33 Campanella, *Antiveneti*, I, lamento 6, ed. by Firpo, pp. 38–39.

which carries on board Cam and his progeny. Venice is no longer the chaste niece of Rome, but a virgin on her way to becoming a prostitute; the winged lion holding the Gospel of St Mark, protector of Venice, has transformed into a dragon, who chose Machiavelli as his new Holy Scripture.[34] Finally, Venice is no longer a 'saggia scuola' and the mother of the 'eroi chi ponno e sanno', but a nest of schismatics and heretics.

The doxography offered in the *Antiveneti* generally refers to Marsilius of Padua as one of the inspirations for Venice's laws on ecclesiastical property and associates him with Luther and Wycliff.[35] Campanella proposes a parallel in terms of employer/employee between Ludwig the Bavarian/Marsilius and Venice / a 'sell-out theologian' ('teologo venduto', otherwise referred to as 'cantanbanco del demonio'), who employed his pen at the service of the Venetian claims. The spokesman for this comparison is the Parisian chancellor Jean Gerson (1363–1429), who takes the floor in the imaginary dialogue between him, St Mark, St Paul, St Chrysostom, and St Thomas Aquinas found in *Antiveneti*, I, lamento 9. The aim of Gerson's speech is to defend his own reputation after his doctrines concerning the limits of papal power — together with those of Soto and Covarrubias, and (due to bad interpretation) those of Chrysostom and Aquinas — had caused scandal in Venice.[36] Gerson's character probably refers to the publication and circulation in Venice of two tracts authored by him and translated into Italian by Paolo Sarpi dealing with the abuse of excommunication.[37]

It has been hypothesized that the anonymous 'sell-out theologian' condemned in the *Antiveneti* was Sarpi himself.[38] Another possibility, however, is that Campanella was referring to the 'modern theologian' (otherwise indicated as a 'certain theologian' or a 'pseudo-theologian')[39] who represented the main polemical target of *La monarchia del Messia*, namely,

---

34 Campanella, *Antiveneti*, I, lamento 8, ed. by Firpo, p. 49.

35 Campanella, *Antiveneti*, I, lamento 6, ed. by Firpo, pp. 36–37; but see also *Antiveneti*, II, discorso 8, p. 114, where Campanella condemns the laws issued by Venice as possible causes of disruption between the Christian rulers and the pontiff, a consequence of which would be the loss of the Spanish conquests in the New World. For an analysis of this passage with regard to the theme of the utility of religion in Campanella, see Piaia, *Marsilio da Padova nella Riforma e nella Controriforma*, p. 352.

36 Campanella, *Antiveneti*, I, lamento 9, ed. by Firpo, pp. 114: 'e a che serve il papa e li concilii se i laici possono esplicare il ius divino con qualche loro teologo venduto, come fe' il Bavaro con Marsilio padovano'.

37 For considerations on Gerson's legacy in the framework of the interdict, see Oakley, 'Complexities of Context'.

38 Piaia, *Marsilio da Padova nella Riforma e nella Controriforma*, p. 351.

39 Campanella never mentions the name of Giovanni Marsilio in *MDM*; according to Frajese, Campanella himself played on the homonymy of Giovanni with the Paduan, referring to him as a 'modern(certain/pseudo-) theologian', but adding the further reference to Marsilius of Padua as a red flag suggesting the real name of the author (cf. 'Introduzione', p. 7).

Giovanni Marsilio. In 1, lamento 6, Campanella polemicizes against the circulation of writings with no name, place, or date of publication, as was the case with Giovanni's pamphlet. Moreover, Giovanni made large use therein of the authority of Soto and Covarrubias — that is, two of the authors that in the dialogue between saints portrayed in the *Antiveneti* were accused of having created scandal in Venice.

The two professors of Salamanca were not the only Counter-Reformation authors whose *auctoritas* Giovanni tried to use in his favour. Another name appearing in the *Risposta d'un dottore in teologia* is that of Cardinal Robert Bellarmine, who was a supporter of the theory of the 'indirect power' of the pope in temporal matters. Giovanni's use of Bellarmine's *auctoritas* in his pamphlet is one of the triggers which caused the cardinal's reaction and started the paper quarrel between the two.[40] Bellarmine's discomfort at seeing his own positions used against the Roman prerogatives might have been enhanced by the fact that Giovanni was not the only one who used his authority in defence of Venice. Paolo Sarpi similarly supported the Venetian claims by referring to the theories on the papal *potestas indirecta in temporalibus* and on clerical exemption found in Bellarmine's *Controversiae* (esp. *De summo pontifice*, *De laicis*, and *De clericis*).[41] Being quoted by those who were accused of defending the Marsilian heresy did not help Bellarmine's reputation within the Roman Curia, especially among those who did not share his theory of indirect power.[42]

From Castle Sant'Elmo, while polemicizing against Giovanni Marsilio in *La monarchia del Messia*, Campanella himself did not squander the opportunity to include in his criticism the theory of *potestas indirecta*. Taking over Giovanni's doxography, Campanella gathered into his critique — with the due qualifications — Marsilius of Padua (together with the aforementioned heretics and reformed theologians), Giovanni Marsilio, Soto, Covarrubias, and Bellarmine himself.[43] From the point of view of Campanella, who supported the idea of a *potestas directa* of the pope

---

40 For the list of the texts composed for the quarrel, see note 25 above.

41 On the Sarpi–Bellarmine relationship, see Tutino, *Empire of Souls*, pp. 88–101.

42 The controversial character of Bellarmine's ecclesiological and political theory vis-à-vis the theoretical framework of the post-Tridentine Church is the focal point of the recent Tutino, *Empire of Souls*; for the 'internal battle in Rome' on Bellarmine's *potestas indirecta*, see pp. 101–10. For further literature on Bellarmine's political thought, see Höpfl, *Jesuit Political Thought*; Motta, *Bellarmino*; and Frajese, 'Una teoria della censura'. See also Giacon, *La seconda scolastica*.

43 While composing *MDM* Campanella had read Bellarmine's first answer to Giovanni, the *Risposta a due libretti*. Similarly, he was acquainted with Domingo de Soto's *De iustitia et iure*. Campanella does not directly associate Bellarmine with Marsilius of Padua, but he critically discusses the cardinal's theories in several places of *MDM* (cf. pp. 74, 83, 142). Campanella's attitude towards Bellarmine and Domingo de Soto is still under-researched. Among the recent contributions dealing with his relationship with some major representatives of the

in both temporal and spiritual affairs and hoped for the realization of a universal Christian monarchy ultimately lead by Christ through his vicar, none of the aforementioned authors understood the true nature of *dominium* and the papal political role. The three passages in which Campanella refers to Marsilius of Padua in *La monarchia del Messia* are useful *loci* for understanding his perspective.

Petrine Primacy and Papal Power in temporalibus

The first reference to Marsilius of Padua is found in *MDM*, VI, where Campanella deals with the 'different heretical opinions and those of the Catholics about Christ's Kingdom, the power of the High Pontiff, and of lay rulers'. After having presented the positions of Muhammad and of those who denied Christ's divinity and refused to ascribe to him any temporal or spiritual lordship, Campanella distinguishes between three heretical positions among Christians: (1) that of the Anabaptists, who believed the Church to be like a 'popular republic' with no supreme spiritual head and 'almost an anarchy'; (2) that of the Lutherans and the Calvinists, who thought clergy should be submitted to secular rulers, that each Christian was a priest, and that one should 'live in a democracy'; (3) that of Wycliff, Hus, Marsilius, and the Waldensians, who

> affirm that the pope is as a priest, a preacher, and a minister of the sacraments. But some, as the Lutheran heretics and Calvinists, assert that the pope is as such only with respect to his own diocese; others, such as Marsilius of Padua, that the pope is above all others, but that he does not have any secular power except insofar as the secular rulers give it to him or allow him to have it. This is affirmed by Marsilius, and by a modern theologian who wrote against the excommunication of Pope Paul V issued against the Republic of Venice, and they prove it, because Christ did not take any temporal lordship neither before nor after his resurrection; thus, he did not leave it to Peter; and he said: *My Kingdom is not of this world* [John 18. 36] and that he was only a spiritual king; and he paid the tribute as a vassal of the empire, and he acknowledged Pilate as his superior [...]. He did not used the material sword, but reproached Peter for that.[44]

Second Scholastics and of the 'tomismo rinascimentale', see De Lucca, '*Ius gentium*'; Sgarro, *Un inquieto domenicano*; and Moiso, 'La libertà e la grazia'. On the presence of Bellarmine, Soto, and Covarrubias in *MDM*, see Frajese, 'Introduzione', pp. 34–35.

44 *MDM*, VI, pp. 71–72: 'Wicleffo poi et Marsilio Padovano, et Giovanni Hus, et li valdensi asseriscono, il papa essere come curato, predicante, et ministro de sacramenti; ma altri dicono solo della sua diocesi, come gli heretici lutherani, et calviniani, altri de tutti sopraintendente [*MM: super omnes dioceses episcoporum esse in spiritualibus*], come Marsilio [Vatican City, Biblioteca apostolica Vaticana, MS Chigi F VI 131: *Marsilio Padovano*], ma

The outline of Marsilius of Padua's ecclesiology and understanding of the relationship between *regnum* and *sacerdotium* sketched by Campanella in this passage mirrors those Marsilian theses which had been condemned in the *Licet iuxta doctrina* — especially nos. 2–5, asserting that Christ did not transmit to Peter any special authority, mandate of vicariate, or jurisdiction compared to the other apostles, and that the Church, pope included, did not have any coercive power unless granted by the emperor.[45] In *DP*, II, 22, Marsilius had indeed defined the leading role of the 'Roman bishop' within the Church as a simple *principalitas* with no coercive jurisdiction intrinsically attached to it. The direct target of Campanella here was, however, the 'modern theologian' — that is, Giovanni Marsilio, the 'new Marsilius from Naples' who in his pamphlet had reported the heresy of the Paduan by readapting it to the Venetian context.

Most probably, Campanella did not come up with this doxographical picture by himself. His choice of wording shows close similarities to a passage in Bellarmine's response to Giovanni's pamphlet. Therein one finds — in reply to Giovanni's proposition IV on the limits of papal power in matters of excommunication — the same accusation of 'Marsilian heresy' and the same doxography.[46]

Indeed, here and throughout *MDM*, VI, the *Risposta del cardinal Bellarmino* to propositions III and IV of Giovanni Marsilio seems to represent one of the main sources used by Campanella for building his own argument — yet, Campanella applies an ideological turn to it which goes against the original intent of the cardinal. A few lines after having associated Giovanni Marsilio with Marsilius of Padua, Campanella in fact places Bellarmine on the enemy's side. After having listed the seventeen

---

che non habbia potestà secolare se non quanto li prencipi secolari li donano, o permettono. Questo dice Marsilio, et un theologo moderno [*MM: Theologus quidam*], che scrisse contro la scomunica di papa Paolo quinto fulminata contro la Repubblica di Venetia, et lo provano, perché Christo non pigliò signoria temporale né prima, né doppo la resurettione; dunque neanco la lasciò a Pietro, et disse: *Regnum meum non est de hoc mundo*, et che era solo spirituale re, e pagò il tributo come vassallo dell'imperio, e riconobbe Pilato per suo superiore [...] Non usò il gladio materiale, ma ne riprese Pietro'; cf. *MM*, VI, p. 128.

45 For the condemned proposition, see Denzinger, *Enchiridion symbolorum*, p. 213; for the whole text, see Du Plessis d'Argentré, *Collectio judiciorum de novis erroribus*, I, cols 304a–311b.

46 Bellarmine, *Risposta a due libretti*, p. 24: 'Questo Autore va tanto sminuendo la Potestà del Sommo Pontefice, che si rende sospetto di credere, che il Papa sia un semplice Sacerdote o Curato, che non habbia iurisditione alcuna, né possa fare altro, che essortare all'osservanza della legge di Dio, come fanno i Predicatori, battezzare, & confessare, come fanno i curati, & cosi pare che voglia rinovare l heresia dei Valdensi, di Vicleffo, di Marsilio di Padova, & di Giovanni Hus, quale hoggi è abbracciata da tutti li heretici moderni'. Bellarmine provides a similar doxography in *De summo Pontifice*, ed. by Fèvre, I, pp. 456–57, while tracing the history of those who rejected the papal primacy in the West. Here, he adds the name of Jandun to the list, associating him with Marsilius among those 'qui Romano Pontifici non modo Episcopos omnes, sed omnes etiam Presbyteros pares fecerunt'.

arguments used in support of the position according to which the pope has no temporal power whatsoever, which are for the most part taken from Giovanni, Campanella treats the divisions internal to the Catholic Church.

On the one hand, Campanella lines up the 'party' of Bellarmine, Navarro, Juan de Torquemada, Soto, and Covarrubias, who maintain that (1) the pope has only an indirect power in temporal matters — that is, he has power in temporal matters 'insofar as the temporal deviates from the spiritual, in order to correct and lead politics [*MM*: the governants] towards religion'; (2) the power of secular rulers comes directly from God; and (3) ecclesiastical exemption is *de iure humano*.[47]

On the other, there stand the canonists, who all agree that the pope is 'lord of the entire world, in both spiritual and temporal matters as he is the vicar of Christ, who, being God, has all power'. Among the many *auctoritates* cited as belonging to this tradition, one finds Thomas Aquinas, his *discipulus* Giles of Rome, and Augustine of Ancona.[48] Clearly, this is the position that Campanella favours.

Also in this case, Campanella's doxography comes from the polemical exchange between Giovanni and Bellarmine. In III, Giovanni had used the authority of Bellarmine and Domingo de Soto to support his claim that Christ did not exercise the authority of a temporal prince, and thus he did not bestow this authority to Peter and his successors. According to Giovanni's account, both illustrious doctors of the Roman Church

> marvelled at the canonists, who dared to claim, with no reason or authority from the New Testament, that the pope is *Dominus totius orbis directe in temporalibus*, which is a scandalous doctrine and little grounded indeed.[49]

Bellarmine's animosity against Giovanni is quite understandable: his name had been used by a pro-Venetian writer to support a position which smelled dangerously of 'Marsilianism'. He accused Giovanni of intellectual dishonesty in quoting his sources and, especially, in presenting Soto's and his own positions on papal power. Bellarmine remarked that he had never denied that the pope had a *potestà suprema* in temporal matters — only heretics (like Marsilius and Giovanni) would affirm that. He acknowledged, however, the existence of divergences within the canonist tradition

---

47 Cf. *MDM*, VI, pp. 74–75; cf. *MM*, VI, pp. 134–36. The references cited slightly change in the two versions. On the issue of clerical exemption, see 'Paying the Tribute', below.

48 Cf. *MDM*, VI, pp. 76–77; cf. *MM*, VI, pp. 136–42. This part is more developed in *MM*: the references to Giles of Rome and Augustine of Ancona are not present in *MDM*. The fact that Campanella refers to Giles of Rome — the medieval champion of an absolute view of papal *plenitudo postestatis* — as the 'disciple' of Aquinas in political matters reveals much of his own interpretation of Aquinas. It is the same as asserting that good Thomists believe in the direct papal power *in temporalibus*.

49 Giovanni Marsilio, *Risposta d'un dottore*, p. [B3ʳ].

with respect to the modality with which the pope has this power. For some, 'the pope has that power in the same manner of the secular rulers', namely, a *potestas directa in temporalibus*. Others, including himself, Soto, Torquemada, and Navarro, held that the papal power per se is spiritual, but that the pope can intervene in temporal matters insofar as they are dependent on spiritual matters. It is thus from Bellarmine that Campanella took his outline of the two contrasting positions among the Catholic doctors — siding, however, with the opposite party.

Campanella uses a similar strategy while presenting Aquinas as a defender of the *potestas directa*, in particular when he quotes the *De regimine principum*, III, 18–20 to demonstrate that Aquinas 'rendered the pope the universal lord in temporal and spiritual matters, without gloss'. To date it is well known that Aquinas was not the author of that part of the *De regimine*, which was instead written by Ptolemy of Lucca. This attribution was questioned also in Campanella's time, as in III, 20 one finds the story of the successions of Adolf, count of Nassau, and Albert of Habsburg as emperor-elects, which happened more than twenty years after Aquinas's death. Campanella acknowledges the philological problem; however, he maintains that the story of Adolf and Albert is a simple case of interpolation, and in his opinion, that interpolation does not change the force and authority of those chapters: if the author of the book was not Aquinas himself, Campanella states, the book was certainly written by someone equally as learned as him.[50] But once more, Campanella is here implicitly reproposing a debate which happened between Giovanni and Bellarmine, and taking his own stance on it. In his pamphlet Giovanni had dismissed the arguments of the papalists based on the third book of the *De regimine* by reminding the readers that the text was not authored by Aquinas; as a source for this philological information, he referred to Bellarmine.[51] Also in this case the cardinal contested Giovanni's improper use of his own name. He claimed that he had never denied Aquinas's authorship with certainty, but only reported the existence of doubts concerning the attribution based on that piece of text. It was, however, a case of interpolation which did not change the authoritative value of the passage. In his *Risposta*, Bellarmine uses it as an entirely legitimate *auctoritas* — regardless of whether it was written by Aquinas or by the author of the interpolation ('ò sia S. Tomaso, ò l'altro').[52] Nonetheless, he interprets it as an authority in defence of his own theory of the *potestas indirecta*. In this case, Campanella

---

50 *MDM*, VI, p. 76: 'San Thomasso nel opuscolo *De Regimine Principum* fa il papa signore universale in spirituale et temporale, et benché non paia suo quel libro per una historia inserta accaduta dopo lui [...]. Questo è poco argomento, ma il libro è dotto d'authore eguale a san Thomasso, se non è lui'; cf. *MM*, VI, p. 140.

51 Giovanni Marsilio, *Risposta d'un dottore*, p. [B3ʳ].

52 Bellarmine, *Risposta a due libretti*, pp. 20–21.

therefore draws part of his counterargument from Bellarmine's text: (C1) the interpolation does not discredit the overall validity of that passage, and it reflects the true position of Aquinas (although perhaps written by someone else). Then, he takes a turn and shifts back to the interpretation originally proposed (but contested for its inauthenticity) by Giovanni: (C2) that part of the *De regimine* supports the universal lordship of the pope *in temporalibus*. As a result, Campanella can claim that that passage is a valid *auctoritas* (C1) and supports the theory of the *potestas directa* (C2). Thus, he uses the authority of Aquinas (or Pseudo-Aquinas) in his own favour, against both the Marsilian position endorsed by Giovanni and that of Bellarmine himself.

To sum up, it appears that, in *MDM*, VI, Campanella took Bellarmine's doxographical setting: on the one side of the spectrum, Marsilius of Padua and Giovanni Marsilio; on the other, the canonists (and himself) supporting a 'princely' idea of the papacy; in the middle, the theologians endorsing the theory of the *potestas indirecta*. What changes in the scenario is the placement of Aquinas, whom Campanella brings into his own fold.

Paying the Tribute

The second passage of *La monarchia del Messia* in which Campanella refers to Marsilius of Padua is a discussion about the origin of clerical exemption revolving around the exegesis of the verses of the Gospel of Matthew on the tribute to Caesar and the temple tax. It is helpful to summarize Marsilius's position on the matter. These two passages are discussed in *DP*, II, 4.9–11, in support of the claim that

> not only [Christ] refused the principate of this world or coercive judgement in this world [...] but also taught in words and showed by example that all men, priests as much as non-priests, should be subject in goods and person to the coercive judgement of the princes of this world.[53]

After having reminded his readers of Christ's laconic answer, 'Render therefore unto Caesar the things which are Caesar's; and unto God the things that are God's' (Matthew 22. 21), Marsilius links the episode of the payment of the tribute to the Roman emperor to that, narrated a few chapters earlier, on the payment of the temple tax:

> When they reached Capernaum, the collectors of the temple tax came to Peter and said, 'Does your teacher not pay the temple tax?' He said, 'Yes, he does'. And when he came home, Jesus spoke of it first, asking, 'What do you think, Simon? From whom do kings of the earth take

---

53 *DP*, II, 4.9, trans. by Brett, p. 166.

toll or tribute? From their children or from others?' When Peter said, 'From others', Jesus said to him, 'Then the children are free'. However, so that we do not give offense to them, go to the sea and cast a hook; take the first fish that comes up, and when you open its mouth you will find a coin; take that and give it to them for you and me.[54]

One of the problems of this passage was the understanding of the cryptic answer 'the children are free'. A possible interpretation, supported by Jerome and reported by Marsilius, was that Christ, being a descendent of King David was exempt from paying the tax; however, he paid it out of humility. Commenting on this solution, Marsilius remarks that even if Christ was of royal stock, this was not the case for Peter, and thus Peter had no justification for being exempt, nor did Christ wish for him (and, by extension, for his successors) to be exempt:

And if Christ had thought it inappropriate for his future successors in the office of priest to pay tribute, and for their temporal goods to be subject to the princes of this world, he could [...] have ordained or proceeded in a different way with those collectors of tribute; for example, by removing from them their intention of asking for it, or in some other appropriate way. But he did not consider it appropriate to do any such thing; on the contrary, he wanted to pay it, and of the apostles he singled out Peter to be associated with him in this, Peter who [...] would be the foremost teacher and shepherd of the church: so that by such an example none of the others would refuse to do it.[55]

Marsilius aligns instead with Origen's exegesis according to which the tax discussed in Matthew 17. 24–27 was a specific toll asked of foreigners, from which the inhabitants of Judea, the 'sons of the land', were free.[56] This kind of exemption, however, would not have been extended to the tribute to Caesar, which should be paid by anyone with no exceptions. Marsilius then concludes that

what Christ wanted was to pay tributes even if they were at certain places and times not due, rather than contend about such things; and to teach the apostle and his successors to pay them too. For this was the justice of counsel, not of command: a justice that Christ, in the humility of the flesh he had assumed, willed to carry out and taught should be carried out. And the Apostle also taught that this should be done, in the likeness of Christ.[57]

---

54 Matthew 17. 24–27.
55 *DP*, II, 4.10, trans. by Brett, p. 168.
56 *DP*, II, 4.11, trans. by Brett, p. 169.
57 *DP*, II, 4.11, trans. by Brett, p. 170.

Marsilius does not explicitly claim here that Christ 'in the humility of the flesh' was obliged to pay the tribute to Caesar — he just says that it was the just thing to do. However, it was in a most radical sense that his critics understood his position. The first of the propositions ascribed to Marsilius and condemned by John XXII in the *Licet iuxta doctrina* is indeed the claim that Christ did not pay the tribute 'by condescension, liberality, or piety', but because he was 'forced by necessity'.[58]

In the context of the interdict pamphlet war, the exegesis of these two passages from the Gospel was a hotspot, since it was linked to the issue of the legitimacy of clerical exemption from political authority. Establishing the reason why Christ paid the tribute and whether he was obliged to do so was relevant in determining whether Venice had the right to impose its laws on the goods and members of the clergy.[59] In this regard, Giovanni Marsilio had claimed that the exemption of clerics and ecclesiastical property from the secular authority was not *de iure divino* but *de iure humano*, and thus granted by the secular ruler. In support of his position, he had referred to the authority of the same authoritative personalities (Gerson excluded) whom Campanella had imagined in conversation in the *Antiveneti*, I, lamento 9: St Paul, John Chrysostom, Thomas Aquinas ('master of all theologians, only sun of the Catholic School'),[60] Domingo de Soto, and Diego de Covarrubias.[61]

To demonstrate that there was no evidence from the Gospels in support of the divine origin of clerical exemption, Giovanni proposed his own interpretation of Matthew 17. 24–27. Against the position of those who maintained that Christ and Peter were not obliged to pay the tribute to the temple based on Christ's words 'the children are free' (assuming that for 'children' one should intend 'clerics'), Giovanni presents two possible readings: either (G1) Jesus meant that the Jews, as 'sons' of that land, were free from paying the tribute, and thus Christ and Peter, who were Jews, were not obliged to pay it; or (G2) Jesus was not obliged to pay 'insofar as he was the son of God', but so as not to create scandal among the tax collectors of the secular princes, he paid anyway.[62] Neither of the

---

58 Denzinger, *Enchiridion symbolorum*, p. 213: 'Quod illud quod de Christo legitur in Evangelio beati Matthaei, quod ipse solvit tributum Caesari, quando staterem, sumptum ex ore piscis, illis qui petebant didrachma, iussit dari, hoc fecit non condescensive et liberalitate sive pietate, sed necessitate coactus'.

59 On the debates over clerical exemption in Rome, see Prodi, *Il sovrano pontefice*; and Frajese, 'Regno ecclesiastico e Stato moderno'.

60 Giovanni Marsilio, *Risposta d'un dottore*, p. [A4^v].

61 Giovanni Marsilio, *Risposta d'un dottore*, p. [C^{r-v}].

62 Giovanni Marsilio, *Risposta d'un dottore*, pp. [B^v–B2^r]: 'volle accennare la sua divinità, et dire, che come figlioulo di Dio non era obbligato a pagare il tributo. Ma perché il rendere questa ragione era troppo alto, et profondo Sacramento, del quale erano incapaci quelli essattori del Principe, disse, *sed ne scandalizentur*. Dove si vede quanto conto fece il Salvatore di non

two interpretations support the claim that clerical exemption has a divine origin. G1 would only imply that Jesus and Peter, as Jews, were exempt from a specific toll meant for foreigners. According to G2, the exemption would only apply to Jesus due to his divinity, and not to Peter or his successors.

Bellarmine's reaction was particularly strong on this point — maybe, also in this case, for personal reasons. The cardinal might have been sensitive regarding the issue of clerical exemption, since in his 1586 version of the controversies, *De clericis*, he himself had claimed that the origin of the exemption was *de iure humano*.[63] He had not gone as far as to deny the legitimacy of the special treatment traditionally destined to the clergy. However, he had maintained that ecclesiastical privileges were granted by princes and papal decrees, not by divine law. In the 1599 version of the controversies, perhaps due to pressures from the Roman Curia, Bellarmine changed his theory by stating that clerical exemption was *de iure humano et de iure divino*. With *ius divinum* in this case he did not mean a precept expressly found in the Scriptures (*ius divinum positivum*), as some canonists maintained, but something deduced by way of analogy (*de iure divinum naturali* or *de iure gentium*). According to this perspective, clerical exemption was not explicitly granted by Jesus; yet it could be deduced from the Holy Writ — for instance from the passage on the temple tax — and natural law, and could not be modified by temporal rulers.[64]

Despite Bellarmine's change of heart, his old theory of clerical exemption was an attractive source for the pro-Venetian writer, as witnessed by the way in which Sarpi exploited it to support the Venetian rights over ecclesiastical goods.[65] In his *Risposta* to Giovanni, Bellarmine was thus particularly driven to insist on his distance from his opponent's position. Bellarmine accused Giovanni of 'being fond of Marsilius of Padua, who said that Christ paid the tribute not out of condescension but because he was obliged to do so (*non condescensione, sed necessitate coactus*)', which, as mentioned above, was the first among the Marsilian propositions condemned by Pope John XXII. In connection to this, Bellarmine adds the authority of Torquemada, who reported the list of condemned theses in his *Summa de Ecclesia* (IV, pt. 2, ch. 37).[66] According to Bellarmine, both exegeses of Matthew 17. 26 proposed by Giovanni were problematic. (G1), stating that the Jews were free from the tribute because they were 'children

---

scandalizzare i ministri de Principi secolari, con allegare una vera, et reale, ma non da loro intesa esenzione'.

63 Bellarmine, *De clericis*, Ingolstadt 1586 edn, I, cols 1535–42. For Bellarmine's theory of clerical exemption and its development, see Tutino, *Empire of Souls*, pp. 82–88.

64 Bellarmine, *De clericis*, ed. by Fèvre (based on the 1599 edition), II, p. 489.

65 On this, Tutino, *Empire of Souls*, pp. 88–101.

66 Bellarmine, *Risposta a due libretti*, p. 18. Torquemada's account of Marsilius's errors can be found in Izbicki, 'The Reception of Marsilius', p. 333.

of the land', was a 'frivolous and useless' argument. According to Exodus 30, the Jews were not exempt from paying the tribute but in fact were the only ones obliged to pay it. (G2), on the other hand, would have possibly implied that, even if Christ were not obliged to pay the tribute insofar he was as the son of God, he was obliged to as a man. The fact that Giovanni had not tried to find arguments rejecting this latter position might have been a signal, according to Bellarmine, that Giovanni shared Marsilius's error:

> The second argument posits that Christ was exempt [from paying the tax] due to his divinity, not his humanity, and that as a man, he was obligated [to pay]; and this is what Marsilius of Padua maintained [...]. Now, I ask you: As a man, was or was not Christ obliged to pay the tribute? If you say he was obliged to, you declare yourself a companion of Marsilius, condemned as a heretic; if you say that he was not obliged to, you confess that your argument has no strength at all and you speak out of turn.[67]

Returning to this point while answering Giovanni's proposition v, Bellarmine argues that clerical exemption was not *de iure humano*, but *de iure divino*, as had been finally established by the Council of Trent (1545–1563). It looks like Bellarmine took a further step here towards a more conservative position. However, in a passage where he clarifies the meaning of the expression '*de iure divino*', his explanation aligns with what he had maintained in 1599:

> And one does not mean by *ius divino* the Holy Writ alone, but also the natural light (*lume naturale*), or, to better say, reason, and natural law: and so Giovanni Diedrone [... claims] that ecclesiastical exemption is *de iure divino* because it is taught and dictated by reason and natural light, as everyone naturally understands that the people and things consecrated to God are of God and there is no reason to support [the claim] that secular princes have power over them. And that this is a *lume naturale* can be known by the fact that in all religions — both the true and the false ones — this law of exemption was observed.[68]

Replying to Bellarmine's allegations, Giovanni counter-accused Bellarmine of not having understood his point or having deliberately distorted it,

---

67 Bellarmine, *Risposta a due libretti*, pp. 18–19: 'La seconda ragione fa Christo esente in quanto Dio, non in quanto huomo, et però in quanto huomo secondo te era obligato: & questo è quello che diceva Marsilio da Padova [...]. Hora io ti domando, Christo, come huomo era obligato, o non era obligato a pagare il tributo? Se dici che era obligato, ti dichiari compagno di Marsilio condennato per heretico, se dici che non era obligato, confessi che la tua ragione non ha forza veruna, & non parli a proposito'.
68 Bellarmine, *Risposta a due libretti*, pp. 31–32.

bending the laws of grammar and fighting dirty. Bellarmine, who blamed Giovanni for endorsing heretical positions, had actually espoused those very doctrines himself:

> All of this is taken *ad verbum* from *De clericis* I, ch. 28, of the *Signor Cardinale*, from which one understands the extent of the presumptuous ignorance or negligent malignity of he who claimed that in the doctrine of the author [i.e. Giovanni] one could find *Brentianate, Calviniate*, and *Marsiliate da Padova*. But the author does not say with Marsilius of Padua that Christ paid the tribute as forced by necessity — granted that Marsilius himself said this thing (*se pur egli disse quella opinione condannata*) — but that he paid so as not to create scandal.[69]

Before finally presenting Campanella's position on this matter, it is interesting to notice how here Giovanni Marsilio mentions *en passant* the idea that Marsilius himself had never defended the proposition of which he was accused by his adversaries — that is, that Christ paid the tribute *necessitate coactus*. This has been read as a clue that, contrary to many of his contemporaries, Campanella included, Giovanni had indeed read the *Defensor pacis*.[70]

Campanella's critique of Giovanni in *MDM*, XIII shares similarities with that of Bellarmine, including the association of the 'modern pseudo-theologian' with Marsilius of Padua.[71] As for *why* Christ and the clergy were *not* obliged to pay tribute (against what 'Marsilio dannato' believed), Campanella's position nevertheless diverged from that of Bellarmine. Like Bellarmine, Campanella argued that the only reason why Christ paid the tribute was to avoid scandal among those who would not have understood the concepts of clerical exemption or natural and divine law. However, he firmly believed that the origin of the clerical exemption was *de iure divino* (i.e. *de iure divino positivo*).[72] In some historical circumstances throughout history, popes and members of the clergy, despite being exempted *de iure divino*, had indeed allowed secular rulers to impose, *de facto*, secular jurisdiction over them. The imposition of a secular ruler happened, however, with 'usurpation of power, and not with power'; and the popes and clerics

---

69 Giovanni Marsilio, *Difesa*, p. 60.

70 On this point, see Piaia, *Marsilio da Padova nella Riforma e nella Controriforma*, p. 393, n. 57. For further exchanges between Bellarmine and Giovanni Marsilio on this matter, I refer to the analysis provided by Piaia at pp. 390–95.

71 *MDM*, XIII, p. 118: '[against G1:] e solo i giudei erano obbligati a questa guisa. Dunque non erano essenti essi soli, come dice il Pseudo Theologo. Ma di nullo modo era obbligato Christo pagare, se non come pare a Marsilio dannato'; cf. *MM*, XIII, pp. 302–04.

72 For the theory of the origin *de iure divino*, Campanella refers to Soto's *De iustitia et iure*, VI, q. 5 and q. 6, art. 7, remarking, however, that Soto changed his mind in his *In IV Sententiarum*, where he stated that the exemption is *de iure humano*; cf. *MDM*, XIII, p. 118 and *MM*, XIII, p. 302.

allowed it only *permissive* and through dissimulation, to avoid scandals.[73] 'Christ paid [the tribute]', Campanella remarks, 'as today our clergymen [living in the Turkish Empire] pay it to the Turks'.[74]

When, in *MDM*, XIV, Campanella returns to the verse, 'Render therefore unto Caesar the things which are Caesar's; and unto God the things that are God's', he bluntly concludes: 'but everything is God's and nothing Caesar's, if not insofar as it depends on God; therefore, since the pope represents God, everything depends on him'.[75] Campanella's theory of *dominium* takes seriously the idea that *dominus*, understood in an absolute sense, is only God, while human beings are only *domini secundum quid* or *per partecipationem*, as *dominium* is granted by God or his vicar, who can decide to withhold it *ratione peccati*.[76] This applies retrospectively as well to the kingdoms that came before the Incarnation, or to those people who did not know about the coming of Christ. It is not coincidental that in his Latin version of the *Monarchia del Messia* Campanella would include the Latin translation of *Discorso delle ragioni che ha il re cattolico sopra il nuovo emisfero*, where he applies the results of his theories on *dominium* to the theologico-juridical issue concerning the rights of the Spanish over the New World.[77] Needless to say, Marsilius of Padua's theory was diametrically opposed to Campanella's on this matter. But Campanella's perspective would also have been unacceptable to Bellarmine, both according to his theory of *dominium* (based on the *ius gentium*), and to his understanding of the papal office as endowed with only an indirect power *in temporalibus*.

After the Order of Melchizedek

The last passage in which Campanella refers to Marsilius is another *locus classicus* for the discussion of the relationship *regnum-sacerdotium* and the nature of the papal office. Specifically, it addresses the question of whether the pope was a priest according to a priesthood of exclusively spiritual nature, like that of Aaron and the Levites, or a priesthood that combined spiritual and temporal powers, like Melchizedek's.[78] Defined in Genesis 14. 18 as the King of Salem and 'priest of God Most High',

---

73 *MDM*, XIII, p. 118; cf. *MM*, XIII, p. 302.

74 *MDM*, XIII, p. 118: 'E [Christo] pagò, come hoggi li clerici nostri pagano al turco. E nota, che per se e per Pietro pagò, non per gli altri apostoli, perché solo Pietro rappresenta Christo con tutte le potestà del Messia, e soffre quel che Christo soffre per l'edificazione del christianesimo'; cf. *MM*, XIII, p. 304.

75 *MDM*, XIV, p. 133; cf. *MM*, XIV, pp. 371–72.

76 *MDM*, I, pp. 47–48.

77 *MM*, Appendix (*Sermo de iuribus regis catholici super novum Hemispherium*), pp. 424–60.

78 For the use of the figure of Melchizedek in medieval political discussions, see Ullmann, 'Frederick II's Opponent, Innocent IV, as Melchisedek'; Pennington, 'Pope Innocent III's

Melchizedek was identified as a 'type' of Christ in Hebrew 7. 17, where the claim of Psalm 110, 'You are a priest forever according to the order of Melchizedek', was referred to as a prophecy of Christ. In *Per venerabilem*, Pope Innocent III extended the use of this reference to Christ's vicar, using it to justify the papal exercise, *casualiter*, of secular jurisdiction.

While defending his own understanding of the pope as a priest 'according to the order of Melchizedek', Campanella associates the name of Marsilius, alongside Dante Alighieri, to the two doctors of Salamanca:

> Dante was greatly mistaken when he said that the pope must have no temporal dominion because he was of the lineage of the sons of Levi; for the pope is not Levitical but Melchizedekkian [*melchisedecchio*]. And the disregard of this point leads Covarrubias, Soto, Marsilius, and the 'ultramontane' heretics to err. And, while disputing with one of them, I forced him to say that the pope was a priest according to Aron, to defend their wickedness.[79]

Marsilius had discussed the figure of Melchizedek in relation to the papal office in *DP*, II, 28.22 while answering an argument by authority brought by the supporters of the secular jurisdiction of the pope and his role of head of the Church. This argument consists of a passage from *De consideratione ad Eugenium III papam* (II, 8), reported by Marsilius in *DP*, II, 27.11, in which Bernard of Clairvaux defended the highest role of the pontiff by associating him with several figures from the Old Testament, Melchizedek included.[80] According to Marsilius, such a 'highest role' advocated by Bernard should not be understood as belonging to the pope 'by direct divine ordination or by a command of divine law' but rather 'by human election or institution'.[81] As regards the association with Melchisedek, Marsilius remarked that

> this is so with regard to the priesthood, in which Melchisedech prefigured Christ; and in the same way so too are all other priests. But it is not so with regard to the realm, because in this respect Melchisedech, who was both king and priest, was the figure only for Christ and for no other priest. Neither moreover did he prefigure Christ in respect of worldly kingdom, because Christ did not come, nor did he wish, to reign in this way, as shown in chapter 4 of this discourse. Rather, Melchisedech, who was at once priest and worldly

---

Views on Church and State'; Kuehn, 'Melchizedek as Exemplar for Kingship'. For Melchizedek in Campanella, see Headley, *Tommaso Campanella*, pp. 247–314.

79 *MDM*, IX, p. 85; cf. *MM*, IX, p. 164.

80 For Bernard of Clairvaux's position, see Kuehn, 'Melchizedek as Exemplar for Kingship'.

81 *DP*, II, 28.22, trans. by Brett, p. 505.

king, prefigured the priesthood of Christ and his heavenly kingdom, not any worldly kingdom.[82]

According to Marsilius, Bernard's reference to Melchizedek was thus to be understood simply in terms of a spiritual priesthood, shared equally by the Bishop of Rome and the other priests, and not to secular jurisdiction. Similarly, the correct understanding of the figure of Melchizedek as Christ-like was not a claim concerning Christ's kingship in this world but in the heavenly kingdom. Campanella held an opposite understanding of the figure of Melchizedek. He saw Melchizedek as a prefiguration of both spiritual and secular priesthood and kingship, applicable to both Christ and his vicar.

Returning to the passage of the *MDM* where Campanella mentions Marsilius concerning this point, it is interesting to consider who might have been the 'one of them' with whom Campanella had a discussion on this matter. The mysterious interlocutor could have been neither Soto nor Covarrubias for chronological reasons. He might certainly have been an unidentified reformed theologian. Frajese, however, proposes an intriguing (though not demonstrable) hypothesis: that the reference to 'Marsilio' in this passage might also refer, perhaps covertly, to Giovanni Marsilio himself, and not to the Paduan.[83] Giovanni indeed explicitly supported the priesthood according to Aron and the Levites in his pamphlet.[84]

Setting this riddle aside, whether Campanella was referring here to Marsilius of Padua or to Giovanni Marsilio with the name 'Marsilio' does not have much consequence, especially for how the two authors were ideally juxtaposed in the pamphlet war. What is relevant is that Campanella believed that Covarrubias and Soto (as well as Bellarmine, although Campanella does not mention him here) shared the same mistake made by both Dante and Marsilius in not acknowledging the pontiff as supreme *rex et sacerdos*. According to Campanella, the theory of the indirect power of the pope *in temporalibus* is just as erroneous as the doctrine of those who denied it completely.

With regards to the papacy 'after the order of Melchizedek', it is interesting to see, once again, how Giovanni, Bellarmine, and Campanella understood the *auctoritas* of Aquinas on the matter — that is, II *Sent.*, dist. 44, q. 2, a. 3, where Aquinas claims that the pope is the *apex* at which both the secular and the spiritual powers unite, and is eternally *rex et sacerdos*, *secundum ordinem Melchisedech*. According to Giovanni, here Aquinas was exclusively referring to the power of the pope over his own lands.[85] On

---

82 *DP*, II, 28.22, trans. by Brett, p. 506.
83 Frajese, 'Introduzione', p. 8.
84 Giovanni Marsilio, *Risposta d'un dottore*, p. [A3^v].
85 Giovanni Marsilio, *Risposta d'un dottore*, p. [B3^{r-v}].

the other hand, Bellarmine held the view that, according to Aquinas, the pope was really the *apex* of both powers, but in different ways — that is, directly in spiritual matters and indirectly *in temporalibus*. Thus, Christians should obey *in temporalibus* the pope more than the secular rulers, insofar as the temporal matters in question regarded the *salus animae*.[86] Discussing this point in the Latin *MM*, vi, Campanella took Aquinas's passage in the strongest sense, namely that the pope and heir of Melchizedek had a direct power in both domains.[87]

Potestas directa, Thomism(s), and Aristotle's Blindness

In May 1621, Campanella submitted three of his books to the *Congregazione dell'Indice* — the *Quod reminiscentur*, the *Atheismus triumphatus*, and *Monarchia Messiae* — for the attention of Cardinal Bellarmine and three other censors who would decide whether their publication should be allowed.[88] Despite the mildly benevolent judgement given by Bellarmine, the three censors denied the authorization and listed nine objections to Campanella's doctrines: the last one concerned his adherence to the theory of direct papal power in temporal matters. In the *Apologeticum*, composed to respond to the accusation and addressed to Bellarmine, Campanella acknowledged that he had maintained the censored position and reaffirmed that stating the contrary was an error. He supported his stance with historical evidence and biblical passages proving that the pope was *rex et sacerdos secundum ordinem Melchisedech*, citing the authority of Aquinas and Pope Boniface VIII's *Unam sanctam*.[89] The *Apologeticum* was later incorporated as an appendix to *Monarchia Messiae*, xiii in a version containing a richer portfolio of *auctoritates* and a more developed counter-accusation against his censors: denying that the pope had power in temporal and spiritual affairs *directe* was an error in *philosophia* and in *theologica politia*.[90] Furthermore, it was a matter concerning the true understanding of Aquinas and of Thomistic identity, which to Campanella represented quite a personal concern: 'for I belong to the Thomist chorus [*in thomistarum choro*]', he claims, 'I could not agree with those who affirm

---

86 Cf. Bellarmine, *De summo Pontifice*, v, 5, ed. by Fèvre, ii, p. 153.

87 *MM*, vi, p. 141.

88 Ernst, 'Il ritrovato "Apologeticum"'. On the vicissitudes around this examination and around the publication more than ten years later of the *Monarchia Messiae*, see also Ponzio, 'Introduction', pp. 16–20.

89 Ernst, 'Il ritrovato "Apologeticum"', pp. 585–86.

90 *MM*, xiii, Appendix, p. 328.

BETWEEN VENICE AND SANT'ELMO   349

that the pope has power over the secular kings indirectly, including in temporal matters'. As for Bellarmine:

> although he might have a good understanding of the matter, he does not speak well according to the intention of St Thomas, nor with a fitting vocabulary [...]. If within the Thomist doctrine I say that the pope rules the laymen in temporal matters indirectly, and directly only in spiritual matters, I would render him neither a lord *per se*, nor *per accident*, but much less.[91]

According to Campanella, recognizing the absolute fullness of papal power means interpreting Aquinas correctly — that is, in light of a total identification of *regnum et sacerdotium*, nature and grace, politics and religion.[92] This idea of unity — which transcended the categories employed in human logic and was centred in the figure of Christ as *prima ragione* and supreme leader — was already present in one passage of the aforementioned letter addressed to Pope Paul V in September 1606:

> Those who say *directe, indirecte, in temporalibus, in spiritualibus, per se, per accidens*, say something about power, but they express themselves through human and not divine logic, which would say instead the following: Christ is first reason, wisdom, word of God, father. Thus, all things of the world, being guided by the first reason, are subject to him, in heaven and earth. [...] Thus, the vicar of first Reason and first Wisdom is Head and Shepherd of all human beings endowed with reason, and therefore of all mankind. Included also are the Turks, the infidels, who are rebellious members and subjects.[93]

One can easily recognize that the targets of this critique include Soto, Covarrubias, and Bellarmine; one can also see that they were targets of a criticism found in *La monarchia del Messia*, XIV, where Campanella claims that those who do not recognize the truth of the absolute power of the pontiff

---

91 *MM*, XIII, Appendix, p. 331. A similar reproach to Bellarmine is found in Campanella, *Discorsi universali del governo ecclesiastico*, ed. by Firpo, p. 478: 'E in ciò predicheranno a' prencipi la potestà papale sopra tutti *de iure divino et naturali et positivo*, come prova S. Tomaso nel libro *De regimine principum*; e si guardino da quel che scrive Bellarmino e altri, venduti a' prencipi secolari'.

92 In this regard, Frajese uses the expression 'consumazione della filosofia di Tommaso', cf. 'Introduzione', p. 37.

93 Campanella, *Lettere*, no. 13, ed. by Ernst, pp. 71–72. This point was further restated throughout *MDM*, whose subtitle recites: 'Dove con *philosofia humana et divina* si mostrano le raggioni del dominio universale del Sommo Pontefice sopra tutto l'universo in temporale et spirituale, e (del)le ragioni de prencipi ecclesiastici e secolari sopra vassalli loro, con modo mirabile *non inteso dalli scrittori sin hora* per confonder gli heretici e scismatici e smorzare le discordie de prencipi' (italics mine).

do not consider Christ as a humanized God and as first reason who is architect and ruler of everything, but as a promotor of a restricted and not universal dominion; and they confined Christ by binding him to the rules of Aristotle, who did not know what providence was, nor of the age to come, nor the virtue of religion, nor the universal monarchy, which he believed to be impossible.[94]

To summarize: Christ, the first Reason, who held both temporal and spiritual power, handed such power completely to his vicar — and this over all the world and since the beginning of time, even before Incarnation, even over those kingdoms who were not yet evangelized. Those who denied this twofold universal power of the pope (like Marsilius of Padua, but also those doctors of the Catholic Church who did not understand Aquinas's doctrine correctly) spoke only from a human perspective, and reduced Christ to the rules of Aristotle, who did not know revelation and could not have had an eschatological perspective.

According to Campanella, this lack of prophetic vision in Aristotle is not only due to the fact that the Stagirite lived before the Incarnation, but also consists in his incapacity to see the bigger picture in the political matter and go beyond what exists in the present. For instance, Aristotle was not able to conceive of the possibility of a universal kingdom;[95] most importantly, Aristotle was not capable of understanding the strength of the political vision offered by Plato in the *Republic*, which he criticized as counterfactual and impossible to be put into practice in the second book of the *Politics*.

Campanella made this point explicitly in the fourth *quaestio* in defence of his most famous work, the *City of the Sun*, where he upholds the utility of writing about non-existent commonwealths.[96] Against the opinion of those who 'philosophize in the Aristotelian manner', Campanella maintains that writing *utopie* (or *eucronie*)[97] is helpful and licit for two reasons. First, because the image of a perfect society might serve as a model, an inspiration for improvement, although that perfect goal may remain unattainable. Second, because the perfect commonwealth that he portrayed in the *Optima republica*, which actually existed in the Edenic state, is in part still put into practice within some religious communities in the present, and will be fully realized again at the end of the time after the fall of the Antichrist, when humanity will be united as *unum*

---

94 *MDM*, XIV, p. 127; *MM*, XIV, p. 346.

95 *MDM*, III, pp. 63–64; *MM*, III, pp. 102–04.

96 Campanella, *Quaestio quarta de optima republica*, q. 4, a. 1, ed. by Ernst, pp. 96–122.

97 According to Frajese (cf. 'Introduzione', *Profezia e machiavellismo*, and elsewhere), the *City of the Sun*, while being written in the style of utopian literature, is actually a messianic text since Campanella portrays there the kind of society which he believed would come into existence at the end of times.

ovile under *unus pastor*, under the rule of Christ.[98] It was thus in going beyond the 'blindness' of Aristotle that Campanella imagined his utopian (or, more accurately, messianic) society in the *City of the Sun*, redefined the relationship between *regnum* and *sacerdotium* and the extent of papal power, and conceived his *nova philosophia*.

At the beginning of his *Defensor pacis*, when defining the purpose of his work, Marsilius of Padua speaks of a 'darkness' within which the people 'have been plunged as a result of [some] discord or strife among themselves'. He presents the aim of his work as an unfolding of the 'highly contagious' cause of that discord that had infected the Roman Empire and political communities generally, and of which 'neither Aristotle nor any other philosopher of his time or earlier could have recognised the origin and species'.[99] According to Marsilius, the cause of the disease, hidden to Aristotle and unfolded by the *Defensor pacis*, was the dangerous ambition of the Holy See on secular matters. The 'Aristotle' which is at the centre of Campanella's critique was equally blind concerning the future office of the pontiff and its functions, his blindness, however, prevented him from seeing something which, in Campanella's opinion, was not a disease but a remedy.

Conclusions

Reconsidering the presence of Marsilius in Campanella's work, this chapter has re-examined the two (interconnected) categories under which the name of the Paduan was understood and employed: Marsilius the Aristotelian, and Marsilius the critic of the pontiff's claims *in temporalibus*. The combined image that emerges turns out to be the negative of Campanella — who was in contrast a champion of direct papal power both *in spiritualibus et temporalibus*, and the promoter of a 'new [anti-Aristotelian] philosophy'. We have then analysed Campanella's references to Marsilius in the *Antiveneti* and in *La monarchia del Messia* more closely, and we have put them into dialogue with the positions — and the modalities to refer to *auctoritates* or anti-*auctoritates* — of Giovanni Marsilio (a modern *avatar* of the Paduan) and Robert Bellarmine (a champion of the *potestas indirecta*, representing a middle-way between the anti-papalism of the pro-Venetian writers and the ultra-theocratic vision endorsed by Campanella himself). This analysis showed how Campanella conceived of his theologico-political vision not only as opposed to the positions of the *Novus Marsilius* from Naples, but also to those authors belonging to the Thomistic tradition who, in his view, did not understand Aquinas

---

98 Campanella, *Quaestio quarta de optima republica*, q. 4, a. 1, ed. by Ernst, pp. 110–12.

99 *DP*, I, 3, trans. by Brett, p. 5.

properly and who, by defending the theory of the *potestas indirecta*, failed to recognize the real power of Christ's vicar. In this story, the figure of Marsilius of Padua played the role of a suitable anti-*auctoritas*, useful to Campanella as a rhetorical weapon to reinforce his stance against his most direct polemical targets.

Works Cited

Primary Sources

Bellarmine, Robert, *De clericis*, in Robert Bellarmine, *Opera Omnia*, ed. by Justin Fèvre (Paris: Vivès, 1870), II, pp. 415–97

——, *De clericis*, in *Disputationes de Controversiis Christianiae fidei*, 3 vols (Ingolstadt: David Sartorius, 1586–1589), I (1586), cols 1416–1542

——, *De summo Pontifice*, in Robert Bellarmine, *Opera Omnia*, ed. by Justin Fèvre (Paris: Vivès, 1870), I, pp. 449–615; II, pp. 5–185

——, *Risposta alla difesa delle otto propositioni di Giovanni Marsilio Napolitano* (Naples: Tarquinio Longo, 1606)

——, *Risposta del Card. Bellarmino a due libretti, Uno de' quali s'intitola Risposta d'un dottore in theologia [...] Et l'altro, Trattato, & risolutione sopra la validità delle Scomuniche di Gio. Gersone Theologo [...]* (Viterbo, Girolamo Discepolo, 1606)

Campanella, Tommaso, *Antiveneti*, ed. by Luigi Firpo (Florence: Leo S. Olschki, 1945)

——, *Apologeticum = Resposta all'opposizioni del Bellarmino non sue, ma referiteli d'altri, chi solo li titoli lessero delli libri miei, perché solo pensaro d'impedir la stampa come che potessero*, in Germana Ernst, 'Il ritrovato "Apologeticum" di Campanella al Bellarmino in difesa della religione naturale', *Rivista di storia della filosofia*, 47.3 (1992), 571–86

——, *Avvertimenti a Venezia*, in Germana Ernst, 'Ancora sugli ultimi scritti politici di Campanella: II. Gli *Avvertimenti a Venezia* del 1636', *Bruniana & Campanelliana*, 5.2 (1999), 452–65

——, *La città del sole / Civitas solis*, ed. by Tonino Tornitore (Turin: Aragno, 2008)

——, *De gentilismo non retinendo*, in *Ludovico justo xiii Regi christianissimo [...] dedicat Fr. Tommaso Campanella [...] tres hosce libello [...]* (Paris: Toussaint Dubray, 1636), 63 pp.

——, *Dialogo politico tra un Veneziano, Spagnolo e Francese, circa li rumori passati di Francia*, in Tommaso Campanella, *Opere*, ed. by Germana Ernst, introd. by Nicola Badaloni (Rome: Istituto Poligrafico e Zecca dello Stato, 1999), pp. 955–93

——, *Discorsi universali del governo ecclesiastico*, in Giordano Bruno e Tommaso Campanella, *Scritti scelti*, ed. by Luigi Firpo (Turin: Utet, 1949), pp. 465–523

——, *Discorso terzo a Venezia = Discorso terzo, come corollario del primo e del secondo, a Venezia per l'union sua col papato per ben suo proprio e del cristianesimo d'Italia*, in Germana Ernst, 'Ancora sugli ultimi scritti politici di Campanella: I. Gli inediti *Discorsi ai principi* in favore del papato', *Bruniana & Campanelliana*, 5.1 (1999), 149–53

————, *Lettere*, ed. by Giovanna Ernst, based upon preliminary unedited material by Luigi Firpo, with Laura Salvetti and Matteo Salvetti, Le corrispondenze letterarie, scientifiche ed erudite dal Rinascimento all'età moderna, 12 (Florence: Leo S. Olschki, 2010)

————, *La Monarchia del Messia*, ed. by Vittorio Frajese, Temi e testi, n.s., 35 (Rome: Edizioni di storia e letteratura, 1995)

————, *Monarchia Messiae*: Tommaso Campanella, *Monarchie du Messie*, ed. by Paolo Ponzio, French trans. by Véronique Bourdette, Fondaments de la politique (Paris: Presse Universitaire de France, 2002)

————, *Le Poesie*, ed. by Francesco Giancotti (Milano: Bompiani, 2013); English trans. *Selected Philosophical Poems of Tommaso Campanella: A Bilingual Edition*, trans. by Sherry Roush (Chicago: University of Chicago Press, 2011)

————, *Quaestio quarta de optima republica*, in Tommaso Campanella, *La città del sole: Questione quarta sull'ottima repubblica*, ed. by Germana Ernst (Milano: BUR, 2006; repr. 2007), pp. 96–173

————, *Quod reminiscetur et convertentur ad dominum universi fines terrae (Psal. xxi). Libri I & II*, ed. by Romano Amerio (Padua: Ex officina libraria Cedam, 1939)

[Giovanni Marsilio], *Difesa di Giovanni Marsilio a favore della Risposta dell'otto Propositioni contro la quale ha scritto l'illustrissimo et reverendissimo sig. cardinal Bellarmino* (Venice: Roberto Meietti, 1606)

————, *Essame sopra tutte quelle scritture, che sin hora sono state mandate alle stampe da alcuni, parte senza nome di autore, parte sotto finti e suppositi [...] contro la giustissima causa della Serenissima Repubblica di Venezia* (Venice: Roberto Meietti, 1607)

————, *Risposta d'un dottore in theologia ad una lettera scrittagli da un Reverendo suo Amico, sopra il Breve di Censure dalla Santità di Papa Paolo V pubblicate contro li Signori Venetiani, et sopra la nullità di dette Censure, cavata dalla Sacra Scrittura, dalli Santi Padri, & da altri Cattolici Dottori* ([n.p.]: [n.pub.], 1606)

Marsilius of Padua, *The Defender of the Peace*, trans. by Annabel Brett, Cambridge Texts in the History of Political Thought (Cambridge: Cambridge University Press, 2005)

Secondary Works

Addante, Luca, 'Campanella e Machiavelli: Indagine su un caso di dissimulazione', *Studi Storici*, 45.3 (2004), 727–50

Amabile, Luigi, *Fra Tommaso Campanella, la sua congiura, i suoi processi e la sua pazzia*, 3 vols, (Naples: Morano, 1882)

————, *Fra Tommaso Campanella ne' castelli di Napoli, in Roma ed in Parigi*, 2 vols (Naples: Morano, 1887)

Benzoni, Gino, 'I teologi minori dell'interdetto', *Archivio veneto*, Ser. 5, 91 (1970), 31–108

Bouwsma, William J., *Venice and the Defense of Republican Liberty: Renaissance Values in the Age of the Counter Reformation* (Berkeley: University of California Press, 1968)

Cassell, Anthony K., *The 'Monarchia' Controversy: An Historical Study with Accompanying Translations of Dante Alighieri's 'Monarchia', Guido Vernani's 'Refutation of the "Monarchia" composed by Dante', and Pope John XXII'S Bull 'Si fratrum'* (Washington, DC: Catholic University of America Press, 2004)

Caye, Pierre, 'Campanella critique de Machiavel. La politique: De la non-philosophie à la métaphysique', *Bruniana & Campanelliana*, 8.2 (2002), 333–51

Condren, Conal, 'Democracy and the *Defensor Pacis*: On the English Language Tradition of Marsilian Interpretation', *Il Pensiero Politico*, 13 (1980), 301–16

Cozzi, Gaetano, *Paolo Sarpi tra Venezia e l'Europa*, Piccola biblioteca Einaudi, 365 (Turin: Einaudi, 1979)

De Lucca, Jean Paul, '*Ius gentium*', in *Enciclopedia bruniana e campanelliana*, II: *Giornate di studi 2005-2008*, ed. by Eugenio Cantone and Germana Ernst (Pisa: Serra, 2010), pp. 134–40

De Mattei, Rodolfo, *Il pensiero politico italiano nell'età della Controriforma*, 2 vols (Milano: Ricciardi, 1982)

Denzinger, Heinrich, *Enchiridion symbolorum definitionum et declarationum de rebus fidei et morum* (Freiburg: Herder, 1911)

Duplessis d'Argentré, Charles, *Collectio judiciorum de novis erroribus*, 3 vols (Paris: Cailleau, 1728)

Ernst, Germana, 'Ancora sugli ultimi scritti politici di Campanella: I. Gli inediti *Discorsi ai principi* in favore del papato', *Bruniana & Campanelliana*, 5.1 (1999), 131–53

——, 'Ancora sugli ultimi scritti politici di Campanella: II. Gli *Avvertimenti a Venezia* del 1636', *Bruniana & Campanelliana*, 5.2 (1999), 447–65

——, 'Introduzione: Storia di un testo', in Tommaso Campanella, *L'ateismo trionfato ovvero riconoscimento filosofico della religione universale contra l'antichristianesmo macchiavellesco*, vol. I (Pisa: Scuola Normale Superiore, 2004), pp. vii–lv

——, 'La mauvaise raison d'Etat: Campanella contre Machiavel et les Politiques', in *Raison et Déraison d'Etat: Théoriciens et Théories de la Raison d'Etat aux XVIe et XVIIe siècle*, ed. by Yves-Charles Zarka (Paris: Presses universitaires de France, 1994), pp. 121–49

——, 'Il ritrovato "Apologeticum" di Campanella al Bellarmino in difesa della religione naturale', *Rivista di storia della filosofia*, 47.3 (1992), 565–86

——, *Tommaso Campanella: Il libro e il corpo della natura* (Rome: Laterza, 2002); English trans. *Tommaso Campanella: The Books and the Body of Nature*, trans. by David L. Marshall (Dordrecht: Springer, 2010)

————, ed., *Tommaso Campanella e la congiura di Calabria* (Stilo: Comune di Stilo, 2001)

Firpo, Luigi, 'Campanella contro Aristotele in difesa della "Città del Sole"', *Il Pensiero Politico*, 15 (1982), 375–89

————, 'Non Paolo Sarpi, ma Tommaso Campanella', *Giornale Storico della Letterature Italiana*, 158 (1981), 254–74

————, *I processi di Tommaso Campanella* (Roma: Salerno, 1998)

Fournel, Jean-Louis, *La cité du soleil et les territoires des hommes: Le savoir de monde chez Campanella* (Paris: Albin Michel, 2012)

Frajese, Vittorio, 'Campanella a Sant'Elmo nell'estate 1606: Due documenti e alcune considerazioni', *Studi Storici*, 40.1 (1999), 263–78

————, 'Cultura machiavellica e profezia messianica nella riflessione politica di Tommaso Campanella: Dalla congiura all'interdetto', in *Repubblica e virtù: Pensiero politico e monarchia cattolica fra XVI and XVII secolo*, ed. by Chiara Continisio and Cesare Mozzarelli (Rome: Bulzoni, 1995), pp. 243–79

————, 'Introduzione', in Tommaso Campanella, *La Monarchia del Messia*, ed. by Vittorio Frajese, Temi e testi, n.s., 35 (Rome: Edizioni di storia e letteratura, 1995), pp. 5–41

————, 'La "Monarchia del Messia" di Tommaso Campanella: Identificazione di un testo tra profetismo e controriforma', *Quaderni storici*, 3 (1994), 723–68

————, *Profezia e machiavellismo: Il giovane Campanella* (Rome: Carocci, 2002)

————, 'Regno ecclesiastico e Stato moderno: La polemica fra Francisco Peña e Roberto Bellarmino sull'esenzione dei clerici', *Annali dell'Istituto Storico Italo-Germanico in Trento*, 14 (1988), 273–339

————, *Sarpi scettico: Stato e chiesa a Venezia tra Cinque e Seicento* (Bologna: Il Mulino, 1994)

————, 'Una teoria della censura: Bellarmino e il potere indirettto dei papi', *Studi Storici*, 25.1 (1984), 139–52

Giacchi, Orio, 'Osservazioni sulla fortuna delle idee di Marsilio da Padova nell'età del giurisdizionalismo', in *Marsilio da Padova: Studi raccolti nel VI centenario della morte*, ed. by Aldo Checchini and Norberto Bobbio, Pubblicazioni della Facoltà di giurisprudenza dell'Università di Padova, 3 (Padua: CEDAM, 1942), pp. 167–90

Giacon, Carlo, *La seconda scolastica*, III: *I problemi giuridico-politici: Suarez, Bellarmino, Mariana*, Archivum philosophicum Aloisianum, s. 2, 6 (Milan; F.lli Bocca, 1950)

Headley, John M., *Tommaso Campanella and the Transformation of the World* (Princeton, NJ: Princeton University Press, 1997)

Höpfl, Harro, *Jesuit Political Thought: The Society of Jesus and the State, c. 1540–1630* (Cambridge: Cambridge University Press, 2004)

Izbicki, Thomas M., 'The Reception of Marsilius', in *A Companion to Marsilius of Padua*, ed. by Gerson Moreno-Riaño and Cary J. Nederman, Brill's Companions to the Christian Tradition, 31 (Leiden: Brill, 2012), pp. 305–34

Kuehn, Evan F., 'Melchizedek as Exemplar for Kingship in Twelfth-Century Political Thought', *History of Political Thought*, 31.4 (2010), 557–75

Moiso, Marta, 'La libertà e la grazia: Campanella critico di Bellarmino', *Bruniana & Campanelliana*, 14.1 (2008), 127–35

Motta, Franco, *Bellarmino: Una teologia politica della Controriforma* (Brescia: Morcelliana, 2005)

Mulieri, Alessandro, 'Against Classical Republicanism: The Averroist Foundations of Marsilius of Padua's Political Thought', *History of Political Thought*, 40.2 (2019), 218–45

Oakley, Francis, 'Complexities of Context: Gerson, Bellarmine, Sarpi, Richer, and the Venetian Interdict of 1606–1607', *Catholic Historical Review*, 82.3 (1996), 369–96

Panichi, Alessio, *Il volto fragile del potere: Religione e politica nel pensiero di Tommaso Campanella* (Pisa: ETS, 2015)

Pennington, Kenneth, 'Pope Innocent III's Views on Church and State: A Gloss to *Per venerabilem*' in *Law, Church, and Society: Essays in Honor of Stephan Kuttner*, ed. by Kenneth Pennington and Robert Somerville (Philadelphia: University of Pennsylvania Press, 1977), pp. 49–67

Piaia, Gregorio, '"Averroïsme politique": Anatomie d'un mythe historiographique', in *Orientalische Kultur und europäisches Mittelalter*, ed. by Albert Zimmermann and Ingrid Craemer-Ruegenberg, comp. by Gudrun Vuillemin-Diem, Miscellanea Mediaevalia, 17 (Berlin: De Gruyter, 1985), pp. 288–300

——, 'Dalla *Politica* di Aristotele all'"averroismo politico": Una vicenda paradossale', *Mediterranea: International Journal on the Transfer of Knowledge*, 3 (2018), 19–34

——, *Marsilio da Padova nella Riforma e nella Controriforma: Fortuna ed interpretazione*, Pubblicazioni dell'Istituto di storia della filosofia e del Centro per ricerche di filosofia medioevale, Università di Padova, n.s., 24 (Padua: Antenore, 1977)

——, 'La "presenza" di Marsilio da Padova in Tommaso Campanella', in *Logica e semantica ed altri saggi*, ed. by Carlo Giacon, Pubblicazioni dell'Istituto di Storia della Filosofia e del Centro per Ricerche di Filosofia Medioevale, n.s., 17 (Padua: Antenore, 1975), pp. 183–98

Pirillo, Diego, '"Questo buon monaco non ha inteso il Macchiavello": Reading Campanella in Sarpi's Shadow', *Bruniana & Campanelliana*, 20.1 (2014), 129–44

Pirri, Pietro, *L'Interdetto di Venezia del 1606 e i gesuiti: Silloge di documenti con introduzione*, Bibliotheca Instituti historici Societatis Iesu, 14 (Rome: Institutum Historicum S.I., 1959)

Plouchart-Cohn, Florence, 'Il "Dialogo tra un veneziano, spagnolo e francese" di Tommaso Campanella fra storia e profezia', *Bruniana & Campanelliana*, 10.2 (2004), 319–32

——, 'Venezia', *Bruniana & Campanelliana*, 13.2 (2007), 589–95

Ponzio, Paolo, 'Introduction', in Tommaso Campanella, *Monarchie du Messie*, ed. by Paolo Ponzio, French trans. by Véronique Bourdette, Fondaments de la politique (Paris: Presse Universitaire de France, 2002), pp. 9–36

——, *Tommaso Campanella: Filosofia della natura e teoria della scienza* (Bari: Levante, 2010)

Prodi, Paolo, *Il sovrano pontefice: Un corpo e due anime; la monarchia papale nella prima età moderna* (Bologna: Il mulino, 1982; repr. 2013)

Ricci, Saverio, *Campanella: Apocalisse e governo universale* (Rome: Salerno, 2018)

Sgarro, Tommaso, *Un inquieto domenicano: Temi e figure della Seconda scolastica nella filosofia di Tommaso Campanella*, Biblioteca filosofica di Quaestio, 28 (Bari: Edizione di Pagina, 2018)

Simonetta, Stefano, *Dal Difensore della pace al Leviatano: Marsilio da Padova nel Seicento inglese*, Testi e studi, 155 (Milan: UNICOPLI, 2000)

——, *Marsilio in Inghilterra: Stato e Chiesa nel pensiero politico inglese fra XIV e XVII secolo*, Il Filarete, 195 (Milano: LED, 2000)

Tutino, Stefania, *Empire of Souls: Robert Bellarmine and the Christian Commonwealth* (Oxford: Oxford University Press, 2010)

Ullmann, Walter, 'Frederick II's Opponent, Innocent IV, as Melchisedek', in *Atti del Convegno Internazionale di Studi Federiciani: VII centenario della morte di Federico II imperatore e re di Sicilia (10–18 Dicembre 1950)* (Palermo: Stabilimento d'Arti Grafiche A. Renna, 1952), pp. 53–81; repr. in *Law and Jurisdiction in the Middle Ages*, ed. by George Garnett (London: Variorum Reprints, 1988), pp. 53–81

CARY J. NEDERMAN

Papacy, Peace, and Political Science

Collective Action Problems in Marsilius of Padua's Defensor pacis

It is widely, although not universally, accepted that the thought of Marsilius (aka Marsiglio) of Padua represents the apotheosis of medieval scholastic Aristotelianism, even if the conclusions he drew therefrom were highly unorthodox. At the core of Aristotle's political philosophy (and the moral ideas with which it is intertwined) was a conception of the systematic study of politics (as he understood the topic) that he termed *politikē epistēmē*, a phrase ordinarily translated into English as 'political science'. In Marsilius's time and well beyond, Aristotelian political science, expressed in its Latinized form *scientia politica*, shaped inquiry into the theory and practice of politics.[1] Scholars ordinarily regard Marsilius of Padua as a paragon of such scholastic *scientia politica*. For instance, Antony Black writes that Marsilius fully embraced

> Aristotle's conception of political science (*scientia politica*) as a distinct area of human understanding, indeed an 'architectonic' one, with its own store of knowledge and equipment of concepts and methods. [...] Marsilius was able to write the first modern systematic treatment of political philosophy in the belief that he was discovering the true essence of polity and authority. Political science had become part of the human being's creative exploration of the world.[2]

---

1 The best general account of the historical process described may be found in Scattola, *Dalla Virtù alla Scienza*. Dauber, 'The Invention of Political Science' covers the period from the thirteenth to the seventeenth century. Also useful are Coleman, 'The Science of Politics', and Ramis-Barceló, 'El concepto de *cientia politica*'.

2 Black, *Political Thought in Europe*, pp. 20–21.

> **Cary J. Nederman** is Professor of Political Science at Texas A&M University and author most recently of *The Rope and the Chains: Machiavelli's Early Thought and its Transformations* (2023).

Marsilius of Padua, ed. by Alessandro Mulieri, Serena Masolini, and Jenny Pelletier, Disputatio, 36 (Turnhout: Brepols, 2023), pp. 359–382

Scholars have disputed the extent to which Marsilius modified the precise features of the Aristotelian epistemic paradigm in light of the Philosopher's differentiation between different conceptions of 'science'.[3] But inasmuch as Aristotelian political science constituted the dominant medieval paradigm for investigation into the realm of politics,[4] Marsilius is held up as its practitioner par excellence.[5] It seems odd, then, that Marsilius employs the word *scientia* relatively seldom in his masterwork, the *Defensor pacis*, and never, so far as I can tell, conjoined with *politica*.[6]

Why might Marsilius have distanced himself from the term 'political science'? I contend that there are two distinct yet intertwined reasons. The first of these is purely historical, insomuch as it identifies a plausible explanation for the divergence of Marsilius's thought from the core of Aristotelian political science that stems from his overarching anti-papal agenda. My other thesis may seem, by contrast, highly anachronistic, inasmuch as it attributes to Marsilius an intellectual position more congenial to certain features of contemporary social science. These two claims converge in making the point that the foundations on which his version of political science rests cannot be properly characterized as *Aristotelian*. The chapter bolsters this claim by initially examining the primary features of Aristotle's own account of political science, as articulated in the *Politics* as well as the *Nicomachean Ethics*. I then analyse the political project — namely, opposition to papal intrusion into secular affairs — that informs the basic rationale for writing the *Defensor pacis*. Finally, I suggest an alternative paradigm for what it might mean to associate Marsilius with political science in a manner that resonates with many key elements of the twenty-first-century version of the discipline. My conclusion may appear rather odd: by extracting Marsilius from the mire of medieval Aristotelianism, he offers far more incisive insights into dilemmas posed by the civic affairs of his own time.

---

3 E.g. Gewirth, *Marsilius of Padua*, pp. 45–49; Quillet, *La philosophie politique de Marsile de Padoue*, pp. 52–53; Olivieri, 'Teoria Aristotelica dell'opinione e scienze politica'; Merlo, *Marsilio da Padova*, pp. 13–14.

4 Although the Roman law language of *scientia civilis* persisted among the lawyers in the medieval universities. See Viroli, *From Politics to Reason of State*, pp. 53–70, and Coleman, 'The Science of Politics'. Alessandro Mulieri has commenced a project to bring Averroist scientific thought to bear on the understanding of the premises of Marsilian political 'science'; see Mulieri, 'Marsilius of Padua and Peter of Abano' and Mulieri, 'Against Classical Republicanism'.

5 A recent exception to this tendency worthy of note is Syros, *Marsilius of Padua at the Intersection*.

6 I have produced a census of his usage in 'Beyond Aristotelian Political Science', p. 495, n. 11.

Aristotelian Political Science

Aristotle's moral and political philosophy begins with the claim that political science is the 'master science of the good', meaning that human fulfilment at the level of virtue is only achieved when knowledge of the proper organization of human community is realized. Short of guidance provided by correct knowledge of political arrangements (the properly organized constitution (*politeia*)), human beings will necessarily and inevitably fall short of the complete fulfilment of which they are capable (*NE* 1094a27–1094b12).[7] Specifically, Aristotle says, the overarching good sought by political science is justice (*Pol.* 1282b16). In turn, 'the just is some sort of equality [...]. For justice is something to some people, and they say that it should be something equal to those who are equal. But what sort of equality and what sort of inequality [...] involves a puzzle for political philosophy', that is, political science (*Pol.* 1282b19–22). To the extent that political science achieves its goal of determining the proper meaning of justice — that is, the correct definition of (in)equality — it affords a standard to distinguish between good and bad constitutions and the laws congruent with them: 'Laws must necessarily be base or excellent, just or unjust, at the same time and in the same way as constitutions [...]. It is clear that the laws in accord with correct constitutions must be just, and those in accord with deviant constitutions not just' (*Pol.* 1282b7–12). The role of the Aristotelian political scientist is to discover and promote the principles constitutive of justice itself, especially by judging which constitutions, and likewise laws, may be declared just. Consequently, 'justice is something political. For justice is a political community's order, and justice is judgment of what is just' (*Pol.* 1253a36–37). Political science is not an abstract enterprise; its end is action (*praxis*), not knowledge for its own sake. Therefore, the good which Aristotelian political science pursues pertains to human flourishing (*eudaimonia*) by means of the activities in which men engage.

Much of the *Politics*, of course, is taken up with the exposition and evaluation of various constitutional systems.[8] For present purposes, I concentrate on Books V and VI, which address Aristotle's concern about actually existing constitutions, based on his observance of historical events in numerous Greek *poleis*, specifically *stasis*, a word variously translated as 'faction', 'revolution', 'civil disorder', and 'class conflict'. Simply stated, *stasis* refers to a process according to which one constitution is replaced by another only for the original system of government to be restored. This

---

7 References to the *Nicomachean Ethics* and the *Politics* are embedded in the text with the abbreviation *NE* or *Pol.*, followed by the Bekker number. I follow the translations by C. D. C. Reeve of *NE* (2014) and *Pol.* (2017).

8 See Polin, *Plato and Aristotle on Constitutionalism*, pp. 183–268.

occurs especially in the relationship between democracies and oligarchies; one oftentimes turns into the other for a while but then is supplanted by the previous regime. Aristotle notes that this instability appears to be more or less permanent (*Pol.* 1301b4–9). In Book v, he investigates the reasons for this repeated pattern, and in Book vi he attempts to provide some concrete suggestions for remedying the seemingly unending conflict.

At present, the first of these topics demands our attention. Recall that the main focus of Aristotelian political science — the ultimate good towards which it is oriented — is justice and that justice pertains foremost to equality and inequality, that is, to determining the appropriate distribution of whatever resource is under consideration. Aristotle's diagnosis of the ill of *stasis* is that the contending parties fail to share the same conception of equality and thus do not agree upon a common principle of justice. Rather, oligarchs believe that their wealth and social status uniquely qualify them to rule; hence they embrace a constitutional system in which an unequal allocation that reflects their superiority counts as just. Aristotle terms this 'proportionate' equality. By contrast, democrats adhere to a 'numerical' idea of equality, which is to say that they believe that men are fundamentally the same and hence that no one may properly lay claims to special or differential authority. Justice in democracy is built on the notion that neither wealth nor occupation nor education nor any other external quality affords one group preference in the exercise of political rights (*Pol.* 1301a20–1302a7). Clearly, the oligarchic and the democratic principles of allotment are incommensurable as they stand. Each of the sides regards the other's perception of equality as irredeemably unjust and will thus fight in order to return to a system reflective of what they perceive to be *real* equality. In Aristotle's view, this explains *stasis*. Note that the process he describes is purely internal to institutional factors; while *stasis* can be triggered by many causes, all of them are ultimately rooted in relative perceptions of constitutional fairness or unfairness to interested parties (*Pol.* 1302a33–1303b17) Having come to understand the bases of *stasis*, Aristotle recommends in Book vi a number of potential resolutions to such conflicts. Justice (or at least a semblance thereof) lies in breaking down the antithesis between competing ideas of equality by the reform of the political order through the incorporation of features of each system into its opposite. It seems to me that Aristotle's highly pragmatic proposal for quelling the problem of *stasis* by means of mixing constitutional principles of equality epitomizes Aristotelian political science.

Marsilius versus Aristotle

One of the most significant elements of political science arising from the diffusion of Aristotelian thought was recognition of the connections between strife and imperfect institutions. Theorists sought to remedy this defect by reference to constitutional mechanisms of renovation through which faction and discord might be remedied and peace secured.[9] Later medieval authors who analysed *stasis* through an Aristotelian lens normally hewed close to the methods and conclusions found in the *Politics*, as Vasileios Syros has documented.[10] According to Quentin Skinner, this project involved a mere updating of Aristotle's proposals to eliminate *stasis* in order to apply to the circumstances of violent disharmony within, especially, many late medieval Italian cities.[11] The 'scientific' account in the *Politics* of *stasis* and how to achieve its elimination proved, in other words, extremely relevant to the concerns of thirteenth- and fourteenth-century Europe, especially the Italian cities, in which strife posed a persistent threat.[12]

Not so for Marsilius of Padua, who, according to *Defensor pacis*, insisted that the crisis of stability confronting his own times arose from a very different source than that of Aristotle's era.[13] Specifically, whereas Aristotle identified the cause of political instability as the inherent defects of various constitutional systems, Marsilius's theory finds nothing internally problematic in the organization of various secular regimes that would account for the strife he encounters in Europe. Indeed, he expresses more or less complete indifference to the evaluation of 'best' and 'worst' constitutions, beyond acknowledgement of the three 'temperate' (kingship, aristocracy, polity) and three 'diseased' (tyranny, oligarchy, democracy) forms of government distinguished by Aristotle (1, 8.3–4). His view seems to be that a well-ordered community (the 'perfected city or kingdom') of whatever type is relatively stable and tranquil in its internal workings so long as its citizens keep their attention focused on their shared interest in attaining a 'sufficient life' (1, 4.5). Unlike the Aristotelian explanation of *stasis*, the threat to peace which disturbs Marsilius is entirely external to the problem of conflicting conceptions of (in)equality stemming from the constitutional organization of a given political system.

Unique among his contemporaries, such as William of Ockham, who also vehemently criticized the papal pretention to earthly power, Marsilius concentrates on the purely temporal threats at stake. In particular, he focuses his analysis on the civil intranquillity that he observes across Europe,

---

9 Black, *Church, State and Community*, p. 356.
10 Syros, *Marsilius of Padua at the Intersection*, pp. 48–52.
11 Skinner, *The Foundations of Modern Political Thought*, I, pp. 54–57.
12 As documented by Hyde, 'Contemporary Views on Faction and Civil Strife'; Rubenstein, 'Some Ideas on Municipal Progress'.
13 All references to the *Defensor pacis* will be embedded in the text, citing the Discourse, Chapter, and Section numbers, relying on the version by Alan Gewirth in preference to that of Annabel Brett. I have also consulted the Latin critical edition by Richard Scholz, which I find superior to that by Charles Previté-Orton.

especially in the so-called *Regnum Italicum*, that is, the northern Italian urbs under the (at least nominal) authority of the Roman emperor (I, 1.2). His references to Aristotle's account of *stasis* are qualified and muted. Throughout the first *dictio* (out of three) of the *Defensor pacis*, Marsilius repeatedly remarks that

> although strife has many original causes, almost all of those which can emerge in the usual ways were described by the foremost of the philosophers in his *Civil Science* [i.e. the *Politics*]. Beside these, however, there is one singular and obscure cause by which the Roman Empire has long been troubled. This cause is very contagious and prone to creep up on all other cities and kingdoms; in its greediness it has already tried to invade most of them. Neither Aristotle nor any other philosopher of his time or before could have discerned the origin and species of the cause. [...] This sophistic opinion, wearing the guise of the honorable and the beneficial, is utterly pernicious to the human race and, if unchecked, will eventually bring unbearable harm to every city and country. (I, 1.3)[14]

Marsilius waits until the final chapter of *Dictio* I to reveal this unique and singular cause that not even Aristotle could have anticipated, because he lived in the time before the birth of Jesus, let alone the emergence of the institution of the priesthood and the formalization of an organized universal Church. The cause, he says, centres on the claim asserted by the Bishop of Rome — the pope — that he possesses a 'plenitude of power' that stretches to 'jurisdiction over all kings, princes, communities, groups and individuals [...] limited by no human law' (I, 19.9). The pope stands above and outside of the self-governance (Marsilius sometimes calls it 'liberty' (I, 1.2)) that earthly political systems — kingdoms and cities, as well as the empire — rightfully exercise. Consequently, the papacy asserts that it may legitimately interfere with secular politics, which leads to the disturbance of temporal peace.

Much of the rest of the *Defensor pacis* delimits the scope of ecclesiastical authority as it extends into the realm of the terrestrial use of power by governments. For Marsilius, such power is inherently coercive; it pertains to the creation and enforcement of public law, the violation of which may be validly punished. According to him, the Church and its agents (up to and including the pope) lack an endowment that permits the same sort of exercise of coercion. Clerical authority is merely advisory, existing for the sake of shepherding souls towards salvation (I, 6). Of immediate interest to us, the cause of the specific intranquillity that Marsilius so vehemently opposes in his own era does not reside in a tension internal

---

14 This position is reiterated in *DP* I, 1.7, I, 15.10, and I, 19.1.

to conflicts among the conceptions of equality that lead proponents of various constitutional arrangements into *stasis*. The Church is purely external to the organization of secular affairs, whether republican or monarchic or imperial. Hence, it matters not to him how a regime is organized, since all forms of government are equally endangered by the external threat posed by the attempt to impose a papal plenitude of power (I, 9.11). Simply stated, Marsilius steps away from key elements of the Aristotelian explanation of *stasis*. Might the absence of reference to political science reflect the recognition (perhaps implicit) that the study of politics for him stood at considerable remove from the Aristotelian conception of it as 'the master science of the good'? We need not speculate how to answer this question, so long as we acknowledge that factors central to the approach identified in the *Politics* to explain the vicissitudes of political strife are utterly irrelevant to Marsilius's analysis.

A Marsilian Science of Politics

If Marsilius is not a political scientist in an Aristotelian sense, then should he be regarded as a political scientist at all? I wish to propose a response to this question that might seem to be an anachronism, but that is rather, on a close reading of the *Defensor pacis*, altogether quite plausible. Permit me to state my thesis forthrightly: the ecclesio-political problematic within which Marsiglio is embedded leads him to employ, even if inadvertently, several basic elements that are fundamental to political *scientific* research today. By no means am I claiming Marsilius as a 'precursor' to or 'anticipator' of the methodology of modern social science inquiry, but rather that the logic of the circumstances with which he writes yields the opportunity to engage with premises shared with my colleagues in modern political science departments. Specifically, Marsilius evinces an implicit understanding of three primary elements endemic to the framework within which contemporary political scientists — or more particularly the large number of those committed to a so-called rational choice paradigm — conduct their investigations.[15] I do not suggest that Marsilius grasped the technical intricacies of rational choice — or could have done so — only that he subscribed to the intellectual foundation on

---

15 The literature on rational choice theory and related topics is prodigious. An especially clear and useful overview (explaining concepts as well as recounting the field's historical evolution) may be found in Hindmoor, *Rational Choice*. Jon Elster has also produced two introductions to rational choice theory that are slightly more technical but still articulate its leading ideas in a manner comprehensible to a lay reader: *The Cement of Society* and *Nuts and Bolts for the Social Sciences*.

which that theory is constructed. The three salient features I have in mind are the following:

1 **Rational choice**, which posits that aggregate behaviour in society reflects the sum of the choices made by individuals. Each agent, in turn, makes decisions based on personal preferences and the constraints (known as a 'choice set') that she faces. The agent chooses the most preferred outcome. In a case in which outcomes can be evaluated in terms of costs and benefits, a rational individual chooses the outcome that provides the greatest net benefit, which is understood to be the maximization of her perceived self-interest. An outgrowth of rational choice is termed the 'collective action problem', that is, why self-seeking people would voluntarily work together in order to achieve goals that profit all yet require the sacrifice of immediate interests. Points (2) and (3) afford two examples of just such dilemmas.

2 **The free-rider problem**, which arises when those who benefit from resources, public goods, or services do not pay for them, which results in an underprovision of those goods or services. For example, someone who declines to pay income tax, yet still takes full advantage of the boon provided by government, is a free-rider. The free-rider problem is common with goods which are non-excludable, to use the technical economic term, meaning that they are equally available to everyone (such as public safety functions).

3 **Rent-seeking**, which connotes the use of private access to public power in order to obtain economic gain without regard for any benefits that might accrue to society at large. For instance, rent-seeking occurs when someone uses favoured differential inclusion in a governmental decision-making process such as the framing of legislation, either directly or through a proxy (what we call a lobbyist). The rent-seeker employs this special position to improve his own condition at the expense of those who lack the ability to guide legislative or policy decisions in order to suit his personal interests.

Insofar as Marsilius's analysis of the foundations of human conduct shares these elements, it stands at arm's distance from Aristotle's view that 'the good' is a moral achievement (i.e. 'living well') rather than merely biological/physiological ('living') (1, 4.2). Marsilius constructs his science with the very clear goal of demolishing the papal pretension to a plenitude of power in order to undermine its very premises by providing an account of secular political community that decidedly supports the value of a way of life unencumbered by extraneous religious intrusions. I do not subscribe to the oft-asserted position that Marsilius was somehow modern, a man before his time. But detaching his thought from the common ascription of orthodox medieval Aristotelian political science opens up new avenues for exploration.

An obvious objection based on the historical plausibility of my proposed reading of Marsilian political science immediately suggests itself.[16] Why would a presumably convinced Christian, even if a somewhat eccentric one, find it necessary or useful to appeal to a key principle associated with rational choice (that is, self-interest) and its attendant issues as the legitimate basis for social and political relations? I maintain that there are demonstrable historical reasons for Marsilius to adopt the position I attribute to him. Indeed, an appeal to the self-interest of citizens as the yardstick according to which the public welfare should be judged emerges quite reasonably from the polemical and intellectual circumstances in which he composed the *Defensor pacis*. As already indicated, the *Defensor* took as its central aim the stinging and comprehensive rebuke of assertions of a 'plenitude of power' made on behalf of the papacy. Marsilius responded by denying to the pope — and indeed to the clergy as a whole — any competence to judge or act upon the temporal good of human beings. This is a far more extreme claim than that made by contemporaries also critical of clerical pretensions to earthly power, who generally accorded to the papacy and others in the ecclesiastical hierarchy a 'casual' (*in casu*) authority to intercede for the sake of the public good when secular rulers were unable to perform their duties.[17] Marsilius rejected such a position and thereby completely undercut the moral force of the priesthood as a spiritual office competent to define standards external to the political realm itself against which the common good might be measured. For him, any determination of public utility could only issue from the consent of citizens; the expression of civic assent formed his check against the unwarranted interference and influence of clerics. But on what basis, according to what criterion, might citizens judge what is good for the community which they inhabit? It could not be rooted in spiritual or moral authority, over which the priesthood claimed a monopoly. Marsilius answers that citizens should refer to a standard that was purely internal to the secular realm and that all could equally comprehend: their conception of personal advantage. If a communal decision was judged by each individual to be beneficial — or at least not harmful — to himself, then it must by definition be good for all.

Marsilius's ecclesio-political predicament thus led him to propose an innovative way to uphold a principle of the common good on the basis of personal calculations of self-interest. According to the *Defensor pacis*, human beings by their nature always seek their own physical preservation as well as spiritual well-being (1, 4.2–3). They do so best when they are able to live cooperatively in order to engage in exchange relations.

---

16 The present project is not entirely *sui generis* in its effort to bring rational choice principles to bear on medieval political theory; see Spindler, 'Politics and Collective Action'.

17 An overview of these issues may be found in Wilks, *The Problem of Sovereignty*.

Hence, society should be arranged so as to promote the goal of private advantage, since the fulfilment of this goal ultimately serves (indeed, defines) the temporal welfare of the community understood as the collective realization of personal gain on the part of its members. Interference with the pursuit of self-interest is justified only in the case of 'externalities' such as causing intentional or inadvertent harm to others. In this sense, Marsilius builds the foundations for the view that personal material advantage constitutes the valid source for the attainment of the good of all. In turn, he also recognizes some of the problems inherent in the model of cooperation among self-interested beings. Without naming them, of course, he confronts such dilemmas identified by modern rational choice theory as free riding and rent-seeking. Moreover, Marsilius attempts to redress the paradoxes stemming from problems of collective action within the constraints of rational choice by appeal to a theory of consent. In his view, the interests of private persons and the benefit of the community as a whole merge precisely insofar as the legal and institutional manifestations of political power only command obedience to the extent that each and every citizen publicly acknowledges that they either further or pose no injury to his own advantage.

Foundations of Self-Interest

Marsilius's ability to adopt a line of reasoning consonant with modern rational choice theory depends on his postulation of a sharp distinction between temporal and spiritual realms in the *Defensor pacis*. He starts with the claim common for this time that human ends 'fall into two kinds, of which one is temporal or earthly, while the other is usually called eternal or heavenly' (I, 4.3). But the resemblance between his view and more conventional medieval thought is largely superficial. According to the *Defensor pacis*, temporal ends are for the most part indifferent to spiritual goals. The term 'spiritual', Marsilius says, 'refers to every immanent action or passion of human cognitive or appetitive power' (II, 2.5), where 'immanent' acts are understood as 'actions or passions' that 'do not pass over into a subject other than the doer, nor are they exercised through any external organs or locomotive members; of this kind are human thoughts and desires or affections' (I, 5.4). Because they are wholly internal and self-regarding, immanent acts are not susceptible to public inspection and control; they are spiritual in the sense that they do not transgress the boundaries of the soul, and hence are invisible to human observation and are known only to God.

By contrast, Marsilius defines temporal matters in three possible senses: first, in connection with the physical world other than humankind, the objects of which 'are ordered toward [human] use, needs, and

PAPACY, PEACE, AND POLITICAL SCIENCE   369

pleasures in and for the status of worldly life'; second, as denoting 'every human habit, action, or passion, whether in oneself or directed toward another for a purpose in this world or the present life'; and third, and most narrowly, as stemming from 'those human actions and passions which are voluntary and transient, resulting in advantage or disadvantage (*commodum vel incommodum*) to someone other than the agent' (II, 2.4). The temporal activities of a human being, Marsilius believes, are only of concern to someone else to the extent that they are 'transient', that is, have an impact on others. Consequently, 'transient' acts — 'other-regarding' may be the best modern equivalent — are the proper object of regulation by the laws and governors of the political community (I, 5.7). When transient behaviour is performed 'in due proportion', it results in benefits to others as well as to oneself. When transient action is 'excessive', however, it disadvantages another person.

To the extent that the temporal conduct of human beings does not 'cross over' and impact upon the life of their fellow creatures, no external regulation is justifiable (I, 5.4). Just as other people cannot properly interfere with 'immanent' acts of the soul, so they cannot intrude in the case of non-transient forms of physical conduct, such as producing what is necessary for survival and exchanging goods with their fellows. When the pursuit of self-interest remains in due proportion, society has no claim upon the individual. Marsilius therefore enshrines temporal advantage as a fundamental and entirely legitimate goal of human conduct. Indeed, he establishes as his 'starting-point (*principium*) that all human beings not deformed or otherwise impeded naturally desire a sufficient life, and avoid or flee what is harmful thereto, which has been acknowledged not only with regard to humanity but also with regard to every genus of animal' (I, 4.2). The advantage of human beings is achieved by gaining those conditions of existence which confer upon them a physically adequate life. Although Marsilius makes passing mention of the Aristotelian conception of a higher 'good life', constituted by the exercise of the practical and theoretical virtues (I, 4.1), material sufficiency receives the overwhelming measure of his attention.

Since temporal satisfaction forms Marsilius's operative principle in the argument of the first discourse of the *Defensor pacis*, we may grasp the key premise for the reconciliation of self-interest with the common benefit. He contends that human beings invariably prioritize their own good: 'Everyone is prone to pursue one's own advantage (*commodum*) and to avoid what is disadvantageous (*incommodum*)' (II, 8.9). Marsilius judges this to be a natural and unavoidable condition of physical human existence, rather than a vice to be condemned and reviled. The pursuit of personal advantage follows directly, in fact, from the principle of self-preservation. Since we are enjoined by nature to preserve our material survival, it is entirely unnatural for us to undertake any action that would injure or disadvantage ourselves. This seems to be the rationale behind Marsilius's striking insistence that 'no one knowingly harms or wills injustice to oneself' (I, 12.8). Marsilius apparently grants that, at least in regard to temporal matters, human beings are fundamentally (to employ modern terminology) strategic actors or rational choosers — self-seeking calculators of their own physical well-being. Indeed, this conception of advantage corresponds quite directly to the first two senses of the word 'temporal' already mentioned: it pertains to the use of the non-human physical world by human beings to fulfil their own earthly ends. Marsilius's vocabulary in this connection, especially his use of *commodum*, is extremely precise. Surprisingly, scholars have paid no substantial attention to *commodum* and related terms in the *Defensor pacis*, comparable to the analysis of *conferens* and similar words that convey the 'common' or 'public' good.[18] Yet Marsilius consistently employs the word *commodum* in the *Defensor pacis* in order to address private advantage, benefit, profit, and similar terms connected with self-interest. *Commodum* seems to be a morally neutral term for Marsilius, suggesting that self-interest is a purely natural and instrumental fact of life. This is reinforced by a passage of the *Defensor pacis* in which *commodum* describes that which naturally benefits an animal (I, 17.8). The term appears recurrently throughout the *Defensor pacis* and carries important implications for Marsilius's understanding of human motivation and choice. Specifically, *commodum* consistently connotes the physical or material benefits and comforts that individuals seek in order to preserve and enhance their lives.[19]

If human beings could live in isolation, and if their activities were entirely self-directed, it would be unnecessary to set limits on behaviour, since each person, looking out for himself, is best qualified to determine what is required for self-preservation. But Marsilius recognizes that the material advantage of human beings also (and perhaps primarily) encompasses 'transient' acts, the third category of temporal affairs. This is the case, in the first place, because the self-interest of individuals is achieved most fully and 'naturally' under conditions of human cooperation in the context of an ordered and organized community. Marsilius holds that 'human beings came together in the civil community in order to pursue

---

18 See the terminological analyses provided in *DP*, trans. by Gewirth, pp. lxvi–xci; *DP*, ed. by Kunzmann and Kusch, I, pp. xxxix–lxxxiii; Di Vona, *I Principi de Defensor Pacis*; Damiata, *'Plenitudo potestatis' e 'universitas civium'*; *DP*, trans. by Brett, p. xliii.

19 Similar usage is adopted by Marsilius in his other main writing, the *Defensor minor*, in which he speaks of 'achieving *commodum* or avoiding *incommodum* in the present world'. Moreover, he insists, in connection with excommunication, that 'no one is to be deprived of one's civil *commodum* in relation to one's person or property by a precept of divine law', where such 'civil *commoda*' includes 'purchasing bread, wine, meat, fish, pots or clothes [...] [and] the rest of functions and *commoda*'. See Marsilius of Padua, *Defensor minor*, IX, 3, XV, 6, ed. by Nederman, pp. 28, 57.

advantage (*commodum*) and a sufficient life and to avoid the opposite' (1, 12.7). The claim that human beings associate primarily on account of self-interest grounds the account of the origins of communal life in the *Defensor pacis*. The 'perfected community' emerges along with the differentiation of the functions necessary for a materially sufficient existence, these tasks being defined by the various arts created by humankind in order to redress their physical infirmities (1, 3.2–5). The human creature, Marsilius observes, 'needs arts of diverse genera and species to avoid the aforementioned harms'. Given their infirmities, 'it was necessary for human beings to assemble together to obtain advantage (*commodum*) from [these arts] and to avoid disadvantage (*incommodum*)' (1, 4.3). Marsilius thus posits that the commission of 'transient' acts that impact others in the context of a communal setting is absolutely necessary for human beings to attain a sufficient life. A 'perfected' civil association requires

> the mutual association of citizens, their intercommunication of their functions with one another, their mutual aid and assistance and, in general, the power, unimpeded from without, of exercising their particular and common functions, and also the participation in common benefits (*commodorum*) and burdens according to the measure appropriate to each. (1, 19.2)

The occupations necessary for achieving a sufficient temporal life, including farmers, merchants, craftsmen, and warriors, make valuable (indeed necessary) contributions to the community (1, 5.6–9). Indeed, citizenship is conferred on a strictly functional basis, judged according to the usefulness of various human activities for the meeting of material human needs.

Paradoxes of Collective Action

By no means does it follow, however, that one's commission of transient actions will invariably benefit both oneself and others at the same time. Marsilius acknowledges that it is entirely possible that people, by seeking their own benefit, may in fact harm the interests of others. 'Transient acts', he observes, 'can be done for the advantage (*commodum*) or for the disadvantage (*incommodum*) or injury of a person other than the agent for the sake of one's condition in the present life' (1, 5.7). The problem, of course, is that should human beings seek their own interests at the expense of their fellows, conflicts would readily emerge within the community:

> Among human beings assembled together, disputes and quarrels arise which, if not regulated by a norm of justice, would cause men to fight and separate [...]. Without correction, the excesses of [transient] acts would cause fighting and hence the separation of citizens, and finally

the destruction of the community and the loss of the sufficient life. (I, 4.4, I, 5.7)

Here we re-encounter Marsilius's central preoccupation in the *Defensor pacis*: the maintenance of civil peace. He closely identifies his main objective — peace — with advantage in an individual as well as a collective sense. In the opening sentence of the *Defensor pacis*, he lauds 'the advantages (*commoditates*) and fruits of the tranquillity or peace of civil regimes', chief among which is 'the sufficient life, which no one can obtain without peace and tranquillity' (I, 1.1). At the close of the first *dictio*, he returns to the same theme. His purpose, he says, is to identify the causal factor — the papacy — that in his own day 'has deprived and is still depriving the community of peace or tranquillity and of the above-mentioned advantages (*commodis*) that follow therefrom, and has vexed it and still vexes it with every kind of disadvantage (*incommodo*)' (I, 19.4). Peace for Marsilius is not an end in itself, but a prerequisite for the realization of stable intercourse within the community by means of which individuals seek and obtain their own self-interest.

Thus, Marsilius is confronted with a salient paradox endemic to rational action in a cooperative setting. On the one hand, all who desire to fulfil their own advantage ought, naturally and logically, to seek peace (and, presumably, oppose disturbances of social tranquillity). Yet, on the other hand, even as individuals are motivated by self-interest to work together, their self-interest may also lead them to take advantage of their fellows, rendering cooperation itself unworkable. Expressed in Marsilian terms, the peace is disturbed when the partial interests of certain individuals (Marsilius has in mind, particularly, the papacy and its supporters) are permitted to govern the communal association to the detriment of the advantage of other of its members. Logically speaking, the constraints supposedly attaching to collective action within the rational choice paradigm disappear insofar as every actor recognizes the same existential threat to their individual well-being, in this instance, the papal claim to a plenitude of power. The realization of such complete ecclesiastical dominance over the material goods of individuals, as well as the political jurisdiction exercised by 'cities or kingdoms' (which Marsilius sometimes couches in the language of liberty (e.g. I, 1.2, I, 17.4)), represents the very antithesis of the contention that in matters of a sufficient temporal existence reference to individual advantage offers the most reliable guide to decision-making. Simply stated, rational people will cooperate when their personal interests are collectively at stake.

Does this entail that, presuming Marsilius's anti-papal agenda is realized, collective action problems would begin to appear? I am of two minds about the answer to this question. On the one hand, a papacy chastened in the fashion that he proposes would no longer pose a threat to the denizens and governments throughout the world beholden to the Church of Rome. Free from submission, there would seem to be no reason for all of the negative elements of collective action to emerge. Yet, on the other hand, there is no assurance that the forces supporting ecclesiastical domination will have been vanquished permanently, even in light of the proposal in the *Defensor* to place the priesthood under the authority of the secular communal order (I, 8.9). If we take Marsilius at his word, the very nature of Christianity, with its inherent potential for a special group capable of coercively enforcing the determination of those who will and will not attain salvation, creates an inevitable obstacle to a final resolution. Insofar as Europe remained unified by a Christian faith and thus by a single institutional Church subject to the administration (however marginal) of a clerical hierarchy with the pope at its top, citizens must collaborate in their vigilance against the renewal of the claims to authority that led to the crisis that Marsilius confronts.

Free Riding

A community can only function for the good of all when its operations serve the interests of each. Yet some members of the community may be tempted to engage in 'transient' deeds that directly or indirectly harm others, thereby threatening the existence of the entire social process. This is doubtless why Marsilius points out how various claims on behalf of clerical exemptions from public regulation result in calculable advantage to the class of religious while doing material harm to the community. Faced with a version of the 'free rider' dilemma, Marsilius notes that the papacy has pronounced decretals that exempt not simply the priesthood, but even lay orders such as the Beguines, Knights Templar, and Hospitallers, from regulation by public authority.

> If all such persons are thus exempted from the jurisdiction of rulers in accordance with these decretals, which also grant certain immunities from public or civil burdens to those who are thus exempted, then it seems very likely that the majority of people will enter these orders, especially because both literate and illiterate persons are accepted without distinction [...]. But with the greater number or majority of people entering into clerical orders, the jurisdiction and coercive power of rulers will become ineffective, and the number of those who have to bear burdens will be reduced to almost nothing; these are the greatest of inconveniences and destructive of the polity. For whomsoever enjoys civil honors and advantages (*commodis*), such as peace and the protection of the human legislator, must not be exempt from the civil burdens and jurisdiction. (II, 8.9)

CARY J. NEDERMAN

To combat the socially corrosive effects of 'free riding', Marsilius invokes something resembling the 'fairness principle' employed by modern philosophers, namely, the idea that those who share in the benefits of a co-operative scheme are obligated to share in equal measure in its burdens.[20] Papally proclaimed exemptions and similar ecclesiastical licenses that bestow a benefit on some members of the community while disadvantaging others violate the very purpose of mutual advantage for which human association was formed.[21]

In order to escape from the dilemma posed by the free rider, Marsilius insists upon the singular legitimacy of a very specific set of boundary conditions for communal participation. First, all whose interests are served or affected by a community must be conceded full membership in it and must consent to the conditions of association (i.e. law and rulership). Second, having so consented, all such citizens are absolutely bound to obey the law and the determinations made by rulers in accordance with it. In other words, people must individually as well as collectively submit to the terms of their cooperation, after which they can be held strictly accountable for 'transient' actions detrimental to the advantage of fellow citizens. Marsilius regards the defining characteristic of citizenship to be the ability to express one's will in the political venue, by judging for oneself the validity of prospective rulers and laws. All matters 'whose proper institution is of the greatest importance for the communal sufficiency of citizens in this life, and whose depraved institution impends communal detriment, must be instituted only by the whole body of citizens' (I, 12.7). This implies for Marsilius not merely formal, corporative assent, but an extensive privilege on the part of each individual citizen to examine prospective laws and rulers.

> Common measures must be laid before the assembled whole body of citizens for their approval or disapproval, so that if any citizen thinks that something should be added, subtracted, changed, or completely rejected, he can say so [...]. For, as has been said, the less learned citizens can sometimes perceive something that must be corrected in a proposed law even though they could not have discovered the law itself. (I, 13.8)

Each and every member of the community reserves to himself final judgement about all matters of public regulation. This is required, Marsilius contends, because a government's very legitimacy depends upon its congruence with the voluntary acquiescence of those over whom it rules. And the only way to assure such congruence is by an initial act of explicit consent on the part of citizens, ratified in effect by the acceptance of the

---

20 Hart, 'Are There Any Natural Rights?'.
21 Marsilius draws essentially the same conclusion at *DP*, II, 2.3 and II, 21.15.

PAPACY, PEACE, AND POLITICAL SCIENCE   375

benefits attendant upon such agreement. Then, should the private conduct of some citizen lapse over into an 'excessive transient' deed — one that harms another person — the execution of the law by the ruler will be seen to be authorized by the community (including, indeed, the offending citizen himself). Hence, Marsilius asserts that no one can protest against the enforcement of a law to which that person has already assented (I, 12.6, I, 13.8). The peace is best upheld when it is regarded as an expression not of the power of the government but of the will of the civil body.

Rent-Seeking

A reasonable question remains: According to what criteria, what point of reference, do citizens discern the worthiness of legislative measures and candidates for rulership? Most medieval thinkers would probably have responded that the selection of laws and rulers depends on right reason or natural justice or divine inspiration in order to reach the correct determination.[22] The wisest, or most virtuous, or most holy, were best qualified to promulgate legislation and to appoint rulers. Polemically, Marsilius cannot abide this, for it potentially positions the priesthood over the processes of decision-making within the secular community. But perhaps because Marsilius emphasizes the self-interested character of human judgement, he also recognizes that permitting a segment of the communal body — *any* segment — to decide for the whole creates opportunities for serious abuse.

> The few would not discern or desire the common benefit equally as well as would the entire multitude of the citizens. Indeed, it would be insecure [...] to entrust the making of the law to the discretion of the few. For they would perhaps consult therein their own private benefit, as individuals, or as a group, rather than the common benefit, as is quite clear in those who have made the decretals of the clergy. (I, 13.5)

Left to their own devices, in other words, people occupying positions of power will quite naturally and unavoidably create laws and make decisions that favour themselves. This behaviour is precisely what modern political scientists mean by 'rent-seeking': the use of public means to pursue private ends. Behind the claims to moral and intellectual superiority that drive the view that the many should defer to the few, Marsilius detects the possibility of naked self-interest intruding into the political process in such as way as to favour those who hold power.

According to Marsilius, the best way to deter rent-seeking is to insist on broadly based consent, the terms of which are not moral reason or spiritual

---

22 One example is Nicholas of Cusa, *The Catholic Concordance*, trans. by Sigmund, pp. 98, 205–09.

illumination but direct impact upon one's own advantage. Every person correctly and adequately evaluates laws and rulers when he measures them against the yardstick of his own self-interest. Marsilius asserts, 'Those matters, therefore, that can touch upon the advantage and disadvantage (*commodum et incommodum*) of everyone ought to be known and heard by everyone, so that they can obtain advantage (*commodum*) and repel its opposite' (I, 12.7). Marsilius cleverly recasts a conventional (and highly elastic) *dictum* of medieval political and legal thought: 'What touches all must be approved by all' ('quod omnes tangit omnem approbatur').[23] The vague term 'tangere' is rendered noticeably concrete by Marsilius: it now refers to the material well-being designated by *commodum*. Citizens must be accorded a role in consent to law and government inasmuch as statutory dictates and execution of them impact upon their direct interests.

Consequently, the common good for Marsilius comes to be coextensive with the aggregate advantage of each of the individuals within the community. No power may legitimately be imposed upon the polity that is inconsistent with the interests of its citizens (where, again, such 'interest' is understood in terms of the value of a materially sufficient life). Therefore, by consulting one's own direct benefit in the evaluation of public affairs, one simultaneously discovers the communal benefit.

> The common utility of a law is better noticed by the whole community, because no one knowingly harms oneself. Anyone can look to see whether a proposed law leans toward the advantage (*commodum*) of one or a few [citizens] more than of the rest of the community and can protest loudly in opposition; this would not be so, however, if the law were to be made by one or a few [citizens], attending more to their own private (*proprium*) advantage (*commodum*) rather than the common [benefit]. (I, 12.5)

If every citizen considers a statutory proposal (or prospective governor), and none finds any detriment to his own interests, then the decision must indeed merit promulgation since it withstands the ultimate test of the common good as conceived by Marsilius: Can this measure harm me in any discernible way? Or will I instead derive some tangible benefit (or at least no injury) from it? When laws and officials are evaluated according to the principle of symmetrical determination of personal welfare, opportunities to rent-seek are extremely limited, if not entirely eliminated.

---

23 On usages of this phrase, see Post, *Studies in Medieval Legal Thought*, pp. 163–238.

Conclusion

The purpose of this chapter has not been to transform Marsilius of Padua into a modern social scientist. Instead, I wish to highlight two points. First, by the early fourteenth century, the narrow constraints imposed by the academic community of the medieval university had been stretched to a breaking point. Marsilius's reticence to refer to political science in some Aristotelian sense suggests, at least to me, a somewhat self-aware recognition that he had burst the bonds of the philosophical orthodoxy of his time. By the definition he knew, he was *not* a 'political scientist' and thus never laid a claim to be. To remain within the confines of strict Aristotelianism was never, I speculate, an option once he had determined to pursue his anti-papal agenda. Admittedly, Marsilius's response to the perceived threat was unconventional. His account affords a systematic and comprehensive explanation of how a well-ordered political community can coexist with the pursuit of material self-interest on the part of its individual citizens. This theoretical framework represents a direct and compelling challenge to the belief — present in the fourteenth century little more than in the religious fanaticism increasingly common in the present day — that a single all-encompassing and unchallengeable conception of 'the good' must subordinate all others. This seems to me to offer one further example of the distance between Marsilian thought and his alleged republican commitments.[24]

My second point in some ways pushes in another direction. I maintain that Marsilius is comfortable with the position that when one judges public matters according to the measure of one's own advantage — which is, at any rate, far easier to do than to contemplate an abstract 'common good' — one will arrive at a precise calculation of the communal benefit. Despite the fact that I detect echoes of certain Marsilian teachings in the public choice doctrines widely embraced by recent social scientists, I deem it crucial to emphasize that he adopts a response to the dilemmas raised by private interests in relation to public goods that in some respects diverges significantly from central tenets of rational choice theory. For instance, Marsilius does not regard the self-regarding motivations of individuals to be irrelevant to or incompatible with the responsibilities of a robust civic life. Modern rational choice theorists often denigrate civic participation (at least implicitly) and point to the irrationality of expressions of political involvement (such as voting).[25] Marsilius insists that engaged citizenship cannot be detached from the communal order and public peace that form the context for the pursuit of personal benefit. That is to say, he assumes

---

24 As I suggest in 'Post-Republicanism and Quasi-Cosmopolitanism'.
25 The classic statements of these views are Downs, *An Economic Theory of Democracy*; Olson, *The Logic of Collective Action*; and Buchanan and Tullock, *The Calculus of Consent*.

that individual choice about self-interest always necessarily refers to the social setting in which it occurs: a community only functions adequately for him when its parts are mutually advantaged, in a physiological (rather than moral or spiritual) sense. Thus, Marsilius's vision of self-interest is much less radically individualistic than that propounded by the rational choice school. He believes that in a peaceful and harmonious community, the correct choice about matters of public welfare will also always be right for each fellow citizen. Ultimately, the separate self-interests of each and every person do not conflict with one another or with a single common good. Marsilius merely posits that no group (particularly not the priesthood or ecclesiastical hierarchy) enjoys any privileged access to the nature of that common good in advance of a public process of obtaining consent. Marsilius advocates a belief that rational beings will (and ought to) come together and stay together in stable and mutually beneficial sociopolitical relationships without the necessity of enduring an irresolvable conflict because they refer in their autonomous decision-making processes to their perceived interests.

Works Cited

Primary Sources

Aristotle, *Nicomachean Ethics*, trans. by C. D. C. Reeve (Indianapolis: Hackett, 2014)

——, *Politics*, trans. by C. D. C. Reeve (Indianapolis: Hackett, 2017)

Marsilius of Padua, *Marsilius of Padua: The Defender of Peace, II: The Defensor Pacis*, trans. by Alan Gewirth (New York: Columbia University Press, 1951; repr. 2000)

——, *The Defender of the Peace*, trans. by Annabel Brett, Cambridge Texts in the History of Political Thought (Cambridge: Cambridge University Press, 2005)

——, *Defensor pacis*, ed. by Richard Scholz, Monumenta Germaniae Historica: Fontes iuris germanici antiqui in usum scholarum separatim editi, 7, 2 vols (Hannover: Hahn, 1932–1933)

——, *The Defensor pacis of Marsilius of Padua*, ed. by Charles W. Previté-Orton (Cambridge: Cambridge University Press, 1927)

——, *Der Verteidiger des Friedens*, ed. by Walter Kunzmann and Horst Kusch, 2 vols (Berlin: Rötten & Loening, 1958)

——, *Writings on the Empire: 'Defensor minor' and 'De translatione Imperii'*, ed. and trans. by Cary J. Nederman, Cambridge Texts in the History of Political Thought (Cambridge: Cambridge University Press, 1993)

Nicholas of Cusa, *The Catholic Concordance*, trans. by Paul Sigmund (Cambridge: Cambridge University Press, 1991)

Secondary Works

Black, Antony, *Church, State and Community: Historical and Comparative Perspectives* (Aldershot: Ashgate/Variorum, 2003)

——, *Political Thought in Europe, 1250–1450* (Cambridge: Cambridge University Press, 1992)

Buchanan, James, and Gordon Tullock, *The Calculus of Consent* (Ann Arbor: University of Michigan Press, 1962)

Coleman, Janet, 'The Science of Politics and Late Medieval Academic Debate', in *Criticism and Dissent in the Middle Ages*, ed. by Rita Copeland (Cambridge: Cambridge University Press, 1996), pp. 181–214

Damiata, Marino, *'Plenitudo potestatis' e 'universitas civium' in Marsilio da Padova*, Biblioteca di Studi francescani, 16 (Florence: Studi Francescani, 1983)

Dauber, Noah, 'The Invention of Political Science' (unpublished doctoral dissertation, Harvard University, 2006)

Di Vona, Piero, *I Principi de Defensor Pacis* (Naples: Morano, 1974)

Downs, Anthony, *An Economic Theory of Democracy* (New York: Harper, 1957)

Elster, Jon, *The Cement of Society: A Study of Social Order* (Cambridge: Cambridge University Press, 1989)

——, *Nuts and Bolts for the Social Sciences* (Cambridge: Cambridge University Press, 1989)

Gewirth, Alan, *Marsilius of Padua: The Defender of Peace*, I: *Marsilius of Padua and Medieval Political Philosophy* (New York: Columbia University Press, 1951)

Hart, Herbert L. A., 'Are There Any Natural Rights?', *Philosophical Review*, 64.2 (1955), 175–91

Hindmoor, Andrew, *Rational Choice* (Hound Mills: Macmillan, 2006)

Hyde, John K., 'Contemporary Views on Faction and Civil Strife in Thirteenth-and Fourteenth-Century Italy', in *Violence and Disorder in Italian Cities, 1200–1500*, ed. by Lauro Martines (Berkeley: University of California Press, 1972), pp. 273–307

Merlo, Maurizio, *Marsilio da Padova: Il pensiero della politica come grammatica de mutamento* (Milan: FrancoAngeli, 2003)

Mulieri, Alessandro, 'Against Classical Republicanism: The Averroist Foundations of Marsilius of Padua's Political Thought', *History of Political Thought*, 40.2 (2019), 218–45

——, 'Marsilius of Padua and Peter of Abano: The Scientific Foundations of Law-Making in the *Defensor Pacis*', *British Journal for the History of Philosophy*, 26.2 (2018), 276–96

Nederman, Cary J., 'Beyond Aristotelian Political Science: *Scientia civilis* and Romanism in Marsiglio of Padua's *Defensor pacis*', *International Journal of the Classical Tradition*, 27 (2020), 493–512

——, 'Post-Republicanism and Quasi-Cosmopolitanism in Marsiglio of Padua's *Defensor pacis*', in *Al di là del Repubblicanesimo: Modernità politica e origini dello Stato*, ed. by Guido Cappelli, with the assistance of Giovanni De Vita, Quaderni della ricerca, 5 (Naples: UniorPress, 2020), pp. 131–46

Olivieri, Luigi, 'Teoria Aristotelica dell'opinione e scienze politica in Marsilio da Padova', *Medioevo*, 6 (1980), 223–35

Olson, Mancur, *The Logic of Collective Action: Public Goods and the Theory of Groups* (Cambridge, MA: Harvard University Press, 1965)

Polin, Raymond, *Plato and Aristotle on Constitutionalism* (Aldershot: Ashgate, 1998)

Post, Gaines, *Studies in Medieval Legal Thought: Public Law and the State 1100–1322* (Princeton, NJ: Princeton University Press, 1964)

Quillet, Jeannine, *La philosophie politique de Marsile de Padoue*, L'Église et l'État au Moyen-Age, 14 (Paris: J. Vrin, 1970)

Ramis-Barceló, Rafael, 'El concepto de *cientia politica* en el siglo XVI', *Revista de Estudios Políticos*, no. 185 (2019), 75–104

Rubenstein, Nicolai, 'Some Ideas on Municipal Progress and Decline in the Italy of the Communes', in *Fritz Saxl (1890–1948)*, ed. by James D. Gordon (London: Thomas Nelson, 1957), pp. 165–83

Scattola, Merio, *Dalla Virtù alla Scienza: La fondazione e la transformazione della disiplinia politica nell'età moderna* (Milan: FrancoAngeli, 2003)

Skinner, Quentin, *The Foundations of Modern Political Thought*, 2 vols (Cambridge: Cambridge University Press, 1978)

Spindler, Anselm, 'Politics and Collective Action in Thomas Aquinas's *On Kingship*', *Journal of the History of Philosophy*, 57 (2019), 419–42

Syros, Vasileios, *Marsilius of Padua at the Intersection of Ancient and Medieval Traditions of Political Thought* (Toronto: University of Toronto Press, 2012)

Viroli, Maurizio, *From Politics to Reason of State: The Acquisition and Transformation of the Language of Politics, 1250–1600* (Cambridge: Cambridge University Press, 1992)

Wilks, Michael, *The Problem of Sovereignty in the Later Middle Ages* (Cambridge: Cambridge University Press, 1963)

FRANK GODTHARDT

The *Defender of Peace* during the Third Reich

Many, possibly most, scholars agree that Marsilius of Padua is a proponent or forerunner of republicanism, popular sovereignty, or even democracy.[1] During the Third Reich, however, some scholars believed that they had discovered similar ideas in, or affinities between, Germany's new political order and Marsilius's political theory. In this historiographical essay, I will discuss three German scholars' views on Marsilius and his political theory at the time of the Third Reich.[2]

These three German academics differed in their subject, age, academic reputation, and attitude towards National Socialism, as well as in their assessment of Marsilius's political importance and their interpretation of the *Defensor pacis*. First, the young philosopher Wilhelm Schneider-Windmüller who dedicated his short monograph on the *Defensor pacis* to the then new National Socialist government. Second, Richard Scholz, the renowned editor of the *Defensor pacis*, who gradually adopted the view that there were affinities between the political order of the Third Reich and Marsilius's political thought. Finally, Friedrich Bock, a fervent member of the Nazi party and the deputy director of the German Historical Institute in Rome throughout the Third Reich, who published extensively on Emperor Ludwig IV (the Bavarian) and presented a new assessment of Ludwig's advisor, Marsilius.

---

1 Most recently Peonidis, 'Marsilius of Padua as a Democratic Theorist'; Sullivan, 'Democracy and the *Defensor Pacis* Revisited'; for a discussion of this, cf. Condren, 'Democracy and the *Defensor Pacis*'.

2 A shorter, German version of this chapter was published in 2020 as Godthardt, 'Die Interpretation des *Defensor pacis*'. I want to thank Thomas Izbicki, Barbara Molony, and Thomas Turley as well as the editors of this volume for their helpful comments on this chapter.

Dr Frank Godthardt received his doctorate in medieval history from the University of Hamburg. He is a senior archivist at the Bundesarchiv in Berlin.

Marsilius of Padua, ed. by Alessandro Mulieri, Serena Masolini, and Jenny Pelletier, Disputatio, 36 (Turnhout: Brepols, 2023), pp. 383–408

BREPOLS ❧ PUBLISHERS   10.1484/M.DISPUT-EB.5.132919

FRANK GODTHARDT

What aspects of Marsilius's political theory attracted these scholars during the Third Reich? How did they each interpret it? And finally, what do we learn about Marsilius's political theory and its possible deficiencies from a discussion of its interpretation during the Third Reich?

Wilhelm Schneider-Windmüller (1908–1969)

Wilhelm Schneider-Windmüller received a doctorate in philosophy from the University of Freiburg im Breisgau in 1929 for his dissertation, 'Die *Quaestiones disputatae de veritate* des Thomas von Aquin in ihrer philosophiegeschichtlichen Beziehung zu Augustinus', supervised by the Catholic philosopher Martin Honecker.[3] When Adolf Hitler became German Reich chancellor on 30 January 1933, Wilhelm Schneider-Windmüller was only twenty-four years old. At that time, he taught philosophy as a lecturer at the Pädagogische Akademie Bonn that had been founded in 1926 by the Prussian state government as a college for the education of male Catholic primary school teachers.

In 1934, Schneider-Windmüller published his *Staat und Kirche im Defensor Pacis des Marsilius von Padua*. As he states in its preface, he had already written the monograph by the end of 1931. However, he had obviously not revised it for publication, which is evident from the fact that he had not updated its bibliography. He mentions only the 1928 edition of the Englishman Charles William Previté-Orton, although the German Richard Scholz had published his critical two-volume edition of the *Defensor pacis* more recently in 1932 and 1933.[4] Prior to its publication, Schneider-Windmüller only added a one-page preface with the date of 30 January 1934 — the first anniversary of the National Socialists' 'seizure of power'. In this short foreword, he relates the politics of the emerging Third Reich to Marsilius's political theory:

> The following treatise on 'State and Church in the "Defensor Pacis" of Marsilius of Padua' was already written at the end of the year 1931. If the author has now decided to publish it, this has happened because similar ideas, especially about the relationship between State and Church, have been revived today. Since the National Socialist revolution, we have finally obtained a unified and

---

3 The dissertation was printed in 1930, Schneider, *Die Quaestiones disputatae de veritate des Thomas von Aquin*. No later than April 1933, he also assumed his mother's maiden name (Windmüller), possibly because Schneider is quite a common name in Germany. For his mother's maiden name, see his later university records, Bonn, Universitätsarchiv, MNF-Prom 172.

4 This had already been pointed out in 1938 by Wolf, 'Neuere Arbeiten zur Kirchengeschichte', p. 240 n. 3.

THE *DEFENDER OF PEACE* DURING THE THIRD REICH   385

purposeful leadership of state, which Marsilius also calls for despite his democratic standpoint. National Socialism has also now accomplished the repatriation of the churches to actual ecclesiastical interests. This was one of Marsilius's main concerns as well. With regard to the position of the clergy in the state, Marsilius drew the boundaries much tighter than is the case today.[5]

Schneider-Windmüller states that he has discovered two affinities between the political order of the Third Reich and the *Defensor pacis*. Regarding the Third Reich, his points of reference are its 'unified and purposeful leadership of state' and its policy of 'repatriation of the churches to actual ecclesiastical interests'. Apparently, he wants to relate the Third Reich's 'unified leadership of state' to Marsilius's call for the *unitas* of the supreme government. Marsilius's call for only one supreme government of a political community is a central element of his political theory, which comprises in particular the categorical exclusion of any stake in, or interference with, a political government by the Church and the pope.[6]

In Schneider-Windmüller's adaptation, Marsilius's *unitas* appears as the 'unified and purposeful leadership of state', which refers to the dictatorial rule of the Third Reich. This seemingly contradicts Marsilius's 'democratic standpoint', but Schneider-Windmüller strives to resolve this contradiction by characterizing the National Socialist takeover as a 'revolution'. With the term 'revolution' he sanctifies the on-going process of the Nazi expansion of power by implying that 'the people' is its legitimate originator.

How does this relate to the actual emergence of the Third Reich and its 'unified leadership of state'? Hitler's appointment as chancellor on 30 January 1933 was followed by a process that the National Socialists later termed the 'legal revolution'. In the subsequent months the new coalition government led by Hitler took steps to transfer and delegate political powers and competences to the Reich government and, eventually, to Hitler alone. The first important measure was the *Ermächtigungsgesetz* ('Enabling Act') of 24 March 1933. After the last semi-democratic elections on

---

5 Schneider-Windmüller, *Staat und Kirche im Defensor Pacis*, p. 3: 'Die folgende Abhandlung über "Staat und Kirche im 'Defensor Pacis' des Marsilius von Padua" wurde schon zu Ende des Jahres 1931 geschrieben. Wenn der Verfasser sich jetzt zur Herausgabe entschloß, so geschah dies, weil ähnliche Gedanken, besonders auch über das Verhältnis von Staat und Kirche, heute wieder lebendig geworden sind. Eine einheitliche und zielbewusste Staatsführung, wie sie auch Marsilius trotz seines demokratischen Standpunkts verlangt, haben wir ja seit der nationalsozialistischen Revolution endlich erhalten. Die Rückführung der Kirchen auf die eigentlichen kirchlichen Belange hat der Nationalsozialismus ja nun auch bewirkt. Es ist dies schon eine Hauptsorge des Marsilius gewesen. Bezüglich der Stellung des Klerus im Staate hat Marsilius die Grenzen viel enger gezogen, als es heute der Fall ist'.

6 *DP*, I, 17, ed. by Scholz, pp. 112–21. Marsilius even includes this point in his list of conclusions at the end of his work, III, 2.11, p. 605.

5 March 1933, the new *Reichstag* as the representative of the German people transferred its authority as a legislator for federal laws to the Reich government. Other constitutional bodies involved in legislating, namely the Reich president and the *Reichsrat* (representation of the federated states), were ruled obsolete for the enactment of new laws.

In addition, the Reich government successively eliminated the autonomy of the different German *Länder* (federated states like Prussia, Bavaria, or the city state of Hamburg). Just one week after passing the Enabling Act, the first law concerning the intended *Gleichschaltung* (coordination) of the *Länder* with the Reich ruled that all parliaments of the federated states and all city councils had to adopt the results of the Reich parliament election for their own representative bodies.[7] Shortly thereafter, the Reich government appointed Reich Commissioners to every state who installed and controlled new *Länder* governments. Ultimately, the state legislatures were dissolved, and all authority of the federated states was transferred to the supreme level of the Reich. The *Reichsrat*, as the representation of the federated states' governments, consequently, was abolished. By July 1933, all political parties except for the Nationalsozialistische Deutsche Arbeiterpartei (NSDAP) had been forbidden. When Reich president Paul von Hindenburg died on 2 August 1934 a referendum was held that conferred to Hitler the office of Reich president. The *Gleichschaltung* had now been perfected. The authority delegated to the 'Reich chancellor and *Führer*' was in effect omnicompetent and unlimited. In this way, a 'unified and purposeful leadership of state' had been achieved. And in this respect, the Third Reich's political order corresponds to Schneider-Windmüller's reading of the *Defensor pacis* and was also supposed to be in harmony with Marsilius's 'democratic standpoint'.

The second affinity between the Third Reich's political order and Marsilius's theory is the 'repatriation of the churches to actual ecclesiastical interests'. With that phrase Schneider-Windmüller addresses the first measures of National Socialist church policy.[8] With the association of the *Deutsche Christen* (German Christians), the German Protestant Churches already had a considerable proportion of National Socialists in their ranks. In its first year, the Reich government took steps towards a *Gleichschaltung* of the twenty-eight autonomous *Landeskirchen* (regional churches) and intended to replace them with a united Reich Church subjected to National

---

7 Evans, *The Coming of the Third Reich*, p. 381, aptly explains *Gleichschaltung* as 'a metaphor drawn from the world of electricity, meaning that all switches were being put onto the same circuit, as it were, so that they could all be activated by throwing a single master switch at the centre'.

8 Most historical studies and accounts are limited to just one denomination. The two predominant churches in Germany are dealt with together by Scholder, *Die Kirchen und das Dritte Reich*, vol. 1; Blaschke, *Die Kirchen und der Nationalsozialismus*; Strohm, *Die Kirchen im Dritten Reich*.

THE *DEFENDER OF PEACE* DURING THE THIRD REICH   387

Socialist control. To this end the new office of a leading *Reichsbischof* was soon established.[9] But the establishment of the Protestant Reich Church failed later in the year 1934 — only after Schneider-Windmüller's book had been published — due to the opposition of the *Landeskirchen* whose autonomy was firmly anchored in German history.

Things were different with the Catholic Church in Germany. In July 1933, after previous contracts with individual German *Länder* like Bavaria (1924), Prussia (1929), and Baden (1932), the Holy See finally concluded a concordat at the level of the Reich that is still controversial today.[10] With this treaty, the Nazis wanted to eliminate the Catholic Church's influence by restricting all its organizations and clergy to purely religious activities. For the German Catholic Church, the concordat was to guarantee its rights, its property, and its independence from state interference regarding its personnel and organizational matters.[11]

It is the latter that Schneider-Windmüller points to as falling short of the demands of Marsilius of Padua concerning the 'position of the clergy in the state'. Schneider-Windmüller calls for a more consistent subordination of the Church to the State and the use of Marsilius as a guide in that matter. In his preface, Schneider-Windmüller continues:

> One thing seems to me to be very noteworthy from his [Marsilius's] discussions for our time too, that it is the same people who are grouped together as the people of the State and as the people of the Church. If, therefore, the welfare of the people is to be the supreme goal of the rulers of the State, then the Church can have no other goal than to work for the welfare of the people. There are, of course, great differences in detail between the time of Marsilius of Padua and our time today. But both are times of spiritual awakening and spiritual reorientation. So, it is worthwhile to look for related ideas.
>
> *Bonn, 30 January 1934!*[12]

Dated on the first anniversary of the National Socialist 'seizure of power', this seems a bold appeal for a young lecturer — that is, to recommend

---

9 Evans, *The Third Reich in Power*, pp. 223–24.
10 Cf. Scholder, *Die Kirchen und das Dritte Reich*, I, pp. 482–524; Wolf, *Papst und Teufel*, pp. 172–203.
11 Excerpts in Blaschke, *Die Kirchen und der Nationalsozialismus*, pp. 96–97.
12 Schneider-Windmüller, *Staat und Kirche im Defensor Pacis*, p. 3: 'Eines scheint mir auch für unsere Zeit aus seinen Erörterungen sehr beachtenswert, dass es doch die gleichen Menschen sind, die als Staatsvolk und als Kirchenvolk zusammengefaßt sind. Wenn deshalb das Wohl des Volkes höchstes Ziel der Staatslenker sein soll, so kann auch die Kirche kein anderes Ziel haben, als zum Wohl des Volkes zu wirken. Im einzelnen bestehen natürlich starke Unterschiede zwischen der Zeit des Marsilius von Padua und unserer heutigen Zeit. Aber beide sind Zeiten geistigen Aufbruchs und geistiger Neuorientierung. So lohnt es sich schon, einmal nach verwandten Gedanken zu suchen. Bonn, 30. Januar 1934!'

a medieval thinker to correct the church policy of the Nazi government. However, Schneider-Windmüller's study of 1931 contrasts strikingly to the 1934 preface. In the monograph itself, we find virtually no commitment to, or sympathy for, National Socialist ideology, nor can we infer any from what he writes. Moreover, there is no indication that Schneider-Windmüller is particularly attracted to Marsilius's concept of the relationship between Church and State. At the end of the book, Schneider-Windmüller concludes rather reluctantly: 'According to the previous statements, Marsilius seems to subordinate the Church completely to the State. But he does not advocate a complete submission of the Church under the supremacy of the State'.[13] After acknowledging that Marsilius wants to subordinate the Church to the State, Schneider-Windmüller tries to put this into perspective by contrasting subordination with the concept of submission. For the rejection of a 'complete submission of the Church', Schneider-Windmüller draws in his treatise, as in its preface, on Marsilius's basic idea of the identity of citizens with believers in a *communitas fidelium perfecta*.[14] However, quite differently from the preface, he states in the monograph's text: 'Thus, the relationship of State and Church in Marsilius is ultimately determined by his doctrine of the sovereign democratic State and by his democratic concept of the Church'.[15]

The difference in statements between the 1931 text and the 1934 volume's preface raises questions. Schneider-Windmüller must have been fully aware of this difference but chose to let the original study appear in print unchanged, without adapting it to his new, political interpretation. Why did he choose to do so? It is easy to imagine that he simply changed his political convictions to a National Socialist alignment like so many other Germans did in the years between 1931 and 1934. But a different explanation is possible. Right at the beginning of the Third Reich, the Nazi government tried to get a tight grip on pedagogical institutions. In its first months, the *Pädagogische Akademien* were renamed *Hochschulen für Lehrerbildung* throughout Prussia, and the minister for education wanted their professors and lecturers to hold National Socialist views. On 7 April 1933, two months after the Nazis' 'seizure of power', the Reich government enacted the so-called 'Law for the Restoration of the Professional Civil Service', which allowed the dismissal of 'non-Aryan' civil servants and those conceivably 'politically unreliable' from the Nazis' point of view.

---

13 Schneider-Windmüller, *Staat und Kirche im Defensor Pacis*, p. 29: 'Nach den bisherigen Ausführungen scheint Marsilius die Kirche völlig dem Staate unterzuordnen. Aber er vertritt doch keine völlige Unterwerfung der Kirche unter die Oberhoheit des Staates'.

14 *DP*, II, 17.9, ed. by Scholz, p. 363.

15 Schneider-Windmüller, *Staat und Kirche im Defensor Pacis*, p. 32: 'So ist das Verhältnis von Staat und Kirche bei Marsilius in letzter Linie bestimmt durch seine Lehre vom souveränen demokratischen Staat und durch seinen demokratischen Kirchenbegriff'.

On 1 May 1933, Schneider-Windmüller was accepted as a member of the National Socialist party, like so many Germans who had applied for a membership in the early months of the Third Reich.[16] For the new National Socialist government, the education of primary school teachers was of particular importance, and during the Third Reich, the proportion of members of the National Socialist party among the professors and lecturers at these colleges was even higher than in other state institutions.[17]

Later that year, Schneider-Windmüller was one of about nine hundred signatories of a collection of political texts that were published under the title *Bekenntnis der Professoren an den deutschen Universitäten und Hochschulen zu Adolf Hitler und dem nationalsozialistischen Staat*.[18] The texts of this pamphlet go back to a convention of German professors and academics in Leipzig on 11 November 1933, the eve of the referendum on Germany's withdrawal from the League of Nations. By 19 October 1933, the German government had left both the international disarmament negotiations in Geneva and the League of Nations in response to the British and French refusal to allow parity to Germany in armament. The referendum of 12 November 1933 was held in order to demonstrate the German people's approval of these steps. It received 95 per cent yes votes due to massive intimidation and electoral manipulation, but even a free election would probably have turned out with an overwhelming majority.[19]

The central part of the pamphlet was a modest manifesto entitled 'Ein Ruf an die Gebildeten der Welt'.[20] The editors added the texts of the speeches by several prominent professors, including the prominent physician Ferdinand Sauerbruch and the philosopher Martin Heidegger, that had been delivered at the Leipzig convention. These speeches were more National Socialist in tone. The pamphlet was edited to support and explain the Nazi government's policy and addressed scholars and professors outside Germany. To this end, it was translated into English, Spanish, French, and Italian. The list of German professors and academics

---

16 Berlin, Bundesarchiv (BArch), R 9361-IX Kartei (NSDAP-Gaukartei) / 38920163; R 9361-VIII Kartei (NSDAP-Zentralkartei) / 20471255.

17 Hesse, *Die Professoren und Dozenten der preußischen Pädagogischen Akademien*, pp. 90–92. In his comprehensive list of all full-time teachers Hesse does not include Schneider-Windmüller who probably only had a part-time appointment.

18 *Bekenntnis der Professoren an den deutschen Universitäten und Hochschulen zu Adolf Hitler*, ed. by Nationalsozialistischer Lehrerbund Sachsen. The title's English translation in that pamphlet has a much stronger message than the original: 'Vow of Allegiance of the Professors of the German Universities and High-Schools to Adolf Hitler and the National Socialist State' ('Hochschulen' must, however, be translated as 'colleges').

19 Evans, *The Third Reich in Power*, pp. 618–19.

20 The pamphlet's own translation: 'An Appeal to the Intelligentsia of the World'.

who had declared their support, organized by university and *Hochschule*, concluded the pamphlet.[21]

However, in July 1934, less than six months after his publication, Schneider-Windmüller was removed from his job as lecturer at the Hochschule für Lehrerbildung Bonn. A considerable number of professors and lecturers at these institutions throughout the Reich were dismissed during the initial period of the Third Reich for presumed lack of genuine National Socialist conviction. Many had joined the NSDAP on 1 May 1933. Once dismissed, Schneider-Windmüller immediately declared his withdrawal from the NSDAP, stopped paying his member fees, and was officially excluded from the party in August 1934.[22]

Was Schneider-Windmüller in 1934 a convinced Nazi or rather an opportunist who pretended to be one?[23] He would have known from the very beginning of Nazi rule that his employment at the Hochschule für Lehrerbildung was at risk. His decision to join the Nazi party and his declaration of consent to the *Bekenntnis der Professoren und Hochschullehrer* when the personnel decisions were imminent should have helped him be regarded as a loyal National Socialist. This would explain why he explicitly identified himself as a lecturer at the Hochschule für Lehrerbildung Bonn on the title page of his Marsilius monograph. And it would also explain why he hastily drew up a commitment to the new state that he simply added to his original text while refraining from reworking the text either from lack of time or because of a conviction that was in fact contrary.

With regard to Schneider-Windmüller's interpretations of the *Defensor pacis* during the Third Reich, it does not matter much whether he was a National Socialist or an opportunist. As a Nazi, Schneider-Windmüller would have been convinced that Marsilius *should* be interpreted as he was in the 1934 foreword; as an opportunist he could well have thought Marsilius *might* be interpreted that way. Either way, in Schneider-Windmüller's view, in 1934 in Nazi Germany, the *Defender of Peace* allowed for these different kinds of interpretation.

---

21 *Bekenntnis der Professoren an den deutschen Universitäten und Hochschulen zu Adolf Hitler*, ed. by Nationalsozialistischer Lehrerbund Sachsen, p. 129 (Schneider-Windmüller's name).

22 BArch, R 9361-II / 1125817.

23 The decision of the denazification tribunal of 23 August 1947 categorized Schneider-Windmüller as *Mitläufer* (follower), and he was sentenced to a fine of 360 reichsmarks. The former director of the Pädagogische Akademie Bonn, Professor Georg Raederscheidt, who was himself deposed as director for political reasons, had stated in a letter to the denazification tribunal of 10 April 1947 that Schneider-Windmüller was dismissed for the same reasons in July 1934 by officials of the NSDAP: Freiburg, Landesarchiv Baden-Württemberg, Abteilung Staatsarchiv Freiburg, D 180/2, no. 210406. On Raederscheidt, cf. Hesse, *Die Professoren und Dozenten der preußischen Pädagogischen Akademien*, pp. 593–95.

THE *DEFENDER OF PEACE* DURING THE THIRD REICH 391

Without a job, Schneider-Windmüller decided to study again. This time he chose to study chemistry, a subject that was more suitable to making a living and more appreciated by the new regime. After he had received his degree and when he needed employment he applied for readmission to the NSDAP, which was finally granted to him retrospectively on 22 January 1937, after payment of the accrued membership fees since June 1934.[24] He received his second doctoral degree only much later due to adverse circumstances in the middle of the war in 1943.[25] After the war he started his own company, a chemistry laboratory near Freiburg, and later he again taught at a teacher training college in Freiburg with an appointment in science.[26] He never again published anything on Marsilius or in the field of philosophy. He died at the age of sixty-one in 1969.[27]

Richard Scholz (1872–1946)

The second scholar I want to discuss is — by contrast — one of the most renowned experts on Marsilius of Padua, the historian Richard Scholz. Before he published the two volumes of his critical edition of the *Defensor pacis* in 1932 and 1933, he had already published a monograph in 1903 on *Die Publizistik zur Zeit Philipps des Schönen und Bonifaz' VIII.: Ein Beitrag zur Geschichte der politischen Anschauungen des Mittelalters*, and — after two years of research as a fellow of the Prussian Historical Institute in Rome — in 1911 and 1914 his still useful two-volume work *Unbekannte kirchenpolitische Streitschriften aus der Zeit Ludwigs des Bayern (1327–1345)* that included a great number of editions of fourteenth-century political treatises. Many articles and books in that field of study, especially regarding the era of Emperor Ludwig, followed. When Hitler came to power in 1933 Scholz was already sixty-one years old. He worked at the University of Leipzig in Saxony as a senior librarian and as an adjunct professor until he retired in 1937. Unlike Schneider-Windmüller and Friedrich Bock, Scholz was never a member of the NSDAP.[28] But like Schneider-Windmüller, he was one of the about nine hundred signatories of the *Bekenntnis der*

---

24 BArch, R 9361-II / 1125817.
25 Schneider-Windmüller, 'Beitrag zur Kenntnis reaktionsträger Carbonylgruppen'.
26 Pädagogische Hochschule Freiburg im Breisgau, ed., *Vorlesungsverzeichnis Sommersemester 1968*, p. 5.
27 Görres-Gesellschaft, ed., *Jahres- und Tagungsbericht der Görres-Gesellschaft für 1969*, p. 52 records his death in 1969.
28 In the NSDAP card files (both central and regional) no record card exists relating to Scholz. The reason for this could be (as in other cases) that it was lost. However, in a correspondence with public authorities Scholz himself did not make an entry in the NSDAP box in the attached form, BArch, R 4910-13276. This is a reliable indicator that he was not a member of the NSDAP at that time.

Professoren an den deutschen Universitäten und Hochschulen zu Adolf Hitler und dem nationalsozialistischen Staat.[29] As a resident of the city, Scholz was probably present at the Leipzig convention on 11 November 1933.

In Scholz's scholarly publications up to 1933 and sometime thereafter, nothing obvious indicates that he felt sympathy for National Socialism. But later he wrote articles closer to the new state ideology. This is a little-known fact that the renowned medievalist Hermann Heimpel concealed in his obituary for Scholz.[30] Scholz died in February 1946, soon after the war ended, but his obituary in an academic journal was not published until 1951 due to the desolate condition of German academic publishing at the time. In that obituary, Heimpel states at one point that Scholz had continued to publish articles 'up to the threshold of the Second World War'.[31] In other words, Scholz did not publish anything, according to Heimpel, after the war began in 1939. But Heimpel's seemingly innocuous assertion is false.

Scholz did publish after the beginning of the Second World War. Among his publications are two books from 1941 and 1944 with editions of treatises by Conrad of Megenberg and William of Ockham.[32] More telling, however, regarding Heimpel's assertion, are the articles that Scholz wrote for a new academic journal, the *Zeitschrift für Deutsche Geisteswissenschaft* that had been established in 1938 and followed an emphatically National Socialist line. Heimpel, the author of the obituary, knew this perfectly well, since he himself wrote the opening article in the journal's first volume.[33] In its foreword, the editors state that they 'feel deeply connected with the new German reality of the united people and the resurrected Reich and receive from there all the decisive impulses of their work'.[34] It published articles concerning history, philosophy, poetry, arts, and music, and also *Volkskunde* (folklore studies) and *Rassenkunde* (racial theory).[35] Scholz contributed three articles, up to the 1941/1942 volume. The first, which appeared in its first volume of 1938/1939, was

---

29 *Bekenntnis der Professoren an den deutschen Universitäten und Hochschulen zu Adolf Hitler*, ed. by Nationalsozialistischer Lehrerbund Sachsen, p. 136 (Scholz's name).

30 Heimpel, 'Nachruf Richard Scholz'. From 1934 until 1941 Heimpel was professor at the University of Leipzig.

31 Heimpel, 'Nachruf Richard Scholz', p. 265.

32 Konrad von Megenberg, *Planctus ecclesiae in Germaniam*, ed. by Scholz; Scholz, *Wilhelm von Ockham als politischer Denker*.

33 Heimpel, 'Das erste Reich'.

34 [Anonymous editors], 'Zum Geleit', p. 2: '[dass sie sich] zutiefst mit der neuen deutschen Wirklichkeit des geeinten Volkes und des wiedererstandenen Reiches verbunden wissen und von dort her alle entscheidenden Antriebe ihrer Arbeit empfangen'.

35 [Anonymous editors], 'Zum Geleit', p. 1. However, only one article, a review essay, was published on racial theory, Kleiner, 'Erb- und Rassenkunde'.

THE *DEFENDER OF PEACE* DURING THE THIRD REICH   393

related to Marsilius of Padua: 'Politische und weltanschauliche Kämpfe um den Reichsgedanken am Hofe Ludwigs des Bayern'.[36]

In this article, Scholz shifts to a new paradigm for understanding the decades of Emperor Ludwig's reign from the old concept of 'emperor and pope' to his new concept of *Kaiser und Reich*. He wants to portray a historical development that started, as he says, with the attempts of Marsilius and other 'foreigners' to revolutionize the political order of the empire with the support of the emperor himself. But thanks to the German nobility's counteraction and their willingness to reform the Reich's political order from 1338 until the Golden Bull of 1356, this development ended with the 'restoration of the German state', as Scholz puts it, and the reconciliation of the emperor and the German political powers.[37] In other words, Scholz's new narrative is how fourteenth-century Germany found new strength through internal unity, for which the empire's struggle with the papacy deserves attention only as its external cause.

Arguing that the Roman-German Empire is, after all, not the ideal nor even the main subject of the *Defender of Peace*, Scholz presents possibly the earliest account of the generic nature of Marsilius's theory. Marsilius's theoretical 'political system', Scholz says, can be applied to political communities other than the empire and even to non-Christian states. What really matters to Marsilius is, according to Scholz, the 'idea of the autonomous, authoritarian state' that is based on a sovereign people that chooses its own political order.[38] And, Scholz says, what scholars have believed so long to be 'popular sovereignty' or '"democratic" ideas' in Marsilius's theory is actually in harmony with the 'idea of the authoritarian Führer-state under one all-powerful Roman emperor' or a city constitution in the manner of the Italian *signorie*.[39]

Like Schneider-Windmüller, Scholz wants to attribute to Marsilius the idea of an authoritarian or unified government and reconcile it with Marsilius's concept of a sovereign people. And like Schneider-Windmüller, Scholz draws a line from Marsilius to the Third Reich, in his case by

---

36 The other two articles are Scholz, 'Germanischer und römischer Kaisergedanke im Mittelalter' and Scholz, 'Weltstaat und Staatenwelt in der Anschauung des Mittelalters'.

37 Scholz, 'Politische und weltanschauliche Kämpfe um den Reichsgedanken', pp. 298–99.

38 Scholz, 'Politische und weltanschauliche Kämpfe um den Reichsgedanken', p. 301: 'Denn was ihn ganz erfüllt, das ist die Idee des autonomen, autoritären Staates, dessen Grundlage das souveräne Volk ist, das sich selbst seine Verfassung gibt und die Gewalten bestimmt, die regieren sollen nach seinem Willen'.

39 Scholz, 'Politische und weltanschauliche Kämpfe um den Reichsgedanken', p. 301: 'Die vielgerühmte Lehre von der Volkssouveränität, zu deren Schöpfer man völlig irrig Marsilius hat machen wollen, und die "demokratischen" Gedanken über Volkswille, Majoritätsbeschlüsse, Wahlen zu den Ämtern usw. vertragen sich im Ganzen des Systems doch sehr gut mit der Idee des autoritären Führerstaats unter einem allmächtigen römischen Kaiser oder auch einer Stadtherrschaft nach Art der italienischen Signorien'.

394   FRANK GODTHARDT

attributing the National Socialist concept of *Führerstaat* to the medieval empire. The two authors differ, however, in the way they respectively reconcile the Third Reich's 'unified leadership of state' with Marsilius's 'democratic standpoint' and a medieval 'Führer-state' with Marsilius's concept of a sovereign people. Schneider-Windmüller asserts this reconciliation without any further explication by referring to the modern concept of revolution, an idea that is, of course, alien to Marsilius. Scholz, by contrast, makes use of Marsilius's theory. Through a series of commissions and delegations, Scholz claims that the sovereign authority of the *universitas civium* is eventually transferred to a single supreme legislature, either the *princeps* or a supreme corporation.[40] Although Scholz does not explicitly relate this to the Third Reich, but rather to the Middle Ages, the process he describes appears to resemble some elements of the Third Reich's 'legal revolution' discussed above.

Scholz also addresses Schneider-Windmüller's other theme, the subordination of the Church to the State. He pointedly interprets Marsilius's doctrine as *Staatskirchentum* without independent ecclesiastical authority.[41] In this article, however, Scholz attributes less relevance to Marsilius's political theory for Ludwig the Bavarian's politics in Italy and Rome than most historians and Scholz himself have — for example in his introduction to the *Defensor pacis*.[42] While still acknowledging Marsilius's importance as an advisor to the emperor, Scholz here states that Ludwig's church policy, in Rome and elsewhere, can be explained without the influence of the *Defensor pacis*. Rather, Ludwig's measures can be seen as a resumption of the so-called imperial church system of the Ottonian and Salian rulers that Scholz identifies as genuinely German *Staatskirchentum*, which he claims already existed in the earliest Germanic legal ideas.[43] Scholz's new account

---

40 Scholz, 'Politische und weltanschauliche Kämpfe um den Reichsgedanken', p. 301: 'Durch eine Reihe von Kommissionen und Delegationen, durch Korporationen und Repräsentanten des Volkswillens wird die souveräne Gewalt der Gesamtheit der Bürger schließlich übertragen auf einen obersten Gesetzgeber, auf den Fürsten oder *princeps*, der die *persona publica* des Staats darstellt, oder auf eine oberste gesetzgebende Korporation'.

41 Scholz, 'Politische und weltanschauliche Kämpfe um den Reichsgedanken', p. 302: 'Das Staatskirchentum des Marsilius kennt keine selbständige kirchliche Autorität'.

42 Scholz, 'Einleitung', p. lviii: 'Die Ereignisse in Rom sind wesentlich von Marsilius mitgeleitet worden; sie schienen der Sieg der Theorien des Defensor Pacis zu sein'.

43 Scholz, 'Politische und weltanschauliche Kämpfe um den Reichsgedanken', p. 303: 'Vieles erklärt sich wohl ohne Einfluß des Defensor Pacis als Wiederaufnahme der salisch-staufischen Kirchenpolitik, d. h. jenes ursprünglich deutschen Staatskirchentums, wie es in den ältesten germanischen Rechtsanschauungen über das Verhältnis von Kirchlichem und Weltlichem schon vorhanden zu sein scheint'. However, new research shows that Ludwig's church policy in Rome and elsewhere cannot be explained without the influence of Marsilius and his writings; see Godthardt, *Marsilius von Padua und der Romzug Ludwigs des Bayern*, pp. 147–76 (on Marsilius's ecclesiology), pp. 214–21 (Ludwig appoints Marsilius as *administrator* of the Archdiocese of Milan), pp. 313–419 (Marsilius has significant influence

THE *DEFENDER OF PEACE* DURING THE THIRD REICH   395

of Emperor Ludwig's church policy in Italy was certainly welcomed by National Socialist readers of his article, but it made Marsilius's genuine ecclesiology look much less important.

Like Schneider-Windmüller, Scholz in this 1938 article saw some affinities between Marsilius's theory and the Third Reich's political order, especially regarding an authoritarian form of rule, which he now clearly welcomed. But unlike Schneider-Windmüller, he did not point out affinities regarding the relationship of State and Church. Consequently, he made no recommendations inspired by Marsilius's political theory to the National Socialist government regarding its church policy. However, one year earlier, in 1937, Scholz mentioned Schneider-Windmüller's monograph on State and Church in the *Defensor pacis* in an article in the *Historische Zeitschrift* where he apparently had taken a somewhat different view. Here Scholz criticizes the 'small work' as 'but a modest contribution that cannot do justice to the historical problem'. On the other hand, he expressly praises Schneider-Windmüller, with obvious reference to the monograph's preface, for drawing 'lively lines of connection to the needs and views of the present'.[44] This was an ambivalent reference to the much younger scholar, but it might be the first hint of Scholz's sympathy for the new regime in his academic writings.

Scholz's adaptation to the prevailing *Zeitgeist* and the new political reality, which we can see in his publications after 1937, contrasts with his previous convictions. In his 1908 article on 'Marsilius von Padua und die Idee der Demokratie' he states that Marsilius has a political ideal, which is 'democracy with a monarchical head'.[45] Specifically, Marsilius's theory of the political community is 'a consistent, democratic construction, the doctrine of popular sovereignty with its utmost consequences'.[46] Thirty years later, Scholz obviously has a very different view of Marsilius. He now considers Marsilius to be a theorist with a remarkably elastic concept of the state that apparently allows the *Führer* of the Third Reich to occupy the position of Marsilius's *pars principans*.

---

on how Emperor Ludwig deposes John XXII, how he elevates a new pope, and how John of Jandun is appointed Bishop of Ferrara by the emperor).

44 Scholz, 'Marsilius von Padua und die Genesis des modernen Staatsbewußtseins', p. 93: 'Die kleine Arbeit von W. Schneider-Windmüller [...] ist doch nur ein bescheidener Beitrag, der dem historischen Problem nicht Genüge tun kann, so dankenswert der Versuch ist, lebendige Verbindungslinien zu ziehen zu den Bedürfnissen und Anschauungen der Gegenwart'.

45 Scholz, 'Marsilius von Padua und die Idee der Demokratie', p. 68: 'Es ist bekanntlich eine Demokratie mit monarchischer Spitze, die Marsilius als politisches Ideal vorschwebt'.

46 Scholz, 'Marsilius von Padua und die Idee der Demokratie', p. 71: 'eine konsequent durchgeführte, demokratische Konstruktion, die Volkssouveränitätslehre mit ihren äußersten Konsequenzen'.

Some years later, in 1942, in the middle of the war, Scholz travelled to the first scholarly conference on Marsilius, on the occasion of the six-hundredth anniversary of the philosopher's death organized by the Faculty of Law of the University of Padua. Due to the war, only participants from the German-Italian 'Axis' were present. Scholz, the only German scholar, was awarded an honorary doctorate by the University of Padua. In his paper, under the historically broad title 'Marsilius von Padua und Deutschland', Scholz discusses the political influence and impact of the Italian Marsilius during his lifetime and in later German history. He places his topic in the context of the bond between Italians and Germans referring to the long-lasting *Schicksalsgemeinschaft* (community of destiny) between these two peoples and emphasizing the importance of 'Germanic blood' for 'building the Italian people' since the fourth century.[47]

In this paper, Scholz changed his mind on one important point from the position taken in his article in the *Zeitschrift für deutsche Geisteswissenschaft* four years earlier. Regarding the political importance of Marsilius, Scholz asserts that the Italian philosopher and his specific political theory did have a great influence on Emperor Ludwig the Bavarian during the Italian expedition and the Roman stay, especially on the central questions about the relation of empire and papacy.[48] And this time Scholz refrains from giving any interpretation of Marsilius's theory that would support a medieval *Führerstaat*. He continues his discussion by giving a nuanced account of the philosopher's dwindling importance in the last years of the emperor's reign in Germany and an overview of the impact of the *Defensor pacis* in the centuries up to the Protestant Reformation and beyond.[49]

Only in the conclusion does Scholz pursue his topic into the twentieth century. In his summary of the *Defensor pacis*'s political theory, he stresses Marsilius's teaching of a church without legitimate authority — an authority exclusively held by the state.[50] In 1942, after the failure of National Socialist church policy and when some segments of the German churches were resisting and opposing the Third Reich, Scholz related the *Defensor pacis* to his own time: 'Even today it [*Defensor pacis*] can still provide insight into state authority, about protecting the state from harmful forces

---

47 Scholz, 'Marsilius von Padua und Deutschland', p. 3: 'Das germanische Blut, das seit dem 4./5. Jahrhundert gotische, langobardische, fränkische, schwäbische und andere deutsche Stämme in Italien, wo sie zum Teil eine neue Heimat gefunden hatten, verbreiteten, ist nicht spurlos verloren gegangen beim Aufbau des italienischen Volkes'.

48 Scholz, 'Marsilius von Padua und Deutschland', esp. pp. 10–11.

49 Scholz, 'Marsilius von Padua und Deutschland', pp. 11–32.

50 Scholz, 'Marsilius von Padua und Deutschland', p. 34: 'Aber die herrschende Zweigewaltenlehre des Mittelalters war unter seiner Feder gegenstandslos geworden: Gewalt ist nur im Staat, niemals in und durch die Kirche'.

THE *DEFENDER OF PEACE* DURING THE THIRD REICH   397

and the separation of what is due to the state from what is not due to it.'[51] In this historical context, Scholz's implicit statement becomes clear. Scholz was attracted by the authoritarian regime of the Third Reich for several years, and in 1942 he, like Schneider-Windmüller had under different circumstances in 1934, also advocated the subordination of the churches to this state.

Friedrich Bock (1890–1963)

The historian Friedrich Bock had the strongest affiliation of these scholars with National Socialism, but he differed from them in his appraisal of Marsilius and the *Defensor pacis*. In 1925, after some years teaching at a *Volksschule*, he finished his doctoral thesis on Emperor Ludwig's foundation of the monastery of Ettal in Upper Bavaria.[52] After that he worked again as a teacher, this time at a *Gymnasium* in Falkensee near Berlin, where he was soon promoted to principal. At about the same time, he started editing the constitutions and charters of Emperor Ludwig the Bavarian from the year 1331 on behalf of the Monumenta Germaniae Historica. However, Bock would never publish a single volume because of disputes with consecutive directors of the Monumenta.[53]

When Hitler came to power, Bock was forty-three years old. Like Schneider-Windmüller, he became a member of the Nazi party on 1 May 1933.[54] In October 1933, however, Bock moved to Rome where he served as *Zweiter Sekretär* (deputy director) of the Prussian Historical Institute, which was renamed German Historical Institute four years later. He ran the day-to-day business of the institute since its director, Paul Fridolin Kehr, who also served as president of the Monumenta Germaniae Historica, resided in Berlin.[55] In Rome, Bock focused his research on the

---

51 Scholz, 'Marsilius von Padua und Deutschland', p. 35: 'Auch heute, so scheint mir, ist der Defensor Pacis noch kein totes, nur für den Historiker lebendig werdendes Buch, auch heute noch kann er Erkenntnis geben über staatliche Autorität, über Bewahrung des Staats vor schädlichen Kräften und die Scheidung dessen, was dem Staate gebührt, von dem Nichtstaatlichen'.

52 Cf. Opitz, 'Nachruf Friedrich Bock'; Bock's doctoral dissertation was printed as Bock, 'Die Gründung des Klosters Ettal'.

53 Interestingly, the documents from the period Bock had been working on were finally edited by Ruth Bork of East Berlin who worked for the German Democratic Republic branch of the Monumenta and published them as late as 1989, the year the Berlin wall came down; Müller-Mertens, 'Nachruf Ruth Bork'.

54 BArch, R 9361-IX Kartei (NSDAP-Gaukartei) / 335187; R 9361-VIII Kartei (NSDAP-Zentralkartei) / 2890811.

55 For the history of the German Historical Institute in Rome during Bock's term of office, see the brief accounts of two of its subsequent directors: Holtzmann, 'Das Deutsche Historische Institut in Rom', pp. 32–33; Elze, 'Das Deutsche Historische Institut in Rom', pp. 19–21.

political and administrative history of the popes and Italy in the time of Emperor Ludwig.[56] Bock never published specifically on Marsilius, but in his extensive research on Emperor Ludwig and Pope John XXII he naturally referred to Marsilius many times. His highly specialized historical research led to a series of articles that are, even by today's standards, serious and sober publications and, in most cases, would not reveal their author's political commitments.

This was different with his comprehensive monograph from 1943: *Reichsidee und Nationalstaaten: Vom Untergang des alten Reiches bis zur Kündigung des deutsch-englischen Bündnisses im Jahre 1341*. In this work he wanted to provide a conclusion to his individual essays and give a general interpretation of the history of the Roman-German Empire within its European context during the thirteenth and fourteenth centuries. The book was dedicated to the German ambassador to the Kingdom of Italy, Hans Georg von Mackensen, on his sixtieth birthday and was apparently inspired by Bock's political convictions.

Bock mentions the Paduan philosopher several times with respect to Ludwig the Bavarian's politics. He considers the emperor to have been a strong and prudent ruler, not weak and malleable as so many scholars had previously contended. Marsilius, accordingly, had barely any influence on the emperor's politics, even during their momentous stay in Rome.[57] These assertions were considerable departures from the mainstream scholarly view during the Second Reich, the Prussian-Protestant German *Kaiserreich* of 1871. Bock's account of this period is a history of the struggles of peoples and powers. The general theme of his book is his notion of French expansionist politics towards the Roman-German Empire in the late thirteenth and early fourteenth centuries. The French popes in the time of Emperor Ludwig, Bock suggests, like Scholz in 1938/1939, were merely willing tools of the French kings. And like Scholz, Bock abandons the common paradigm of empire and papacy. The issues Marsilius raises in the *Defender of Peace* are thus inevitably neglected.

Bock's account of Marsilius's minor importance as an advisor to the emperor corresponds with his disinterest in the philosopher's political theory. Bock frankly admits his disinclination to deal with the arguments and discussions of the *Defender of Peace*.[58] Not interested in matters of

---

56 Cf. Tellenbach, 'Nachruf Friedrich Bock'.

57 One year earlier, Wimmer, *Kaiser Ludwig der Bayer im Kampfe um das Reich*, who portrays the emperor in a similar way with even more national pathos, hardly mentions Marsilius at all, referring to him tellingly as a Franciscan friar.

58 Bock, *Reichsidee und Nationalstaaten*, p. 239: 'Von Anfang an sei betont: Wir haben hier nicht auf die geistigen Grundlagen dieses berühmten Werkes einzugehen, wir werden uns nicht damit beschäftigen, was aus Aristoteles oder aus der mittelalterlichen Philosophie und Theologie stammt, wir wollen auch das Problem beiseite lassen, was der eine oder der andere Verfasser zu dem gemeinsamen Werk beigetragen hat'.

THE *DEFENDER OF PEACE* DURING THE THIRD REICH   399

religion and ecclesiology, Bock never mentions important concepts from the *Defensor pacis* such as the *legislator fidelis* or the *communitas fidelium perfecta*, and asserts that the emperor's church policy in Rome had nothing to do with religion.[59] Rather, Bock portrays the *Defensor pacis* essentially as a presentation of Ghibelline political theory: 'One thing is certain: there are no significant differences between the state theory of the *Defensor pacis* and that of the Ghibellines'.[60] Unfortunately, Bock, who writes so strongly in favour of Ghibelline political theory, does not explicate this concept more precisely.[61] The most important elements of Ghibellinism for Bock are its bond with the Roman-German emperors and its fundamental idea of the respective autonomy of State and Church.[62] According to Bock, the *Defensor pacis* seems redundant: 'Everything we know of the views of the Ghibelline leaders finds a counterpart in the book of Marsilius'.[63] But obviously not everything in the *Defensor pacis* finds a counterpart in what we know of Ghibelline political thinking, since Marsilius's theory is much wider in scope and allows for its application to many more political challenges. Marsilius calls for a subordination of ecclesiastical institutions and offices to the political communities and thus directly contradicts Ghibelline political theory in one of its basic ideas.[64] Thus, Marsilius's political thought naturally had correspondences with Ghibelline thinking, but the *Defensor pacis* is certainly not equivalent to Ghibelline political theory.

As a consequence of Marsilius's alleged lack of genuine influence on the emperor, Bock portrays Marsilius as a mere man of action who simply fitted into the existing Ghibelline orientation of Ludwig's policy and 'did not shy away from harsh measures': a useful enforcer of Ludwig's will, but

---

59 Bock, *Reichsidee und Nationalstaaten*, p. 259.

60 Bock, *Reichsidee und Nationalstaaten*, p. 240: 'Eines ist sicher: wesentliche Unterschiede zwischen der Staatstheorie des *Defensor pacis* und der der Ghibellinen lassen sich nicht feststellen'.

61 Bock, *Reichsidee und Nationalstaaten*, pp. 147–50.

62 For a more comprehensive account of Ghibelline political theory cf. Gianluca Briguglia's chapter in this volume.

63 Bock, *Reichsidee und Nationalstaaten*, p. 240: 'Alles, was wir von den Ansichten der Ghibellinenführer wissen, findet eine Entsprechung in dem Buch des Marsilius'.

64 In his more systematic approach Kölmel, *Regimen christianum*, esp. pp. 491–92 and 503–04 in his chapter on Ghibelline theory, adds little to what Bock presents. He does not share Bock's enthusiasm for Ghibelline theory and points out that it rather emphasizes the respective autonomy of the temporal and spiritual spheres. In contrast to Bock, Kölmel, *Regimen christianum*, p. 531, concludes in his chapter on Marsilius that the latter's doctrine of Church and State for that reason departs from Ghibelline theory. Marsilius, therefore, was not a Ghibelline theorist.

not an inspiring or idea-giving advisor.[65] This portrait, however, contrasts strangely with Bock's later account of Marsilius as a 'stylist' for the imperial chancery in the period after the Italian campaign.[66] Due to his general narrative, Bock cannot acknowledge that Marsilius had significant political importance and influence in his lifetime. This corresponds with his total disinterest in any possible affinities between the *Defender of Peace* and the Third Reich. Bock was not inclined to adapt the *Defensor pacis* to the Third Reich as Schneider-Windmüller and Scholz did for two further reasons. Bock, of course, was not a specialist on Marsilius. He had no reason to make research on Marsilius relevant in new political circumstances. His protagonist was Emperor Ludwig, and if he had drawn any explicit line from the Third Reich to the fourteenth century it would have been to the German ruler and not to the foreign philosopher. Furthermore, Bock did not feel compelled to prove his National Socialist affinity. No one would have doubted his conviction. And he would not have feared losing his job, as Schneider-Windmüller had, or his opportunity to keep on publishing, as Scholz might have done after his retirement. Thus, the most convinced National Socialist of the three German scholars presented here draws the thinnest line between Marsilius and Germany from the time of Emperor Ludwig to the Third Reich.

After World War II, Bock was 'denazified' and lost his job. As a private scholar, he then turned to regional history. Among the few publications connected to his earlier research interests is a short article from 1960 about the recently published literature on Emperor Ludwig.[67] In that article, he stoutly defended his 1943 monograph for the last time. He died in 1963.

Bock's monograph was reviewed by Richard Scholz, and this review is interesting. It was published posthumously as late as 1951 but had been written presumably before the end of the war. Scholz objected to almost every central point of Bock's book. With that review, Scholz rejected Bock's narrative of this period of German history as a struggle between peoples and powers (and his own temporary paradigm of *Kaiser und Reich*) in favour of a return to the older paradigm of a dispute between papacy and empire. He also returned to his former convictions about

---

65 Bock, *Reichsidee und Nationalstaaten*, p. 241: 'Auch vor Härten schreckte er nicht zurück. Wenn wir auch seine Persönlichkeit nur recht verschwommen sehen, so zeichnen sich doch die sympathischen Züge eines klugen und entschlossenen Mannes ab'.

66 Bock, *Reichsidee und Nationalstaaten*, p. 397. However, Bock and other scholars' presumption that the *Defensor pacis* was used by the imperial chancery as a work of reference for the wording and style of the *arengae* of Ludwig's charters is not justified. This conclusion is the result of my analysis of all *arengae* in question, Godthardt, *Marsilius von Padua und der Romzug Ludwigs des Bayern*, pp. 421–30.

67 Bock, 'Bemerkungen zur Beurteilung Kaiser Ludwigs IV. in der neueren Literatur'.

THE *DEFENDER OF PEACE* DURING THE THIRD REICH   401

the significance of Marsilius as both a major theorist and an important advisor to the emperor. Scholz concluded: Bock 'has by no means properly recognized the *Defensor pacis*'s originality and fundamental meaning'.[68]

Conclusions

For some time now, since the studies of Conal Condren and Cary Nederman, the view that Marsilius's political theory is generic in nature has become widespread.[69] It is much less known, however, that Richard Scholz had already pointed out in 1938/1939 and again in 1942 that the principles of the *Defensor pacis* could 'be applied to a wide variety of constitutions'.[70] Quite different political orders can be legitimized by Marsilius's theory. The study of the interpretations and adaptations of the *Defensor pacis* during the Third Reich, however, leads to questions that have barely been addressed so far. How is it that Marsilius's political theory enables various political orders that are so different from one another, even though his origin of political authority, which is the *universitas civium*, is the same? And how do different constitutions come about? To understand this, we need to focus our attention on something in Marsilius's theory that has been underestimated in previous research: the many and manifold transfers and delegations of authority and political powers from the body of citizens to various institutions of the political community.

Regarding the political system of the medieval Holy Roman Empire, Marsilius offers two important examples to which he applies his theory: first, the delegation of the right to elect the supreme government of the political community, the king and emperor, from the original *universitas civium* to only seven princely electors; and second, the transfer of the power to enact laws for the entire political community from the body of

---

68 Scholz, Review of Bock, *Reichsidee und Nationalstaaten*, pp. 333–34: 'Die Formeln "guelfische" und "ghibellinische" Lehre treffen m. E. überhaupt nicht den Kern der Fragen, das völlige Absehen von den kirchlich-religiösen Gesichtspunkten in der damaligen Politik und politischen Doktrin geht nicht an. Die ganze Tiefe der Wandlung der Weltanschauung seit dem 13. Jh. und ihrer Wirkung auf Politik und Politiker wird nur schwach erkennbar; eine Schrift wie Dantes Monarchia und vollends der Defensor Pacis des Marsilius von Padua sind in ihrer Originalität und grundsätzliche Bedeutung bei weitem nicht richtig gewürdigt'.

69 Condren, 'Democracy and the *Defensor Pacis*'; the concept 'generic political theory' goes back to Nederman, *Community and Consent*, esp. pp. 19–21.

70 Scholz, 'Marsilius von Padua und Deutschland', p. 34: 'Das Volk soll nicht herrschen, sondern nur die Herrschenden autorisieren, nichts anderes besagt diese Lehre von der sogenannten Volkssouveränität bei Marsilius. Seine Neigung gehört der Monarchie, der Führung der Gemeinschaft durch einen Einzelnen oder einer Gruppe mit Zustimmung der Gesamtheit. Das entsprach aber ebenso gut germanischen, wie römischen Anschauungen und konnte auf die verschiedensten Verfassungsformen, auch in Deutschland, angewandt werden'.

citizens to the emperor. However, Marsilius omits or avoids discussing or analysing the acts of delegation of powers and authority that are fundamental to the design of a political constitution. It is hardly clear from any of Marsilius's writings who exactly in the name of the *universitas civium* delegates what powers, to what extent, according to which procedures, when, and why. On these crucial points, I would argue, Marsilius's account remains obscure.

The benefit of Marsilius's generic theory and its failure to detail procedure is that it allows a wide range of very different political systems. The downside is the same — that it allows this wide range of very different political systems. But does it allow the Third Reich? Are the interpretations of the *Defensor pacis* by Schneider-Windmüller and Scholz justified, according to which Marsilius's theory should also encompass the concept of a 'Führer-state' and be able to justify National Socialist church policy? The alleged 'legal revolution' of the initial phase of the Third Reich, which led to a comprehensive 'co-ordination' of the entire political system, seems to these authors to be compatible with Marsilius's theory of the manifold delegations of political powers. But there are difficulties with this interpretation. While it may seem that the extent of the omnicompetent and unlimited power the *Führer* obtained in the Third Reich could be valid within Marsilius's theory, the circumstances of its manifold delegations are in fact not legitimated by Marsilius's theory.

An important characteristic of the so-called 'legal revolution' was that the National Socialists deployed massive propaganda, intimidation, violence, and electoral manipulation in almost every act of transfer of political authority from the people or its representatives to the Reich government. Although it is unclear in Marsilius's theory how exactly a delegation of political power should take place, the consent of the *universitas civium* is obviously understood as free from violence and fraud. Moreover, it is a fundamental doctrine in Marsilius that once conferred, political competences can generally be revoked, while it is a major characteristic of the National Socialist state that a revocation is to be excluded — by any means. The Third Reich was designed according to the *Führerprinzip* (leadership principle), the idea that once omnicompetent and unlimited political authority has been irrevocably transferred to the top of the state, authority henceforth can only be delegated — in harmless particles — from the top down to the bottom.

There are similar problems with using Marsilius's theories to justify National Socialist church policy. Marsilius's idea of the Church as a subordinated or integrated part of the political community applies only to a *communitas fidelium perfecta* — a faithful Christian people and a faithful Christian *pars principans*. While this may not have been the case in every European political community in Marsilius's time, it was most certainly not true in the Third Reich. After the Protestant Reformation, the unity of the Church in the Holy Roman Empire and then Germany had ceased to exist. By the twentieth century, especially during the Third Reich, a significant minority of Germans had left the churches. And Adolf Hitler was by no means a devout Christian (and certainly not a new Constantine or Ludwig the Bavarian), but rather an adversary of Christianity. Thus, by Marsilian standards, the Nazi leadership, which was committed to neo-paganism, was not allowed to have authority over the German churches, and these, like the pre-Constantinian Church, were entitled and obliged to self-government.[71]

However, the elasticity — and deliberate vagueness — of Marsilius's political theory, which Richard Scholz called attention to and which Wilhelm Schneider-Windmüller made use of, was not immune to a Nazi reading. Marsilius of Padua certainly could not have foreseen such an interpretation of his medieval political theory in a distant and alien future.

---

71 Cf. *DP*, II, 17.15, ed. by Scholz, p. 370.

404 FRANK GODTHARDT

Works Cited

Archival Sources

Berlin, Bundesarchiv (BArch), R 4910-13276; R 9361-II / 1125817; R 9361-VIII
Kartei (NSDAP-Zentralkartei) / 20471255 and 2890811; R 9361-IX Kartei
(NSDAP-Gaukartei) / 335187 and 38920163
Bonn, Universitätsarchiv, MNF-Prom 172
Freiburg, Landesarchiv Baden-Württemberg, Abteilung Staatsarchiv Freiburg,
D 180/2

Primary Sources

*Bekenntnis der Professoren an den deutschen Universitäten und Hochschulen zu Adolf
Hitler und dem nationalsozialistischen Staat*, ed. by Nationalsozialistischer
Lehrerbund Sachsen (Dresden, 1933)
Konrad von Megenberg, *Planctus ecclesiae in Germaniam*, ed. by Richard Scholz,
Monumenta Germaniae Historica: Staatsschriften des späteren Mittelalters,
2.1 (Leipzig: Hiersemann, 1941)
Marsilius von Padua, *Defensor pacis*, ed. by Richard Scholz, Monumenta
Germaniae Historica: Fontes iuris germanici antiqui in usum scholarum
seperatim editi, 7.2 (Hanover: Hahn, 1933)
Scholz, Richard, *Die Publizistik zur Zeit Philipps des Schönen und Bonifaz' VIII.: Ein
Beitrag zur Geschichte der politischen Anschauungen des Mittelalters*,
Kirchenrechtliche Abhandlungen, 6/8 (Stuttgart: Enke, 1903)
——, *Unbekannte kirchenpolitische Streitschriften aus der Zeit Ludwigs des Bayern
(1327–1345)*, I: *Analysen*; II: *Texte*, Bibliothek des Königlich-Preussischen
Historischen Instituts in Rom, 9–10 (Rome: Löscher, 1911–1914)
——, *Wilhelm von Ockham als politischer Denker und sein Breviloquium de
principatu tyrannico*, Schriften des Reichsinstituts für ältere deutsche
Geschichtskunde, 8 (Leipzig: Hiersemann, 1944)

Secondary Works

[Anonymous editors], 'Zum Geleit', *Zeitschrift für deutsche Geisteswissenschaft*, 1
(1938/1939), 1–2
Blaschke, Olaf, *Die Kirchen und der Nationalsozialismus*, Reclams
Universalbibliothek, 19211 (Stuttgart: Reclam, 2014)
Bock, Friedrich, 'Bemerkungen zur Beurteilung Kaiser Ludwigs IV. in der neueren
Literatur', *Zeitschrift für Bayerische Landesgeschichte*, 23 (1960), 115–27
——, 'Die Gründung des Klosters Ettal: Ein quellenkritischer Beitrag zur
Geschichte Ludwigs des Bayern', *Oberbayerisches Archiv*, 66 (1929), 1–116

————, *Reichsidee und Nationalstaaten: Vom Untergang des alten Reiches bis zur Kündigung des deutsch-englischen Bündnisses im Jahre 1341* (Munich: Callwey, 1943)

Condren, Conal, 'Democracy and the *Defensor Pacis*: On the English Language Tradition of Marsilian Scholarship', *Il Pensiero Politico*, 13 (1980), 301–16

Elze, Reinhard, 'Das Deutsche Historische Institut in Rom, 1888–1988', in *Das Deutsche Historische Institut in Rom, 1888–1988*, ed. by Reinhard Elze and Arnold Esch (Tübingen: Max Miemeyer Verlag, 1990), pp. 1–31

Evans, Richard J., *The Coming of the Third Reich: How the Nazis Destroyed Democracy and Seized Power in Germany* (London: Allen Lane, 2003)

————, *The Third Reich in Power: How the Nazis Won Over the Hearts and Minds of a Nation* (London: Allen Lane, 2005)

Godthardt, Frank, 'Die Interpretation des *Defensor pacis* während des Dritten Reichs', in *Von Hamburg nach Java: Studien zur mittelalterlichen, neuen und digitalen Geschichte. Festschrift zu Ehren von Jürgen Sarnowsky*, ed. by Jochen Burgtorf, Christian Hoffarth, and Sebastian Kubon, Nova Mediaevalia: Quellen und Studien zum europäischen Mittelalter, 18 (Göttingen: Vandenhoeck & Ruprecht Unipress, 2020), pp. 349–64

————, *Marsilius von Padua und der Romzug Ludwigs des Bayern: Politische Theorie und politisches Handeln*, Nova Mediaevalia: Quellen und Studien zum europäischen Mittelalter, 6 (Göttingen: Vandenhoeck & Ruprecht Unipress, 2011)

Görres-Gesellschaft, ed., *Jahres- und Tagungsbericht der Görres-Gesellschaft für 1969* (Cologne, 1970)

Heimpel, Hermann, 'Das erste Reich: Schicksal und Anfang', *Zeitschrift für deutsche Geisteswissenschaft*, 1 (1938/1939), 3–25

————, 'Nachruf Richard Scholz', *Deutsches Archiv für Erforschung des Mittelalters*, 8 (1951), 264–66

Hesse, Andreas, *Die Professoren und Dozenten der preußischen Pädagogischen Akademien (1926–1933) und Hochschulen für Lehrerbildung (1933–1941)* (Weinheim: Deutscher Studien Verlag, 1995)

Holtzmann, Walther, 'Das Deutsche Historische Institut in Rom', in *Veröffentlichungen der Arbeitsgemeinschaft für Forschung des Landes Nordrhein-Westphalen*, Geisteswissenschaften, 46 (Cologne: Westdeutscher Verlag: 1955), pp. 7–43

Kleiner, Hans, 'Erb- und Rassenkunde', *Zeitschrift für deutsche Geisteswissenschaft*, 1 (1938/1939), 556–62

Kölmel, Wilhelm, *Regimen christianum: Weg und Ergebnisse des Gewaltenverhältnisses und des Gewaltenverständnisses (8. bis 14. Jahrhundert)* (Berlin: Walter de Gruyter, 1970)

Müller-Mertens, Eckhard, 'Nachruf Ruth Bork', *Deutsches Archiv für Erforschung des Mittelalters*, 47 (1991), 373

Nederman, Cary J., *Community and Consent: The Secular Political Theory of Marsiglio of Padua's 'Defensor Pacis'* (Lanham, MD: Rowman & Littlefield, 1995)

Opitz, Gottfried, 'Nachruf Friedrich Bock', *Historische Zeitschrift*, 201 (1965), 522–24

Pädagogische Hochschule Freiburg im Breisgau, ed., *Vorlesungsverzeichnis Sommersemester 1968* [Freiburg im Breisgau, 1968]

Peonidis, Filimon, 'Marsilius of Padua as a Democratic Theorist', *Roda da Fortuna: Revista Eletrônica sobre Antiguidade e Medioevo / Electronic Journal about Antiquity and Middle Ages*, 5 (2016), 106–24

Schneider[-Windmüller], Wilhelm, *Die Quaestiones disputatae de veritate des Thomas von Aquin in ihrer philosophiegeschichtlichen Beziehung zu Augustinus*, Beiträge zur Geschichte der Philosophie und Theologie des Mittelalters: Texte und Untersuchungen, 27.3 (Münster: Aschendorff, 1930)

Schneider-Windmüller, Wilhelm, 'Beitrag zur Kenntnis reaktionsträger Carbonylgruppen' (unpublished doctoral thesis, University of Bonn, 1943)

——, *Staat und Kirche im Defensor Pacis des Marsilius von Padua* (Bonn: Ludwig Röhrscheid, 1934)

Scholder, Klaus, *Die Kirchen und das Dritte Reich*, I: *Vorgeschichte und Zeit der Illusionen 1918–1934* (Frankfurt am Main: Propyläen, 1977)

Scholz, Richard, 'Einleitung', in Marsilius von Padua, *Defensor pacis*, ed. by Richard Scholz, Monumenta Germaniae Historica: Fontes iuris germanici antiqui in usum scholarum seperatim editi, 7.2 (Hanover: Hahn, 1933), pp. v–lxx

——, 'Germanischer und römischer Kaisergedanke im Mittelalter', *Zeitschrift für deutsche Geisteswissenschaft*, 3 (1940/1941), 116–42

——, 'Marsilius von Padua und Deutschland', in *Marsilio da Padova: Studi raccolti nel VI centenario della morte*, ed. by Aldo Checchini and Norberto Bobbio, Pubblicazioni della Facoltà di giurisprudenza dell'Università di Padova, 3 (Padua: CEDAM, 1942), pp. 3–35

——, 'Marsilius von Padua und die Genesis des modernen Staatsbewußtseins', *Historische Zeitschrift*, 156 (1937), 88–105

——, 'Marsilius von Padua und die Idee der Demokratie', *Zeitschrift für Politik*, 1 (1908), 61–94

——, 'Politische und weltanschauliche Kämpfe um den Reichsgedanken am Hofe Ludwigs des Bayern', *Zeitschrift für deutsche Geisteswissenschaft*, 1 (1938/1939), 298–316

——, Review of Bock, *Reichsidee und Nationalstaaten*, *Deutsches Archiv für Erforschung des Mittelalters*, 8 (1951), 332–34

——, 'Weltstaat und Staatenwelt in der Anschauung des Mittelalters', *Zeitschrift für deutsche Geisteswissenschaft*, 4 (1941/1942), 82–100

Strohm, Christoph, *Die Kirchen im Dritten Reich*, C. H. Beck Wissen, 2nd edn (Munich: C. H. Beck, 2017)

Sullivan, Mary Elizabeth, 'Democracy and the *Defensor Pacis* Revisited: Marsiglio of Padua's Democratic Arguments', *Viator*, 41 (2010), 257–70

Tellenbach, Gerd, 'Nachruf Friedrich Bock', *Quellen und Forschungen aus italienischen Archiven und Bibliotheken*, 42/43 (1963), xi

Wimmer, Karl, *Kaiser Ludwig der Bayer im Kampfe um das Reich* (Munich: Hoheneichen, 1942)

Wolf, Ernst, 'Neuere Arbeiten zur Kirchengeschichte des Mittelalters (Schluß)', *Theologische Rundschau*, n.s., 10 (1938), 221–42

Wolf, Hubert, *Papst und Teufel: Die Archive des Vatikan und das Dritte Reich*, 2nd edn (Munich: C. H. Beck, 2009)

GREGORIO PIAIA

Marsilius of Padua in *The Name of the Rose**

Between Historical Fiction and Post-1968 Ideology

Conceived as a powerful doctrinal weapon in the conflict between Louis the Bavarian and the Avignon Pope John XXII, the *Defensor pacis* lent itself to being used in the controversies between religious authority and worldly power that punctuate the history of the Latin West. It is hardly surprising, therefore, that the practice of rendering Marsilius's highly topical politico-religious thought and its ideological use emerges recurrently dating back to the translation of the *Defensor pacis* into the Florentine vernacular in 1363, the period preceding the long, expensive but ineffectual War of the Eight Saints between Florence and the Avignon Papacy (1375–1378).[1] This translation was not based on the Latin text of the *Defensor pacis* but on an earlier French translation, which we no longer have. In the same period, Marsilius's political theories aroused considerable interest in France, as confirmed by the *Songe du Vergier* (1378), written when Pope Gregory XI resolved to abandon the Avignon seat in 1377, resulting in the Western Schism.[2] During the schism, the *Defensor pacis* was clearly recognized by some supporters of conciliarism and was a source for the third book of Nicholas of Cusa's *De concordantia catholica* (1433).[3]

The editio princeps of the work, which was edited in Basel in 1522 by a group of intellectuals oriented towards Erasmus's spirituality and close to the Reformation movement, obviously represents a fundamental step in the interpretation and use of the *Defensor pacis*. In the subsequent translations into English (1535) and German (1545), Marsilius's text underwent

---

* Translated by Raffaella Roncarati.
1 Cf. Marsilius of Padua, *Difenditore della pace*, ed. by Pincin; Tromboni, 'Filosofia politica e cultura cittadina'. On the historical context, cf. Najemy, *A History of Florence*, chs 5 and 6.
2 Cf. Quillet, *La philosophie politique du Songe du Vergier*, pp. 51–60.
3 Cf. Piaia, 'Marsilius von Padua († um 1342) und Nicolaus Cusanus († 1464)'.

> **Gregorio Piaia** (b. Belluno, 1944) is Professor Emeritus in the History of Philosophy at the University of Padua.

Marsilius of Padua, ed. by Alessandro Mulieri, Serena Masolini, and Jenny Pelletier, Disputatio, 36 (Turnhout: Brepols, 2023), pp. 409–430
BREPOLS ❧ PUBLISHERS
10.1484/M.DISPUT-EB.5.132920

considerable deletions and adaptations, which distorted its original framework so as to make it useful for Henry VIII of England and the politico-religious aspirations of Evangelical-Lutheran Protestantism. The complete insertion of Marsilius into Matthias Flacius Illyricus's *Catalogus testium veritatis* (1556) sanctioned the image of the Paduan as a precursor of the Reformation on a religious as well as a political plane for the following centuries. In his works *Ordinum Hollandiae ac Westfaliae pietas* (1613) and *De imperio summarum potestatum circa sacra* (1647), Hugo Grotius availed himself of Marsilius's doctrines in order to support the secular authority's power to intervene in the religious sphere, to endorse tolerance, and to oppose the more intransigent Calvinist circles.[4]

Municipal pride and the tradition of Venetian jurisdictionalism underlie the measured judgement that Abbot Melchiorre Cesarotti expressed in 1796 on the heretic Marsilius, polemically contesting the *Considérations d'un Italien sur l'Italie* by Abbot Carlo Denina.[5] But it was in the nineteenth century that Marsilius was rediscovered and particularly praised for his modernity: in Germany, the philosopher of law Friedrich Julius Stahl identified 'the traces of the modern theory of the sovereignty of the people' in the *Defensor pacis*,[6] whereas in France Adolphe Franck underlined Marsilius's closeness to Rousseau, both of whom held that only the laws issued from the whole community can guarantee the obedience of all citizens.[7] In Italy, Francesco Fiorentino observed that Marsilius had maintained 'the absolute independence of the State', whose origin lies exclusively in the 'free choice exercised by peoples', and therefore the Paduan 'performed in the science of the State that which Pomponazzi was later to perform in philosophy'.[8] Pasquale Villari too, in his monograph on Machiavelli, presented Marsilius as a 'prophet of the future', while pointing out, however, that he had remained tied to the method and 'abstract idealism' of scholasticism.[9] Francesco Scaduto showed greater attention to Marsilius's historical context, recognizing the innovation and significance of having given theoretical form to the idea of the sovereignty of the

---

4 On these themes, see my volume *Marsilio da Padova nella Riforma e nella Controriforma*. In particular, as concerns the use of Marsilian thought in English authors, see Passerin d'Entrèves, 'La fortuna di Marsilio da Padova in Inghilterra'; Stout, 'Marsilius of Padua and the Henrician Reformation'; Condren, 'Democracy and the *Defensor Pacis*'; Condren, 'George Lawson and the *Defensor pacis*'; Simonetta, *Marsilio in Inghilterra*; Simonetta, *Dal Difensore della pace al Leviatano*; Koch, *Zur Dis-/Kontinuität mittelalterlichen politischen Denkens*.

5 Cf. Piaia, 'Il padre Zaccaria', pp. 343–52. But see also Giacchi, 'Osservazioni sulla fortuna delle idee di Marsilio'.

6 Stahl, *Storia della filosofia del diritto*, pp. 62–63 and 74–75. On the figure of Marsilius as a 'precursor', see Russi, 'Letture e valutazioni di Marsilio da Padova'.

7 Franck, *Réformateurs et publicistes de l'Europe*, pp. 135–51.

8 Fiorentino, *Pietro Pomponazzi*, pp. 149–50.

9 Villari, *Nicolò Machiavelli e i suoi tempi*, II, pp. 501–02.

MARSILIUS OF PADUA IN *THE NAME OF THE ROSE*   411

people, a customary practice in Italian free cities inspired by him, and of having defended not so much the empire but rather 'the State in itself'.[10]

In the same years, Baldassare Labanca, a former priest who taught moral philosophy at the University of Padua from 1879 to 1881, published the first Italian monograph on Marsilius, in which the Paduan heretic is exalted as a 'prophet of the future', a forerunner of the 1789 French Revolution and of socialism itself in its most genuine form. Indeed, Labanca notes, in the *Defensor pacis*,

> the tyrannical papal and imperial authority is replaced by popular authority, not the kind of ignorant authority, which also results in tyranny, and even worse, in anarchy, but the intelligent authority of the people, which represents it [and corresponds to] the prevailing part of citizens.[11]

A few years before, in 1876, Napoleone Pietrucci, a scholar of local history, had written a letter to the mayor of Padua in which he proposed that a monument to Marsilius should be erected, presenting him as the figure who anticipated Count Cavour and his idea of a 'free Church in a free State', which is at the basis of modern liberalism.[12]

Labanca's interpretation was taken up again and developed by Erminio Troilo at the conference held in Padua in 1942 on occasion of the sixth centenary of Marsilius's death. Troilo, who was himself professor of theoretical and moral philosophy at the University of Padua, emphasized the philosophical weight of the *Defensor pacis*, linking its political theses back to Latin Averroism. Inspired by the latter, Marsilius appears to have performed a radical transformation of the political perspective. Indeed, according to him,

> the double truth has its political equivalent in the double authority (religious and political), which dialectically attains its final result in only one authority, understood in the historical and political sense of a pure humanity or worldliness (or, which comes to the same thing, of pure rationality): the State.

Furthermore, in a daring theoretical passage, Troilo considered the Averroistic doctrine asserting the unity of a separate Intellect as the foundation of Marsilius's 'populism', so that the State, the ultimate expression of

---

10 Scaduto, *Stato e Chiesa negli scritti politici*, p. 244.

11 Labanca, *Marsilio da Padova riformatore*, p. 222. Cf. Piaia, 'Baldassare Labanca'.

12 Piaia, 'Baldassare Labanca', p. 370. The proposal of erecting a monument to Marsilius was taken up again by Labanca in the dedication of his volume to the mayor of Padua, but was not carried out.

412   GREGORIO PIAIA

human community, is seen as 'a sort, we might say, of agent Intellect made immanent in the form of collective understanding and will'.[13]

Moving on into the later twentieth century in the post-conciliar climate of the Catholic world, the proposal of reversing the traditionally negative image of Marsilius as a heretic emerged and was officially recognized.[14] By contrast, in more traditionalist circles, Marsilius's doctrinal position was expanded and projected forward to the point that he was considered the initiator of a process that culminated in the twentieth-century 'theory of the totalitarian State' owing to the 'absolute fullness of power' that he grants to the 'activity of the State'.[15]

We are thus faced with a subtle network of interpretation and ideological exploitation that renders the fortune of the Paduan heretic particularly complex but also fascinating,[16] a fortune that obviously relates to the history of political thought but, in the case of the world-famous novel by Umberto Eco, *The Name of the Rose*, crosses over into the wide territory of fiction. Eco considers fiction to be multivalent: there is a first level, which pertains to mass literature and is aimed at the common reader who is chiefly interested in the plot and wishes to know how the story ends; the second level concerns the historical setting, which allows the culturally less unprepared reader to grasp at least some of the historical and cultural references that are scattered throughout the work; then there is a third level that refers to the philosophical and political message conveyed by the novel that a discerning reader can perceive here and there in the conversations held by the characters.

In his novel, Eco mentions Marsilius several times and skilfully follows the path, already abundantly and variously trodden, of the ideological and political use of the Paduan thinker. But Eco adds a new angle to Marsilius in the narrative of *The Name of the Rose*. What is this new angle? It consists, first, in the literary genre itself, namely that *The Name of the Rose* is a work of fiction that is both a historical novel and a mystery story rather than a theoretical or polemical text, and, second, in the role of Marsilius in the overall economy of *The Name of the Rose*, a role that is barely evident and certainly ambiguous at first glance. This role not only appears to concern the narration as such from the point of view of its autonomous structure,

---

13 Troilo, 'L'averroismo di Marsilio da Padova', pp. 62–63. On the interpretative trajectory of so-called political Averroism, see Piaia, 'Dalla *Politica* di Aristotele all'"averroismo politico"'.

14 Cf. Leonardi, 'La riforma della Chiesa nel progetto di Marsilio' and Leonardi, 'La centralità dei problemi ecclesiologici nel *Defensor pacis*'; Damiata, '*Plenitudo potestatis*' e '*universitas civium*'; Battocchio, 'Marsilio da Padova, la politica, il Vangelo'; Piaia, '"Sancte Marsili, ora pro nobis?"'.

15 Galvão de Sousa, *O totalitarismo nas orígens da moderna teoria do Estado*, pp. 212–13.

16 Cf. Ménard, 'L'aventure historiographique du *Défenseur de la paix*'; Bayona Aznar, 'El periplo de la teoría política de Marsilio de Padua'; Ancona, *Marsilio da Padova*.

MARSILIUS OF PADUA IN *THE NAME OF THE ROSE*   413

but also to involve (how and to what extent?) the person of the author himself. Indeed, in the novel, the historical figure of Marsilius is repeatedly mentioned, but appears to be marginal and subordinate when compared with the figure of William of Ockham, who takes up, so to speak, the lion's share of the reader's attention. Here a question emerges: What if the apparent marginality of Marsilius's character were nothing but a means of camouflaging his strongly political presence? A presence potentially much more explosive than the *epistemological* and more widely *philosophical* presence of Ockham, whom Eco overtly proposes as a herald of modern, or rather postmodern, thought.[17]

Let us proceed systematically. It is well known that various historical figures of the later Middle Ages converge in the character of Brother William of Baskerville, the protagonist of *The Name of the Rose*. The philosopher William of Ockham obviously, who inspired Eco to name his strange and mysterious protagonist along with Arthur Conan Doyle's detective novel *The Hound of the Baskervilles* (1902). But another Englishman is also present, that is, Roger Bacon, who towards the end of the thirteenth century had maintained the importance of mathematics in the study of natural phenomena. And then there are the Spiritual Franciscans like Michael of Cesena, who asserted the principle of 'meritorious poverty' and opposed the pope, and finally our Marsilius de' Mainardini, better known as Marsilius of Padua.[18]

In Eco's novel, the Paduan appears for the first time in the Prologue, where the already old monk Adso of Melk recalls the extraordinary events that he had witnessed 'toward the end of the year of our Lord 1327, when the Emperor Louis came down to Italy to restore the dignity of the Holy Roman Empire' against the 'usurper, simoniac, and heresiarch' Jacques of Cahors, who wrongfully sat on the papal throne at Avignon. The father of the young Adso, a German baron 'fighting in Louis's train', had wanted his son, a Benedictine novice, to accompany him on the expedition beyond the Alps, so that he could become acquainted with 'the wonders of Italy' and attend the coronation of the emperor in Rome. Adso recalls that in Tuscany his parents,

> on the advice of Marsilius, who had taken a liking for me, decided to place me under the direction of a learned Franciscan, Brother William

---

17 This interpretative approach has already been concisely presented in my article 'Postille storico-filosofiche', p. 168. The critical literature on *The Name of the Rose* is very extensive, such as to rival that on Marsilius. Of relevance to the theme examined here are the following essays: Zecchini, 'Il Medioevo di Umberto Eco'; Bausi, 'I due medioevi del *Nome della rosa*'.

18 On the character William of Baskerville, see in particular the essay by Miethke, 'Der Philosoph als Detektiv'.

of Baskerville, about to undertake a mission that would lead him to famous cities and ancient abbeys.[19]

Marsilius, who — a few lines earlier — is counted among the 'imperial theologians' together with the Parisian Averroist John of Jandun, reappears in the 'Sext' of the 'First Day', during the conversation between the two Franciscan friars Ubertino of Casale and William of Baskerville, which is centred on the delicate and captivating connection between mysticism and lust, and hence between the spiritual and corporeal dimensions. This theme, developed by Eco with subtlety, fascinates those readers who are more receptive to psychological depth, and so William's autobiographical allusion risks going unnoticed: 'I studied, I met some very wise friends', William tells Ubertino, who asked him what he had done in recent times, after renouncing the task of inquisitor. William responds,

> Then I came to know Marsilius, I was attracted by his ideas about empire, the people, about a new law for the kingdoms of the earth, and so I ended up in that group of our brothers who are advising the Emperor. But you know these things: I wrote you.[20]

Marsilius reappears in the 'Second Day. Nones' during another dialogue which is of central importance in the theoretical structure of *The Name of the Rose*. It is the dialogue between William of Baskerville and the abbot of the monastery, who embodies the cultural tradition inherited from the early Middle Ages and influenced by Augustine of Hippo and Pseudo-Dionysius the Areopagite, that is, before the rediscovery of Aristotle in the Latin West completely changed the outlook on the world, on nature, and on social and political relationships. Marsilius is mentioned here at two places in the text. The first occasion is when William discusses with the abbot the matter of a possible although difficult negotiation with the pope. William attributes to Marsilius the idea of sending to Avignon 'an imperial envoy who would present to the Pope the point of view of the Emperor's supporters' along with Michael of Cesena.[21]

The second occasion is of greater significance, since it suggests that Marsilius's position in support of the emperor is only a means to achieve quite another purpose. Those who supported Louis the Bavarian in fact had different motivations, interests, and perspectives. Although their ways of looking upon the wealth and poverty of the Church, upon war and heresies are opposed to each other, William and the abbot agree in their support of 'the rights of Louis, who is also putting Italy to the sword', even

---

19 Eco, *The Name of the Rose*, pp. 13–14.
20 Eco, *The Name of the Rose*, p. 61.
21 Eco, *The Name of the Rose*, p. 147.

MARSILIUS OF PADUA IN *THE NAME OF THE ROSE*   415

if they do so for different reasons. William seems aware of this paradoxical situation, which involves Marsilius too:

> I, too, find myself caught in a game of strange alliances. Strange the alliance between Spirituals and the empire, and strange that of the empire with Marsilius, who seeks sovereignty for the people. And strange the alliance between the two of us, so different in our ideas and traditions.[22]

Therefore, according to Eco's account, the *Defensor pacis* was not only an extraordinary and complete dossier containing philosophical and theological arguments in favour of the emperor and more generally of the civil *potestas* against the papal claim to the *plenitudo potestatis*, but was also and above all a clever attempt to circulate the idea of the sovereignty of the people under the cover of the controversy between Louis and John XXII.

The principle of the sovereignty of the people, only briefly mentioned here, is in truth fundamental to the position of Brother William of Baskerville (alias Umberto Eco) concerning life in society. It re-emerges more evidently in the conversation between William and the young Adso ('Third day. Nones'), where the political theme is meaningfully associated with the theme of the birth of the 'new science' and of the 'new natural magic', which Roger Bacon had proposed as an 'enterprise directed by the church', but that William thinks should be an operation managed directly by the intellectual community. He almost foreshadows the eighteenth-century *république des lettres*:

> So I think that, since I and my friends today believe that for the management of human affairs it is not the church that should legislate but the assembly of the people, then in the future the community of the learned will have to propose this new and human theology which is natural philosophy and positive magic.[23]

In this passage, which sounds like an announcement of the modern process of secularization, where science and politics replace religion, Marsilius is not mentioned although he is evidently included among William's 'friends'. But the doctrinal position of the Paduan reappears vigorously in the 'Fifth day. Prime', during the 'fraternal [in fact rather turbulent ...] debate regarding the poverty of Jesus', which takes place between the delegation of Pope John XXII and that of Louis the Bavarian. While the delegates on either side wrangle and exchange insults, the novice Adso asks Brother William to enlighten him on the question of the poverty of Christ. Here we come to William's answer, which is certainly of a political rather than theological character, and presents Marsilius as a double-crosser who uses

---

22 Eco, *The Name of the Rose*, p. 153.
23 Eco, *The Name of the Rose*, p. 206.

his support for the imperial cause as a screen to promote a democratic conception of power:

> 'But the question is not whether Christ was poor: it is whether the church must be poor. And "poor" does not so much mean owning a palace or not; it means, rather, keeping or renouncing the right to legislate on earthly matters.'
> 'Then this', I [= Adso] said, 'is why the Emperor is so interested in what the Minorites say about poverty.'
> 'Exactly. The Minorites are playing the Emperor's game against the Pope. But Marsilius and I consider it a two-sided game, and we would like the empire to support our view and serve our idea of human rule.'[24]

But immediately afterwards William declares himself quite doubtful — thus resembling Buridan's ass — about the policy to be adopted in the current debate and, like a good Englishman, professes his adherence to realism and pragmatism, acknowledging that Marsilius's plan is not feasible at the present time: 'The time is not ripe. Marsilius raves of an impossible transformation, immediately; but Louis is no better than his predecessors, even if for the present he remains the only bulwark against a wretch like John.'[25]

The character of Marsilius, therefore, seems to exit the scene almost as though he were a dreamer far removed from reality. In fact, he is merely placed out of view, and as in a hide-and-seek game, his doctrines take centre stage. Once the squabble is over and the two delegations resume their dealings, William mentions Marsilius's doctrines explicitly when it is up to William to 'expound the theses of the imperial theologians', addressing those present with a discourse on 'a strange concept of temporal government' ('Fifth Day. Terce'). Starting circuitously from creation and from Adam, William, with a leap forward, comes to the central thesis of *Dictio* I of the *Defensor pacis*:

> Considering also that the Lord had given to Adam and to his descendants power over the things of this earth, provided they obeyed the divine laws, we might infer that the Lord also was not averse to the idea that in earthly things the people should be legislator and effective first cause of the law. By the term 'people', he said, it would be best to signify all citizens, but since among citizens children must be included, as well as idiots, malefactors and women, perhaps it would be possible to arrive reasonably at a definition of the people as the better

---

24 Eco, *The Name of the Rose*, pp. 345–46.
25 Eco, *The Name of the Rose*, p. 346.

part of citizens, though he himself at the moment did not consider it opportune to assert who actually belonged to that part.[26]

After having distracted and bewildered the audience with a long and erudite digression on the power of *impositio nominum* that God conferred to Adam, William can therefore conclude the first part of his speech by proclaiming, in a pure Marsilian style:

> Whereby [...] is it clear that legislation over the things of this earth, and therefore over the things of the cities and kingdoms, had nothing to do with the custody and administration of the divine word, an unalienable privilege of the ecclesiastical hierarchy.[27]

The doctrines of the *Defensor pacis* are thus explained. As concerns the character of Marsilius, he reappears a little further on in William's long discourse almost as though on the sly and not in reference to a conception of the state — as one would expect — but in connection to the dispute about poverty. It is as if Eco's intention was to separate the first *dictio* of the *Defensor pacis* from its author, making it autonomous and valid in itself and in abstraction from historical circumstances:

> As for the connection with the dispute about poverty, William added, his own humble opinions, developed in the form of conversational suggestions by him and by some others such as Marsilius of Padua and John of Jandun, led to the following conclusions.[28]

In *The Name of the Rose*, Marsilius is mentioned again with reference to his activity as imperial vicar in ecclesiological issues in Rome, to which we will return below. Two short mentions contained in the 'Fifth Day. Vespers' are also noteworthy, where William of Ockham's ecclesiological and political doctrines are characterized as even more radical than those of Marsilius and where William of Baskerville recognizes the cleverness of the Paduan as an 'imperial adviser'.[29] But of greater interest in these pages is how Michael of Cesena, minister general of the Franciscan order, distances himself from the political positions just illustrated by William of Baskerville. In this case too, Marsilius is not named but remains veiled:

> You, William, spoke very clearly today, and you said what you would like. Well, that is not what I want [...]. I want the Franciscan order to be accepted by the Pope with its ideal of poverty. [...] I am not

---

26 Eco, *The Name of the Rose*, p. 352 (cf. *DP*, I, 12.3–4). At the end of the same page, there is another point that echoes the Marsilian text: 'Well, then, William continued, if one man can make laws badly, will not many men be better?' (cf. *DP*, I, 11.3).

27 Eco, *The Name of the Rose*, p. 353.

28 Eco, *The Name of the Rose*, p. 355.

29 Eco, *The Name of the Rose*, pp. 292 and 294.

418 GREGORIO PIAIA

> thinking about the assembly of the people or about the law of nations. I must prevent the order from dissolving into a plurality of Little Brethren.[30]

We have thus completed the picture of Marsilius's 'presence' and his political theories in *The Name of the Rose*. So, one might ask: Well, what is problematic about Eco's presentation of Marsilius, since the novel is interwoven with references to historical figures and quotations drawn from a wide diversity of literary sources from the Middle Ages, sources that Eco has explored and used with such accuracy and enthusiasm? The problem lies in the fact that his representation of Marsilius's thought, which is centred on the principle of the will of the people, turns the Paduan into a convinced and resolute forerunner of modern democracy, and this appears anachronistic today.[31] Such a representation is the result of a forward projection that disregards Marsilius's historical context, although as we have seen it enjoyed wide success in the nineteenth and early twentieth centuries. Indeed, the reference to the *universitas civium* in the *Defensor pacis* does not arise from Marsilius's adherence to a democratic ideal (as it might seem on the basis of *The Name of the Rose*), but from the need to find an autonomous and authoritative theoretical basis for the exercise of political power, so as to rescue the latter from the 'perverted' doctrinal circuit of theocratic thought, which rested on the mighty philosophical and theological system formerly elaborated by pseudo-Dionysius.

At the beginning of the fourteenth century, the basis for an alternative to the Neoplatonic tradition was sought in Aristotle, the *Philosophus* par excellence. Aristotle's political theory, which is little inclined to recognize the primacy of democracy, was interpreted and bent by Marsilius in a definitely democratic direction (the 'immediate cause' of government and law is the people, whereas God is only the 'remote cause'), thus depriving the representative of God on earth, that is, the *romanus episcopus vocatus papa*, of all claim to temporal power. But in Marsilius — and this is the point at issue — the sovereignty of the people should not be understood in today's sense, nor in a sense prevalent during the Enlightenment, and to be accurate, neither in the sense of the medieval free cities. Rather, Marsilius's sense of the sovereignty of the people should be understood in the sense of a 'seigneurial' regime, which was in the process of replacing the regime of the free cities at the time of the Paduan. The seigneurial regime formally rested on a double investiture: first, on the part of the *populus* through

---

30 Eco, *The Name of the Rose*, p. 391 (the last sentence appears to have been omitted in the English translation).

31 On the issue of 'republicanism' in Marsilius, see, in particular, Gewirth, 'Republicanism and Absolutism'.

election, and second, on the part of the emperor with the conferment of the title of 'imperial vicar'.[32]

Being a citizen of Padua, Marsilius certainly had a clear view of the regime governing that free city, which in those years was undergoing a deep crisis that would result in the seigniory of the Carraresi. But he also knew the seigneurial regime well, with which he had established close personal contacts. It suffices to mention the seigniories of Matteo Visconti in Milan and of Cangrande della Scala in Verona, the two main Ghibelline exponents in northern Italy who, in 1319, had charged Marsilius with a mission to France in order to propose that Charles de La Marche (the future King Charles IV of France) take over the helm of the Ghibelline league.[33] The mission was unsuccessful, and we know that on 29 April 1319 Pope John XXII wrote a letter to Charles de La Marche urging him to reject the proposal put forward by Marsilius — the very same Marsilius who, one year before, on 5 April 1318, had received assurances from Avignon that he would obtain the first canonical benefice that would become vacant in Padua. Marsilius had been awaiting this benefice for at least a year and a half, which meant that he had not yet openly sided with the Ghibellines. It is not unlikely that, tired of waiting for the benefice, Marsilius decided to serve the Ghibelline party publicly, a choice entirely legitimate in itself, but one that had little to do with a supposed predilection for democracy.

Regarding this last point, let me raise a question of method, which pertains to the job of being a historian of ideas: In order to better understand an author, is it more important to place him in his time or to project him forward, following the developmental or progressive model that found its ultimate expression in Hegel and the various forms of Hegelianism that appeared in the nineteenth and twentieth centuries? From a methodological point of view, and without trespassing into the philosophy of history and political philosophy, it is important to distinguish between what an author wrote in a certain epoch and in a certain milieu from the way in which that author has been subsequently read, interpreted, and used (in a word, his legacy). The latter perspective is undoubtedly interesting, but it should not overly influence the work of contextualizing an author. Going back to Marsilius, we might ask: Have those scholars who insist on the democratic orientation of his thought ever asked themselves why his contemporaries,

---

32 On these questions, see Quillet, *La philosophie politique de Marsile de Padoue*, pp. 23–48, where the author examines the statutes of the city of Padua and the relations between the seigniory and the empire as well as the meaning acquired by the imperial vicariate, with reference to the emblematic case of Matteo Visconti. See also Piaia, 'The Shadow of Antenor'; Collodo, 'Scienze della natura e ricerca politica', pp. 44, 123, 133, 202–03, 226–27.

33 On the 'Ghibelline component' of the *Defensor pacis*, see Briguglia, *Marsilio da Padova*, pp. 48–50.

even those who wrote against him, did not pay much attention to this aspect? They may reply that Marsilius was too advanced, that his critics were not able to see the theoretical potential contained in his doctrines. But we can retort: Is this *our* Marsilius or the historical Marsilius who lived at the turn of the fourteenth century?[34]

Let us consider now the structure of the *Defensor pacis*. Thanks to a more accurate historical contextualization, it seems possible to dispel to some extent the problematic transition from the *legislator* of the first *dictio*, which coincides with the *universitas civium seu eius valentior pars*, to the *legislator supremus superiore carens* of the second *dictio*, which corresponds to the person of the Holy Roman Emperor. This is a transition that apparently constitutes a real regression when considered from the point of view of nineteenth-century interpretations of the *Defensor pacis*. Indeed, rather than a sudden leap, the transition seems to indicate a shift in perspective that can be explained by the passage from the domain of the city-state (the Greek *polis* evoked by Aristotle and the *civitas* of central and northern Italy) to the much wider domain of the Holy Roman Empire. The second *dictio* can thus be legitimately reintegrated into Marsilius's thought, resolving the apparent dissimilarity or dichotomy between the supposedly modern *Dictio* I and the medieval *Dictio* II. Many scholars of Marsilius have pointed out this dichotomy, and its most visible effect can be seen in the 1991 reprint of the Italian translation of *Dictio* I alone. Quite intentionally, the publisher chose to omit the far more voluminous *Dictio* II as if it were nothing but a hindrance, an embarrassment from which the original and modern message of the Paduan should be cleared.[35] Simply from the point of view of form, this practice brings to mind the opposite but nevertheless similar manoeuvre performed in 1545, when the German translators of the *Defensor pacis* omitted the whole translation of *Dictio* I in order to enhance the ecclesiological and political message of *Dictio* II. They also did so because of the frequent references to Aristotle in *Dictio* I, which reminded them of the scholastic method that they abhorred.

At this point, we should ask: Why did Eco appeal to an obsolete and now outdated interpretation of Marsilius's political thought? An easy answer would be that Eco, as a novelist, was free to make use of the historical sources available to him as he thought best and was certainly not required to bring himself up to date with the extremely vast critical

---

34 In this regard, see Piaia, 'L'idea di sovranità popolare', in particular, pp. 114–15, where it is observed that Guglielmo Amidani, one of the first to refute the *Defensor pacis*, had himself recourse to the principle of the sovereignty of the people although with the purpose of curbing the power of the emperor, which is a testament to the neutral character of that principle that lent itself to opposite applications.

35 Marsilius of Padua, *Il Difensore della Pace*, ed. by Vasoli; in his 'Introduzione' (p. 46), Vasoli declares that the second 'discourse' (*dictio*) of the *Defensor pacis* 'is not reproduced here by reason of evident publishing expediency'.

MARSILIUS OF PADUA IN *THE NAME OF THE ROSE*   421

literature on Marsilius. Far be it from me to think that the eminent Professor Umberto Eco was mistaken. The image of a 'democratic' Marsilius he provides in *The Name of the Rose* is not the result of a lack of up-to-date bibliographic knowledge but of a definite choice. Not only is this choice due to the demands of the narrative, but it has an ideological and existential nature. Indeed, Eco's decision to represent Marsilius as he does is intimately connected to the very genesis of the novel. That is, the figure of Marsilius plays a particular role in the novel that finds its inspiration in the politico-cultural climate of the late 1970s. This climate was deeply affected by the terrorism that took place in the so-called *anni di piombo* ('years of lead'), which disrupted and destabilized the progressive front. The kind of atmosphere that permeated the 1970s was incisively and clearly evoked by Pierluigi Battista in 2019, when the arrest of the terrorist Cesare Battisti gave rise to widespread and contrasting reactions:

> That deadly decade [i.e. the seventies] attained a level of political violence and abuse unknown in peacetime. There were over 370 dead, victims of that gloomy and mournful period of terrorism and *stragismo* [strategy of massacres], and over one thousand injured, besides countless cars set on fire, shop windows broken, roads unpaved, lives ravaged. But, in addition, everyday life was submerged in a climate of omnipresent and threatening violence, which turned into an endless string of night ambuscades, beatings, retaliations, armed assaults, brutal pranks perpetrated by death squads of various political colours which filled with blood the streets of cities and small towns.[36]

The *anni di piombo* brought about a crisis in the movement of renewal that the cultural avant-gardes had started in the early 1960s (and in which Eco had actively taken part as a member of the Gruppo 63)[37] and was to explode as a global phenomenon involving students and workers after the fateful 1968, the year of global protest. The movement seemed relentless, like a flooding river, and strangely enough, was halted by its more radical fringes, passing from protest to armed struggle in order to speed up 'the revolution'. Over the course of all these events, Eco did not hesitate to commit himself personally. In 1971 he was one of the 757 people who signed an open letter to *L'Espresso* concerning the Pinelli case,[38] taking a stand against the police officer Luigi Calabresi who was killed the following year by several militants of Lotta Continua. Eco was also among those who signed a letter of self-accusation in sympathy with the editors of the

---

36 Battista, 'Quei terribili anni Settanta'.
37 For an intellectual portrait of Eco, see Merrell, *Umberto Eco*.
38 The anarchist Giuseppe Pinelli died falling from a window in the night between 15 and 16 December 1969 in the police headquarters of Milan, where he had been questioned after the massacre in Piazza Fontana (12 December 1969).

newspaper of Lotta Continua who had been accused of inciting violence. However, when events came to a head, he distanced himself from the armed struggle and criticized acts of terrorism in the pages of *L'Espresso* and *La Repubblica*.[39]

The most striking event of the *anni di piombo* was the 16 March 1978 kidnapping and the following assassination of Aldo Moro, leader of the Christian Democratic Party. At the time, Moro was in favour of a government promoting national solidarity, which was supported by the Communist Party as well. We should not forget that other sad, politically motivated murders punctuated the years in which Eco produced his first novel, which, as he declared, he began to write precisely in March 1978.[40] The preface to *The Name of the Rose* is dated 5 January 1980; a month later, on 12 February, at Rome's historical University 'La Sapienza', the Red Brigades killed the vice-president of the Magistrates' Governing Council, Professor Vittorio Bachelet. On 2 August 1980, a bomb attack perpetrated by the far-right NAR group on the Bologna railway station claimed the lives of eighty-five people. One year before, on 24 January 1979, the Red Brigades had killed the Genoese worker and trade unionist Guido Rossa, blaming him for having identified a supporter of the Red Brigades in his factory. In 1979 terrorist attacks perpetrated by different groups reached their height, with 659 attacks.[41]

When confronted with these events, progressive intellectuals felt passed over and laid aside. The *anni di piombo* not only led to the killing of people. The predominance of violent over political action meant that an entire cultural and political programme was jeopardized. Hence the 'silence of the intellectuals',[42] and their migration to other shores, such as fiction. It is precisely here that the genesis of *The Name of the Rose* — and in particular of the function assigned to Marsilius and to his political theories — is to be found. But this migration was not a mere escape from the present and from political commitment. Eco was perfectly aware of this aspect; so much so that, in his *Postscript to 'The Name of the Rose'*, he observed: 'For two years I have refused to answer idle questions. [...] The most idle has been the one raised by those who suggest that writing about the past is a way of eluding the present.'[43] Indeed, in the case of Eco, the shift to the field of fiction was inspired by his intention to sublimate

---

39 These articles were later collected by Eco in the volume *Sette anni di desiderio*. A detailed biography of Umberto Eco is available on <https://it.wikipedia.org/wiki/Umberto_Eco> [accessed 21 August 2021].

40 Eco, *Postscript to 'The Name of the Rose'*, p. 13.

41 With regard to this dramatic period, see Galli, *Storia del partito armato*; Zavoli, *La notte della Repubblica*; Baldoni and Provvisionato, *Anni di piombo*; Oliva, *Anni di piombo e di tritolo*.

42 Cf. Attal, 'Gli intellettuali italiani e il terrorismo'; Lupo, 'Il silenzio degli intellettuali?' (on Eco see p. 69).

43 Eco, *Postscript to 'The Name of the Rose'*, p. 73.

the defeat that he suffered on the ideological-political plane; he made the genre of fiction, even popular fiction (and actually thanks to it), a means of somehow reasserting a programme centred around the ideas of democracy and equality.

So, let us return to the 'double crossing' performed by Marsilius and Brother William. Over the course of the statements taken from the *Defensor pacis*, which at first glance seem to be casually inserted and without any concrete outcome, there appears, in fact, the much more substantial and murderous movement of the Dulcinians. Eco recalls this movement in a crescendo starting from the early years of the fourteenth century and leading, ultimately, to the most tragic contemporary events. Let us read, for example, several highly significant passages from the account given by the former follower of Brother Dolcino of Novara and now cellarer, the character of Remigio of Varagine:

> And we burned and looted because we had proclaimed poverty the universal law, and we had the right to appropriate the illegitimate riches of others, and we wanted *to strike at the heart* of the network of greed that extended from parish to parish, but we never looted in order to possess, or killed in order to loot; we killed to punish, to purify the impure through blood. Perhaps we were driven by an overweening desire for justice: a man can sin also through overweening love of God, through superabundance of perfection.[44]

Here we have the overlapping, almost imperceptible, of contemporary and medieval reality, as in a hall of mirrors: the expression 'to strike at the heart' is evidently modelled on the message released by the Red Brigades the day after Aldo Moro's kidnapping ('To strike at the heart of the State'). The cellarer's avowal sounds tragically applicable to the present time when he ardently proclaims:

> We wanted a better world, of peace and sweetness and happiness for all, we wanted to kill the war that you brought on with your greed, because you reproached us when, to establish justice and happiness, we had to shed a little blood [...] there was our own blood, too, we did not spare ourselves, our blood and your blood, much of it, at once, immediately, the times of Dolcino's prophecy were at hand, we had to hasten the course of events.[45]

On the one hand, the reference to Dolcino's millenarianist prophecy takes us back in time to the medieval period and, on the other hand, the emphasis laid on 'a better world', on 'justice', and even more on 'our blood and your blood', echoes the language used by the Red Brigades and their

---

44 Eco, *The Name of the Rose*, 'Fifth Day. Nones', p. 384. My italics.
45 Eco, *The Name of the Rose*, 'Fifth Day. Nones', p. 384.

supporters. 'Everyone mourns for their own dead' was scrawled in block capitals in the entrance hall of the Faculty of Education at Padua on 5 July 1981, the day when the bullet-riddled body of the engineer Giuseppe Taliercio was discovered in the boot of a car near the petrochemical plant of Marghera after being held hostage for forty-six days. Eco's novel was published the year before, but the words of the former Dulcinian Remigio sound like a bitter harbinger.

One may therefore ask whether the political project that Eco, in the words of William of Baskerville, ascribes to Marsilius is merely theoretical (thus remaining a message whose fulfilment may come to pass in the future, as William himself affirms) or whether, if we move from theory to praxis, it had already found its turbid and murderous equivalent in the vicissitudes of Brother Dolcino, which took place fourteen years before the *Defensor pacis* was written. According to the latter hypothesis, Umberto Eco appears to be ambiguously present in both characters, in Brother William (i.e. Marsilius) as well as in the cellarer Remigio, and it is thanks to the avowal of the latter, who is a grotesque but after all pleasant character, that the bloody adventure of the Dulcinians (alias the Red Brigades) is sublimated and explained, even justified, at least within the bounds of good intentions, by implicitly referring to the theories of Marsilius of Padua in order to elucidate the reasons for those excesses, however deplorable and blameworthy.

At first glance, it seems risky to associate Marsilius's theoretical position with the boisterous and violent action of Brother Dolcino, but it is Eco himself who welds together these two characters through the words of the young Adso. In recounting his dialogue with Ubertino of Casale, Adso attributes a clear and solemn principled declaration to the latter:

> It is characteristic of heresy, or of madness, that it transforms the most upright thoughts and aims them at consequences contrary to the law of God and man. The Minorites have never asked the Emperor to kill other priests.[46]

So, everything is alright, isn't it? Not really, for immediately afterwards Adso mentions a concrete example of the gap that separates theoretical declarations from practical action, and it is here that we find Marsilius again who, together with the Minorites in Rome, finally incurs — how strange! — the same mistake as Dolcino:

> He was mistaken, I know now. Because, a few months later, when the Bavarian established his own order in Rome, Marsilius and other Minorites did to religious who were faithful to the Pope exactly what

---

46 Eco, *The Name of the Rose*, 'Third Day. After compline', p. 227.

Dolcino had asked to have done. By this I don't mean that Dolcino was right; if anything, Marsilius was equally wrong.[47]

This statement of fact induces Adso to meditate on the problematic relationship between theory and praxis, obviously in relation to the case of the Dulcinians but more generally on the role and responsibility of the politically committed intellectual: Where is the boundary between the intellectual who theorizes a political and social revolution and the 'bad master'? And, moreover, does the responsibility for excess rest with the intellectual who speaks and writes or with those who try by any means, even by acts of violence, to translate his theoretical message into reality?

> But I was beginning to wonder, especially after that afternoon's conversation with William, if it were possible for the simple people who followed Dolcino to distinguish between the promises of the Spirituals and Dolcino's enactment of them. Was he not perhaps guilty of putting into practice what presumably orthodox men had preached, in a purely mystical fashion? Or was that perhaps where the difference lay? Did holiness consist in waiting for God to give us what His saints had promised, without trying to obtain it through earthly means? Now I know this is the case and I know why Dolcino was in error: the order of things must not be transformed, even if we must fervently hope for its transformation. But that evening I was in the grip of contradictory thoughts.[48]

This conclusion may be appropriate for those who, like the good Adso, trust divine providence. But if we view the conclusion as a superimposed image and consider it as referring to the project of deep political, social, and cultural transformation that Eco too had supported, then it appears disconcerting; it sounds like an announcement of the failure of the relationship between theory and praxis, or at least as an announcement postponing its fulfilment to an indefinite future time. Here William's judgment about Marsilius's thought re-emerges: 'The time is not ripe. Marsilius raves of an impossible transformation, immediately'. This would seem, then, to be a hopeless and at the same time self-ironic attempt, by means of an apparent escape into the historical novel, to retrieve something from that movement of politico-cultural renewal of which Eco had been a spokesman and had tragically failed in the *anni di piombo*. In this fiction, whose story is set in the early fourteenth century, this 'something' finds its expression in the most famous passage of the *Defensor pacis* (1, 12.3):

---

47 Eco, *The Name of the Rose*, 'Third Day. After compline', p. 227. The persecutory acts fulfilled by Marsilius when he was spiritual vicar in Rome are mentioned again at the end of the novel ('Last Page', p. 498).

48 Eco, *The Name of the Rose*, 'Third Day. After compline', pp. 227–28.

'Nos autem dicamus [...] legislatorem seu causam legis effectivam primam et propriam esse populum seu civium universitatem aut eius valenciorem partem'.

Several years ago, I had the opportunity of debating my interpretation of another one of Eco's novels with Eco himself.[49] This is no longer possible today (Umberto Eco left this world on 19 February 2016), so we have to confine ourselves to an interpretative hypothesis prompted by this new episode, certainly not the last,[50] in the fortune and legacy of Marsilius of Padua.

---

49 Cf. Piaia, 'Il padre Athanasius'.

50 This is confirmed by the use of Marsilius's figure and thought in another and more recent historical novel, which is clearly inspired by *The Name of the Rose* and whose protagonist is a son of Peter of Abano, i.e. Peter *junior*. Cf. Paccagnella, *Il figlio del Grande Eretico*, pp. 164–66 (in particular p. 165, where Marsilius's theories are defined as 'rather revolutionary'), 188–90, 202, 215, 254, 268, 272–73, and 305 (where the 'participative republic' illustrated by Tommaso Campanella in his *The City of the Sun* is associated, on the one hand, with Marsilius of Padua and, on the other, with Karl Marx).

Works Cited

Primary Sources

Eco, Umberto, *The Name of the Rose*, trans. by William Weaver (London: Picador, 1984)

——, *Postscript to 'The Name of the Rose'*, trans. by William Weaver (San Diego: Harcourt Brace Jovanovich, 1984)

——, *Sette anni di desiderio: Cronache 1977–1983* (Milan: Bompiani, 1983)

Marsilius of Padua, *Defensor pacis*, ed. by Richard Scholz, Monumenta Germaniae Historica: Fontes iuris germanici antiqui in usum scholarum separatim editi, 7.2 (Hannover: Hahn, 1933)

——, *Difenditore della pace, Defensor pacis, nella traduzione in volgare fiorentino del 1363*, ed. by Carlo Pincin (Turin: Fondazione Luigi Einaudi, 1966)

——, *Il Difensore della Pace: Primo discorso*, ed. and commented by Cesare Vasoli (Venice: Marsilio, 1991)

Secondary Works

Ancona, Elvio, *Marsilio da Padova: Indagine su un enigma storiografico* (Padua: CEDAM, 2012)

Attal, Frédéric, 'Gli intellettuali italiani e il terrorismo', in *Il libro degli anni di piombo: Storia e memoria del terrorismo italiano*, ed. by Marc Lazar and Marie-Anne Matard-Bonucci, Ital. trans. by Cristian Delorenzo and Francesco Peri (Milan: Rizzoli, 2010), pp. 131–34

Baldoni, Alberto, and Sandro Provvisionato, *Anni di piombo* (Milan: Sperling & Kupfer, 2009)

Battista, Pierluigi, 'Quei terribili anni Settanta', *Il Corriere della Sera*, 21 January 2019, p. 15

Battocchio, Riccardo, 'Marsilio da Padova, la politica, il Vangelo: Tra "archeologia" e "teologia"', *Studia Patavina*, 42 (1995), 279–87

Bausi, Francesco, 'I due medioevi del *Nome della rosa*', *Semicerchio: Rivista di poesia comparata*, 44.1 (2011), 117–29

Bayona Aznar, Bernardo, 'El periplo de la teoría política de Marsilio de Padua por la historiografía moderna', *Revista de Estudios Políticos*, no. 137 (2007), 113–53

Briguglia, Gianluca, *Marsilio da Padova*, Pensatori, 31 (Rome: Carocci, 2013)

Collodo, Silvana, 'Scienze della natura e ricerca politica: La civitas terrena nel *Defensor pacis* di Marsilio da Padova', in *Filosofia naturale e scienze dell'esperienza fra medioevo e umanesimo: Studi su Marsilio da Padova, Leon Battista Alberti, Michele Savonarola*, ed. by Silvana Collodo and Remy Simonetti, Contributi alla storia dell'Università di Padova, 47 (Treviso: Antilia, 2012), pp. 15–240

Condren, Conal, 'Democracy and the *Defensor Pacis*: On the English Language Tradition of Marsilian Interpretation', *Il Pensiero Politico*, 13 (1980), 301–16

——, 'George Lawson and the *Defensor pacis*: On the Use of Marsilius in Seventeenth-Century England', *Medioevo*, 6 (1980), 595–617

Damiata, Marino, *'Plenitudo potestatis' e 'universitas civium' in Marsilio da Padova*, Biblioteca di Studi francescani, 16 (Florence: Edizioni Francescane, 1983)

Fiorentino, Francesco, *Pietro Pomponazzi: Studi storici su la scuola bolognese e padovana del secolo XVI* (Florence: Le Monnier, 1868)

Franck, Adolphe, *Réformateurs et publicistes de l'Europe: Moyen Âge, Renaissance* (Paris: M. Lévy Frères, 1864)

Galli, Giorgio, *Storia del partito armato* (Milan: Rizzoli, 1986)

Galvão de Sousa, José Pedro, *O totalitarismo nas orígens da moderna teoria do Estado: Um estudo sobre o 'Defensor pacis' de Marsílio de Pádua* (São Paulo: Saraiva, 1972)

Gewirth, Alan, 'Republicanism and Absolutism in the Thought of Marsilius of Padua', *Medioevo*, 5 (1979), 23–48

Giacchi, Orio, 'Osservazioni sulla fortuna delle idee di Marsilio da Padova nell'età del giurisdizionalismo', in *Marsilio da Padova: Studi raccolti nel VI centenario della morte*, ed. by Aldo Checchini and Norberto Bobbio, Pubblicazioni della Facoltà di giurisprudenza dell'Università di Padova, 3 (Padua: CEDAM, 1942), pp. 167–90

Koch, Bettina, *Zur Dis-/Kontinuität mittelalterlichen politischen Denkens in der neuzeitlichen politischen Theorie: Marsilius von Padua, Johannes Althusius und Thomas Hobbes im Vergleich*, Beiträge zur Politischen Wissenschaft, 137 (Berlin: Duncker & Humblot, 2005)

Labanca, Baldassare, *Marsilio da Padova riformatore politico e religioso del secolo XIV* (Padua: Fratelli Salmin, 1882)

Leonardi, Giovanni, 'La centralità dei problemi ecclesiologici nel *Defensor pacis*: Risposte caduche e istanze perenni', in 'Marsilio ieri e oggi', ed. by Gregorio Piaia, special issue, *Studia Patavina*, 27 (1980), 343–49

——, 'La riforma della Chiesa nel progetto di Marsilio', in 'Marsilio ieri e oggi', ed. by Gregorio Piaia, special issue, *Studia Patavina*, 27 (1980), 303–07

Lupo, Giuseppe, 'Il silenzio degli intellettuali? Parte dagli anni Ottanta', *Vita e Pensiero*, 102.5 (2019), 63–69

Ménard, Jacques, 'L'aventure historiographique du *Défenseur de la paix* de Marsile de Padoue', *Science et Esprit: Revue théologique et philosophique*, 41 (1989), 287–322

Merrell, Douglass, *Umberto Eco, the Da Vinci Code, and the Intellectual in the Age of Popular Culture* (Cham: Palgrave Macmillan, 2017)

Miethke, Jürgen, 'Der Philosoph als Detektiv: Wilhelm von Baskerville, Zeichendeuter und Spurensucher, und sein "alter Freund" Wilhelm von Ockham', in '...eine finstere und fast unglaubliche Geschichte'?: Mediävistische Notizen zu Umberto Ecos Mönchsroman 'Der Name der Rose', ed. by Max Kerner (Darmstadt: Wissenschaftliche Buchgesellschaft, 1987), pp. 115–27

Najemy, John M., *A History of Florence, 1200–1575* (Oxford: Blackwell, 2006)

Oliva, Gianni, *Anni di piombo e di tritolo, 1969–1980: Il terrorismo nero e il terrorismo rosso da piazza Fontana alla strage di Bologna* (Milan: Mondadori, 2019)

Paccagnella, Renzo, *Il figlio del Grande Eretico* (Rome: Cromografica, 2012)

Passerin d'Entrèves, Alessandro, 'La fortuna di Marsilio da Padova in Inghilterra' [1940], in Alessandro Passerin d'Entrèves, *Saggi di storia del pensiero politico dal Medioevo alla società contemporanea*, ed. by Gian Mario Bravo, 'Gioele Solari' / Dipartimento di studi politici dell'Università di Torino, 10 (Milan: Franco Angeli, 1992), pp. 169–86

Piaia, Gregorio, 'Baldassare Labanca interprete ottocentesco di Marsilio da Padova', in Gregorio Piaia, *Marsilio e dintorni: Contributi alla storia delle idee*, Miscellanea erudita, 61 (Padua: Antenore, 1999), pp. 353–87

——, 'Dalla *Politica* di Aristotele all' "averroismo politico": Una vicenda paradossale', *Mediterranea: International Journal for the Transfer of Knowledge*, 3 (2018), 19–34

——, 'L'idea di sovranità popolare in Marsilio da Padova e Guglielmo Amidani', in Gregorio Piaia, *Marsilio e dintorni: Contributi alla storia delle idee*, Miscellanea erudita, 61 (Padua: Antenore, 1999), pp. 104–17

——, *Marsilio da Padova nella Riforma e nella Controriforma: Fortuna ed interpretazione*, Pubblicazioni dell'Istituto di storia della filosofia e del Centro per ricerche di filosofia medioevale, Università di Padova, n.s., 24 (Padua: Antenore, 1977)

——, 'Marsilius von Padua († um 1342) und Nicolaus Cusanus († 1464): Eine zweideutige Beziehung?', *Mitteilungen und Forschungsbeiträge der Cusanus-Gesellschaft*, 24 (1998), 171–93; Italian edn: 'Marsilio da Padova e Niccolò Cusano: Un rapporto ambiguo?', in Gregorio Piaia, *Marsilio e dintorni: Contributi alla storia delle idee*, Miscellanea erudita, 61 (Padua: Antenore, 1999), pp. 202–19

——, 'Il padre Athanasius, l'atomista canonico e l'isola-del-giorno-prima: Divagazioni sul Seicento filosofico di Umberto Eco', *Rivista di storia della filosofia*, 51.2 (1996), 333–40; repr., together with a letter by Umberto Eco, in Gregorio Piaia, *Talete in Parnaso: La storia della filosofia e le belle lettere*, La filosofia e il suo passato, 49 (Padua: CLEUP, 2013), pp. 357–69

——, 'Il padre Zaccaria, l'abate Cesarotti e l'attualità di Marsilio nel secolo dei Lumi', in Gregorio Piaia, *Marsilio e dintorni: Contributi alla storia delle idee*, Miscellanea erudita, 61 (Padua: Antenore, 1999), pp. 328–52

——, 'Postille storico-filosofiche a Umberto Eco narratore', *Philosophia: Rivista della Società Italiana di Storia della Filosofia*, 12–13 (2015, but published in 2017), 159–81

————, '"Sancte Marsili, ora pro nobis?": Sulla dimensione religiosa in Marsilio da Padova', in Gregorio Piaia, *Marsilio e dintorni: Contributi alla storia delle idee*, Miscellanea erudita, 61 (Padua: Antenore, 1999), pp. 118–35

————, 'The Shadow of Antenor: On the Relationship between the *Defensor pacis* and the Institutions of the City of Padua', in *Politische Reflexion in der Welt des späten Mittelalters / Political Thought in the Age of Scholasticism: Essays in Honour of Jürgen Miethke*, ed. by Martin Kaufhold, Studies in Medieval and Reformation Traditions, 103 (Leiden: Brill, 2004), pp. 193–207

Quillet, Jeannine, *La philosophie politique de Marsile de Padoue*, L'Église et l'État au Moyen-Age, 14 (Paris: J. Vrin, 1970)

————, *La philosophie politique du Songe du Vergier (1378): Sources doctrinales*, L'Église et l'État au Moyen-Age, 15 (Paris: J. Vrin, 1977)

Russi, Luciano, 'Letture e valutazioni di Marsilio da Padova: Analisi di un topos letterario tra letteratura della liquidazione e retorica dell'anticipazione', *Il Trimestre*, 13 (1980), 3–28

Scaduto, Francesco, *Stato e Chiesa negli scritti politici dalla fine della lotta per le investiture alla morte di Ludovico il Bavaro (1122–1347): Studio storico* (Florence: Le Monnier, 1882)

Simonetta, Stefano, *Dal Difensore della pace al Leviatano: Marsilio da Padova nel Seicento inglese*, Testi e studi, 155 (Milan: UNICOPLI, 2000)

————, *Marsilio in Inghilterra: Stato e Chiesa nel pensiero politico inglese fra XIV e XVII secolo*, Il Filarete, 195 (Milan: LED, 2000)

Stahl, Federico Giulio, *Storia della filosofia del diritto*, Italian trans. by Pietro Torre (Turin: Favale, 1853)

Stout, Harrey, 'Marsilius of Padua and the Henrician Reformation', *Church History*, 43 (1974), 308–18

Troilo, Erminio, 'L'averroismo di Marsilio da Padova', in *Marsilio da Padova: Studi raccolti nel VI centenario della morte*, ed. by Aldo Checchini and Norberto Bobbio, Pubblicazioni della Facoltà di giurisprudenza dell'Università di Padova, 3 (Padua: CEDAM, 1942), pp. 47–77

Tromboni, Lorenza, 'Filosofia politica e cultura cittadina a Firenze tra XIV e XV secolo: I volgarizzamenti del *Defensor pacis* e della *Monarchia*', *Studi danteschi*, 75 (2010), 79–114

Vasoli, Cesare, 'Introduzione', in Marsilio da Padova, *Il difensore della pace: Primo discorso*, ed. by Cesare Vasoli, translation with parallel text (Venice: Marsilio, 1991), pp. 9–62

Villari, Pasquale, *Nicolò Machiavelli e i suoi tempi*, 2nd edn, 2 vols (Milan: Hoepli, 1895–1897)

Zavoli, Sergio, *La notte della Repubblica* (Rome: Nuova ERI, 1992)

Zecchini, Giuseppe, 'Il Medioevo di Umberto Eco', in *Saggi su 'Il nome della rosa'*, ed. by Renato Giovannoli (Milan: Bompiani, 1985), pp. 322–69

Index of Names, Places, and Events

Aaron: 345

Acciaiuoli, Angelo: 241, 243

Adam: 60, 416–17

Adolf of Nassau, King of the Romans: 338

Adso of Melk: 413, 415–16, 424–25

Agamben, Giorgio: 292–93, 295

Aichele, Alexander: 16

Albert I of Habsburg, King of the Romans: 338

Albert the Great: 36, 38–39, 82 n. 26, 87–88, 90, 94, 133 n. 41, 137, 152, 221–22, 254 n. 5, 327

Albertano da Brescia: 226

Alcuin of York: 50

Aldobrandini, Cinzio: 331 n. 27

Alexander of Aphrodisias: 36 n. 24, 326–28

Alexander the Great: 260

al-Fārābī, Abū Naṣr Muḥammed: 22

Alighieri, Dante: 19, 50, 125, 133 n. 41, 139 n. 65, 204–05, 209, 216–17, 253, 255–56, 259–61, 266–67, 278, 285, 287–307, 313–14, 326, 328–29, 346–47, 401 n. 68

Alighieri, Jacopo: 289–90

Alighieri, Pietro: 289–90

Alleluia (the Great Devotion) movement: 225

Althusser, Louis: 78 n. 8

Álvaro Pelayo: 219 n. 16

Ambrose of Milan: 54, 243

Amidani, Guglielmo: 420 n. 34

Anabaptists: 253, 335

Andrea da Bologna: 242

Andrea da Perugia: 220

Andrea de Pace: 220 n. 21

Anni di piombo: 421–22, 425

Annibale (Annibaldo) di Ceccano: 94

Anonymous of Milan: 76, 80–82, 85

Anselm of Canterbury: 87 n. 47, 156 n. 19

Antichrist: 253, 258, 268–69, 302, 304, 350

Antonius Andreae: 94

Apocalypse *and* apocalyptic thought: 15, 19, 253–56, 258, 261, 264–69, 272–73, 277–78, 289

Arezzo: 222

Aristotle *and* Aristotelianism: 11–12, 15, 17–22, 31–43, 52–54, 56–57, 75–96, 105, 107, 109, 111, 113, 117–19, 123–42, 149, 151, 153, 157–59, 161 n. 35, 169–71, 180–81, 188, 202, 205, 208, 218, 220–25, 227–29, 233, 236–37, 241–45, 254–55, 261–62, 266–67, 269, 273–74, 276–78, 296, 311, 324–28, 348, 350–51, 359–66, 369, 377, 398 n. 58, 414, 418, 420

Arnaldus of Brescia: 326, 328–29

Arnold (Arnaldus) of Villanova: 258

Asti: 243 n. 127

Augustine of Ancona: 219, 337

Augustine of Hippo *and* Augustinianism: 17, 19, 31, 49–70, 78, 87 n. 47, 115, 119, 125, 162, 169, 208, 220 n. 22, 227, 231, 238–39, 243, 285–88, 295,

297 n. 91, 299, 302, 305, 313–14, 384, 414

Augustinians: 56, 219, 229

Augustus, Roman emperor: 259

Averroes *and* Averroism: 17, 22, 87 n. 47, 124–25, 132–33, 135–36, 140–42, 254 n. 5, 326–28, 360 n. 4, 411–12, 414

Avicenna: 87–88, 94 n. 74, 153, 160 n. 34, 161 n. 35

Avignon: 10, 12, 216, 239, 241, 243, 409, 413–14, 419

Bachelet, Vittorio: 422

Bacon, Roger: 223, 413, 415

Baden: 387

Badoer, Marino: 220

Baldo degli Ubaldi: 238

Bale, John: 223

Bartholomew of Bruges: 11, 21, 94

Bartholomew of Varignana: 89 n. 51

Bartolo da Sassoferrato: 238

Bartolomeo da San Concordio: 19, 218, 223, 225, 234–35, 243

Bartolomeo da Urbino: 220 n. 19

Basel: 409

Battista, Pierluigi: 421

Battisti, Cesare: 421

Battocchio, Riccardo: 15

Battuti: 225

Bavaria: 9, 386–87, 397

Beatrice: 297

Beguines: 373

Bellarmine, Robert: 19, 324–25, 331, 334–39, 342–45, 347–49, 351

Benevento, Battle of: 226

Benso, Camillo: 411

Benvenuto da Imola: 290

Bergamo: 243 n. 127

Berlin: 397

Bernard Gui: 198, 268 nn. 64–65, 269 n. 66

Bernard of Clairvaux: 17, 50, 63–65, 69, 236, 346–47

Bernardi della Mirandola, Antonio: 326–27

Bertrand de la Tour: 198

Bertrand du Pouget: 198, 329 n. 17

Black, Antony: 16, 359

Blythe, James: 236

Bobbio: 243 n. 127

Boccaccio, Giovanni: 290, 305

Bock, Friedrich: 20, 383, 391, 397–401

Boethius (Anicius Manlius Severinus Boethius): 236, 241

Bologna: 89 n. 51, 222, 239, 242, massacre of: 422

Bonagratia of Bergamo: 16

Bonaventure: 141, 223

Boniface VIII, Pope: 10, 230, 256–57, 268, 294, 348, 391

Bonn: 384, 387, 390

Brandolini, Aurelio Lippo: 78

Brenet, Jean-Baptiste: 16

Brescia: 243 n. 127

Brett, Annabel: 16, 52, 152, 271–76

Briguglia, Gianluca: 16, 31

Brutus (Marcus Junius Brutus): 203

Bulgakov, Mikhail: 49–50

Burkhardt, George *see* George Spalatin

Calabresi, Luigi: 421

Calabria, Conspiracy of: 327 n. 12, 331 n. 26

Calvinists: 326, 328, 335, 344, 410

Campanella, Tommaso: 19, 323–52, 426 n. 50

Canning, Joseph: 264

Capodilista, Bartolomeo: 223

Cassiodorus (Magnus Aurelius Cassiodorus): 181, 255 n. 7

Cato (Marcus Porcius Cato 'Uticensis'): 187, 192, 194, 233

INDEX OF NAMES, PLACES, AND EVENTS 433

Catto, Jeremy: 226
Celestine V, Pope: 289–92
Cesarotti, Melchiorre: 410
Charles de La Marche (Charles IV,
  King of France): 198, 419
Charles I of Anjou, King of Sicily:
  200–01
Charles II of Anjou, King of Naples:
  218
Christian Democratic Party, Italian:
  422
Chrysostom, John: 50, 53, 61, 68,
  236, 333, 341
Cicero (Marcus Tullius Cicero) *and*
  Ciceronianism: 18, 31, 78, 125,
  149, 152, 155 n. 18, 157–58, 160,
  187–88, 201, 208, 223, 227, 231
  n. 69, 233, 236, 241–42
Clement V, Pope: 10, 236
Clement VI, Pope: 13 n. 17, 218, 241,
  243
Colombini: 225
Colonna, Giovanni: 241,
Colonna, Landulphus: 13, 266
Communist Party, Italian: 422
Como: 243 n. 127
Condren, Conal: 15, 31, 51, 53, 78,
  401
Conrad of Megenberg: 392
Constantine I, Roman emperor: 65,
  268, 285, 292, 403
  Donation of: 266, 300–03, 307
Constantinople: 300
Corrado d'Ascoli: 222
Costa Ben Luca: 90
Count of Cavour *see* Benso, Camillo
Counter-Reformation: 306, 324, 329,
  334
Courtenay, William: 79, 94
Cova, Luciano: 239
Covarrubias, Diego de: 324–26, 329,
  333–35, 337, 341, 346–47, 349
Cranz, Ferdinand: 80–81

Crema: 243 n. 127
Cremona: 243 n. 127
Cremonini, Cesare: 326–27
Cromwell, Thomas: 306

Damon and Pythias: 233
David, Hebrew king: 340
Della Bella, Giano: 291 n. 40
Della Scala, Cangrande: 12, 198, 305,
  419
Denina, Carlo: 410
Diocletian, Roman emperor: 289–92
Dionysius of Syracuse: 233
(Pseudo-)Dionysius the Areopagite:
  414, 418
Dolcini, Carlo: 40
Dolcino of Novara: 268–69, 423–25
Domenico da Peccioli: 234 n. 87
Dominicans: 19, 202–03, 215–45,
  313, 324, 329
Donatists: 69
Dondino da Pavia: 216
Doyle, Arthur Conan: 413
Dulcinians: 423–25
Durand de Champagne: 219 n. 16

Eco, Umberto: 20, 412–26
Edward the Confessor, King of
  England: 258
Eight Saints, War of: 409
Eiximenis, Francesc: 219 n. 16
Emiliano da Spoleto: 222

Engelbert of Admont: 205 n. 22
Enlightenment: 418
Enrico da Rimini: 19, 217, 235–39,
  243
Erasmus of Rotterdam: 409
Erfurt: 223
Esau: 290, 292 n. 47
Ettal, Monastery of: 397
Eustratius of Nicaea: 87 n. 47

INDEX OF NAMES, PLACES, AND EVENTS

Fabricius (Gaius Fabricius
    Luscinus): 187, 192, 203, 233
Falkeid, Unn: 301, 305
Falkensee: 397
Fano: 241
Farnese, Odoardo: 331 n. 27
Ferrara: 236, 395 n. 43
Fieschi, Luca: 216
Fiorentino, Francesco: 410
Flagellants: 225
Florence: 19, 200–03, 217–18, 222,
    229–35, 239–41, 243, 409
    Santa Croce, Convent of: 224
    Santa Maria Novella, Convent of:
        218, 230, 233–35, 239–40
Flüeler, Christoph: 38, 81
Frajese, Vittorio: 324, 347
France: 10, 216, 327 n. 12, 389, 398,
    409–10, 419
Franciscans: 16, 141, 179, 184–85,
    219–20, 223–24, 227, 305, 398
    n. 57, 413–14, 416–17, 424
Franck, Adolphe: 410
Franconi, Federico: 218
Frederick II Hohenstaufen, Holy
    Roman Emperor: 9, 253
Frederick (III) of Aragon, King of
    Sicily: 198, 268
Frederick von Aubsburg: 9
Freiburg im Breisgau: 384, 391
French Revolution: 411

Galen: 16, 87–88
Galilee: 297
Galvano Fiamma da Milano: 216,
    218, 222, 225, 243–44
Garnett, George: 15, 19, 255–56,
    263–78
Gauthier de Brienne: 243
Gelasius I, Pope: 300, 303, 314 n. 187
Genet, Jean-Philippe: 219
Georg Spalatin: 302
Gerald Odon see Guiral Ot

German Historical Institute (Rome):
    383, 391, 397
Germany: 9, 20, 22, 384–403, 410
Gerson, Jean: 333, 341
Gewirth, Alan: 14, 52, 81, 273–74
Ghibellines and Ghibellinism: 10, 12,
    16, 18, 21, 39 n. 40, 197–205,
    207–08, 226, 240, 305, 313, 328,
    399, 401 n. 68, 419
Giacomo da Viterbo see James of
    Viterbo
Giles of Orleans: 86
Giles of Rome: 12 n. 9, 38, 42, 50, 56,
    64, 75–76, 78, 81–82, 86, 89–90,
    94, 161 n. 35, 203–04, 219–20,
    222–24, 226, 229, 256, 337
Gilson, Étienne: 299
Giordano da Rivalto: 234
Giovanni da San Gimignano: 218
Giovanni da Viterbo: 226
Giovanni Guerrisco da Viterbo: 222
Giovanni Regina da Napoli see John
    of Naples
Godfrey of Fontaines: 21, 107–08
Gramsci, Antonio: 78 n. 8
Great Western Schism: 409
Green, Louis: 244
Gregory VII, Pope: 264
Gregory IX, Pope: 10, 253
Gregory X, Pope: 200
Gregory XI, Pope: 409
Gretser, Jacob: 330 n. 22
Grotius, Hugo: 410
Guelphs and Guelphism: 10, 197,
    199–205, 208, 226, 401 n. 68
    Blacks: 218, 230, 235
    Whites: 204, 230
Guglielmo da Sarzano: 220
Guibert de Tournai: 219 n. 16
Guillaume Peyraut (Guillelmus
    Peraldus): 219
Guiral Ot: 223

INDEX OF NAMES, PLACES, AND EVENTS   435

Hake, Johann: 94
Hegel, Georg Wilhelm Friedrich: 419
Heidegger, Martin: 389
Heimpel, Hermann: 392
Henry IV, King of France: 329
Henry of Germany: 76 n. 3
Henry VII of Luxemburg, Holy
    Roman Emperor: 9, 198, 205–06,
    220, 239
Henry VIII, King of England: 278,
    306–07, 410
Herod Antipas: 297
Herod I, the Great (the Elder): 59–
    60, 257 n. 19
Hesiod: 188–89
Hildegard of Bingen: 258
Hindenburg, Paul von: 386
Hitler, Adolf: 384–86, 389, 391–92,
    397, 403
Hobbes, Thomas: 16, 22, 306
Honecker, Martin: 384
Hospitallers, Knights: 373
Hugh III, King of Cyprus: 226
Hus, Jan: 276–77, 326, 328, 335–36
Hutten, Ulrich von: 302

Ibn Rushd see Averroes
Ibn Sina see Avicenna
Innocent III, Pope: 10, 346
Innocent IV, Pope: 10
Isaac: 290
Isidore of Seville: 241
Italy: 9–10, 12, 18–22, 62, 76 n. 3, 79,
    198–207, 215–45, 292–95, 297,
    305, 332, 363–64, 393–96, 398,
    400, 410–11, 413–14, 419–20
Izbicki, Thomas: 278

Jacopo da Cessole: 217, 235–37
James of Viterbo: 86, 219, 256
Jean de Pouilly: 11, 21
Jerome of Stridon: 55, 340

Jesus Christ: 17, 19, 49–51, 53, 57–
    61, 63–70, 103, 105, 110–15,
    119–20, 179, 183–88, 194, 203–
    04, 218, 228, 237, 257, 267–68,
    270–72, 275, 277, 285–88, 291–
    314, 330, 335–37, 339–52, 364,
    415–16
Joachim of Fiore: 258–59
Johan von Erfurt: 223
Johannes de Fonte: 223
John, St (Evangelist): 49–51, 53, 55–
    59, 61–69, 116, 183, 255, 286–
    88, 296–97, 299, 307–08, 310–
    13, 335
John Dinsdale: 94
John Duns Scotus: 94, 141
John of Durazzo: 218
John of Jandun: 10–14, 17, 21–22,
    92, 94, 189 n. 32, 305 n. 144,
    326–27, 336 n. 46, 395 n. 43, 414,
    417
John of la Rochelle: 152
John of Naples: 76 n. 3, 216, 218
John of Paris: 12 n. 9, 19, 216, 244,
    253, 255–59, 261, 263, 266–67,
    278
John of Salisbury: 235–36
John of Wales: 235 n. 94
John Wyclif: 326, 328, 333, 335
John XXII, Pope: 9–10, 12, 197, 216,
    220, 266, 305 n. 144, 326 n. 10,
    331, 341–42, 395 n. 43, 398, 409,
    415–16, 419
Juan de Torquemada: 337–38, 342
Juan García de Castrojeriz: 219 n. 16
Juan Gil de Zamora: 219 n. 16
Judaea: 285, 287
Julian the Apostate, Roman
    Emperor: 65
Juvenal (Decimus Junius Juvenalis):
    241

Kantorowicz, Ernst: 298–99

Kautsky, Karl: 78 n. 8
Kaye, Joel: 16
Kehr, Paul Fridolin: 397
Knuuttila, Simo: 153

Labanca, Baldassare: 411
Labriola, Ada: 236
Lactantius: 50, 285–86, 288, 292–93, 295, 313
Lagarde, George de: 13–14, 52
Lambertini, Roberto: 16, 89
Landino, Cristoforo: 290–92
Lanza, Lidia: 21, 34, 38
Latini, Brunetto: 200–02, 209, 226
Leipzig: 389, 391–92
Leonino da Padova: 220 n. 19
Leopold of Bebenburg: 205 n. 22
Levites: 330, 345–47
Locke, John: 22
Lodi: 243 n. 127
Lombardi, Baldassarre: 290 n. 38
Lombardy: 198, 243
Lorenzetti, Ambrogio: 238
Lorenzo de' Monaci: 236
Lotta Continua: 421–22
Louis IX, King of France: 219
Louis X, King of France: 218
Lovati, Lovato: 11
Ludwig IV the Bavarian, Holy Roman Emperor: 9, 12–13, 16, 35, 54, 198–99, 205, 215, 220, 239, 244, 266–67, 278, 305, 333, 383, 391, 393–400, 403, 409, 413–16, 424
Lukács, György: 78 n. 8
Luke, St (Evangelist): 58–59, 112–13, 295–97, 325
Luther, Martin: 301–02, 304, 326, 328, 333
Lutherans: 326, 328, 335, 410

Machiavelli, Niccolò: 22–23, 326–28, 333, 410

MacIntyre, Alasdair: 78 n. 8
Mackensen, Hans Georg von: 398
Macrobius (Macrobius Ambrosius Theodosius): 187–88, 241
Magdeburg: 223
Maimonides, Moses: 22, 87 n. 47
Malatesta, Galeotto: 217, 239
Malatesta, Malatesta III: 217, 239–41
Mannelli, Luca: 217–18, 239–43
Maramauro, Guglielmo: 290
Marcus Curtius: 203, 233
Marcus Atilius Regulus: 203, 233
Mark, St (Evangelist): 61 n. 71, 325, 333
Marshall, William: 307
Marsilio, Giovanni: 19, 323–26, 329–31, 333–34, 336–39, 341–44, 347, 351
Martin of Braga: 236
Martinus Polonus: 215
Matthew, St (Evangelist): 58–59, 114, 272, 295, 325, 339–42
Matthias Flacius Illyricus: 410
Melchizedek: 325, 345–48
Mende: 224
Michael of Cesena: 16, 413–14, 417
Miethke, Jürgen: 14, 31, 264
Milan: 12, 198–99, 206–07, 218, 243–44, 305 n. 141, 394 n. 43, 419, 421 n. 38
Sant'Eustorgio, Convent of: 222
Mineo, E. Igor: 244
Montaperti, battle of: 201
Montpellier: 223
Monumenta Germaniae Historica: 397
Moreno-Riaño, Gerson: 15, 31, 55
Moro, Aldo: 422–23
Moses: 105, 190 n. 36, 330
Muhammad: 105 n. 8, 335
Mulcahy, Daniel: 51–54, 56
Munich: 10, 12–13, 16, 95
Münster: 253

INDEX OF NAMES, PLACES, AND EVENTS   437

Murray, Alexander: 221
Mussato, Albertino: 11–12, 198

Naples: 198, 230 n. 64, 325, 336, 351
  Castel Sant'Elmo: 331
Narbonne: 224
Narni: 222
National Socialism: 20, 383–92, 394–
  97, 400, 402
Nebuchadnezzar: 267
Nederman, Cary J.: 15, 31, 55, 401
Nero, Roman Emperor: 233
Niccolò di Ceccano: 94
Nicholas of Cusa: 301 n. 125, 375
  n. 22, 409
Nicholas V, Anti-pope: 10, 304
Niphus, Augustinus: 326 n. 10
Noah: 332
Novara: 243 n. 127
Nozick, Robert: 78 n. 8
NSDAP (Nationalsozialistische
  Deutsche Arbeiterpartei) *see*
  National Socialism

Olivi, Peter of John: 224
Origen of Alexandria: 55, 340
Orosius, Paulus: 297 n. 91
Osimo: 241
Ottaviani, Didier: 15
Ovid (Publius Ovidius Naso): 236

Padua: 9–12, 16, 21, 79, 124–25, 141,
  223, 396, 411, 419–20, 424
Paolino da Venezia: 220
Paris: 9–12, 21–22, 32–33, 35, 57, 79,
  86–87, 89–90, 94–95, 124–25,
  129, 141–42, 216, 223, 226, 229
  n. 64, 258, 304
  Saint-Jacques, Convent of: 221
Parma: 243 n. 127
Pascoli, Giovanni: 292–94
Paul V, Pope: 19, 324, 329, 331, 335,
  349

Paul, St (Apostle): 50–51, 55–56, 59,
  61–65, 68–69, 104, 110, 276, 296
  302, 333, 341, 346
Pecock, Reginald: 301 n. 124
Pedro de Castrovol: 224
Peña, Francisco: 330 n. 22
Peralta, Nicolò: 220 n. 21
Peter, St: 58, 335–37, 339–42
Peter (Pedro) I, King of Castile and
  León: 219 n. 16
Peter of Abano: 11–12, 16, 21, 87,
  124–25, 131–32, 135, 138, 141–
  42, 152–54, 426 n. 50
Peter (Pere) of Aragon: 219 n. 16
Peter Auriol: 94
Peter of Auvergne: 17, 21, 34, 36–39,
  76, 78–95, 124–25, 129, 131, 133
  n. 43, 135, 139 n. 65, 222–24
Peter of Spain: 296 n. 81
Peter Comestor: 236
Peter Lombard: 52, 54, 222 n. 27,
  255 n. 7
Petrus de Trabibus: 224
Philip I, Prince of Taranto: 218
Philip IV, King of France (Philip the
  Fair): 218, 229–30, 256–57, 294,
  391
Piacenza: 243 n. 127
Piaia, Gregorio: 14, 324, 326
Pierre de la Palud: 216
Pietro dell'Aquila: 223
Pietrucci, Napoleone: 411
Pighius, Albertus: 326 n. 10
Pincin, Carlo: 14
Pinelli, Giuseppe: 421
Pisa:
  Santa Caterina, Convent of: 234
  n. 87
Pistoia:
  San Domenico, Convent of:
  240–41
Plato *and* (Neo/)Platonism: 37, 68,
  290, 350, 418

INDEX OF NAMES, PLACES, AND EVENTS

Pompey the Great: 294

Pomponazzi, Pietro: 326–28, 410

Pontius Pilate: 19, 49–51, 57, 59, 62–70, 270, 285–88, 291–301, 304–14, 330, 335–36

Ponzio, Paolo: 324

Porzio, Simon: 326, 328

Possevino, Antonio: 330 n. 22

Previté-Orton, Charles William: 384

Proclus: 87 n. 47

Prussia: 384, 386–88, 398

Prussian Historical Institute see German Historical Institute

Ptolemy of Lucca: 19, 75, 203–04, 209, 216–17, 229–34, 237, 338

Pufendorf, Samuel: 306, 310

Puritans: 326, 328

Pythagoras: 188–89

Pythias see Damon and Pythias

Quidort, Jean see John of Paris

Quillet, Jeannine: 14

Quintillian (Marcus Fabius Quintilianus): 241

Quirini, Lauro: 78

Radulphus Brito: 11, 21, 86, 94

Raederscheidt, Georg: 390 n. 23

Raimundus Acgerii: 224

Rawls, John: 78 n. 8

Red Brigades (*Brigate Rosse*): 422–24

Reformation: 306, 324, 396, 402, 409–10

Remigio de' Girolami: 19, 202–03, 216–18, 222, 225, 229–34, 239–40, 244

Remigio of Varagine: 423–24

Rimini: San Cataldo, Convent of: 239

Robert de Cruce: 223

Robert Grosseteste: 111 n. 35, 128, 223

Robert of Anjou, King of Naples: 198, 218, 220

Roman Empire:

Ancient: 51, 67, 204–05, 259–61, 266, 268, 278, 288, 290, 295–98, 300, 303, 313

Holy: 9–10, 18, 53, 197, 204–08, 216, 260, 266, 277, 296, 298–300, 305, 306, 314, 351, 364, 393–94, 396, 398, 401, 403, 411, 413–16, 419–20

Roman Republic: 187–88, 192, 203–04, 233

Rome: 10, 12, 265, 300, 332–34, 341 n. 59, 383, 391, 394, 396–99, 413, 417, 422, 424–25

Rosadi, Giovanni: 292–94

Rosen, George: 53

Rossa, Guido: 422

Rousseau, Jean-Jacques: 410

Sachsenhausen Appeal: 9

Salamanca, School of: 329, 334, 346

Sallust (Gaius Sallustius Crispus): 82, 218 n. 12, 223, 227, 233, 236, 241

Sánchez de Arévalo, Rodrigo: 78

Sancho IV, King of Castile, León and Galicia: 219 n. 16

Sanglier, Henri: 64, 69

Sarpi, Paolo: 326, 329, 333–34, 342

Sauerbruch, Ferdinand: 389

Scaduto, Francesco: 410

Schneider-Windmüller, Wilhelm: 20, 383–91, 393–95, 397, 400, 402–03

Scholz, Richard: 20, 35, 383–84, 391–98, 400–03

Scipio (Publius Cornelius Scipio Africanus): 187–88, 192

Scott, Joanna: 55

Seneca (Lucius Annaeus Seneca): 155 n. 18, 218 n. 12, 223, 233, 236, 241–42, 302

Servanzi, Gregorio: 330 n. 22

Shogimen, Tagashi: 16

Siena: 238

Siger of Brabant: 189 n. 32

Simplicius: 87 n. 47

Skinner, Quentin: 201–02, 363

Soto, Domingo de: 324–29, 333–35, 337–38, 341, 344 n. 72, 346–47, 349

Spain: 327 n. 12, 333 n. 35, 345

Spini, Geri: 218, 235

Stahl, Friedrich Julius: 410

Stoics *and* Stoicism: 154–56, 160 n. 34

Strabo *see* Walafried Strabo

Susemihl, Franz: 34–35, 37, 40

Sylvester I, Pope: 300–03, 307

Syros, Vasileios: 14, 16, 22, 38, 363

Tagliacozzo, battle of: 226

Taliercio, Giuseppe: 424

Templar, Knights: 373

Themistius: 326–27

Theophrastus: 326–27

Theophylact: 50, 53, 61, 67–68

Third Reich *see* Germany

Thomas Aquinas *and* Thomism: 17–19, 34, 36, 38, 50, 52–54, 61, 68, 75, 80, 87 n. 47, 89, 94, 103–04, 106–08, 114–20, 124–26, 133 n. 41, 135–42, 152, 160 n. 32, 161 n. 35, 167 n. 55, 216–17, 219–23, 226–33, 236–37, 239, 241–44, 254, 257, 275–76, 286, 313–14, 325, 327–28, 333, 337–39, 341, 347–51, 384

Thomas de Bailly: 11, 21

Thomas Wilton: 11, 21

Thompson, Augustine: 221

Tiberius, Roman emperor: 286, 297

Tierney, Brian: 16

Titus, Roman emperor: 294, 297 n. 91

Tolomeo Fiadoni da Lucca *see* Ptolemy of Lucca

Torrigiano de' Cerchi: 290 n. 38

Torquatus (Titus Manlius Imperiosus Torquatus): 203

Tortelli, Giovanni: 302

Tostado, Alonso: 78

Toste, Marco: 21, 31, 38, 158

Trent: 305
Council of: 343

Trial of Jesus, Roman: 17, 19, 49–51, 53, 57–70, 285–314

Troilo, Erminio: 411

Ubertino of Casale: 414, 424

Ullmann, Walter: 14

Valerius Maximus: 223, 227, 233, 235–36, 239, 241–42

Valla, Lorenzo: 19, 285, 288, 301–05, 307, 314

Vasoli, Cesare: 41

Vegetius (Publius Vegetius Renatus): 236

Venice: 19, 235–39, 323, 325, 329, 331–35, 341
(Venetian) Interdict: 20, 22, 325, 329–33, 341
Santi Giovanni e Paolo, Basilica of: 236

Venturino of Bergamo: 225

Vercelli: 243 n. 127

Vergil (Publius Vergilius Maro): 218 n. 12, 241, 288

Vernani, Guido: 216–17, 222, 225, 239–40, 243, 261, 329 n. 17

Verona: 198, 305, 419

Vieri de' Cerchi: 291 n. 40

Villari, Pasquale: 410

Vincent of Beauvais: 219, 235 n. 94

440 INDEX OF NAMES, PLACES, AND EVENTS

Viroli, Maurizio: 236
Visconti, Azzone: 218–19, 243–44
Visconti, Bruzio: 218, 241–43
Visconti, Federigo: 221
Visconti, Giovanni: 218–19, 243
Visconti, Luchino: 218–19, 243
Visconti, Matteo: 12, 198–99, 206–07, 419

Walafried Strabo: 54
Waldensians: 257 n. 19, 326, 328, 335

Walter Burley: 11, 21, 38, 326–27
Walter de Bosevile: 224
William Bernard of Narbonne: 11
William of Baskerville: 413–17, 423–25
William of Moerbeke: 34–38, 41, 83, 221
William of Ockham: 16, 34, 38, 141, 220, 306, 363, 392, 413, 417
World War II: 392, 400